PRAISE FOR THIS BOOK

"I commend to the faithful Fr. Perricone's collected essays, which speak with a clarity and forthrightness so urgently required in our times, reminiscent of the voice of the Fathers in their unwavering fidelity to the deposit of faith. In an age that witnesses the eclipse of perennial truths, Fr. Perricone stands as a steadfast herald of Christ's immutable doctrine and the luminous beauty of Sacred Tradition, draws souls into the radiant heart of Catholic worship, inspires a holy zeal in defending the rights of Christ's Church, and rekindles the flame of supernatural hope and charity that animates the saints. All who seek spiritual nourishment amidst the confusion of our times would do well to return, again and again, to *Torches Against the Abyss*, so that, with fortitude and humble trust renewed, they may cleave ever more closely to Our Lord Jesus Christ and His holy Bride, the Church."
—✠ATHANASIUS SCHNEIDER, Auxiliary Bishop of the Archdiocese of St. Mary in Astana

"Father John A. Perricone is an international Roman Catholic treasure. Only a few contemporary scholar-priests have defended the teachings of Holy Mother Church with such total fidelity, tactical brilliance, and warm wit. Fr. Perricone's writing incarnates the truism that truth doesn't change, because, as the Master said, *portae inferi non praevalebunt*. In *Torches Against the Abyss*, he has given us in one volume a lifetime of his articulate and masterful defenses of the faith. Encyclopedic in its scope, fearless in its embrace of truth, and satisfying of the reader's thirst for understanding, *Torches* is his masterpiece. It should be in every Catholic home and library in the English-speaking world."
—JUDGE ANDREW P. NAPOLITANO, *NY Times* best-selling author, TV commentator, host of *Judging Freedom* Podcast

"'Blessed are those who mourn' (Matthew 5:4). As the reader will see in this volume, Father John Perricone mourns—but why? 'They shall look upon him whom they have pierced' (Zecheriah 12:10). Father Perricone, a man of prayer and study, mourns as he has witnessed in his own lifetime the piercing of the betrayed Christ. With Rossetti, he can cry out, 'Am I a stone, and not a sheep, That I can stand, O Christ, beneath Thy cross, To number drop by drop

Thy blood's slow loss, And yet not weep?' But this book is no litany of despair. The words (rightly or wrongly) attributed to Tertullian may rightly be attributed to Father Perricone: 'Hope is patience with the lamp lit.' These essays are a light in the darkness, or, better said, a reflection of the Light Who is Christ, Who cannot be defeated by this present darkness (Ephesians 6:12)."

—**FR. ROBERT MCTEIGUE**, S.J., host of *The Catholic Current* and author of *Christendom Lost and Found*

"In *Torches Against the Abyss*, Fr. Perricone takes readers through the darkness of sin and error into the light of faith, weaving history, theology, and lived experience into a powerful testament of hope. He confronts the cultural void of our times with the eternal truths of the Catholic religion, illuminating a path forward. If you have ever heard his speaking voice, you can almost hear him preaching the words off the page!"

—**STEVE CUNNINGHAM**, *Sensus Fidelium*

"Fr. John Perricone is a thinker unlike any other in our times: precise, penetrating, and pugilistic. His wisdom and—yes!—his wit are just what our troubled times need. He has a singular knack for diagnosing what our troubles are, while never failing to prescribe the exact remedy. It is the remedy of a rolled-up shroud in an empty tomb, of tongues of fire in an upper room—the medicine of a merciful God working through His Church. Take, read, and see why Fr. Perricone is among today's foremost Christian apologists."

—**PIETER VREE**, editor, *New Oxford Review*

"Fr. John Perricone is one of the most gifted Catholic essayists of our time. His writing is faithful to the Church, strikingly relevant, and expressed with luminous force. With prophetic clarity and a pastor's heart, he confronts the confusions of our age and calls Catholics to courage, fidelity, and joy. *Torches Against the Abyss* is not just a collection of essays, it's a rallying cry for the Church on earth and for all who long to see her shine with the light of Christ."

—**MARK LAMBERT**, *Catholic Unscripted*

TORCHES AGAINST THE ABYSS

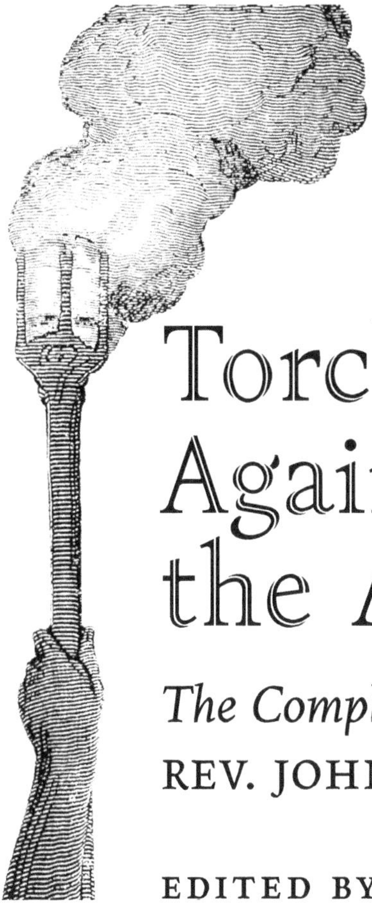

Torches Against the Abyss

The Complete Essays of
REV. JOHN A. PERRICONE

EDITED BY DAN MARENGO

Copyright © 2025 by Rev. John Perricone

All rights reserved.

No part of this book may be reproduced, stored in a retrieval system, or transmitted in any form, or by any means, electronic, mechanical, photocopying, or otherwise, without the prior written permission of the publisher, except by a reviewer, who may quote brief passages in a review.

Os Justi Press
P.O. Box 21814
Lincoln, NE 68542
www.osjustipress.com

Send inquiries to
info@osjustipress.com

ISBN 978-1-965303-42-9 (paperback)
ISBN 978-1-965303-43-6 (hardcover)
ISBN 978-1-965303-44-3 (ebook)

Layout by Michael Schrauzer
Cover by Julian Kwasniewski
Cover image: Adolph von Menzel,
Studentenfackelzug (1859),
Alte Nationalgalerie, Wikimedia Commons
Frontispiece photograph by Jon Stulich,
used with permission.

To Venerable Fulton Sheen,
timeless light of Catholic intellects,
fearless warrior of the Holy Faith,
consummate preacher rivaling Bossuet and Lacordaire,
creator of earthquakes in the souls of men.
Especially in the soul of this priest.

For Zion's sake I will not keep silent,
and for Jerusalem's sake I will not rest,
until her vindication goes forth as brightness,
and her salvation as a burning torch.
Isaiah 62:1

But you, O Lord, will endure forever,
and your name from age to age.
You will arise and have mercy on Sion:
for this is the time to have mercy.
Yes, the time appointed has come,
for your servants love her very stones,
are moved with pity even for her dust.
Psalm 101[102]:12–14

Though an army encamp against me,
my heart would not fear.
Though war break out against me,
even then would I trust.
Psalm 26[27]:3

CONTENTS

PREFACE xv

ACKNOWLEDGMENTS xxi

PART I: A CHURCH IN CRISIS 1

  1: TIMELY TRUTHS AND EGREGIOUS ERRORS 3
    Always the Same 5
    All You Need Is Love? 7
    It's Not Your Education, Stupid 10
    Aren't We All Going to Heaven? 13
    St. Thomas Aquinas, Anyone? 18
    The Beginning of the End of Recreational Catholicism 22
    Apocalypse or New Dawn? 27
    The Strange Case of the Catholic Anti-Catholic 31
    All About ME 35
    Monsters at Hallmark 40
    Catholicism's Ghost 42
    Is Christ a Magician? 47

  2: OF POPES, CARDINALS, AND BISHOPS 53
    Where is Today's Pope St. Pius X? 55
    A Fearful Homage 58
    Joseph Cardinal Bernardin, R.I.P. 63
    Apologize? For What? 65
    Something to Apologize For 67
    A Scene from Raphael 70
    Millstones Galore 73
    (Bad) Business as Usual 76
    The Remarkable Papacy of Pope Benedict XVI 79
    Cardinal Cupich's Uncertain Trumpet 84
    Archbishop Viganò's Letter: Now What? 89
    Archbishop Cordileone vs. Sisters of Perpetual Indulgence 92
    Looking Backward in the Diocese of Charlotte 96
    May Pope Francis Rest in Peace—
      And May Peace Return to Mother Church 101

3: OF COUNCILS AND SYNODS   107
  The Council of Nicaea at 1,700 Years Old   109
  Vatican II at 60: Stop the Cheerleading   113
  Down the Rabbit Hole of Synodality   118
  Synodal Fallout: Putting Light Under Bushel Baskets   122
  The Navel-Gazing of Synodal "Listening"   126
  The Synodal Comedy: Act II   130
  The Time of Magical Thinking   134

4: OF PRIESTS AND PRIESTHOOD   139
  The Greatness of the Priesthood   141
  In Praise of Heroic Priests   144
  In Praise of the (Former) Society of Jesus   148
  Saint Mychal Judge?   153
  Paulist Fathers: Disassembling the
    Catholic Faith for Decades   157
  Why I Love the *National Catholic Reporter*   161
  Nunsense, Redux (Part I)   165
  Nunsense, Redux (Part II)   169
  Black Power!   173
  Of Healing Priests and Other Strange Intrusions   178
  Clothing the Naked Catholic Square   183
  Beware the Priest as Clown   190
  The Priest as Hercules   195

PART II: ANCIENT BEAUTY, EVER NEW   199
  5: DIVINE WORSHIP   201
    Not for Liturgists But for Men   203
    Active Participation: Truths and Counterfeits   205
    Latin in the Mass   208
    Together, Turning to God   211
    An Embarrassment of Riches   214
    Why the Extraordinary Form is Truly
      Extraordinary   217
    Which Liturgy Appeals to Catholic Youth?   223
    Lex Orandi, Lex Aedificandi   227
    A Rumbling   229
    Traditionis Custodes: A Setback, not a Defeat   235
    A Berlin Wall–Again   239
    Rome, We Have a Problem   243

6: THE MOST HOLY EUCHARIST   247
   Returning to Our Knees   249
   A Radical Proposal for Eucharistic Revival   254
   A Modest Proposal to End the Vocations Crisis   259
   Fable-Time in Chicago   263
   Where Eucharistic Revival Goes to Die   268

7: BEAUTY IN THE CHURCH   273
   The Preferential Option for the *Poor Sinner*   275
   Warning: This Music May Be Harmful to Your Soul   281
   Whither Our Catholic Churches?   285
   What in the World is a "Worship Space"?   291
   Modernist Churches: Lies Set in Stone   295
   Why the Walls of Notre-Dame Are Groaning   299
   Awake in Paradise   303

PART III: FOLLOWING OUR KING TO HEAVEN   307

   8: DEATH AND RESURRECTION   309
      Whatever Happened to Lent?   311
      Union with God or Union with the World   315
      Haunted by Passiontide   319
      The Ecstasy and Terror of Holy Thursday   322
      Good Friday: The Start of a New Beginning   325
      A Friday Unlike Any Other   328
      Lift High the Cross   331
      Escaping the Cross: The Ugliest Temptation   334
      O Death, Where Is Thy...Tickle?   337
      Purgatory   342
      Resisting a Counterfeit Easter   344
      Easter: Launching the Revolution of the Cross   347
      Heaven is Only in Heaven   350

   9: SPIRITUAL COMBAT   353
      Love's Violence   355
      Catholics as "Strangers"   359
      An Embarrassing Feast for a "Reimagined Church"   363
      Catholicism Is About Swords   367
      The Properly Angry Catholic   371
      The Place of Joy in Times of Crisis   375
      The Bashfulness of Sin   380

Mercy on the Cheap   383
Does Jesus Love You Just the Way You Are?   387
"Bless Me, Father, for I Have Sinned"   391
Christmas and Nietzsche's Abyss   395
Abandon All Pride Those Who Seek the Kingdom   397
The Holy Spirit Makes Men of Steel   400
Never Let a Crisis Go to Waste   404

10: LESSONS FROM THE SAINTS   407
Our Lepanto Moment   409
Catholicism, the World, and a Warrior Angel   412
"Re-enchanting" the World   415
St. Mary Magdalene   421
A Medieval Remedy for Modernity's Ills   424
Black Lives Really Mattered to St. Peter Claver   430
The Paradoxes of Auschwitz: Barbarity
   and Beatitude   434
St. Mother Teresa: Loving the Poor Catholic Style   438
On Not Keeping the Poor Poor   441

11: MARRIAGE AND THE FAMILY   447
Fathers, Rise to Your Greatness   449
How Long, O Lord?   453
Motherhood and Civilization   456
Why Valentine's Day is Named After a Saint   460
The Holy Family and Holy Families   463
Modernity's New Drink: Marriage on the Rocks   466

PART IV: A WORLD UPSIDE-DOWN   471

12: OUR FRAYING CULTURE   473
God Bless America?   475
"Render unto Caesar...": To Vote or Not to Vote   479
The Tightening Noose of Diversity Ideology   483
RIP, DEI: The End of Our Captivity   487
Christ Was a Brown Jew   492
The Obsolete Human   494
The Tragedy of Legal Positivism   499
Three Cheers for Inequality   502
Three Cheers for Smokers   505
Censorship   509

Our Brave New (Woke) World 512
Thank God, Governor Cuomo 516
Lawmakers Declare War on the Church 520
Christianity & Islam: Morally Equivalent? 524
Marin County Meets the Tiber 528
All of Vienna Is Giddy About Nanya 531
The Paris Olympics: Caligula Redux 533
Bill in the Hotel Room with Paula 537
Occupy Harvard 539
So Much for *Veritas* 544
Hell in Manhattan 547
In Praise of Land Mines 550
I ♥ Texas 552
Is Opposition to Illegal Immigration a Sin? 555
Radical Chic Redux 560

EPILOGUE 565

SOURCES 567

ABOUT THE AUTHOR 571

PREFACE

All right, I am a thief. The title of my book was taken from a speech that was delivered by the famed French writer, Francois Mauriac, to a group of Catholic college students at the Sorbonne in the young years of the Twentieth century. It was a time of a devouring secularism which was tearing at the very fabric of that Eldest Daughter of the Church, as well as the once impregnable pillars of Christian civilization. To this time of promethean Secularist confidence, the reach of Mother Church was weakening.

To wit, a burgeoning Modernism was afoot. It promised a Catholicism more amenable to "Man Come of Age." Modernism represented a retiring embarrassment at the Church's bold and passionate trumpet announcing the primacy of the supernatural. It found antediluvian the Church's ancient invitation to embrace the delights of sanctity to fill the hollow hearts of Modern Men.

This dual assault upon the foundations of western civilization disturbed one of the century's premier poets. To the surprise of the reigning intelligentsia, one they thought their own, T. S. Eliot, would pen an erudite wakeup call in 1922, *The Waste Land*. It was a stinging rebuke to Secularism's decadence. As though that were not enough, Eliot followed it by an equally withering indictment in his poem, "The Hollow Men." Eliot's entire oeuvre was a *cri de coeur* to a wheezing culture which had made a fatal pact with Modernity.

Against this invading army, faithful Catholics felt besieged. Especially the young. Multiplying their confusion were some of the most prominent Catholic intellectuals of the day encouraging compromise, not resistance.

Against this swirling sea of melancholy and accommodation, Mauriac spoke. It was a trumpet blast. Rousing and fortifying, the great French novelist begged the disorientated young Catholics to be "Torches Against the Abyss." It was a call to arms, an address of surging hope and confidence. Refusing to belittle the frightening darkness, he felt obliged to inflame his audience against it. He reminded them of their great patrimony. As Roman Catholics they enjoyed supernatural fire from Heaven, and it fell upon them to be the light for a world which had come to love the Darkness.

Indeed, they were to be blazing torches against the Abyss. Their exhilaration was palpable. Mauriac had trumpeted the summons to march, and march they did.

Our world and Mother Church today face a similar abyss over one hundred years later. Only worse. Not only do we stare into a civilizational abyss, but that abyss has wound its way into the Church herself. The Bride of Christ has confronted abysses before, the Roman Empire, for instance. But then she fought that challenge with an arsenal of saints and inspired doctors. They made her impregnable, even as the abyss hurled its most lethal thunderbolts. In fact, her strength deepened, and her resolve stiffened the more the Roman Imperium attempted to smother her, hence, Tertullian's, *"sanguis martyrum, semen christianorum."*

Today, however, a more grueling task confronts us. We face a culture inured to God. Hatred can easily be handled, but indifference? Weariness with God ultimately leads to an ennui with truth itself. It is no surprise that the very nature of the sexes is called into doubt. Chesterton summarizes with piquant insight, "Take away the supernatural, and what is left is not the natural, but the unnatural."

C. S. Lewis penned a brilliant assessment of our besieged culture in his essay, Modern Man and his Categories of Thought. As with all of Lewis, it shimmers with insight:

> I sometimes wonder whether we shall not have to reconvert men to real Paganism as a preliminary to converting them to Christianity. If they were Stoics, or Orphics, Mithraists, or (better still) peasants worshipping the earth, our task might be easier.

Lewis's diagnosis was recently on full display. Shivers of shock were felt by Americans in a recent Senate confirmation hearing for the nominee for the Supreme Court, Ketanji Brown Jackson. During that March 2022 hearing, Miss. Jackson was asked by Senator Marsha Blackburn to provide a definition for the word "woman." Jackson responded, "I can't..."

Were there howls of disbelief? No. At least groans? No. Only a genteel silence. Her nomination was approved by the Senate.

Without doubt, the Abyss had now migrated to the highest chambers of the land. Moreover, its effete *bien pensant* proceeded to stamp it as *de fide*. The few Americans who registered protest were treated like screaming lunatics in an asylum.

Take a bow for your prescient insight, Mr. Lewis.

The Herculean Church of Tertullian and St. Cyprian would never have let such degeneracy stand. But that once mighty Church has faded. Tragically, she has become a limping invalid after her own choosing. She has hammered out a whole new credo, replete with compromise and accommodation. Now, she is barely a shadow of her former self.

Conquering religious Orders who once roamed the world claiming new souls for Christ, now beg to be vassals of that unredeemed world. Bishops who once carried crosiers boldly crushing the enemies of Mother Church, now preach a non-confrontational church who no longer sees any enemy as enemy. A once daunting Catholic educational system which fashioned students into intellectual Catholic Olympians, has now become one more accessory in the advancement of secularist hegemony.

Added to this is a strange new historical twist. Past slippages into heterodoxy were often caused by higher clerics enjoying lives of leisurely pleasure. Pope Leo X comes to my mind. When he assumed the Chair of St. Peter in 1513, he made the casual statement: "Since God has given us the papacy, let us enjoy it." This, while the Roman Church was splitting at the seams.

Not today. Many a worthy higher prelate prefers subservience to the zeitgeist rather than leisurely pursuits. Most pretend that no dire crisis presently strangles the Church. They are the "see no evil, speak no evil, hear no evil" episcopacy. They persist in their kitsch Catholicism. They rush to multiply pointless offices to their chanceries, zealously believing that bloated bureaucracies are remedies to their galloping collapse. They turn the other way at parishes contorted into left-wing NGOs, with liturgies that more resemble soothing chat rooms than the cosmos transforming Liturgy of Paradise. They seem dumbfounded at the sight of empty parishes and ghost-town seminaries, resorting to Fortune 500 companies to advise them on solutions. Faced with terminal loss of clergy and sinking morale, they corral them into *de rigeur* obligatory "convocations" at tony resorts sans clerical dress for sterile exercises in self-absorbed navel-gazing.

They are bishops of the pampering touch, not the strong hand of the Lion of Judah. Any mention of an existential crisis is met with concerned stares reserved for the mentally unbalanced. They remain marooned in a sterile theological paradigm inherited from a Sixties hellscape. Rather than give their charges Bread from Heaven, they have them feast on sawdust. In Churchill's words, "They are sheep, in sheep's clothing."

Yes, we face a dark and menacing abyss, whose very acknowledgment risks marginalization. With his usual panache, Chesterton captures the dizzying absurdity,

> The great March of destruction will go on. Everything will be denied. Everything will become a creed. It is a reasonable position to deny the stones in the street; it will be a religious dogma to assert them. It is a rational thesis that we are all in a dream; it will be mystical sanity to say that we are all awake. Fires will be kindled to testify that two and two make four. Swords will be drawn to prove that leaves are green in summer.

Interesting. That was written in his book, *Heretics*, published in 1907.

For sixty years the Church has carried on a love affair with the World. Most if its leaders crave to be like it, risk anything to be loved by it, and covet its applause. Pope Leo XIV's predecessor took glee in inviting to the Vatican the principal enemies of the Church, basking in the gaze of their approval.

This is nothing less than wooing the Abyss.

Yet, *we* must be torches. Isn't this the mandate of Our Savior? "No man, when he hath lighted a candle, covereth it with a vessel, or put it under a bed? But setteth on a Candlestick that they which enter may see the light" (Lk 8:16). "Therefore whatsoever you have spoken the darkness shall be heard in the light and that which you have spoken in the ear in closet shall be proclaimed upon the housetops" (Lk 12:3).

We have been given the torches of Holy Church's infallible truth and conquering graces. We must be on the front lines of that Light to the nations. In Auden's words, "stumbling forward, rejoicing." As we march, we must rescue those Catholics who lie wounded through the negligence of so many of their leaders.

These essays should not be looked upon as funeral dirges, but as a call to arms. No doubt they focus the gaze upon

fatalities in the Church and society, but only to better redress them.
We each must become a new Athanasius, willing to suffer exile after exile for the sake of Christ the Incarnate Word. We must not fear walking side by side beneath the well-earned "Athanasius *contra mundum*." We each must become the new St. Nicholas rising up to strike the imposters who deny the Holy Faith. We each must become the new St. Boniface, who battled barbarians as he felled the Germanic Donar's Oak. We must recapture the thrill of being those blazing torches who give light to the Darkness.

St. Bernard of Clairvaux preached one of his most electrifying sermons at Vezelay, a little city of Burgundy, on Palm Sunday, March 31, 1146. It was in response to a request of Pope Eugene III, who himself was a monk in Clairvaux. The Pope called upon his spiritual father to preach a Second Crusade to bring succor for the distressed condition of the Holy Land. Here, a small part of that classic sermon:

> How can you not know that we live in a period of chastisement and ruin? The enemy of mankind has caused the breath of corruption to fly over all regions; we behold nothing but unpunished wickedness. Neither laws of men nor the laws of religion have sufficient power to check the depravity of customs and the triumph of the wicked. The demon of heresy has taken possession of the chair of truth, and God has sent forth his malediction upon his sanctuary.
>
> O, he who listens to me, hasten then to appease the anger of heaven. But no longer employ his goodness by vain complaints; clothe not yourselves in sackcloth, but cover yourselves with your impenetrable bucklers. The din of arms, the dangers, the labors, the fatigues of war are the penances that God now imposes upon you. Hasten then to expiate your sins by victories over the infidels, and let the deliverance of holy places be the reward of your repentance.
>
> Fly then to arms! Let a holy ire animate you on the fight, and let the Christian world resound with these words of the prophet, "Cursed be he who does not stain his sword with blood!"...
>
> Remember that their triumph will be a subject for grief to all ages and an eternal opprobrium upon the generation that has endured it. Yes, the living God has charged me to announce to you that he will punish them who shall not have defended him against his enemies.

Christian warriors, He who gave his life for you, today demands yours in return. These are combats worthy of you, combats in which it is glorious to conquer and advantageous to die.

Illustrious Knights, generous defenders of the Cross, remember the example of your fathers, who conquered Jerusalem, and whose names are inscribed in heaven. Abandon then the things that perish, to gather unfading palms and conquer a king that has no end

There fell upon the thousands of young crusaders a hypnotic silence. Then all the barons and Knights applauded the eloquence of St. Bernard and were persuaded that he uttered the will of God. Louis VIII, deeply moved by the words he had heard, cast himself at the feet of St. Bernard and demanded the Cross. Then clothed with this sign, he exhorted all those present to follow his example

The hill upon which this vast multitude was assembled resounded for a long period of time with the cries, *Deus Vult!* The Crosses that the Abbot of Clairvaux had brought were not sufficient for the great number who asked for them, so he tore his vestments to make more.

Yes, St. Bernard's words bring embarrassed smiles to an enfeebled Catholicism, but to us, it is the truth that makes the blood of Catholics run hot.

Fellow Catholics, raise your torches!

There is an Abyss to be conquered.

ACKNOWLEDGMENTS

It is honor to have Os Justi Press publish this book of my essays. Dr. Peter Kwasniewski, its head editor, is one of the most accomplished scholars of our day. His oeuvre is beyond tracking. With that intellectual arsenal, he has refuted the most cherished theological and liturgical mythologies of the past seventy-five years. Scores of priests and bishops are indebted to Dr. Kwasniewski for the courage to topple those sacred cows, hitherto unchallenged.

Editors are to writers what spectacles are to a near-sighted man. They furnish his original prose with a sparkle he might have missed. If I stand as a writer at all, it is upon the shoulders of men who assist my writing with those expert editing skills. For this I am indebted to Daniel Marengo and Dr. Mario Romagnoli for always elevating my writing with their indefatigable skills.

I wish to thank Daniel Marengo again, but also Frank Minishak for the formidable task of assembling my original manuscript to meet the exacting standards of publication. For their countless hours of work, I find no adequate words. To Frank Minishak a singular note of gratitude. Without his encyclopedic grasp of all things technical I would be like a deer in the headlights.

Finally, I wish to thank the publications that have published my essays over the past thirty years; their gracious permission allowed these to be published within two covers. To Eric Sammons of *Crisis*, Pieter Vree of *New Oxford Review*, and Marcia Maranski of *Latin Mass Magazine*, my sincerest gratitude.

Any errors you find in this book are my own, and not attributable to the sterling staff of publishers and editors who have assisted me.

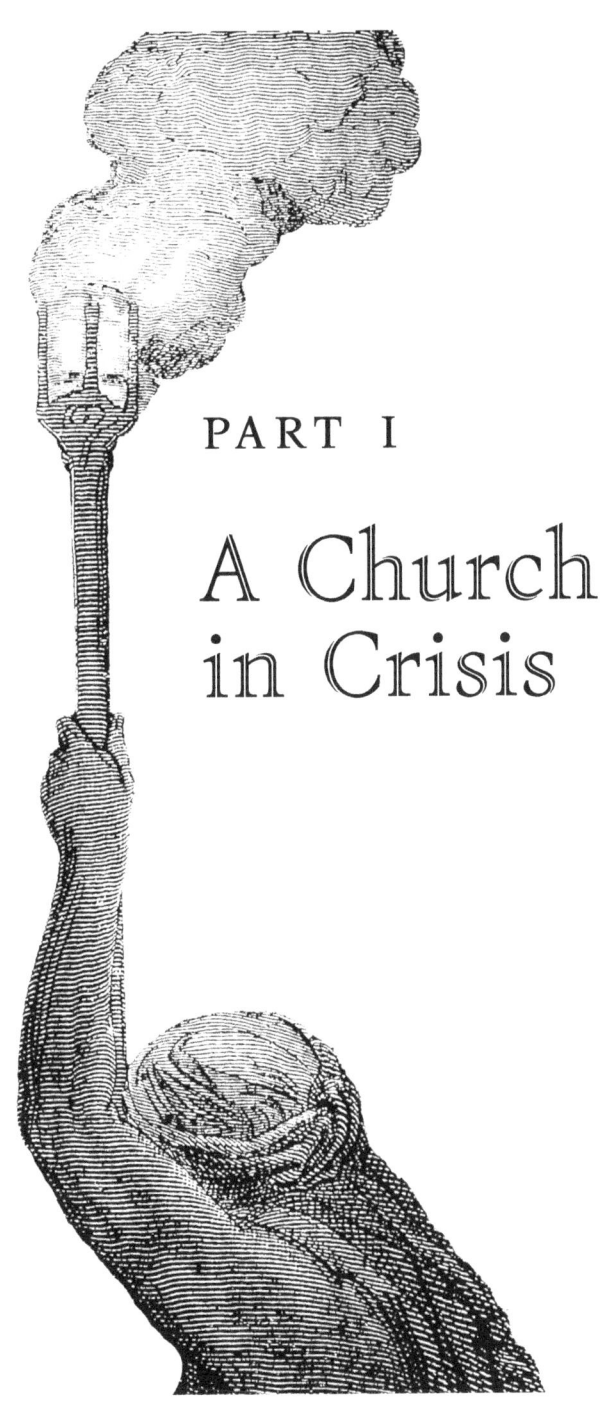

PART I
A Church in Crisis

1
Timely Truths and Egregious Errors

ALWAYS THE SAME

Time can make idiots of us all. Look how promptly a man adopts an aversion to the past, thinking all things having transpired before him to be antique and irrelevant. Nothing can be more demeaning today than to be called behind the times and a position is sure to perish when it is called medieval. Similarly, the same man worships the cult of the future. He intones the word progress with a chorus blaring that only tomorrow will bring something better. Universities compete by pitching themselves as forums for new ideas and science's latest discoveries. The dreaded Dead White European Male is cleansed from curricula simply because he is Yesterday.

There was a time when men of more common sense were vigilant against time's seductions. What mattered most to them was truth, or the permanent things. Time's passage had no claim with them because truth never changes. Most important for each generation was to imitate the best in the one before. Change could only come slowly, because the presumption always favored the past, and the truths upheld there. "Change is absolutely unnecessary, unless it is absolutely necessary to change," said Edmund Burke. He knew that the accumulated reflections of the past are more valuable than the fleeting moment where we happen to stand. Thus tradition.

No longer treasured by men, tradition is compass and light. Walking into the future was never a fear, but walking without eyes is. Tradition is always the eyes of men. Our future is our past because the truth is enshrined there. The Modern sees the past as a heap of skeletons, while men of common sense see the past as living shoulders whereon we stand, the better to see. Truths are owned by no age, they are ageless. But the past, as that splendid torrent of truths, is what makes life both steady and noble.

It is not Darwin and Hegel, with their newest is best evolutionism, that advance civilization, rather it is St. Paul. In *First Corinthians* he vowed that he could only "deliver to you what I also received" (1 Cor 15:3). He admonished Timothy to "guard what has been entrusted to you" (1 Tim 6:20). No one loves man more than the Church, because it is Her timeless truths which steady man as he bounces from day to day. "Jesus Christ is the same yesterday, today and tomorrow" (Heb 13:8) is the Holy Ghost teaching us that God never changes and His truths don't either. Truth is semper idem... always the same. St. Augustine confirmed this when he exclaimed in the *Confessions*, "O God, ancient beauty and ever new."

One of the greatest of the Church's princes and Prefect of the Holy Office during the term of three twentieth-century popes, Cardinal Ottaviani, emblazoned *Semper Idem* on his coat of arms because he loved the truth, as any good Catholic should. We embrace the *Semper Idem*, not because we hate the new, rather because the only thing that is ever really new is the truth.

ALL YOU NEED IS LOVE?

This past half-century or so has seen the word love dragged through the mud. Once a queen; now a harlot.
No surprise that beneath this strain the word has lost its luster. Repeated blows have so flattened its majesty that it can mean anything; and thus, it means nothing. In the past few years, this emasculation has reached new depths.

LGBTQ+ agitprop has only buried love more deeply. What is it that they mindlessly chant? *Love is love.* Love has been invoked so promiscuously as to make it a veritable lie. This gives cognitive dissonance a new dimension. Imagine groups in 1943 reacting to Auschwitz and Dachau by joining in marches screaming more love.

Hardly a solution to the Final Solution. More like *Alice Through the Looking Glass.* Such is this latest folly, reminiscent of those drug-addled hippies in 1967 placing daisies in the barrels of the guns of National Guard soldiers.

In the end, this gauzy antinomianism leads only to more death: the death of truth. If this be love, let us have no part of it.

Such mindless groupthink, a witch's brew of Leftist ideology and therapeutic couture, profoundly eviscerates love and is a profound danger to society itself. The Roman Catholic Church will have none of it—because she alone shows the world the truth about love, for her Bridegroom is Love Incarnate.

Therein lies the answer: truth *and* love.

All the virtues are regulated, guided, and ordered by truth. So it is that the cardinal virtues take their lead from prudence, an act of the intellect which applies truth to the exercise of all the rest. Of all the virtues, St. Thomas devotes the most time to prudence, citing no less than eight integral parts. Without truth, a virtue is like a spinning wheel unhinged from its axis—it wreaks destruction as it takes its pell-mell course.

Love is no exception. Truth bridles its formidable power. The Greeks recognized love's fearsome wildness in plays like Euripides's *The Bacchae.* Their revered Oracle at Delphi not only warned Greeks to Know Thyself, but the often forgotten, yet no less important, mandate Nothing to Excess. Aristotle's *in medio stat virtus* essentially bowed to truth alone to know the path to the good, thus raising virtue to the impressive heights of *arête* (excellence).

Love is not some homogenized virtue, one size fitting all. Its legitimate expressions fan out like a rainbow, and that array of lights is dictated by truth. Sometimes love demands severity. Sometimes tenderness. Still other times, it translates as indifference. T. S. Eliot wrote in *Ash Wednesday*: "Teach us to care and not to care."

That enigmatic verse attests to the strict dependence of virtue upon truth. Otherwise, how can man know when to love and not to love except to consult the unerring standard of truth. Ecclesiastes dramatically confirms the multilayered vernacular of love in its third chapter: "a time to kill, and a time to heal...a time to love, and a time to hate."

These sacred words are spoken by God the Holy Spirit, and while bracing to pious ears, they must be maddening to the dispositions of sentimentalized Catholics who have surrendered to all the pieties of the Secular Left.

Interesting, how Henri de Lubac, he of the suspicious conclusions of *Surnaturel*, wrote presciently about trends like these in the Church, making it a hostage to The World:

> There is nothing more demanding than the taste for mediocrity. Beneath its ever-moderate appearance, there is nothing more intemperate... It suffers no greatness; shows beauty no mercy. When the ecclesiastical world is worldly, it is only a caricature of the world. It is the world, not only in greater mediocrity, but even in greater ugliness.

War, for instance, is an act of love for the injured parties of the aggressor to be able to live in peace. Chesterton declared, "The soldier goes to war not because he hates the enemy in front him, but because he loves those he has left behind him."

Penalties for crimes: these are acts of love for those who might be victimized by the incursions of the miscreant, to say nothing of the miscreant himself. Or, more according to the mind of St. Thomas, they are a loving redress of the fabric of the common good torn by the unjust.

Parental punishment of their children is love's act, securely building the foundations of character. A student's failing grade stings, but it is a teacher's act of love, not only to the student's future success, but a tribute to the demands of truth. In a way, it is all about love, but love dressed in the clothing which truth demands.

Chesterton put his characteristically deft finger precisely on the problem when he wrote in *Orthodoxy*:

> The modern world is full of the old Christian virtues gone mad. The virtues have gone mad because they have been isolated from each other and are wandering alone. Thus some scientists care for truth; and their truth is pitiless. Thus some humanitarians only care for pity; and their pity (I am sorry to say) is often untruthful.

Malcolm Muggeridge undoubtedly read this text when he wrote about the inhumanity of the humane in a 1978 *New York Times* editorial. Humanism without truth does indeed become inhuman because truth has ceased to be its compass. Today's young guerillas call for love as an answer to the *rigidities* of the moral law.

Tragically, some of the highest-ranking hierarchs in the Church take delight in mimicking them.

Truth takes the world as it is, not as we wish it would be. From there it fashions strategies that truly serve the ends of love, though reaching it not by naiveté's straight line. Love is seldom a straight line. Straight lines are only for tyrants. It is not an accident that St. Bernard of Clairvaux summons the Second Crusade, St. Joan of Arc leads the armies of France, and Catholic chaplains ready men's souls for war. Those closest to God know best love's splendidly refracted shafts of light.

When love is carefully encased in truth it radiates peace, men scale the heights of perfection, and societies prosper.

Without truth, love is a silk noose strangling the soul of men and squeezing the life from society.

Flannery O'Connor slices through the hardened carapace of our post-Christian age with chilling logic:

> If other ages felt less, they saw more, even though they saw with the blind, prophetical, unsentimental eye of acceptance, which is to say, of faith. In the absence of this faith now, we govern by tenderness. It is a tenderness, which, long since cut off from the person of Christ, is wrapped in theory. When tenderness is detached from the source of tenderness, its logical outcome is terror. It ends in forced labor camps and in the fumes of gas chambers.

Be careful when the din of the masses fills your ears with *love, love, and more love*. Translated, it really means, the end is nigh.

IT'S NOT YOUR EDUCATION, STUPID

Headlines out of the *Wall Street Journal* on May 14, 2002 were no surprise to Catholics. The respected newspaper reported the U. S. Drug Czar, Mr. John Walters, declaring that the U. S. drug advertising campaign of recent years has failed. After $929 million dollars Mr. Walters confessed that the pricey project to stem drug use among the young actually was shown to have increased it.

So much for the messiahship of education. Knowledge can do many things, but not everything. Indeed, it cannot provide the most important thing. What is that? True happiness, of course. Only virtue can deliver happiness. But Catholics know that. Or, do they? Perhaps not.

Another news story from the pages of the New York City papers confirmed this. It was reported that several seminarians from a major East Coast seminary were routinely using the library computer to access pornography. To further complicate the story, the Seminary was immediately recognized as one of the top five in orthodoxy. How can this be? Again, the knowledge myth. As long as the teaching is sound, the boy will be sound. Not true, or rather half true. If the discipline necessary for the inculcation of priestly habits is absent, the knowledge remains merely noetic.

The cognoscenti (even the conservative ones) will protest that this is treating men like children. But it just so happens that in the cultivation of the highest virtues all men begin like children. Do young men protest the rigors (sometimes humiliating) of Parris Island in training to be Marines? Does the graduate student grouse beneath the yoke of a mentor who demands conformity to his every eccentricity? Of course not. Complaints are not heard, because there is a recognition that important habits must be learned. A thick tangle of reckless appetites and pampered desires must be tamed so that they can be placed in service to a noble end. Edmund Burke appreciated this task when he wrote, "Men qualify for freedom in exact proportion to their dispositions to put moral chains upon their own appetites."

Society cannot exist unless a controlling power is put somewhere on will and appetite, and the less of it there is within, the more there must be from without. Those chains are only forged upon the anvil of sacrifice.

Similar disciplines (if not more) must punctuate the formation of seminarians, especially in this culture. Mere learning is not sufficient. Sports coaches would never stand for the players spending their time in libraries reading about their sport; winning happens only when they practice it. It can be no different for the training of priests. Monitoring of time, recreation, companions, comings and goings, are of the highest importance. Just as vice has the power to seep into any part of man's life, so the seminary must take reasonable precautions to regulate every part of a man's life. Of course, no system will ever succeed in protecting candidates from every vice or making every man a good priest. It will however make most men good priests. The rest is in the hands of God. At least God (or men) cannot accuse the Church of not doing her very best.

This intoxication with *sola scientia* is not restricted to Catholic elites or the cultural clerisy. It is a far more democratic thing. It would seem that most Catholics thrill to the zeitgeist of anointing knowledge-as-perfection. It is a temptation as old as the hills, and at least as old as the Acropolis hill. Plato was convinced that character was based on knowledge, and vices merely represented some kind of mistake or omission in education. Part of Plato's notion was correct. Being good does entail knowing what goodness is. That, however, is only half the battle. Plato would need Aristotle to furnish the other half. Aristotle insisted that for knowledge of the good to work, a man has to work on doing the good things he knows he should. Without the work, the knowledge is worthless.

We call that work virtue. It is derived from the Latin word *virtus*, which means strength. Virtue is that sine qua non which gives goodness muscle. Virtues are the ligaments connecting the bones of the bare knowledge of goodness. A man full of knowledge is a genius; a man full of virtue is a hero, even better a saint. Whom would you prefer?

Let us put it differently. The genius knows all the reasons why he should try to save you from a burning building, but does not because he is a coward. The hero, on the other hand, might not know all the reasons why he should save you, but knows he must, and does, because he is brave.

Virtue is the deep gulf which separates these two gentlemen. Given their druthers, most men would take the hero, and certainly the heroic priest. Excommunicate Fr. Alfred Loisy tellingly remarked after hearing of his condemnation, "There is only one man more stupid than the Curé of Ars, and that is Pius X." Ah, the blindness of those who see redemption as simply knowledge. It can be pure hell.

Something tells me that we are all a little weary of geniuses and experts and the black paths down which they have led us. It may be the time for heroes again. Leon Bloy said that the only tragedy in life was not to be a saint. He is absolutely right. All you have to do is take a look at a world without them.

Like ours.

AREN'T WE ALL GOING TO HEAVEN?

Nine out of ten Catholics would probably answer yes to the question: "Aren't we all going to Heaven?" And the reason is clear. Theologians and obedient hierarchs have carefully been constructing a Big Tent Catholicism for over six decades, which pins salvation upon mere sincerity or the self-realized person. The whole conceit of the Spirit-of Vatican-II dreams were spun out this controlling lie. Lives and treasure depended upon propagating this novum. This tale of easy redemption swept away millennia of carefully defined doctrine like a mighty tidal wave. Bonhoeffer contemptuously called this fraud easy grace, showing that even a Protestant spotted deceit when he saw it. But when unchecked in the Church, it eventually creating a mythology that has fashioned the spanking-new, Spirit-of-Vatican-II Church in which we dwell. Truth to be told, outré and common theologians alike, and most of the Catholic intellectual class, constructed one of the most byzantine houses of cards in the Church's history.

A suffering church has been waiting for respite from this long and persistent ruse, and it has come. Mr. Eric Sammons has written *Deadly Indifference*, a learned, yet accessible, book which finally furnishes chapter and verse to this half-century-old theological subterfuge. To use Karl Jasper's descriptive term, Mr. Sammons book will be seen by history as axial: unique moments which close one part of history and begin another. A similar term might be pivotal. Therefore, it threatens the regnant theological paradigm of almost three-quarters of a century. Like the fairy tale, *The Emperor's New Clothes*, it compels Catholics to see that the new soteriological clothes since 1965 are no clothes at all. It has been, to use a colloquialism, the grandest theological con game of the past century.

Be forewarned, this book is not meant for the faint of heart, or those wedded to the status quo. Strong stomachs are called for. Mr. Sammons brings Catholics back to the immemorial and unchanging teaching of the Catholic Church. And that might be too bracing for weaker souls. Mr. Sammons's theological reasoning is executed with the meticulous care of a seasoned theologian. It is like a surgeon's scalpel, carefully excising the cancerous growth, while leaving surrounding vital nerves intact. No mean task. The critical teaching at issue is extra *Ecclesiam nulla salus* – outside the Church, no salvation.

In the past fifty years certain theologians have weakened that teaching quite cleverly by nesting it among truths, half-truths, and disguised error. *Deadly Indifference*'s adroit navigation of this complexity is done with admirable care and unusual exactitude, disentangling fraud from truth. His theological virtuosity makes this book axial. It also delivers the *coup de grâce* to towering lies that have been the mother's milk of Catholics universally for decades upon decades. The result being the attenuation of their Faith, the flattening of their zeal, and the literal loss of their supernatural identity.

In the first pages of the book there is set before us the ancient teaching of the Church: *extra Ecclesiam nulla salus*, no salvation outside the Church. This theological formula is first articulated by St. Cyprian of Carthage (c. 200–258). Ever since, it has been the cornerstone of Catholic doctrine, enshrined in infallible granite by Lateran Council IV (1215), "There is indeed one universal Church of the faithful, outside of which nobody at all is saved." Then there is the adroit assemblage of all the relevant Magisterial texts supporting the teaching. The graphic clarity of the teachings might startle not a few Catholics as they are slowly nudged from their forced slumber.

May I whet your appetite? "For it must be held by Faith that outside the Apostolic Roman Church, no one can be saved; that this is the only ark of salvation; that he who shall not have entered therein will perish in the flood."[1] "Those who do not belong to the visible Body of the Catholic Church... We ask every one of them to correspond to the interior movements of grace, and to seek to withdraw from that state in which they cannot be sure of their salvation."[2]

After the citation of many more magisterial texts than these, the author concludes, "Of all the teachings of the Catholic Church, few have been taught more consistently throughout her history than *extra Ecclesiam nulla salus*."

---

[1] Pope Pius IX, *Singulari Quidam*, December 8, 1854.
[2] Pope Pius XII, *Mystici Corporis*, June 29, 1943.

Having set forth the ancient teaching, this book launches into its most impressive part. It confronts the problem of what is deftly named the Emphasis Shift. With the Second Vatican Council various theologians begin to soften the teaching of extra *Ecclesiam nulla salus*. They never flatly deny the teaching, but they surround it with so many qualifications that it was killed by a thousand cuts. Or they played a game of legerdemain, as when they confidently cited Vatican II's *Lumen Gentium* 16:

> But the plan of salvation also includes those who acknowledge the creator. In the first place amongst these are the Muslims, who, professing to hold the faith of Abraham along with us adore the one and merciful God, who on the last day will judge mankind. Nor is God far distant from those who in shadows and images seek the unknown God, for it is he who gives to all men life and breath and all things, as the Savior wills that all men be saved. Those who also can attain to salvation who through no fault of their own do not know the gospel of Christ or His Church, yet sincerely seek God and moved by grace strive by their deeds to do His will as it is known to them to the dictates of conscience. Nor does Divine Providence deny those helps necessary for salvation to those who, without blame on their part, have not yet arrived at an explicit knowledge of God and with his grace strive to lead a good life.

All well and good. But the same confident theologians fail to cite the final paragraph of that passage, which dramatically changes the whole tone of giddy optimism into the more sobering classical teaching of the Church:

> But often men, deceived by the Evil One, have become vain in their reasoning's and have exchanged the truth of God for a lie, serving the creature rather than the Creator. Or some there are who, living and dying in this world without God, are exposed to final despair. Wherefore to promote the glory of God and procure the salvation of all of these, and mindful of the command of the Lord, "Preach the gospel to every creature," the Church fosters the missions with care and attention.

When speaking of *extra Ecclesiam nulla salus*, to be sure, the Church was not insensitive to the innocent parts of the human race who, through no fault of their own, never came to a knowledge of the Catholic Church. For them the term invincible ignorance applied. Over the centuries, the Church has refined this teaching so that it reached a doctrinal clarity and perfection. Essentially it was twinned with Trent's teaching on the kinds of Baptism – water, blood, and desire. Baptism of water is self-evident on its face. Baptism of blood, applying to those who die for the Faith, though not having received Baptism. However, Baptism of desire was the form that required the lion's share of the Church's doctrinal illumination. It applied to those who, never hearing of Christ or His True Church, endeavor to live according to the lights that the good God has given them, few and poor as they might be. Those lights would essentially be the precepts of the Natural Moral Law, joined to the belief in God, who rewards good and punishes evil (cf. Rom 2:5).

Clearly, in that state they are not barred from Heaven (however, if such a happy state should result, it is only through the Catholic Church). However, the Church has perennially taught that this circumstance is both precarious to salvation and begs redress whenever possible. She takes her lead from St. Peter (1 Pet 4:18), "If the righteous man is scarcely saved, where will the impious and sinner appear?" Put another way, if the Catholic, with all the supernatural aids supplied by Mother Church, pursues his salvation "in fear and trembling" (Phil 2:12), what of non-Catholics? Here is the infallible truth that inspired the heroic missionary efforts of the Saints, often resulting in grisly martyrdoms. It is the stuff of such as these that has driven the driving passion of the most ordinary Catholics to "convert all nations" (Mt 28:19). It is also the conviction that has made apostasy so dreaded a sin, indeed the one earning Our Lord's most ominous condemnation, the "sin against the Holy Spirit" (cf. Mk 4:12; Lk 12:10).

Here is where *Deadly Indifference* shines. While the theologians dared not deny this infallible truth, they subtly weakened it with impermissible expansions, resulting in a rump residue, a mere shadow of the former teaching's grandeur. The consequences were catastrophic. Where the Church made the qualifications to Baptism of desire all but improbable, the Emphasis Shift makes them normative. This Shift is more tragic than its abstraction would suggest. It eventually devolved into the general Catholic conviction that a sincere life is sufficient for salvation. No surprise, therefore, that most contemporary Catholics react to the forceful expression of *extra Ecclesiam nulla salus* as though seeing footage of Auschwitz's crematoria. When the full-throated millennial doctrine is properly proclaimed it appears to ordinary pew-sitting Catholics as alien as a piece of Ku Klux Klan propaganda.

Mr. Sammons expertly details the fallout from this seemingly benign Emphasis Shift with empirical scrupulosity and theological grace. Suffice it to say that this oft-thought anodyne shift has set its tentacles around every aspect of Catholic life with deadly effect. Even orthodox bishops find themselves shying away from the explicit expression of the teaching, with some even embracing an Origenist ἀποκατάστασις (*apocatastasis*). Deadly Indifference chronicles some of the more egregious examples. This article will leave you to that in the quiet of your study.

No, not everyone is going to heaven. That is not an insouciant judgment, but the Holy Spirit speaking through the teaching of the Church. Unless it is once more proclaimed boldly and fearlessly, even more will lose the chance of salvation. Our Savior did not die on the Cross so that the well-meaning could gain heaven. He died so that every man would have the opportunity to hail the Blood He shed on the Cross. That Precious Blood is only touched through His Holy Catholic Church.

Belittle that staggering mystery, and salvation simply disappears.

ST. THOMAS AQUINAS, ANYONE?

Ferment in the Church appears to have reached a peak at the Amazonian Synod. *Outré* theological positions crafted fifty years ago were anointed as a New Normal for a *novum* named the Synodal Church. With each synod of the Bergoglio papacy the Church inches toward an Anglican church model. But the Amazonian synod broke new and shocking ground. It strained for nothing less than the replacement of the Eternal *Logos* with the pagan *mythos*, resulting in chilling echoes of the abomination of desolation in the book of Maccabees.

But surprisingly, this new theological inversion seems to be serving transcendent Providential designs. This undisguised embrace of syncretism, at best, or full-blown paganism, at worst, is like ice water splashed in the face of a long somnolent Catholic Faithful. Scales are falling from the eyes of scores of Catholics who once were willing to let the spirit blow where it will, or accommodate the Church to the spirit of the times. They now see where that wind was intended to blow. Included amongst these are more and more of the Catholic intelligentsia, as well as the effete theological Brahmans seated in seminaries and universities, not a few who spent the past decades playfully flirting with daringly new theological paths. Even Catholics of a more cautious stripe have been given pause. These, once quite certain that the mere glorious exposition of the beauty of the Faith would be sufficient to bring the Church's enemies to their senses, have been shaken. These Catholics are the ones once loathe to speak ill of error, to punish or to ever use prohibition from the Holy Communion as a weapon, or punishment. Yes, even such as these are waking to the bitter price of irenicism. Hands-off toleration is showing its real face, and those dear Catholics are regretting their half century exercise of naiveté. It seems they never learned the lessons given at our mother's knee: God helps those who help themselves. Ignoring that truism leads down the road of presumption. Irenicism only feeds the theological beast, and soon the beast begins to feed on the innocent.

St. Thomas Aquinas, Anyone?

Perhaps it is time for the Church to unchain her own Slayer of Theological Beasts: St. Thomas Aquinas. For too long the Common Doctor has been relegated to an inglorious exile. For well-nigh half a century the conventional theological class has sedulously censored St. Thomas, when not vilifying him. Even when invoked (cf. Transcendental Thomism and the *nouvelle théologie*), it was only through the lenses of Kant and Heidegger, effectively neutering him. To their mind, for good reason. These *au courant* theologians knew well that this Angelic Doctor is the thick steel wall protecting the Faith against the seepage of Modernity. Tear it down and the Faith is fatally exposed. That is not hyperbole, it is the Magisterium.

After citing six hundred years of Pontifical praise for St. Thomas, Leo XIII concludes a section of *Aeterni Patris* (1879):

> While to these judgments of great pontiffs on St. Thomas Aquinas comes the crowning testimony of Innocent VI: "His teaching above that of others...enjoys such an elegance of phraseology, a method of statement, a truth of proposition, that those who hold it are never found swerving from the path of truth, and who dares assail it will always be suspected of error." (no. 16)

As an intriguing aside, the same encyclical reveals:

> For it has come to light that there were not lacking among the leaders of heretical sects some who openly denied that, if the teaching of St. Thomas Aquinas were only taken away, they could easily battle with all Catholic leaders, gain the victory, and abolish the Church. A vain hope indeed, but no vain testimony. (no. 48)

To repeat, this was written in 1879. Over fifty years of Thomistic deprivation gives ringing confirmation to these Leonine monita.

If there be still any so starry-eyed to doubt this effective Modernist strategy, they need only roam the writings of the Modernists themselves. Abbé Huvelin, the nineteenth-century vicar of Paris's St. Augustin, was the mentor of Baron von Hügel, both vintage Modernists. Huvelin once solemnly cautioned von Hügel, "Scholasticism clarifies things by impoverishing them...(They) do not understand that life, all life, escapes analysis. What they dissect is the dead body... Pass by then with a gentle, very gentle, smile; pass them by." Etienne Gilson remembers trolley rides with the censured Modernist Laberthonnière when he was a student at the Sorbonne. Over and over the embittered heretic inveighed against the evils inflicted upon the Church and upon mankind by St. Thomas Aquinas.

For these early Modernists, the dream of burying St. Thomas would have to await a more propitious time. It would arrive seventy years later in the 1950s when the Modernists gained sufficient seats in seminaries and universities. That time reached its full moment a decade later when the Shepherds of the Church let the Modernists have their way beneath the banner of ressourcement and a new historical consciousness (to that scheme, *Aeternis Patris* no. 67 replies: "Among the Scholastic Doctors, the chief and master of all towers Thomas Aquinas, who, as Cajetan observes, because 'he most venerated the ancient doctors of the Church, in a certain way seems to have inherited the intellect of all'"). St. Thomas was shunned, and the Faith withered.

Modernism stands upon two pillars. The first is subjectivism: truth is merely a construction of the individual mind, requiring the replacement of truth as *adequatio mentis ad rem* (conformity of the mind to the thing) with the fatal *adequatio mentis ad vitam* (conformity of the mind to life). The second follows from the first as its logical consequence. The individual "me" is the center of the world with his experience critical to the enterprise of life and religion. Every inch of St. Thomas's being would be repulsed by these claims. Every dot and comma of his metaphysics shriek against solipsism of this sort. To him it is the cyanide of the intellect. Each of the ten million words of his theology and philosophy revolts against the idea that man is the center of the cosmos. The Angelic Doctor would have instantly recognized that thinking like that is nothing less than standing reality on its head. Think of it this way: St. Thomas's teachings line up like an army of ten thousand armored tanks poised for attack against the Modernist enormity. Against the Church's Thomistic might, there is no contest. Modernists grasped this perfectly. St. Thomas is the Church's Samson. Modernism is her Delilah.

St Thomas teaches that *reality* is the thing, not what is in our minds. Our minds are given to us only that they might conform themselves to reality. That, in fact, is Thomas's definition of truth. What is inside the mind only counts if it precisely reflects what is outside the mind, which is exactly why St. Thomas's philosophy is called Realist. No Ph.D. necessary to appreciate that. No wonder the Modernists squirm beneath that kind of talk. They intend to remake the world according to their image and likeness. God must be tossed from the picture, so they could become the picture. What a shock to the Canadian bishops in 1969, flush with the appetite for *aggiornamento*, when they asked Dr. Marshall McLuhan how they could better understand the modern communications revolution. He promptly replied: "Read St. Thomas's *De Spiritualibus Creaturis.*"

For a good part of the last century a Catholic student's only dip into philosophy consisted in a pell-mell look at diverse philosophical opinions. Never would one be declared better than another, since one outlook/perspective is as good as another. Truth is simply one's own story/narrative, and the real crime against humanity is believing your story more true than another. This is that much touted mosaic, or to a more Catholic ear, the seamless garment. How far this is from the lucid words of St. Thomas: "The end of philosophy is not to know what men have thought but in what consists the truth of things." Leo XIII was aptly named. Only a Lion could roar the dictates of *Aeterni Patris* like this one: "Let teachers be carefully chosen to do their best to instill the doctrine of St. Thomas Aquinas into the minds of their hearers; and let them clearly point out its solidity and excellence above all other teaching. Let this doctrine be the light of all places of learning which you may have already opened, or may hereafter open. Let it be used for the refutation of errors that are gaining ground."

For St. Thomas the whole world of reality was made *by* God, *for* God and reaches its only fulfillment *in* God. Man is created by God to *find* God so that he might find *himself*, and so find happiness. Man is not made to look into himself, but always to look at God. When he wants to hear God, he doesn't listen to his "inner voice," he listens and surrenders to the voice of His Bride, the Holy Catholic Church. That Voice is normatively heard in the public worship of the Church – the Holy Mass. That Voice is muffled when Catholics are tutored in the liturgy – as canvas school: created anew with the palette of the community's need. But where is God?

St. Thomas knew. Catholics must begin to lean their heads upon the wisdom of St. Thomas, as he often leaned his head on the tabernacle as he wrote. Catholics must guard the walls of the Sacred City of the Church. But they stand strong only when bearing the arms of Aquinas.

If not, the City falls.

THE BEGINNING OF THE END OF RECREATIONAL CATHOLICISM

Recreational Catholicism? Let me explain. It is an attribution identifying the current stage of collapse in the Roman Church. Its coinage is meant to convey the tangled knot of the therapeutic, political, theatrical, and ego-massaging trend besetting the Church, all of which produces a kind a zombie Catholic, who is daily fed on what Huxley called in Brave New World the feelies: engineered pleasures that maintain their victims in a state of floating euphoria.

Its principal vehicle is the liturgy, where Sunday celebrations are carefully planned by Liturgy Committees for maximum effusions of non-threatening messages of welcoming. While normal men gag on its oozing sentimentality, certain kinds of Catholics crave it. Sunday after Sunday. It is like a narcotic, you see.

Music is meticulously chosen to leave participants in swoons of gratified self-absorption. Toxic language, such as defined doctrine or the moral law, are proscribed. In fact, not a few bishops insist that the communion line (deliberate lower case for accuracy) be absolutely non-discriminatory. One and all come forward, the shepherds intone, because the sacrament is not a place of judgment but a place of warm fellowship.

All of this is topped by celebrant priests who see their roles as talk show hosts. Each is vested shabbily enough (a requirement) to telegraph a casualness consistent with sipping margaritas. Added to this are churches resembling airport lounges. Of course, the Recreational bureaucracy is always intent upon improvement. So now churches are equipped with jumbo screens guaranteeing the mood of a sports bar.

Other vehicles exist to proffer Recreational Catholicism. The entire educational apparatus of the Catholic Church, for instance. What was once an unprecedented tool for the inculcation of Catholic truth and devotion has become a factory of counter-Catholicism. Every facet – from grammar schools, high schools, universities, and colleges, to seminaries and houses of formation – have become appendages of a sprawling Recreational Catholicism. Even the once-named "convert classes" (labeled RCIA and now OCIA) are immersions in an inverted Catholicism with familiarity of the Nicene Creed as foreign as Sanskrit.

At the highest levels of church governance, defense of the Faith is now replaced by another tentacle of Recreational Catholicism — the Synodal Listening sessions. These are sandbox exercises where participants babble about redesigning a Catholic Faith more suited to a modern, woke sensibility. Breezy conversation stands in place of granite doctrine, producing a Catholic Church stretched into forms barely resembling historic Christianity. Various dicasteries of the Holy See concoct a no-fault Catholicism where the repeal of the moral law proceeds apace by a thousand cuts, and traditional Catholic dogma suffers the blows of intentional ambiguity.

This Recreational Catholicism is merely the next iteration of historic Modernism. The 1907 heresy was a more subtle version of Renan's 1893 *Vie de Jésus*, a shocking reinterpretation of the New Testament, blanched of any trace of the supernatural. Or, in the charged words of his disciple C. A. Sainte-Beuve, "we have forced Jesus to hand in His resignation from the Godhead." This was nothing less than a take-no-prisoners assault on doctrinal Catholicism. By the closing years of the nineteenth century, the Catholic Modernists appeared. Fathers Loisy, Tyrrell, et al. insisted upon a more spiritual Catholicism, where the object of Faith was not the crude intrusions of Divine Revelation and its doctrines, but a gentler spiritual faith. Doctrinal Catholicism was to be surrendered to a religion of personal élan. This Recreational Catholicism is merely the next iteration of historic Modernism.

G. K. Chesterton remarked: "Beware those who clamor for the spirit of Christianity, for what they really want is the ghost of Christianity."

Modernism is Christianity's ghost.

Recreational Catholicism is Catholicism's ghost.

Just as the same Chesterton spoke of the five resurrections of the Church, in his memorable *The Everlasting Man*, we are on the cusp of a sixth. Or, to borrow from the *First Letter* of the first-century Pope Clement, the Church is like the phoenix rising from the ashes. Look carefully, and you will see it. And it's happening today. Before our very eyes. With the headwinds of crisis still whipping against our faces, many might miss it. Moreover, its beginnings are small, like all great things. But it possesses remarkable strength. It is showing itself on every continent—but, surprisingly, strongest in America.

First, and most importantly, this renaissance is manifesting itself among the faithful—especially the young. They have witnessed Recreational Catholicism and find it like feasting on sawdust. Many of them have awakened and are discovering the riches of the Faith in classic theology and philosophy once thought to be safely buried by elite mandarins of Modernism. They are thrilling to such old authors as Fathers Garrigou-Lagrange and Ambroise Gardeil, Msgr. Ronald Knox and Fr. Gerald Vann, Fathers Basil Maturin and Edward Leen. To say nothing of Lewis, Chesterton, Pieper, Daniel-Rops, Gilson, and Maritain. Add to these Msgr. Robert Benson, Fr. C. C. Martindale, and Hilaire Belloc.

Other Catholics are founding publishing houses (such as Sophia Institute Press, Ignatius Press, Os Justi Press, Emmaus Road, Arouca Press, Cluny Media, and Angelico Press, to name a few), online magazines (like *Crisis*, *LifeSiteNews* and *OnePeterFive*), creating routine podcasts and daily radio shows (like *The Catholic Current* with the imitable Fr. Robert McTeigue)—all of whom can be likened to the pre-Soviet era Radio Free Europe. With skill and ingenuity, they are broadcasting the message of Doctrinal Catholicism over the heads of the cadaverous ecclesial bureaucracy that sits like a massive beached whale on the Mystical Body of Christ. These dynamic New Catholics have become the lean and diminutive David, slinging the tiny polished stones of the Victorious Christ against the massive and dollar-bloated Goliath of the conventional leadership.

This high-powered group of young Catholics is impassioned with an electrifying love of the Old Faith, and they are aborning a renaissance before our very eyes. Coming from their numbers are priests. Scores and scores of them. Many are entering the Traditional orders of the Fraternity of St. Peter or Institute of Christ the King. Both seminaries are at their maximum capacity, training young men in the fashion of the seminaries from the Council of Trent to 1965.

Catholics owe it to themselves to visit these impressive battlegrounds of sanctity and learning. Their superiors appreciate that they are sending newly anointed priests as sheep in the midst of wolves. To that end, their training has the feel of Parris Island, with order and discipline sitting upon the crown of their ascetical/ theological/philosophical formation like jewels set in a golden diadem. After eight years of this blessed rigor, they are launched, in the words of Henri Daniel-Rops, to bring to the world and the Church *a revolution of the Cross.*

Even some dioceses have begun to imitate the seminary classical program, and they are reaping astonishing results. Discretion prohibits naming them due to the present climate in which the Church finds herself. But Catholics can rest their heads more securely upon their pillows at night knowing that legions of young men are being summoned by the Holy Spirit to lead this New Renaissance.

It should not surprise us that these newly ordained priests are becoming pastors in record time. A proper supernatural attitude can see how the vocation dearth acts as a blessing. It permits priests who normally would wait decades to be pastors to take on that role in seeming minutes.

Unafraid of the spiritual, doctrinal, and liturgical ruins that face them, they meet the challenge with creative, careful, and heroic swiftness, sometimes verging on the dramatic. In 2024, a very young pastor in southern New Jersey read that a local church was shuttering its doors. He wasted no time in hiring engineers to devise a plan to transport all of its marble sanctuary altars and altar rails and reset them in his church. After several months of meticulous moving and repositioning, a church conceived in the seventies to appear like a dentist's waiting room underwent a miraculous transformation in marble. In fact, the extraordinary pastor named his renaissance Faith Moves Marble. But he is not finished. He is now in the planning stages of constructing a medieval tower to adjoin his church.

This new phalanx of wondrous priests does not act in half measures. They recognize that the faithful have hungered without bread long enough.

Amid this astonishing good news, there is still more. The Traditional Mass grows in leaps and bounds, all the more striking given the circumstance of its three-year suppression. Again, only a supernatural attitude will do. In many ways, this explosive growth depended upon scores of young Catholics exploring the internet to investigate what they were told was a malignancy growing in the womb of the Church. Investigate they did. What they found did not fit the cautions of malignancy about which they were cautioned. And they rushed to the Traditional Mass. In fact, very soon in the Washington, D.C., area a group of young Catholics will march for the preservation of the Traditional Mass.

All this to the consternation of these young people's betters. To quote Graham Greene in *Brighton Rock*: "I cannot understand, nor can you, the appalling strangeness of God's Mercy."

Sorrow and wrath over the wreckage of the past sixty years will not do. A New Springtime is about, albeit so very small; but a Springtime, nonetheless.

APOCALYPSE OR NEW DAWN?

See then that ye walk circumspectly, not as fools, but as wise, redeeming the time, because the days are evil.
Ephesians 5:15

O tempora! O mores!
Cicero

Certain grumblings of some Catholics should shock good Catholics. None more than when a Catholic whines that these atrocious days in which we live are signs of the end times. Those despairing Catholics are guilty of three sins. In the first place, pride, for they are claiming a knowledge that not even Our Savior claimed, "But of that day or hour knoweth no man, no, not the angels of heaven, but my Father only" (Mt 24:36).

In the second place, presumption, assuming that our scant intellects can plumb the impenetrable Providential arrangements of our Triune God. "O the depth of the riches of the wisdom and of the knowledge of God! How incomprehensible are his judgments, and how inscrutable his ways! For who hath known the mind of the Lord? Or who hath been his counsellor?" (Rom 11:33).

Finally. despair, believing that the times are beyond redemption, while refusing to believe that God grants us the grace to vanquish any obstacle in attaining our true good here on earth or the perfect happiness of Heaven. When we pray Psalm 118, "This is the day the Lord has made; Let us rejoice and be glad in it" we are affirming the doctrinal truth that God in His wisdom has placed us in this time as the best time for us to achieve our sanctification and accomplish His glory. Not yesterday, not tomorrow; not there, rather than here; not later but not now.

Jean-Pierre de Caussade fittingly names this divine truth the sacrament of the present moment and enjoins us to an abandonment to Divine Providence. This great eighteenth century spiritual master writes:

> Thus when we thirst for holiness, curiosity for theoretical knowledge of it can only drive it further from

us. We must put speculation on one side, and with simplicity drink everything that God's designs present to us in actions and sufferings. What happens to us each moment by God's design is for us the holiest, best, and most divine thing.

With signature clarity Venerable Fulton Sheen augments Caussade: "The inscrutable will of God (is something) which we cannot understand, anymore than a mouse in a piano can understand why a musician disturbs him by playing."

Our joy is in the doctrinal truth that God has placed us in the time and place most propitious for both our happiness and our sanctification. Imperfect understanding of this truth leaves us prey to the varied impairments delivered by the devil. One instance of his artifice is the aching wish for a better time or place; to live in a more felicitous past or future. Tempting indeed, but damning. When the Vandals were making their hellish march to Hippo (present-day Algeria), St. Augustine lay dying in his bed. The people were succumbing to hysteria. Some made their way to the residence of the failing Bishop, moaning; "O Bishop, these times! These times!" To which St. Augustine sternly replied, "Who made these times? Who placed you in these times? When you change yourselves, the times will change!"

Augustine was merely repeating the words of St. Paul, "Redeem the time." No doubt our treacherous times are fraught with danger because they are scorched with Satan's fire. Airbrushing that fact is lunacy, and lunacy is never a program for faithful Catholics. Any attempt to sideline the invisible powers behind all of it demean St. Paul's chilling warning, "For we wrestle not against flesh and blood, but against principalities, against powers, against the rulers of the darkness of this world, against spiritual wickedness in high places" (Eph. 6:12).

Equally parlous is overreaction. Good Catholics cannot consume their days ransacking books and websites for special prayers of deliverance. The Catholic response to this spectacle of civilizational and ecclesial collapse must always a be traditional one: the Holy Rosary and St. Michael the Archangel. Otherwise we sink into the quicksand of delirium.

Take Our Lord's own words seriously: "Unless ye become converted and become like little children, ye shall not enter the Kingdom of heaven" (Mt 18:3); and "Consider the lilies of the field how

Apocalypse or New Dawn?

they grow; they toil not, they spin not; and yet I say unto you, that Solomon in all his glory was never thus arrayed" (Lk 12:27).

No toiling: with exertions of worry and idle chatter. Rather childlikeness—which is following the example of the saints. The Word Made Flesh gave us the road to heaven and peace. Why must we insist that we have a better idea? Alas, here are the marching orders of Catholics. Here stands the action plan for us. With each prayer in these wretched times, there must be a corresponding apostolic action. The eyes of Faith permit us to see the errors, but the virtue of fortitude inspires us to attack the errors. The enemies of Christ in the Church have mightily struggled for decades to persuade us that there is no enemy. All are our friends. Even if we should recognize an enemy, he ought never to be fought, only accompanied and listened to. This etiolated position calls to mind the unsettling words of Hilaire Belloc:

> We sit by and watch the barbarian, we tolerate him. In the long stretches of peace, we are not afraid. We are tickled by his irreverence. His cosmic inversion of our old certitudes and fixed creeds refreshes us; we laugh. But as we laugh we are watched by large and awful faces from beyond; and on these faces, there is no smile.

The stench of this suicidal attitude is epitomized in the trope, "the altar rail is not a battlefield." This is a flagrant violation of the Savior's teaching, "Think not that I come to send peace on earth; I came not to send peace, but a sword" (Mt 10:34). Or, "And from the days of John the Baptist until now the Kingdom of heaven suffereth violence, and the violent take it by force" (Mt 11:12).

These words of Christ do not recommend bellicosity; they demand strength in fighting the enemy. False irenicism is a mockery of this divine injunction, and faithful Catholics have every obligation to resist it no matter who says it or what they wear. When analyzing the virtue of fortitude (a varied, rich, and polyvalent virtue), St. Thomas Aquinas speaks of the obligation it imposes, *to pounce upon evil*.

This is our vocation. To stand with the heroism of our martyrs. To unloosen our tongues. We have been given the fire of the Holy Spirit to cast a fire upon the earth. Woe to those who befriend the shadows.

But what of St. Paul's injunction: circumspection and be not unwise? Simply put, consider each action carefully before it is made. Courage is marching fearlessly against the enemy, but each march is designed for a particular enemy. Moreover, each soldier of Christ marches with a slightly different step. For each Catholic this response of fortitude varies with circumstance and state in life. For each it requires deploying all God's gifts and talents, intellectual and otherwise, to enter the fray. Be sure the action be strategic, smart, and tactical, without being brash or counterproductive. Here the faithful Catholic is guided by prudence. Recall that prudence does not counsel pusillanimity; its object is effectiveness. Wars are lost by stupid and overly zealous soldiers; so are supernatural ones.

The overarching key to St. Paul is found in the words of Chesterton in his *Lunacy and Letters*: "Christianity establishes a rule and an order. The chief aim of that order is to give room for good things to run wild."

Now, that sounds like a plan.

THE STRANGE CASE OF THE CATHOLIC ANTI-CATHOLIC

Journalism's favorite bullseye is the Catholic Church, and their most prized journalist is the Catholic anti-Catholic. This species of journalist has a unique pedigree. He or she has been educated, for the most part, in the toniest Catholic universities, where they have been carefully weaned on a Catholicism bearing as much resemblance to historic Catholicism as astronomy does to astrology. After all, except for a few notable exceptions, Catholic colleges and universities have become assembly lines for the production of reliable Catholic anti-Catholics. These journalists have cultivated a deep resentment to a Church which dares to claim it teaches the truth, especially in matters moral. Being Catholic themselves, they have a perfect feel for the Catholic issues prone to the greatest ambiguity and adroitly exploit them.

No American newspaper excels in Catholic anti-Catholics more than the *New York Times*. Their pages are a veritable Who's Who of Catholic anti-Catholics. Day after day they prove right the mordant comment of Richard John Neuhaus, "For the New York Times, the only good Catholic is a bad Catholic." To the list of Catholic anti-Catholic notables, at whose top is Maureen Dowd, we must now add the name of Frank Bruni. His anti-Catholic oeuvre in the *New York Times* has been impressive, but on January 27, 2013 he reached a new high (or should we say low). His column's title was *Catholicism's Curse*. Any guesses? According to Mr. Bruni – it is priests. This is more than going for the jugular; this is lopping off the head.

Actually, Mr. Bruni is using his column as a paean to Gary Willis latest book *Why Priests? A Failed Tradition*, which Mr. Bruni breathlessly calls provocative. Mr. Willis, a former *National Review* columnist (late '50s–early '60s, before he defected to a totalizing Left-wing political and ecclesial creed which has since consumed him like a crack addiction) and brilliant classicist who taught at Yale till his retirement, has devoted the last nearly half century to fevered tantrums against the Catholic Church. This latest volume is the most recent of dozens in this genre. Before reading even one of its pages one knows what to expect.

For instance, he drags out the dreary failed Higher Criticism claiming that the Apostles created a power structure nowhere in the mind of Christ (altogether ignoring John chapters 13 through 18, to say nothing of 1 & 2 Timothy and Titus, and the Church's constant and consistent Magisterium for 2000 years: *oops!*). Then there is the hoary argument (recycled more often than that nasty old Inquisition) that Constantine helped solidify this clerical caste system as a convenient support for imperial power (happily overlooking the loud protests to imperial power by the likes of St. John Chrysostom, St. Athanasius, St. Nicholas, St. Cyril of Alexandria, St. John Damascene, et al). Of course, no attack on the Church would be complete without the boring recitation of perverse clerical sexual and political abuse during the Middle Ages and Renaissance (happening to accidentally omit that for every pope there were a thousand Savaranolas, Fra Angelicos, Bonaventures, Francis of Assisis, and Thomas Aquinases; for every Medici and Julius II, there were innumerable Charles Borromeos, Peter Canisiuses, Robert Bellarmines, and Philip Neris).

It must be admitted that Willis and Bruni have a certain literary flair; but it is a flair for dishonesty, hungrily lapped up by the half-educated masses. They trade in half-truths and skewed interpretations easily swallowed with their chaser of a cleverly turned phrase. Behind all this artifice is an earnest agenda indicting a Church which persists in the business of exhorting men to moral goodness, indeed, sanctity itself. To the Catholic anti-Catholic this is hubris at its worst. Venerable Cardinal Newman identified their problem with his usual precision:

> Men persuade themselves, with little difficulty, to scoff at principles, to ridicule books, to make sport of the names of good men; but they cannot bear their presence: it is holiness embodied in personal form, which they cannot steadily confront and bear down.

Contrast Willis's tendentious scholarship with the sterling scholarship of Dr. Robert Louis Wilken in his latest book, *The First Thousand Years: A Global History of Christianity*. R. R. Reno gives us a snapshot of this magisterial treatise of church history when he writes, "In telling the story through its many twists and turns of theological controversy, political intrigue, and spiritual striving, Wilken often returns to the culture-shaping power of the Christian Faith."[3] Wilken's seasoned scholarship presents the reader with the Church in all her glory, while hiding none of her flaws. But he helps us see that the flaws are of flawed men, not a flawed Church. One can add to Wilken any number of towering scholars on whose shoulders he sits, such as Christopher Dawson, Henri Daniel Rops, Philip Hughes, and Jean Danielou. Against the melodious symphony of these formidable scholars, Wills comes off as a foghorn.

But the taunts of a Willis and Bruni do not take shape in a vacuum. For every fire, there must be fuel. The fuel stoking these Catholic anti-Catholic fires is the last decade of clerical abuse and its appalling cover-up, culminating in the unprecedented disgrace of the retired Roger Cardinal Mahoney, now banned from executing a single public priestly duty. His humiliation is richly deserved. This failed Successor of the Apostles, and scores like him, used the past forty years to carefully sow the seeds of the present chaos, all the while couched behind the façade of the Spirit of Vatican II. Catholic anti-Catholics took to this like a kitten to a saucer of milk. But soon it left them in a bind. How could they continue applauding the Mahoney leftism, yet distance themselves from its poisonous fruits? It remained only a dilemma for a time, before they settled upon a plan: say Mahoney liberalism didn't go far enough. *Perfect!* We shall have our cake and eat it too.

Enter Messieurs Willis, Bruni, and their tribe. Tired of pederast priests? Scrap the priesthood. Want to strengthen marriage? Admit same sex marriage. Eager to bolster Church membership? Lift all those strangling prohibitions on sex. Very simply: cure the disease by injecting more of the disease.

Unlikely as it may seem, there is happy news. The Brunis and Dowds, Willses and Mahoneys are all fading into irrelevance. The *It* Catholics are the hundreds of young habited nuns and cassock-clad priests in their twenties. Upon the Catholic horizon appears a blazing new dawn congested with legions of thirty-something scholars excitedly bringing St. Thomas Aquinas to the Twenty-First Century, and a bursting crop of newly married

---

[3] *First Things*, January 2013, p. 4.

Catholic couples having armies of babies. Their fidelity and goodness is making the Catholic anti-Catholic a fossil. They are the new sounds of Christ Victorious. Those glorious sounds will very soon bury the old noise of infidelity and betrayal. Truth to be told, some of us never thought we would hear such sweet sounds again.

Shame on us.

ALL ABOUT ME

People of a certain age will probably remember the Esalen movement of Big Sur, California. For those whose memories might fail them (or who simply want to forget), Esalen was a part of the larger self-actualization movement that clogged the decade of the Seventies like sludge. It was the sepia afterglow of the exhausted Enlightenment project, where the emancipated human person is unburdened by the nooses of religion, morality, nationality, custom, or even gender to finally be all that they wanted to be. It is what Philip Reiff called the unencumbered self, or Rousseau's noble savage who roams the world like some free-floating energy burst, unmoored to anything except whimsy. It was the Hiroshima of Western culture, whose radioactive fallout we yet breathe.

Esalen was ground zero of this societal detonation. It took the eccentric ivory tower theories of Maslow and Rogers and transformed them into digestible spoonfuls of countercultural toxin fitted for the hoi-polloi. Remember the anarchic novels of Herman Hesse and the subversive poetry of Alan Ginsburg? Esalen was Hesse and Ginsburg for dummies. Alas, Esalen is celebrating the 50th Anniversary at their idyllic headquarters perched along that storied Pacific coastline, with a fat cultural victory under its belt. Know Esalen or not, still you bump into it all around you.

Look no farther than Occupy Wall Street. If you're wondering about the cause of its loathing for all that is good, true, and rational (read Christianity) – I blame the runoff of Esalen. Every time you listen to some Hollywood cipher step forward to accept an award and say "I thank the Universe," there's Esalen. Each time you watch a chic unmarried Hollywood couple purchasing their seventh (or so) adopted third-world child as a symbolic raised fist against Western (read Christian) Civilization, there's Esalen. When you find your child returning home from school boasting identity as a citizen of the world, you're looking at the long smoke tail of Esalen. Judge for yourself as you listen to Miguel

Angel Vergara, a Mayan shaman, speaking rhapsodically about the return of Kukulkan, the snake deity, who will inaugurate a new age of spiritual enlightenment in 2012:

> The cosmos is talking to us—we need to listen, Kukulkan shines in the infinite. Kukulkan is the sacred energy beating in every atom. Kukulkan is the feathered Serpent living in your heart forever.[4]

Even though Kukulkan might not be on the tip of your tongue each day, it doesn't mean the Spirit of Esalen is not breathing down your neck. Esalen has served the purpose of relativizing all truth and downsizing the superiority of Western Civilization (read Christianity). You might not worship Kukulkan, but Esalen has made you afraid to criticize him. Part of that entrenched Spirit of Esalen has imposed the taboo of even suggesting that Kukulkan might be inferior to Christ. After Esalen such a commonsense judgment is not merely gauche, it is downright evil. Post-Esalen America sees such judgements of truth as reeking of bigotry. Esalen has rendered common sense mute and neutered the nobility of Christianity, consigning it to an embarrassing backwater for the shallow and uneducated. Wasn't it some prominent Post-Esalen cultural figure who, in 2014, referring to such unreconstructed types, remarked that "they cling to their guns and their religion"? The contempt is palpable and the ruin wrought by the Esalen elite and its disparate acolytes is on clear display.

Esalen popularized the now well-worn (though still powerfully attractive) stupidity, "spiritual but not religious." This fatuous slogan has become so ubiquitous that you can even hear it intoned in schoolyards and sandboxes. Of course, it is amazingly protean. After all, to have spirituality simply means to possess a spiritual soul, with powers of intellect and will, guaranteeing no particular outcome, good or bad. As Balzac remarked, "each man's soul is capable of becoming either a sewer or a sanctuary." Any firmly held conviction can become one's spirituality. As a form it is indeterminate enough to carry any content: Roman pagans were spiritual; Druids were spiritual; Persian Zoroastrians were spiritual; and so were Epicurean hedonists, as well as Aztec high priests ripping out the hearts of men and hurling

---

[4] *New York Times*, August 20, 2012.

them skyward to Huitzilopochtli, their sun god. Being spiritual leads nowhere except to the cul de sac of the unbounded Imperial Self, tethered to nothing but its own rationalizations. Being "spiritual" is nothing more than fidelity to self; and to God, only when convenient.

It is a perilous enterprise, and terribly unsettling, when we find its laissez faire relativism creeping into the highest reaches of our culture. Alarm is in order when we find it manifestly enshrined in the highest court of our land, as when the majority of the Supreme Court wrote, "At the heart of liberty is the right to define one's own concept of existence, of meaning, of the universe, and of the mystery of life" (*Planned Parenthood v. Casey*, 1992). The Esalen elan was lurking about almost a century before its appearance when Walt Whitman fulsomely lauds its spirit in *Leaves of Grass*, "Nothing, not God/ Is greater to one/ than one's self is."

Most tragically, it took very little time for Esalen's roots to set themselves securely in Roman Catholicism. Its unmistakable mark is a neuralgia to any set truth or dogma: antinomianism writ large. It is a frame of mind that evacuates the concept of God of any traditional meaning and the utilizes it as an effective vehicle for self-expression. Some know it by the name New Age, but it is hardly new. Its roots snake far back into the mists of ancient religious history: Hinduism, Buddhism, Manicheanism, Gnosticism, and Albigensianism. One need only reread Monsignor Ronald Knox's magisterial *Enthusiasm* to appreciate the full range of this error's reach. When Esalen speaks of spirituality it is really referring to the ego in all its self-enclosed splendor. To Esalen, and its Catholic variants, one becomes fully spiritual when the *summum bonum* is no longer God, but the self, and personal contentment usurps individual sacrifice. In the Esalen lexicon the truly spiritual person is the one who manages to snap all the links to societal/religious expectations, norms, and laws. The self then exists in a blessed stillness, loosed from the racket of moral obligation, and fulfilling all the fancies of the liberated self. The self swoons on an apotheosis high: God is within Me: God is Me Happy. Chesterton saw this monstrousness of the airbrushed atheism when he wrote: "Of all the horrible religions, the most horrible is the worship of the god within... That Jones shall worship the god within him turns out ultimately to mean that Jones will worship Jones."

It is distressing to observe that the past forty years of much Catholic talk about spirituality has been this veiled Esalen spirit. Finding oneself has replaced finding God's Holy Will; listening to the Holy Spirit has been corrupted into carefully listening to your inner voice. Saving your soul is never mentioned in the new Catholic spiritual growth lingo (or in Catholic preaching, for that matter), for the growth they're preaching has nothing to do with saving your soul. The inexhaustible treasure of the lives and teachings of the Saints is a dead letter except to spin them to some Esalen purpose.

Tis a thousand pities that the most prominent order of women religious were gutted by this decadent ideology of egoism, shamefully exhibited in 2014 by the LCWR's bitter conflicts with the Holy See. If you were to dig deeply under the layers of this past half century of our religious orders, you would find the sediments of Esalen ideology, like the traces of some meteoric strike that left all these orders ghosts of their former selves. This alien ideology has settled like some virus in the once robust religious bodies of the Catholic Church.

The Franciscans, for instance. This venerable Order, in so many places, has subverted their founder's intentions by insisting that their solitary charism is the fraternity of the friars. But what that fraternity is fraternal about is never mentioned. For it is to tolerate and affirm the brother no matter his thoughts or actions. Alone forbidden is a judgement upon the brother. So much for St. Francis's utter submission to the mind of the Church and the devotion of his stigmatized body to the Passion of Christ. Similarly for the Jesuits. They have twisted the crystalline intentions of their founder St. Ignatius into gauzy pronunciamentos on standing with the dispossessed of the world and discerning their roles in an ever-changing global community. Gone is *ad maiorem Dei gloriam*, to say nothing of the absolute obedience to the Church which was the bedrock and taproot of the Society of Jesus's founding genius (in fact, the fourth vow of the Jesuit priest is obedience to the Roman Pontiff, whom St. Ignatius taught they must obey like corpses). These two Orders, whose priests once strode the world like spiritual Titans, now lie supine like some drugged adolescent. Where once their orotund voices announced the name of Christ the King down the corridors of the world, they now intentionally stunt their voices, pathetically mumbling only the drivel of the age.

Man flourishes with holiness, not spirituality. It is man's sanctification that God wills, not his self-affirmation. It is not looking inside that will bring man happiness, but looking outside to the Cross. Is it not self-realization that lets man soar to heaven, only self-forgetfulness. Yes, the ancient Greeks did exhort us to "know thyself," but only so that our self-knowledge would startle us into admitting how small we are when we are content with being me.

Falling on our knees before the crucifix is the way to bliss. In our Holy religion alone does Christ send His Holy Spirit. In that enveloping fire of the Paraclete alone are men forged into that unique and privileged blessing called spiritual.

MONSTERS AT HALLMARK

If you are anything like me, you don't expect to find monsters in a Hallmark store. Well, I did. Look again, and you will too. Last May I was scrambling for a friend's First Communion Card. After long minutes of wading through the banal, the insulting, the crass, and the treacly I thought I had finally come upon a fairly inoffensive card. Until I opened it. The initial verse was mindless but serviceable. Then came the closing line: "may you always nurture the inner God within you."

What?! "The inner God within you"?! Was this a card for some New Age California cult? Certainly not a First Communion. But that was the intention. Who knows how many purchased the card thinking it was cute. Worse still, believed it expressed the mind of the Catholic Church. That's monstrous. As is the case with any monster, it devours you. Here it is not your body that dies, but your soul. Truth to be told, this noxious sentimentalism has become the new orthodoxy in most Catholic parishes through their etiolated religion programs, and their Liturgy Committee designed liturgies. The mighty force of the Faith has become a simpering whimper. No surprise that beneath such an oppressive regime most Catholics would think such a card cute. After all, the lounge music they are treated to each Sunday at Mass has the effect of rotting the soul, like sugar rots teeth.

Earnest Catholics struggling daily to remain mainstream or moderate might think this an overreaction. It isn't. The most effective way to avoid an attack is to know when it is coming: To be forewarned is to be forearmed. But this greeting card was a stealth attack: a spiritual 9/11. Its very cuteness is the *coup de grâce*. Most Catholics (the audience for this type of card) would likely read it and be fine. Talks about God. That's good. Then, the God inside you. Sounds like the soul, maybe even sanctifying grace. Okay. But it's not okay. It's TNT. Before you know it, it explodes, with its shrapnel tearing at the soul.

Catholics of a few generations ago would spot this sentimentalization of their Faith and recognize it to be toxic. Our Catholic

Faith does not rest on gauzy sweet nothings, but on majestic and towering Truths. If a soul is fed on spiritual muzak, it becomes superficial (and weak) as what it consumes. Soon it can do nothing but crave its next fix. It is locked in a circle of self-absorption. It can no longer love, or hope, or believe o sacrifice. It can only indulge. Chesterton was at his best when he remarked on this subtle subversion of religion: "Of all the horrible religions the worst is the religion of the God within. For when Mr. Jones is talking to the God within, Mr. Jones is merely talking to Mr. Jones."

This is the sad plight of our culture, and these cultural fumes have seeped into the Catholic Church. It is particularly devilish, for this sentimentality does not come dressed in the sharp and easily spotted edges of the Catholic Dissident. Howling heresy has been replaced by a maudlin slop. Better fit for the Catholic masses, but none less parlous. Notice how well it's working. How many bitter complaints were received from Catholics indignant at that First Communion Card. Probably only mine.

Many Catholics today don't realize that God is not me. God is Himself. He must come to me. Catholics must receive Him. There is no inner God that I nurture. Inside of me there is only me. By myself I am empty, God must fill me with His grace. Thus, every day I must seek to follow Christ; to die to myself; "to take up my Cross." Yes, the life of sanctifying grace is the indwelling of the Blessed Trinity in the Catholic soul. But that is not my inner God. Anyone who manufactures a phrase like that is not talking Catholicism, but some other alien ism, quite fearful to the survival of man's soul.

Little Catholics (and adult ones as well) should be carefully taught that the point of life is loving God. Not very difficult. In fact, children thrill to that prospect. Especially when they see Him hanging on the Cross.

Give them cards encouraging them to nurture the God within and that beautiful Divine romance is swept way. The only romance left is with themselves.

Now, that's monstrous.

CATHOLICISM'S GHOST

Today's new spirituality, often found within the Church, is an ugly caricature of the millennial truths of union with God set forth by the Church, her saints, and her Doctors. One of Hollywood's more sybaritic starlets solemnly announced the other day that she was embarking on a 30-day spiritual cleanse in India. Since neither ecumenism nor eco-enthusiasms are my métier, I was bewildered. Could it be some novel Gnostic excrescence? Or a twenty-first century variation of Stoic *apatheia*? Perhaps a new twist on commonplace pantheism? Knowing Hollywood, it is most likely some terribly *au courant* exercise in self-absorption.

No doubt it is indeed that epiphenomenon of Modernity — namely, being spiritual without being religious. But without religion, the spiritual is a vain voyage into the self. Common error sees the spiritual as merely the non-physical. That is like saying a Titian is merely the absence of white. Both are missing the fuller picture, in fact, missing it entirely. When spirituality departs the moorings of religion, it becomes anything that suits one's fancy. Chesterton pointedly remarked: "Anytime one speaks about the spirit of Christianity, they are speaking about the ghost of Christianity." Same song, in a different key.

This parlous error is not confined to the pampered denizens of Hollywood. It has long taken up residence in the Church herself. No surprise, since it is the softer side of a hard-knuckled Modernism which has been galloping through the Church for over one hundred years, now reappearing with a greater virulence than ever before. What are its signs?

- A conspicuous absence of doctrine
- A decided tincture of Freudian/Rogerian self-stroking
- A marked identification of spiritual progress with self-aggrandizement
- A not so veiled contempt for the millennial Catholic tradition of perfection
- A studied attempt to reconfigure a Catholic figure, when admitted of mention at all

This new spirituality litters the contemporary Catholic landscape, leaving any naïve Catholic searching for God swallowed whole by its ideology. This highly-organized tribe suffers no lack of handsome facilities, usually identified as spirituality centers, an Orwellian term whose irony is lost upon its partisans. Essentially therapeutic depots with a thin veneer of Christianity, they are monuments to what Dr. Philip Rieff called The Triumph of the Therapeutic. Visitors are met with a sunny ambience, practitioners wearing carefully affirming smiles with a Potemkin village manner. All of it a genteel descent into a Dante demimonde.

The Church has suffered eruptions of this faux spirituality many times over the millennia, but heretofore she has mustered the will to condemn them. That will has yielded to an irenic torpor. This ugly blotch upon the Bride of Christ has many origins. Its remote predicates lay in the first century with the Gnostics, the Manichees of the fourth, Joachim of Fiore and the Spiritual Franciscans of the thirteenth, the questionable Cloud of Unknowing and ambiguous Meister Eckhart of the fourteenth, the Alumbrados of sixteenth-century Spain, and the Jansenist *Petite Église* and the Quietists of seventeenth-century France.

But the proximate one can be traced to a Cistercian monk, Fr. Louis, whose name in the world was more recognizable – Thomas Merton. This world-famous convert of *Seven Storey Mountain* fame produced works on Catholic spirituality which can be rightfully called classics. By the late 1940s, he had become for many an iconic figure, fit to beckon souls to the delights of the interior life of sanctification as few others in the century had. More than a few thrilled to the lines of *Life and Holiness*, *Seeds of Contemplation*, *The Sign of Jonas*, *Bread in the Wilderness*, and *The Last of the Fathers*.

These works were part of a stellar period immediately following his entrance into Cistercian seclusion in 1949. It lasted until the very early '60s. Then Merton strayed.

Permitted to leave his Cistercian cloister (a shocking departure for that ancient Order of St. Bernard of Clairvaux), he began to rub shoulders with the emerging Catholic Left and gradually shed his old Catholic skin. His written works became hostage to the antinomian spirit of the '60s. The ancient Catholic spiritual/ ascetical/mystical tradition, which Merton passionately loved and propagated so eloquently, began to dim in his writings, only then to finally disappear. Replacing it was a faddish syncretism which spoke of Lao Tzu rather than John of the Cross and Karma instead of Calvary. Tragic for Merton; even more tragic for the Church. Effects of this subtle inversion soon rippled out to every corner of the Church. Beneath its heavy hand, Catholic institution after institution surrendered to its sweet song of emancipation: seminaries, convents, houses of formation, schools, and parishes. In the '60s and '70s, it was a Daring New Thing, a tantalizing rupture from two thousand years of a Catholic ascetical tradition which had forged saints and mystics. By the '80s, it had become standard operating procedure, a New Orthodoxy for a reimagined Church.

Consider this freshmen retreat being conducted at a New York Catholic high school in just a few weeks. Each parent was asked to answer the following questions, which will then be read to the retreatants. Recall, this is a spiritual retreat.

- Express support for him/her despite all the misgivings, fights, and mistakes
- The unique qualities you admire about your child
- Reflect on your child's growth and maturity in the past year and transition into high school
- Your belief in them, dreams, and support for the future
- Importance to keep values such as kindness and love
- Anything unique to your child and your relationship with them

If this seems to you part of a routine therapy session, you are right. But any mention of God here? Any reference to the Catholic Church or her teachings? What about adherence to the commandments? Confession? Prayer? Sacrifice? Virtue? Christ Crucified? All these clear markers of Catholic perfection are buried beneath an oleaginous Newspeak designed to sterilize the soul of any of its natural or supernatural aspiration.

Perhaps this is the real child abuse which deserves prosecution.

This descent into solipsistic reverie takes its cue from a serious and long-mounted reconceptualization of God. The *Ascent of Mt. Carmel* and the *Interior Castle*, propounded by Doctors of Prayer like St. John of the Cross and St. Teresa of Avila respectively, are preempted for a feckless journey into the Freudian landscape of the inner consciousness. Any identification with the classical Catholic touchstones of perfection is treated as retrograde and atavistic.

Yet, no matter all their theological legerdemain, one truth remains: union with God is won only on the Cross through the

Tabernacle. True holiness possesses one litmus test: a deeper devotion to the doctrinal truths of the Catholic Church. Not merely detached nods to abstractions but flights of passionate love. All other roads are ruses perpetrated by the Prince of Lies. St. Augustine warned against this foray into the self-as-god because he once fell victim to its titillations. He was lured into a Manichean universe and a Plotinian Absolute, which left man unanchored from moral norms or any contact with a personal God.

After famously reading the 13th chapter of St. Paul's letter to the Romans, "put on the Lord Jesus Christ," Augustine exalts, as though a heavy boulder has been lifted from his chest. He writes: "The Light of certainty flooded my heart and all dark shades of doubt fled away." The Doctor of Grace concluded, "You had converted me to yourself."

At his baptism, on Easter 387, he enters the Ambrosian basilica in Milan, and in the words of Dr. Pecknold:

> Singing hymns, experiencing a miraculous healing, touching the relics of martyrs, breathing in the fragrance of the Holy Eucharist, he knows the altar of his heart has been turned around by God. He knows that it's only God who can draw together all the scattered and fragmented elements of our lives, but we must offer all of ourselves to be forged in the fires of divine charity.

By the end of Book Ten of the *Confessions*, he is writing as the Bishop of Hippo: "I am mindful of my ransom. I eat it, I drink it, I dispense it to others and as a poor man, long to be filled with it." This alone is the soaring summary of the life of spiritual perfection, thoroughly grounded in the doctrine and tradition of the Church. Compare it to the new spirituality. Exactly. There is none. The Church proffers a royal road to Christ's heart on Golgotha; the other, a narcissistic *cul-de-sac* of cloying conceit.

As soon as any soul seeks another path other than the one set out by the Catholic Church, he soon finds himself in a spiral of deceptions. St. John of the Cross tartly replied to those given to this temptation:

> (it) outrages Our Lord, that you not merely glance at your crucifix. God would have a right to say, "Here you have my Beloved Son, in Whom I am well pleased. Hear Him, and do not seek for new modes of teaching. Because in Him, and by Him, I have told you and revealed all that you

can desire and ask me, – giving Him to you as a brother, as a master, as a friend, as a ransom and as a reward."

The new spirituality is an ugly caricature of the millennial truths of union with God set forth by the Church, her saints, and her Doctors. It is a blueprint for a soul's demise, a perilous mimicry of modernity's folly.

Whether it be the strange god of Hollywood's invention or the still stranger god of Modernism's excreta, Catholics should flee. For God is to be pursued only as God, the Thrice Holy God of Hosts. For that, one need go no further than one's crucifix, then the Tabernacle.

Anything else is Catholicism's ghost.

IS CHRIST A MAGICIAN?

Don't laugh. Over the past sixty years, such questions were taken quite seriously. In the 1970s, Christ was depicted as a clown in a runaway-hit Broadway musical, *Godspell*, and as a hippy guru in *Jesus Christ Superstar*. These strange renderings became *de rigueur* in not a few Catholic parishes. All these enormities were not to be outdone by the Dominican (now Anglican) Matthew Fox with his bestselling book *On Becoming a Musical, Mystical Bear*, presenting the Savior as a drug-addled sage in hallucinatory stupors.

Those times seemed apocalyptic.

But, to our more serious question above. We should preface these words by God's: "It is a wicked and perverse generation that asks for signs and wonders" (Mt 16:4).

To Catholics of every stripe, those words of Our Savior are unsettling. Why is God here so very dire? Isn't the wish of most Catholics that Our Lord will show us favor by manifesting signs and wonders? Even in the Church's better days, a preponderance of Catholics looked in their prayers to Christ for prodigies of explicit gifts.

While Christ did indeed enjoin us to ask and to knock, we must not mistake that for the essential mission for which His Father dispatched Him. For that we look to St. Matthew: "For I have not come to call the righteous, but sinners to repentance" (Mt 9:13).

As it states in the Nicene Creed, which we pray fervently each and every Sunday, repeating over and over again: "for us men and for our salvation, He came down from heaven." Of course, we plead before His throne for every one of our needs, great and small. But our greatest need is salvation from our sins. This has become *déclassé* in these past few decades, with sermons spilling over with calls to self-realization, equity, and mutual listening. This is understandable, considering how much more of a labor it is to change our lives than posture about the woeful status quo.

Making the matter of salvation even more remote is the near disappearance of insisting upon the state of sanctifying grace for the reception of Holy Communion. If the Communion rail (*oops*, I meant to say the Communion line – it's so tiring to remember the flattened and desacralized argot), is merely a welcoming line for the friendly display of inclusiveness, then salvation from sin has become not only a fossil but an insult.

Even once reflexive Catholic bullet phrases like "poor sinners" and "saving your soul" have become incomprehensible, almost taboo. Christ's salvific mission has become reconfigured. He has come to save us from environmental depredation, impolitic talk of right and wrong, right-wing political structures (read: conservative government), or, worst of all, the unreconstructed pre-Conciliar liturgy.

It appears that more than a few of the Church's shepherds are leading Catholics into a Brave New World, but not a Christian one. The once dazzling world of Catholic mystery, with its whole topography of exquisite art and architecture, has slowly vanished. Is this what Hegel meant by the "fury of disappearance"? Even a benighted philosopher like him spoke truth once or twice.

Adding more force to Christ's words is St. Paul's own in 1 Corinthians 1:22: "For both the Jews require signs; and the Greeks seek after wisdom. But we preach Christ crucified; unto the Jews indeed a stumbling block, and unto the Gentiles foolishness."

Even when Our Lord did perform miracles, it was only as a recognition of Faith and often accompanied by a stern admonition to tell no one (Mk 7:36; 8:26; Lk 5:14; 9:21).

But, alas, herein lies the *raison d'être* of Christ's divine work: that men would have Faith in Him:

- "When Jesus heard it, he marveled, and said to them that followed, verily I say unto you, I have not found so great faith in Israel." (Mt 8:10)
- "Daughter, be of good comfort; thy faith hath made thee whole." (Mt 9:22)
- "If ye have faith as a grain of mustard seed, ye shall say unto this mountain, remove hence to yonder place: and it shall remove: and nothing shall be impossible unto you." (Mt 17:20)
- "And the apostles said unto the Lord, increase our faith." (Lk 17:5)
- "Nevertheless, when the Son of Man cometh, shall he find faith on the earth?" (Lk 18:8)

Faith is defined as that unshakeable certitude in the truth of what God has revealed because He has revealed it. St. Thomas teaches that this theological virtue is a perfection of the intellect because it concerns the amplitude of knowledge. Faith does not preclude a thirst for greater understanding. In fact, we are obligated to spend our lives deepening our knowledge of the Faith through greater study, for its riches are so vast.

So it is that Cardinal Newman wrote regarding the Faith, "ten thousand difficulties do not make one doubt." Difficulties regarding the Faith are inevitable for probing and fertile intellects. How else will our minds revel in the full beauty of the Faith except by its perpetual unveiling through our questions? But this intellectual quest is a virtue, as opposed to doubt. Doubt is a moral failure, the rejection of the Church's prerogative to teach the salvific truth.

Still, why is Our Savior so frightful about those seeking signs and wonders? For these are the demands of those men who seek the compensations of this world rather than the rewards of the next. It is the downfall of men who have wearied of things supernatural and find their only interest in the titillations of the here and now. When the enthusiasms of the culture become the new Religion of Man, then man has truly lost God. The estimable scholar Daniel J. Mahoney calls this the worshipping of the Idols of the Age. In his book of the same name, he writes pungently,

> The religion of humanity in its dominant forms is not productive of community. Good works, humanitarian works, are welcomed, of course, but one can love Humanity through a vague and undemanding sentimentality. Loving real human beings is another matter altogether. It involves the exercise of the cardinal and theological virtues, which have little or no place in the new humanitarian dispensation. In its own way, humanitarianism is neither politically nor morally demanding. It makes the avant-garde of humanity feel smug and self-satisfied, needing neither grace nor the full exercise of the moral or civic virtues. It creates a world that has no place for either magnanimity, the supreme virtue of Plutarch's heroes, or a Churchill or a de Gaulle, or humility, the defining trait of Mother Teresa or St. Francis. Secular humanitarianism posits a world without heroes or Saints, a world in which the capacity to admire what is inherently admirable is deeply undermined.

Dr. Mahoney continues with an almost damning apocalyptic force when he expertly exegetes the final temptation of Christ in the desert,

> He resists the demonic temptation to become a servant of power and to bend to the requirements of a Kingdom that loses sight of almighty God and his purposes for humanity. Christ's Kingdom is ultimately not of this world, even if the seeds of the Kingdom (like the mustard seeds of the parables) are announced in multiple ways through Christ's preaching and miracles. Unlike Barabbas, Christ is no robber, no zealot, no freedom fighter. The salvation the Son of Man offers is not a political liberation, not emancipation in this world from the terrible challenges of sin and death. His is a call to repentance and not a project to promote political liberation. Pope Benedict is quite taken by the 19th century Russian philosopher and theologian Vladimir Soloviev's portrait of the Antichrist, who announces with great fanfare the need to give priority "to a planned and organized world." Soloviev's Antichrist is a thoroughgoing humanitarian...one who promises humankind a perverse "secular salvation" and a Kingdom without Christ the King.

Lucifer's intentions are clear in Christ's temptations in the desert. He wants Him to be a magician, pulling out of His hat signs and wonders.

Turn stones into bread! How the crowds will shriek.

Jump off that high building! How their jaws will drop.

Even on Calvary, "If Thou art the Son of God, come down from that cross!" This would be a feat that would awe them.

But all He shows is a man led like a sheep to his slaughter. The world wants signs and wonders. All the Savior gives is Heaven.

In a classic 1944 article, *The Humanitarian versus the Religious Attitude*, the philosopher Aurel Kolnai crowns Dr. Mahoney's words with a similarly anguishing cameo of a world without the supernatural grace of Christ:

> Man does indeed stand in great need of religion: wherefore, whenever the traditional religion of a civilization is weakening, and irreligious patterns of thought acquire ascendancy in men's minds, a secondary appearance of semi-religious or para-religious attitudes can be observed. We are faced with a heretical watering-down of the traditional religion, arbitrary qualifications of the

humanitarian creed, semi-scientific fads and fashions, autochthonous or imported superstitions actually believed or flaunted as a matter of diversion and political ideologies assuming a religious tinge and fervor.

Do we not witness this in the Church today? The endless drone of political things, not supernatural ones. The shocking encouragement of "accompanying" sinners rather than changing them. The sophomoric exercise of "listening" to the world, not teaching it. The saccharine summons to be happy just the way we are, not the sharp call to die to ourselves. Or the sweet invitations to make accommodations to the self, not the unsavory call to carry one's cross.

This impatient craving for signs and wonders represents a troubling collapse of the Church's doctrine of Divine Providence. The balm of this doctrine lies in the acceptance of events as permitted by Christ for our purification; purification for our sanctification; and sanctification so we can do great things. No doubt we suffer daily the appalling plunder of our Church and civilization, but to waste a moment of time interpreting their trajectory or seeing them as premonitory is as vain an exercise as the ancient Romans inspecting the entrails of animals to predict the future.

Our only wonders are the supernatural ones of our Faith. The wonder of ordinary water and a priest's words making clean the soul of an infant in Baptism. The wonder of being washed of sins in the sacrament of Confession, or the presence of Calvary each time Holy Mass is celebrated. What of the wonder of possessing the Incarnate God reigning in our tabernacles, announced only by the flickering, red sanctuary lamp standing like a perpetual sentinel.

It is easy for even the best of Catholics these days to hanker after signs and wonders.

That is the stuff of magicians, not the Thrice-Holy God.

Of Popes, Cardinals, and Bishops

WHERE IS TODAY'S POPE ST. PIUS X?

At the beginning of time a snake slithered into a Garden called Eden. He entered quietly and quite unobtrusively, as is his wont. And he wreaked havoc on the human race. That same serpent slithered into the supernatural Garden of Eden, which is the Holy Catholic Church, in the waning years of the nineteenth century. Again, he did so unnoticed and blending quite naturally into the human landscape. This Ancient Serpent had oft-times crawled into the sacred precincts of Holy Church since that first entry. But this time it was different. Dramatically different. His havoc this time would strike a thousand blows to the Mystical Body of Christ. These were blows that cut more deeply than any in the two millennia that Christ's Body trod the earth. Truth be told, those wounds have now been freshly reopened in a cruel twist of the serpent's ingenuity.

Back in 1907, one man possessed the grace to spot the serpent. This man was a priest and a pope. More importantly, he was a saint. Giuseppe Melchiore Sarto was baptized on June 8, 1835, and was crowned Roman Pontiff as Pius X in August 1903 and died on the eve of World War I. Four decades later, Pope Pius XII raised Pope Pius X to the altars, the first pope to be canonized since Pope Pius V in 1712.

This saint named the serpent: Modernism. The title is easily misunderstood as a censure of all things contemporary, but it was chosen because this new heresy was a veritable cornucopia of philosophical and theological errors festering since the Enlightenment. He wasted no time in promulgating on September 8, 1907, a fierce and unambiguous condemnation in an encyclical, *Pascendi Dominici Gregis* (Tending the Flock of Our Lord). The encyclical's title summarized the entire office of the Roman Pontiff, and indeed every successor of the Apostles: to feed, protect, and defend the little ones, like you and me. This saint understood, despite his meek and self-effacing manner, that Our Lord was summoning him to be a strong Father, by jealously guarding the *depositum fidei* which alone nurtures the souls of men. Papa

Sarto recognized that the little ones would not be able to rise to the heights of Holy Charity if their souls were riddled with the toxins of heresy.

Pope Pius X understood that the easy religion Modernism proposed would tickle the ears of modern man like the sirens that seduced Odysseus's soldiers. Modernism drained the life from Catholicism, leaving only an embalmed Church. Under cover of becoming more friendly to the world, Modernism would wed the Church to the world leaving its Savior as only a noble historical footnote. The great pope would have none of this and set about purifying the Church. From Peter's throne he hurled thunderbolts that shook the Church east to west, north to south.

The encyclical's dense 87 pages exposed a heresy of startling depth, prompting the Pontiff to tag it the synthesis of all heresies. Where other errors in the Church's history had threatened branches of the supernatural vine, Modernism attacked the trunk and root. Over and over, the Modernist partisans protested that an obscurantist Rome was once again impeding progress. A peasant pope lacked the sophistication to delicately parse anew a revised Gospel more congenial to men come of age. When the excommunicated Father Alfred Loisy (one of Modernism's founders and most brilliant defenders) was approached at the end of his life for the Last Rites and rapprochement with the Church, he snapped: "Reconciled to the Church of Rome? To Pius X? A man more stupid and embarrassing than the Curé of Ars? No!"

Distilling the rich analysis of Pius X's encyclical would be as much a miscarriage as recommending Cliff Notes for *Hamlet*. A few highlights must suffice: Modernism insisted that religion is simply a matter of a subjective movement of man's élan, or, more idiomatically, a transaction of feelings. God was not outside, administered exclusively by a paternalistic Church; God was within, or, in Bergson's phrase, God was man's *élan vital*. This Modernist novelty earned one of Chesterton's choicest quips: "The most horrible of all religions is the religion of the god within. When Mr. Jones says that he is talking to the god within, all that Mr. Jones is doing is talking to Mr. Jones."

Modernism didn't stop there. It held that the Church's immemorial teachings had been mummified in a lifeless ahistorical irrelevancy, like a flea in amber. The Modernist prescribed historical consciousness, so that each doctrine is seen as only useful for the time in which it was written. Christ and his truth must evolve. Their meaning must depend upon the zeitgeist of each age. Finally, Modernism's lodestar was its stress upon individual human experience. This was to become the gravamen of Revelation. A rebooted Christ was to be refashioned into the image of each individual man. No longer was man made in the image and likeness of God; God was remade in man's. Or, in the words of that *de rigueur* theologian of the 1960s, John Robinson of *Honest To God* fame, "In order for Christ to be saved, Christianity must die."

Truly, the synthesis of all heresies. Not just one aspect of the Faith was threatened, but the very Faith itself. Not just one aspect of God's truth disappeared, but God himself. No wonder Pius X knew he must count no cost too great in addressing this malignancy. He mandated every one of his bishops around the globe to hunt down this heresy and crush it. The saint commanded that every priest solemnly proclaim an oath against Modernism as a prerequisite for reception of Holy Orders. That oath remained in effect till 1978, when it was thought to be an embarrassing fossil from a crouched and paranoid Catholic past, a relic of a Fortress Church. Today, echoes of Modernism resound in not a few parishes and university lecture halls. Its resuscitated apologists preach an open church that will make possible the easy dissemination of the old theological errors along with their newer variations.

During the Modernist crisis, Pope Pius X was approached by some cardinal advisers to reconsider his condemnation of the Modernist heresy. Shouldn't he adopt a more conciliatory tone? Wouldn't the Church be better served by fruitful dialogue? The humble yet Herculean pope famously retorted: "You want them to be treated with oil, soap and caresses. But they should be beaten with fists. In a duel, you don't count or measure the blows, you strike as you can." Isn't this how we expect fathers to sound when his children are at risk? Especially Holy Fathers? Wouldn't it be nice to think that Winston Churchill was inspired by that remonstrance of Pius X when, faced with advisers who pleaded negotiation with Hitler, he bellowed, "One does not reason with a tiger when one's head is in his mouth!"

Someone, please tell me on this his feast day, where is Pius X today?

A FEARFUL HOMAGE

No Catholic must ever allow himself to be second to anyone in his loving homage to the Roman Pontiff. Few have expressed this obligation with more force and majesty than Pope St. Pius X. It was on November 18, 1912, and the saint was addressing the priest members of the Apostolic Union upon the Golden Jubilee of their founding. He began by posing to himself the question, "How must the Pope be loved?," then continued,

> The Pope is the guardian of dogma and morals; he is the depository of the principles which insure the integrity of the family, the grandeur of the nations, the sanctity of souls. He is the councilor of princes and peoples; he is the chief under whose sway none feels tyrannized, because he represents God Himself. He is par excellence, the Father, who unites in Himself all that is loving, tender, and divine...
>
> When we love someone, we seek to conform ourselves in everything to his thoughts, to execute his will, to interpret his desires. And if Our Lord Jesus Christ said: "If anyone loves Me, he will keep My word" (Jn 14:23), then to show our love for the Pope we must obey him...
>
> We do not oppose to the Pope's authority that of other persons—no matter how learned—who differ from the Pope. For whatever reason may be their learning, they are not holy; for where there is holiness there cannot be disagreement with the Pope.

Pope St. Pius X spares no weight of expression to convey the obligation of every Catholic in discharging his homage to the Vicar of Christ. Our faithful bonding to the Roman Pontiff is the measure of our binding to Christ's Holy Church, and to Christ Himself. This is built into the DNA of every Catholic, or at least it should be. It was a Catholic philosopher, Dr. Frederick Wilhelmsen, who wrote an essay in January 1971, "The Pope as Icon." In this piece he presented a deeply rooted and richly rhapsodic commentary on Pope Pius's own words:

(In our modern world) the presence of the Pope imposes as he anneals the faithful in their burden of constituting the cosmos in being and returning all things to the Father through the Spirit. The Pope will teach and exhort but he will principally be. Giving eternal blessing, Urbi et Orbi, arms stretched out in white cross that will embrace all creation, the Pope will iconically impose Christ lovingly on the world more simply by being than by what he may say. In Christ and through His Vicar men will then enter a peace and repose that have fled the earth, taste a promised eternity, heal the wounds of contingency, find an exit from pure immanence, and come to know the one high adventure to which they have been called.

Of course, both the stirring words of Pope St. Pius and the profound depths of Dr. Wilhelmsen assume all that Mother Church has defined regarding the Pontifical Office. Whilst the highest obeisance is to be paid to his person, and obedience to his teachings, that specific guidance of the Holy Spirit does not extend to every waking moment or every decision of the Successor of St. Peter. This is where the characteristic complexity and subtlety of the Catholic Faith enters. In matters of strict faith and morals, a Catholic must give unwavering assent. In matters of discipline, a Catholic must cede absolute obedience, but can legitimately pose questions as to expediency and effectiveness. In matters of prudential judgment (such as comments on economy, politics, or administration of justice), only respectful attention is required: disagreement here is neither unseemly nor unfitting.

Even as every Catholic holds all this without the slightest question, still he possesses a mind. And that mind rightfully roams over questions which cannot help but plead consideration. One can be a faithful Catholic and still wonder aloud as to pontifical gestures and actions that strike a discordant chord to the astute Catholic eye.

Without slighting the operations of the Holy Spirit in the election of Pope Francis, we cannot discount our obligations to reason. This compels taking the measure of the man based upon what the man has done. The office of Roman Pontiff is not magical, and while it protects the Faith from any injury, it does not guarantee that the Faith flourishes. We would therefore be obtuse in not forecasting the future of Pope Francis's pontificate from the lens of his past actions. A few relevant facts (in order of importance):

1. He is a Jesuit, which no one even slightly awake over the past fifty years, recognizes that this is a religious order racked by dramatic departures from fidelity to the Faith. Francis's age also suggests that he was ordained in the thick of Jesuit restiveness. Hmmm.

2. He has cast his episcopal reign as service to the poor ("social justice"). What does this mean? Does it suggest something beyond the compassion that marks the soul of any simple Catholic? As a touted philosophical/theological project, it may. In the light of the past half century it has meant that the primary concern of Christ and His Church for the salvation and sanctification of souls is replaced by the political work of improving society. In this view, men are not seen as sinners before the mercy of God, but as separate victim groups protesting before the nanny state.

3. While eschewing the trappings of office pulls our sentimental heart strings, it comes dangerously close to arrogant preening.

4. The choice of a pontifical name vividly departing from two thousand years of tradition is something that can be seen as trivial but could also be seen against a wider attitude of disdain for precedent, custom, and tradition. This is a sign that might not be welcome in an iconoclastic age contemptuous of the past.

5. As we speak, reports are already teaming out of Buenos Aires regarding Bergoglio's deeply troubling policies of governance, and attitudes toward the programs of his predecessor.

Perhaps we had become spoiled with Benedict's philosophical/theological genius, his penetrating diagnosis of secularism and his clarion calls to absolute resistance using our principal weapon—the Holy Mass. While I applaud Francis's adherence to Mother Church's moral teachings, perfect fidelity to moral teachings is not the *telos* of Christ's Holy Church. Sanctification is. Otherwise, the moralism of the Quakers or Salvation Army would be sufficient for man. We are not called to be good persons (*ugh!*) but saints. Thus the exquisite and transporting beauty of Holy Church's Divine Liturgy, celebrated in Churches of such staggering loveliness as to leave men without breath. All of this bespeaks how grace clothes our souls, mortality being only its necessary skeleton (cf. "be ye therefore perfect as my Heavenly Father is perfect," Mt 5:28).

For the first time since the magisterium of Pius X and XII, Benedict taught these truths with fire and supreme clarity. He

A Fearful Homage

reminded me of St. Bernard of Clairvaux. Mothers would cover the ears of their sons when this 12th Century mystic saint came to their towns to preach, afraid that his words would so inflame their hearts that they would leave all and follow him. Benedict was our Bernard of Clairvaux. Francis will be absolutely orthodox (the Holy Ghost guarantees that), but he will not be a Benedict. But – how we swooned to Benedict's teachings and actions. Where Benedict ignited conflagrations, Pope Francis sets off sparks of concern. Little things, such as his persistent reference to himself as the Bishop of Rome. True, of course. Conspicuous, however, is the absence of the traditional reference to himself as Successor of St. Peter – a more ample and sharper attribution. Caviling? Perhaps. But in the Theological Wars of the past half-century, the Bishop of Rome title was code for diminution of Papal prerogatives. Again, this may be paranoia. But a theologian of Bergoglio's stature doesn't speak or act accidentally. Good reason for a savvy Catholic to become, shall we say, nervous.

Then there is the clear evidence of what we have hitherto seen with our own eyes. Francis's pontifical Masses. They seem to telegraph a rupture with the liturgical project of Pope Ratzinger. The supreme law of *lex orandi, lex credendi* which Benedict was so painstakingly re-teaching the Church has stalled. With that, the only hope of the new evangelization (a term which makes me shudder, for all its overtones of *sola scriptura*) is postponed. The Holy Ghost will protect the *depositum* from harm, but Francis can most certainly construct impediments to its propagation. Already, his preaching, while hardly offensive to pious ears, is vapid and pointless. No harm will be produced, but no fervor either.

Then, of course, there is the humility. Let us glance at the humility of our fondest saints, St. Francis of Assisi, for instance. Il Poverello lived a life of radical poverty, but when deacon at Mass, was scrupulous to use only the finest vestments produced by human hands. He never spoke of the poor as a political class, or as a victim group, or a segment of humanity deserving privileged treatment. Mother Church never countenances a "preferential option for the poor" (a Marxist slogan; as well as the upending project of the Society of Jesus since 1964, which has separated it entirely from the spirit of its founder, to say nothing of erasing its supernatural character. The magnificence of this four-century old glorious Order is now reduced to the ignoble condition of a forgettable secular movement soon to find itself on the ash heap of history). Christ died on Cavalry not that the poor could become rich, but that poor sinners could enjoy the riches of Redemption. Mother Church does not look at us in terms of economic condition, but as poor banished children of Adam and Eve. All of us – the same.

Thus, Pope St. Pius X. He loathed the sumptuous trappings of Office. But in true humility, recognized they were not his to reject. True humility compelled never drawing attention to himself. So he assumed all the pomp of Office, not only as signs of supreme authority as Vicar of Christ, but also for the edification of us poor sinners, who seeing that beauty would see reflected the Beauty of the Saviour. And John Mary Vianney, who wore a threadbare cassock for the whole of his priesthood yet would solicit donations from the rich and poor alike so that his church, and all the accoutrements of Holy Mass and the Sacraments, would be the most splendid in all of France. He would often say, "For me, nothing; for the King of Kings, everything!" I am afraid we are entering a Borgia papacy – inside out. Borgia flaunted his decadence with prideful abandon. Bergoglio will flaunt his repudiation of prerogatives of Office with prideful abandon.

Again, none of us should be second to any Catholic in devotion, love, respect, and homage to the Vicar of Christ. But we cannot help but surrender that homage with eyes wide open. And slightly fearful.

JOSEPH CARDINAL BERNARDIN, R.I.P.

P raise stretched itself to its limits in the obsequies of Joseph Cardinal Berdardin. Newspaper after newspaper was jammed with fulsome raves of the late Archbishop of Chicago, right down to the editorial pages where, curiously, even the usually anti-Catholic wolf pack in the mainstream press mourned like First Communicants. From these odd sources mere words seemed inadequate in the expression of gratitude to this Episcopal giant who bestrode the American Catholic Church for so long. Did they sense here a kind of fellow traveler?

Further, how did he manage to keep his fellow bishops in his thrall for well on thirty years? It is apparent that the Catholic Church in America bears the Bernardin imprint. Even casual observes quickly note that Episcopal style of almost every American bishop mimics Bernardin's cool yet mushy style. Has any other bishop of the century exerted more influence than he? Hardly. Let's inspect the record.

By the late 1960s this youngest consecrated bishop of the American hierarchy (36 years old) had deeply imbibed the spirit of the Second Vatican Council's theological experts, the so-called *periti*. What was this spirit? Mostly it was talk. Lots of it. They called it dialogue. Endless dialogue.

His first task was immediately to reconfigure the corporate agency of the American bishops, dividing it between the National Conference of Catholic Bishops and the United States Catholic Conference. Both would embody the new *periti* spirit. Gone was the old authoritarian model. Gone, too, the certitude. In its place, the Conciliar *periti* modus demanded a ceaseless breezy style that engendered mounting questions and confusion. Certitude did exist, of course, but only theoretically.

With his fetching "I am Joseph, your brother" Bernardin tutored his fellow bishops in an informal leadership hitherto unknown to that high Apostolic office. Cleverly, he recast *gravitas* as pretense – have you tried kissing a Cardinal's ring lately? – and reserve as insouciance. This became the operative principle for everything in the NCCB, from pastoral letters to the reformation of the liturgy. He wielded a powerful veto on any *episcopabili* who did not meet the strict pastoral criterion.

Midway through his ecclesiastical tenure, the Cardinal joined major figures of the American hierarchy in sponsoring the pernicious Call to Action. This assembly of dissenters was the culmination of his beloved dialogic process. Call to Action boldly proclaimed an empowered laity to announce a renewed conversation on such issues as priestly celibacy, divorce and remarriage, and contraception. Of course, such as this caused alarums in the halls of the Vatican, but he charmed them. He told them these were simply growing pains. They backed down. But there was still more to come.

When the Cardinal promulgated his Seamless Garment doctrine, the applause was deafening. He managed to stitch together all the pressing issues of liberal justice — nuclear weapons, the homeless, capital punishment, the aged — together with the problem of abortion. Crude preoccupation with abortion would now seem atavistic against this noble sweep of life-issues. The chattering elites called him a genius, and abortion assumed its relative place amongst other breaches of justice. No longer was abortion such an eyesore for striving Catholics.

To say such accomplishments are impressive means simply that they made a deep impression. The Church in America is surely the Church that Bernardin built. But to say his accomplishments deserve praise is quite another matter. That judgment presupposes an agenda very different from the classical Catholic one. We can say with certainty and with no fear of dishonoring the dead, that all he did to the Catholic Church in America is something for which he must now render account before Divine Justice. *Requiescat in pacem.* And may God help him.

APOLOGIZE? FOR WHAT?

After reading *We Remember* a formidable priest-historian complained to me, "Did we do anything right?" One might wonder in light of the flurry of apologies occupying the time of the Holy See. Not in two millennia had the Roman Church pounded its breast with such unseemly acts of contrition. Is the Church of 1998 possessed of more moral sensitivity than any other epoch of the Church? Hardly.

Contrition for one's personal sins is an act that transforms the soul. Contrition for the sins of the Catholic Church is frankly an impossibility. While the Catholic Church is constituted of individual Catholics, no Catholic is the Church. "We are Church" is a leftist slogan angering us so deeply because it is so deeply false. The perennial tendency of her children to sin is not due to that tendency to sin in the church, for one of her marks is holiness. Catholic apologies therefore strike the faithful Catholic as untheological and indiscreet. Nor because Catholics can never be wrong, but because the Catholic Church (in Faith and Morals) is always right.

An admirable humility showed itself in the critical reaction of pew-sitting Catholics protesting, "I might act stupidly and sinfully, but my Church does not." *Mea culpas* only obscure the consciences of the Faithful, and emboldens her enemies. After all, the world will always hate the Church. When the Church gives it an inch the world will always take a foot. With apologies like this, the world will easily conclude that if the Church was wrong in this matter, she probably has been wrong in many others. The world does not see with careful theological distinction. Only Roman dicasteries do.

The Pontifical Commission for Religious Relations with the Jews sincerely believed that their document *We Remember: A Reflection on the Shoah* would shed light by murmuring *mea culpas*. But its rush to contrition caused them to miss the importance of some of the very truths that they applauded.

The truth is that most Catholic bishops and many of the ordinary Catholic faithful acted with great solicitude toward the Jews in World War II, many times at personal risk to themselves, their families and their positions. One need only recall the Dutch Bishops (whose bold condemnation of the Nazi programs backfired with a vicious Nazi counterattack which, incidentally, was the very one that claimed the life of Edith Stein, later canonized as Teresa Benedicta of the Cross).

What of the obedient superiors of convents? They quickly responded to Pius XII's order to provide protection to the Jews. Of course, *We Remember* takes special note of Pacelli's exceptional gestures on behalf of the Jews. In the middle of a paragraph toward the end of the document they note the expressions of gratitude Jews extended to Catholics for all they did for them, "including what Pius XII did personally or through his representatives to save hundreds of thousands of Jewish lives." This afterthought treatment of one (and, perhaps, only) of the major figures in the alleviation of the agony of the Jews seems sweepingly remiss. Like speaking of World War II with FDR in a footnote. The full truth of that ugly episode was not served well.

We Remember takes note of Pius XI's early, and fearless, condemnations of Nazism in *Mit Brennender Surge* (the first time that an encyclical was *not* promulgated in the Latin tongue, giving it even greater force). No institution or religion in the world registered such indignation. Yet what should have become that document's prolonged boast quickly became an act of repentance. Are such reversals of logic excusable in a major Roman document?

Retroactive fits of contrition may win the scattered applause of some progressives, but it dishonors the heroism of Catholics who acted outstandingly in a terribly conflicted time. When that lesson is fully appreciated, acts of contrition will be too late.

SOMETHING TO APOLOGIZE FOR

To a superficial world the magnanimous acts of Pope John Paul II are met with superficiality. His carefully crafted apologies, for instance. Each was an open admission that sometimes sons of the Church did not behave as faithful sons. Some of their actions brought embarrassment to the Church by falling short of the Church's perfect teachings. It was a reproach to you and to me. Peter's successor was saying to us, "Be the faithful sons you ought to be." Of course, I am always the unfaithful one, the Church is utterly faithful. I am the one who acts wrongly; her actions are always perfect. I am the sinner, she is immaculate. Leave it to a superficial world to see it backwards. To think the Church is sometimes wrong, often a sinner, responsible for infidelity.

Apologies are nothing new for the Church. Peter embarrassed Our Lord in Gethsemane by cutting off the ear of the slave boy. Our Lord restored the severed organ as a kind of apology. Not an apology for anything the Savior did. But from the Savior, for something that His apostle did. Christ's Vicar is acting similarly. In fact, Papa Wojtyla was doing this at the very beginning of his reign. Remember *Domenicae Cenae*? Catholics enjoyed great consolation when they heard their Holy Father say:

> I would like to ask forgiveness-in my own name and in the name of all you, venerable and dear brothers in the episcopate – for everything which, for whatever reason, through whatever human weakness, impatience or negligence, and also through the at times partial, one-sided and erroneous application of the Second Vatican Council, may have caused scandal and disturbance concerning the interpretation of the doctrine and the veneration due to this Most Blessed Sacrament. And I pray the Lord Jesus that in the future we may avoid in our manner of dealing with this sacred mystery anything which could weaken or disorient in any way the sense of reverence and love that exists in our faithful people.[1]

---

[1] *Domenicae Cenae*, no. 12.

Simply stunning. And I am sure the generosity of this Pontiff's heart is not finished. Be prepared for still more. Maybe ones like these:

"Since we have already extended apologies to the Faithful for all the depredations imposed upon the Holy Mass, especially indignities perpetrated to the Most Blessed Sacrament, we now desire to ask forgiveness of God for all the churches that have been utterly destroyed and disfigured under the guise of a new liturgy. Holy Church shall forever call this dark period the Neo-Iconoclasm, recalling that bitter period of the seventh and eighth centuries. But that first Iconoclasm was inspired by a disordered reverence for God that believed His ineffable majesty sullied by human artistic expression. The Neo-Iconoclasm espouses no such love of the Divine Majesty, for it hardly believes in a Divinity, except, of course, the one within us. That is not religion, but idolatry. Its architecture and design (like the theology from which it draws) is sterile because its whole object is man. Since its homage is no longer to God but to man, it forces art to become anti-art. Suddenly, transcending inspiration turns to self-absorption. Sadly, we confess and admit that the last forty years have seen the annihilation of more churches than under the barbaric regimes of Stalinist and Maoist Communism. It is certainly not intemperate to confess that more Catholics suffered a kind of martyrdom at the hands of this Neo-Iconoclasm than all those noble Catholics who died in camps and gulags. At least those martyred souls had the consolation of last visits to their Savior, in His glorious churches. Our many apologies.

"Can we stop here? The heart of the Pope reaches out to the children. Our Lord exclaimed, "Suffer the little children to come unto me," and so does His Holy Church. But may we say, for one-third of a century our children have been banned from Christ. Almost every diocese in the world has instituted catechetical programs drained of the Church's truth—programs that have dragged children from Christ and from His Church. No voice has been louder in defense of the unborn than the Church's. But in the protection of the souls of our born children, many of our bishops have raised no voice. No apologies from this throne are strong enough to repair this damage. It will always remain Mother Church's holocaust. Her Dachau. Generations of Catholics walk with hollow souls because so many of our bishops did nothing. How can we apologize for other holocausts when this holocaust shatters the

Something to Apologize For 69

Pope's heart? Peter's successor cannot groan loudly enough for all the children bereft of the beauty of purity. All because of the sex education in Holy Church's own schools which has aborted our children's innocence before it ever had a chance to breathe. Parents gave us their children with absolute trust. Who but the Church would love their children as much as they? Then, to their horror, they watched their children smothered. And when they sought redress in the open hearts of their shepherds, they found only the stony silence of walls. How can the Sovereign Pontiff apologize enough? How can the Vicar of Christ ever give proper comfort to the broken heart of so many mothers who, like Rachel, weep for their children, for they are no more? This time not through a physical slaying, but through a spiritual one. Will these mothers be comforted if the Roman Pontiff assures them that our heart is broken as well? To the children, our apologies. To the fathers of the children, our apologies. To the mothers, all our apologies are not enough."

"The Pope's heart is filled with much more sorrow. A sorrow that compels us to go even further. But it would be unseemly to proceed. Love is proved by deeds. Your Pope will demonstrate sorrow through deeds. Watch. Soon you will see us wield our supreme power to halt the things that have smothered your hearts in such sadness."

Of course, that is not what Pope John Paul II actually said. Well, not yet. Get down on your knees and pray. *Who knows?*

A SCENE FROM RAPHAEL

England may have the impressive trappings of her queen, but the Roman Catholic Church will always have the real splendor of the Supreme Pontiff. The glory of the Petrine Office shone in St. Patrick's Cathedral on June 19, 2000, in the person of the papal nuncio, Archbishop Gabriel Montalvo. In the place of the Sovereign Pontiff, the Archbishop sat upon the vacant Episcopal throne of the New York Archdiocese—where no person (save the Pope or his representative) could sit since the passing of its last occupant, John Cardinal O'Connor. Next came a page from the medieval *Très Riches Heures* of the Duc de Berry. Even the *New York Times* gasped: "It might have been a scene from Raphael or Titian: the cathedral bathed in Florentine light, arches within arches, vaulted stone pillars, Soaring stained glass, the rapt faces of priests, nuns and laity arrayed in the vase, gray drafty interior, and at the focus a bishop radiant in white vestments." Jaded journalists don't write that way about jerrybuilt new/renovated churches "adapted to the new liturgy."

Then the piercing moment. In phrases of unbearable majesty, not much different from the time of Aquinas, Montalvo read from the papal parchment: "John Paul, Bishop, Servant of the Servants of God, to our Venerable Brother, Edward Michael Egan... In the fullness of Our Apostolic Authority, we now appoint you Archbishop, Pastor and Leader of the Archdiocese of New York, bestowing upon you all the rights and privileges, together with the duties and obligations, which that administration entails in accordance with the Sacred Canons... We have no doubt that, in keeping with their zeal for the Catholic religion and their proved love for the Church and the Roman Pontiff, they will welcome you as their leader and will readily comply with your directives and decisions... Given in Rome, at St. Peter's, on the eleventh day of May, in the year of Our Lord 2000, the twenty-second of Our Pontificate." Takes your breath away. You could almost feel the updraft of the Holy Ghost skimming across your cheek.

A Scene from Raphael

Against that scene heavy with the Church's richness, it might have been easy to miss the significance of another. This one was almost hidden, like the exchange of some cherished secret. As the new Archbishop crossed the Fifth Avenue threshold of his new cathedral, he stopped. The Vicar General approached, showed Archbishop Egan a large crucifix, and then pressed it to the lips of the Archbishop, who kissed the crucified feet of the Savior. Immediately after that act of homage, the Vicar General handed the Archbishop the *aspergillum*, and he sprinkled the entrance of the cavernous Gothic cathedral with the soft rain of Holy Water.

Why mention these nearly hidden gestures? Because, as with all the signs in the Church's ritual arsenal, they are like golden darts tipped in fire. They illuminate our life's darkness. The Archbishop's veneration of the crucifix signifies his submission to the reign of Christ. Even in the midst of this dazzling ceremony – the transferal of vast, heavenly authority – every man is finally the same: a beggar naked in his sins before the Cross, utterly dependent on the mercy of Christ. The Holy Water? Echoes of our Baptism and all the sacraments to which we cling that we might not perish. Let it be clear, only those sacraments set us safely in the wounds of Our Savior.

One detail about this narthex ritual shouldn't be overlooked – it is no longer performed. Most bishops over the past few decades have elected to ignore it. Some kind of gracious nod to modernity. Archbishop Egan did not. A Catholic would be remiss to overlook this gesture. Even if he had, he couldn't possibly have overlooked some other things. Like the Archbishop's repeated refrain about increasing priestly vocations. To stress vocations is to emphasize the centrality of the priest in the life of the Catholic. It is to paint the supernatural role of the Church in thick, bold letters followed by an exclamation point.

That is remarkable – for *these* times. Just beneath the actual text is the unspoken subtext: the priest is essential to the Church – not the mushrooming faux lay ministries. The priest saves the world by saving souls – not parroting political agendas. Man is truly sated by the priest feeding him the Bread of Angels – not the world's bread that leaves him hungry tomorrow. That's quite a dose of clarity for Catholics wandering in the wilderness of half-truths and "have-a-nice-day" liturgies. No wonder Peter's successor wrote in his letter to Archbishop Egan: "You never disappointed the hope or expectation of Mother Church... [So] we naturally and spontaneously choose you... to fill the vacant see of New York."

Everything in that triumphant Mass of installation routed the Left—leaving not a single doubt about Archbishop Egan's path. His entire sermon was framed by the story of the Roman martyrs St. John and St. Paul who died for the Holy Faith exclaiming, "Our lives are in the service of the emperor. But our souls belong to God. Gladly would we die rather than forsake the truth of Our Lord and Savior." Then like a smithy forging a strong chain with the pounding of his hammer on the anvil, the Archbishop declared his "uncompromising acceptance of all that the Lord has revealed. This is our foundation. Our strength is grounded in our faith." Then again: "[We must] be relentlessly committed to announcing the Gospel completely, clearly and courageously." Each of those phrases exploded in St. Patrick's like thunderclaps. Lest he leave the slightest question in anyone's mind, he concluded, "We kneel before the Son of God whom we adore, we creatures whom He redeemed. There can be no hesitation, no compromise." Them's fighting words. Move over, St. Athanasius.

Some months have already passed since that momentous day at St. Patrick's Cathedral and the Church is still up to her neck in problems. No surprise. Only a fool ever thought that Archbishop Egan would solve them overnight. Or even by the time he retires. But just having someone here who speaks like that makes the Continuing War easier to fight. He might not be an angel, but he's on their side. For these days, that's a lot.

MILLSTONES GALORE

Dreadful as it is, words cry out to be spoken about the hemorrhaging sexual misconduct among priests. Priests who struggle to be good find this subject nauseating. Even when the facts are true and exposed to the public, we demure comment. Words, even analytic ones, seem only to add infection to an already oozing wound. Moreover, to good Catholics mere passing comment seems to violate the sacred Pauline injunction, "But immorality and every uncleanness or covetousness, let it not even be named among you" (Eph 5:4).

All of that being said, the horror is so deep and touches so many, it demands jeremiads. It is raw corruption of a child's innocence whose "angels gaze upon the face of God." It is committed by a priest and therefore the highest blasphemy that could be perpetrated against the Divinity. It is a spastic laceration of the face of Christ by the consecrated hands of *alter Christus* (another Christ). It is willful and shocking embrace of the frightening condemnation of Christ, "But he that shall scandalize one of these little ones that believe in me, it were better for him that a millstone be hanged about his neck, and that he should be drowned in the depth of the sea" (Mt 18:6). The sin is unworthy to even cry out to heaven for vengeance. It is not murder; it is worse. Not genocide; it is *far* worse. Those atrocities destroy only bodies and races, this one sucks out the soul of its victims. It leaves them to a life of near suffocation, like some cruel circle in Dante's Hell. Living men with nearly dead souls gasping for, but never quite able to breathe, the air of God. It is horror compounded by disgrace enveloped in shame.

But speak we must, if for nothing than to have our revulsion on record. As we speak, other things must be noted for the record. Let it be said that priestly misconduct does not appear in a vacuum. A congenial atmosphere must be actively or passively cultivated for such things to proper. Those conditions became fertile with the collapse of the traditional disciplines that surrounded the Priesthood.

No more savvy analysis of human nature exists than the Roman Church. Since her wisdom is Revelation fused deftly with the *philosophia perrenis*, it is quite perfect. That wisdom was especially brought to bear upon the training of priests. Holy Church knows Man; his darkness, his lights, his inclinations, his potencies, and his aspirations. Seminary time was a template where strengths could be perfected and weaknesses shaved away. This constituted a formational ensemble unparalleled in the West. Yes, it was not perfect. No attempt of man here on earth can be. But given the complexity of man and the high ideals to which Holy Church calls her priests, it was nearly perfect. It furnished the priest with two things: an arsenal of discipline which would tame whatever needed training and the reason for it: sacerdotal identification with Christ Crucified. No sacrifice too great for Him. It never pretended to create perfect priests, only priests who knew they ought to *strive* to be perfect.

All of this collapsed nearly overnight. Between 1965 and 1970 the majority of Bishops thought it a divine mandate to dismantle brick by brick the classical seminary structure. Many invoked the Second Vatican Council, not realizing that it was a vain invocation. Not a sentence of *Optatam Totius*[2] furnished warrant for anything but the slightest refinement and re-emphasis.

More tragic still was their shift in thinking about man. The classical seminary model correctly saw man as Poor Sinner; the bishops' new model was man as Promethean Dreamer. The former engaged man in daily battle against the *fons concupiscentiae*, the latter invited man to the celebration of the Imperial Self. Consequences of this shift are seen in the moral ruins about us. Even priests shaped by the classical system eagerly jettisoned the reliable disciplines which guaranteed fidelity to Christ, and stepped onto the new terrain of the Emancipated Self which insured fidelity only to me.

Many bishops recast the whole moral index: the hero's mantle was bestowed upon priests felled by vice, which was now reconfigured as a fruitful resolution on the way to Authenticity. While punishments for priests did not entirely disappear, they became reserved for those clerics who persisted in the dated thinking of the Old Church.

---

[2] *Declaration on the Formation of Priests*, October 28, 1965.

This brief historical context aids in understanding things otherwise incomprehensible. Take the remark of a prominent Ordinary of a major Northeastern diocese made shortly after the Boston disclosures. When asked how Bishops could allow this clerical misconduct to go unpunished, he defensively snapped, "Bishops are not policemen; they are shepherds." Is that so? Did it perhaps escape His Excellency's attention that shepherds *also* police, lest any harm come to the sheep? Why would the Bishop chafe at the suggestion of performing a task executed so ably by his predecessors? Could it be that his impatience at policing comes from a skittishness about an unblurred gasp of right and wrong? Perhaps he has become too cozy with the attenuations of moral new-think. A Bishop is *alter Christus*, after the true Christ Who rebuked as robustly as He loved. It was this episcopal confusion that invited John O'Sullivan's trenchant inditement:

> Christ Himself would have spoken far more harshly to John Geoghan and the other priests who destroyed the innocence of those in their care. Yet in speaking harshly He would have loved them more. For He might have turned them away from the sins that corrupted their souls and attacked the bodies of children in their charge. Geoghan can only hope to find in prison the stern but loving Christ whom he evaded all too easily in the Boston Archdiocese.[3]

The preposterous remark of the Bishop shall be preserved alongside the equally fatuous, "It all depends upon what you think the meaning of 'is' is." Both remarks shamelessly try to defend the indefensible. It is such a scandal that Catholics will now rank Bishops alongside an impeached president when they choose whom it is they will believe.

Charles Péguy remarked over a century ago, "We shall never know how many acts of cowardice have been motivated by the fear of seeming not sufficiently progressive." Ah, Mr. Peguy, yes, we will. What we never wanted to know was that the cowards would be Bishops.

---

[3] *National Review Online*, January 31, 2002.

(BAD) BUSINESS AS USUAL

Just when you thought it was safe to begin trusting the Bishops, Dallas 2002 came along. This was the alleged moment when the Bishops would address the tidal wave of scandals threatening to drown them. The most jaded Catholic observers thought that this was The Moment. Perhaps now the deep sadness of the past thirty-five years would be over. A thirty-five years when most of the bishops had dutifully genuflected to the zeitgeist, treating any other viewpoint (including pro-Papal ones) as recidivist. It was seemingly endless three decades when they tragically squandered their dignity and credibility and zealously fed the bottomless appetite of a leftist Leviathan which now devours them.

Alas, The Moment's great promise died. With all the obtuseness of a Leo X refusing to face Fr. Martin Luther, they too marched backward. We all watched incredulously when we saw whom they had selected to tutor them on staying the crisis. None other than R. Scott Appleby of Notre Dame and Margaret O'Brien Steinfels of *Commonweal*. Both credentialed brahmans of leftist Catholicism. Each of their institutions have been roaring engines of the theological dissent that barked the marching orders for the American Episcopacy. They might as well have invited Bill Clinton to lecture them on character. If they wanted lay input, why did they lean on laymen whose viewpoints have created the crisis? Couldn't at least one of the laymen have a reputation for orthodoxy? Ralph McInerny? Charles Rice? Deal Hudson? James Hitchcock? Paul Likoudis?

No, The Moment came and went. And any who still held on to the possibility of The Moment had their hope dashed when Bishop Bruskewitz spoke. He respectfully asked the Bishops to consider the role theological dissent or clerical homosexuality might have had in the crisis. The Bishops promptly voted the proposal down. Of course, these are the Bishops whose name is Dialogue. You know, every viewpoint bears a hearing etc., etc. Their Excellencies ought to be careful, lest it appear that all along they embraced a double standard. With dissenters, yes. With the orthodox, no. Tsk, tsk.

(Bad) Business as Usual 77

We cannot overlook the good things about Dallas 2002. Oh, not the things that the Bishops did, but what happened on account of what the Bishops did not do. No one should be fooled by the diversionary tactics of The Charter for the Protection of Children and Young People or the much-touted Office for Child and Youth Protection under the leadership of Governor Frank Keating. These measures are carefully constructed to quell the media howling and adroitly move the scandal off center stage. Like putting a Liz Taylor mask over the Wolf Man. It is truly business as usual. A razzle-dazzle PR solution where there should be a rigorous top-to-bottom reassertion of earthshaking orthodoxy. This is not the time for slick Madison Avenue posturing but for the severe glance of St. Pio of Pietrelcina. The Bishops should have adopted a policy of zero tolerance for committees and action items, status quo and old buddy network, winking at dissent and stonewalling the Vatican. They should have ordered the Catechism of the Catholic Church for every Catholic classroom and require instant conformity to *Ex Corde Ecclesiae* in every Catholic college. Those things would have gutted the crisis, not zero tolerance a la Dallas 2002.

But the good news. That took place after the Dallas conference. When all the cameramen went home and the boom mikes were shut off, a group of Catholics convened with Bishop Bruskewitz as their principal speaker. Bruskewitz there performed a memorable and historic act: he dared to lift his voice against his brother bishops. With the steeliness of Churchill he declared the men of Dallas 2002 to be, "this hapless bench of Bishops." Only a spare five words, you say. But a mere five words that history will translate as, *Charge!* And history will show that other brother bishops followed.

One more piece of good news. It is Michael Novak. This savage crisis seems to be changing his neo-conservatism into a paleo one. This brilliant writer's erstwhile perfectly manicured sentences of balance and calm seem to have given way to loaded pistols of indignation. As with so many faithful Catholics, he is fed up with making excuses for bishops who have acted (or not acted) inexcusably. Novak may be a trumpet for many fence-sitting orthodox Catholics. Catholics who for too long have believed the battle against dissent slightly indelicate or vocal complains about bishops *déclassé* (or, even worse, impious). How can they listen to the words of the new Novak-as-he-Man and not reconsider:

Everything the bishops did in Dallas showed how fearful they still are of being thought conservative. That is why they refuse even to touch the one issue that John Paul II had told them is central: fidelity to the whole Catholic teaching on married love and sexuality.

That would have meant antagonizing the secular, liberal press. That would have meant preaching Catholic doctrine straight. The bishops didn't want to touch that task.

They refused by voice vote a motion to study the role of dissent in the present scandalous developments. They were afraid to probe that deep, neuralgic nerve.

Even the choice of two liberals to speak of Catholic laywomen and men displayed the bishops' remarkable fear of being thought conservative. In that respect, the bishops still don't get it.

The bishops need to understand that what we Catholics love and respect is the Catholic Faith, not them. If they lack courage to speak up for the Faith, what are they good for except to be thrown out and trodden upon, salt without savor?

I don't know about you, but I hear more and more people saying that they should throw out the whole bench and get a new team. A few exceptions aside, this one doesn't seem to be completely serious.

But my advice is to give them a little bit more time. And pray that one or two dead leaders among them will step forward for the good of the Church. Enough of Avignon. It's time to take the Church back to Rome.[4]

Well, ladies and gentlemen, it seems the time has come to put on your gloves. Our bishops may not want a war but we are giving them one anyway.

CHARGE!

---

[4] *National Review Online*, June 18, 2002.

THE REMARKABLE PAPACY OF POPE BENEDICT XVI

Entering the conclave on Sunday evening, every Catholic had his papal wish list, especially priests. For priests of my disposition there was only one cardinal who stood far above all the rest: Joseph Cardinal Ratzinger. As obvious as was his superiority above the rest, so was our certainty that he was absolutely unelectable.

So many reasons were stacked against him. Since 1981 he had ruled the Holy Office (the Sacred Congregation for the Doctrine of the Faith), the watchdog for the purity of Catholic doctrine. This successor department to the Office of the Holy Inquisition is deputed to cast a roaming universal eye over the correct teaching or writing of the Catholic Faith. Where it finds deviation, it conducts inquiry, solicits retraction, and exacts complete fidelity. In the face of the recalcitrant, the Holy Office escalates its response proportionate to the gravity of the error or the obduracy of the theologian: warning, condemnation, withdrawal of license to teach, and, *in extremis*, excommunication.

The Holy Office is not anonymous; it has a face. For twenty-four years the face was that of Joseph Cardinal Ratzinger. Need we look further for un-electability? Discharge of these duties was not exactly endearing.

The eminent German cardinal of stratospheric intellect was as intrepid as any NYPD detective. During his prefecture he silenced dozens of theologians who threatened the integrity of the Faith. Some of them were famous, Hans Kung, Charles Curran, Jeanne Gramick, Ernesto Cardenal, and Jacques Dupuis. Some Catholics of a certain mind deemed this stifling and backward. Right-minded Catholics saw it as the necessary corollary of charity: the protection of the innocent from the rapacious. Cardinal Ratzinger was simply heeding the warning of his Divine Master: "But he that shall scandalize one of these little ones that believe in me, it would be better for him that a millstone should be hanged about his neck and that he should be drowned in the depth of the sea" (Mt 18:6).

Though this could suffice it to secure his un-electability, still other issues contributed. Take his literary oeuvre. Joseph Cardinal Ratzinger published an average of a major theological volume every two years over the time of this prefecture. Each was a magisterial work of erudition and originality. For instance, in *Salt of the Earth* and *The Ratzinger Report*, he clarified his intellectual journey from progressive leftist in the early '60s to unflappable defender of the Faith. *The Spirit of the Liturgy* and a *New Song for the Lord* were groundbreaking studies in the sacred liturgy. These works boldly stepped beyond the stale platitudes of a disingenuous post-conciliar liturgical paradigm. Within exciting flights of theological and philosophical brilliance, Cardinal Ratzinger introduced a fresh blueprint resurrecting the bright promise of the Conciliar Fathers as well as re-infusing into liturgical studies a new purposefulness rooted in the stunning beauty of the Transcendent. With the publication of *God in the World*, the now Benedict XVI forthrightly diagnosed the mendacity of secularism and its escape from God. He direly warned of an enveloping darkness if men did not return to Christ and His Holy Church.

With each new book dissidents howled like men suffering boiling acid over their skin. This was the paper trail *par excellence*. It had to doom any hope of the papacy. Or so we thought.

The *coup de grâce* was to come on April the 18th. Cardinal Ratzinger, as Dean of the College of Cardinals, offered the Mass of the Holy Spirit and preached. The sermon was like fire from heaven. An earnest candidate for the throne of St. Peter would have preached a carefully moderate sermon.

Cognizant of his audience, the exquisitely censorious multitude of 115 cardinal electors, he would have fashioned a sermon of proper flatness saying right things while saying nothing. Not Cardinal Ratzinger. He preached with the theological elegance of St. Athanasius and the tart urgency of Savonarola. He sharply warned the assembled Princes of the Roman church that "a dictatorship of relativism" threatened Western culture and Christ's Church itself. Unless the Church recollected its strength and moved forcefully with the ammunition of the *depositum fidei*, grim consequences would follow.

Good gracious! Between the lines of that invective one could hear, *don't elect me!* Clarity such as Ratzinger's is almost unknown amongst the Church's scarlet-clad Princes. Usually, their preference is non-imputable ambiguity. No one gets blamed; nothing gets done.

As the doors of the Sistine Chapel closed majestically on Monday afternoon, we had one certainty: Ratzinger would *not* be our Pope.

With speed known only one other time in 100 years, the world heard the ancient announcement, *habemus papam!* Cardinal Ratzinger emerged onto the balcony of St. Peter's Basilica as Pope Benedict XVI.

All of us could almost hear the words of Christ after He had stilled the storm on the Sea of Galilee, *O ye of little Faith.*

On April 24, 2005 the new Pope begged: "My dear friends – at this moment I can only say: pray for me, that I may learn to love the Lord more and more. Pray for me, that I may learn to love His flock more and more – in other words, you, the holy Church, each one of you and all of you together. Pray for me, that I may not flee for fear of the wolves." Only a week or so before, with Pope John Paul II dying, Cardinal Ratzinger performed the traditional papal Way of the Cross in the Roman Coliseum. There, at the Third Fall, he exclaimed, "How much filth is there in the church, and even among those in the priesthood, who ought to belong entirely to Him." He knew with painful clarity that he would now be fighting against the Gates of Hell.

How did this happen? This priest and his friends have asked this of ourselves hundreds of times since that Tuesday afternoon.

Only on our knees, staring at the crucifix, did we realize how.

Our new Pope wasted no time. Barely ten days into his young papacy and already he had cast the first shot across the bow of Peter's Barque. From Rome, it reached far across the Atlantic and into the editorial offices of *America* magazine. Benedict XVI's target was that magazine's editor, the Jesuit, Father Thomas Reese. In the coarser vernacular of battle, we might say Benedict's shot took Father Thomas Reese out. In the more genteel vocabulary of the Church, he was silenced. In any language Father Reese S.J. was removed as editor. The old saying comes to mind: The wheels of Rome grind slowly, but grind they do.

So what? What indeed! *America* magazine is one of the oldest and most influential Catholic journals in this country. Founded by the Jesuits at the beginning of the last century, it was the gold standard of Catholic writing. For decades it collected the blue-ribbon Catholic intellectuals of its day into its formidable arsenal. When *America* spoke, everyone listened – Catholic and non-Catholic. In its daring and intellectual muscularity, it very much reflected the spirit of the order which founded it.

The Society of Jesus had its origin in the warrior heart of St. Ignatius Loyola in the sixteenth century. This former soldier of fortune turned his heart to Christ during a long convalescence following one of his military campaigns. After many months in solitary retreat he decided to found a religious order. While there was nothing new in that, there was something entirely new in Ignatius's Society.

This Basque saint saw it as a military garrison in the service of Christ the King: Priests at prayer for the sake of war. War against the enemies of the Church taking orders from His very own Vicar on earth, the Supreme Pontiff. Ignatius envisioned this new Order as an elite corps of the Marines. Eager to fight in any part of the far-flung empire of the Church in perfect obedience to Christ's Vicar. In fact, Ignatius chose as the name of this revolutionary new order the Company of Jesus – leaving no doubt as to how they saw themselves. While that name was finally changed by Pope Paul III in 1540 to the Society of Jesus as the official recognition by the Church, their spirit did not. Warriors were how they were conceived, and warriors they remained. To further deepen their high purpose, St. Ignatius added a fourth vow to the traditional three of poverty, chastity, and obedience. That fourth was absolute fidelity to the Pope. As Ignatius expressed it, "If the Roman pontiff tells me that this is black, though with my eyes I see it to be white, I will say that it is black." In another place he taught, "We shall obey the Roman Pontiff like corpses." A bit of the Spanish extravagance there. Extravagance or not, Jesuits lived that obedience to the tee.

The whole sixteenth century church gasped in amazement at this radical new family in their midst. Their Parris Island training of soul and intellect was set down by the founder in a classic work (second only to the *Imitation of Christ*), the *Spiritual Exercises*. This was the Society's war manual – against Satan and his pomps. So profound was the saint's insights into the human soul and its struggles that the Church embraced it as her own. If men asked how to become a saint, Holy Church routinely handed them the *Spiritual Exercises*. Through the crucible of the Exercises combined with the unique spirit of Ignatius, these ordinary priests became giants. They bestrode every continent across the globe in search of souls for God. In their wake they transformed education, politics, science, art, music, and architecture. Without exaggeration, the world was not the same after the Jesuits. And for that the world was grateful.

Four hundred years later, this Society of Jesus has virtually disappeared. Oh yes, there are still Jesuits and Jesuit universities, but there are very few Jesuits of the spirit of St. Ignatius Loyola. They are imposters at best. They have mutated into an epicene wing of the political Left, with nary a shred of the supernatural spirit that once was their glory. For centuries they were the Church's Praetorian Guard, and now they are her Fifth Column.

For the past forty years *America* magazine has become the principal agent in that Fifth Column. Its chic attacks upon the teachings of the Church reached new sophistication under the urbane editorship of Father Thomas Reese. Week after week he proffered Catholic dissent under the rubric of intellectual inquiry, all the while saying between the lines that a new Catholic maturity allowed the faithful to take their pick.

Benedict XVI would have none of it. This Pope, who promised us to be "The rock upon which all could stand safely," has already made the Church in America slightly safer by the expulsion of Father Reese from *America*. I suspect that *a la carte* Catholicism is not in the plans of the Holy Spirit.

This might only be a small beginning, but every long journey begins with a small first step.

CARDINAL CUPICH'S UNCERTAIN TRUMPET

Ghosts from the 1970s were stirring at Catholic University in Washington, D.C., this past November – at the Catholic Theological Union, to be exact. His Eminence Blase Cardinal Cupich, Archbishop of Chicago, was the guest speaker, and his speech was steeped in some of the most beloved argot of that bygone era. It seemed to be an exercise in superannuated enthusiasms, all of the relevant to theologians of a certain age but risible to the millennial audiences of today. This new generation seeks a robust and dynamic existential Catholicism. Instead, what they heard was a hoary, hallucinatory Catholicism long relegated to the landfills of toxic theological experiments. Is this too harsh? Judge for yourself.

The good cardinal began his Murnion Lecture, titled "Dialogue in the Key of Pope Francis" (November 2, 2017), by quoting the Holy Father: "The flock...has an instinctive ability to discern the new ways that the Lord is revealing to the Church." Francis is, Cupich said, "trying to figure out where the Lord is taking us," and the growing disquiet in the life of the Church today "is due to the unfamiliarity with the method of discernment that Pope Francis often uses." Cupich then let forth with a stunning volley of provocative invitations: "It is our job," he said, "to take up that discernment," and that "takes time. It involves discipline. Most importantly, it requires that we be prepared to let go of cherished beliefs and long-held biases."

Hmm. What could His Eminence have meant? The most cherished beliefs of Catholics usually mean the articles of the Creed and the moral law. Cardinal Cupich could not possibly have been referring to these, right? Then what? The uncertainty was unsettling.

And what of long-held biases? Headstrong secularists deploy this epithet against the Church's teachings, particularly those concerning marriage and the family. What for secularists is bias, is for Catholics fidelity to God – fidelity not only to divine revelation but to the revelations of reason available to all men.

Take any man on the street. He is a metaphysician, whether he knows it or not. Why? Because he believes his eyes. He sees the anatomy of a man and a woman and instantly understands the moral law—not exactly, and not at once. But because he believes his eyes, those eyes bring his intellect to the truth that men and women are naturally what they are physically. Wittingly or not, the ordinary fellow in the street arrives at the ontological truth of man's nature. Calling it anything other than what his eyes see is simply unnatural. It is this commonsense conclusion that effete cultural elites call bias. Surely, that's not what the good cardinal meant.

Just because faithful Catholics battle against this type of unnaturalness doesn't make them haters. Hating the disease never means hating the patient. In fact, the most notable act of love is to comfort the afflicted by helping to cure his disease. Upholding traditional Catholic teaching doesn't make Catholics villains but heroes. The great Thomist Fr. Reginald Garrigou-Lagrange expressed this eloquently when he wrote, "The Church is intolerant in principle because she believes; she is tolerant in practice because she loves. The enemies of the Church are tolerant in principle because they do not believe; they are intolerant in practice because they do not love." No one understands this more than the good cardinal, yet his words have justifiably caused dissonance.

There was more in Cardinal Cupich's address that was perplexing. "Catholics must have a change of heart if dialogue is to be successful and common ground is to be found," he asserted. Catholics "must come to an understanding that Jesus Christ is always doing something new." So not true. Our Lord proclaims, "Behold, I make all things new" (Rev 21:15). Few words of Christ are more comforting. But make no mistake: His Church has consistently understood this easily malleable phrase in one way. The newness of Christ's divine grace, pouring forth from His wounds on Cavalry. Washed in His precious blood, we are made new. This is wondrous. The newness is made ever more evident as we enter deeper into the truth of Christ, who is "the same yesterday, today, and tomorrow." In the economy of salvation, we are called to change every day, to be converted, to become new, so we may become more like Him who is unchangeable. "O beauty ever ancient, ever new," in St. Augustine's memorable words. Indeed, it was St. Augustine who expressed the traditional reading of the verse: "Rid yourself of what is old and worn out, for you know a new song. A new man, a new covenant; a new song. This new song does not belong to the old man. Only the new man learns it; the man restores from the fallen condition through the grace of God... To it all our love now aspires and sings a new song."

Similarly, Christ's Church: She changes so she may ever remain the same. Through the centuries, the Church has rightly been wary of those who are eager to translate Our Lord's summons to newness as permitting novelty. Bringing novelty into the Church is usually an attempt to make the faith more congenial to the age and less demanding of believers. But the Savior's mandate is the exact opposite: The times change, not the Church. Clearly, a prince of the Church ought to realize that an imprecise use of the phrase making all things new subjects it to the perils of protean manipulations. Firm clarity is demanded. But Cupich's address lacked that firmness, leaving his intentions unclear.

His Eminence's language then became even more tendentious. "We are not a Church of preservation, but rather a Church of proclamation," he said. "To achieve this end, we must be open to significant, if not revolutionary changes." The cardinal seems to want to construct a false dichotomy between preservation and proclamation. But there is none. If the Church has not preserved, what is it that she has to proclaim? Isn't preserving what St. Paul meant when he wrote, "I delivered unto you first of all that which I also *received*" (1 Cor 15:3), and "O Timothy, guard what has been *entrusted* to you" (1 Tim 6:20)?

Moreover, Cupich continued, "Discerning dialogue will be key to unburdening ourselves from the temptation of settling for the ways things are, the familiar, the comfortable way, because it offers the hope that God is doing something new in our time." The elasticity of the term *something new in our time* is concerning. Every age thinks of itself as the best, looking down its nose at times past. This is the bumptious vanity of which C. S. Lewis warned when he cautioned against chronological snobbery. Shiny new things are the invariable prelude to bitter old catastrophes. St. Paul is unmistakable in his suspicion of the present times: "Be not conformed to this world: but be ye transformed by the renewing of your mind, that ye may prove what is that good, and acceptable, and perfect, will of God" (Rom 12:2).

But if that conformity is not to an eternally preserved Truth proclaimed by Mother Church, to what does it tend? Clearly, the Church shapes the applications of her irreformable teachings to the exigencies of the age. But she never reshapes her teachings to its tastes. Is this not what Our Lord meant when He said, "Every scribe which is instructed unto the kingdom of Heaven is like unto a man that is a householder, which bringeth forth out his treasures things new and old" (Mt 12:52)? Cardinal Cupich's words run the grave risk of having the proclamation depends only on the whim of an age. In fact, this has been the regnant interpretation of those who abandon the hermeneutics of continuity. Such a reading has always brought Holy Church to the edge of a cliff.

Then there is Cupich's use of the word revolution. For men of all ages, particularly men living in the shadow of Marx's enormities, the word suggests chaos, disequilibrium, unsteadiness. It is a word conspicuously absent from the conventional theological conversations of the Church—and for good reason. Revolution is an overturning of the present order; it is dreadful in any society. But it is impossible in the perfect society of the Holy Catholic Church. Overturning the sacred order of the Church Christ Himself constituted is nothing less than an overturning of Christ Himself: "Heaven and earth shall pass away, but my words shall not pass away" (Mt 24:35).

Disquieting too these words of Cardinal Cupich: "We must continue to develop the spiritual and other resources needed... to be leaders in a synodal Church that is reimagining itself." These words would make many a Catholic scratch his head. A synodal Church? Of course, the cardinal was referring to the ancient tradition of each bishop ruling sovereignly in his own diocese. But a bishop's sovereignty depends on his fidelity to the unity of the Church, guaranteed by union with the Vicar of Christ, who guards and defends Tradition. *Cum Petrus, sub Petrus* (with Peter, under Peter). But Cupich's rendering could easily be construed as meaning something different. It could easily be taken to mean that local Churches should be left to themselves, each at liberty to alter Tradition according to standards entirely their own. This kind of synodality quickly devolves into classic Protestantism.

Against this parlous interpretation, the esteemed Fr. Thomas Weinandy, O. F. M. Cap., in 2018 took issue. The former head of the U. S. Bishop's Committee on Doctrine and a member of the International Theological Commission, wrote in his now-famous letter to Pope Francis, "Encouraging a form of "synodality" that allows and promotes various doctrinal and moral options within the Church can only lead to more theological and pastoral confusion. Such synodality is unwise and, in practice, works against collegial unity among bishops." The Church's woeful experience with false interpretations of inculturation attests to this. When local custom is permitted to refashion Catholic teaching, Catholicism slowly withers.

Cardinal Cupich might also want to reconsider his generous use of the word reimagining. His intentions are no doubt benign, but the word is the routine vernacular of iconoclasts. It suggests openness to horizons entirely untethered to the normative or natural.

We live in days where the ground is constantly shifting beneath us. Every certitude is questioned, and metaphysical shelters are few, most having long been blown away by the hostile winds of secularism. The only refuge is the Rock of the Holy Catholic Church. Uncertain trumpets like Cupich's will not do.

ARCHBISHOP VIGANÒ'S LETTER: NOW WHAT?[5]

Beloved, do not be startled at the trial by fire that is taking place among you, as though something strange were happening to you.
1 Peter 4:12

Well, what now? Where do we go from here? It is obtuse of any priest or prelate not to speak of the dark crisis enveloping the Church. Even more obtuse to airbrush its severity, or call it a rabbit-hole as did one of the Church's Princes. The crisis metastasized a week ago with the publication of the history-making letter of the esteemed Papal Nuncio and former Governor of the Vatican State, Archbishop Carlo Maria Viganò.

Similarly, only the most indifferent Catholic cannot be deeply concerned. Of course, there will be those "spiritual" Catholics who remain above this fray, tsk-tsking at those febrile Catholics who worry endlessly of such things. Then there are those besotted Catholics soaked in the spirit of Vatican II, who find that all this talk of sexual inappropriateness a distraction from the burning issues of the environment and migrants (again, a remark by one of the Church's Princes.) Such a breathtakingly shocking statement merely confirms Chesterton's chilling, albeit prescient, warning, "The great march of destruction will go on. Everything will be denied... Fires will be kindled to testify that two and two make four. Swords will be drawn to prove that leaves are green in summer."

But, where do we go from here? To the only place we can go—to Christ and His Holy Church. We take refuge in her unchanging teachings, while stubbornly ignoring those teachers who lobby for changing the eternal Word for words that express better ideas. After all, a half century of that fatal tradeoff has produced the fertile ground for this Crisis to blossom, like a mushroom cloud.

---

[5] The letter in question is the testimonial of August 2018 on the complicity of the pope and other Vatican officials in the rehabilitation and protection of Theodore McCarrick.

Isn't it odd that some of the highest authorities in the Church have chosen to call Catholics utterly faithful to Christ's permanent truth, ideologized. Crisis, indeed.

For us ordinary Catholics, five jeweled divine Catholic truths will be our manna in this desert.

1. Our Faith is in Christ, not in priests or bishops, or even popes. As faithful Catholics we depend upon those priests for the grace of the Sacraments. Without the Pope, whom St. Catherine of Sienna teaches holds the Key of the Blood, we are bereft of the comforts of Christ. But our Faith does not rest on them. Our Lord guides us: "The scribes and the Pharisees sit in Moses's seat: All therefore whatsoever they bid you observe, that observe and do; but do not ye after their works; for they say and do not" (Mt 23:1-3). It is a luxury to have holy priests and bishops. Yet sometimes it pleases God to withdraw that luxury. He has, many times in the course of the Church's history. This is one of those times.

2. We must cease staring at the crisis. Staring at it injures the soul. Not that Catholics should retreat into a childish and pietistic see-no-evil posture. That is neither mature or Catholic. But they should avoid an obsessive curiosity about the details of this grotesque plague. Catholics should remain informed, judicious and intelligent as they pursue the facts. Then, calmly make their judgments. Unafraid. But dwelling upon this Crisis leaves a Catholic exposed to the kind of penalty suffered by Sarah, Lot's wife. As they fled from the destruction of Sodom and Gomorrah, God commanded that they not look back. Sarah did, and she turned to salt. Beware.

3. We are obliged to come to the assistance of our Holy Church. There are clearly three ways to support her. First, prayer and penance. The second form of assistance, prayer and penance. But there is a third way: prayer and penance. Aside from this, many of us are called by God to do more. Our Lord expects some of us, maybe more than some, to act and act dramatically. That will depend upon one's obligations to state in life. Those acts should be courageous, prudent, measured, smart and respectful. If Our Lord is indeed summoning a Catholic to such an apostolic labor, shirking it would be a betrayal.

4. We serve as the humble servants of God's pleasure. But that Divine pleasure depends upon His timetable, not ours. There is not a single Catholic who does not want this Crisis to be settled

tomorrow. Why not? The wounds to Mother Church are unbearable. But this may not be God's pleasure. His wise Design may have it differently. So we wait upon His pleasure, though it may not be ours. This commits us to a heroic form of patience, a virtue not foreign to faithful Catholics. T. S. Eliot gives this Catholic mandate poetic beauty in Burnt Norton: "For us there is only the trying/ the rest is not our business." However, we are not called to a dour endurance, but a joyous expectation. Joy is a fruit of the Holy Spirit—therefore it is our birthright. It is rooted in an absolute certainty that Mother Church is headed toward a new springtime of beauty and holiness. But when? That's not our business.

5. We must consider ourselves privileged. From all eternity God willed that you and I be present at this crushing moment in the life of His Church. Our thrice Holy God foresaw that it would only be the likes of you and me who would best serve the Church, at this time and in this circumstance. Such a thought is incomprehensible. Me? But nothing happens by accident. All is ordained by God's Providence. In that case, we are indeed privileged. To recognize that God brought us to this time, precisely you and me, should make us eager to accomplish great things for His Church. Overlooking this privilege would not only be ingratitude, but a sin.

In *A Tale of Two Cities*, Charles Dickens wrote the memorable first sentence, "It was the best of times; it was the worst of times." For Catholics, this is the worst of times. Few moments in two thousand years has such ugly corruption reached to the commanding heights of the Church. But, at the same time, it is the best of times. Nothing could be better than the God given opportunity to show Him heroic fidelity. To be present, as we watch Our Lord show us what He meant when he proclaimed, "Behold I make all things new."

ARCHBISHOP CORDILEONE VS. SISTERS OF PERPETUAL INDULGENCE

Pentecostal fire still burns brightly in San Francisco. It blazes from the episcopal throne of Archbishop Cordileone, in his 2023 exceptional editorial in the *Wall Street Journal*. He trumpets a sanguine defense of the Church, so unusual for his kind. But it is not the first time he has broken ranks with the greater number of his episcopal confreres (the Pelosi affair comes to mind).

Not to put too fine a point on it, but with studied prudence and a marked fidelity to the duty of a Successor to the Apostles he has governed the See of San Francisco with the steadiness of St. Cyprian or St. Denis. With the Apostolic persistence of St. Athanasius, the meticulous scholarship of Aquinas, and the sonority of Bossuet he boldly inserts the voice of Mother Church into the ears of a diseased secularism.

In that bracing editorial for the *Wall Street Journal*, he calmly called to task the Los Angeles Dodgers' decision to give a community hero award to the Sisters of Perpetual Indulgence, who are, in the Archbishop's words, "a group that perversely dresses up as nuns while encouraging lewd and sacrilegious behavior." Cordileone names this appalling gesture for what it is: "The latest example of mainstreaming derision of the Catholic Faith."

These are the kinds of episcopal words that make Catholic hearts race. His temperate, albeit firm, tone sunders the decades-long inertia that seems to have entrapped much of Catholic officialdom. Cordileone's words are like Kafka's axe, when the existentialist novelist wrote in another context, "The purpose of the novel is to take an axe to the frozen sea inside us." Cordileone wields not the novel's axe but the Church's.

San Francisco's archbishop precedes those words by reciting a long list of anti-Catholic bigotry in America's past, among them:

- In 1834, a frenzied mob attacked and burned to the ground a convent of Ursuline nuns outside of Boston. The act was the culmination of years of anti-Catholic preaching and

Archbishop Cordileone vs. Sisters of Perpetual Indulgence

aggression toward the Church's property. None of the firemen present intervened, and some reportedly joined the riot.
- Later that century, the Know Nothing party emerged to suppress the rights of German and Irish Catholic immigrants, fearful of a Catholic conspiracy to take over the country.
- Not long after that, the Ku Klux Klan began to terrorize black Americans, Catholics, and Jews. In 1921, an enraged Klansman fatally shot Fr. James Coyle after the priest celebrated the wedding of the gunman's Catholic-convert daughter to a Puerto Rican man. The killer was acquitted at trial by a Klan-filled jury at a trial presided over by a Klansman judge.

The archbishop then reminds his audience that the United States Conference of Catholic Bishops reports that "at least 260 incidents" – attacks on Church property – "have occurred across 43 states and the District of Columbia since May 2020." He continues,

> Catholics in the San Francisco area have weathered our share of attacks in October 2020, protesters trespassed on to the property of Mission San Rafael carrying paint, tools and rope with the intention of desecrating and destroying a beloved statue of St. Junipero Serra. Five perpetrators were later charged with felony vandalism.

All these facts have been reported and, for the most part, forgotten. Little known was that on May 25th, the Marin County district attorney's office decided to resolve the case through "an innovative restorative justice solution" reducing the charges to a misdemeanor if the defendants were willing to say "I am sorry" and pay an unspecified sum toward restitution. The archbishop concludes, "Worse yet, officers from the San Rafael Police Department saw the crime in real time and decided to "observe the demonstration and not intervene' for fear of escalation."

With rare clarity of mind and even rarer common sense for these times, Cordileone summarizes,

> history teaches that when we don't treat religiously or racially motivated crime seriously, we will see more and more worse aggression. Already we are witnessing what such laxity has wrought across America. Transgender activists on social media have threatened heinous violence against Christian transphobes who don't subscribe to their ideology.

Bravo, Archbishop Cordileone! He brings to mind the stirring words of St. John Chrysostom: "Let us then come back from that altar like lions breathing out fire, thus becoming terrifying to the devil, and remaining mindful of our Head and of the love which He has shown us."

One wonders why similar outrage was not expressed by ordinary Catholics across the country. If such acts were committed against Muslims or Jews there would have been howls of indignation. And rightly so. Why have Catholics been mute to such attacks on their Holy Religion? Could it be that they no longer consider their Religion holy? Could it be that a half-century of diluting Catholic identity has taken its toll? Could we be harvesting the fruits of decades of pulpits and Catholic schools teaching that nothing defines Catholics except a treacly "God loves you" catechesis?

For most Catholics, the rich content of the Faith has been leveled to a saccharine do-goodism that stands for nothing. Catholic doctrine is as unknown to most Catholics as the Bhagavad Gita. For most Catholics, the rich content of the Faith has been leveled to a saccharine do-goodism that stands for nothing.

Moreover, our once mighty Catholic university/college system has been transformed into a reliable feed for the Woke Left. Their classrooms have been turned over to a steady diet of anti-Catholic grievance at best and hearty draughts of transgressive Catholic theology at worst. Such students would have no reason to defend their religion. Likely, we would find them leaping upon the bandwagon that Archbishop Cordileone deftly decries.

Aside from all of this, there is the scandalous silence of a good part of the American hierarchy to such anti-Catholic bigotry. Catholics have long been taught to obey their leaders. I suppose they do.

What is a Catholic to think when so many of their leaders have been mired in hopeless deadlock over such an obvious issue as entrance of pro-abort politicians to the Holy Eucharist. Or the muddled problem of admitting divorced and remarried Catholics to Holy Communion? Or the generally deafening quiet on the burning issue of transgenderism and the nature of Christian Marriage between a man and woman?

Catholics are not fools. They learn by silence, or near silence. No surprise that many Catholics reading Archbishop Cordileone's intellectually coherent words might believe them to be harsh or overwrought. Such remarks are déclassé to the newly-minted Catholics of a redressed religion of accommodation rather than doctrine.

An example of this attenuated Catholicism is the one that Cordileone cites in his editorial. Of course, he reports the incident with exquisite charity and cultivated Romanitas. With all that, he does report it. To the disgrace of the Los Angeles Dodgers' award to the anti-Catholic group, the Archbishop of Los Angeles "has asked us to respond to the outrage in a deeply Christian fashion: namely, ridding any resentment in our hearts and reaching out to our communities' Catholic sisters." Now, now. Isn't that kind of pusillanimity tantamount to watching an old lady being mugged and responding by taking out your rosary? We love the Rosary, but the situation calls for much more.

Cordileone responds to such a thin response with a thoroughly measured priestliness, "That's important, but faithful Catholics would also do well to warn their political leaders from becoming modern Know Nothings." A perfect riposte.

It is time for trumpets, not whispers. The time for détente has ended. Cordileone has set the match to the rotting timbers of a post-Vatican II kneeling before the world. Other lit matches must follow.

LOOKING BACKWARD IN THE DIOCESE OF CHARLOTTE

Any Catholic with a pulse recognizes that something strange is happening in the Diocese of Charlotte. It has taken a *volte-face* and decided to walk backward.

Strange, for nothing irks Synodal Catholics more than being accused of looking backward. To them, anything in the Catholic Church that preceded 1965 is anachronistic, in fact, a very offense against God. They kneel at the altar of novelty, embracing its controlling dogma of Progress with its central tenet: tomorrow's ideas are always superior to yesterday's. An excrescence of Hegel, you may say.

Perhaps. But you must look further back to the French Revolution. Those cretins sought a bloody do-over of history, daring even to create an entirely new calendar. Their remote inspiration was Jean-Jacques Rousseau who declared, with jagged irony, "sometimes you must force men to be free." Robespierre and his fellow Jacobins followed that counsel with every thump of the guillotine.

The Modern credo dutifully worships at the shrine of the New. They chant always a New Beginning, death to the past, never look back. No surprise that every modern dictator sings out of this songbook. Pol Pot wished to bring Cambodia into the glorious Present by declaring 1974 year one. He then sadistically decimated one quarter of his population to insure that prized liberation. Not too far away, in China, Mao Zedong embraced that deadly dream even if it meant brutally slaughtering millions of his fellow Chinese to make the point.

Only one thing from the "past" do the Moderns cherish: repression, quick and thorough. Echoes of that contradiction can be seen in America today: law-fare, virtue signaling, free-speech repression, organized pillaging, and exacting conformity. Any trace of the Old Ways is met with swift retribution and social shunning. Anyone esteeming the Past earns Hawthorne's scarlet letter—but with a cruel twist: not for disobeying God's Law but for obeying it.

Invariably, this metaphysical vacuum eventually spawns dissenters—namely: Orwell, Huxley, Solzhenitsyn. Something in the soul of men eventually stirs. A brave few remember. And what they remember is our noble Past—that Past with its truth, its wisdom, its solidity, its beauty, and its conformity with the soothing truths of human nature. A few quickly turn into an army. No longer do they want to worship the advance of time. They crave the Timeless.

This return to the timeless is appearing in shocking numbers, to the chagrin of the aging gatekeepers of the Dead Past. One intellectual light is John Mac Ghlionn of *The Catholic Herald*, who recently gave this growing trend explosive expression:

> We were told the future would be limitless, utterly empowering. We were told we would be happiest with fewer rules, fewer roles, fewer traditions. Just vibes. But the experiment failed. We're lonelier. Sicker. Spiritually starved. In place of meaning, we got algorithms. In place of transcendence, we got TikTok therapy. And beneath the saccharine haze of self-care, many young people feel the gnawing presence of something missing.

If ever there was a punch in the gut of the myth of the Modern, this is it.

Which brings us to the Diocese of Charlotte.

Its new successor to the apostles is one of few remaining devotees of a Dead Past—not the ever-new past of truth, beauty, and goodness but a warrior of a past beginning in 1965. He has drunk deeply at the springs of the Modern Project. For him, every single token of the Church's Tradition, especially in the Sacred Liturgy, is a noose around the Catholic neck, something to be censured. He looks upon it as an obstacle to that ever-evolving Omega Point. Those in the know tell us that he has mastered transactional techniques so emblematic of the Modern Man. For him, all is process, dialogue, performance. With the Moderns, such leaders abhor finality in being. All must be open to perpetual revision lest the Process be frustrated.

This whole sterile and discredited enterprise is on full display in the bishop's carefully organized assault on the traditions of the Sacred Liturgy. As with all devoted Moderns, his teeth were set on edge when he arrived in Charlotte a year ago (after the premature and mysterious exit of the esteemed Bishop Jugis) and beheld a diocese returning itself to theological, liturgical, and disciplinary sanity.

It is imperative to understand the world that shaped the bishop's temperament and perspective: his Franciscan Order. While every religious Order in the Church sealed its compact with Modernity, none did it with as much gusto as the Franciscans (except, of course, the Jesuits). Franciscan formation was (and is) a thorough, unrelenting, and comprehensive program in the abhorrence of the Church's past—theological, moral, liturgical, and artistic. After years of that steady indoctrination, a priest is launched with the zeal of invading paratroopers. As they mount their offensive, their battle plan is a simple one: take no prisoners.

As with all Moderns, these priests will embrace only one part of the pre-1965 Church: its disciplinary machinery. This works well especially with recalcitrant clergy firmly wedded to the timeless traditions of the Church. Esteeming obedience (to be frank, an unnuanced obedience), they instantly conform. Modern bishops depend upon this knee-jerk conformity.

It must be carefully noted that these Modern priests themselves (and bishops) adhere to a highly selective obedience. In the past twelve years, they shouted obedience to the Holy See, while they have routinely disobeyed the Holy See for all the decades preceding. Aside from this self-serving obedience, they would consider obedience to the Church's doctrinal, moral, and liturgical tradition to be dangerously retrograde.

Many bishops adhere to this Modern mindset. But none match the ferocity of the new bishop of Charlotte. For a bishop who subscribes to the free-floating, give-and-take, non-committal Synodal Listening, he governs like a medieval bishop—with one glaring difference: medieval bishops wielded the sword against those who *lapsed* in their Catholic beliefs; the Modern bishops wield it against those who do *not*. Look at the granular intensity of his liturgical bans. It bespeaks an *idée fixe* which undermines his celebrated, indiscriminate openness to all things. Not him. My, even Mao ruled, "let a thousand flowers bloom."

Tsk, tsk, Bishop Martin.

The bishop of Charlotte labors beneath the carapace of a hollow and spent theological past. He does not seem to notice that the young people today have rejected his fondness for a Woodstock hippy past, now embracing a Chartres pilgrimage future.

Let me return again to the rousing prose of Mr. Mac Ghlionn:

> Catholicism offers what the modern world cannot: structure. Discipline. Mystery. It doesn't whisper that you're perfect just the way you are. It demands transformation. It demands submission – to something older, wiser, and greater than you. To be Catholic is to live inside a story. A two-thousand-year-old, blood-soaked, gold-threaded, world-shaping story. It has martyrs and miracles. Saints and scoundrels. Architecture that makes you weep. A God who became man. A carpenter who suffered for your sins. A virgin mother crowned in heaven. Try fitting that into a 15-second Instagram reel....
>
> You don't walk into a traditional Catholic Mass and feel like you have stumbled into a self-help seminar with hymns. You feel the weight of two millennia settle on to your shoulders. There are no mood boards, no fog machines, no pastors in skinny jeans offering life hacks. There is only the priest, the altar, the sacrifice, and the silence. A silence that, for many, is more honest than any sermon....
>
> In a culture obsessed with identity, Catholicism offers identity through surrender. Not the curated, performative kind, but a cruciform kind – dying to self to live in Christ. It's everything the modern self recoils at, which is precisely why it is so powerful.

My goodness! Move over Chesterton.

The bishop of Charlotte may have forced a turning point. His high-handed absurdities will alert even somnolent Catholics at how utterly passé his draconian pogroms truly are. They will look at his dreams of Modernity and recognize it has produced "bare ruined choirs," politicized septuagenarians, shuttered churches, vacant seminaries, and whole continents that have drifted from the Faith.

On the other hand, normal Catholics – and even normal non-Catholics – will notice in the Diocese of Charlotte:

> Crammed Traditional Masses overflowing with young people and families with armies of children
>
> A newly-built, multi-million-dollar seminary bursting at the seams with young men, all of whom are born North Carolinians (!)
>
> Parishes and schools teaching the Catholic Faith in all its richness.

Any sane man will ask: Why does this need fixing? At that moment, they will come face-to-face with the lunacy of the Modern Project. It runs against the grain of man's very nature: a thirst for the rootedness of truth, beauty, and goodness. While many hold on to the Modern project for dear life, it is fading and will eventually die on the vine.

Alas, many more dioceses will continue to march backward. For us who will only march foreword, there are the spirited words of Msgr. Ronald Knox.

In the late 1950s, he was asked to speak at St. Edmund's college in Ware, England. His summons to those students was typically restrained in the inimitable manner of Knox, but underneath there was an earthquake:

> It is becoming a clear issue in our day, the Church or nothing.
> So it is with the religion you are taught here: there is none other than but this. The doctrines which you are taught in apologetics or Christian doctrine class are not a sort of continuation of the gender rhymes; the practices of piety in which you are encouraged are not a tiresome regulation made for you by housemasters. They are the world's last hope which is committed to your keeping.
> They are the giant's sword... If thou will take this, take it, for there is no other than this. We are a College of outlaws; those who have gone out from us were men who could set their face against the false standards of the world they lived in, who could stem the current of their times instead of being carried away with it.
> ...we must learn to hold and to wield our boyhood's sword, the religion of the Catholic Church. If thou wilt take this, take it, for there is none other than this.

You must say: give it to me.

And we shall. Again and again, we shall.

Though Charlotte saddens us, we must not stare at it too long, lest what happened to Lot's wife happens to our souls.

Remember, we are Catholics of the future.

We march *forward*, having on our lips the words of one great bishop: *Our future is the past.*

MAY POPE FRANCIS REST IN PEACE— AND MAY PEACE RETURN TO MOTHER CHURCH

Not even months into his new pontificate, Pope Francis declared, to a group of young people in Paraguay, "Go out and make a mess." A puzzling remark from the Successor of St. Peter. As the years of his papacy went on, we witnessed what he meant. Year after year, he kept his promise. And the Church descended into an unprecedented chaos.

Recall St. Augustine's classic definition of peace: the *tranquillitas ordinis* (the tranquility of order). During Pope Francis's reign, there was nothing of order and certainly no tranquility. Upheaval followed upheaval; shock gave way to more shock; ambiguity was compounded by ambiguity. Each episode met by the *cri de coeur* of faithful Catholics. More than a few prestigious theologians otherwise known for their bookish detachment and academic reserve were signing onto international statements fearful that Pope Francis had fallen into heresy.

Good Catholics were confused.

Promulgation of his first encyclical, *Amoris Laetitia*, sent a chill through the Church universal. The Guardian of the Deposit appeared to be changing the immemorial teaching of the Church by permitting divorced remarried Catholics to Holy Communion.

Good Catholics were confused.

Papal apologists twisted and turned in their attempt to fit the square peg of rupture into the round hole of orthodoxy. Nothing worked. The words meant what the words said. Nor was there any backtracking on the part of Pope Francis.

Good Catholics were confused.

No reconsiderations for Pope Francis. He dug in his heels and published a reiteration in the official *Acta Apostolicae Sedis* granting the questionable departure from traditional doctrine on Marriage a quasi-magisterial approval. This perilous admission precipitated the now historically famous intervention of the so-called *Dubia*

Cardinals: Walter Brandmüller, Raymond Burke, Carlo Caffarra, and Joachim Meisner. Such a careful request for doctrinal clarification – from not one but four prominent cardinals – was extraordinary. It seemed the worry of Catholics was justified. And they waited. And waited. Many months later, the pontiff granted a reply, but it was as muddled as the concerning encyclical. This was puzzling given the pope's appetite for transactional governance. Good Catholics were confused.

Then there was Pope Francis's penchant for draconian disciplines. Even his apologists became embarrassed. Clerics of a more progressive bent long thought these instruments unfashionable in a dialogical Church. Especially one marked by the *laissez-faire* air of synodality. Yet he punished, silenced, and sacked bishops and clerics with abandon. It seemed curious that a pope of such purported non-judgmentalism should behave as one of the most judgmental. His *modus operandi* appeared like that of medieval popes. Odd, to say the least.

Good Catholics were confused.

Even the most unbiased observer could see that Pope Francis enjoyed an appetite for the *de rigueur* ideological fashions of the day rather than the unfashionable rigors of the Deposit of Faith. Even that anointed Pauline phrase was mocked and proscribed by the papal nuncio to the United States, Cardinal Christophe Pierre, in a discussion with the then-deposed Bishop Strickland.

Good Catholics were confused.

No pope in recent memory removed as many bishops from their dioceses, even excommunicating seemingly innocent priests. It appeared as though only those upholding Revealed teachings were in his crosshairs. This was hard to justify given his passivity in the face of the significant apostasy of the German bishops and other such prelates throughout the world.

Good Catholics were confused.

Catholics scratched their heads as he brought pagan idols into St. Peter's Basilica. He happily welcomed known enemies of the Church into his audiences, and he promoted *du jour* Progressive causes such as eco-justice and transsexual rights. Yes, let us engage the Church's enemies. But what of the optics? Everyone knows that a picture is worth more than a thousand words.

Perplexity settled upon Catholics as he exhibited an unusual passion for tiny, sexual niche minorities while being utterly indifferent to faithful Catholics suffering the whiplash of ecclesial tremors. One dramatic example comes to mind: Chinese Catholics, among them cardinals, bishops, and laity who presently suffer persecution and rot in dungeons.

Good Catholics were confused.

Bewilderment settled upon Catholics as he promoted equality of religions and misrepresentation of the rights of nations to defend their borders from aliens. He trumpeted assorted causes dear to the Left and often scolded Catholics for excessive proselytization, leaving them in a dazed wonderment. Whose mandate should they follow, Christ's or his?

Again, it seemed as if dissent was rewarded and fidelity penalized. Like Sherman's March to the Sea, Pope Francis seemed intent upon crushing any growth of the authentic Faith.

Good Catholics were confused.

Most disconcerting was his unrelenting attack upon the Traditional Mass. This is a mushrooming movement in the Church. In surprisingly large numbers, it is becoming the home of large families, robust fidelity to the Faith, and scores of vocations to the priesthood and religious life. Sincere Catholics were baffled as Pope Francis mounted a pogrom of complete exclusion to a group of Catholics who showed the greatest respect to his Office as well as perfect loyalty to the articles of the Faith.

This program of abolition represented a determined and pronounced rupture with both *Ecclesia Dei Adflicta* and *Summorum Pontificum*, his predecessors' correctives to the Montini/Bugnini prohibitions of the ancient Traditional Mass.

He was clearly wedded to a liturgically discredited paradigm which had acted as a vehicle for the wildly secularist motifs of the first half of the 20th century. Just as the Johann-Pauline/Benedictine liturgical recalibrations were taking form, Pope Francis chose to bury them.

Good Catholics were confused.

In speech after speech, he ranted against seminarians and priests who preferred the classical vesture for Holy Mass or the donning of the cassock. Again, odd. Firstly, that he gladly cast a pall over the enthusiasm of new seminarians and freshly ordained priests (of which there is a dearth, if he had not noticed). Secondly, he was expressing an unconcealed contempt for a liturgical expression venerated in the Church for centuries.

Good Catholics were confused.

He promoted bishops who deployed oppressive disciplines against traditional expressions of the Faith while aggressively promoting ideologies at odds with it. Pope Francis granted approval of new liturgical forms, such as an Amazonian Rite, which, at the very least, obscured the Faith. Pope Francis seemed to have left us in a collapsed mine shaft, with only teaspoons to dig out.

Good Catholics were confused.

Pope Francis indeed kept his promise of creating a mess. With that mess arrived the demise of peace in the Church. Factionalism ensued. Heightened tensions erupted. Not a few Catholics embraced eccentric notions of sedevacantism.

But one of the greatest tragedies of this period is the silence. Silence from the shepherds. Suffering Catholics looked toward them for guidance and received only bromides and anodyne preachments. They either evaded the issue of the tumult altogether or intoned all is well, a refrain they have perfected. Their shameful silence left Christ's little ones to roam helplessly, falling through the fissures caused by the doctrinal turmoil. Will history treat these mute prelates as it did the bishops in Henry's sixteenth-century England, or 1930s Germany?

Good Catholics were confused.

While many Catholics felt themselves adrift in a sea of disorientation, the grace of God endured. Impressive numbers of admirable Catholics permitted the free-fall to steel their Faith. With heroic perseverance, they remained loyal to the immutable teachings of Mother Church and her timeless practices of piety. Futures generations will applaud these heroic souls and write testaments praising them. They were faithful when infidelity was the coin of the realm.

Could they have been inspired by the affecting poetry of T. S. Eliot in his *Four Quartets*: "For us there is only the trying/ the rest is not our business"?

Or perhaps, St. John Henry Newman in his stalwart words:

> The whole course of Christianity from the first is but one series of troubles and disorders. Every century is like every other, and to those who live in it seems more worse than all times before it. The Church is ever ailing, religion seems ever expiring, schisms dominant, the light of truth dim. Its adherents scattered. The cause of Christ

is ever in its last agony... But the Church is like Noah's ark, which did not hinder or destroy the flood but rode upon it, preserving the hopes of the human family within its fragile plan.

Let us all pray for the immortal soul of Pope Francis. Let us respectfully keep the nine days of his obsequies. Let us have Mass after Mass offered for his happy repose. Still, after all that, Pope Francis leaves us confused.

But not God.

3
Of Councils and Synods

THE COUNCIL OF NICAEA
AT 1,700 YEARS OLD

Perchance, you haven't noticed. But for the past sixty years or so a pitched battle has been waged in the Church, something close to Jacobin revolution. Of course, its birth was simultaneous with a most prominent event. But even mentioning it would earn immediate censure, so, I will not. (So much for Synodal listening. I suspect Orwell was correct in *Animal Farm*: "All animals are equal, but some animals are more equal than others.")

On the one side, there are heroic Catholics who treasure the riches of their Church, from its metaphysical foundations, its infallible teachings, and its ancient liturgy and piety. On the other, we have a coterie of zealots bent on redefining the Faith, leaving it barely a shadow of its former self. Faithful Catholics have suffered greatly for over a half-century beneath the heavy jackboot of this band of agitators. Their project was a grand redesign of the Nicene Creed, if not casting it whole and entire into the dustbin of history. Need proof? Watch Cardinal Tagle spinning about a stage in dance garb chanting John Lennon's "Imagine."

This is the denouement of the Modernist project.

Nicaea is a decisive blow to this fey counterfeit of Faith. Its articles stand like a mighty Alpine range, each peak more imposing and elegant than the next. How many parishes this year will celebrate this auspicious anniversary? Rejoice in its muscularity? Celebrate its summons to heroic struggle to defend it? Stand in rapt awe of the saints of millennia who embraced unspeakable deaths to defend it? Eagerly imitate St. Nicholas in coming to blows with Arius, the archenemy of the salvific Nicaean Catholic Faith?

If they will not, we must!

Raise your fiery torches and lift your voices till they grow hoarse. All in gratitude for the Nicaean articles which are the sure steps of our ladder to Paradise.

If you were present at Nicaea in May of 325, you likely would have shed tears.

Standing with throngs of other Catholics, you would have witnessed lines of regally clad bishops filing into the great Cathedral of Nicaea. Eusebius of Caesarea estimates that 318 bishops solemnly processed into the principal Church and central Hall of Emperor Constantine where the Council would transpire.

That, however, would not have been quite the cause of your tears. It was the sight of bishops who had suffered sadistic brutalities for the Holy Faith at the hands of the Roman Imperium of Maximin and Licinius. Many of them limped, their limbs having been torn out by the torturers. Your stare would have been frozen as you witnessed Bishop Paphnutius from Upper Thebes, whose eye sockets were hollow, his eyes having been torn out by the Roman soldiers of the Praetorian Guard because he refused to deny the Holy Faith.

This procession into the Church in Nicaea was the march of spiritual titans. They cared little for the approval of the world or secure positions. The only security they coveted was the comfort of Christ.

Long deliberations ensued. Very long deliberations. For the Council Fathers appreciated that the salvation of the human race hung upon the absolute precision of each and every word of their doctrinal formulations. These singular bishops understood that their holy obligation was simply to pass on "what they had received" (in the Latin construal *traditio*: see 1 Cor 4:7 and 15:1, Phil 4:9, 2 Thess 3:6). They would not dare change it, add to it, subtract from it, dilute it, or mute it.

This solemn obligation clung to their conscience with terrifying consequence, lest the priceless treasure of the Faith be obscured. They recognized that the doctrinal formulae were chiseled into what would forever be the foundation of the Catholic Faith. This held all of them in frightful thrall.

Paul Claudel gives memorable, poetic expression to the earth-moving gravity of what these Nicaean bishops accomplished:

> When in my village church I hear the Credo being recited, one article after another, by the harsh voice of the soloist, to which the naive whine of the little girls' response, I tremble with an inner ecstasy: it seems to me that I am present at the creation of the world. I know the cost of each one of those formulae printed in eternal truth. With what rending of heaven and earth, what rivers of blood,

by what effort, what mental travail, and with what overflowing grace they came to be born.

I see those great masses of dogma emerge and take form before my eyes one after the other; I see man struggling painfully and finally succeeding in tearing out of his own heart the final affirmation. It is like a cathedral, immovable and yet advancing with all its columns from porch to choir.

Claudel is only to be outdone by Chesterton. Here are his soaring words in *Orthodoxy*. Every Catholic has likely read these sentences over and over, causing their hearts to race. His prose is so beautiful, so electrifying, that they not only deserve repetition but memorization:

> Last and most important, it is exactly this which explains what is so inexplicable to all the modern critics of the history of Christianity. I mean the monstrous wars about small points of theology, the earthquakes of emotion about a gesture or word. It was only a matter of an inch: but an inch is everything when you are balancing.
>
> The Church could not afford to swerve a hair's breadth on some things if she was to continue her great and daring experiment of the irregular equilibrium. Once, let one idea become less powerful, and some other idea would become too powerful.
>
> It was no flock of sheep the Christian shepherd was leading, but a herd of bulls and tigers, of terrible ideals and devouring doctrines, each one of them strong enough to turn into a false religion and lay waste the world. Remember that the Church went on specifically for dangerous ideas: she was a lion tamer.
>
> The idea of birth through a Holy Spirit, of the death of a divine being, of the forgiveness of sins, or the fulfillment of prophecies, are ideas which, anyone can see, need but a touch to turn them into something blasphemous or ferocious.

He continues with historical and theological precision wedded to arresting insight:

> The smallest link was let drop by the artifices of the Mediterranean and the lion of ancestral pessimism would burst his chain in the forgotten forests of the north.
>
> ... It is enough to notice that if some small mistake were made in doctrine, huge blunders would be made in human happiness. A sentence phrased wrong about the nature of symbolism would have broken all the best

statues in Europe. A slip in the definitions might stop all the dances: might wither all the Christmas trees or break all the Easter eggs.

Doctrines had to be defined within strict limits, even in order that man might enjoy general human liberties. The church had to be careful, if only that the world might be careless.

Then he concludes with bombastic crescendo, like the clanging of cymbals:

This is the thrilling romance of orthodoxy. People have fallen into a foolish habit, of speaking of orthodoxy as something heavy, humdrum, and safe. There was never anything so perilous or so exciting as orthodoxy.

It was sanity: and to be sane is more dramatic than to be mad.

It was the equilibrium of a man behind madly rushing horses, seeming to stoop this way and to sway that, yet in every attitude having the grace of statuary and the accuracy of arithmetic. She swerved to left and right, so exactly as to avoid enormous obstacles.

... She left on the one hand the huge bulk of Arianism, buttressed by all the worldly powers to make Christianity too worldly. The next instant she was swerving in to avoid an orientalism, which would have made it too unworldly. The orthodox Church never took the tame course or accepted the conventions: the orthodox Church was never respectable. It is easy to be a madman: it is easy to be a heretic. It is always easy to let the age have its head: the difficult thing is to keep one's own.

To have fallen into any one of the fads from Gnosticism to Christian Science would indeed have been obvious and tame. But to have avoided them all has been one whirling adventure: and in my vision the heavenly chariot flies thundering through the ages, the dull heresy sprawling and prostrate, the wild truth reeling but erect.

As we heartily celebrate the 1,700th anniversary of this epoch-making Council, let us repel the silliness that has struggled to replace doctrinal Catholicism. The Nicaean Fathers arrived at the Council maimed, trophies of their heroic defense of the Faith.

Contrast that with too many of our hierarchy today who wear the sunny smile of compromise, hoping the world will love them, even as they show no love for the truth.

Not us. Never us.

VATICAN II AT 60: STOP THE CHEERLEADING

On October 4th, Basic Books released George Weigel's latest work, *To Sanctify the World: The Vital Legacy of Vatican II*. It left much of the Catholic world slightly confused, except for that dwindling minority still starstruck by Vatican II's promise of a new Pentecost. Far be it for any faithful Catholic to call into question its legitimacy or validity.

With that full disclosure out of the way, isn't it possible – after sixty years – to ask some quite relevant questions about its expediency or its design? It seems Mr. Weigel is of a generation that accepted uncritically the *weltanschauung* of a mid-20th century European Catholic elite still swooning over Roncalli's mirage of *aggiornamento*.

Call to mind that it was entirely of a piece with that dizzying headiness of going to the moon, supercomputers, and the Age of Aquarius. A time of the intoxications of Teilhard de Chardin and his beloved Noosphere, Rahner and his Anonymous Christian, and Hans Urs von Balthasar's *apokatastasis*. And even more: Sr. Corita Kent's "damn everything but the circus," Harvey Cox's *Secular City*, Rogerian Self-actualized Man, and, who can forget the new frontiers of John Robinson's *Honest to God*. Ah, they were times that left men dreaming dreams. And every one of them became a nightmare.

Out of this fanciful period was Vatican II convened. Sadly, it allowed its antinomian exuberance of the age to fall like magical dust on more than a few of the Council's principal architects. When Pope John XXIII announced his intention to summon the Council, Cardinal Heenan of London warned, "This is tempting the Holy Ghost!" Why such a monition from an otherwise prim and circumspect British Prince of the Church?

Councils were only convened to confront great crises threatening the Church. Where was the crisis compelling this one? No Catholic could see one, but an elite illuminati did.

It seems as though Mr. Weigel has been swept up in the dreamscape of that Catholic cognoscenti. After citing Pope John's opening address about the "council's greatest concern" presenting more fully "the sacred deposit of Christian doctrine," Mr. Weigel goes on to say, "That would not happen, however, if the Church merely guarded this (then quoting Roncalli again) "precious treasure... as if we were only concerned with an antiquity."

Weigel proceeds to explain, "Nor would it suffice to repeat familiar formulas of faith, like those in the simple question-and-answer catechisms that Catholics had long known." For an otherwise sterling orthodox Catholic thinker, those are strange words indeed. How else can one explain them except to wonder that perhaps he inhaled too much of the questionable assumptions of the European *bien pensant*?

How else to comprehend this counterintuitive and utterly ahistorical defense of Roncalli's myopic vision?

> John XXIII knew that the defensive Catholicism of the Counter-Reformation, however successful a salvage operation, had run its course. It was time to raze the bastions that Catholicism has erected and turn its robust institutions into platforms for evangelization and mission in order to engage a deeply troubled modern world. The Church, he believed, existed to proclaim and compassionately witness the Christian truth for the world's healing and sanctification. It could not hide that truth like the frightened servant in Christ's parable of the talents.

Mr. Weigel seems to be parroting the Old Thinking of the septuagenarian and octogenarian Shepherds in the Church. This Old Guard is presently splenetic at the cry of young Catholics for the undiluted Ancient Faith rather than the Synodal Way that is so giddily embraced (and tightfistedly enforced) by their betters.

How could someone as gifted as Mr. Weigel repeat without embarrassment Roncalli's indictment of 500 years of Post-Reformation Catholicism as "guarding a precious treasure as though it were an antiquity"? He knows better than most St. Paul's mandate to Timothy: *custodi depositum* (guard the deposit). Yes, the Church jealously guards so that she can boldly proclaim. And, indeed, she did. And she did it with supernatural gusto during all those centuries to which Mr. Weigel happily bids a fond farewell.

Then there is this: "It was time to raze the bastions that Catholicism has erected and turn its robust institutions into platforms for evangelization and mission in order to engage a deeply troubled

Vatican II at 60: Stop the Cheerleading

modern world." We expect this kind of cant from self-loathing Catholics, but not from a gifted Catholic intellectual of Mr. Weigel's rank. Was that summons due to a momentary memory lapse? Mr. Weigel pleads for a Church "to proclaim and compassionately witness to Christian truth for the world's healing and sanctification." Surely Mr. Weigel recalls the global and prodigious efforts of the Church in the past centuries doing just that. To name a paltry few:

- The Jesuits' monumental missionary efforts in South America, to say nothing of their staggering accomplishments in covering all of Europe with its finest educational institutions
- St. Isaac Jogues's heroic efforts to bring the Holy Gospel to the Indians of North America
- Fr. Junipero Serra's breathtaking missionary work and foundations in California
- The Holy Ghost Fathers' dazzling missionary accomplishments in Africa
- The Maryknoll Fathers' dauntless work in China, which accumulated for that Order countless numbers of martyrs
- Innumerable Religious Orders of Women who marched into Africa to open hospitals and schools
- St. Katherine Drexel's founding of the Sisters of the Blessed Sacrament specifically to bring the Gospel to Native Indians and Blacks
- The St. James Society, which sent scores of priests to work in the missions of South America.
- Mother Teresa's missionary work in India

Was all of this evidence of a Church obsessed with guarding antiquity? Perchance Mr. Weigel was thinking of a Church insufficiently engaging the world on high intellectual matters? In that case, he certainly must know the amazing philosophical and theological work of Catholic scholars in those fortress years who transformed the intellectual landscape. To cite just some:

- Jacques Maritain's guest professorships at Columbia, Princeton, and the University of Chicago, all the while publishing some of the most significant works on St. Thomas Aquinas and influencing the entire academic world.
- Etienne Gilson's guest professorships at Harvard and the Sorbonne, as well as delivering the esteemed Gifford Lectures at the University of Aberdeen in Scotland.
- Fr. Stanley Jaki's impressive oeuvre in reconciling physics and the sciences with the truths of the Faith.

- Fr. Garrigou-Lagrange's work in Thomistic philosophy and his polemical works engaging the philosophies of the day.
- Learned Catholic academic societies in every major scientific, literary, philosophical, and theological discipline.

Add to this impressive work of evangelization the fact of thousands of Catholic schools with an average student population of one thousand children; seminaries filled to capacity, and novitiates as well; religious brothers conducting some of the finest schools in America.

Does all of this sound like a Church enclosed in upon itself? This ever-mushrooming evidence of Catholic universal reach prompted the imitable Karl Adam to write in his memorable 1934 *Spirit of Catholicism:*

> What [the Church] wishes to establish is the fact that human reason, while remaining true to itself, can by its own principles advance to a point where God becomes visible as the fundamental basis and ultimate meaning of all reality, and where knowledge passes over into faith, philosophy into theology. Whenever men have doubted or denied the capacity of the human mind to transcend the limits of experience, whenever they have attempted to paralyze or kill man's profound yearning for absolute truth, then the Church has come forward in defense of reason, whether against Averroes and Luther or against Kant. And the more our own age becomes weary of subjective idealism and seeks to rediscover the objective world, the more grateful will it be to Pope Pius X that in his much abused anti-Modernist Encyclical *Pascendi* he denounced all positivism, pragmatism and phenomenalism and defended the power of reason to transcend and surpass experience, thus exorcising those twin bugbears of solipsism and skepticism which menace all knowledge.

If Vatican II deserves all the encomia showered upon it by the Old Thinking, then how does one explain the censorious comment of Pope Paul VI, in 1972, that "The smoke of Satan has entered the Church." Lest I be accused of violating *post hoc ergo propter hoc*, we must be clear that there is no cause-effect between Montini's lament and Vatican II. But their uncomfortable proximity raises eyebrows. To quote Mark Twain, "History does not repeat itself, but it rhymes." Clearly, the smoke of Satan was not a consequence of Vatican II, but it does seem to rhyme.

Moreover, the vigorous stretching that Pope Benedict XVI performed in articulating a hermeneutic of continuity is demonstration that Vatican II could not stand alone. It contained undeniable weaknesses. They could only be redressed by supplying the necessary unambiguous statements made by the Church's Magisterium. Other ecumenical councils never required such embarrassing backtracking. Their reasoning was as tight as a drum and the meaning of their words as clear as the sun.

Isn't it time to move past the Old Thinking that lauded Vatican II? With all due respect to the Second Vatican Council, it does not meet the demands of a secular world. For that we need a virile, unequivocal, and full-throated Catholicism.

Yes, take from Vatican II what was good, but stop the cheerleading. It is simply unseemly of an intelligent and faithful Catholic.

Mr. Weigel, isn't it time to admit that the bloom has come off the rose?

DOWN THE RABBIT HOLE OF SYNODALITY

"When I use a word," Humpty Dumpty said, in rather a scornful tone, "it means just what I choose it to mean—neither more nor less."
"The question is," said Alice, "whether you can make words mean so many different things."
"The question is," said Humpty Dumpty, "which is to be master—that is all."
Lewis Carroll, *Alice in Wonderland*

Worlds upside down seem to be rather commonplace these days. Alice's world of Mad Hatters, Humpty Dumpty, and topsy turvy Tea Parties have become the norm. Meanwhile, the men who spot these forays into Wonderland are looked upon as the odd ones.

Examples are too numerous to count. Defending men as men and women as women is now indictable hate speech. Coming to the defense of natural things like husbands and wives bearing children is looked upon as atavism. Priests redefining disordered sexual desires as merely differently ordered have become a new orthodoxy winning kudos from many bishops and earning them honored places in the pantheon of a Brave New Theological World. Excellence as a fundamental human aspiration has been outlawed as a term of oppression. Critical Race Theory is now going so far as to say that Mathematics is a source of white supremacy. This nonrational blather mushrooms daily, and sanity is reaching the point of disappearance. Humpty Dumpty would blush.

Creating Wonderlands will always be a human temptation. As Eliot wrote in *The Four Quartets*, "Humankind/cannot bear/too much reality." It is easier to create worlds within worlds out of the whole cloth of our ideas than to live in the sometime unsettling world of the real. The Gnostics reveled in the concoction of imagined worlds that only a chosen illuminati would have access to. It became the first mortal threat to the infant Catholic Church in the first century, precipitating St. John to write his Gospel. In the first majestic lines he insists, "In the beginning was the Word." He was commanding attention to the Truth who is the Word made Flesh, to which man must prostrate.

This calls to mind St. Thomas, who teaches us that the only purpose of the intellect is to know the real which carries us to the Real. Before that divinely sculpted truth, Wonderlands tumble into nonsense. But fallen man will persist in trying. For the Serpent's temptation "Ye shall be as gods" will always enjoy an irresistible attraction. Our times are a time of unparalleled Gnostic ascendancy. Never have men been so willing to dwell in a world of Humpty Dumptys and Mad Hatters as they are today. Proof is found in the sheer fear of normal folks to speak truths of ordinary common sense. Chesterton was prescient when he wrote in *Heretics*:

> The great march of destruction will go on. Everything will be denied. Everything will become a creed. It is a reasonable position to deny the stones in the street; it will be a religious dogma to assert them. It is a rational thesis that we are all in a dream; it will be a mystical sanity to say that we are all awake. Fires will be kindled to testify that two and two make four. Swords will be drawn to prove that leaves are green in summer.

Quite chilling. Yet, so very true. One does not have to be a Catholic to be alarmed at the insatiable appetite for Wonderland. Take Orwell, for instance. He saw modern man's descent into Gnosticism when he wrote, "We have now sunk to a depth at which the re-statement of the obvious is the first duty of intelligent men."

Flannery O'Connor saw her work as a novelist a Catholic vocation calling men back to their senses. She beckoned them to abandon the comforting confines of their Wonderlands by the shocking use of grotesque violence. She explains, "I have found that violence is strangely capable of returning my characters to reality and preparing them to accept their moment of grace. Their heads are so hard that almost nothing else will do the work."

As grim as this cultural Gnosticism is, the circumstance is even grimmer when it seeps into the sacred precincts of the Catholic Church. The ancient adage applies: *corruptio optimi pessima* "the corruption of the best is the worst of all." The past half-century has demonstrated this, with its bizarre theological speculation and liturgical surrealism.

Almost every Catholic university and college (with few exceptions), to say nothing of learned theological societies (calling them learned strains credulity), has become a petri dish of Gnostic whimsy. Enter most Catholic collegiate classrooms or the annual symposia of the Catholic Theological Society of America, and it seems as though you have landed in the Mad Hatter's Tea party. Language is twisted, ideas are psychedelic, and fidelity to Church teaching is the only proscribed thought.

After the pontificates of John Paul II and Benedict XVI, Catholics believed that the bitter years of Newspeak and Wonderland had abated, and sanity was on the horizon. No such respite. Theological Wonderland has returned with a vengeance from the lips of the hierarchal upper crust. The past seven years has reached shocking new depths, but all of them seem to have been surpassed by a new species called Synodality.

Before Church historians crouch to their attack mode, let us assure them that any Catholic is aware of the venerable institution of local Councils in the ancient Church (infrequently called synods). Each one of these enjoyed a noble purpose: to clarify Church discipline or teaching and to refute heresy.

The present Synodality fever bears no such pedigree. For proof, merely look at Synodality in the German Catholic Church. Even third graders recognize that the German Church is in full meltdown before our very eyes, unmoored from any of the Church's millennial magisterial teaching. Yet this same pseudo-Catholic energy is on full display in the Holy See's promulgation of a *Preparatory Document* and companion *Enchiridion*. Read them at your own risk. In the words of Matthew Cullinan Hoffman, both documents "serve up a mix of group-therapeutic catchphrases and ideological chic." This is a Gnosticism that would make Marcion envious.

Let a sampling serve as a prima facie case:

- "We must remain open to the surprises that the Spirit will certainly prepare for us along the way. Thus, a dynamism is activated that allows us to begin to reap some of the fruits of a synodal conversion, which will progressively mature."
- "Openness to conversion and change: We can often be resistant to what the Holy Spirit is trying to inspiring us to undertake. We are called to abandon attitudes of complacency and comfort that lead us to make decisions purely on the basis of how things have been done in the past."

- "The task before us includes accrediting the Christian community as a credible partner in paths of social dialogue, healing, reconciliation, inclusion and participation, the reconstruction of democracy, the promotion of fraternity and friendship, living a participative and inclusive ecclesial process, exploring participatory ways of exercising responsibility in the proclamation of the Gospel and in the effort to build a more beautiful and habitable world, and bringing to light and trying to convert prejudices and distorted practices that are not rooted in the Gospel."
- "True and proper conversion is the painful and immensely fruitful passage of leaving one's own cultural and religious categories."

After wading through the Orwellian Newspeak muck of those few passages, you come squarely face to face with Gnosticism in its fullest bloom: anarchic, antinomian, transgressive, and destructive of rationality and human coherence. The document proposes a *Weltanschauung* that is as far removed from classical Christianity as astronomy is from astrology. The eminent philosopher Aurel Kolnai seemed to be commenting on this document when he wrote in 1944: "The worshipers of Baal professed a more genuine religion than many present adherents of a vague and modern religion soaked in humanitarianism." Roman Catholicism is supernatural and redemptive, not protean and therapeutic.

Ordinary Catholics must be prepared to walk away from this Gnostic Wonderland. This will not be easy. For the avatars of this New Land will use all the punitive mechanisms of the Old Church to propagate and enforce their dreams.

Alice in Wonderland is a fairy tale that ends happily. Synodality is indeed a fairy tale, but it ends in a nightmare. To be forewarned is to be forearmed.

SYNODAL FALLOUT: PUTTING LIGHT UNDER BUSHEL BASKETS

Lower the *Vexilla Regis*. Raise the white of flag of surrender. The Synodal Church has arrived. Where Christ once declared victory in the red blood of His Cross, the Synodalists bleat in the pastels of accommodation. Their white flag was a shameless admission that the Church of 2024 no longer has anything to say. Of course, much was said. And said. And said again. But it was "a tale told by an idiot, full of sound and fury, signifying nothing."[1]

Sad that the whole world should witness the once mighty Roman Church reduce itself to such self-parody. Rather like a grown man reverting back to thumb-sucking. The Synodalists were engaged in the serious business of reducing the Church to irrelevance. Inured by decades of such failed rapprochement with the pieties of the age, most Catholics stopped listening decades ago.

Proof abounds. Diocese after diocese is announcing the closure and mergers of more churches. They correctly announce that Catholics are no longer coming. One wonders if for one fleeting moment they might consider that vapid religious education and impotent liturgies for sixty years might have something to do with it. Apparently not. So, the dance with irrelevance continues.

Still, enough Catholics are content to applaud this waltz with insignificance. It is, after all, a no-fault Catholicism where one can have one's cake and eat it too. Enough high-ranking prelates protect it as though it were the *sancta sanctorum*, happy to deepen the paralysis of an already paralyzed church. These are men who prize process over certitude, the *bien pensant* over truth, diversity over excellence, and the zeitgeist over tradition.

The roots of this paralysis run deep, stretching back to the early twentieth century. Then, a wildly popular Sorbonne professor named Henri Bergson thought he was toppling the idols of a sterile scientism with his free spirited intuition. So alluring was

---

[1] *Macbeth*, Act 5, Scene 17.

this untethered intuition that it even captured the intellectually-starved Raissa and Jacques Maritain, until they discovered the richly oxygenated air of St. Thomas Aquinas. Other Catholics were not so fortunate.

Blondel's *L'Action* and Pierre Rousselot's *L'intellectualisme de Saint Thomas* pushed more strenuously the assault on truth, seeing it as insulting, with its strutting as something quite definite and propositional. In Blondel's world, truth was a straitjacket to the *élan vital* of action. Rousselot proposed that the Church's doctrinal expression of sacred revelation was stifling and should yield to the fresh formulations of each age. These are not to be cast aside as figures of an inconsequential academic debate. They are the tendons upon which was fashioned the leviathan being experienced today.

For the Synodalist, the call to sanctity is displaced by the call to action. (Historical footnote: this was the name of a *de rigueur* experiment of the late 1970s, eventually cast into the landfill of failed experiments.) The Church's traditional firmament of piety and devotion is replaced by political fervor, and humble submission to the will of God collapses before a careful attention to the Self.

Relativism reigns supreme. The Synodalist's functioning rubric casts the whole of the Church's doctrinal and spiritual tradition aside as outdated and harmful. The 2024 purges of the Traditional Mass are proof of their zealotry. Its increasing ferocity only proves how much of a mortal danger it is to their project. Just as the Jacobins erased history with the adoption of a new calendar, so the Synodalist's earnest desire to have the Church's beginning be 1965. The problem with relativism is that in due course today's relativism falls victim to relativism. When truth disappears, so does the steadiness of any position. Even false ones. All are eventually cast into the devouring fires of the Relativist Moloch.

In the Synodalist world, justice must bow to an all-devouring authoritarianism. It is always amusing to watch men who detest authority wield it so lustily. With the abandonment of truth, its gentle sway is no longer an incentive – only the sheer exercise of power. Nietzsche recognized this with unflinching candor. So did Machiavelli. In both instances, men must be compelled to conform, whether by the lash of *The Prince* or of the Übermensch. Rousseau put it succinctly in *The Social Contract:* "Sometimes men must be forced to be free."

Contrast this with the elegant formulation of the great Dominican Thomist Fr. Reginald Garrigou-Lagrange:

> The Church is intolerant in principle, because she believes; but is tolerant in practice, because she loves. The enemies of the Church are tolerant in principle, because they do not believe; but are intolerant in practice because they do not love.

Pure Thomistic genius: balanced and piercing.

It shouldn't surprise us that the Synodalists' methods are arbitrary and crushing. Since they have long left the bright uplands of virtue and doctrine, their weapons leave behind the delicacy of those instruments which once were the arsenal of Mother Church. Interesting that this attribution for the Church has long been abandoned by the Catholic Left. They passionately argue that it is the paternalism of a dead past. Closer to the truth, it is one of the most ancient terms for the Church, beginning with St. Cyprian in the third century: "no one can have God as their Father, who does not have the Church as their mother."

The *Catechism of the Catholic Church* elaborates:

> It is in the Church, in communion with all the baptized, that the Christian fulfills his vocation. From the Church he receives the Word of God containing the teachings of the law of Christ. From the Church he receives the grace of the sacraments that sustains him on the way. From the Church he learns the example of holiness and recognizes its model and source in the all-holy Virgin Mary; he discerns it in the authentic witness of those who live it; he discovers it in the spiritual tradition and long history of the saints who have gone before him and whom the liturgy celebrates in the rhythms of the sanctoral cycle. (no. 2030)

Yes, even justice frays beneath the yoke of the Synodalist. Yes, they drone on about peace and justice, but always there lurks behind their high dudgeon Orwell's devastating words in *Animal Farm*: "All pigs are created equal, but some are more equal than others."

Oh yes, the Synodalist's white flag. It is raised aloft to signal to the World that it has won. It is a self-flagellation, a *mea culpa* for two thousand years of offensive doctrinal rigidity. The highest churchmen are waving that flag with statements insisting that all religions are paths to God. Or the Synodal bishop at one of the many press conferences, who pontificated, "We have much to learn from other religions." Only a few days ago, a prominent Jesuit at the Synod posted a picture of two women, with the caption: "For All Soul's Day: How a Catholic woman's faith provided comfort after the loss of her wife."

What Synodal ingenuity. Using an ancient solemn feast of the Church to undermine the Church's ancient Faith.

Alas, the white flags. Recall where Dante placed cowards in the *Divine Comedy*: at the very gate of Hell's entrance – neither in Hell nor in Heaven because their cowardice makes them repulsive to both the saved and the damned. They are consigned to run incessantly, waving white flags.

If that doesn't make the Synodalist's skin crawl, maybe God's words might; "Neither do men light a candle, and put it under a bushel, but on candlestick; and it giveth light unto all that are in the house" (Mt 5:15).

Or, if that doesn't do, perhaps this: "but whoso shall offend one of these little ones which believe in me, it were better for him that a millstone were hanged around his neck, and that he were drowned in the depth of the sea" (Mt 18:6).

Take comfort, little ones. God's justice grinds slowly, but it grinds.

THE NAVEL-GAZING OF SYNODAL "LISTENING"

That which I tell you in the dark, speak ye in the light: and that which you hear in the ear, preach ye upon the housetops.
Matthew 10:27

It seems as though navel-gazing is quite the fashion these days—even in the Church, if Synodal listening is any indication. The problem with navel-gazing, a fortiori Synodal listening, is that it prefers solipsistic reverie to the bold injunctions of Christ Our Savior. Rather than considering ways for Holy Church to bring the fire of her divine teachings to a wheezing culture drawing its last breath, it chooses the exhausted psychobabble of the transgressive seventies. This world of ours, to say nothing of Catholics themselves, yearns for the truths of dogma, but what it receives from the likes of Synodal listening is vaping. Romano Guardini strikes the right tone,

> In dogma, the fact of absolute truth, inflexible and eternal, entirely independent of a basis of practicality, we possess something which is inexpressibly great. When the soul becomes aware of it, it is overcome by a sensation as of having touched the mystic guarantee of universal sanity: it perceives dogma as the guardian of all existence, actually and really the rock upon which the universe rests. "In the beginning was the Word—the *Logos*."

This is what a world in meltdown needs to hear: the bracing message for which we must climb to the housetops. Toothy bromides will not work. Michael Hanby (*Communio*, Winter 2021) puts his finger precisely on the menace of Synodality 2022:

> There is considerable danger that the implementation of synodality will become the occasion for replacing what remains of the church's Sacramental, organismic, and Marian self-understanding with bureaucratic and political understanding... This would be the most tragic of ironies: promoting, in the name of anticlericalism, the

The Navel-Gazing of Synodal "Listening"

most clericalist conception of the church imaginable – the Church of pure administration, though with its functions now distributed more democratically among various parties and agencies.

Pretending that a positive spirit will solve all ills is illusory. Time has come for the "see no evil, speak no evil, hear no evil" clerics to make their exit. These men do not embrace the Faith; they are hopelessly dancing with shadows. How else to describe the ten *thematic nuclei* detailed in the *Preparatory Document of the Synod on Synodality* (got that?) written under Cardinal Hollerich's direction. (Yes, this is *the* Cardinal Hollerich who declared that the Church must change its teachings on homosexuality, assuming, I suppose, that he has a better idea than God. In the words of His Eminence: "I believe that the sociological-scientific foundation of this teaching is no longer correct." Hmmm. Quite bold even for a member of the cadaverous Society of Jesus.)

Ah yes, the thematic nuclei (Orwell's Newspeak can't hold a candle to this):

- To whom does our particular Church need to listen?
- What space is there for the voice of minorities, the discarded, and the excluded?
- Do we identify prejudices and stereotypes that hinder our listening?
- How do we listen to the social and cultural context in which we live?
- How does the Church dialogue with and learn from other sectors of society, the world of politics, economics, culture, civil society?
- What tools help us to read the dynamics of the culture in which we are immersed and their impact on our style of church?
- How do we discover "new" ways of showing God's love?

So encased is this agitprop in its own world that its breathtaking audacity can only be captured by the artistry of Lewis Carroll in *Alice in Wonderland*. I give you Alice's fantasy:

> If I had a world of my own everything would be nonsense. Nothing would be what it is because everything would be what it isn't. And contrariwise, what it is, it wouldn't be, and what it wouldn't be, it would. You see?

When rational analysis reaches its tipping point, only the words of savvy fiction can embrace the folly. Carroll renders Synodality's surreal nature perfectly. I suppose the writer of fiction's pictures is worth more than a thousand words of a theologian. Aside from the embarrassment to thinking Catholics, what of the world's verdict on such escapes from reality?

The more serious poetry of T. S Eliot is our recourse when tongues are tied before the spectacle of Synodality. His *Hollow Men* seizes the shallowness: "diseased by life without principle." This is nothing less than *The Triumph of the Therapeutic*, a chilling consummation of Philip Rieff's direst predictions. The Catholic Faith is not a gauzy affair of the heart, it is romance with the Cross. Neither are the gymnastics of clinical self-awareness but a conquering of the self. Synodality is the starburst of Modernism not the dust of Calvary.

Many wise men have raised the alarm about the rising tide of this nihilistic spirit. One of them is the gifted Thomist, Gerald Vann, O. P.

> The humanist world is a shallow world; a world of false and facile optimism, inasmuch as it forgets the fact of sin, or tries to ignore it. But you cannot ignore the underworld of life with impunity. Either you must go down into it, suffer it, understand it, and overcome it: or you can try to forget it for a time, and then, sooner or later, it will rise up against you and destroy you. And when the whole civilization tries thus to forget the sense of depth it may live very placidly on the surface for a while; it may make immense progress, but still only on the surface; and then its nemesis too will come upon it, and it will find itself driven back to the darkness of the cave.

The same Dominican seems to be speaking to blinkered clerics today when he writes in *Eve and the Gryphon*:

> The humanist world is roofed in low by its self-imposed limitations, and stifles men who perhaps without knowing it long for a sight of the infinite skies; And its programs of social reform are apt to end in arrogance, because it lacks the dimension of worship, and to end in a progressive mechanizing and regimenting of human nature itself because it fails to realize that the endless upward striving of humanity is not in the last resort toward material ends, however beneficent, but towards the supernatural destiny of the sons of God.

The Synodal listening sessions can easily be dismissed as another parlor game, most certainly passé by tomorrow. But that would be naïve. It is far darker. These sessions are a capitulation to the zeitgeist on a universal scale. It is the tip of the iceberg, concealing beneath a massive project of deconstruction. While many Catholics may not appreciate its true danger, it still seeps into their souls like a colorless, odorless gas that kills.

The Church's divine mission is to give humanity a contemplative gaze into the Most Holy Trinity, not to embrace the secular causes *du jour* or sterile programs of self-realization. Tragically, these have already seeped into the bloodstream of most Catholics who know nothing of the Nicene Creed but everything about inclusivity; Catholics who have been weaned on the burlesque titillations of flattened liturgies and homilies of anemic bonhomie rather than on the majestic Masses which bring men's hearts to the Heart of God.

Catholics deserve more of St. Bernard of Clairvaux and less *thematic nuclei*. Listen to him in 1146, when he preached the sermon at Vézelay, launching the Second Crusade:

> Fly then to arms! Let a holy ire animate you in the fight... Could God have not sent twelve legions of angels or breathed one word and all his enemies would crumble away into dust? But God has considered the sons of men, to open for them the road to His mercy. His goodness has caused to dawn for you a day of safety by calling you to avenge His glory in His name.
>
> Christian warriors, He who gave His life for you, today demands yours in return. These are combats worthy of you, combats in which it is glorious to conquer and advantageous to die.
>
> Illustrious knights, generous defenders of the Cross, remember the example of your fathers, whose names are inscribed in heaven.
>
> Abandon then the things that perish, in order to gather unfading palms, and conquer a Kingdom that has no end.

To those impassioned words, thousands of knights knelt and famously shouted, over and over, *Deus Vult!* (God wills it!).

Now, it is our time to climb to the housetops and begin to shout. Too much time has passed; too much damage suffered. Indeed, *Deus Vult! Deus Vult!*

THE SYNODAL COMEDY: ACT II

Assaults on the city of Rome have not been infrequent over the course of the millennia.

Attila attempted, but failed, when coming into the formidable presence of Leo called the Great, resulting in a dramatic *volte face*.

Napolean conquered Rome in 1809.

The Italian Nationalists of the Risorgimento mounted attacks upon Rome in 1848, forcing Blessed Pius IX to flee in a simple black Roman cassock to Gaeta in the Kingdom of the Two Sicilies.

Hitler subdued Rome on June 4, 1943.

Yet none of these can compare to the assault being suffered by Rome today. This time the foe is Synodal Listening – II, and it is nothing less than the squandering of Christ's salvific inheritance. To witness princes of the Church and assorted empurpled prelates parade about as though in some Rogerian self-actualization exercise makes a Catholic shudder. If not for Christ's words, "And the gates of Hell shall not prevail against it," a Catholic would be tempted to think he was witnessing the end of Catholicism.

This ruling elite behaved as though they were fanatical participants in a Maoist Struggle Session. Those historic monstrous displays dragged Chinese citizens into the semblance of a court and gratuitously accused them of being class enemies. They were then humiliated, accused, beaten, tortured, and put to death.

In the Synodal Sessions, it is the Faith that is so treated. Its majesty trampled upon, then traded for the cheap trinkets of the best psychobabble money can buy. All the more chilling is the gleeful willingness with which the successors of the apostles participated. Imagine. On the very ground consecrated by the blood of Peter and Paul and countless other martyrs, their successors are performing like a troupe of vaudevillians. They exhibit the gravitas of scarecrows.

One hesitates to accuse these synodalists of heresy, for there is far too little there to deserve the weight of such opprobrium.

Heresy requires probity and purpose. It is the stuff of serious men. These synodalists are giddy pallbearers for the corpse of a spent Catholic Left.

Before the Synod began, a retreat was mandated. You see, the insipid requires preparation. To fool the Catholics masses, folly requires mimicking Old Catholicism, though it be only a hollow shell. Hence the otherwise respectable guise of retreat. The Synodal Retreat was as close to an authentic retreat as astronomy is to astrology.

Take a quick glance at a copy of the agenda and prepare to cringe. It begins:

> The penitential liturgy is intended to direct the work of the Synod towards the beginning of a new way of being Church. In St. Peter's Basilica, the penitential celebration, presided over by Pope Francis, will include time to listen to three testimonies of persons who have suffered sin: the sin of abuse: the sin of war: the sin of indifference to the dramas present in the growing phenomena of migrations all over the world. They will confess the:
>
> - Sins against peace
> - Sins against creation, against indigenous populations, against migrants
> - Sins of abuse
> - Sins against women, family, youth
> - Sins of using doctrine as stones to be hurled
> - Sins against poverty
> - Sins against synodality/lack of listening, communion and participation of all

This is the din of Babel. Where does one begin? The task is akin to nailing down raindrops. The most obvious question: What is the sin of using doctrine as stones to be hurled? Could this refer to the defense of the Revelation of Christ? If so, one wonders what then is there to believe? If doctrine is something hurtful, then the purpose of Christ's Church evaporates. Doctrine is the unchanging teaching of the Faith. If that cannot be used as our buckler and shield, then what is?

That very query calls into question the purpose of martyrdom. Did St. John Fisher go to his death because he hurled doctrine against his enemies? Was his beheading then futile? Indeed, a sin? Was the Council of Trent a nefarious episode because it defined doctrines as ways to quell the fires of Protestant heresy?

Reason here stands stupefied. Theological analysis screeches to a halt. Against such stream of consciousness platitudes there is no egress. In his *Metaphysics*, Aristotle remarks that trying to argue with a man who has taken leave of reason is like speaking to a vegetable. Is this our predicament?

Any Catholic not embarrassed by this fog must look to see if their baptismal character has faded. Pachamama ceremonies along with the new Mayan and Amazonian rites of the Mass were only faint preludes to the soaring inanities of the Synod Retreat. These synodalists fashion themselves a pack of new Moses promulgating a terribly *au courant* list of sins. It used to be that Modernist theologians of the past years were busy burying any mention of sin. This new crop is now busy reviving it. But sins of a different color. A color bearing no resemblance to Christianity.

Readers of *Crisis* might smile at all of this. As they should. The tragedy is that ninety percent of the Catholic world will hang on this Synod's every word and treat it with the reverence of the Gospel.

Perhaps they, and the synodalists, should read St. Gregory the Great's *Pastoral Guide* of 599:

> To advance against the foe involves bold resistance to the powers of this world in defense of the flock. To stand fast in battle on the day of the Lord means to oppose the wicked enemy out of love for what is right. When a pastor has been afraid to assert what is right, has he not turned his back and fled by remaining silent? Whereas if he intervenes on behalf of the flock, he sets up a wall against the enemy in front of the House of Israel...
>
> The word of reproach is a key that unlocks a door, because the reproach reveals a fault of which the evildoer is himself often unaware. That is why Paul says of the bishop: he must be able to encourage men in sound doctrine and refute those who oppose it...
>
> Anyone ordained a priest undertakes the task of preaching, so that with a loud cry he may go on ahead of the terrible judge who follows. If, then, a priest does not know how to preach, what kind of cry can such a dumb herald utter? It was to bring this home that the Holy Spirit descended in the form of tongues on the first pastors, for he causes those whom he has filled, to speak out spontaneously.

Is St. Gregory the Great "using doctrine as stones to be hurled"? What dangerous ground these synodalists have chosen to tread.

But all this must not be met with either rancor or desperation. No room for those exertions in authentic Catholic hearts.

Call to mind the occasion of St. Ignatius's visit shortly after the approval of the Society of Jesus in 1540 by Pope Paul III. He traveled to Spain to meet with the Cardinal Archbishop of Toledo, Juan Pardo de Tavera, to ask permission for his newly erected Society to work in his archdiocese. The cardinal flatly refused. The saint then returned to his small band of new priests and announced the news. They were crestfallen. Immediately, St. Ignatius encouraged them, "I know that you are sad, this simply means that Our Lord expects great things of us."

St. Ignatius repeats that same exhortation to us today from Heaven. In the teeth of unprecedented crisis, there stands an invitation from Christ Victorious. Over two millennia, His Holy Church has risen from far greater crises. She will today. But not without inspired laymen like the readers of *Crisis* and their friends.

Be assured, the crisis will deepen, and the time for redress will drag on even longer.

But alert and intelligent Catholics have no recourse now except prayer. Each must examine their actions against the deeply affecting words of Our Savior in the *Book of the Apocalypse*: "But because thou art lukewarm and neither cold nor hot, I will begin to vomit thee out of my mouth" (Rev 3:16).

These must be looked upon as times for Catholics to do great things.

Get started.

THE TIME OF MAGICAL THINKING

J oan Didion's 2005 bestseller, *The Year of Magical Thinking*, left her readers a bit shaken. The rending account of her husband's death was cast in a demimonde of disturbing shadows. For quite a time it tossed her into a twilight existence of strange disconnections and fantasy expectations. Hence her tantalizing title. Her mourning bore no resemblance to reality, only a loose pastiche of semi-mad concoctions.

Didion's book came immediately to mind when reviewing the results of last October's Synod on Synodality. It was a moment of Magical Thinking, bearing no resemblance to historic Christianity. Even critiques became challenging, like trying to nail down snowflakes. But such has been the project of Modernism for well over a century. Its lodestar is a carefully crafted ambiguity expressed in an argot both bewildering and malleable.

Read carefully this excerpt from their document *"Synodal Church in Mission"*:

> Synodality can be understood as the walk of Christians with Christ and toward the Kingdom, together with all humanity mission-oriented, it involves coming together in assembly at the different ecclesial levels of life, listening to one another, dialogue, communal discernment, consensus building as an expression of Christ's making himself present alive in the Spirit and decision-making in differentiated co-responsibility.

Any educated individual would find this hallucinatory. Normal human beings do not speak in this kind of disconnected cant. This is a kind of degraded speech that would make Orwell blush. It is a language trapped in a specialized gnostic world foreign to normal men. Attempting to parse is vain, for it enjoys no correspondence to a reality familiar to most rational men.

Any Catholic would be hard put to find any likeness to the mandate of Christ: "Go ye therefore, and teach all nations, baptizing them in the name of the Father and of the Son and of the Holy Spirit. Teaching them to observe all things whatsoever I have commanded you" (Mt 28:19-20).

Where is there the thundering certitudes of the Creed? Where is the summons to heroic sanctity? Where is mention of saints who alone change the world and perfect the Church? Where is the desire to inflame the world with love of Christ? Where is the command to embrace the Cross and die to self? These are the badges of authentic Catholic identity.

No Roman gathering in two thousand years has reveled in the vacuous jargon on display at Synod 2023.

But this was carefully diagnosed by Pope St. Pius X in his *tour de force* 1907 encyclical *Pascendi Dominici Gregis*. In an encyclical of encyclopedic range, he exposed every facet of the Modernist heresy. In one part, he famously names Modernism the synthesis of all heresies. In the beginning of the encyclical, he explains his reason for that damning epithet:

> [their] danger is present almost in the very veins and heart of the church, whose injury is the most certain, the more intimate is their knowledge of her. Moreover, they lay the axe not to the branches and shoots, but to the very root, that is to the faith in its deepest fires. And having struck at this root of immortality, they proceed to disseminate poison to the whole tree, so that there is no part of Catholic truth from which they hold their hand, none that they do not strive to corrupt.

Because *Pascendi* identified the disease of Modernism with such penetration and surgical accuracy, the document has been reviled as a fossil. Its mere mention serves for purposes of derision, if remembered at all.

The Modernist basks in the shadows of indeterminacy. This better serves their purposes of plying their designs. They lobby for a reimagined Church existing only to mimic the antinomies of Secularism. They covet the political, while making the supernatural seem eccentric. Ask your parish priest to comment on *Pascendi* and prepare for a condescending smirk, or, more likely, a blank stare of ignorance.

All that is definite, defined, and certain is held in suspicion by the invitees of the Synod. More to their taste were Magical Thinking inanities such as:

- In this time of profound encounter and dialogue we offer the invitation to journey together, creating spaces for everyone so that we may live unity in diversity

- Catholics must experience the Synod, must do Synod; Conversation in the spirit is a new way of being church, so enlarge the space of your tent
- The Synod mothers ask for a kenotic de-centralizing since listening and dialogue inspire decision-making processes in an authentically synodal manner
- The lived experience that has been shared through a listening church respects the protagonism of the spirit in God's surprises

To convict this as an assault upon the Gospel would be confusing, due its gaseous construal. Studied ambiguity does not deal in the language that ordinary men utilize. It occupies a wholly different world than ordinary men. To mention adherence to dogma or the moral law would raise eyebrows. This is far worse than heresy, for heresy deals with the denial of truth.

The Synodal Way considers truth an intrusion.

These Synodal trailblazers have successfully erected a new Tower of Babel. Their breezy debasement of language, and the words which are its glue, is ultimately a defiant mockery of the Word.

Herein lies the deepest problem. If truth is discarded, there is nothing about which to argue. Aristotle declares in his *Metaphysics* that attempting to speak to a man who has taken leave of the laws of right reason is akin to speaking to a vegetable. There is no receptivity on the part of the listener because he has abandoned the signature mark of man – rationality.

So it is that the Church since the Council of Trent has insisted that its candidates for the priesthood spend as much time in studying philosophy as theology. For any lapse in thinking correctly guarantees howling errors in believing correctly.

This is proven by Cardinal Hollerich, the relator-general of the Synod. The cardinal explained that the Synod is "the experience of the journeying together of the people of God... to bring the synodal church into sharper focus as a comprehensive vision."

Is this the comprehensive vision that allowed the same Cardinal Hollerich to state in an interview, "The teaching of the Catholic Church must change in regard to homosexual acts, keeping it more in line with the findings of contemporary science"? One suspects that the "synodal comprehensive vision" has not much room for Christ's eternal teachings on the nature of man and his acts. The comprehensive vision must mean having better ideas than God.

Of course, we are already seeing the results of the Synod's Magical Thinking. The 2023 document of the Dicastery of the Doctrine of the Faith, *Fiducia Supplicans*, in the typical patois of Synodality (saying nothing, so anything can be said) declares blessings can be given for sin (excuse the graphic language). After ploughing through the Synodal Newspeak, that is exactly what a blessing for those in irregular unions means. Despite the dancing and handstands attempted by many bishops, priests, and even laity to put a best face forward, the blessing is for sin. It's impossible to square a circle.

Catholics of stout mind and soul will welcome the 2023 Synod with appropriate response – laughter. But those kinds of sensible Catholics are miniscule in number. The vast amount of the faithful will fall to the siren song of the Synodal Way. Why not? It is no-fault Catholicism.

Only recently, a Catholic contender for the presidency declared that he has changed his views on same-sex marriage because of the Vatican's sea change on the issue. Incidents like this will proliferate, portending a fallout that will be catastrophic.

Henry VIII's *Oath of Supremacy* is child's play compared to what Synod 2023 has rolled out.

Ah, for the good old days of the Church behind the Iron Curtain. Those heroic Catholics enjoyed the luxury of suffering a clear enemy outside the thick walls of Mother Church. We do not.

Woe to the Shepherds who treat this Synodality and its fruits with a genteel and calculated silence.

Will they ever have their John Fisher moment?

If not, aren't they afraid of millstones?

4
Of Priests
and Priesthood

THE GREATNESS OF THE PRIESTHOOD

The Priesthood and the Holy Eucharist are bound in as intimate a union as you and your body. Reasons for this are as clear to a Catholic as his own name. The Holy Eucharist is Our Lord's very own Body and Blood, soul and divinity, under signs of bread and wine. Just as it was *only* Our Lord Who could create this Sacrament, so it is *only* Our Lord Who can repeat it. But where is Christ today to repeat this wondrous transformation?

No need to search far and wide. Find a priest, and you have found Christ. Perhaps that dogma of the Church bears some clarification. It is not that Father So-and-So stops being himself and starts to be Christ. That would be rather preposterous. Correctly understood, when the priest offers Holy Mass or performs any of the sacraments he acts with the power of Christ. In fact, at that moment the priest is Christ. Amazing, isn't it? Far more amazing than we shall ever know. Such a mystery required the Church to mint a very technical formula to express with absolute precision that wondrous fact. She tells us that the priest acts *in persona Christi* (in the person of Christ Himself). As unique is Christ, as unique is the priest. As indispensable to the human race is Christ, so is the priest. As essential is Christ to the salvation of all men, so is the priest. As central is Christ to the hope of the world, so is the priest.

All of this is true because Christ has willed it so. Our Savior has deigned that His redemptive presence in the world depend upon His priests. No priest, no Mass. No priest, no forgiveness of sins. In recognition of this staggery mystery everything about the priest separates him from the rest of men: his Roman collar/cassock replaces ordinary dress; his clothing during the sacraments or Holy Mass is distinctive. Even his form of address bespeaks his high dignity: Father (he gives life to our souls in the supernatural order). Abandoning any of these signs of the priest's vocation is to chip away at the priest's vocation itself.

As the priest is one with the Holy Eucharist, so is he one with the Holy Mass. The work of the Holy Mass explains him. It is his definition. It is his reason for existence. Holy Mass for the priest is the same as words for the English teacher or numbers for the mathematician. Without it the priest is inexplicable, as the English teacher would be without his words, or the farmer without his soil. It is true that the priest is there for men on scores of other occasions outside of Mass. However, that fact ought never to obscure the primary purpose of why he exists: to offer Holy Mass and forgive sins. All those other things that he does, as good and noble as they are, cannot compare or replace what he does at Holy Mass.

Every inch of the Traditional Mass bursts its seams with its regard for the priest. Lest anyone mistake that the Mass is the work of Christ with the priest *in persona Christi*, she crowds the *actio Missae* with tokens of that deep truth. Since the priest is ordained principally to offer sacrifice his hands are consecrated with Sacred Chrism. His hands are literally set aside and infused with the powers of transforming bread and wine into the Body and Blood of Christ. Those consecrated hands become the ordinary way by which the consecrates species are to be handled. No other hands must touch the Body of God, save his. For this reason laymen are *never* to handle the sacred host in any fashion, in any circumstance. A supreme reverence for the Holy Eucharist inspires this prohibition. This same reverence inspires the faithful to loving compliance.

Nothing less but inexpressible love for the Savior in the Sacred Host brings the faithful to their knees to receive Him in Holy Communion. It is a gesture of their submission to Christ the King. In the very act of doing it, the faithful soar the heights of pure joy. It is like the kiss of a husband for his wife, or of a mother for her children. This gesture of kneeling for Holy Communion is a moment of deepest satisfaction. Few acts of man bring him closer to experiencing the closeness of God.

Similarly for the priest. You will observe what seem like endless genuflections of the priest. For a man of no faith they seem endless and merely repetitive. Love tells a different story. Each genuflection is a detail of reverential affection. Endless, indeed. Does the lover want his physical affections for the beloved to ever end? Does the mother carefully count the kisses for her infant lest they become too repetitive? As Blaise Pascal reminds us, "Love has reasons that the reason knows not of." We are justly suspicious of those who judge the genuflections of the priest to be excessive during the Traditional Mass. One rightly wonders if they have ever been in love.

Each time you step into the Traditional Mass you enter a swirling new world of grandeur, reverence, love, splendor, mystery, and intimacy. Each one of those things accompanied by proper signs and symbol which intoxicate us. Such explosive things are too much for many modern men to bear. But that will always be the problem of some modern men. Never, ever of the Old Mass.

IN PRAISE OF HEROIC PRIESTS

Amidst the dark clouds of crisis that surround Mother Church, it is well to take notice of God's rays of hope. Not that we should fail fortitude and pretend that circumstances are not as grave as they are. Nor should we fail justice and lessen our efforts against those who would harm our Holy Church. Withal, humility demands we see things as they are. One of those clear and radiant realities are the good priests about us. Some not merely good but heroic, and not merely heroic but stunning. A few of these have their names in lights, but the vast number are anonymous, quietly caring for souls in places whose names we shall never know. Added to their quotidian fidelity, is often the opprobrium of their fellow priests for not fitting in. Those captious priests have chosen the easier path of least resistance or capitulation. Their muzzled voices uphold the compromised status quo, and the pointed words of Chesterton are apropos: "A dead thing can go with the stream, but only a living thing can go against it." As though this is not enough, to many of those sterling priests comes the sting of watching those much less worthy than they rise to positions of honor and rank, while they are relegated to the least desirable of stations.

But still this band of noble priests persist, through God's grace and the company of the steadfast Catholic faithful. They are young and old, but amazingly today, they are overwhelmingly young. Like God's pied pipers, disproportionate numbers of young men follow them. They are flocking to orthodox dioceses and traditional orders like the Fraternity of St. Peter and Institute of Christ the King, the Benedictines of Norcia and Clear Creek. They are eager to leave behind the cadaver of the *spirit of Vatican II* to the superannuated Old Guard who still embrace that spent ideology like some cult of necrolaters. Their motto is the St. Augustine's from his *Confessions*, "O Ancient Beauty, and Ever New." They burn with passion for the Church and her ancient teachings and ancient liturgy. Prepare your heart to race when you read the August 6th edition of the *Catholic News Herald* of the Diocese of Charlotte, North Carolina. It's remarkable St. Joseph College Seminary, begun only a few years ago, just admitted their Fall Freshmen class of eight men. They are called the Delta Class. These young candidates for the priesthood will join 16 men already in formation. All of them clad in the Roman Cassock, looking like a Navy Seal battalion. These elite young men stand at the exceptional leadership of their Rector, Father Matthew Kauth, assisted by the adjoining parish pastor, Father Timothy Reid. All together they constitute one of the most explosively exciting developments of the last two decades. Their drive is for sanctity, their passion for the doctrine of the Church and their zeal the salvation of souls. They are the tip of Mother Church's glistening new silver spear. These impressive young men call to mind the memorable line of St. Columbanus to his missionary monks of the fifth century, "We are God's fire!"

But they do not stand alone. Several hundred miles north in Washington D. C. is the Dominican House of Studies. It has become a literal assembly line of young men taking the Dominican habit. This St. Joseph Province boasts some of the brightest minds in the Church's theological firmament. This freshly invigorated Province is singlehandedly breathing new life into the study of St. Thomas Aquinas. They are clearly rivaling the first revival of St. Thomas Aquinas post *Aeterni Patris*. They have established footholds in major secular universities and mirror the successes of the first Dominicans of the Thirteenth century. All of these new priests and seminarians seem to have made the stirring words of Romano Guardini their own:

> In dogma, the fact of absolute truth [is] inflexible and eternal... we possess something which is inexpressively great. When the soul becomes aware of it, it is overcome by a sensation of having touched the mystic guarantee of universal sanity; it perceives dogma as the guardian of all existence, actually and really the rock upon which the universe rests. "In the beginning was the Word" – the *Logos*.

While the headiness of these new priests may daze us, we cannot forget the veteran priests who have been dogged in their fidelity. These have managed to keep their heads above the theological sludge that has drowned their clerical brethren. They have stood fast to the classical principles of Catholic doctrine and liturgy. Fad never lured them nor did the fatal appetite for ambition, a flaw that has curdled the soul of many a good priest. Sound theology for these priests, in most cases, did not come from their seminary training but in spite of it. Thanks to exceptional parents, a good priest mentor, or the sheer operation of the Holy Spirit, these priests enjoyed a reliable *sensus theologicus* that steered them past the perilous shoals and eddies of Accompaniment Church, against which they might suffer shipwreck. They are often sidelined by some of the Church's governing elites. But this leaves them unfazed: Fidelity comes at a steep price. Their days are filled with carrying starved souls to the torrents of grace. They have no time to fret over the trivial pursuits of clerical apparatchiks who, in the evocative lines of Eliot's Burnt Norton, spend their days "distracted from distraction by distraction."

These singular priests can instantly sniff the poisoned air of secularism or of sentimentalized Catholicism a hundred miles away. They have stared down the maw of modernity and armed themselves against every one of its subterfuges. Its sound bites don't fool them. Its seductive logic does not tempt them. Every stock epithet in the Modernist quiver has been hurled at them like javelins, and they have dodged all of them. While the clerical *bien pensant* scold, "You can't go back", these good priests reply, "Our future is the past." Growling again, "You must change with the times," their smart riposte, "No, priests must change these times." You see, this brave company of priests is bright, gifted and bristling with vibrant fidelity to Holy Church. They will not be duped by Dupes.

These priests, whether oils still wet upon their palms or long dried, draw from the depths of the Church's teachings and tradition. Their dependence is not only upon St. Thomas Aquinas and magisterial dogma, but all the golden threads that are the Church's past. Wondrously, these priests have multiplied their own kind, in either inspiring fresh bands of young men or shaping new waves of the Catholic Faithful in a fighting force for God's Truth and His Holy Church. They speak supernatural Truths over and over again, each time clothing them with new luster. Like those Old Testaments priests who blew their horns to bring down Jericho's walls, so will these heroic priests of Jesus Christ bring down walls as well. Their horns are eternal truths, and the walls they topple are the ones made NewChurch lies.

When that day comes Catholics will look back at these times of great crisis and weep at the catastrophe. But they will also see that the Great Crisis was the Holy Spirit's fiery forge. And only on that anvil could He have shaped these glorious priests – titans among us. Sometimes heaven's ways are hard to understand. But they are always the sure ways.

IN PRAISE OF THE (FORMER) SOCIETY OF JESUS

Not so long ago, giants roamed the earth. They were called Jesuits. Of course, our Holy Church has produced giants for millennia, not only Jesuits. Forged in the fires of grace and sculpted by the divine artistry of the Holy Spirit, they have adorned the Church, as gleaming jewels in her crown. These giants changed the course of history, civilizations and, most critically, men's hearts. But of these Catholic giants few stand out as dramatically as the Society of Jesus. Even a jaded world is compelled to credit this supernatural force of giants with astonishing accomplishments. The sheer power of their spiritual and intellectual might confounds the imagination. Their grandeur is singular, causing wonderment in the eyes of most men.

All this startling triumph lies at the feet of one diminutive Basque soldier, Ignatius of Loyola. After a young life of vain derring-do, a battle injury sustained in 1521 confined him to a hospital where his preferred tales of love and chivalry were absent, leaving him with only a volume of the lives of the saints. With some reluctance he took up the book, and with the suddenness of a thunderclap, the Holy Spirit invaded his heart. He saw his past exploits of heroism as quite vain and sterile. A new kind of valor struck him, a valor for the cause of Christ and His Holy Church. His noble Spanish blood found a new purpose, a new call to arms, a wholly different passion, and a heroism beneath the banner of Christ the King. This is the soldiering that made his heart soar, and he would delay no longer.

Aware that he required a whole new orientation he made his way to a solitary redoubt called Mt. Manresa wearing only a sackrobe. In the moving words of the historian Henri Daniel Rops, "Christ laid in wait." After ten months of grueling fasting and intense prayer he knew what God was calling him to do. With haste charged with high purpose, he then bathed, trimmed his nails, cut his hair, found suitable clothes, and marched forward. Christ had revealed to him that he was to continue his role as soldier, but now in a divine army, vanquishing the Savior's enemies and ransoming souls for Him. Part of this revelation was that he must employ everything the earth offered for this mission, as long as it was not sinful. Here he made his own what would be the motto of his new corps of soldiers, and of every Catholic, *ad maiorem Dei gloriam*. With this as his banner, he ultimately recognized that his new elite army would have to be the forward phalanx in defense of the Faith. For that noble aspiration the highest level of sanctification would be necessary. That could only be achieved with the highest level of a knowledge of the Faith. Again, Rops, "Ignatius understood that the fiery passion for God had to be tempered by study and hard work." With this conviction, he traveled to Paris and received the doctorate in 1534.

A dramatic turning point was reached August 15th, 1534. St. Ignatius, with four companions, among whom was Francis Xavier, Francis Borgia and Peter Faber, ascended Montmarte in Paris and made an act of consecration to the Mother of God. Only five years later Pope Paul III established the Society of Jesus as a religious order with the bull *Regimini Militantis Ecclesiae*. Clearly, its very title trumpets the genius of the new order: they were to be the militant regiments of the Church. The opening lines of their Founding Document tell the story: "This Society was founded for whomever desires to serve as a soldier of God, to strive especially for the defense and propagation of the Faith and for the progress of souls in Christian life and doctrine."

And what feats of valor would adorn their ranks. Such prodigies could only have appeared because of Ignatius. The secret of their supernatural success was the saint's *Spiritual Exercises*, a never ceasing torrent that would produce breathtaking results both in the men who joined Ignatius ranks, as well as in every part of the world where their feet would take them.

The *Spiritual Exercises* set down two markers: (1) sanctification (2) in the service of Mother Church. The blueprint of sanctification would follow the ancient traditions of the Church. Each member would travel the Purgative-Illuminative and Unitive way. First, an awareness and conquest of their sins; second, a heroic cultivation of the virtues in imitation of the Life of Christ; finally, a union with Christ Crucified, so intimate, that "Nevertheless I live; yet not I, but Christ liveth in me" (Gal 2:20). His masterpiece was not named the *Exercises* for the sake of poetic flourish. Ignatius intended for his men to know that sanctification was not flights of treacly self-absorption, but the rigors of conquest: the conquest of the self. Relentless stripping is demanded, tearing away at all the layers of self-regard that pride so sedulously constructs. Individualism dies, so that individuality can flourish. Sanctification does not bury the self that God has been pleased to create, but only the self-love which has distorted the man (cf. *gratia fecit naturam*). Ignatius knew that unless self-love was expelled, the Holy Spirit could not fashion His masterpiece. Only then can his supernatural thunder resound throughout the world. Indeed it did, with every member of the Society of Jesus. They made their appearance in the Church like a rolling tidal wave, a seeming endless series of triumph after triumph.

Of their monumental accomplishments, their presence in Elizabeth's sixteenth-century England was the most stunning. Wasting no time, Fr. Allen, as the newly appointed rector, established a seminary in Douai, France, for the education and formation of Jesuit priests bound for care of persecuted Catholics in England. As these Jesuit heroes crossed the English Channel, they knew they would be facing ghoulish torture and certain death. Yet they sailed. And with the eagerness of lovers soon to meet their beloved. By 1594, 450 Jesuit priests were dispatched to England. Countless numbers were executed, Edmund Campion amongst the most famous. On his deathbed, Fr. Allen lamented that he should die in his bed while, "by his persuasion so many had borne imprisonments, persecutions and martyrdom in England." As Joseph Pierce notes, "His own unworthiness to die a martyr's death was seen by him as being what his sins deserved." While they could not end the march of Protestantism in England, they did route it in Poland, Lithuania, and Southern Germany.

Upon St. Ignatius's death in 1556 his Society had founded 74 colleges on three continents. His famous *Ratio Studiorum* — Latin, Greek, classical literature, poetry and philosophy, science, the arts, vernacular languages, and rhetoric — became the educational template for the transformation of boys into colossal men of learning and stalwart Catholicism. By 1600, the apostolic works of the Society exploded:

- Francis Xavier was baptizing thousands in India
- Jesuits reached Latin America with missions in Peru, Columbia, and Bolivia

In Praise of the (Former) Society of Jesus 151

- By 1603, 345 Jesuits were working in Mexico
- By 1716 Jesuits were baptizing in Tibet, gaining an exceptional mastery of the Tibetan language and culture producing long and detailed accounts of the country and its religion as well as treatises in Tibetan that attempted to refute key Buddhist ideas and establish the truth of Christianity

Each religious Order has produced similar results. But the Society of Jesus seems to tower over them all, with their accomplishments staggering the imagination. Indeed, all Catholics should be chanting the praises of this Order on this feast of St. Ignatius. An Order whose accomplishments stupefies both Catholic and non-Catholic alike.

Then something happened.

Around 1964 a kind of apocalypse devastated the Society, dividing it into a before and after, like B. C and A. D. Led by the General, Fr. Pedro Arupe, the Society decided that the past four hundred years were somewhat of an embarrassment. They needed to refashion their purposes to make it more congenial to a secular world. They decided to trade their sublime supernatural purpose for *au courant* programs that would win kudos from a revolutionary Knowledge Class. They leapt upon the careening juggernaut of Marxism and made it the *raison d'être* of their sprawling educational network. To make it palatable they called it social justice. The result? Their seminaries became gulags of reprogramming and their universities, factories of anti-Catholic fury. Where once their prodigious intellectual gifts produced Catholic titans, now they created shills for a debased culture. They reached new lows by applying Modernist hermeneutics to Catholic doctrine, rendering the *depositum fidei* a rotting carcass.

Shamelessly they proselytized a strange religion bearing little resemblance to historic Christianity. How else explain the deeply disturbing words of the newest Superior General, Fr. Arturo Sosa Abascal. When asked about the Christ's teaching regarding the indissolubility of marriage, he replied: "Human reality is much more nuanced and never black and white... At the time no one had a recorder to take down His words... Over the last century in the Church there has been a great blossoming of studies that seek to understand exactly what Jesus meant to say... which attests that the word is relative." Even a second grader could see that this has Modernism written all over it. And Modernism is arsenic to the Faith.

Then there is the outgoing president of Fordham University, Fr. Joseph McShane. In a 2022 piece in the *Wall Street Journal*, he made this gaseous remark: "There is still a real demand for a university that includes a reverence for the divine." That is porous enough to include, well, anything. But he truly reveals the new Society of Jesus in this: "Colleges and universities are well-placed to promote a culture of encounter rather than a culture of pronouncements." Translation, please. Actually, no translation necessary. You know what he means. Today, one ironclad rule alone governs the new Society: the proscription of any doctrinal, moral, ascetical or liturgical tradition that existed before 1970.

All of this confirms the ancient Roman adage: *corruptio optimi pessima*, the corruption of the best is the worst. Tragically, the Society of Jesus has become the lackey of the zeitgeist. God's Marines have become God's embarrassment.

Only God knows what will come of this once powerful Order. Their numbers are in dramatic free-fall and their provinces shrink with each passing day.

Know this. There are still exemplary faithful Jesuits. They know who they are. Some of you may know them.

With their heroism, perhaps the Society will make St. Ignatius smile from heaven someday. It will take a Herculean effort.

Who knows? God's Marines may still return.

SAINT MYCHAL JUDGE?

After eighteen years of remembering 9/11, distance should bring greater clarity. Of course, some of the details of that cataclysm will likely seem ancient history to younger generations, such as the name Fr. Mychal Judge. But such reflection might cast fresh light to those who recall that name well, but also presenting an uncanny parallel to today's fraught times.

By this time Father Mychal Judge is renowned the world over for his priestly ministrations and tragic death on September 11th, 2001. Images of Father Judge being carried by New York firemen, head slumped, bearing his slightly tilted fire helmet, are now iconic. Long after concerns raised by columns like this, the priestly body of Father Judge carried in makeshift procession will rise as one of the riveting moments of American history, like the Marines raising the flag at Iwo Jima. It will act as a woodcut memorializing the heroism of Catholic priests, pressed like a palimpsest against the Priestly Crises of our times.

Even so, it would be remiss for Catholics to leave unaddressed certain anomalies regarding the public priestly persona of Father Judge. Accompanying all of Father Judge's acts of mercy was his not so hidden homosexuality. One ought to carefully note the paean in New York's *Village Voice* of September 19–25, 2001:

> To friends he was known as a gay man who appreciated the Gay USA show and celebrated the City's "gorgeous men" by saying, "Isn't it wonderful?!" When his close friend, gay activist Brendan Fay, started a St. Patrick's parade in Queens last year that included gay groups, Judge helped him fund it and showed up in his brown friar's robes to put the church on the side of the oppressed, even as Catholic officialdom was urging a boycott. He frequently donated clothes to the Out of the Closet Thrift Shop for gay and AIDS causes on East 81st Street. He was a long-time member of Dignity, the gay Catholic group. In recent years, he came out to many of those he loved, including Fire Commissioner Tom von Essen, who warmly accepted him.

Most certainly, in matters of this sort a sharp clarity and careful delicacy is required. No man is without sin, or its inclinations. Priests are no different. Struggles against our sins is the arena of sanctity, priests not excepted. Soaring drama has frequently been created out of such struggles: Bernanos's *Diary of a Country Priest*, Greene's *The Power and the Glory*, J. E. Powers's *Morte d'Urban*. Common to all of these is the priest's passionate love of Catholic truth. Dramatic tensions arise from his keen awareness of how distant his personal life has strayed from that truth. In that tension lies his agony, but also his triumph. No drama can be present in the life of a priest who desires to only rewrite the truth, not die for it.

In Father Judge's decision to publicly disclose his homosexuality, it is feared that noble struggle mutated into vain performance. Father Judge crossed a moral Rubicon. Heroism against volcanic carnality seemed to become complacency in a corrosive gay ideology. Moreover, the *Catechism* declares homosexuality to be objectively disordered (no. 2358); elsewhere it is called "a more or less strong tendency ordered toward an intrinsic moral evil."[1] All attempts at theological legerdemain notwithstanding, these magisterial pronouncements still obligate filial submission.

Perplexing, isn't it, that Father Judge would allow that moral weakness to be advertised? Unless, perhaps, to make it more palatable. One wonders. It must be made absolutely clear that no imputation of sin is being made against Father Judge. No one but God knows those things. All that is being imputed here is a witting (or unwitting) collapse to ideology. For a priest, that is almost as bad as sin. Arguably, it is sin.

Sufficient evidence exists for such claims. The *New York Times* cited a friend of Father Judge: "What his life says is 'Yes, you can be gay and good, you can be homosexual and holy," said Brendan Fay, a gay rights advocate who was a friend of the priest's" (September 27, 2001). The next paragraph of the same story reports: "Friends recall how Father Judge had invited the AIDS ministry of Dignity, a gay Catholic organization, to operate out of St. Francis. Mr. Fay said Father Judge marched in an alternative St. Patrick's Day in Queens that included gays."

---

[1] Congregation for the Doctrine of the Faith, *Pastoral Care of Homosexual Persons*, no. 17.

How very curious, a priest in a gay pride parade? Ought not priestly compassion for those oppressed by vice, or even injustice, be applied in the confessional box? Of course, the rabid anti-Catholicism alone of such parades ought to proscribe the participation of any priest. Did this obvious fact elude Father Judge?

And what of Dignity? How could Father Judge not have known about the anti-Catholic posturing of Dignity? Dignity is a misnamed Catholic organization lobbying for some 30 years for the Church's accommodation of the gay ideology: that homosexual acts are gestures of love and therefore stand squarely alongside the sexual acts of marriage. Dignity's agenda differs not an iota from the secularist gay one. It fails to understand that the Catholic Church opposes the gay agitprop, not the homosexual person. Dignity, along with the secular gay front and fellow travelers, does not. This is a flagrant affront to Catholic sexual teaching. It dares not be taken lightly. Could it have missed the attention of Father Judge?

Father Judge's missteps seems to fit into a more general pattern noticeable in not a few areas of mainstream Franciscanism (for this reason, many reform Franciscan groups have appeared.) For example, Father John Felice, accepting an award on behalf of the fallen FDNY fire chaplain in April 2002, seemed to speak in coded ambiguity: "There is a rush to canonize Mychal these days and I think that is a mistake. In making saints out of people we often shove them away from our experience and place them on a pedestal. He was a very human, flawed, complex person just like the rest of us." QED.

One is tempted to dismiss all of this as caviling, at best, a violation of *de mortuis nihil bonum*, at worst. Yes, that is, until a piece appears like the one in the *National Catholic Reporter* on May 17th, 2001. It contained not an ounce of ambiguity. Brother Jack Talbot, a member of the Capuchin Franciscans, headquartered in Detroit, declared himself "out of the closet", as a gay friar. Might not a Catholic be somewhat wary of the wholesale use of a vocabulary so intimately wedded to a secular movement at war with the Catholic Church? Shouldn't that wariness extend to a boastfulness about an inclination the Catholic Church declares gravely disordered? What of those more tender Catholic souls who smart at such bold admissions, or even suffer scandal? But Brother Talbot is not finished: "Human sexuality is the font of all that centers and propels us. I invite our gay brothers and sisters to 'come out.' Tell your sacred stories to others." In hindsight, don't we see where this has led?

Now, all of that may be New Age coated Freudianism, but it isn't Catholicism. Any alert Catholic cannot help but note the direction of the evidence. He would not be acting tendentiously, only clearheadedly.

May Father Mychal Judge rest in peace, and we leave him to the sweet mercies of the Savior, on Whose mercies we all depend. But *Saint* Mychal Judge. Isn't that a bridge too far? That would be canonizing an alternative Catholicism. Let us be clear, an alternate Catholicism is *not* Catholicism. It is certainly not the stuff of saints. Nor, dare I say it, of faithful priests.

PAULIST FATHERS: DISASSEMBLING THE CATHOLIC FAITH FOR DECADES

Headlines blared in New York City last week: "Manhattan Catholic Church declares God is Trans." They referred to a banner hanging on the façade of the venerable St. Paul's Church in Manhattan, sitting right outside Lincoln Center for the Performing Arts. This historic Church, founded by the Paulist Fathers, was once a fabled mecca for conversions to the Catholic Faith; now, it's a tomb for a bloodless Catholic ghost.

Those of us familiar with the Catholic landscape of Manhattan were not surprised at this latest salvo against the Faith. The Paulist Fathers, for the past forty years, have made this glorious architectural wonder the busy workplace for disassembling the Catholic Faith. Their own Paulist Press, once a publishing engine for scores of books explaining and defending the Catholic Faith, is now more of an abattoir for All Things Catholic.

An alert Catholic may ask: But why has such a Catholic anomaly been permitted to exist? To that question, one must ask the forty-year span of Cardinal Archbishops of New York. Live and let live, I suppose.

A damning strategy, for sure.

A New York newspaper inquired of a number of St. Paul's parishioners their thoughts of the subversive slogan. One remarked: "St. Paul's is a place of welcome. It's also a place to question one's own path."

Hmm. Almost sounds hallucinogenic. That, or maybe a text from an ancient gnostic gospel. What makes it so unsettling is that it expresses what might be the feeling of a majority of Catholics today, where typical parishes reprocess them to speak in such jargon. They have been disconnected from historic Christianity and float in a solipsistic ether of the self, with an occasional sprinkle of god-talk. Wouldn't Feuerbach be proud!

Because the dissemblers have been busy at their work, most Catholics today have only the leanest idea of what being a Catholic means. They certainly possess even less understanding of what the word religion means.

It is derived from the Latin *religio*, and buried in that word is the Latin term *ligatus*. Ligatus is defined as a binding, or an intimate connection, from which we receive our English words ligament and obligation. That enables us to appreciate the depth of the meaning of the word religion. It is a binding to Almighty God: to His Revelation, His teachings, and most sublimely, to God Himself. While this generic definition can be applied broadly to any entity fulfilling its terms, it can only be applied perfectly to Roman Catholicism.

Now, to our St. Paul's parishioner.

The Roman Catholic Church is indeed welcoming. But welcoming to all those who are prepared to embrace, with full and unreserved obedience, her supernaturally revealed truths. The Church welcomes all into a glorious objective world of winged divine mysteries. She welcomes all those who possess the valor to adhere unquestionably to virtue and sacrifice. The Church offers a welcoming to enter the life of the Bride of Christ, in all her spiritual and physical splendor. A welcoming to all who want possession of a "pearl of great price" (Mt 13:46), whose value exceeds all things human. A welcoming to all those who are willing to shout "from the housetops" (Mt 10:27) that the only path to fulfillment and glory is found in the Roman Catholic Church.

The Church does not exist to find one's own path. The Church *is* the path. Chesterton put it dramatically:

> Modern man is more like a traveler who has forgotten the name of his destination, and has to go back whence he came, even to find out where he is going. Modern Man has not only forgotten the name of his destination, he has even forgotten he has a destination.

For poor Wandering Man the Church is his destination, where he can find his true home in Heaven.

This privilege is enjoyed solely by Catholics. Here we enter upon the greatest mystery of our holy religion. Not a mystery as a riddle or a clever problem to solve. That is not mystery at all. True mystery is a truth so dazzling that not even the greatest of human intellects could fully grasp it. Mystery is not intimidating but, rather, intoxicating. It is like looking at the wondrous expanse of the oceans: even as one gazes at its lovely immensity, one is seeing only a scintilla of what is there.

So, mystery: one sees, but mostly, one does not see.

Once in the arms of the Church, men understand why she is called Mother. She feeds not only with truth but with God. The colossal mystery of our religion lies in our binding to God in intimate friendship. How can this be? Friendship entails equality. Friends holding each other. Even Aristotle, in the *Metaphysics*, when asking himself if men can be friends with God, answers no. Applying pure logic, there is simply no proportion between an infinite being and man.

So how can a man be God's friend? How does God approach, so man can hold Him? Here we arrive at the ineffable mystery of our Holy Faith: its deepest center, its loftiest height, its unfathomable richness. Somehow, somewhere, in some way, God holds us so that we can hold God. This only happens in Christ. It is Christ who surrendered the invisible splendor of His divine nature to have it be joined to the visible poverty of our human nature. For Christ, even this Incarnation is not sufficient for friendship. Before He dies, He leaves to us a divine way that He can bind Himself to us and we to Him: the Holy Eucharist.

Catholics do not bind themselves to a Christ who is out there or up there but, rather, to God who is *right here*, in the very midst of us. In our tabernacles. So it is that Roman Catholicism is the true religion—because God is right here.

Yes, other religions might honor God. But other religions can only honor God out there. Catholics actually have God. Each time you receive Christ in the Holy Eucharist, God holds us, and we hold Him. Mother Church fittingly calls this mutual holding Holy Communion.

For God and man hold each other in a common union. A union so intimate that words collapse before the mystery.

This recalls Graham Greene in his *The Power and the Glory*. When the whiskey priest is distributing Holy Communion to the poor Mexican peasants kneeling on a dirt floor in one of their hovels, the narrator remarks: "And the priest was amazed as he placed God on the tongues of men."

'Tis a pity that the St. Paul's parishioner is blind to this supernatural grandeur.

When men want religion without God, they enclose themselves in a claustrophobic world. Things are left with gaping metaphysical holes. They are not what they are supposed to be. And since nature abhors a vacuum, that metaphysical hole is filled by the whims of men. Those whims are the stuff of terror.

Again, Chesterton: "Take man away from the supernatural, and he is not left with the natural, but with the unnatural." Apart from God man does not die. Much worse. He becomes a monster. Oh, he looks the same; but his soul, like Dorian Gray's attic portrait, becomes disfigured, twisted and grotesque.

Look around. No lack of evidence for that.

We fully appreciate the remark of St. John of the Cross in his *Spiritual Canticle*: "Outside of God everything is narrow."

My poor St. Paul's parishioner, what riches have been stolen from you. What a grand theft of cosmic proportions. You see, the closer we are to Christ in the Holy Eucharist, the more He sends us His Holy Spirit. The Holy Spirit lets us see the finger of God in all things. He lets us see through circumstances to the ways of God, where other men see only circumstances. He lets us see with eyes of charity, which can see the reasons for all things – even things which violate charity. Thus, Richard of St. Victor: "*ubi amor, ibi oculus*" (where there is love, there is the eye).

The typical Catholic, like the one at St. Paul's, is missing the vast horizons of our Holy Religion. He has been sold a basket of lies, and now he chokes on them. Without the bracing air of the Church's truths, he chases after each and every deceit *du jour* served up by a wheezing secularist culture. And as a man at sea trying to slake his thirst with salt water, each draught brings on a maddening and unquenchable yearning.

Such yearnings will not be satisfied with bizarre concoctions such as "God is trans." Those inventions are the clacking approach of the Gates of Hell.

There is only one place where the Gates of Hell do not prevail. Leave St. Paul's and come home.[2]

---

[2] After the publication of this article, a representative of the Paulist Fathers requested that information in this article be corrected. He noted: "The sign in question was a small sign giving the name and description of one artist's display in the eight-artist exhibit 'Vessel: A Spiritual Art Experience.' The exhibit was curated by a Duffy Fellow from the Fordham University Center on Religion and Culture. The exhibit is a partnership between the Fordham University Center on Religion and Culture and the Openings Collective, a visual artists collective that often exhibits at the Church of St. Paul the Apostle. The exhibit was supervised by the staff of the Fordham University Center on Religion and Culture and Paulist Fr. Frank Sabatté, director of

WHY I LOVE THE NATIONAL CATHOLIC REPORTER

Yes, I confess it. Before all the readers of *New Oxford Review*, I stand accused. My vice is shocking because the *National Catholic Reporter* has been the paper of record for the spirit of Vatican II faux Catholicism for the past 50 years. It has been the *Congressional Record* of the Catholic Left, chronicling the steamrolling of the Faith with breathless ardor. Of course, spirit of Vatican II Catholicism has as much to do with Catholicism as a firefly has to do with fire. Resemblances in names are only skin deep. The *National Catholic Reporter* (hereafter, *NCR*) bears as much truthfulness in their name as the People's Republic of North Korea has in theirs.

NCR boasts for half a century of being the cutting edge of a reimagined Catholicism – that project which seeks going further even than the condemned Modernism of 1907. For these avatars of All Things New, the trailblazers Fathers Loisy, Tyrrell and Sullivan did not blaze far enough. *NCR* has been compulsory reading for many of the pace setting episcopal *nomenklatura* and the regnant *bien pensant* who have held a death grip on most Catholic institutions of learning and chancery offices for too many decades to count.

How could any faithful Catholic love such a thing? How can I? You see, *NCR* is the canary in the mineshaft: disclosing sure signs that something is coming hitherto unnoticed by others. Their keenly developed sense of heterodoxy's dominance make them perfect predictors to emerging and credible threats to their

---

the Openings Collective. The pastor of the Church of St. Paul the Apostle and the leadership of the Paulist Fathers did not approve the original title of the display. The original title of the display was that one artist's opinion. It did not reflect any opinion of the parish or of the Paulist Fathers. When the original title of the display was brought to the attention of the leadership of the Paulist Fathers, it was changed. There was never a banner with the original title of that one artist's display on the facade of the Church." When asked multiple times by *Crisis* whether the statement *"God is Trans"* is blasphemous, the Paulist Fathers representative refused to answer.

long-held hegemony. *NCR*'s reportage of cracks in its supremacy become causes for glee amongst faithful Catholics; any alarms on *NCR*'s part, approaching triumph for us. I suppose one man's poison is another man's food. For these reasons this writer combs through the pages of *NCR* in the hope of discovering rumblings of *NCR*'s discontent.

Its issue of February 5-18, 2021 delivered a bonanza. The frontpage headline screeched: "Charlotte's rad-trad pastors." Caption underneath: "In came Latin, incense and burned books, out went half the parishioners." The byline: Peter Feuerherd. Factoring in journalistic hyperbole (the Catholic Left's penchant for hurling the slur "book-burning" is the equivalent of the Secular Left's calling someone racist: a conversation stopper, with another notch in the victory belt of the Left). A certain hermeneutic is required here. *NCR*'s operating assumption, as well as a majority of the reigning apparatchiks in the Church, is that the successful understanding and transmission of the Gospel has been impeded by two thousand years of the Church's cadaverous tradition and scholastic theology. It deems these things accretions. For them, devotion to eternal truths has mutated into a devotion to the zeitgeist.

NCR's real terror was disclosed in the image atop the panicked headlines. It was of Bishop Peter Jugis, the exceptional Ordinary of the Diocese of Charlotte, North Carolina. He is flanked by some 30 seminarians. That bears repeating: 30 seminarians. Numbers that large for a relatively small Diocese like Charlotte is startling. The top ten Archdioceses in the country, indeed of North America, cannot report such numbers. Some have no seminarians at all, leaving them with the grim task of shuttering their seminaries, or merging them. St. Joseph's seminary sings *Te Deum*: most others intone the *Dies Irae*.

But back to the photograph. Behind them the façade of the spanking new St. Joseph's College Seminary built at a cost of $19 million dollars, sitting there like a medieval building just floating down from the campus Oxford University. All of this striking accomplishment the brainchild of one of the most gifted priests in America, Fr. Matthew Kauth. His achievement cannot be overstated. He is not only responsible for raising all the monies for the construction of the seminary, but also the inspiration for the thirty young men now studying for the priesthood for the Diocese of Charlotte. Each of his seminarians look like they were pulled from a seminary brochure of 1956 or the graduation photo of the latest class of Navy Seals: ebullient, hale and clothed in the Roman cassock, bespeaking their passion for the Church's tradition, her immemorial teaching and an admirable awareness of the Church's millennial understanding of the *romance of the symbol*. If you think this too good to be true, go to the many videos on YouTube. There you will not only see and hear the seminarians, but also their gifted rector, Fr. Kauth.

All of this sits quite uneasily for NCR. Seems as though these signs of the Church's approaching springtime are too much to take, like sunlight on a vampire. So, Mr. Feuerherd went hunting for Franciscan Sr. Katarina Smith, professor emerita of the Seminaries of St. Paul Minnesota for an interpretive coda. This had to be quite a labor for him, for this unregenerate band of dissenting theologians have become curious fossils for today's forward-looking generation of seminarians. Her rich comments bespeak a coming apocalypse.

Most revealing was her description of the Charlotte seminarians and all the many like them: "They want certainty. They want answers." Mind you, for Sr. Katrina this is an indictment, not a recognition of the nature of the human person which has marked man's nature for as long as there was man. It is as much a trait of man *qua* man as air is for breathing. It is the longing that summoned forth the genius of Socrates, Plato and Aristotle. Her and her kind are not only chasing after a reimagined Church but a reimagined man. Sr. Katrina's grievance is against nothing less than truth in general and dogma in particular. This kind of nihilism we expect of Michel Foucault and Nietzsche, not a professed religious, and seminary professor to boot.

She laments further, "These seminarians gloss over complicated issues in moral theology." May I translate? Objective good and evil are too constricting for the ever-expanding self. Sounds like Nietzsche's *Beyond Good and Evil*, you say. And you would be right. Then the good sister goes in for the kill: "(they) latch onto traditional modes and symbols like the wearing of elaborate cassocks" (cassocks we know; "elaborate cassocks" escape us!). *O my!* You can almost hear Voltaire screaming: *"écrasez l'infâme!"* After these fulminating warnings, Sr. Katrina delivers this bone chilling prediction: "Their small numbers are not insignificant because they tend to be active" (Like a mutant strain of the Covid virus, I suppose). Then, "They will exert influence on the Church as more are ordained." Bravo, Bishop Jugis!

Mr. Feuerherd remarks that these New Seminarians labor beneath the opprobrium of Pope Francis barb of being little monsters. There must be some mistake. The Roman Pontiff would never malign an emerging group of young, robust, immovably orthodox and virtuous seminarians as little monsters. More journalistic hyperbole, to be sure. But there was no hyperbole in the comments of Fr. Tim Kelly, pastor in the Diocese of Tyler, Texas, and former professor of homiletics and patristics at St. Mary's Seminary in Houston.

The former professor whines that these New Seminarians are advancing an alternate magisterium. *Hmm*. What magisterium can that be, esteemed professor? Perhaps, the two-thousand-year young Magisterium of the Catholic Church with clearly demarcated lines of truth and error? He concludes, "These men have been coming out of the cult of John Paul II." Now the good professor has shown his hand. Not necessarily to include Fr. Kelly, but this kind of language usually comes from priests who have not bowed a moment to the Church's Magisterium, yet suddenly drag the term out now for their own purposes. Similarly, those who now piously invoke obedience to authority. For fifty years these Keepers of the Modernist Flame made it their vocation to dismiss both authority *and* obedience. A curious reversal is at play here, and faithful Catholics should stand warned.

No, I shall not apologize. I do love the *National Catholic Reporter*, and I do thank Mr. Feuerherd. Where else could we find the reliable signs of our coming triumph?

NUNSENSE, REDUX (PART I)

Be sure to keep your eyes peeled for the next few weeks, because the Nuns on the Bus may be rolling into your neighborhood. Nuns on the Bus? It is a project of *Network*, a nun's group which lobbies for social justice (read: Leftist causes, with special emphasis on the Catholic Church's oppression of its members, especially women). Before going any further, these are not your father's nuns. Oh no, these nuns are slightly to the left of Jane Fonda. In fact, don't think you'll spot them on the street, they are unspottable. Back in the seventies these gals decided the religious habit was a ball and chain that kept them vassals of the patriarchal Catholic Church. Moreover, habits had to go to better identify with the suffering masses smarting beneath the thumb of a capitalist first world. Finally disrobed, these ladies could take their place on the front lines of societal change, free of the straight-jacket of a God shamefully distorted by two-thousand years of Catholic lies. These Nuns on the Bus nuns saw it as their job to hasten the demise of an institution better left on the ash heap of history. Their attitude was deftly expressed by Gary Wills, in his 1970s book, *Bare Ruined Choirs*, which he hoped would be the long-awaited obituary of the Catholic Church:

> The church was enclosed, perfected in circular inner logic, strength distributed through all its interlocking aspects; turned in on itself, giving a good account of itself to itself – but so vulnerable, so fragile, if one looked outward, away from it. It had a crystalline ahistoricity; one though of change or time could shatter it – and did.

Wills was the Tom Paine of the radicalization of the Catholic Church, and these nuns were his willing Minutemen loaded for bear. Swinging their once-proud wimples and rosary beads over the heads like some tribe of Huns carrying the skulls of their victims, these emancipated nuns would teach the Catholic Church a lesson it would never forget. While hordes of them abandoned schools, hospitals, and cloisters, enough of them remained and, like Sherman's March to the Sea, leveled everything Catholic in their path. It can safely be said without fear of contradiction that the ruin the Church faces today in every corner of its life is, in large part, the malignant fruit of their work. As effectively as the nuns of the nineteenth and first of half of the twentieth century gave the Catholic Church such glory, similarly effective has been the Nuns on the Bus been in undoing that work and creating the numbing devastation the Church has endured in the last half century.

Let us return to Network. It is part of a wider conglomeration of progressive nuns called the Leadership Conference of Women Religious (LCWR), which has been the corporate battering ram of the radical Catholic agenda. It has had clear sailing for the past half century, challenged by no one in their scorched earth campaign. Until now. Several weeks ago, Pope Benedict XVI, through his Sacred Congregation for the Doctrine of the Faith, barked, *No More*. Well – the nuns were absolutely blindsided – and outraged. Top strategist Sister Simone Campbell, who spent the last eighteen years of her religious life representing poor people at a community law center in Oakland, California, was not standing for this intrusion. In her words, "I've been a faithful religious woman for over forty years, and some guy who's never talked to me says were a problem? Ooh, that hurts." Just in case you missed it, the guy Sister Campbell refers to is the Holy Father. Get the picture? We are looking at a group of women religious more hostile to the Church than the Church's secular enemies.

Why is the Holy See making such a fuss? Could it be, in its communication with the LCWR, that the nuns have allowed radical feminist themes to permeate its meetings and hosted speakers who have espoused a rejection of the faith and silence on abortion? Yes, that could be it. Of course, that is only the tip of the iceberg. Add to that the Yale professor, Sister Margaret Farley, and her book *Just Love*, which mockingly rejects every aspect of the Church's teaching on sexual morality. Oh yes, Sister Farley is seventy-seven and has been teaching and writing stuff like this for oh, forty years. Two months ago, the Holy See censured her, to the groans of the *New York Times*, *Time* magazine, and every self-respecting member of the liberal firmament. These punitive actions are of one piece with the overall strategy of Pope Benedict XVI.

The first part of the Benedictine reforms are principally liturgical, and rightly so. He is re-teaching the Church that the liturgy is impressive not expressive: its purpose is to impress man's soul with the grace of Christ, so that, more and more, "It is no longer I who live, but Christ lives in me" (Gal 2:20). For too long, liturgy underwent a debasement insofar as it was seen as expressive: the vehicle for the individual (or a particular cultural/social group) to exhibit himself or his aspirations. The Mass *versus populum* (facing the people) captured this disorientation. As the Pope wrote when he was Cardinal, the Mass facing the people had deplorable effects:

> Less and less is God in the picture... The turning of the priest to the people has turned the community into a self-enclosed circle. In its outward form, it no longer opens out on what lies ahead and above, but is closed in upon itself. The common turning toward the East... did not mean that the priest "had his back to the people": the priest was not regarded as so important... A common turning to the East during the Canon remains essential... looking at the priest has no importance. What matters is looking together at Our Lord.[3]

The second and more crucial Benedictine reform is making religious about God again. The LCWR nuns, along with their allied priests and bishops, moved to take God out of religion. It was truly that dramatic. Pope Benedict strongly emphasizes that we don't feed the poor as a social act, but as the way of carrying out God's will. We don't shelter the homeless because some have no home, but because Our Lord commanded us. We do all that we do for the *maiorem Dei gloriam*, not to make some political or social point.

St. Catherine Drexel went to the black and Indian peoples not as a social justice cause, but as an act of oblation to her Divine Spouse. St. Francis Xavier Cabrini did not go into the New York slums to care for immigrants to speak truth to power, she did it to please her Lord and King. St. Elizabeth Ann Seton founded school after school not to meet some social need, but to bring the souls of the young to God. St. Jean Jugan established an impressive network of homes for the aged because she saw the image of the Crucified in the elderly; and Blessed Mother Teresa carried the destitute poor in her arms, not as a protest against government inaction, but because she saw Christ her Master in the distressing guise of the poor.

---

[3] *The Spirit of the Liturgy* (Ignatius Press, 2000), 80-81.

Contrast this supernatural feast of love of God through love of neighbor with the shrill iconoclasm of the nuns of the LCWR. Compare that resplendent band of women saints, who drew strength from Christ Crucified and their vowed consecration, with the rogue guerillas of LCWR who feed off hatred of the Church and seek inspiration from Marx and Betty Freidan. Look at these women saints' stunning good works, flowing from hearts utterly obedient to their beloved Mother Church, then look at the political lobbying and protest marches of the LCWR quickened solely by a frenetic loathing of all settled human and religious traditions.

So keep your eyes open for that Nuns on the Bus tour. And as those white-haired septuagenarians wave at you from their bus windows, know that you are seeing a fading, albeit tragic, chapter in our Church's history. We are happy to see them limping into the sunset, but brokenhearted that countless souls were lost till they did.

NUNSENSE, REDUX (PART II)

South Hampton's typical hollow chatter came to an abrupt halt last week. Well, not altogether. It just switched subjects, but the subject these pampered mandarins turned to was quite unusual – a nun. Sister Jacqueline Walsh had been struck and left dead by a hit-and-run driver of an SUV as she was walking in front of the retreat house where she was spending some time. So very tragic. Especially when one of God's own is taken from us when there are so few.

Even more tragic was what Sister Walsh had become. Let's start with the press photo. It must have left most readers scratching their heads. Sister Walsh was in no way identifiable as Sister Walsh. In her street dress she blended very nicely into any ordinary crowd as simply one of the crowd. Nothing special. Nothing unique. Of course, her consecration as a Sister of Mercy some 44 years ago set her aside as extraordinarily unique. She was wedded to Christ and His Holy Church with the privilege of being able to stand out amidst a crowd. Odd, that Sister Walsh would want to surrender that high dignity by trading her stately religious habit for a Kmart party dress. In desperately trying to fit in, she ironically shut herself out. The religious habit made her a magnet for souls hungry for signs of God's love in a starved secular world. Souls thirsty for transcendence find a veritable fountain in a nun's habit. The veil covering the head of the religious is equally a cover for man in escaping the pelting rain of our culture's lies.

Though some Catholics may take this as an eccentric perspective of some by-gone day, it is the constant teaching the Church's Magisterium. Thus Pope John Paul II at St. Patrick's College in Maynooth, Ireland:

> To you... religious: I say: Rejoice to be witnesses to Christ in the modern world. Do not hesitate to be recognizable, identifiable, in the streets as men and women who have consecrated their lives to God... Believe that contemporary men and women set value on the visible signs of the consecration of your lives. People need signs and reminders of God in the modern secular city, which has

few reminders of God left. Do not help the trend towards "taking God off the streets" by adopting secular modes of dress and behavior yourselves. (1 October 1978)

The Saint returned to the subject of the religious habit once more in a major address to Mothers General in Rome:

> A special witness is... that of a religious garb. It constitutes, in fact, an evident sign of complete consecration to the ideals of the Kingdom of Heaven... It is also a sign of definitive detachment from merely human and earthly interests; it is a sign, furthermore, of poverty lived joyfully and loved, in confident abandonment to God's providential action. (November 30, 1979)

Not content with two major mandates to retain the religious habit, the same Pope John Paul II returned to it again. Since frequency of repetition invests greater force to magisterial commands, no doubt should exist in any Catholic mind as to the Church's definitive charge on the wearing of the religious habit:

> The modern city, where the sense of the sacred is considerably diminished, needs to find people who are inspired by faith and love; it is not indifferent to a message that is clearly identifiable. Therefore, do not be slow to show your consecration in a visible way, by wearing your religious habit, simple and poor; it is a silent but eloquent testimony. (February 2, 1987)

Perhaps Sister Walsh was distracted when these pontifical directives were promulgated? Maybe she thought them ambiguous? Open to many interpretations? Any of these benign interpretations seems to stretch credulity. One is only left with the conclusion that Sister Walsh was directly defiant of the wishes of the Roman Pontiff. Truth to be told, Sister Walsh was not alone in the contumacity, it spread like a brushfire through almost every one of the two hundred and fifty-three or so religious congregations in North America. As with any wildfire, the flames of their disobedience left the faith of many souls scorched and forever disfigured.

Once the good sisters departed from the exquisite drama of the religious habit, all manner of anomalies rushed in. Some were epitomized in the reportage of Sister Walsh's long religious life. One of the more disturbing episodes was reported in the press. Sister Walsh assisted in St. Edward the Confessor (Syosset,

NY) as a pastoral associate. Try finding pastoral associate in any official document of the Holy See, and you will search in vain. It is another one of those dead concepts that rose from the carcass of the spirit of Vatican II. While it has no true Catholic substance, it nonetheless acts as a toxin to any true Catholic parish, and it is almost always a progressive nun. Sounds rather laudable. After all, for time immemorial Holy Church has depended upon the good nuns and the generous faithful to carry out her Divine work. But this is not what the pastoral associate was up to: the pastoral associate was the camel's nose under the tent. It soon became a perfect vehicle for effectively eroding the office of the priest.

To the surprise of no one, this has been the leitmotif of progressive nuns for the last quarter of the Twentieth Century. Not that priests were unwilling hostages. Many of these self-loathing clerics consorted happily in their theological emasculation. Triumphantly standing side by side and hand in hand with priests, the pastoral associates could almost taste the realization of their revolutionary dream of women priests. With the greatest caution, they walked a kind of juridical tightrope, carrying out as many duties as are not strictly priestly ones (and, not infrequently, some of those as well). Though not as egregious, the same purposes were being effected by the proliferation of so-called ministers littering the landscape of nearly every parish. The net result of all of this was devastating. Slowly, but most surely, the faithful fell like toy soldiers right into the groove methodically planned for them. This whole new Brave Catholic World was embraced as a new normal. By the time the laity awakened to the deformity, it was too late. As Lenin reminded us, tell a lie often enough and the people finally accept it as the truth.

All of this is ample evidence of the slow war of attrition the Catholic Left has waged over the past half century. And, sad to report, they have nearly won. What concessions they could not arm-wrestle from the Holy See, they cleverly won by legerdemain, gaining what they wanted without ever having to call *it* what it actually *is*. This has been the record of the past forty years: what begins as a scandalous rupture with the Church's teaching is slowly accepted as mainstream convention. Case in point. Sister Walsh was described by one parishioner as organizing parish festivals and dancing up a storm. Organizing parish festivals is perfectly wonderful, but a consecrated religious dancing up a storm? *Hmmm.*

All of us felt the jolt of Sister Jacqueline Walsh's untimely death. Sadly, we have also suffered the jolt of her unseemly conduct as a religious. More sadly, she, and all religious like her, has left a spiritual wreckage of such magnitude that it will take an army of saints dozens of years to repair.

May God be merciful to Sister Walsh. But bruised Catholics like us will not find it easy to show mercy. Not because we are heartless, but because of the heartless ways that the new Nuns have so deeply wounded the Church we so love.

Blows to the Church from her enemies are expected, but blows to the Church from her own are unbearable.

BLACK POWER!

I know what you're thinking. It's not that at all. Black Power is, of course, priests in their cassocks. Can there be any greater power than that? They present the great drama of the Holy Gospel. A priest merely in black suit is prosaic; in the cassock, he is poetry. Perhaps this is why the Archbishop of Washington, D.C. a few weeks ago implored his priests to gather in questionable demonstration in their cassocks. Such an episcopal summons for the donning of cassocks had not been heard for over a half century. Interesting. Could there be a rediscovery of the cassock in the offing? Then there is the incident in St. Louis a few days ago. Two cassocked priests leading a large group of young Catholics in the recitation of the Rosary before the statue of St. Louis. Rioters were enraged; normal folks were moved. The Hurons of Canada called the St. Isaac Jogues and his missionary Jesuits blackrobes. The cassocks of these saints piqued the interest of the Indians. Though unlettered, they sensed they were in the presence of the extraordinary.

But there is the nagging question: Why are young men not breaking down the doors of our seminaries in restless desire for the graces of Holy Orders? Why are they not enthusing to march in the divine uniform of the cassock? Some of the answer lies at the steps of secularity. Its delights are like the sirens that seduced Odysseus. Their insistent song seems no contest to the muted whisperings of the Holy Spirit that excites the hearts of those young men. Having said that, modernity's enticements cannot match the Church's. She possesses an ensemble of potent supernatural symbols that no earthly force can compete. They are ancient in their lineage, but modest compared to the blinding glare of secularism's allurements. Their simplicity should not deceive. It is the emblematic manner of the Holy Spirit who woos souls rather than dazzle them. Under such subtle inspirations the soul responds slowly but surely, guaranteeing a response not born of fleeting enthusiasm but unwavering conviction.

Many in the Church have intentionally permitted this formidable magnet for the young to collect dust. The perennial lessons of the Church seem to have been lost upon not a few Catholic leaders who fall to the seductions of Madison Avenue and the slick sheen of pyscho-babble's ephemera. When elites within the Church decide that she is a corporate affair and not a mystical one, she is dragged to unworthy stratagems. Several years ago, the Archdiocese of Los Angeles announced that it would hire a top-flight public relations firm to handle its image. Around the same time the Diocese of Albany followed suit. Glaring anomalies are apparent here. No surprise that the evidence shows that the Church has reached a dangerous critical mass in the decline of vocations. Looking only at a sliver of the East Coast reveals a situation of grave concern. This year the Diocese of Bridgeport, CT ordained not a single man. The Archdiocese of New York, 2; Diocese of Brooklyn, 3; Rockville Center, 2. In the Province of New Jersey: Archdiocese of Newark, 10; Paterson, 3; Metuchen, 3; Trenton, 1 and Camden, 2. Other dioceses are following similar trends. Not to put too fine a point on this, but there does seem to be a cause for concern. To be sure, exceptions stand out amongst this grim picture. The Fraternity of St. Peter and the Institute of Christ the King. Of the conventional Orders, the amazing Dominicans of the St. Joseph Province. Of diocesan seminaries, one alone stands out: the spanking newly built Minor Seminary of the Diocese of Charlotte, North Carolina under the extraordinary leadership of Fr. Matthew Kauth. Their high volume of vocations is wildly disproportionate to the small number of Catholics in that growing diocese. But the other diocesan seminaries of the United States remain crippled.

The secret of overcrowded seminaries? Only the millennial old prescription the Church has always employed.

The Roman Church began advertising for priests thousands of years before Madison Avenue was even a twinkle in the eye of East Coast moguls. She didn't need glossy magazine copy or sixty second television bites. Saints did the trick. Put them out in front of young men and you will have a stampede on your hands. The lure of sanctity is irresistible. Only the saint can speak to the depths of the human person, the depths that beg for happiness. All the stirrings of young men—their passions, strivings, aspirations, dreams and virile energies—are electrified in the presence of the saint. In fact, without saints the souls of young men become enervated, leaving only a metaphysical ennui which entombs them. Chesterton's wisdom tells of this mystery: "When the young man knocks on the door of the brothel, he is looking for God."

Look at St. Bernard of Clairvaux in the twelfth century. This ascetic went about the French countryside and mesmerized the young men who heard him speak about the love of God and the renunciation of self. They rushed after him as though he were giving them gold. But he was giving them much more — Christ Crucified. And they swooned. Legend has it that when mothers found their boys listening to the saint they would run and cover their boys' ears.

Or St. Philip Neri. Who could have imagined that this seemingly half-mad priest who levitated during Mass could be any match for the lubricious delights of Renaissance Rome? But when Philip strolled through the Eternal City he was like a Pied Piper. Rich young men accustomed to gorging themselves on the whatever they desired, now desired only the company of this happy saint. They could have a dozen boudoirs, but after being with Philip, they craved only the Tabernacle. St. Philip turned their hunger for carnal pleasures into a hunger for heaven. Amazing. And it didn't cost the Church a dime or a hundred vocation board sharing sessions.

Only Christ calls men to the priesthood and His voice passes through Christ-like priests. Not merely through their voices, but through their actions, bearing and dress. Chesterton once remarked that when he saw Cardinal Manning walking through London, his scarlet cappa billowing in the wind, he thought of thousand Arabian nights. No surprise. Look at how we thrill to the sight of a Marine in his dress blues. Woven into man's nature is a thirst for the romance of the symbol. Most certainly it is the example and words of the priest which seduce the heart of a young man. But his cassock announces his high office and makes a man's heart dance. Here is the truest Black Power. All these gestures of the priest conspire together to prompt a man to throw everything away for Christ. Priest in their cassocks stand out like a Colossus of Rhodes. It leaves Madison Avenue green with envy. Oddly, it leaves many a bishop stone cold, even angry. There is something deeply amiss here, leaving any literate Catholic profoundly disturbed.

Most importantly, however, is not the priest, but the priest *at Mass*. Holy Mass envelopes the whole panoply of heaven with Christ Immolated reigning at its center. No greater wonder falls upon a man's soul than to watch a priest attend to the hundred glorious details coalesce to produce the supernatural beauty of the Mass. It is a beauty not theatrical, but theological. It is not spectacle, but mystery. It is not born of clever liturgical workshops, but of the Church's ancient tradition. Too many of the jerry-built "liturgies" of the average parish are either so fatuous or mawkish that they summon not the noble in man, but the shallowest. A normal man is repulsed by them. And if, per chance, he is attracted, it is because he is being entertained, as though it were a performance of My Fair Lady. If there are men willing to devote themselves to that type of meretricious exhibition, they are only men of a certain disposition for flair and flamboyance. Men who see the Mass as their stage. The Church in 2020 has recently reaped the bitter harvest of men like that. Ignatius Loyola and Isaac Jogues would not approve.

The priest at Mass attracts men and makes them. The Mass is a manly act because it is the act of the Perfect Man. It is a heroic act because Christ at every Mass is at war slaying Satan. This Divine Tumult rivets a young man's heart more than any sermon or book. Alexander the Great, Hannibal and General Patton are trifling compared to this Divine Captain. C. S. Lewis wrote once that the vestments of a priest must always be heavy or at least look heavy. It is because the priest carries the weight of war at Mass, as well as the grandeur of Divine Victory. Tissue weight polyesters simply will not do. Only jewel encrusted cloth of gold can fully tell the tale. As the Polish philosopher Leszek Kolakowski rightly remarked, "Religion is not a set of propositions, it is the realm of worship, wherein understanding, knowledge, the feeling of participation in the ultimate reality and moral commitment appear as single act."

On September 21, 2001, Pope John Paul II punctuated this indispensable solemn awe that is constitutive of the Mass, a dynamic and hieratic visibility which conveys a dazzlingly ineffable invisibility:

> The Liturgical Celebration is an act of the virtue of religion that, consistent with its nature, should characterize Itself by a profound sense of the sacred. In it, man and

the community should realize that it is, in a special way, before Him Who is three times Holy and Transcendent. Consequently, the behavior called for should be permeated by a reverence and by a sense of amazement that pours forth from one knowing that he is in the presence of the Majesty of God. The People of God need to see in the priests and deacons a behavior full of reverence and of dignity, capable of helping them penetrate the invisible things, even without words or explanations.

That is how the Church advertises. It is a millennial strategy which fills seminaries and produces saintly priests. Other methods may be tried, but we only produce fools. Or worse.

OF HEALING PRIESTS AND OTHER STRANGE INTRUSIONS

But thou, when thou prayest, enter into thy closet, and when thou hast shut thy door, pray to the Father which is in secret: and thy father which seeth in secret shall reward thee openly.
Matthew 6:6

Addressing this subject is a task fraught with danger. For the doctrinal vacuum created in the past sixty years of spirit of the Council convulsions has left not a few Catholics stranded in a kind of no-man's-land. Unanchored by the hallowed Tradition and traditions of the Church's millennial treasures, they find themselves scrounging for scraps off the tables of secularism and therapeutic kitsch. With liturgical offerings that often impersonate third-rate vaudeville, their souls starve.

With good intentions, they find refuge in a kind of hysterical prayer – put another way, a sort of soothing emotional swoon. Since this refuge is born of genuine spiritual longing, it is hard to hold it to strict theological/ascetical standards. But be held to them they must. Otherwise, added to the doctrinal bedlam there will be spiritual decadence, a salve which soothes but does not sanctify. Some may argue that it is a halfway house to authentic prayer, or better than nothing. But this sentimentality is addictive and can render the soul permanently impaired. Raised on a diet of pretzels and beer, the taste of caviar is unendurable.

Msgr. Knox gave this thorny problem of emotion/hysteria in prayer magisterial treatment in his classic *Enthusiasm*. He traces the dark *cul-de-sacs* of emotion in prayer from the early Church to the nineteenth century. Each time it rears its head, a more serious fissure is to blame. Msgr. Knox stated:

> Enthusiasm...[has] at [its] root a different theology of grace. Our traditional doctrine is that grace perfects nature, elevates it to a higher pitch, so that it can bear its part in the music of eternity, but leaves it nature still. The assumption of the enthusiast is bolder and simpler: for him, grace has destroyed nature, and replaced it. The

saved man has come out into a new order of being, with a new set of faculties, which are proper to his state... He decries the use of human reason as a guide to any sort of religious truth. A direct indication of the divine will is communicated to him at every turn, if only he will consent to abandon the arm of flesh – man's miserable intellect, fatally obscured by the Fall.

This serious detachment from the ascetical/spiritual tradition of the Church leaves the soul lost at sea, accountable to nothing but his own excitations. Chesterton names this the god within. In a famous passage from *Orthodoxy*, his scathing assessment:

> Of all horrible religions the most horrible is the worship of the god within... That Jones shall worship the god within him turns out ultimately to mean that Jones shall worship Jones. Let Jones worship the sun or moon, anything rather than the inner light; let Jones worship cats or crocodiles, if he can find any on his street, but not the god within. Christianity came into the world firstly in order to assert with violence that a man had not only to look inwards, but to look outwards, to behold with astonishment and enthusiasm a divine company and a divine captain. The only fun of being a Christian was that a man was not left alone with the inner light, but definitely recognized an outer light, fair as the sun, clear as the moon, terrible as an army with banners.

What is absent in enthusiasm is a humility before the example of the saints, who never prayed with external display or manic delirium but always with a calm and chastened manner. Shall we say, like the Publican: "And the publican, standing afar off, would not lift up so much as his eyes unto heaven, but smote upon his breasts, saying, God be merciful to me a sinner" (Lk 18:13).

St. Cyprian should not be forgotten in his *Treatise on the Lord's Prayer*:

> When we pray, our words should be calm, modest and disciplined. Let us reflect that we are standing before God. We should please him both by our bodily posture and the manner of our speech. It is characteristic of the vulgar to shout and make a noise, not those who are modest. On the contrary, they should employ a quiet tone in their prayer.

It is precisely a waning of that humility which creates the fertile conditions for extravagant and false spiritual phenomena to flourish. If the soul does not take its delight from obeying the

Church and her tradition, it begins only to delight in itself. Sadly, this narcissism leads men out of the Catholic Church. These departures are clearly seen in Catholics who intentionally embrace error.

However, they are no less present in Catholics who revel in enthusiasms clearly contrary to the tradition of the saints. While the intellect is easily seen to be misled by heresies, frenzied emotions mimicking devotion are equally deadly. Both leave men marooned, alone, and without the Church.

Take, for instance, the phenomenon of today's healing priest, making his appearance here and there to the delight of the masses. To be sure, saintly priests with the charism of healing (*gratia gratis data* — grace given for the benefit of others) have always adorned the Church, winning the admiration of the faithful. The glaring difference between these canonized saints and the current crop of pretenders is that saints possessed humility while the latter only an appetite for self-promotion (one wonders if they are aware of John 3:30: "He must increase, but I must decrease").

Memory may fail, but one does not seem to remember St. Padre Pio advertising Healing Masses. Or St. Vincent de Paul. Or any of the saints. This alone should be a monitum for Catholics rushing to star appearances of the healing priest *du jour*. If not that, then Luke 11:29: "It is a wicked and perverse generation that looks for signs and wonders."

The true Catholic soul eschews anything which is novel, meretricious, or idiosyncratic. St. Vincent of Lerins's principle for the recognizability of true doctrine applies also to the realms of prayer and Catholic practice. His test consisted of weighing the conduct against three properties: *semper, ubique, ab omnibus*. In other words, if the practice cannot be verified as having been used *always* in the life of the Church, *everywhere* in all the places that the Church exists, and by *all* Catholics wherever they existed, the practice, or opinion, should be rejected.

More simply, a Catholic ought to flee from any practice not embraced by the saints. True saints with the charism of healing, like St. Pio, loathed the spotlight. Even more loathsome to such men would be the moniker of healing priests. Such a pervasive humility marked their lives that their preferred place of meeting the faithful was in the confessional box and *not* on the stage. Ah, the staginess. What else can we call the hysteria and shouting, the fainting and trembling?

Where in the history of Catholic devotion can we find these manifestations except in periods of doctrinal laxity and disciplinary decline (again, Knox's *Enthusiasm*)? On November 23, 2001, the Sacred Congregation for the Doctrine of the Faith promulgated a seventeen-page *"Instructions on Prayers for Healing."* Therein we find, "anything resembling hysteria, artificiality, theatricality or sensationalism should be absent from such gatherings, above all on the part of those in charge."

Moreover, it goes on further to warn that prayers for healing must remain separate from the celebration of the Mass and the Sacraments. Of course, the *Instruction* was responding to a whole subculture of hysterical movements that have mushroomed in the Church for the past half-century. None of them seems to pass the Vincentian test.

The Church rests her teaching on the canonical writings of two of her greatest saints: St. John of the Cross and St. Teresa of Avila. They stand in the pantheon of doctors of the Church. Indeed, she has called them her Doctors of Prayer. Both are absolutely clear and thoroughly unambiguous about the questions we consider. St. John of the Cross seems like a chemist labeling a bottle with skull and crossbones when he abjures emotion in prayer. Listen to his serious caution on emotional experience and similar phenomena in his *Ascent of Mount Carmel*:

> We must never rely upon them or accept them, but must always fly from them, without trying to ascertain whether they be good or evil: for the more completely exterior or corporeal they are, the less certainly they are from God. It is more proper and habitual for God to communicate to the soul, where there is more security and profit, than to the senses wherein there is ordinarily much danger and deception... So he that esteems such things errs greatly and exposes himself to great peril of being deceived... And thus it may always be supposed that such things as these are more likely to be of the devil than of God, for the devil has more influence on that which is exterior and corporeal, and can deceive a person more easily there by that which is more interior and spiritual... He knows how to insinuate into the soul a secret satisfaction with itself... These representations and feelings, therefore, must always be rejected: for, even though some of them be of God, He is not offended by their rejection, nor is the effect and fruit which he desires

to produce in the person by means of them any the less surely received because they are rejected and not desired.[4]

St. Teresa of Avila is no less harsh in her warning about eccentric displays in prayer or paranormal exhibitionism in priests. She merely stands in an unbroken tradition of saints and magisterial teaching. Perhaps that is the operative word in all this: Tradition, to be understood precisely in the Pauline sense (1 Tim 6:20) as that which has been handed down by the Church of the ages. In her *Interior Castle* she writes:

> Those deceive themselves who believe that union with God consists in ecstasies or raptures, and in the enjoyment of Him. For it consists in nothing except the surrender and subjection of our will, with our thoughts, words, and actions, to the will of God, and it is perfect when the will finds itself separated from everything and attached only to that of God, so that every one of its movements is solely and purely the volition of God.[5]

In a word, we must all try to pray like St. Teresa of Avila or St. John of the Cross and follow priests who act like St. John Bosco or the Cure of Ars. Any deviation from that norm should make any Catholic terribly suspicious.

In these charged times, proper doses of suspicion are in short supply. It might be well for us to remember the sobering warning of Victor Hugo: "To each man there lies the choice to make of his soul either a sanctuary or a sewer."

---

[4] Book 2, Ch. 11, sections 2, 3, 5 and 8.
[5] Book 3.

CLOTHING THE NAKED CATHOLIC SQUARE

Secularized man has succeeded in making himself a shadow. By eschewing every trace of moral absolutes, tradition and, indeed, the very anchor of nature itself, he has made himself a ghost. So etiolated, he can only rely upon the whimsical demands of the gaseous self. In this claustrophobic universe there is no longer need for God or religion. For those without a stomach for so sharp a break with millennia of metaphysical stability, there are the Sentimentalists. These persist in religion but bend religion to their own ends.

Committed to a reverence for the canons of modernity, they busy themselves trimming, accommodating and shaving away those sharp edges of religion that they claim have too long intruded obtrusively on the tender modern sensitivity. To these, sociologist Christian Smith aimed his damning description: moralistic therapeutic deism. W. H. Auden's obloquy of the 1930s can well be attributed to them: low and dishonest. At least Nietzsche had the honesty to follow secularity to its logical *cul de sac* of atheism. No such courage is found in these religious sentimentalists; They arrive at de facto atheism crouched beneath the patina of religion.

Religious Sentimentalists heartily subscribe to the motto of the rioting French students of 1968 in Paris: "It is forbidden to forbid." Strange that such antinomianism would hide under the sheep's clothing of religion. But such dissembling is their mark. In 2017 R. R. Reno wrote pointedly of this furtive wrecking spirit, "everything strong and limiting goes. We must weaken social authority so that we can love more fully. For the radical French thinkers who came to be called 'postmodern,' nihilism offered the opposite of despair. The notion that there are no solid, enduring truth was for them a gospel of freedom." Isn't this the true project of the German bishops? Aren't they and their tribe fashioning a New Religion shorn of religion? This band of happy trailblazers refuses to affirm that truth arrives from gazing wondrously at the Real. They choose manufactured meanings, loosed from Reality, and eventually suffer the all too modern fate of meaninglessness. Ask Sartre. Read Kafka.

Quite tragically more than a few in the Church have chased the chimera of Modernity. Under the severe lash of secularism's hegemony, they welcome a regime of subtractions: in dogma, morality, priestly formation, liturgy and ascetical practice. Like a man taking a buzz saw to an ancient tree, they did the same to the Church's Tradition and traditions. They justified their sordid agenda by posturing that they were clearing centuries of irrelevant accretions. In fact, they were axing the ancient tree of the Church's life-giving traditions, leaving the Catholic faithful scorched by secularism's unforgiving sun.

In the movie *The Great Silence*, on the life of cloistered monks, there is a great moment when a group of monks are chatting and one of them mentions that another monastery had dropped a number of its practices in order to adapt to the times. Quickly an elderly monk replies:

> Our entire life, the whole liturgy, and everything ceremonial are symbols. If you abolish the symbols, then you tear down the walls of our own house. When we abolish the signs; we lose our orientation. Instead, we should search for their meaning... One should unfold the core of the symbols... The signs are not to be questioned. We are.

Libraries have been written on modernity's seepage into the Catholic Church, none better than St. Pius X's *Pascendi Gregis*. But let us be less ambitious and diagnose this penetration through the prism of a seemingly small detail of the Church's array of sacred symbols: the priest's black Roman cassock. Some will surely complain that this is an exercise in the trivial. Yet that very protest is a telling proof of the problem. Such flip demurrals divulge a corrupting superficiality, which cannot recognize an appreciation of the web of crucial symbols that constitute religion, and human life itself. Each strand of that web is critical to the whole, and disturbing even one strikes a blow to its integrity. Wittgenstein recognized these interwoven layers of meaning to human life when he warned that altering this complex tapestry of truths is like trying to repair a spider's web with a boxing glove.

But why a focus upon the Roman cassock of the priest? Isn't this a bit narrow? Not if one sees that the priest is the tip of our Holy Religion's spear. He is the face of the Church's redemptive mission, in all its comforting glory and stirring majesty. The priest is the bearer of God's weighty mysteries, the *dispensatores mysteriorum Dei* (1 Cor 4:1), and this weighty mystical vocation demands a correspondingly weighty sign. It must be noted that the Roman cassock, quite different from the black street suit and Roman collar, is dramatically unique, possessing a voice both dramatic and affecting. It bespeaks the supremely singular role the Catholic priest performs. C. S. Lewis once remarked that even if a liturgical vestment is not heavy, it ought to *look* heavy. Sacred signs bear the heavy weight of the Ineffable Trinity, so should their physical appearance. The Roman cassock does that to a tee.

The priest in the Roman cassock not only represents a divine institution, a legacy of illuminating dogmas, or a prestigious position in a world respected Church. More grandly, the cassocked priest trumpets to the world a dazzling power: to summon the Word Incarnate upon altars for the salvation of the human race; to literally change the souls of men by uttering the words of absolution. Even while performing works of charity, the priest in the Roman cassock sets himself apart from those doing the same. In cassock, the priest adds a supernatural luster which brings to the work a radiance it did not have before. The habited St Vincent DePaul taking a child in his arms, or the cassocked St. John Bosco playing with his boys is poetry; a state official, or even a good Catholic doing the same things is prose.

The priest is not merely a socially significant figure; he is a cultic embodiment. All this goes beyond the words he preaches *in nomine Christi*. More metaphysically profound, he stands *in persona Christi*. Here is the stunning ontology of the cassock, it discloses the power to invoke the supernatural. To this extraordinarily numinous role there must be attached an equally extraordinary sign. A mere business suit and collar, while adequate, is certainly not sufficient. Only the riveting sign of the priest covered in the folds of the cassock will do.

The black Roman cassock identifies the priest with a supernatural universe, a *mysterium tremendans et fascinans*, in the evocative words of the religious phenomenologist Rudolf Otto. It contrasts dramatically with the *mundum*. In a sweet paradox the Roman cassock, by its very strangeness, separating the priest from the ordinary business of the world, simultaneously binds him more intimately to that world.

For as His Divine Master, the priest *exists* for that world. His cassock bids man come back his truest self, and most noble End.

If twentieth century phenomenology, so esteemed by S. John Paul II, has taught us anything it is that man is *homo symbolorum*. Man dwells in a world of rich and beckoning symbols sating his parched soul, as a thirsty man drinking water in a desert. Remove these elaborately embroidered galaxies of meaning and man is choked and existentially emaciated. Psychology tells us that 95% of all communication is nonverbal. Well before this researched psychological conclusion, Holy Church understood this. She is the preeminent herald of the Infinite through millennia of fashioning worlds within worlds of sign and symbol. The simple black Roman cassock is only one of the strands in that imposing firmament. It speaks eloquently *to* the world, but it is not principally *for* the world.

It is chiefly for the priest. It reminds him of his place, his duty, his obligation. Daily it teaches him that without Christ he is nothing; for the sake of Christ he must die to the world. Often the priest falls short of these ideals, and might find the cassock an indictment. Good, that is its purpose. The imitable Fr. Edward Leen, master scholar of dogmatic and ascetical theology of the early twentieth century, addresses this amazing power of external signs to transform interior disposition. In his *Progress Through Mental Prayer* he writes:

> To act then as it becomes us to act, truly to reflect in our conduct what we are, we must in all things comport ourselves as having heavenly tastes and ideals... By the cultivation of a truly spiritual bearing in all things possible to me by ascetical effort aided by grace... the exterior will finally affect the interior.

Leen seems to be echoing the ancient truth about the religious rule: keep the rule, and the rule keeps you. At first, the maxim may seem jejune, but proof of it is found in the fact that the habit is worn by groups such as cloistered Carmelites or Carthusians, whom no one ever sees.

All this being true, the Roman cassock still continues to act as a potent sign to the world. It marks the priest as an Ambassador of the Absolute; a Keeper of the Permanent Things. To a secular age smothered in the ephemeral, the transitory, the soundbite, the cassock is a welcome respite, summoning man to breathe again the pure air of the Transcendent. The oft told story of Alec Guinness is illustrative. In the first volume of his autobiography, *Blessings in Disguise*, Guinness writes about an incident that happened to him while making the *Father Brown* movie in France. After a day of production, he was strolling back to his hotel still wearing the Roman cassock, the costume his role demanded. Out of a hedge darted a small French boy. He ran to Guinness, thinking him a priest, held his hand for a short time, then let go and dashed away, waving to the actor as he did. That little French boy recognized the priest in his Roman cassock as a supernatural shelter in which he could find security, protection, love and goodness. That recognition struck Guinness's soul like an earthquake. Guinness later confessed that the incident was the decisive spark that brought him to the Catholic Church. Soon after his conversion, his Sephardic Jewish wife, followed her famous husband, and entered the Catholic Church as well. One Roman cassock produced more than whole libraries of books. I suppose a picture *is* worth more than a thousand words.

Ah, the irony. Even as Secular Man scours every trace of traditional signs from society, it multiplies signs of its own. After all, Secularity lives beneath the shadow of Marshall McLuhan and cannot escape obedience to his axiom. The famous social philosopher coined the emblematic slogan of our age, the *medium is the message*: *what* we communicate is not as important as *how* we communicate it. Common sense as well as common experience gives confirmation: long hair and the peace sign in the sixties, along with guitar, beads and sandals were explosive signs of rebellion. Aren't passions roused by the flag, a swastika or a coned shaped white hood? Peculiar, isn't it, that just as signs ruled the popular imagination, many in the Church abandoned theirs.

In 1969 Peter Berger authored his groundbreaking little book, *A Rumor of Angels*. There he bemoaned the relentlessly grinding secularization of culture which he viewed as dissolving religion, the crucial glue of human society. He searched desperately for "signals of transcendence", shafts of light for a mankind sinking into a cruel darkness. Of course, the Church possessed all those signals of transcendence, and yet more than a few of her leaders were outlawing them at worst, embarrassed by them at best.

The Roman cassock enjoys its own ontology, a window into worlds upon worlds of rich meaning. Everyone of those worlds leading to God, *esse ipsum subsistens*. Setting it aside blows a gaping hole in that carefully constructed world. Yet this is what seems to have happened in the past half-century. Not only has the minimal clerical uniform of business black suit and collar become a rare sight, but some priests have gone so far as to replace the black clerical front for a variety of colors. This is not mere quirk or eccentricity; it is a statement. Such a clownish display is a deliberate and conspicuous rupture with tradition. And while it makes those who sport such carnival attire only seem like bizarre cartoons, it still delivers its blow.

At the root of this attitude is conformity to the so-called spirit of Vatican II, a concocted parallel world to the Roman Catholic one, confirming a Modernist agenda decisively abjured by the Church. While many clerics have rightly distanced themselves from this aberration, too many harbor an obvious diffidence to the rich traditions of the Church, among them the Roman cassock.

Many a fine cleric falls prey to this embarrassment of the sacred, content to hide behind the thinnest display of religion. Clearly, this is manifested in the nervous fear that many Catholic leaders have in confronting the galloping zeitgeist. If there be paranoia in this essential obligation of the Faith, there should be no surprise at being ashamed of the Church's ensemble of sacred signs.

The gifted essayist Maureen Malarkey wrote,

> I am inclined to believe that, yes, a priest who comes dressed like the yard man or a lumber jack is likely following advice from the chancery to meet people where they are, in the illusory cant of the day. Nevertheless the priest is not a technician, like the appliance repair man or meter reader. He embodies the Omega of our hope; his presence asserts it among those who have surrendered hope and trust. Is confrontation the sole means of bearing witness. That is not for me to answer. I can believe that retreat in advance affirms the very loss of trust... Maimonides said it well: "The beginning of all defeat is retreat." Is not a cassock testimony in itself, a

silent instrument that gives word of what we ourselves might be unable to say? It must not be put aside, mothballed for more congenial times.

Interesting: The abandonment of the simple black Roman cassock as an initial sign of retreat; the first waving of the white flag of surrender. It just might be.

BEWARE THE PRIEST AS CLOWN

Clownishness reached new depths several months ago in the Philippines. Not the Bozo kind, the Catholic kind. Cardinal Antonio Tagle took to the stage, donning a chorus line outfit, microphone in hand, bobbing and swaying as he crooned John Lennon's "Imagine."

For those fortunate to have escaped the cultural junk-littered demi-monde of the '60s and early '70s, this song was a paean to the consolations of atheism. His Eminence held the Filipino Catholic crowd in thrall as they, too, swayed to this spectral reinvention of Catholicism. Yes, this was in the Philippines, where Roman Catholics reach 78.8 percent of the population.

Disturbing as this should be to grounded Catholics, it should not be considered heretical. Heresy is far too respectable to descend to such redoubts of vaudeville religion. Heresy takes the Faith in great earnest, enough to understand its central dogmas and to calculate fatal substitutes. Heresy is a serious business, and it requires serious thinking.

No, what we have in Cardinal Tagle's nightclub gig is making the Faith nothing more than a joke. More menacing, it is an embalming of religion, making it a shadow of itself.

For Catholicism's approved cognoscenti, this approach has become their preferred line of attack for tweaking of the Old Faith. Its ground plan is to infantilize religion to such a degree that it becomes no more demanding than a sandbox exercise. Trying to critique it is rather like attempting to nail down raindrops. Its purpose: that all feel well, all be smiling, no one be unwelcome, and bonhomie fill the room.

Aborning here is no-fault Catholicism, where no one is banned from the reception of the "bread," God loves everybody, and "love is love."

Nightmare? Yes, to most Credal Catholics. But isn't that the aim of most parishes today? In these religious deserts, nothing bespeaks the majesty of God. Every detail is self-referential, viz., the saccharine music along with the swagger of the priest as he descends the middle aisle glad-handing and waving to his fans.

But there is more. The platoons of "ministers" settling in their roles like vendors at a state fair. Not to be overlooked is the modernist design of the new churches which remind one of laundromats. Their sterility would embarrass even Bauhaus and Le Corbusier.

For this comedic enterprise, no detail is neglected. Even the vestments of the priest advertise the message of the banal, the pedestrian, the ordinary, the fatuous. This clowning reaches its peak in the reception of Holy Communion (an expression quite unknown to a deprogrammed laity), where all take a casual stride to the minister to take the bread and drink the cup in a display of good feeling and nonthreatening "connecting."

But beware, vice makes a furtive entrance in the priest as clown. Where the heretic priest might raise the defenses of alert Catholics, the priest of oozing affections is nonthreatening, leaving most Catholics disarmed. Then what enters the soul is religion as a no-threat zone, easily falling victim to the joking priest with his cloying winks and "have a good day" send-off. Along with his studied casualness at the altar, all of this conspires to be a totalizing reconfiguration of Catholicism. Who cannot love the priest as Mr. Rogers and the makeover of God that he peddles?

The priest as clown shrinks the souls of Catholics by making them content with merely the trivial and meretricious. Then the fatal switch. No longer God demanding obedience but a stroking god, bidding all to be themselves. Belloc's ominous warning chills the soul:

> We sit by and watch the barbarian, we tolerate him. In the long stretches of peace, we are not afraid. We are tickled by his irreverence. His cosmic inversion of our old certitudes, and fixed creeds refreshes us: we laugh. But as we laugh we are watched by large and awful faces from beyond; and on these faces, there is no smile.

A similar Taglian performance was conducted by the good Cardinal Cupich at a stadium Mass several weeks ago hailing Chicago's native son as pope. He repeated, like a metronome, the all too familiar, "Jesus loves you just the way you are." Spliced into that incantation was the obligatory "all are welcome," especially those who break the law as illegal immigrants. Add to that the swinging mariachi band and you have the big-top feel of a Barnum and Bailey circus.

Witness here the victory of Man over God. The Secular over the Sacred. The Clown over the Consecrated Priest. The Entertainer over *Alter Christus*.

St. Paul describes priests as the *"dispensatores mysteriorum Dei"* (1 Cor 4:1), an exalted title of transcendent proportions. This sacerdotal status embodies the whole man, body and soul. It would be a truncated Catholicism that sees the indelible mark of Holy Orders as merely interior. This would be a denial of the metaphysical unity of the human person. This unity most surely manifests itself in a kind of resonance, where the soul manifests its highest purposes in the body.

This is why symbols bear such weight in the life of man: they radiate the interior mystery of the human person. So obvious is this truth that the most common man adheres to it reflexively and without question, objecting to its absence. Evidence is ubiquitous: the wedding ring, the policeman's uniform, the salute to a superior, the erect walk of The Old Guard at the Tomb of the Unknown soldier, or a nation's flag.

Abandoning any of them would cause protest, if not a riot—and for good reason. The symbol embodies a truth that lies deep in the soul of man. Setting it aside is eclipsing the truth itself, and man finds himself capsized.

The compelling power of symbols is just as critical to the life of the priest, if not more. He bears in his soul the indelible mark of Holy Orders which demands notice by the world. The priest represents the power of the thrice-Holy God, making the symbols of his soaring Office all the more necessary, all the more communicative.

It is first conveyed in his manner: grave, purposeful, composed, and strong. The word "grave" is not to be understood as forlorn; it is to be understood in its Latin derivative: *gravitas*. It is that quality reflected in seriousness without being ponderous, steadiness without artifice. It communicates joy without frivolity and approachability without an ounce of sentimentality. The priest should bear himself with assurance, never haughtiness; confidence, never swagger; high purpose without pomposity.

All these traits breathe through his dress, as it would with any man. As with any office, this is something quite consequential. When exercising his sacerdotal office at Holy Mass, or in the administration of any of the sacraments, his raiment must bespeak the supernatural wonders he dispenses. It should cause arresting amazement in Catholics. They must look and behold Heaven breaking through.

His vesture must appear as rich and sumptuous as the Divine Mysteries he summons to earth. In C. S. Lewis's words, "the priest at Mass should wear vestments that are heavy, or, at least, look heavy"—heavy with the glories of Paradise. His vestments must act as a tocsin bidding Catholics to come and partake of the riches of the Incarnate Word. Catholics should be left dazed.

Even when he is not administering the surging graces of the Holy Mass or the Sacraments, he is still a priest. Whether he walks the environs of his parish or the streets of New York City, he must always be announcing the glories of the Savior who longs for the souls of men.

Nothing accomplishes this announcement more pointedly than the Roman cassock. Yes, many priests decide to wear the black suit, rabat, and white cuffs on the avenues of the world. But our world has changed. Indeed, it has crumbled. It pleads for a dramatic message. Only the priest can supply it. Yes, many priests decide to wear the black suit, rabat, and white cuffs on the avenues of the world. But our world has changed. Indeed, it has crumbled. It pleads for a dramatic message. Only the priest can supply it.

It is ever more necessary for him to bestride the byways of this fallen world in dress that conspicuously differs from the ordinary and pedestrian life of its citizens. Whether that be a Dominican habit or a Roman cassock, it shouts a divine mission far better than words. The Roman cassock makes him different so men might not fear being different.

The cassock creates a firestorm in the denizens of our wizened culture and a cooling breeze in the hearts of Catholics. For secularized man, the Roman cassock is an irruption of the Supernatural in their desiccated world. It might disturb, it may seem odd, but it always creates a cyclonic appearance and demands a response. The cassock, to borrow the words of Franz Kafka (in speaking of the purpose of the novel), is like "an axe against the frozen sea within us."

For the Catholic, it is like an oasis, where he finds relief from the fetid air of his secular world. It also acts as the strong voice of a Supernatural dominion that he might have forgotten. Forgotten at the hands of men who deliberately set out to make him forget.

The priest set forth here stands as diametric opposite to the priest as clown. That kind of priest considers himself no longer an icon of the sacred but a man like any other. The clown priest does not believe he brings to men the marvels of the Supernatural but only a firmer foundation in the world in which men sink. He does not see himself as the transformative invitation to Calvary but merely a facilitator helping folks be more themselves. He does not see himself as the thunderous voice of the Lion of Judah but simply the pathetic assurance to men that God loves them just the way they are.

An Anglican priest once bemoaned his fate, representing a false religion, when he remarked, "When St. Paul arrived in cities, there were riots. When I arrive in a city, they call for tea." This is the fate of the priest as clown.

Do not fret, dear Catholic. Despite Cardinal Tagle's disco dance, the priest as clown is a dying breed, just as the inanities of the Bergoglio pontificate have become an embarrassing memory. Robust Catholic genius is creating podcasts, publishing houses, and new organizations of laymen that are setting the stage for a bright and rich Catholic renaissance. We are already seeing the fruits of their labors in the appearance of priests pulsating with the fires of Heaven and the splendors of the Supernatural.

Oh, how the architects of the priest as clown are shrieking now.

Catholics still may have to suffer the burlesque of the priest as clown. But not for long.

THE PRIEST AS HERCULES

A perfect metaphor for the classical priest is Hercules. Sadly, the Modern priest happily sees himself as Shirly Temple, steering not the mighty Barque of Peter, but the good ship Lollipop.

Modernity has succeeded in jailing God.

Then it made many of His priests a class of pygmies. Pity. For God's priests are anointed to be a class of Titans.

First, a bit of pertinent background. Virgil's *Fourth Eclogue* was always believed to be a *proto evangelion* by the Church Fathers. It would not be rash to say that an equivalent similitude can be applied to Hercules, a kind of *proto presbyteros*: an ancient allusion of the Catholic priest.

As Hercules, the priest is given strength from Heaven beyond ordinary human capacities.

Hercules willingly embraced his twelve labors, bravely overcoming their wickedness. Similarly, the priest encounters the gates of Hell. Clothed in Christ's sacerdotal armature the priest — as *alter Christus* — vanquishes Hell's terrors with the invincible power of the sacraments. Hercules is always depicted by rippling mounds of muscle. The priest enjoys a more formidable notice, his heroic virtue, which amazes the world more than Hercules's imposing physical frame.

This dogmatic picture of the priest has been obscured by the Great Crisis of the past six decades. In fact, a tragic attenuation of the priest's towering vocation. After the Second Vatican Council many thought the priest's sacred character ill fitted to modernity's Brave New World. The theological class bullied bishops into accepting a new paradigm of the priest as political actor, social activist, and throughout the South American church, guerrilla Marxist.

Every token that bespoke the priest's unique status was thought embarrassing, and a rush ensued to erase any semblance of his supernatural vocation. At that very Council itself not a few *periti* were seen shorn of clerical dress, donning the business suit of the bourgeoisie. Even for those who persisted in identifiable clerical dress, the traditional Roman Cassock was looked upon as a shameful repudiation of Man Come of Age.

This collapse was strengthened by the *Nouvelle Theologie*, an experiment of the early twentieth century which broke ground for a new way of looking at God, resulting in a downsizing of God. At the heart of its mission was to level the Thomistic foundations of theology and philosophy which had protected the Church so effectively. Aquinas was the thick wall that repelled all manner of the Church's enemies. With that gone, chaos would ensue. And it did. Interestingly, one of its principal avatars, Hans Urs von Balthasar, entitled his 1952 work *Razing the Bastions*. A daring and provocative title, to be sure. But one quite fitting for the sea change it envisioned for the Church.

Moreover, the *Nouvelle Théologie* successfully miniaturized the dramatic contours of the priesthood. It debuted a model of the priest that was effete, saccharine, and profoundly secular. This was just showcased this past week when a Paulist priest offered a gay pride Mass in Greenwich Village outside the Stonewall Inn, ground zero of LGBTQ+ aggression.

Official outrage? *None.*

The Herculean priest struggles to make men saints, summoning them to spiritual warfare. He identifies false ideas and firmly condemns them. He is manfully confrontational when necessary, seeing himself as the protector of God's flock—or, in the words of St. Gregory the Great, "Worrying over the incursion of barbarians and fearing the wolves who menace the flock entrusted to my care."

This priest after the heart of Christ is unafraid of the heat of battle because, through grace, his manhood remains intact; it is not shredded by the jagged teeth of the Modernist Leviathan. Chesterton expresses this with his signature panache:

> You cannot love a thing without wanting to fight for it. You cannot fight without something to fight for. To love a thing without wishing to fight for it is not love at all; it is lust. It may be an airy, philosophical, and disinterested lust; it may be, so to speak, a virgin lust; but it is lust, because it is wholly self-indulgent and invites no attack.

Chesterton crowns this ode to love and battle:

> The full value of this life can only be got by fighting, because if we have accepted everything, we have missed something—war. This life of ours is a very enjoyable fight, but a very miserable truce.

Not so the New Post-Conciliar Priest. He preaches self-affirmation, not battle against vice. Dialogue, not refutation. Ambiguity, not truth. He massages feelings, rather than bringing men to the Cross. In the words of one major American prelate in 2019, "Accusations of heresy are simply an inability to deal with ambiguity." This kind of neutered priest was on display in a remark also in 2019. He was bemoaning the use of the cassock. He giddily pontificated that *he* presents himself in lay dress because his role is to bring love. And you thought this kind of drivel disappeared with flower children and Woodstock.

Let's see. Cassocked priests for over a millennium did not? Hercules, meet Timothy Leary.

But this New Priest was foreign even to Hollywood. Old Hollywood, that is. The classic movie *On the Waterfront* proves the point. This Marlon Brando classic is not a movie; it is a sermon. It plumbs the depths of the human heart with Shakespearian flair. It doesn't censure the full range of human experience as does contemporary Hollywood.

Hollywood 2024 is a Puritan Hollywood. A reverse Puritanism: morality banned, religion proscribed, and God taboo, its air as claustrophobic as the kind Hester Prynne breathed in Hawthorne's *The Scarlet Letter*. It wears the high-buttoned collar of Woke ideology so tightly that its restricted air supply of reality makes it impossible to see life as it is. Today's Hollywood might as well be Amish Town West. It fears reality as much as those dear Pennsylvanians fear modernity. T. S. Eliot's verses had to be directed against the likes of the 2024 Hollywood elites when he wrote in the *Four Quartets*, "Humankind cannot bear/very much reality."

All the gifts of Hollywood's spectacular talent are frozen in a spiritual cake of ice. These formidable artists are immobilized by a terror of the real; the search for God and a thirst for virtue. Art thrives upon revealing to us the beauty of reality – *every* part of it.

When artists flinch from this vocation, their art curdles into crudity. Titillation replaces intuition, while debauched man crowds out man ennobled. Hollywood should be our 16th-century Florence – unveiling man in all his splendor and tragedy. Rather, it has become our Babylon – and Babel. It fails us by showing man only as a beast. Hollywood today is Dante's *Inferno* – without the *Purgatorio* or *Paradiso*.

But the Hollywood of *On the Waterfront* was a Hollywood of the whole Dante because it was a Hollywood of the whole man. Proof of this lies in portraying wrenching moral struggle, principally in the person of The Priest. Karl Malden exhibits the Catholic priest as Hercules. His goodness and honesty are drawn in epic lines. The priest is hero in the tradition of Odysseus and El Cid. Men seek him for both light and strength and he supplies both in abundance.

Here is a Hollywood unafraid of the reality of God, holy religion, and fallen man. Against that backdrop we see man for who he is: wretched and pure, flawed and struggling, conflicted and sure, craving God and yet wallowing in sin. Here is the priest calling men to sacrifice after the sacrifice of Christ. Here not only does goodness triumph over evil, it is more attractive than evil. Here the priest calls real men in their real conditions to make real leaps of grace.

This is life as a Caravaggio canvas, not a Popeye cartoon.

Who better serves man?

No one was more Hercules than the Cure of Ars, St. John Vianney. This 19th century saint never left his parish of Ars, France. All he did was offer Mass, hear Confessions, and teach the *Catechism*. Of course, that's like saying all that MacArthur and Patton did was defeat the Axis powers. St. John Vianney engaged men at the only place that matters: the battlefield of their souls. He helped them conquer their sins – and so helped them be men again. No joy compares to *that* joy.

In another time, that was the only kind of priest the world knew. So much so that 1954 Hollywood produced *On the Waterfront*.

The world was richer when such priests strode the earth.

How much poorer it is without them. How much more dangerous.

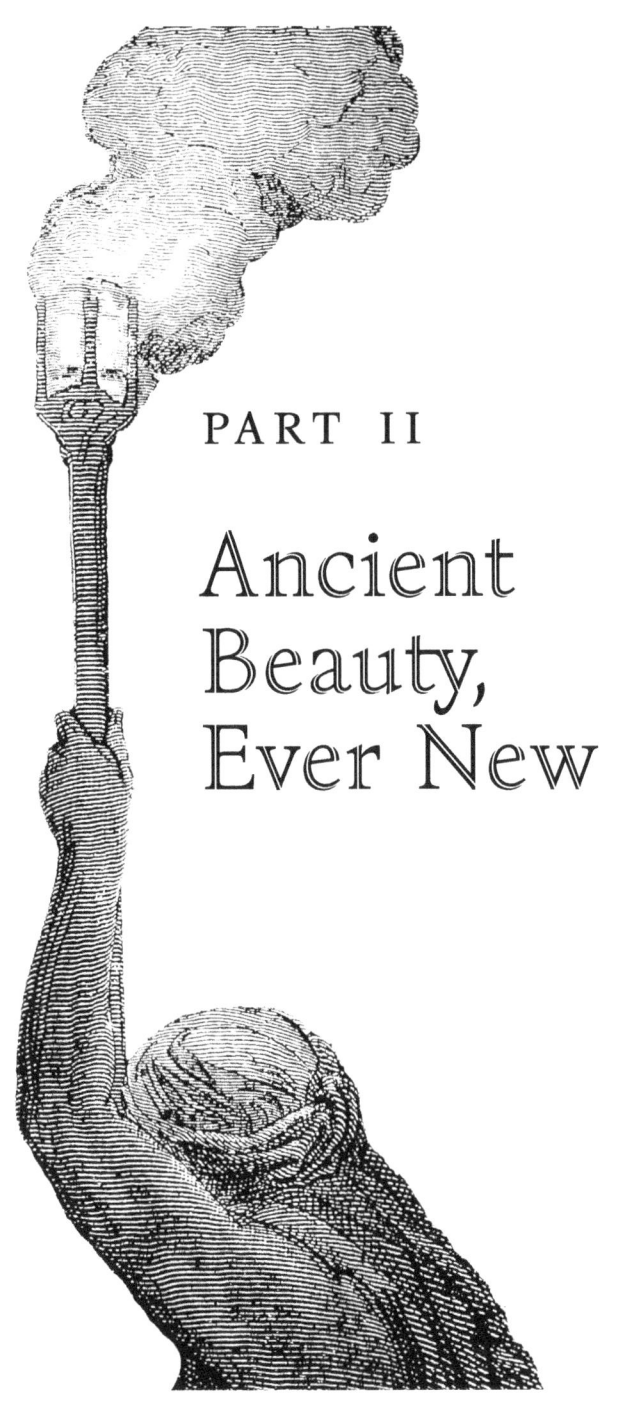

PART II

Ancient Beauty, Ever New

5
Divine Worship

NOT FOR LITURGISTS BUT FOR MEN

Los Angeles, capital of the Left coast, is the launching pad for some of our culture's zaniest trends. Now, the liturgical dreamers of the Los Angeles Archdiocese are hoping to launch their own little project into orbit as well. In 1997, the Archdiocese's head, Cardinal Mahoney, made an announcement calling for de-Europeanizing the liturgy. That's liturgical mumbo-jumbo for further loosening the liturgy from the bond of Roman tradition. Europeanizations include things such as kneeling, genuflections and, of course, Latin. More generally, they mean gestures, words and songs that conventionally suggest reverence for the Divine. Quite a plan. But not the one our Holy Father had in mind for the millennium.

From time immemorial, the traditional Roman form of the Mass has been under attack. For the Gnostics, it was too pure. For the Jansenists, it was not pure enough. Our own century has produced a number of liturgical bushwhackers. Having suckled on the iconoclasm of the sixties, they now decide that rubrics and ritual laws hamper man's unbound creative spirit. The externals of religion in general and liturgy in particular cramp their style. What's inside is what's important. True enough, but it's not the whole story. The interior state of one's soul is indeed an interest that towers above all others. It is standard Catholic dogma that external practices can never substitute for interior grace. Interior grace, on the other hand, doesn't flourish without external actions. Our Lord, in fact, designed the sacraments to be external signs of the granting of invisible graces.

Those primordial sacramental signs have a mighty ripple effect. Every part of Catholic life imitates their divine pattern. Catholicism is never more itself than when it enlists physical things to manifest its invisible mystery. That's why Baroque churches served her purposes so well. Their sumptuous complexity inebriate the senses and impress upon the mind the supernal truth of Christ's conquest over sin and His Kingly reign of grace. Angels do not require the heady lessons of the Baroque. Men do. Their body/soul nature craves grace's fleshly epiphanies. Catholics should never be squeamish when the Faith announces itself to the world in lavish physical forms. After all, we daily bend our Angelus knees at *et Verbum caro factum est* because the Son of God chose to save us through the visibility of human flesh. No Catholic ought to be sheepish with that Divine logic. The Incarnation demands that the Church utilize splendid things for splendid truths.

To de-Europeanize the Mass is to replace magnificent forms with banal ones. Even though the Faith remains intact, when its forms do not measure up to its glory, less than glorious fruits result. Cardinal Newman preached in his Plain and Parochial Sermons:

> No one can really respect religion and insult its forms. Granted that forms are not immediately from God, still long usage has made them divine to us; for the spirit of religion has so penetrated and quickened them, that to destroy them is, in respect to the multitude of men, to unsettle and dislodge the religious principle itself. In most minds usage has so identified them with the notion of religion, that one cannot bear transplanting... Precious doctrines are strung like jewels upon slender thread.

Chesterton remarked once that the shimmering of Cardinal Manning's scarlet robes struck his imagination as the Arabian Nights did, as signs of a glory beyond imagining. Yes, interior things only flourish in the soil of external things. That is why Mother Angelica in full habit is replete with interior invitations of grace without uttering a single word. Priests in Roman cassocks pierce a soul more deeply than ten brilliant sermons, as does the Pope in jeweled tiara or a cardinal in scarlet *cappa magna*; all signs of a glory beyond imagining.

ACTIVE PARTICIPATION: TRUTHS AND COUNTERFEITS

Too many to count are the depredations foisted upon the Roman Liturgy in the last half-century. Many of them perpetrated under the guise of a more active participation in the Mass. Liturgists made it seem as though they had discovered some New Sparking Truth heretofore unknown to the Catholic Church, like unearthing a new Dead Sea scroll. This mendacity must stand in line with all the others that this *nouveau riche* clique thrust upon an unsuspecting Church, such as Holy Mass *versus populum*, Holy Communion received standing and in the hand, the iconoclastic rearrangement and denuding of Catholic Churches (that one, under the guise of noble simplicity). Must I go on? Properly formed Catholics saw through these deceptions and waged a heroic battle against them. But active participation deserves special attention. When Pope St. Pius X enjoined Catholics to "not pray at Mass, but pray the Mass" he was repeating the ageless admonition of the Church. Neglect of the teaching was never the fault of the Mass, but the fault of those attending the Mass. As one newcomer to the ancient Mass once remarked, "After It, I was exhausted. It required such intense participation." Not only are deep supernatural Mysteries revealed here, but even deeper metaphysical ones involving the human person.

Imagine for a moment a mother keeping vigil near the bed of her ill child. Or a Bach devotee listening to a concert of his master's music in immobile attention. Or a woman riveted to a movie's tragic ending as tears roll down her cheeks. Each one of the people in these instances is at the peak intensity of human action. No words are being spoken, no action being performed, no movement taking place. Yet, though each person is brimming with activity, the eye sees no physical activity at all. All of it is happening interiorly, hidden; however, an observer can spot it instantly.

Such clear common sense is a necessary condition for any understanding what the Church means when she asks Catholics to participate fully in the Holy Mass. Any true human participation requires essentially one thing: understanding. Unless a man accompanies an action with a sufficient understanding no real human action can take place. The more profound the understanding, the more perfect the action. When little or no understanding is occurring, we criticize by saying, "He's just going through the motions."

Actions without understanding are empty and hollow. This is why external actions depend upon and follow from internal motions. If they do not, a man becomes a marionette. So it is that common sense (and philosophers as well) asserts that what men first do "inside" (understanding) is far superior to what man does "outside" (physical activities).

But what does this have to do with Holy Mass? Everything. Men are the ones who participate at Mass, not angels. In fact, man's salvation depends upon it. The depth of participation is the measure of grace received. Maximum active participation at Mass is accomplished when the mind is fully engaged in conversation with God, and the will involved in making acts of love. Clearly, those two kinds of acts (understanding and love) can reach breathtaking pitch, and no one be the wiser. That is because what is happening to the Catholic is happening deep within his soul. Only *that* pleases God. Only *that* is active participation. Of course, as with any human acts, oftentimes they are expressed in physical acts. Husbands kiss their wives; audiences applaud for the orchestra; people wave goodbye to their friends. Physical signs are the spillover of abundant interior acts. But they are only spillover.

A Catholic's active participation at Holy Mass is principally his acts of adoration: genuflection, kneeling, bowing, striking of the breast, folding of the hands, the sign of the cross, standing, and sitting. Occasionally the understanding and love of the soul expresses itself in secondary signs like singing and responses. Notice the order of the signs. Especially notice the order of outward signs to interior acts. The Traditional Mass follows these orders precisely. In doing that, it respects man's nature and leaves room for a perfect intimacy with God.

The phrase of St. Teresa of Avila in her Autobiography is telling. She writes: "I would die for even the smallest rubric of the Holy Mass." This celebrated mystic was not merely rendering tribute to her love for the Mass, but disclosing a perfect balance between interior oblation and external expression. The highest regions of prayer must always be grounded in and proceed from the rich ensemble of signs, traditions, and customs that constitute the supernatural armature of the Holy Church. Union with God does not detach souls from the Church's millennial liturgical and devotional life, but immerses them ever more deeply in that life. Many a heretical movement owes itself to a denial of that doctrinal premise. Look no further than the first century Gnostics, fifth century Manichees, twelfth century Albigensians and, of course Joachim of Fiore and his "Eternal Gospel." This false understanding does not peter out in the Middle Ages, it seeps into the twentieth century in the later Thomas Merton and the wide movement today of a quasi-Buddhist "spirituality" currently infecting not a few Trappist and Benedictine monasteries. A cursory glance at the National Catholic Reporter will show their pages filled with advertisements of so-called Spirituality Centers, all of them cloaking this hoary heresy of God without the Church.

Thus an ironclad law: Any human communication, whether with God or man, is empty without its first beginning deep within the soul and is sterile without telling about itself in proper signs. Two images suggest themselves to Catholics as models of active participation at Holy Mass: St. Luke's publican and the Mother of God.

The publican in St. Luke's Gospel (18:10-14) you may recall, is contrasted by Our Lord with the Pharisee. Both publican and Pharisee are praying in the Temple. The Pharisee is standing in the very front, speaking aloud of how good a man he is. The publican is at the darkest back corner of the temple, "standing afar off... not so much as lift(ing) up his eyes towards heaven; but struck his breast saying: 'O God, be merciful to me a sinner.'" Our Lord immediately bursts into remarkable praise of the publican saying, "I say to you, this man went down into his house justified rather than the other."

However, Our Lady is the most perfect example of active participation. She attends the First Mass, Our Lord's suffering and death on Calvary. Look at what she is doing. Look again. Apparently nothing. No speaking, no physical movements, no moving about. She stands looking at her Son; He looking at her. Both transfixed in perfect acts of love. No need to look further for the meaning of "active participation." Other human acts of love after Our Lady's on Calvary are only faint copies. She seemed to be doing nothing, but was actually doing everything.

Please, let us follow Mother Church's command to "fully participate" at Holy Mass. Let us never forget the perfect way to do that: Imitate Our Lady.

LATIN IN THE MASS

Before we speak of Latin in the Mass, we must be sure never to call it the Latin Mass. The Traditional Mass, not made a mainstream part of Catholic life by Pope Benedict's decree *Summorum Pontificum*, is not distinguished by the fact that it is in Latin (though that is one of its principal characteristics) but that it is traditional. Since 1969, the Novus Ordo (the New Mass with which the Catholic world is most familiar) was always permitted to be said in Latin. No permission needed. Why? Because the Church has always considered the Latin language to be the normative tongue for not only the Holy Mass, but also as the vehicle of her most solemn dogmatic pronouncements as well as all her official business. Thus, in *Sacrosanctum Concilium*, the Second Vatican Council's document on the liturgy, we read: "The use of the Latin language... is to be preserved in the Latin rites" (no. 36, 1), and "care must be taken to ensure that the faithful may also be able to say or sing together in Latin those parts of the Ordinary of the Mass which pertain to them" (no. 54).

Some may ask the logical question: If the Church has always taught that Latin is the normative liturgical language, why isn't it in every parish? This is an involved question, better left for another time. For now, Pope Benedict has fixed our attention on a happier future course, one more perfectly aligned with the Church's constant tradition. A more fruitful question should be: Why the Church's millennial affection for a dead tongue—Latin?

Our answer should be framed by a remark made by G. K. Chesterton in his little-read book, *The Resurrection of Rome*. He writes, "Rome is a place where everything is buried, and nothing is lost. A city full of tombs, and yet full of life. The mortuary images do not carry the savor of mortality, but rather immortality." The Latin language operates similarly. It is a buried language, precisely so nothing may be lost. Its meanings, nuances, connotations, and suggestiveness, are all frozen, like a prehistoric insect in amber. When it is used, it delivers as unambiguous a meaning as a silver trumpet. It stands above time, so that it can

Latin in the Mass

speak to the men of any time. For a religion whose business is announcing to ever-changing men the never-changing truths of God, Latin is an indispensable tool. Otherwise, her changeless truths would suffer the wear of changing times. For that, man would be all the poorer.

No more important words are uttered than the words of Holy Mass. Shouldn't the Church strive mightily to keep them right? Keeping them right requires a preservative language which guarantees that those words will always stay alive. Only living words can infuse life into living souls.

An even more profound reason obligates Latin in the mind of Mother Church. The Holy Mass is the work of Christ redeeming mankind from the grip of hell. No action on earth can compare. When the Mass is celebrated, all of heaven appears, history changes, God stirs souls, created reality is touched to its foundations. For something so extraordinary, all that surround it should be extraordinary. That should start with its language. For such an unusual act, only an unusual language will do.

St. Augustine described this as *In Dominico eloquio* ("in the Lord's style of language"). Romano Guardini was referring to a strange language bespeaking the strangely exquisite world of the supernatural into which we enter when we participate in the Holy Mass when he wrote in *The Spirit of the Liturgy*: the Holy Mass "creates a universe brimming with fruitful spiritual life." The eminent Patristics scholar, Robert Louis Wilken, expresses it dramatically: "Christianity is a culture in its own right; the Church must insist on its own way of speaking... If we forget how to speak our language, we lose something of ourselves."

Still the persistent question: *But I can't understand it!* But you can! In the very inscrutability of the Latin language, every man – young and old, educated and illiterate – understands the sublimity of Christ saving mankind on the altar. The very uncommonness of the Latin transports the soul into the uncommon act of God – coming down from heaven in the form of a small host to save us from our sins. This is the towering truth that makes our souls explode in wonder. Of course, a Catholic may wish to follow every word. For that he picks up his missal. There he will find appropriately majestic translations of those jeweled sentences shaped by thousands of years of Catholic tradition, like sand compressed by time into pearls.

But beware. Reading the missal will distract you from gazing at the ornate spectacle of the priest summoning God to take up His throne upon our altar. You see, a Catholic may not understand any of the Latin words, but that very Latin imprints upon the Mass the transcendent mystery which helps man to completely understand. Not only does the Catholic understand, but he is stirred, moved, shaken, and stunned. Heaven is before his very eyes.

What more is there to understand?

TOGETHER, TURNING TO GOD

Three things are readily identified when Catholics express unease with the Traditional Mass: the use of the Latin language; the silence of the priest during the Canon; and the posture of the priest at the altar facing God and not the people. Latin in the Mass was discussed in the last essay. Let us turn our attention to the priest's posture of facing God and not the people.

A perfect opening for this discussion is in the very language used by confused Catholics in articulating their objection: "but the priest has his back to us." *Au contraire*, the priest does not have his back to us; rather, he has his body facing God. That posture is as natural as it is for the faithful attending Mass to be facing the altar where God is. Imagine for a moment the faithful attending Mass turning and facing each other. That odd position would be immediately recognized as quite comical. Why? Because any normal Catholic understands that during Holy Mass the attention of everyone is to be on God, not on each other.

Wouldn't it be a peculiar exception to exclude the priest from such a natural position of prayer – facing God, together with everyone else? Yet this is the strange stance of Catholics who make a complaint about the position of the priest during the Traditional Mass. They would ask him to assume a physical position at holy Mass that for themselves they would see as clearly preposterous. At Mass no one would dare say of the person in front of him, "How rude; she has her back toward me!" Isn't it equally silly to say that of the priest offering the Traditional Mass?

During Holy Mass the entire Mystical Body of Christ is turning toward Christ, like men eagerly awaiting the coming of their Divine Rescuer. The priest is one with the pleading faithful as he, *in persona Christi*, is begging the Father for His mercy as he holds before His Divine Majesty the precious Body and Blood of His Only-Begotten Son. This stands as the critical theological reason for the priest to face the same direction as the faithful. Moreover, for a culture that craves solidarity and community, isn't this the perfect sign? The priest, one with his people, as he pleads before

Almighty God, just as Our Lord is one with us through His Sacred humanity as He pleads before His Father.

Still more layers of meaning suggest themselves when we look closely at this posture of the priest facing God with the people. Our Lord calls Himself the Good Shepherd (Jn 10:11). The shepherd carefully guides his flock by leading them. The shepherd proceeds forward ahead of them, bravely confronting the darkness, avoiding the obstacles, discovering the disguised traps, and preventing stumbling into deep ravines. The sheep follow the shepherd's lead, lest they perish. Similarly, the Good Shepherd leads us through the thickets of this valley of tears, so that we safely arrive in Paradise. He does not lead walking backwards. He leads by erectly walking forward – unafraid to face enemies lest you and I, whom He loves, become their prey.

The structure of each Church building is seen by Mother Church as a kind of ship. So it is that the main body of each Catholic Church is called the nave – the very Latin word for ship. Why the symbol of a ship? Because it is the Church with her Holy Mass and Sacraments which act as a ship sailing upon the often treacherous seas of life, navigating each and every one of us to the safe port of heaven. Who is steering this Ship of Grace? Our Lord Himself. He is the Divine Captain Who, like any good captain, is looking ahead at the deep ocean lest the ship veer off course. Our confidence is in the very position of the Divine Captain – looking straight ahead so that the ship does not deviate from its path.

From the infancy of the Church the priest always leads the Church at Holy Mass, symbolized by him facing God with the people in his care. Oftentimes, this posture of the priests was called was called facing East, that is, in the physical direction from whence the sun rises. The Church recognized that Christ the Son was the world's New Sun – our true light. Its rising in the east was a daily reminder that Christ Our Redeemer comes to us as faithfully each day as that rising sun, with the grace of Holy Mass and the Sacraments. Moreover, Christ Our Lord will one day come to meet us at the hour of our death. But, most dramatically, Our Lord will come to meet us at the end of the world when, accompanied by throngs of Cherubim and Seraphim, He will return to this earth in a spectacle of blazing glory. As we begin to open up the Church's liturgical symbolism, we enter worlds within worlds, layers within layers of rich meaning. So it was that from Apostolic times the Church decreed that every altar face east, lest no Catholic have escape from his mind the opulent symbolism pointing him to Emmanuel – God coming to us at Holy Mass; and everyone, priest and people, gaze at Him in wonder.

In the many years of the writings of Benedict XVI, no liturgical gesture has been emphasized more than this one. Long chapters in dozens of his books are devoted by the Roman Pontiff (then-Cardinal Ratzinger) to the grand fullness of the symbolism of the priest facing God with his people. How blessed we are to have a Church who wraps us in the profound comfort of such symbols. And how poor are those Catholics who fail to understand them. Or worse, who simply do not want to.

AN EMBARRASSMENT OF RICHES

Strange, times have befallen us. Strange, indeed, when, once millennia of Catholics saw the details of the Traditional Mass as privileged portals to the Eternal, now suddenly are viewed by not a few Catholics as insufferable burden. To name just a few: The Mass's majestic and sonorous silence, the priest facing God in earnest pleading, and a Latin language creating the thick air of mystery and salvific transcendence. But this distaste rose not spontaneously from the Catholic soul, but was the systematic project of a professional theological class that can only be aptly described in the fitting obloquy of W. H. Auden, as low and dishonest. Truly, this corrupting enterprise was the consummate *trahison des clercs*.

Hostage to this deracinated clique of conciliar Liturgists, ordinary Catholics were meticulously tutored to prefer dining on the dry sands of secularism, than the haute cuisine of the supernatural. So in these strange times, truths once as obvious as breathing seem now utterly inscrutable. Hence, the obligation to present them afresh. George Orwell profoundly observed of our strange times: "We have now sunk to a depth at which the restatement of the obvious is the first duty of intelligent men."

To that important task, let us review some rich details that festoon the grandeur of the Ancient Mass.

Consider the subject of *ad orientem* (priest facing God). It goes without saying (or perhaps these days it does not) that the Holy Mass is about Christ – not us. Catholic common sense, right? Would that it were so. In 1998 a priest friend was preaching a sermon about the very subject of the Mass being essentially about Christ. After his sermon, an eightyish couple approached him, pillars of his parish. Without irony they remarked to the priest that they had never heard that the Mass is about Christ. I am sure that the dear couple meant to say that it was so long since they heard it, it seemed as though they had never heard it before. Tis sad, isn't it?

Of course, the Mass is about Christ – His sacrifice on Calvary (in an unbloody fashion) for the redemption of the human race. That truth is knitted into every square inch of the Traditional Mass. Of all the gestures that dramatize that mystery, the priest facing God at the altar is paramount. In that posture the Church establishes for the priest a certain anonymity. Clearly, the faithful recognize that it is Father So-and-So, but they actually see very little of Father So-and-So. He is not talking to them because he is talking to God. It is as though we are overhearing the intimate conversation between Christ (in the person of the priest) and His Father.

This anonymity is critical for the Mass. It pointedly ignores the personality of the priest and bows only to the personality of Christ. We are not beholding Father So-and-So's face – with all the particularities, likable or not, that go with Father So-and-So. Holy Mass is not the time for that. At Mass we seek to behold only the face of the Savior. That Divine Face becomes known to us in the stunning unfolding of the words and gestures of Mass itself. It is only through the anonymity of the priest that the full presence of Christ is revealed. The Baptist's words echo through our mind, He must become more and I become less. That is what we crave. This is what the Church knows that we deserve.

For almost ninety percent of the Traditional Mass the priest speaks in hushed tones, seeming to the faithful blessed silence. Not exactly silence for the altar boys and those standing within inches of the priest. But that is unimportant; for all intent and purposes the faithful at Mass find the priest wrapped in a sacred silence. What is important is that all of us know that, like Moses on Sinai, the priest, *in persona Christi*, in the Person of Christ, ascends the altar to speak and offer Himself to His Father. It is the supreme cultic conversation of Lover and Beloved. It is no wonder that such a sublime intimacy is cast by Mother Church in the most hushed exchanges. Yet, through that very silence bellows the staggering reality of the Mystery. Here no Catholic can be mistaken about a uniquely striking moment occurring before his very eyes. A moment that human eyes can find no other place on earth. Once more, as He did two thousand years ago, our Lord is laying His sacrificed Body before the throne of His Beloved Father. All of it happening – for us. For us!

This silence is indeed unsettling, especially in our own culture where sounds (noise?) surround us like a permanent membrane. It leaves us addicts – unable to live without it. This is what T. S. Eliot meant in his poem *Burnt Norton*, when he writes, we live "distracted from distraction by distraction." Modern man so fills his soul with the roiling superficialities of life that the most beautiful ones never have a chance to be heard. For that there must be silence. Silence acts as a ladder whose rungs lead the feet of the soul down to its depths. Only in that place can it properly do what it must – consider, ponder, embrace, and relish the foundational Truth of existence. At that depth, however, there is only the sight of your life and Christ. It can be terrifying. Out of cowardice or fear, most men settle for distraction. Anything to get their minds off the only thing the mind should be about.

Next time you attend the Traditional Mass, sealed by the splendid silence of the priest, do not think you are hearing nothing. Recognize that it is through that very silence that you can hear everything.

WHY THE EXTRAORDINARY FORM IS TRULY EXTRAORDINARY

Sometime in 1970 Pope Paul VI was made an offer which he tragically refused. The Pontiff had just banned the millennial old Roman Missal throughout the world. Forever. The ancient majestic form of the Mass was halted with the suddenness of a bird slamming into a plate glass window. Sir Kenneth Clark, leading a glittering roster of the world's leading artists and intellectuals, offered the Pope their eternal gratitude if he would but rescind his abrogation of the classical Roman Mass. They argued that it fused the Europe we now know. Furthermore, it communicated an ineffable mystery within an artistic liturgical form unsurpassed in aesthetic achievement. History tells the rest. Liturgical technocrats won over art and tradition, and Paul VI delivered to the world his *Novus Ordo Missae*, or the *Missa Paulinus*.

Axiomatic for every Catholic is the dogmatic fact that Christ's sacrifice of Calvary is made present at every Mass. This must never be in question when we compare the value of one liturgical form with another. Justified disgust at enormities at Novus Ordo Masses these days should lead no one to say there is no Mass. Unless certain strict norms for validity are flouted, every Mass is an immolation of the Immaculate Lamb of God for our salvation. Period. Once this is understood, a discussion can develop without fear that certain strong positions suggest disloyalty to the Church.

Fifty years distance from the second Vatican council and its liturgical reforms give all of us sufficient objectivity to weigh them appropriately. For decades growing numbers of scholars have begun a sustained, growing, and pointed critique of the *Novus Ordo Missae*. Chief among them:

- Pope Benedict XVI (*Feast of Faith, The Spirit of the Liturgy*, etc.)
- Monsignor Klaus Gamber (*The Reform of the Roman Liturgy*)
- Father Aidan Nichols, O.P. (*Looking at the Liturgy, Lost in Wonder*)
- Alcuin Reid
- Peter Kwasniewski

- Martin Mosebach
- Catherine Pickstock
- Michael Fiedrowicz

The superiority of the Ancient Mass can be argued from four theological perspectives: mystery, sin, prayer, and adoration. Before beginning this analysis it cannot be stressed enough that every valid Mass contains these properties *ex natura ipsius rei*. What is permissible to argue is which form more effectively communicates these properties. A diamond set within a tangle of weeds communicates less of its value than when it is set in a solid gold engraved encasement. Same diamond; different communication. In one, the beauty of the jewel is obscured; in the other it radiates. So the forms of the Mass.

MYSTERY

By mystery we mean the presence of the Divinity which is incomprehensible and ineffable. Not in the sense of a puzzle, but rather like a sunset: never fully understandable, but irresistibly attractive. Rudolf Otto, the noted religious phenomenologist, aptly expresses it in the phrase, *mysterium tremendans et fascinans* (a mystery overwhelming and simultaneously captivating). The Ancient Roman Mass is saturated with conspicuous mystery. It employs an evocative ensemble of symbols to evoke a thick mood of sacred mystery. Aside from the several dozen precise rubrics executed during the Mass, the central one must be the priest silently praying the Canon.

A psychological separation is effected here, and it strikes dramatically. The muted sacerdotal voice signals the commencement of a stunning Divine Act which is unmistakable by the palpable stillness. Only the ruffling of heavy vestments and the tinkling of silver bells interrupts it. Paradoxically, this stark separation produces a simultaneous intimacy, as well as a heightened longing. It resembles the whispered conversation of lovers, where more audible words would injure the intimacy of the moment. Thus God descends upon our altar by the hushed words of the priest only to take us to Himself, here and unto heaven. This penetrating sense of mystery is only deepened by the priest facing God. He is seen not only as leading the faithful to heaven, as a captain leading men to war, but simultaneously separated from them as he conducts the business of Calvary in persona Christi.

The use of the Latin language consummates this sense of mystery. Not that mystery rests upon incomprehensibility. But its use does rest upon a distance from the commonplace, the ordinary, the pedestrian. A necessary dissimilarity with the familiar is critical in establishing contact with the world of the supernatural. Otherwise, mystery melts into the quotidian and drab imitation of the marketplace.

SIN

The elaborate penitential choreography of the Foot Prayers (Psalm 42) and the nine *Eleisons* immediately ushers priest and faithful into a vivid awareness of their sinful lot. Indeed, the humble and pronounced kneeling, then profound bowing of the servers and priest while they recite these galvanic prayers, drives this point home with thunderous clarity. The Ancient Mass possesses an exquisite series of Offertory prayers which highlight our sinful approach to the thrice holy God. The mandatory striking of the breast is a potent act that accompanies each entreaty for mercy: *Sanctus, Agnus Dei, Domine Non Sum Dignus.* Each time, there is recalled St. Augustine's haunting query: "If Christ were to stand before you now, what would you think, not of Him, but of yourself?"

Instantly there comes to mind the scene of St. Peter pleading with Christ to depart from him, a sinful man. Or, the Magdalene washing Christ's feet with her hair. Yet this searing awareness of sin does not frighten or distance rather, it deepens the aching for the Savior Who alone relieves our sinful misery. Sin's palpable presence in the Ancient Roman Mass acts as magnification of Christ's pity for man brought to its highest pitch on Calvary. The solemn words of the Creed become real, "For us men, and for our salvation He came down from heaven." Though the sorrow for sin envelopes us, the compassion of Christ envelopes all the more. St. Paul's words seem to settle firmly in our souls, "But where sin abounded, grace did much more abound" (Rom 5:20) with an understanding powerfully branded onto men's hearts.

PRAYER

Even a superficial glance at the prayers of the Ancient Roman Mass resonates with a clarity, beauty, and spiritual refinement that sweeps the faithful into the depths of the mystical sacrifice. This prayerful reverence is sustained at every moment. The faithful are never victimized by idiosyncrasy or idiocy, precisely because the inflexibility of the Ancient Roman Mass protects them. No matter that the priest is uninspired or uninspiring, weary or even a simpleton, the Ancient Roman Mass makes each priest do exactly the same thing and that same thing is sublimity itself. It gives flesh to the old Catechism definition, "Prayer is the lifting up of the mind and heart to God." Each of the prayers of the Ancient Mass is an encyclopedia of doctrine; compact, unambiguous, clarifying, and stirring. Take the Collect of the Feast of St. Aloysius Gonzaga:

> Father of love, giver of all good things, in St. Aloysius you combined remarkable innocence with the spirit of penance. By the help of his prayers may we who have not followed his innocence follow his example of penance. Grant this through our Lord Jesus Christ, your Son, who lives and reigns with you and the Holy Spirit, God, for ever and ever.

Each sculpted sentence is a pleading before God's throne for the salvation of our souls and temporal protection from adversity. Each prayer is like a miniature cameo, brevity wedded to doctrinal poetry. Or, perhaps like a range of towering mountain peaks lifting us higher and higher so we can touch the face of God.

Such hieratic vocabulary seems almost alien to the *Novus Ordo Missae*. And by design. The necessary decade long revision of the Roman Missal begun by Pope John Paul II and completed by Pope Benedict XVI is proof that something in the *Novus Ordo Missae* cried out for redress.

For its fabricators intentionally traded sacral expression for a more pedestrian style better suited to their latitudinarian interests. Even the preferred vestments of the *Novus Ordo Missae* exhibit this drab utility. Each resembles items from a neighborhood thrift shop rather than the sumptuous splendor befitting the celestial court of the Immolated Lamb of God. Look at the van Eyck Ghent Altarpiece and see what I mean.

ADORATION

Because we are not angels the Church recognizes that each movement of the soul must be accompanied by an action of the body. The interpenetration of soul and body in man, constituting a whole and undivided person, demands it. While the principal act of man at Mass is adoration, it is stillborn if not joined to physical acts: kneeling, genuflections, bows, striking of the breast. The Ancient Roman Mass is teeming with these gestures. They are directed to Christ present in the Most Blessed Sacrament and to the person of the priest, who acts in persona Christi. If a stranger were to walk in upon an Ancient Roman Mass he would not for a moment think he had walked in a chance gathering of friends. Like a clanging cymbal close to his ear, he would know he had stepped in upon Something unlike anything on earth. For instance, each time the priest moves the Sacred Species, that action is both preceded and followed by genuflection. This is adoration writ large.

No casualness, only strict precision of movements. No improvisations, only perfect adherence to prescribed words. No bonhomie, only attention to God and His grandeur. No performance, only the homage of adoration before the throne of the Savior. All but the dimwitted can see that Someone must be present here beyond human words. These gestures of adoration draw the soul like a magnet, sundering distraction and leaving the soul exposed to the elevations of grace. No doubt, a priest celebrating the *Novus Ordo Missae* can create this ambience of adoration, but this is rare. For its very intrinsic structure does not lend itself easily to such postures of latria. The ethos of the *Novus Ordo Missae* is an informal elasticity, which is anathema to the Ancient Roman Mass.

Jacques Maritain wrote the preface to the 1936 classic, *The Mystery of the Church*, by distinguished Thomistic theologian Father Humbert Clerissac. In it he writes movingly of his attendance at the Masses of Father Clerissac. Read this text of Maritain carefully. Could this have been written of most Masses of the *Novus Ordo Missae*?

> The Mass, said St. Vincent Ferrer, is the highest work of contemplation. I never assisted, and I believe I shall never again assist, at Masses offered with so much perfection, exactitude, completely recollected love, and supreme and almost terrible majesty of those Masses of Father Clerissac which I had the happiness of serving throughout one year. He pronounced the words of consecration in an unforgettable way, in a voice that was low but astonishingly

distinct, in so energetic a tone that it seemed to pierce the heart of God. The sacrifice of the Mass was truly for him the consummation of all things: the supreme action. He often advised people to unite themselves to it in such a way that they put, so to say, their whole life into the chalice of the priest, offering it with him for the four principle ends of this oblation of Jesus Christ through which the work of our redemption is accomplished each time that it is renewed.

So why is the Extraordinary Form extraordinary? Need one even ask?

WHICH LITURGY APPEALS TO CATHOLIC YOUTH?

Washington D. C. is no stranger to making history. This past Saturday was no exception. You would not have found throngs of people marching with angry placards, but hundreds of Catholics on their knees. They were not assembled at the National Mall, but at the Basilica Shrine of the Immaculate Conception. They were not participating in political activism, but fervently adoring Christ at the Holy Sacrifice of the Mass. Hundreds and hundreds of twenty-somethings were not participating in any ordinary Mass, but in a Pontifical Solemn High Tridentine Mass celebrated by one of America's most exceptional Ordinaries, Archbishop Alexander Sample, who governs the Archdiocese of Portland, Oregon. It was nothing less than a spiritual earthquake.

Not only was the nave crowded with young people, but the sanctuary was filled with rows and rows of young priests and seminarians, vested in cassock and surplice. It was a stunning snapshot of, what many thought, was a long buried past. But what was really stunning is that is the wave of a pulsating dynamic future. It was Catholic springtime in the 2018 springtime of Washington, D. C. While the bursting apple blossoms vied for attention, they couldn't compete with the stirring beauty of Catholic young people hungry for God.

Make no mistake, this past Saturday in Washington, D. C.'s Basilica was, in Karl Jasper's portentous phrase, an *axial* moment. A turning point, from which future ages could mark a pivotal change in perspective, a tectonic shift in cultural movement. In Archbishop Sample's sermon: "Maybe the experience of these young people growing up with the ordinary Form did not carry within it the beauty, reverence, prayer, and fullness of the sense of mystery, transcendence and awe that the Traditional Mass has provided for them." Though the archbishop couched his words demurely, words of agreement must be shouted loudly.

Only in the rarest instances have the young observed the Ordinary Form prayed majestically. Ordinarily, even when prayed reverently, it never soars, leaving souls dizzy with the thick air of Heaven. While it is certainly the ineffable unbloody Sacrifice of Calvary, the Ordinary Form is often anemic and flat. Lamentably, in more than a few places the Ordinary Form suffers a bastardization: reduced to a protean stage for performing clerics or inventive liturgy committees. The net result is leaving souls parched. Not surprisingly, the oft-times bombastic, but always perceptive, Dr. Camille Paglia had cause to remark:

> My dissatisfaction with American Catholicism, which partly began during my adolescence in the late '50s, was due partly to its increasing self-Protestantization and suppression of its ancient roots. Within twenty years, Catholic churches looked like airline terminals: no statues, no stained-glass windows, no Latin, no litanies, no gorgeous jeweled vestments, no candles—so that the ordinary American Church now smells like baby powder.

A New Evangelization requires new men and women. Only the effusions of grace in the Divine Liturgy, unencumbered by ambiguous settings, can produce them. The soul's sanctification and the Holy Spirit's "recreating the face of the earth" is the work of a Sacred Liturgy, which sets men ablaze. The grandeur of the Roman Liturgy in its Extraordinary Form does just that. And the Pontifical Solemn High Mass is the consummate vehicle for that supernatural conflagration. As the hundreds knelt at that Pontifical Mass, they could hear the words of the book of the Apocalypse: "... behold, a throne was set in Heaven, and One sat on the throne. And He that sat was to look upon like jasper and a sardine stone; and there was a rainbow round about the throne, in sight like unto an emerald.... And before the throne proceeded lightnings and thunderings and voices... saying... Worthy is the lamb that was slain to receive power, and riches, and wisdom, and strength, and honor, and glory, and blessing" (Rev 4:1-11; 5:12-13). Holy Mass is the royal court of the Slain Lamb, or in Dr. Catherine Pickstock's words, "the sacred polis." Catholics are its royal citizens.

Professor Tracey Rowland expresses this beautifully:

> [The Church] makes it possible for people, poor as well as rich, to transcend their cultural limitations, to rise above their cultural poverty, and be citizens, or rather, subjects, of an eternal city. The effect of the Church on

the culture of the world, and in particular on the life of the "common man," ought to be ennobling, ought to be affirming of a royal status as a child of God, as a member of a royal priesthood, a people set apart. This does not happen when mass culture is baptized by its use in the liturgy, or when its idioms are taken up to wrap the Church's doctrines. Contrary to the rationale behind such pastoral strategies, their ultimate effect is to make the Church relevant to the modern world, but to make it indistinguishable from the modern world, and this in turn makes it completely irrelevant.

The New Evangelization summons Catholics to nothing less than a transformation of our culture of death, akin to the transformation Mother Church affected fifteen hundred years ago in translating the Pagan Roman Empire into triumphant Christendom. For that daunting task, man needs the Mass, the Immemorial Mass which was the engine that built Western Civilization. So, Dr. Catherine Pickstock (an Anglican, and professor at Cambridge) argued in her magisterial *After Writing: On the Liturgical Consummation of Philosophy*. In her densely argued tour de force she set down the case that the Extraordinary Form of the Roman Mass alone can breach the thick walls of Modernity. Pickstock:

> The liturgical city is avowedly semiotic. Its lineaments, temporal duration, and spatial extension are entirely and constitutively articulated through the signs of speech, gesture, art, music, figures, vestments, color, fire, water, smoke, bread, wine and relationality... [all] exalt[ing] a different and salvific formulation of the various dichotomies which have been seen to reside at the heart of immentistic secularity.

Some may have frowned at this Pontifical Mass. But those frowns disguise a shallowness that threatens the life of the soul. Listen to J. B. Bagshaw, in his *Treasure of the Church*: "It is impossible ... for men to believe that Our Lord is amongst them and not lavish on Him their most precious treasures, just as it was impossible for St. Mary Magdalene not to pour out her precious ointment on His feet."

If one required further assistance in understanding the full theological splendor of the Pontifical Mass, there is no better way than through the words of Dr. Peter Kwasniewski:

In the realm of the supernatural mysteries, Christianity is purely and entirely monarchical... we profess that Christ our King, the Lord of heaven and earth, of all times, past, present, and to come, of this world and of the next; that His angels and saints are His royal court; that He deigns to call us friends and brethren, yes, but such that we know that we never cease to be His servants. We long for His courts and tabernacles. The thick politicism of the imagery points to the real, sovereign polity of the Mystical Body, subsisting in the Roman Catholic Church, as a *societas prefecta* and altogether perfected in the Heavenly Jerusalem, the city of the great king. Our ecclesial sacrifice, the Most Holy Eucharist, is a kingly and high-priestly oblation.

Though we still stand knee-deep on the ruins on secularist modernity, a new world is aborning – a marvelously exciting and bright world. Want to hear more about it? Find one of those twenty-somethings that prayed at that Washington, D.C. Mass on April 28th. They will tell you. And your heart will dance.

LEX ORANDI, LEX AEDIFICANDI

In no less than six years the Roman Church will celebrate the centenary of St. Pius X's encyclical *Pascendi Dominici Gregis*. Sarto's encyclical boldly identified and aggressively prosecuted a heresy whose virulence the Church had never seen before. Indeed, the Pontiff was not intemperate in applying to Modernism the epithet, synthesis of all heresies. Its treachery was singled out from all the errors of the centuries because its treachery was unparalleled. Other heresies set out to mangle one or two truths of holy religion. Modernism's goal was to bury religion itself.

As Richard Weaver has taught us, ideas do have consequences. The particularly pernicious idea of Modernism soon began to show its influence upon every portion of the Church's life. Since the principal tenet of Modernism was the apotheosis of man and neutering of dogma, every sign that bespoke the supernatural had to be surrendered. Because one of the most potent signs of the supernatural is the Church building, radical redesigns became *de rigueur*. These new configurations were not mere new modern styles, they were styles proselytizing modernism. They shocked, they disturbed, they intentionally broke with every architectural and artistic tradition that incarnated the Faith of our Fathers. And as the assumptions of modernism became more regnant, so did church architecture become more sterile, more jarring, more unsettling. Just as medieval cathedrals were monuments to faith, many of the new churches of these last hundred years became monuments to the death of faith.

The aggressiveness of this project reached a fever pitch in the last thirty years. Finding itself safely entrenched, an emboldened modernism threw its erstwhile discretion to the wind and proclaimed itself boldly – particularly in art and architecture. That mighty engine which carried the Faith so powerfully would now undermine it just as powerfully.

It is a calamitous story, but some of these calamities' worst enormities were perpetuated against the signs most precious – and in a certain sense, most necessary – to Catholics: their Churches, their art, and – most tragically – their sacred liturgy. This baneful collapse possessed a certain inevitability, because *lex orandi, lex credendi*: what one believes shapes how one prays. And if I may add to the venerable formula – *lex aedificandi*. The way in which one believes and prays determines the shape and style of the places where one prays.

Who would teach this ancient truth to a modern world ossified in its secularity? Children, of course. Not exactly children, but very young men and women. God surprised the world with the voices of young scholars who refused the tyranny of the decadent status quo. These men and women possessed an appreciation of the deep metaphysical and dogmatic truths underlying the symbiotic unity of dogma, prayer, liturgy, and architecture. Like an unexpected army come to rescue prisoners long thought lost, came these troops of young Catholics: terribly bright, spirited, and intending no pause till they achieved triumph for Holy Church. They carried their new Old Wisdom like proud medieval knights on horseback with banners unfurled, flapping against the winds.

These Catholics are conspicuously young because orthodoxy in the twenty-first century is principally a youth revolution – a Woodstock in reverse. Modernism is an ideology of the old seeking eagerly to justify both its vice and its ennui. Orthodoxy is the adventure of the young who are hungry for the adventure which is *ad majorem Dei gloriam*. Those passionate for the truth are always young – *Introibo ad altare Dei, ad Deum qui laetificat juventutem meam*. Each one of this new company of Catholic artists and scholars have devoted much time to articulating the implications of this ontological unity for liturgy, prayer, and art. Each stands in the forefront of a fresh generation of artists, artisans, and thinkers who are excitedly poised to ignite a new Counter-Reformation. They are the advance legions of the Johan Pauline New Evangelization.

Like the Berninis and Michelangelos before them, they have been enchanted by the dogmas and liturgy of the Church and are generously laying before her the bounty of their talents. Each one knows, after all, as goes the Church – so goes our world.

A RUMBLING

Hear that rumbling beneath your feet? It is the sound of the quickly approaching Catholic Triumph. Lest anyone be quick to accuse me of optimism, let the record show that I see Modernism continuing to metastasize. Enough Bishops still salute to the Spirit of Vatican II credo. Others, not wanting to squander the booty of the past third century but wishing to be seen as seizing the role of conciliator, intone the Bernardin hymn of Common Ground. Most of the rest, even those with an orthodox persona, freeze in the face of the modernist apparatus. These otherwise good bishops maintain the stagnating status quo of doctrine-less catholic school/CCD programs, epicene seminary structures, and most damaging, psychologized preaching and burlesque liturgies. No optimism here.

Yet there is still that unmistakable rumbling. We have heard nothing like its sound since the other rumbling which began a whole third of a century ago when there commenced the attempt to strangle Vatican II with the Spirit of Vatican II. It came within an inch of succeeding. Until 1989.

Pure Divine handiwork unfolded. From an unmitigated calamity for the Roman Catholic Church, the excommunication of the Archbishop Marcel Lefebvre and schismatization of his own Society of Pius X, came the Johan Pauline Papal motu proprio *Ecclesia Dei Adflicta*. And God turned darkness into light. With this generous impulse of the Sovereign Pontiff allowing the Traditional Mass, a new corner was turned. Traditional Masses sprouted on every continent. Even more amazing were the congregations, three-quarters of whom were under the age of 40, too young to have even remembered that venerable liturgical form. Before our eyes, a new Youth Movement was aborning. A Pentecost reversed Babel, today's youthful generation of the Ancient Roman Missal was reversing yesterday's generation of Woodstock. *Mirabilia Dei!*

Yet there was more. Everywhere you looked there appeared new religious orders. Every one devoted to the promulgation of the Traditional Mass in keeping with the mind of the Roman Pontiff.

None of this youthful enthusiasm was marred by caustic reaction to the Modernist decadence or an unseemly lack of charity to its supporters. Calm, intelligent and virile buoyancy was the only thing for which these kids could be blamed. And sanctity. Yes, sanctity. We hadn't seen sanctity like that since the Old Days. Their names? The Fraternity of St. Peter, Institute of Christ the King, the Benedictine Monastery of St. Madaleine in Le Barroux, the Dominicans of St. Vincent Ferrer and the Institute of the Holy Cross of Riaumont. Where most bishops were wringing their hands in despair over vocations, the rectors of these Orders were pleading with candidates to hold off their applications. Too many applicants and too few buildings! To this day the tide has not abated. In the past few years there is also the Opus Mariae Mediatricis and the Society of St. John. And this writer knows of a half dozen more that are imminently to be launched.

All of this brings us to St. Peter's Square on October 26th, 1998. Tens of thousands of pilgrims descended upon Rome to festively celebrate ten years of the Roman document *Ecclesia Dei Adflicta*. Aside from the sheer multitudes of the faithful, something astounding met the eyes of onlookers. Hundreds of young men. Each one looking like he stepped out of West Point. Rather than the military uniforms of the U.S. Army they were wearing the military uniform of the Holy Priesthood – the Roman cassock. Some may say, so what? As secularist theological thinking replaced traditional theological thinking, a deep loathing began to appear for the cassock amongst priests. Simply put, the cassock tethered them to a classical thinking they rejected. The cassock symbolized all the Left hated. It represented unswerving commitment to an eternal vocation, devotion to sacrifice, virtue, innocence, and most importantly, the cultic work of saving souls through the sacraments and Holy Mass. That kind of thinking was declared anathema by the Theological Elite. The Roman cassock bespoke a different universe. A love of heavenly things. It was an ode to detachment, to love of God, to the triumph of truth over fashion. It was permanence, first principles, a respite from the City of Man, and powerful invitations to Divine Grace. With this as context, look at those young men in the cassock again. What they were saying without saying a thing was electrifying.

Then the words of the Pope, "I invite the bishops also, fraternally, to understand and to have a renewed pastoral attention for the faithful attached to the Old Rite and, on the threshold of the new millennium, to help all Catholics to live the celebration of the Holy Mysteries with a devotion which may be true nourishment for their spiritual life and which may be a source of peace." Then there was Cardinal Ratzinger. In his address to these pilgrims several days before the speech of Holy Father, this great Prince of the Church praised God for the remarkable fruit of vocations and sanctity that gushed from the papal text, *Ecclesia Dei*. The Prefect went on to deliver an address that stupefied those who listened. It actually won banner headlines in Paris's daily *Le Monde*, which correctly noted that the Cardinal's words would rock the dusty modern conventions of the Catholic world.

No, there is no doubt that there is rumbling beneath our feet. Make no mistake about what it means.

It is the beginning of The Beginning.

No matter what you may say about G. K. Chesterton, he can't be blamed for the present dizzying enthusiasm for the Tridentine Mass. It does seem, however, that his words could have been the preface to the groundbreaking speech by Cardinal Ratzinger in Rome last October. Chesterton presciently wrote, "Again and again we are told by all sons of priggish and progressive persons that we cannot go back, as it cannot go anywhere. Every important change in history has been founded on something historic; and if the world had not again and again tried to renew its youth, it would have been dead long ago."

That is it, of course. Perhaps paradoxical, but so very, very true. It was put so well in the episcopal motto of one of this century's great prelates: Our future is the past. The strength unleashed by *Ecclesia Dei Adflicta* was not nostalgia, it was *gratia*. Yes, grace. For Divine grace is never old or new, but old and new at the same time. It is St. Augustine addressing God in the *Confessions* as, "O ancient Beauty old and ever-new." That was the genius thrust of Ratzinger's address. The Tridentine Mass, which he praised so extravagantly, is not a mummified form. No liturgical form approved by the Catholic church ever is. Rather, the Church approves liturgical forms for their fitness to bear the sublime riches of Calvary's Sacrifice. Thus, those liturgical forms never cease throbbing with life, clothing those who approach them with light and grace. Thus Ratzinger:

The orthodox forms of a rite are living realities... expressions of the life of the Church, in which are distilled the faith, the prayer and the very life of whole generations. The Church has the power to define and limit the use of such rites... but she never purely and simply forbids them.[1]

Larger and larger numbers of Catholic thinkers (cf. Nichols, Ratzinger, Gamber, and non-Catholic Pickstock) are siding with Ratzinger's analysis that the Bugnini liturgical revisions were heavily loaded down by Enlightenment prejudices. And this has occurred at a time when modernity's disenchantment with them is producing the Deconstructionist despair. Modernity's song of giddy progress had for its refrain an abhorrence for the past – an all-too common sentiment in our culture. Its Trojan horse was dragged into the Sacred City of the Roman Rite by grim liturgical experts whose faces drew smiles only at the sound of that new word of intoxicating power – *Change*. As with any intoxication, it robbed them of reason and left only blinding drives. To this day their spirit dominates the once majestic and rich science called Sacred Liturgy. Some will mock that science's former time as riddled with stale rubricism and rigid formulae. Such criticism, of course, is about as valid as rejecting chemistry because it is bound to the Periodic Table of the Elements, or English Literature for its dependence on grammar.

Underlying this criticism are the unquestioned assumptions of Nominalism, where the absence of standards is the only standard. Ratzinger spots all of this with an eagle's eye. In his 1997 autobiography *Salt of the Earth*, he trenchantly observes:

> I am of the opinion that the Old Rite should be granted much more generously to all those who desire it. It's impossible to grasp what could be dangerous or unacceptable about that. A community that suddenly declares that what until now was its holiest and highest possession is strictly forbidden, and makes the longing for it seem downright indecent, calls its very self into question.

So entrenched is this delirium for Change that it provoked Bishop Donald Trautman, former head of the US Bishops Committee on the Liturgy, to make the oracular remark two years ago that the only constant in the liturgy is change. The prospects of burgeoning numbers of young Catholics crammed into Tridentine

---

[1] 24 October 1998, Rome.

A Rumbling

Masses created alarm in a former Bugnini secretary and director of the Concilium, Rembert Weakland. In an article in the tony Jesuit weekly *America*, Archbishop Weakland noted the run away popularity of the Tridentine Mass with dismay and urged watchfulness along with the gravest concern. Strange, you say. But ideological intoxication does strange things. And it dies slowly. No comfort came to the hearts of the Liturgical Establishment when the Holy Office Prefect declared:

> The difference between the liturgy according to the new books, how it is actually practiced and celebrated in different places, is often greater than the difference between the Old Mass and the New Mass, when both these are celebrated according to the prescribed books.[2]

One of the most stunning features of the Ratzinger address was its praise of the Old Rite. His criticism was reserved exclusively to the *Novus Ordo Missae*. Or, more precisely, the whole ensemble of structuralized depredations that have come to be known as the *Novus Ordo Missae*. Of course, Ratzinger has given wide encouragement to the several organizations desiring a reform of the reform, which is all well and good. But while their contributions are most necessary to the life of the Church, their effects shall not be seen for generations. The same animus meeting the Tridentine Mass awaits them as well. With one difference. Catholics may find respite now, in the Tridentine Masses being celebrated today, all throughout the world. What Ratzinger is saying through the lines of his text is that the reform of the reform Mass must await both the demise of the Liturgical Apparatus (controlling almost every Liturgy Office in the world) and the glacial movement of the Holy See. Yes, let a hundred orthodox flowers bloom. But let us not forget that one is already in full blossom.

Dr. Catherine Pickstock reminds us in her theological and philosophical world-moving work, *After Writing: The Liturgical Consummation of Philosophy*, that the Tridentine Mass is a rite so powerful that it is always moving man and his culture to depths that make tomorrow possible. And the Mass does this not by casting off any of Yesterday's splendors, but carrying them forward to meet Tomorrow's needs. And if Tomorrow can add to Yesterday's richness, let it. This is not a cramped achaeologism, nor a

---
[2] 24 October 1998, Rome.

futurism run amuck. The Cambridge scholar also significantly notes that the Mass is the most important Work in the world. For it is the Work of God redeeming man and man adoring God. It is the Work that makes it possible for every other work of man to be accomplished. And that Work has never been presented with such might and beauty than in the Tridentine Mass.

Let the Work begin.

TRADITIONIS CUSTODES: A SETBACK, NOT A DEFEAT

Now the dust has settled from *Traditonis Custodes* (somewhat), it might be a good time to recall Eliot's *Christianity and Culture*, where, he perceptively remarked, "Victories are never permanent, and neither are defeats" Though an unreconstructed Anglican, he possessed a *sensus Catholicus*, which shone through in sentences like that. It is an insight we should take to heart in these post *Traditonis Custodes* days.

Eliot's insights are buttressed by St Augustine's repudiation of fourth century Ososius's *Seven Books of History*, who argued that Christ's final victory had arrived upon the earth with the Emperor Theodosius's proclamation of Christianity as the official religion of the Roman Empire. Augustine scolds sharply in the *City of God*:

> Not only from the time of Christ but from that of Abel, the Church has gone forth on pilgrimage, amid both the persecutions of the world and the consolations of God, and so it will be till the end of time... As far as the prospects for the future are concerned, they remain as uncertain as always, for in the very great multiplicity of human affairs, no people has been granted such security as would free it from the dread of invasions hostile to this life.

It almost seems as though Eliot read St. Augustine's *Letter to Firmus*,

> The life of earthly societies appears not as an orderly progression towards a determinate end, but as a simple process by which the two cities run out their earthly existence with a mixture of successes and failures, but no guarantee of success or salvation in this world.

Though *Traditionis Custodes* was a blow, leaving us quite numbed, St. Augustine's warning should steady us. The temporary pain of gratuitous injustice ought not obscure our memory of past triumphs or future ones. And future ones will come.

Lest anyone accuse me of optimism, let the record show that I see Modernism continuing to metastasize. Enough bishops will still salute the Spirit-of-Vatican-II credo. Others, not wanting to squander the booty of the past half century will intone the sweet music of reaching for the sensible middle (read: avoiding any threat of future advancement). Most of the rest, even those with orthodox persona, will continue to freeze in the face of the sprawling Modernist apparatus.

These otherwise good bishops will maintain the stagnant status quo of doctrine-less Catholic schools/CCD programs, epicene seminary structures and faculties, deracinated Catholic colleges/universities (name even one orthodox Catholic bishop who has stopped any Catholic college/university in his jurisdiction from its relentless exit from Catholic teaching and identity), and most damaging, the psychologized preaching and burlesque liturgies. No optimism here.

For all this, victories will come. Recall past victories which visited us even in the teeth of seeming doom when the Spirit-of-Vatican II desperately attempted to strangle Vatican II. It came within an inch of success. Until 1989. Pure Divine handiwork unfolded. From unmitigated calamities for the Church, not least the excommunication of Marcel Lefebvre and the schismitization of his own Society of Pius X, came the Johan Pauline papal motu proprio *Ecclesia Dei Adflicta*. And God turned darkness into light. With this generous impulse of the Sovereign Pontiff allowing the Traditional Mass, a new corner was turned. This momentous, albeit imperfect and exiguous, document was followed eighteen years later by the bonanza of *Summorum Pontificum*. Traditional Masses sprouted on every continent, and with the help of the internet countless thousands came to discover a Mass whose beauty dazed them. Even more amazing were the congregations, three-quarter of whom were under the age of forty, too young to have even remembered that venerable liturgical form. Before our eyes a new Youth Movement was aborning. As Pentecost reversed Babel, today's Catholic youth of the Ancient Mass were reversing yesterday's Woodstock generation. *Mirabilia Dei!*

Yet there is more. Everywhere you turned there appeared new religious orders, building on the decay of the conventional religious orders who had married the zeitgeist. Everyone devoted to the promulgation of the Ancient Mass in keeping with the mind of the Roman pontiff. None of this youthful enthusiasm was marred by either caustic reaction to the Modernist corruption or an unseemly lack of charity to its supporters. The renaissance was not restricted to religious Orders, conventional dioceses like Charlotte, North Carolina sprouted a new seminary led by a rock-solid visionary like Fr. Matthew Kauth.

Calm, bright and virile buoyancy was the only thing these kids could be accused. And sanctity. A craving for sanctity that had not been seen since the Old Days. Where most bishops were wringing their hands in despair over vocation black winter, the rectors of these Orders and Diocesan seminaries pleaded with candidates to hold off their applicants: too few classrooms for the deluge of young men begging for entrance. To this day the tide has not abated. As an old pastor told his seminarian, "Once the horses have left the stable, closing the doors will not stop the stampede." Not to appear indecorous, but you can't put the genie back in the bottle.

No *motu proprio* will stop the ordinary Catholic marveling at the sight of these New Seminarians. Each one looking like he stepped out of West Point. Instead of the uniforms of the U.S. Army, they are wearing the military uniform of the Holy Priesthood—the Roman Cassock. Some may quip, so what? Or worse. As secular theological thinking replaced traditional theological thinking, a deep loathing set in for the Roman Cassock amongst priests. They saw it as an impediment to the New Gospel of a Re-Imagined Church; an embarrassing throwback to a time of a ritualistic priesthood that had seen its day.

Simply put, the Roman cassock tethered them to a classical thinking that suffocated them like a noose. The cassock represented unswerving commitment to an eternal vocation, devotion to sacrifice, virtue, innocence, and, most crucially, the cultic work of saving souls through the sacraments and Holy Mass. That kind of thinking was anathema to the Theological Elite who had wildly embraced the spirit of the world.

The cassock bespoke a different universe. A love of heavenly things. It was an ode to detachment, to love of God, to the triumph of truth over fashion. It was permanence, first principles, a respite from the City of Man, and a powerful invitation to Divine Grace. With this as context, look at those young men in cassocks again. What they are saying without saying a thing is electrifying.

Though *Traditionis Custodes* gave us a jolt, let our hearts race to the words of John Paul II, words which will perennially tower over the spiteful small-mindedness of that *motu proprio*:

I invite the bishops also, fraternally, to understand and to have a renewed pastoral attention for the faithful attached to the Old Rite and, on the threshold of the New Millennium, to help all Catholics to live the celebration of the Holy Mysteries with a devotion which may be the true nourishment for their spiritual life and which may be the source of peace.

Then there was Benedict XVI (then Cardinal Ratzinger), commenting on the effects of *Ecclesia Dei Adflicta*, praising God for the remarkable fruit of vocations and sanctity that gushed from the papal text. That address stupefied those who listened. It won headlines in Paris's daily *Le Monde*, who correctly noted that the cardinal's words would rock the dusty modern conventions of the Catholic world. In hindsight, it was the beginning of The Beginning.

Catholics must not lose sight of the fact that it is still The Beginning. Even after *Traditionis Custodes* impressive numbers of bishops have permitted the continuance of the celebration of the *Usus Antiquior*, noting its extraordinary fruits. Of course, there are still the gale winds of *Traditionis Custodes* which will batter the fledgling Beginning. As in nature, they will only make The Beginning stronger and more resilient. In this time of vertiginous uncertainty, it might be well for us to recall the words of *Ecclesiastes*:

> To everything there is a season, and a time to every purpose under Heaven:
> A time to break down, a time to build up,
> A time to weep, and a time to laugh; a time to mourn, and a time to dance...
> A time to get, and a time to lose; a time to keep, and a time to cast away...
> He hath made everything beautiful in his time.

This our season for patience; for waiting. Waiting for God to show us clear paths forward in the light of unexpected setbacks, but not defeats. But it is a season that God has permitted. So, we end with Eliot as we began with Eliot. This time, from *Burnt Norton*: "For us, there is only the trying. The rest is not our business."

A BERLIN WALL—AGAIN

Rising, piece by piece, are the bricks of a new Berlin Wall. It is not a physical barrier, like the original Wall, imprisoning captive peoples in a communist hell. This one is a spiritual Wall, separating devout Catholics from a means of adoring God that they love: the Traditional Mass.

It is an unprecedented reversal of the generous indulgences of both John Paul II and Benedict XVI. Both pontiffs were redressing the unjust suppression of the Traditional Mass by Pope Paul VI. In the now historic words of Pope Benedict XVI in the letter to the bishops of the world accompanying his motu proprio *Summorum Pontificum*:

> What earlier generations held as sacred, remains sacred and great for us too, and it cannot be all of a sudden forbidden or even considered harmful. It behooves all of us to preserve the riches which have developed in the Church's faith and prayer, and to give them their proper place.

This document was the culmination of pontifical acts which finally ended the hegemony of a corrupt theological/liturgical nomenklatura that had foisted upon the Church an alien *lex orandi* that, if not deforming the *lex credendi*, most certainly attenuated it. With an intrepid determination, this liturgical *bien pensant* violated the millennial work of the Holy Spirit which fashioned the Traditional Mass whose roots traced back to the first centuries of the Church's existence.

No such intrusion had ever been perpetrated in the history of the Church's sacred liturgy. Ludwig Wittgenstein, eminent linguistic analyst, was correct when he wrote, "Attempting to change the canons of a language is like trying to mend a spider's web wearing boxing gloves."

No description more aptly captures the damage done by these liturgical apparatchiks. Preceding Benedict XVI's providential declaration had been the methodical accumulation of many decades of meticulous theological/philosophical scholarship collecting evidence of the Bugnini/Concilium vandalization of the sacred liturgy.

All of this germinated in the formidable intellect of Joseph Ratzinger. As he sifted the weight of the massive work of theologians, historians, and philosophers, he began a decades-long work of piecing together the proper understanding of the Mass, while producing devastating critiques of the liturgical junta responsible for the fabrication of the Novus Ordo.

With glacial progress, a growing number throughout the Church were convinced of the liturgical arguments of Pope Benedict. In a particularly striking passage, then-Cardinal Ratzinger wrote in a Forward to a groundbreaking work of Dom Alcuin Reid, *The Organic Development of the Liturgy:*

> Growth is not possible unless the Liturgy's identity is preserved... Proper development is possible only if careful attention is paid to the inner structural logic of this "organism": just as a gardener cares for a living plant as it develops, with due attention to the power of growth and life within the plant and the rules it obeys, so the Church ought to give reverent care to the Liturgy through the ages, distinguishing actions that are helpful and healing from those that are violent and destructive... With respect to the Liturgy, the Pope has the task of a gardener, not that of a technician who builds new machines and throws the old ones on the junk pile.

Like the appearance of a new land mass, *Summorum Pontificum* was promulgated by Pope Benedict on July 7, 2007. It released the Traditional Mass from its decades-long captivity. But not without howls from an unreconstructed hierarchy wedded to Old Ideas. Their groaning was joined by a chorus of theological mandarins whose revisionist theology depended upon the elasticity of a Novus Ordo regime.

On February 21, 2023, the Holy See promulgated still another juridical document further restricting the Traditional Mass from its celebration. It comes two years after the initial restrictions of the motu proprio *Traditionis Custodes*. These two documents, both draconian and gratuitous, originated in the discredited thinking that Pope Benedict laid bare.

Both are oblivious to the conspicuous spiritual fruits the Traditional Mass has borne, with scores of single young people and families crowding it. Their attendance is not spawned by resentment of the Novus Ordo nor animus toward a sometimes-ungracious hierarchy. Thus proving that the suppression is one of ideological spite and vindictive reprisal.

Further demonstration lies in the Holy See's indifference to the doctrinal enormities of places like Germany, to say nothing of the shocking remarks of the current Synodal relators.

One wonders where is the accompaniment so beloved by the present pontificate? Where is the going out to the fringes? Where is their listening Church?

Indeed, it must seem to the decent Catholics attached to the Traditional Mass that a kind of Berlin Wall is closing in upon them. Yet, though bewildered and downtrodden, they are not petulant; confused, but not vitriolic; sorrowful, but not inflamed. Their reaction to The Suppression is serene, but not unintelligent. Terribly bright, they appreciate the theological/canonical dynamic at work, and they respond intelligently but never disobediently.

Their response is tempered by respect for rightful authority, but not blinded by it. They strive to be faithful sons and daughters of the Church no matter the persecution *by* the Church. As the great Thomistic scholar Fr. Antonin Sertillanges, O.P., once remarked, "Sometimes Catholics are called to suffer *for* the Church; but there is no greater suffering as to endure suffering *by* the Church."

Even as the height of this new Berlin Wall grows higher, they will accept this suffering as willed by God, deepening their fidelity to Mother Church.

One thing they will not surrender is the Immemorial Mass. To that they are committed *usque ad mortem*. Their inspiration is the English martyrs, especially in the Pilgrimage of Grace of 1547-48, when thousands marched in protest against Henry VIII's frightful abolition of the Roman Mass from every corner of England, a country so soaked in the Faith that for centuries it boasted the title of Our Lady's Dowry. Even as the height of his new Berlin Wall grows higher, they will accept this suffering as willed by God, deepening their fidelity to Mother Church. One thing they will not surrender is the Immemorial Mass.

They take courage from the Catholics behind the Iron Curtain who remained ever faithful to the True Faith in spite of the jackboot of barbaric Communism. They are steeled by the stories of

Polish Catholics in the darkest days of Communist tyranny. Having no priest, they would secretly congregate in the forest and pray the Mass together with their missals. When they arrived at the Consecration, they would fall silent and weep.

Today's heroic Catholics recognize that this cruel season will pass in God's good time. Till then, they will let the fires of their suffering forge more strongly the supernatural virtues of Faith, Hope, and Charity. They will endure the lies patiently because they possess the truth.

If the Holy See forbids their participation at the millennial Traditional Mass, they will not be deterred. They will repair to auditoriums, to open fields, to street corners and alleyways. They will not cease praying the Mass of the Ages. For without this Ancient Mass, their hearts will no longer soar.

You see, love does such things.

ROME, WE HAVE A PROBLEM

If ever there were an emergency message to Rome, this is it. It might have been the SOS a year ago as some bishops witnessed large numbers of other bishops using their pastoral canonical privilege to bypass the iron-fisted prescriptions of *Traditionis Custodes*. But it is certainly the frightened alert in light of the Extraordinary Form Mass held at the U.S. Capitol last Tuesday.

It was a Jericho-Walls-crumbling moment. This time it was not Jewish priests and Israelites circling the city and blowing their horns but Catholics worldwide storming Heaven. Or, a parallel more recent, the cracking of the Berlin Wall by East Germans, but this time by passionate Catholic millennials who will not let the Mass of the Ages become a fossil of past ages. Its significance cannot be overemphasized. This Extraordinary Mass was celebrated at the request of the Speaker of the House, Mike Johnson, in an archdiocese that has witnessed the near abrogation of all Traditional Masses. The irony could not have been sweeter.

Mr. Johnson intended the Mass to mark the anniversary of the FBI's investigation of Traditional Masses as potential nests of domestic terrorism. The House properly investigated this enormity with the interrogation of its Director, Mr. Wray, at an open Congressional hearing. For all his wriggling, he was unable to escape blame for the shocking activity of his agents.

The Mass was originally intended for the Speaker's small dining room—until he discovered that the request for attendance exceeded its capacity. It was then moved to a larger meeting room down the hall from the Speaker's office. A team of young Catholic men and women from various House and Senate offices eagerly offered their assistance in organizing the event.

But mere organization is an understatement. They went to work with the excitement and passion of men on a mission. Not so much on account of the anniversary, but because of the Extraordinary Form Mass being celebrated. The organizers enlisted the help of a priest known only to them, to protect him from any punitive action. The whole affair was executed with military precision and attention to detail.

It captured the attention of the world. No sooner was the makeshift chapel disassembled that the Catholic press roared into action. First, the usual traditional online news organizations, then others. Most intriguing was reportage of *America* magazine, the Jesuit magazine of record for the *avant-garde* Catholic Left. Their headline screamed "Illicit Latin Mass held in the U.S. Capitol." This was rich.

Interesting that the New and Improved Society of Jesus would employ the dated word illicit. After all, their star theologians long banned that term from the theological language of the *bien pensant*. This is the same Society which proscribed anachronisms such as moral absolutes ages ago (except, of course, the new moral absolutes of the Woke Left).

This is the Society whose sprawling university/college apparatus has become the humming factory of anti-Catholic Catholicism. Long ago, this ever-so-modern Society raised the flag of *laissez-faire* Catholicism. Yet here they were with the fury of Puritans hanging the scarlet letter round the neck of Hester Prynne. What might be next for the terribly *au courant* Society? A new iteration of the Salem Witch Trials?

But why would there be alarm in some chanceries? Because this was not the trajectory planned by the foes of the Traditional Mass. After sixty years of the conventional *Novus Ordo* wisdom, its votaries were certain that the Traditional Mass would, by this time, long be forgotten. They were quite certain their efforts over the past half-century or so would have secured its place on the ash heap of history. It would go the way of meatless Fridays, Sacred Heart devotions, novenas, and mortal sin.

They did not plan on a Youth Revolution catapulting the Traditional Mass into full view again.

Two historical accidents contributed to this revolution: a pandemic virus and *Traditionis Custodes*. When Covid struck and churches closed, Catholics eager for Mass turned to the Internet. As search engines purred, thousands, tens of thousands, stumbled upon this strange Traditional Latin Mass hitherto unknown to them. They found its transcendence, beauty, and palpable mystery infectious.

They began their own investigation into its origins. Their inquiry opened new horizons, suggested a host of questions, and created an irresistible hunger. Not lost on them was Pope Benedict's *Summorum Pontificum*, when he shook the very foundations of conventional liturgical praxis of over a half-century:

> What earlier generations held as sacred, remains sacred and great for us too, and it cannot be all of a sudden entirely forbidden or even considered harmful. It behooves all of us to preserve the riches which have developed in the church's faith and prayer, and to give them their proper place.

As the pandemic subsided and churches unlocked their doors, the available Traditional Masses swelled. At last, a religion for grown-ups.

Similarly, the promulgation of *Traditionis Custodes*. Many a curious Catholic wondered what this proscribed rite of Mass could possibly be. What kind of malice did it carry to deserve such a universal condemnation? Its evil must be unprecedented. This banned Mass must embody a fearful danger to souls to earn immediate suppression, like some cancer spreading on the Mystical Body of Christ.

What other conclusion could be drawn? After all, the papacy rolling out its most brutal sanctions against it boasted its non-judgmentalism, going to the peripheries, toleration of practices never before countenanced by the Church for the sake of accompaniment, and affection for creating messes. It was developing new paradigms (like contextual theology) that would make condemnations a thing of an embarrassing medieval past. Mustn't a thousand flowers bloom? For such a papacy to act so out of character had to mean that they were confronting a malignancy beyond words. One could almost hear the wailing of Voltaire, *"écrasez l'infâme!"* (Crush the infamous thing!)

Otherwise, why such a draconian censure? What was this tantalizing and unparalleled new wickedness?

Curiosity was piqued. To the internet for answers. As the eyes of millennials fell upon the illicit practice, they were stumped. This outlawed Mass seemed to speak to them of God, His mysteries, and His love. It bespoke a solemnity that fed their starved hearts. It presented an ordered economy of truths whose power they could not resist. *This* is wickedness? *This* is deserving of the stamp of illicity?

Young minds vowed to dig more deeply. They saw themselves as twenty-first century Columbuses searching for a new world. Even within the claustrophobic boundaries of *Traditionis Custodes* they still discovered the treasure and found themselves transformed. This was not wickedness. This was Heaven.

Officialdom grimaced. Theologians penned diatribes. Liturgists growled.

Rome, we have a problem.

You could almost hear the frightened chancery apparatchiks and approved knowledge class: something is afoot that should never have been. Decades of settled reformed liturgy appeared at risk. Liturgical *terra firma* was shaking beneath their feet. More than a half-century of liturgical scholarship was slipping from their hands.

No worry. After all, the numbers crowding these Masses were minuscule compared to the general Catholic population. Yet this furnished scant consolation. For in these Masses' seemingly insignificant numbers was a passion, a devotion and commitment that was inexplicable. More vexing was their deference to Church authority, their modesty, their irenic spirit, and their, shall we say it, desire to simply be good Catholics.

Rome, we have a problem.

To all this, Graham Greene in *Brighton Rock*; in perfect tones of Catholic orthodoxy, he wrote, "I cannot understand, nor can you, the appalling strangeness of God's mercy."

6
The Most Holy Eucharist

RETURNING TO OUR KNEES

There was one part of the house I had not yet visited, and I went there now. The chapel showed no ill-effects of its long neglect; the art nouveau paint was as fresh and bright as ever; the art nouveau lamp burned once more before the altar. I said a prayer, an ancient, newly learned form of words, and left, turning towards the camp...
 Something quite remote from anything the builder had intended has come out of their work, and out of the fierce little human tragedy in which I played; something none of us thought about at the time: a small red flame – a beaten copper lamp of deplorable design, relit before the beaten copper doors of a tabernacle; the flame which the old knights saw from their tombs, which they saw put out; that flame burning again for other soldiers, far from home, farther, in heart, than Acre or Jerusalem. It could not have been lit except for the builders and tragedians, and there I found it this morning, burning new among the old stones.
 I quickened my pace and reached the hut which served us for our ante-room.
 "You're looking unusually cheerful today," said the second-in-command.

So ends *Brideshead Revisited*. An ending sweetly triumphant. Not only does the *bon vivant* Ryder come to the Faith, but the thing that transfixes him in that manorial house he knew so well was the "burning red flame of the sanctuary lamp." Like a magnet, it drew him. It announced, like a hundred silver trumpets, that the King sat upon His throne again. With the understatement of a true genius writer, Waugh simply concludes: "You're looking unusually cheerful today." Little did the second-in-command know that that singular joy climbed deep from within Ryder's soul. It was the joy of a man meeting his God. It is the joy which fills all of us when we spot the flickering flame in the red sanctuary lamp. No joy on earth matches this joy.
 Corpus Christi is the grand feast that reminds of that great Mystery – man meeting God. This happens only in the Most Holy Eucharist. Yes, man meets God in the inspired words of

the Bible; the infallible teachings of Mother Church; the intimate conversations with God in prayer; and even in the vast sweep of God's marvelous creation. But in all those meetings, we meet God spiritually. In the Most Holy Eucharist, we meet Him physically.

This astonishing mystery causes us to fall to our knees, or should, unless we have suffered a fatal breach of faith. It has prompted the Church to build her breathtaking churches, compelling even unbelievers to stare in wonderment. It has stirred the Holy Spirit to guide the Church in constructing the sublime drama of the Holy Sacrifice of the Mass; as a spiritual monument, ineffable; as a cultural jewel, a *pièce de résistance*. All this for one purpose: homage to the Immolated Lamb who lies upon our altars, and who houses Himself in golden tabernacles.

Make no mistake, this newness is not novelty. Novelty is arsenic to the Mystical Body of Christ. The newness is the standard of glory which now applies for a Reality hitherto not seen by angels or men: Christ with us in the Most Blessed Eucharist.

The blueprints are found in the book of the *Apocalypse*. Sample some of them:

- "Merchandise of gold and silver, and precious stones; and of pearls, and fine linen, and purple, and silk, and scarlet, and all thyine wood, and all manner of vessels of ivory, and all manner of vessels of precious stone, and of brass, and of iron, and of marble." (Rev 18:12)
- "And saying, Alas! Alas! that great city, that was clothed in fine linen and purple, and scarlet, and decked with gold and precious stones and pearls." (Rev 18:16)
- "And the twelve gates were twelve pearls; every several gate was of one pearl, and the street of the city was pure gold, as it were transparent glass." (Rev 21:21)

These verses should leave no doubt at how every Catholic Church, the palace of the King, should appear. Having grasped them, Catholics will understand the thundering verse in Genesis: "And trembling he said: How terrible is this place! this is no other but the house of God, and the gate of heaven" (Gen 28:17).

He promised that He would not leave us orphans. The sacred Host is everlasting testimony to that. With a display of divine condescension that baffles the mind, He who crafted the universe now resides in a tiny room dwarfed by the universe. This disguise of His Kingly majesty is done out of love, lest His ravishing glory make us tremble as It did Moses on Sinai, or the Apostles on Tabor. Our Savior permits nothing to stand in the way of sinful man's approach to the Son of God. Yet, when we plumb the depths of the Mystery of the Tabernacle, we understand Chesterton who confessed to being frightened by that tremendous Reality.

In attempting to shed light upon the doctrine of the Holy Eucharist, the esteemed Thomist Fr. Dominic Hughes unveils the dogma under the rubric of the Gift of Understanding, given us by the Holy Spirit in Baptism and Confirmation:

> Understanding is likewise aware that Christ is not present (in the Holy Eucharist) as in the Upper Room, but substantially and without any distinguishable bodily position. His arms are not outstretched, but His mercy is unrestrained. He is not a captive in the Tabernacle, but rather He captivates the hearts of all who leave the imprisonment of their own selfishness long enough to share His happiness. In the Sacrifice of the Mass, Christ is not some prelate of past ceremonies but the principal priest Who offers the holocaust of Himself to His Heavenly Father. Nor is He passive in the act of Holy Communion; He absorbs the soul to Himself in a union of love which binds the soul to all who share in Him.

When J. R. R. Tolkien was writing to his son Michael during the dark days of the Nazi bombing of London, he told him to bind his heart to the Most Holy Eucharist:

> Out of the darkness of my life, so much frustrated, I put before you the one great thing to love on earth: The Blessed Sacrament... There you will find romance, glory, honor, fidelity, and the true way of all your loves on earth...

Do you find romance when you pray before the Tabernacle? Impulses of greater fidelity? Do all your loves find their way, their perfection, their *raison d'être* when you gaze upon the Holy Eucharist? As you adore Our Savior truly present in the Tabernacle, think of this. Of all God's actions in the economy of salvation, the mystery of the Holy Eucharist is most perfect. In the Creation, God gives us things out of nothing; in the Incarnation, He gives the sight of His Sacred Humanity; on Calvary, He gives us the offering of His life; in the Resurrection, He gives us the manifestation of His power; in the Ascension, He gives us the delight of His glorification. But in the Holy Eucharist, He gives us Himself.

Even hearts stiffened by sin soften before the Eucharistic Mystery. Graham Greene's whiskey priest in *The Power and the Glory* is distributing Holy Communion in a secret hovel to a group of Mexican peasants. As he does, Greene writes hauntingly that the reprobate priest realized that "He was placing God on the tongues of men." Reflecting upon the Holy Eucharist, St. John Henry Newman writes:

> Thou dwellest on our altars, Thou the Most Holy, the Most High, in light inaccessible, and angels fall down before Thee there; and out of the visible substances and forms, Thou choosest what is choicest to represent and to hold Thee. The finest wheat flour, and the purest wine, are taken as Thy outward signs, the most sacred and majestic words minister to the sacrificial rite; altar and sanctuary are adorned decently or splendidly, as our means allow; and Thy priests perform their Office in befitting vestments, lifting up chaste hands and holy hands.

Artists have composed some of the most transporting music to express our homage and devotion to the Most Holy Eucharist. Though they all touch the hem of the Mystery, perhaps the words of the *Divine Liturgy of St. James* capture most fully man's spellbound awe:

> Let all mortal flesh keep silence
> And with fear and trembling stand;
> Ponder nothing earthly minded
> For with blessings in his hand,
> Christ our God to earth descendeth
> Our full homage to demand
> At His feet the six-winged seraph;
> Cherubim with sleepless eye,
> Veil their faces to the Presence,
> As with ceaseless voice they cry,
> Alleluia, alleluia, alleluia, Lord Most High!

After receiving Holy Communion, St. John Chrysostom writes, "We are like lions breathing forth fire, thus do depart from this altar, being made terrible to the devil."

Where are the Catholics that leave the altar rail like lions breathing forth fire? Where are the altar rails? Where are the churches reminding us of the Paradise that every church is because the King of Kings reigns there among us? Why aren't Catholics in rapt wonder as are the Cherubim and Seraphim?

Do you mourn the disintegration of Western civilization? Do you weep at the tsunami of nihilistic rage besetting our beloved America? Do you now know fully the pain of the memorable words of Yeats, when he moaned in "The Second Coming": "The best lack all conviction, while the worst are full of passionate intensity"? Do you retch at wave after wave of every once-reliable institution in America groveling before the Barbarians in our midst?

Then know that on this Corpus Christi 2024 only a return to a robust and visible adoration of this august Sacrament will bring these agonies to an end.

Yes, our enemies are not only outside the Church. But we must brave them all.

Think what hangs in the balance.

A RADICAL PROPOSAL FOR EUCHARISTIC REVIVAL

Ominous. It is the only word which can adequately describe the 2020 Pew Research Study. It polled Catholics on their belief in the Real Presence of Christ in the Holy Eucharist. Almost 70 percent polled said no. Chilling, but not surprising. Even a casual glance at parishioners receiving Holy Communion in most Catholic parishes reveals a nonchalance that is telling.

One need not be a trained phenomenologist to appreciate the importance of symbolic acts in man's self-disclosure. Insouciance in the presence of the Holy Eucharist is a damning sign—not only of the total absence of rudimentary piety, but of a withered belief in the doctrine itself. One flows from the other as certainly as day follows night. If a Catholic shows as much attention to the Holy Eucharist as he does to collecting his order at Starbucks, something is awry.

The American bishops seemed to have noticed this alarming anomaly in the past year. Odd that they should have detected this doctrinal collapse in 2023, since it has been glaringly evident for over a half-century. It is rather like a man being bitten by a shark and only screaming an hour later.

Clearly, this crumbling of the central dogma of the Catholic Church had its conspicuous antecedents—antecedents supported by carefully planned strategies; all of them gestating among the theological grandees for decades. So many, now forgotten, laid deep the foundations for the denuded Catholic Faith now so ubiquitous. To name only a few:

- Edward Schillebeeckx, O.P., and his attenuation of grace through the sacraments
- Karl Rahner, and his supernatural existential; to say nothing of his iconoclastic article *How to Receive a Sacrament and Mean It*
- The whole of the *Concilium oeuvre*
- The sacramental theology of the Theological Society of America, 1965–present

While this list is hardly exhaustive, (actually, quite skeletal) it does suggest the formidable momentum that set down the pillars upon which the present crisis rests.

All of this cerebral theological ground-laying could only be called the handle of the spear. The tip of the spear was two pronged: liturgy and catechesis. Without these, the revolution to undermine the Holy Eucharist would have been stillborn. These two vessels are the ones which bring the Faith to the ordinary Faithful. Liturgy and catechesis instill not only doctrine, but piety and the entire Catholic identity and élan.

The esoteric ruminations of faux Catholic scholars would have collected dust on university/seminary shelves unless they were translated into praxis by the instruments of liturgy and catechesis. This is exactly what was done with impressive and sweeping results. In the case of catechesis, the old *Baltimore Catechism* anchored the Faith firmly in the minds of the young; its successor leaves young Catholics adrift in a sea of passé Sixties flotsam. And all of this has taken place over the past sixty years under the unwatchful eyes of pastors and bishops. Or, shall we say, watchful eye?

So thorough was this transformation of Eucharistic theology that well-meaning Catholics now confidently call the Mass a meal and the Holy Eucharist bread of fellowship. Under this logic, it is quite hostile, to say nothing of actionable, to refuse any man or woman access to the Holy Eucharist. Not a few bishops growl at a priest even publicly repeating the traditional requirements for reception of Holy Communion. So very unwelcoming, you see. This alarming doctrinal breakdown entrenched itself so deeply that it even dictated new architectural forms for churches, confirming the Marshall McLuhan principle: The medium is the message.

This helpful backdrop brings us back to the bishops. The Pew survey was a bit of cold water splashed in their faces, or, some faces. Something must be done. Alas, launch a three-year Eucharistic Revival culminating in a 2024 Eucharistic Congress. Every Catholic prays that it succeeds.

But, toward that end, some proposals should be made. At first glance, they may appear radical. Indeed, they are; but only because they stand so starkly against the blighted landscape of current Eucharistic practice. Some of these proposals may even seem so antediluvian as to be laughable. But this further proves the point, that Eucharistic doctrine has become so debased that such things seem almost taboo, like four-letter words.

First proposal: Tabernacles returned to the center of every church. It is interesting how liturgists commandeered this movement of tabernacle from the center of every church to the side, if not out of the church proper itself. They appealed to Vatican II, the preferred tool in foisting upon the Church novelties which reconfigured the Faith. In point of fact, the relevant 1983 canon (derived from *Sacrosanctum Concilium*) contradicted this: "The Tabernacle in which the Eucharist is regularly reserved should be placed in a part of the Church that is prominent, conspicuous, beautifully decorated and suitable for prayer" (can. 938:2).

Only those of an ill-disposed agenda would interpret this directive as anything more than a maintenance of the status quo of churches before the Council. Period. Any sidelining of the tabernacle transmits the unquestionable message of sidelining Christ Himself. No amount of theological/liturgical dissimulations can conceal this. Liturgists may not abide by the inescapable laws of the natural symbol, but ordinary folks do.

Second proposal: Abolish communion in the hand. This smuggled, early-Sixties practice was an undisguised rupture with a millennial tradition which deeply implanted a reflexive understanding of the Holy Eucharist. With effortless ease, the traditional practice conveyed to both unlettered and gifted alike the ineffable sacredness of the Sacrament of the Altar. No words necessary; no lengthy explanations required. Thus the immediacy of the symbolic act: informing, uplifting, and impassioning.

The Church alone plumbs the power of the symbol with her repertoire of ritual acts, all of it accomplished without theatricality or kitsch, yet embodying every element of authentic drama. What emerges is a unique wedding of man's highest capacity for poetry threaded with the divine strokes of the Third Person.

The early Sixties, that wretched time, rightly deserving W. H. Auden's epithet of the 1930s, "that low and dishonest decade," ushered in the demise of the reverential and critical Communion on the tongue that can be traced to a restive European theological elite bent on retooling the Faith of the Church. They made fatuous appeals to the sacredness of the whole body and the innovation as an ancient practice. Those arguments were mendacious at their first showing, but, by this time, have so outlived their shelf life

A Radical Proposal for Eucharistic Revival   257

that their mere mention should cause embarrassment.

Its deadly spread so alarmed Pope Paul VI that he promulgated *Memoriale Domini* in 1969. Here he confronted the damaging practice illicitly introduced, and he ruled it should cease:

> With a deepening understanding of the truth of the eucharistic mystery, of its power and of the presence of Christ in it, there came a greater feeling of reverence towards this sacrament and a deeper humility was felt to be demanded when receiving it. Thus the custom was established of the minister placing a particle of consecrated bread on the tongue of the communicant. This method of distributing holy communion must be retained, taking the present situation of the Church in the entire world into account, not merely because it has many centuries of tradition behind it, but especially because it expresses the faithful's reverence for the Eucharist.

Third proposal: Eliminate Extraordinary Ministers of the Holy Eucharist. Again, to the common Catholic mind of today, a suggestion such as this sounds like the abolition of the Ten Commandments, only demonstrating how pervasive the distorted understanding of the Holy Eucharist is. The fact that few Catholics refer to Extraordinary Ministers is further proof of the tight grip of doctrinal misunderstanding. In the 1997 document promulgated by the Sacred Congregation for Liturgy and the Discipline of the Sacraments (along with seven other dicasteries) it is made clear the extraordinary nature of allowing laymen to distribute Holy Communion, keenly aware of the easy slippage into doctrinal chaos:

> The Holy Father notes that "In some local situations, generous, intelligent solutions have been sought (to the shortage of priests). The legislation of the Code of Canon law has itself provided new possibilities, which however, must be correctly applied, so as not to fall into ambiguity of considering as ordinary and normal, solutions that were meant for extraordinary situations in which priests were lacking or in short supply.

These dicasteries were clearly adhering to St. Thomas Aquinas in *ST* III, q.82, a.3, "Whether the Dispensing of this Sacrament Belongs to the Priest Alone":

> The dispensing of Christ's body belongs to the priest alone, for three reasons. First, because he consecrates as in the

person of Christ; but as Christ consecrated his body at the supper, he also gave it to others to be partaken of by them. Accordingly, as the consecration of Christ's body belongs to the priest, so likewise does the dispensing belong to him. Secondly, because the priest is the appointed intermediary between God and the people; Hence as it belongs to him to offer the people's gifts to God, so it belongs to him to deliver consecrated gifts to the people. Thirdly, because out of reverence towards this sacrament, nothing touches it, but what is consecrated; hence the corporal and the chalice are consecrated, and likewise the priest's hands, for touching this sacrament. Hence it is not lawful for anyone else to touch it except from necessity, for instance, if it were to fall upon the ground, or else in some other case of urgency.

Fourth proposal: Reception of Holy Communion should always be kneeling. The last few years have seen a war waged on the few Catholics who follow the crystalline interior logic of orthodox Catholic doctrine, kneeling to receive Holy Communion. In their fury to abolish kneeling, the Innovators invoke the hollow excuse of uniformity and local custom. Even the most naïve Catholic sees this for the naked dissembling which it is. One stands to grab a free lunch, not to receive the Bread of Angels (pardon me, that kind of sacral language makes the Old Guard's skin crawl). It is puzzlement that the same shepherds that perpetrated this not so veiled diminution of Eucharistic doctrine desire now to promote Eucharistic doctrine.

Attempting any longer to disguise the causes of the degradation of Eucharistic belief is monumentally disingenuous, on par with the Wizard of Oz ordering Dorothy, "Pay no attention to that man behind the curtain!"

Our good bishops have been unafraid in harboring radical gestures in the past, even when they have jolted the faithful. Why not one more? Or four more?

Excellencies, shake the status quo. Be unafraid to shock. Step upon the third rail.

Be pioneers. Embark on a startling Eucharistic Revival.

A traditional one. The only thing you have to lose is a crisis.

A MODEST PROPOSAL TO END THE VOCATIONS CRISIS

Allow me to touch a liturgical third rail: Communion in the hand.

Before I do, look at the July 4th edition of *La Croix International*. It reports that of the 96 dioceses in the country of France, 58 produced not a single ordination to the Priesthood. Truth be told, this crisis is not restricted to France. It has enveloped all of Europe, some countries suffering even more severe shortages than France.

Europe is not alone. North American ordinations are also in free-fall. One East Coast seminary, which hosts three major metropolitan dioceses, has a seminarian population hovering around 50 – that is, 50 seminarians for more than 7.8 million Catholics. Before 1960, when the seminary served only one Archdiocese, it housed three hundred seminarians.

This is a collapse of historic proportions. A cause for concern, don't you think? Might it have something to do with the precipitous decline of reverence for the Holy Eucharist? To some progressive Catholics, this suggestion may seem somewhat quaint. Then again, to that same set of Catholics (and priests of the new paradigm), belief in the Real Presence itself is quaint. Tolerate slippage in the high reverence owed to the Most Blessed Sacrament (how many Catholics even use that expression any longer?), and the Church suffers a decline in the priests whose vocation it is to be its guardian.

Of course, Communion in the hand is an approved practice, but one which is only juridically tolerated. No matter how antediluvian this may sound, it is the reality. Moreover, no intelligent Catholic would maintain that Communion in the hand alone caused a decline either in devotion to the Blessed Sacrament or in vocations to the priesthood. On the other hand, no intelligent Catholic would deny that Communion in the hand holds a principal place in the constellation of factors that have led to these declines. Any other conclusion is counterintuitive.

Such analysis may seem slightly eccentric to a large portion of Catholics raised in a world constructed by *au courant* liturgists. But let us remember it was a world built from scraps extorted from the Holy See. Ancient history, but true history nonetheless. When the liturgical record of our age is accurately documented, Catholics will marvel at how the courtly procedures of Rome were broadsided time after time by fast-moving liturgists. Like the agile English boats wreaking havoc on the hulking Spanish Armada, so the '60s liturgists ran circles around the stately Roman curia, winning as booty a millennium of rich and sublimely awe-inspiring sacred liturgy.

The issue with Communion in the hand is not a bit of quirky crankiness. The practice arose from the toxic soil of virulent dissent. For some years, youngsters have been instructed that it is another glorious tradition of the ancient Church. This is a plain deception. If not for highly organized pressure groups in the '60s (which simply initiated the practice in a dramatic act of defiance), its regular practice would still be viewed today as shockingly irregular. By the time the dust settled, fatal concessions had been made. In due course, like termites chewing away at a foundation, the once mighty Catholic edifice of Eucharistic piety began to crack. This was quite predictable since Catholics believe as they act (*lex orandi, lex credendi*). When actions are altered, beliefs will inevitably change too—no matter how unintentionally. Trying to defend the novel Eucharistic practice by appealing to its present long fixity in the Catholic mind is no defense. Theological argument is not won by invoking *stare decisis*.

Rome understood this perfectly. In a pointed effort to stamp out false liturgical practices and defend traditional Eucharistic piety, Paul VI promulgated *Memoriale Domini* in 1969. This document eloquently upheld the ancient practice of Communion on the tongue while reluctantly tolerating the new practice. Pope John Paul II, and Pope Benedict XVI, refused Communion in the hand at all Pontifical Masses. Mere papal preference? Not quite. It is a forceful acknowledgement of the ancient principle: the slightest diminution in any of the reverences to the Blessed Sacrament risks significant diminution of belief.

No wonder the 2000 *Institutio Generalis Missalis Romani* contains the pregnant clause (no. 161): "If communion is given only under the form of bread, the priest raises the Eucharistic bread slightly

A Modest Proposal to End the Vocations Crisis

and shows it to each one, saying: 'The Body of Christ'... and [the faithful] receive the Sacrament as they choose, either on the tongue, or in the hand, *where this is allowed*" (emphasis added). In the typically spare manner of Roman documents, a notable truth is conveyed. Communion on the tongue remains normative, with Communion in the hand only tolerated, where permitted by law. This detail might be lost in the din of hammering together a liturgical New World, but it should not be lost on those with a deep love for the Body of Christ. But is linking this change in practice to a decline in vocations a slight stretch? Not really.

Holy Church understands that an intimate ontological bond exists between the Holy Eucharist and the Holy Priesthood: an eclipse in appreciation for the one inevitably leads to a decline in interest in the other. A priest's whole *raison d'être* is the Holy Eucharist. He protects it, as the Bridegroom protects the Bride. All the priest's vigor streams forth from that august sacrament, and it is that sacrament which fashions his priestly personality. His priestly manhood is perfected in the adoration, care, and affection for that sacrament. Apart from it, the heart of the priest withers and his priestly virility falters. Softness replaces heroism and an epicene compromise substitutes for fiery conviction. Soon the priest no longer seeks the sharp strokes of saintly action but is more at home in the safer and softer secular life. Conceal the majesty of the Holy Eucharist and you reduce the once noble class of priests into a tribe of spiritual pygmies. And soon even that inglorious residue disappears. Could the lesson be more clear? No healthy young man aspires to be small. Greatness alone summons him.

France has much company in its crisis of priests. Almost every diocese in North America faces frightening declines in vocations. To their credit they have attempted nearly every possible solution: new vocation offices, new vocation teams, high school rap sessions, internet advertising, highway billboards, Madison Avenue firms, bishops' subcommittees, and even ads in *Playboy*. Nothing seems to have worked. But have they tried everything?

Maybe the solution has been as close as the church around the corner: the Mass and the Holy Eucharist. Look no further than these. However, when you look at the Mass and the Holy Eucharist, be sure you look at them as the Church understands them, not as the liturgists do. Too many well-intentioned priests and bishops have naively embraced the mindset of the Liturgical

Establishment and not that of the Roman Church. This results in *sentire cum periti* (thinking with the experts) rather than *sentire cum ecclesiae* (thinking with the Church). Catholics who think with the Church see the liturgy as an end in itself; the Liturgical Nomenclatura sees liturgy as a means to something else. Holy Church instructs us that the liturgy is the act of Christ redeeming mankind in the re-presentation of his atoning sacrifice of Calvary. Man comes to adore and to love so that he can be filled and sanctified. Man kneels at Mass for no other purpose. Endless needs and petitions crowd his mind as he kneels before the Divinity, but all of those are entirely secondary to that act of adoration, that act of loving self-oblation.

For this reason man delights in surrounding the sacrificial act of the Crucified Savior with all manner of riches, splendor, and grandeur. Not any of it for any other reason than to glorify Christ, just as our love at the moment of Transubstantiation is for no one but him. This is the transcendence of love—his love and ours. It is this Love that makes all other loves possible. It was foreshadowed in the Magdalene's bath of perfume over the Savior's feet. "To what end?" the Traitor protests, then and now. The Savior defends the Magdalene's excess—an excess for no reason save for love of the Savior. This is love's sublimity. This is the liturgy's pinnacle shrouded by ranks of angels. This is the axis upon which creation turns.

Establishment liturgists operate in a smaller world, almost Lilliputian. To them the liturgy is only a means to another thing: self-realization, community, peace, justice, healing, diversity, dignity, et cetera, et cetera. To the liturgist of a Brave New Liturgical World the liturgy is people-work, so it is their solemn law that a plethora of people be found everywhere in its performance. To paraphrase Hamlet: "Man's the thing." Ironically, in this very, very small world of the liturgist there is no room for God, and even less room for men—real men, that is.

Every Catholic should be deeply moved by France's plight. It is our plight, too. Perhaps it is time to experiment with a different remedy. Explore a new paradigm. Maybe a supernatural problem demands a supernatural solution.

It might seem like strange new thinking. But the old thinking doesn't seem to have worked. C'mon, be daring. Try something new. The only thing you can lose is a crisis.

FABLE-TIME IN CHICAGO

For the time will come when they will not endure sound doctrine... But shall heap to themselves teachers, having itching ears. And they shall turn away their ears from the truth, and shall be turned unto fables.
2 Timothy 4:3-4

They say that all clouds have silver linings. Alas, one should suppose it even applies to the United States Catholic Conference of Bishops (hereafter, USCCB). Observe the silver lining as you look at the preparations for the USCCB's Eucharistic Revival announced several months ago (eucharisticrevival.org). Wading through the usual happy-talk typical of most of the work of the USCCB, a Catholic will happily arrive at a bit of seriousness (*mirable dictu!*). Bishop Cozzens, chair of the 2024 National Eucharistic Congress (sanctioned by the USCCB) announced four walking pilgrimages beginning in May 2024, commencing in San Francisco. They continue at the tomb of Blessed Michael McGivney in New Haven, Connecticut, then at the U. S. Mexico border near Brownsville, Texas, and onwards to the headwaters of the Mississippi, in Northwestern Minnesota. They will conclude, shortly before the Congress, which begins in Indianapolis July of 2024.

Bishop Cozzens wrote that the pilgrimage aims "To invite everyone; young people and whoever wants to pilgrimage with Jesus in the Blessed Sacrament across the country from four sides of the country, praying and seeking their own deeper walk with Jesus, as we process the Blessed Sacrament towards Indianapolis." He elaborated upon the plan: "teams will partner with local dioceses to undertake major processions with the canopy and cross and servers and people singing hymns and praying and things like that [sic]."

Quite unprecedented, and deserves applause. Troubling, however, is the pesky little detail that 73% of Roman Catholics do not believe in the Real Presence. So, while some of the 27% will thrill to this important procession, what of the rest of the Catholic population who remains agnostic regarding this doctrine, or in outright denial?

Spokesman for this problem seems to be Cardinal Cupich, Chicago's Prince.

He is a bit chilly to the whole idea of Eucharistic processions in general, and the Church's traditional doctrine in particular. The Chicago Archdiocese has told organizers of the Eucharistic pilgrimage that, while pilgrims may travel through the archdiocese during their processional walk to Indianapolis, they are expected to reserve the Eucharist in a ciborium, rather than process with the Eucharist exposed in a monstrance, as the pilgrimage will do in other areas of the country.

This is a startling departure from a traditional manifestation of devotion to the Holy Eucharist for centuries. And therefore quite concerning. His reservations seem to rest on the *de rigeur* reinventions so dear to the theological knowledge-class of the iconoclastic Seventies. With a deft legerdemain they left Eucharistic doctrine in shambles, smuggling into the Church *nova* (to both the doctrine of the Church and its sacred traditions) as communion-in-the-hand, extraordinary ministers, standing for Communion, tabernacle-less churches and committee designed liturgies appearing more like folk jamborees than the immemorial Sacrifice of Calvary.

The good Cardinal has carefully finessed his position in a short book *Take, Bless, Break: A Strategy for Eucharistic Revival*. He writes: "Although there are many positive elements in eucharistic adoration it can engender narrowness, and even distorted perceptions of the sacrament itself."

This is nothing less than veiled embarrassment of the Church's teaching. His sentences could have been torn from the pages of the revisionist Eucharistic theology that has brought us to the present crisis we are suffering. Through such refined attenuations dissenting theologians over the past decades have crafted a slippery slide away from the exalted Eucharistic theology taught by the Church for millennia. No such protean language has ever been used by the official Magisterium of the Church. Never in two thousand years has she equated a robust and explicit adoration of the Eucharist (or in John Paul II's charming phrase, Eucharistic wonder.) as narrowness. Yet this attitude has become entrenched as "official" church teaching taught in not a few seminaries and houses of formation.

The official teaching of the Church tells quite a different story. Pope Paul VI repeated the ironclad tradition of the Church in

Fable-Time in Chicago

his *Mysterium Fidei*, a document quoted by the *Catechism of the Catholic Church*:

> The Catholic Church has always offered and still offers to the sacrament of the Eucharist the cult of adoration, not only during mass, but also outside of it, reserving the consecrated hosts with the utmost care, exposing them to the solemn veneration of the faithful, and carrying them in procession.

No hedging here, as Cardinal Cupich's statement seems to convey.

Chicago's Cardinal's tepid approach (to put it kindly) to the Holy Eucharist is exhibited by his embarrassment at processing with the Sacred Host enthroned in the Monstrance. This prohibition is a far cry from the sanguine words of Pope John Paul II in his *Ecclesia de Eucharistia*:

> Let us take our place, dear brothers and sisters, at the school of the saints, who are the great interpreters of true Eucharistic piety. In them the theology of the Eucharist takes on all the splendor of a lived reality; It becomes "contagious" and, in a manner of speaking, "it warms our hearts." Above all, let us listen to Mary most Holy, in whom the mystery of the Eucharist appears, more than in any one else, as a mystery of light. Gazing upon Mary, we come to know the transforming power present in the Eucharist. In her we see the world renewed in love. Contemplating her, assumed body and soul into heaven, we see opening before us those "new heavens" and that "new earth" which will appear at the second coming of Christ. Here below, the Eucharist represents their pledge, and in a certain way, their anticipation: *Veni, Domine Iesu* (Rev 22:20).

One is hard put to find Cupich's grave worries about narrowness in the Pope's words. The Cardinal deploys one of the most effective strategies of the Dissenters: invent a problem, then propose a solution. From beginning to end, a parody of Catholic orthodoxy.

But wait. Cupich expresses further concerns: "Eucharistic Adoration can 'privatize' one's relationship to the sacrament and to the Lord Himself, overlooking the communitarian dimension of Eucharistic worship." This statement either betrays woeful lack of understanding of the Church's teaching regarding the Most Holy Eucharist or a carefully designed deconstruction of that teaching. Cupich's strategic muddled thinking is blatantly contradicted by

Pope Benedict XVI in his 2007 Post-Synodal Apostolic Exhortation *Sacramentum Caritatis:*

> With the Senate assembly, therefore, I heartily recommend to the church's pastors and to the people of God the practice of eucharistic adoration, both individually and in community. Great benefit would ensue from a suitable catechesis explaining the importance of this act of worship, which enables the faithful to experience the liturgical celebration more fully and more fruitfully. Wherever possible, it would be appropriate, especially in densely populated areas, to set aside specific churches or oratories for perpetual adoration. I also recommend that, in their catechetical training, and especially in their preparation for First Holy Communion, children be taught the meaning and the beauty of spending time with Jesus, and help to cultivate a sense of awe before his presence in the Eucharist.

The Pope concludes:

> The personal relationship which the individual believer establishes with Jesus present in the Eucharist constantly points beyond itself to the whole communion of the church and nourishes a fuller sense of membership in the body of Christ. For this reason, besides encouraging individual believers to make time for personal prayer before the sacrament of the altar, I feel obliged to urge parishes and other church groups to set aside times for collective adoration. Naturally, already existing forms of eucharistic piety retain their full value. I am thinking, for example, of processions with the Blessed Sacrament, especially the traditional procession on the solemnity of Corpus Christi, the 40 Hours Devotion, local, national and international eucharistic congresses, and other similar initiatives.

The adoration of the Sacrament *is* social for in the Holy Eucharist is Christ's ineffable love for the Church and the whole human race. When a Catholic adores the Sacrament he grows in *caritas* for Christ and all whom Christ loves. What greater social engagement can exist than this. To accuse Eucharistic Adoration of individualism is wholesale denial of Eucharistic doctrine as it has been embraced by the Church for her entire existence.

Cardinal Cupich leans heavily upon Fr. Louis Camelli, his delegate for formation and mission, as well as theological advisor.

He wrote in the March issue of America magazine, "The heavy emphasis that the revival places on Eucharistic devotions, such as processions, adoration, 40 hours and Eucharistic miracles does not capture the heart of the matter."

Actually, the heart of the matter is the instrumentalization of the Holy Eucharist: no longer is It an end in Itself, but only a means to a more worthy end. This serious error is seen in the enthusiasm for theme Masses. Another attempt at instrumentalizing the Holy Eucharist. The Mass and the Holy Eucharist exist only for the adoration of the Blessed Trinity and the salvation of the human race. Even the honor of the saints or the votive Masses for certain intentions are all subordinated and in service to the exclusive purpose for which the Holy Mass and Sacred Eucharist exist.

Theologians like Fr. Camelli have been involved in this long game of prevarication for sixty years. It has clogged their learned theological journals and been standard fare in the mainstream of Roman Catholicism. It has birthed the current sad state of not only crippled Eucharistic practice, but Sacred Liturgy, church architecture and compromised priestly identity itself.

St. Paul's epistle to Timothy gives dire warning about times to come "when they will not endure sound doctrine, but will heap to themselves teachers having itching ears... and shall be turned unto fables." Well, those times are here. And we are up to our ears in fables. It certainly may seem fable-time in Chicago. But I fear fable-time may have arrived in more places than the Windy City.

WHERE EUCHARISTIC REVIVAL GOES TO DIE

For all its good intentions, the grand project of Eucharistic Revival is barely limping to its finish line. Applause is in order, for at least it noticed a precipitous loss of Faith in the central mystery of Catholicism. But its cure was carefully wrapped in the naïve gauze that created the fatal lapse in the first place. Look at its official website: A swirl of puerile slogans, kindergarten art and breathtaking lack of seriousness.

But such grave breaches of Catholic Faith deserve the thunderbolts the likes of Blessed Pius IX's *Quanta Cura* and the *Syllabus of Errors*, not petite entreaties couched in the porous language that delivered us to these desperate straits.

But that seems to be a bridge too far. The Shepherds seem to be strapped into a straitjacket created by the naivete (or malice) of Important Theologians of the past half century. One of their more ambitious projects was retooling the doctrine of the Holy Eucharist. This was then accompanied by a massive dismantling of the whole architectonic devotional ensemble which promoted piety and protected its doctrinal purity.

More serious was the whole mood created by this *Theological Nomenklatura*. By their unchallenged fiat, error was declared to be an antediluvian *cul de sac*. With priggish insouciance, error was now clothed in the gentler philosophical category of difference, which was to stand proudly along truth without prejudice. (O, you say, whiffs of Derrida and Foucalt. And you would be correct.). Standards were to be considered atavistic, and only reverent listening was to stand in in its place.

Those who govern the Church found themselves paralyzed. Who were they to stifle the blowing of the spirit? Strangely, they had no qualms in dragging out the old inquisitorial machinery to discipline those standing in the way of the spirit blowing.

But if a *carte blanche* now reigned, couldn't it apply to those opposed to the ideology of the spirit blowin' where it will? Clearly not. Listening would only be deigned to those whom the ruling class found worthy of being listening to.

Which brings us to Chicago. And its Prince. With Solomonic certitude, in 2025 he mandated new and inflexible rules regarding the reception of Holy Communion. No kneeling. No acts of adoration.

His reasoning rested upon strange new construals. Strange, because this kind of theological reasoning has never been seen in the Church before. He writes: "Our ritual for receiving Holy Communion has special significance. It reminds us that receiving the Eucharist is not a private action but rather a communal one, as the very word communion implies."

Are you raising eyebrows? You should be. Could His Eminence be misunderstanding that communion is with Our Lord Jesus Christ, and the teachings of His Holy Catholic Church? Yes, communion with other Catholic in the Mystical Body of Christ who think with the Church. (*sentire cum ecclesia*). But that is quite secondary to communion with the Kings of Kings. Of course, this might be attributed to poor sentence construction, or an editor's slip. Let us move on.

Then there is this: "For that reason, the norm established by the Holy See for the universal church and approved by the United states Catholic Conference of Bishops is for the faithful to process together as an expression of their coming forward as the body of Christ and to receive Holy Communion standing." But the Universal norm also clearly states that it is a *universal right* of the faithful to receive Holy Communion kneeling.

Puzzled? You are not alone. Look far and wide, it is impossible to find in the Deposit of the Faith that "processing together...is expression of...coming forward as the Body of Christ." Scrutinize as thoroughly as you like, you will be hard put to find this strange reasoning for the reception of Holy Communion. For two thousand years reception of Holy Communion was the act of homage, humility and adoration of the Incarnate Son of God present in the Holy Eucharist.

Of course, *Redemptionis Sacramentum* of 2004 should settle the matter:

> In distributing Holy Communion it is to be remembered that "sacred ministers may not deny the sacraments to those who seek them in a reasonable manner, are rightly disposed, and are not prohibited by law from receiving them." Hence any baptized Catholic who is not prevented

by law must be admitted to Holy Communion. Therefore, it is not licit to deny Holy Communion to any of Christ's faithful solely on the grounds, for example, that the person wishes to receive the Eucharist kneeling or standing. (no. 91)

Against this dogmatic backdrop, the Cardinal's remarks seem hallucinatory

Nonetheless, He continues confidently: "Nothing should be done to impede any of these processions, particularly the one that takes place during the sacred communion ritual." Notice the hand of the Nomenklatura here: cleverly juxtaposing this novelty with the words sacred Communion ritual. The mixing creates sufficient confusion, leading many Catholics to conflate the sacred with the processions, rather than the reverent reception of Christ in Holy Communion. The typical Catholic's head is now spinning. Solid doctrinal practice is replaced with vertiginous confusion.

The good Cardinal is not finished: "No one should engage in a gesture that calls attention to oneself or disrupts the flow of the procession." For over a thousand years Catholics, saints and sinners, have knelt before their God to receive Holy Communion. Now we are told they did this to merely "draw attention to themselves" and (God forbid) disrupt the "flow of the procession." Isn't this elevating banality to the level of virtue?

Layer upon layer of Eucharistic practice was constructed over the millennia as protection against the slightest attenuation of Catholic doctrine regarding the Eucharist. For over sixty years it has been breached. Look at the result.

Clearly, the evidence has taught nothing. Chicago Catholics are to embrace theological thinking that undermines both sound logic, simple common sense and traditional Catholic piety for over one thousand years. The good Cardinal must be quite well intentioned, but this mandate cannot possibly be of any assistance to Eucharistic Revival. It seems to be its death.

Yet hope springs eternal. A bright group of Catholics designed a scientific survey entitled Real Presence Survey (realpresencecoalition.com). It was the single largest survey of lay Catholics ever completed in the United States. It was sent in an Open Letter to all the Bishops of the United States. Its findings would not surprise the ordinary Catholic. Its credibility is supported by the fact that 79% of survey respondents primarily attend the Novus Ordo Mass,

Where Eucharistic Revival Goes to Die

deflating claims that the survey results were skewed by radical traditionalists. 96% of respondents attend Mass on at least a weekly basis. And 97% of the respondents stated that they believed in the Real Presence of Jesus Christ in the Eucharist.

Some other findings may interest you. The top ten issues identified by respondents to the Real Presence survey were:

- Receiving the Holy Eucharist in the hand all standing
- Scandal created by offering Holy Communion to public sinners who obstinately reject Catholic teaching
- Lack of humility and reverence in the presence of the Eucharist
- Clergy's casual attitude towards the Eucharist
- Failure to instruct the faithful on Transubstantiation
- Failure to regularly remind the faithful they must be in a state of grace to receive the Eucharist
- Removal of the Tabernacle from the center of the sanctuary
- Loss of emphasis of the Mass as a sacrifice
- Failure to remind the faithful that the Eucharist is necessary for their salvation
- Loss of the sense of supernatural transcendence

The Survey concludes with some recommendations:

- Encourage the practice of receiving the Eucharist on the tongue while kneeling
- Catechized the faithful (e.g. Transubstantiation, worthy reception, etc.)
- Encourage greater reverence for the Eucharist (e.g., genuflecting, kneeling, prayer, thanksgiving after Mass, etc.)
- Eliminate extraordinary ministers of Holy Communion
- Withhold the Holy Eucharist from public officials who obstinately reject half the teaching (Canon 915.)
- Increase Eucharistic events (e.g., adoration, processions, benediction, etc.)

These recommendations have been cited by many theologians over the decades. Regretfully, each represent a third rail in the governance of the Church. The fear and trembling at implementing them is palpable. You see, Old Paradigms hang like a ball and chain from the necks of many bishops.

Truth to be told, the sincere, albeit thin, attempts at Eucharist Revival have been embraced, or were already embraced, by a notable amount of parishes.. But they are notable in their scarcity. Unless firmer actions are taken, the noble intentions of Eucharist Revival will be stillborn.

One can talk and talk of proper devotion, but if everything a Catholic does in his parish contradicts what is spoken, the result is nihil.

The collapsing West today needs the Church now as surely the decaying Roman Empire did two thousand years ago.

But the Church is only as mighty as the traditional doctrines she preaches. Especially the Holy Eucharist.

The time is short. The parlor games of the Old Catholic Group Think have been shown for their hollowness. Let us boldly set forth a New Thinking, which for authentic Catholics is the Ancient Teaching.

Who knows? Perhaps the typical Secularized Catholic will find it fascinating.

It's at least worth a try, isn't it?

7
Beauty in the Church

THE PREFERENTIAL OPTION FOR THE POOR SINNER

Any alert Catholic paying attention over the past sixty years well knows the familiar slogan of this article's title. Well, almost. That last word in the title was never an original part of the slogan. Therein lies a story – and a lesson.

In the raucous wake of the ending of the Second Vatican Council (1962-1965) a significant number of the theological *bien pensant* executed a doctrinal *coup d'état*. Under the banner of *aggiornamento*, they masterminded a tectonic shift in the *raison d'être* of the Roman Catholic Church. No longer was the Church's mission saving souls; respectable Catholics now spoke of social justice.

In fact, from the '60s to this very day, a Catholic would be hard put to find mention of saving souls in any sermon or part of the voluminous Catholic mainstream academic literature (used in Catholic colleges, universities, seminaries and various houses of formation) accumulated since Vatican II. So thorough was the revolution that the mere mention of the phrase saving souls today in well-heeled circles is met with arched eyebrows or awkward embarrassment.

Overnight, the Church was made to appear as though the plight of the poor was never her concern. Against her alleged callous indifference rose bands of enlightened priests and nuns who would show her a thing or two. This fifth column would spare no shock in proving their point; in fact, shock became a potent weapon in their arsenal. Breaking with the past was their driving passion – especially the despicable past of the Catholic Church before 1965.

Their cause exhibited the utopian furor of the Jacobins and Maoists. Destruction was necessary to soften the soil for the social justice/equity they would usher upon the face of the earth. In the twinkle of an eye, Catholics noticed the difference: St. Vincent de Paul Societies were replaced by social justice committees; Lenten Mite Boxes (touchingly depicted with the suffering Savior of Gethsemane) would be tossed for rice bowl boxes; St. Nicholas drives at Christmastime gave way to Giving Trees.

Add to this something even more troubling. The precious (and oftentimes artistically priceless) liturgical accoutrements used for Holy Mass and the Sacraments were tagged as signs of the oppression of the poor (as well as the detritus of a malign triumphalism that needed to be erased entirely, like the airbrushing of historical photos incommensurate with Communist Party orthodoxy).

With the fanaticism of Bolsheviks, organized bands ransacked sacristy after sacristy for every sacred vessel and vestment they could find. Everything was either sold or burned, lest their contagion ever infect the New Catholics aborning. Similar frenzies were unleashed upon the beloved interiors of churches across the globe. This was all done so that the poor could be served, and a new Reimagined Church could arise. You could not be accused of melodrama for calling to mind Rousseau, who calmly remarked, "Man must be forced to be free."

Scores of ancient religious orders toppled like dominoes before the force of this antinomian juggernaut. Tell-tale signs of these heady rebel groups can be seen in organizations like the Leadership Conference of Women Religious, still waging war against despised past centuries of traditional religious life. Though these religious are now greatly spent by age, one can still spot the revolutionary spark which created the fires that consumed Old Catholic culture. That spark still flickers in the many religious orders that traded saving souls for creating a just society.

Because of the Movement's feral intensity, today's Catholics are forced to walk amongst the scarred remains of a once glorious Catholic Church. Of course, a faithful remnant remains, but they are relegated to roam a spiritual wasteland resembling Berlin after World War II. Shakespeare expresses the tragedy of this cataclysm,

> ...those boughs which shake against the cold,
> Bare ruined choirs, where late the sweet birds sang.
> (Sonnet 73)

Emergent from this troubled period was the slogan, "Preferential option for the poor." One searches in vain for this new concept in the church's treasury of dogma or piety, or in her long and soaring history. Instead of this novel and tendentious category, what one does find is the Law of Charity: which binds each and every Catholic to care for any need.

Our Lord is clear: "Whatever you do to the least of my brethren, you do to me" (Mt 25:40). From this Divine Commission, the Church fashioned the corporal and spiritual works of mercy. Legions of saints, over thousands of years, committed themselves to the selfless care of the poor, leaving the world stammering before their heroic generosity. In every Catholic Church, the Faithful are confronted by the poor box, begging for their supererogation. It could safely be said that the Catholic Church invented active care for the poor. After all, our salvation depends upon it (cf. Mt 25:32–46).

Attention to those in need is part of the Church's supernatural DNA. No Catholic will find a home in Heaven unless they face Christ the Judge marked with their love for those who cry out in need. But these obligations of charity are always discharged within an exquisite order, principally stamped by humility. Order means that everything and every action has its place situated in a carefully ranked hierarchy. That ranking comes from both a natural and supernatural reckoning. Each element not only has its place, but its very place is indispensable to the beauty of the whole.

Think of an artistic masterpiece in music or painting. So many elements conspire to create the spectacle of beauty. Every element is crucial; but it is crucial precisely in the place it occupies, no matter how small. St. Thomas teaches us that the three essential properties of beauty are: *integritas, consonantia,* and *claritas* (integrity, proportion, and radiance). This is order. To be clear, it pertains not only to art but to our sanctification.

The Church's teaching possesses order because our Lord's did. Take the woman's anointing of our Lord with precious perfume (Mt 26:7–13). As Judas reproves the waste as better used for the poor, he receives the Savior's reprimand: "Why do you trouble this woman? For she hath wrought a good work upon me. For the poor you always have with you." His divine teaching bespeaks a marvelous order: while the plight of the poor demands relief, it does not obscure or preempt other more important obligations. However, when the poor become an *idée fixe*, it mutates into a political category usurping the place of God.

This is the problem with any ideology/heresy: it forgets its place in the natural and supernatural order of things. Rather than liberate the human person, it smothers him. Regarding the poor, the urgent point of St. Paul: "For the Kingdom of God is not meat and drink: but justice and peace, and joy in the Holy Ghost" (Rom 17:14). In the very prayer that falls from the lips of Our Savior, we find this luminous order. First, He teaches us to pray "Thy will be done," and only then, we beg, "Give us this day our daily bread." Ecclesiastes, too, memorably enjoins the sacred order,

> All things have their season,
> and in their time all things pass under heaven.
> A time to be born, and a time to die,
> A time to plant, and a time to pluck
> up that which is planted...
> A time to love, and a time to hate. (Eccles 3:1-3)

Msgr. John Ryan, the indefatigable champion of the downtrodden, presciently lectured in 1920 to the New York School of Social Work,

> There is grave danger that assistance to the neighbor for his own sake alone will be converted into the service of society as a whole, and the ignoring of the intrinsic worth of the individual... Supernatural charity is a much more effective motive than love of the neighbor for his own sake or for the sake of society: for the human being in distress assumes a much greater value when he is thought of a relation to God.

Blessed Antoine Frederick Ozanam (1813-1853), founder of the St. Vincent de Paul society, warned sharply,

> The goal of the Society was not to help the poor, this was only a means. Our object was by the practice of Charity to strengthen ourselves in the Faith, and to win others for it... Personal perfection and not the eradication of poverty per se is the primary goal of the Society.

What could be chaotic is made harmonic with the impress of order. No Catholic stands exempt from the eleemosynary injunctions of Holy Charity. However, a natural and Divine order must be obeyed. Each Catholic discharges the duty of charity according to his state, means, and prudently available opportunity: all beneath the hidden cloak of humility, which alone clothes it with merit.

The preferential option for the poor ignored this rich and textured Catholic teaching, thus degenerating into a caricature of charity. It was minted in the desiccated university lecture halls of Western Europe (along with its umbrella term, liberation theology)

The Preferential Option for the Poor Sinner 279

and soon migrated across continents. It found its most congenial home in South America, where it became a battle cry for its priests and bishops.

Decades passed, and the preferential option for the poor ate away at the once robust foundations of South American Catholicism. Eventually, liberation theology was roundly condemned by the magisterium of Pope John Paul II and executed by his deputy, Joseph Cardinal Ratzinger. However, it did not entirely disappear. It mutated into a more benign form but a form still bearing the theological genes of the preferential option for the poor.

Even those clerics who obeyed the Church, rejecting this reprobated ideology, still retained its spirit. To them, all the Church's exterior forms of piety and Office became an embarrassment. Clerical attire became an obstacle to solidarity with the poor. The Church's whole traditional ensemble of Redemption became, for them, an albatross.

Thus, the pedigree of the preferential option for the poor. Truth be told, it is still alive and well; and it has now burrowed into the theological cells of a formidable cross section of the Catholic intelligentsia. It sees the poor through an ideological lens which not only makes the true poor invisible but hides their intrinsic human dignity as well. They are no longer men, like all other men. They are the poor. No longer do they possess the dignity of high aspiration but are relegated to being a permanent underclass feeding off the largesse of their betters.

Rather than the Church's rousing summons to strive mightily to *be more*, the ideologues sedulously teach them how to take more. It thus deafens them to the ancient Roman adage (confirming the timeless Divine lessons), *ad astra per aspera*: reaching the heights always entails struggling mightily. In the ideologues' credo, the poor ought to be pitied, never exhorted. They stagnate beneath the disguised soft discrimination of low expectations.

The preferential option for the poor ideologues design a manipulable tribe called the poor, who are forbidden to thirst for the truth and beauty which is the patrimony and comfort of all human beings. These ideologues insist that all the poor must ever see is their misfortune. Misfortune defines them. Their lack of what others have becomes their identity. Their humanity is eviscerated as ideologues entomb them perpetually as the poor. This is the capital sin of Envy writ large.

This is a tragedy of immeasurable proportions. The Church, in all her interior and exterior beauty, is a treasure from which the poor are banned. If the ideologues truly looked at the poor, they would see not poor men, just men. They would see not the poor but simply poor sinners, no different than the rest of the human race, all in need of the same merciful Christ. All they desire are the sweet beauties only the Catholic Church could supply.

For the poor are like the rest of us, the same as us — not a class apart. Our Lord does not see rich or poor, privileged or unfortunate, low class or high. He sees only fallen men and women whom He loves.

Christ's only preference is for poor sinners. Who dares improve upon that?

WARNING: THIS MUSIC MAY BE HARMFUL TO YOUR SOUL[1]

Only the most myopic would deny that a kind of mushroom cloud has covered the Catholic Church for the past half-century. A small, but quite significant, part of that spiritual nuclear winter has been the profound collapse of Sacred Music.

Votaries of the spirit of Vatican II (in today's *au courant* vernacular, the New Paradigm) knew well the power of music in liturgy. If their reimagining of Christianity was to settle its roots deeply in the souls of Catholics, music was the key. They learned well the perennial wisdom of Plato when he wrote in *The Republic*, "Musical training is a more potent instrument than any other, because rhythm and harmony find their way into the inward places of the soul."

> Emotions of any kind are produced by melody and rhythm; therefore, by music a man becomes accustomed to feeling the right emotions; music has thus the power to form character, and various kinds of music based on the various modes, may be distinguished by their effects on character – one, for example, working in the direction of melancholy, another of effeminacy, one encouraging abandonment, another self-control, another enthusiasm, and so on through the series.

Almost 800 years later, Boethius echoed these great giants of natural wisdom when he wrote, "Music can both establish and destroy morality. For no path is more open to the soul for the formation thereof than through the ears."

Added to these, they observed the great success that Arius enjoyed in winning the masses by composing hymns. Whole populations found themselves praising the Arian Christ, no longer God, but only *like* God. Stevedores sang these Arian hymns as they loaded cargo on ships anchored in the harbors of Alexandria, Carthage, or Thessalonica. In this way, Arius's poisonous

---

[1] A slightly different version of this essay appeared as the Foreword to Peter Kwasniewski's *Good Music, Sacred Music, and Silence: Three Gifts of God for Liturgy and for Life* (TAN Books, 2023).

heresy swept over fourth-century Catholicism like a mighty tidal wave. So swift was this heretical deluge that it prompted the now famous, albeit terrifying, lament of St. Jerome, "The world awoke and found itself Arian."

For all these reasons, we could justifiably add to the venerable theological axiom *lex orandi, lex credendi* a new one: *lex cantandi, lex credendi*. Or, more idiomatically, "We begin to believe, the way that we sing." When Catholics in a typical parish are served lounge music instead of sacred music, their souls suffer a kind of dry rot. They experience not the fear and trembling of Calvary but only the wispy breezes of the musical theater. This is no longer religion but vaudeville. Worse still, when the music descends to mimicking the rock concert, the soul undergoes a proportionate excitation. And not to divine things.

If a Catholic denied traditional music is not allowed to be struck to the depths by the likes of *Let All Mortal Flesh Keep Silence* or Franck's *Panis Angelicus*, then he is left to be drowned beneath the indulgent waves of sentimentality. The former hymns steel the soul for supernatural contest, the latter for mindless self-absorption.

Sacred Music is the indispensable instrument of the Holy Spirit in leading souls in their march toward Heaven: it is gravity and solemnity wrapped in the stunning beauty that only music can offer.

Looking at music in general, or sacred music more particularly, we see two principles at work. One has to do with simply being human, the other, with being a Catholic. Both reasons go directly to the soul of man and his civilization. For those who think narrowly, music in Church is a kind of mood setter, cute but irrelevant. An ampler mind recognizes that music acts like an earthquake upon the soul, unleashing powerful forces for good or ill.

On a purely natural level, music is the sheen that glistens over life's quotidian dreariness. It is a part of beauty. Without beauty, man's life becomes flat and self-absorbed. Music lifts man's soul out of its prosaic circumstance and sends it soaring to heights it would not know without it. Or depths. Music's power is so potent that it can arouse passions able to perform heroic actions or debased ones.

Almost twenty years ago, the Port Authority of New York and New Jersey decided to play only soft classical music throughout its Manhattan Bus Depot because psychologists had proven it would lower crime. On the other hand, nightclub owners know to play loud, percussive music, piquing the passions and producing the emotional abandon that sells liquor and facilitates sexual license. No human heart is exempt from racing to the stanzas of *The Battle Hymn of the Republic* or any march of John Philip Sousa. Music has its own grammar and vocabulary. Differences of language, age, and race cannot impede its impact.

Once again, such an impact was duly noted by Plato. In *The Republic*, he teaches, "No change can be made in styles of music without affecting the most important conventions of society." It was exactly for this reason that he forbade music in his Republic. As Michael Linton expresses, Plato spoke brilliantly to this subject when he taught that "Music does not merely depict qualities and emotional states but embodies them." A performer singing (or a hearer listening) "about the rage of Achilles, for instance, would not only be depicting the emotional states of anger and violence and the personal qualities of Homer's hero, but he would be experiencing those things himself."

In 1570, France's Charles IX created the Académie de Poésie et de Musique. In his *lettres patents*, the King declared,

> It is of great importance for the morals of the citizens of a town that the music current in the country should be kept under certain laws, all the more so because men conform themselves to music and regulate their behavior accordingly, so that whenever music is disordered, morals are also depraved and whenever it is well ordered, men are well-tutored.

Music is not only integral to a full human life, but it possesses the power to shape human life. Though Plato expresses it with philosophical brio, each one of us already knows this. One need only consult your own experience.

Thus, sacred music builds civilization and ennobles character. It does, however, even more. When music is composed to honor the Blessed Trinity at Holy Mass, it is called Sacred. Under that purpose, music consummates its highest end. It not only brings man to the heights of beauty; it brings man to Beauty Itself, Almighty God. Man is never so intoxicated than when he is surrounded by Sacred Music. This music transforms him and pierces man's soul to the core of his being. Often, it produces a contrition so profound that a man's life can take a wholly different course.

St. Augustine attests to this in Book IX of *The Confessions*: "How I wept to hear your hymns and songs, deeply moved by the voices of Your sweetly singing Church! Their voices penetrated my ears, and with them, truth found its way into my heart; my frozen feeling for God began to thaw, tears flowed and I experienced joy and relief."

On these grounds, Mother Church has encouraged the most exquisite Sacred Music known to man. Not only that, she has felt it her grave obligation to protect it. The stakes could not be higher. Man's soul hangs in the balance. If the music is wrong, the teaching of the Church will be wrong, and men will go wrong. So it is that in this century the popes have devoted such energy in defining and carefully regulating the conduct of Sacred Music. They also appreciated the corrupting forces in the last hundred years militating against dogmatic truth and trumpeting sentimentalized subjectivism.

It was this awareness that clearly inspired Pope St. Pius X to promulgate his masterpiece on sacred music: *Tra Le Sollecitudini*, whose one-hundredth anniversary Pope John Paul II honored with an appropriate tribute. In that document, Pope St. Pius X taught that the three properties of Sacred Music are universality, goodness of form, and holiness. He declared that those properties are perfectly fulfilled in the Gregorian Chant of the Church. They also become the paradigm of all Sacred Music. They raise it above the idiosyncratic in cultural forms (universality), possess the high marks of the grand music of the ages (goodness of form), and excite in souls a hunger for God (holiness).

Pope St. Pius X teaches, "The Church has constantly condemned everything frivolous, vulgar, trivial and ridiculous in sacred music—everything profane and theatrical both in the form of the compositions and in the manner in which they are executed by the musicians. Sancta sancte, holy things in a holy manner" (*Tra Le Sollecitudini*, no. 13).

The Church's Sacred Music are the wings that carry Christ into man's soul. Remember that when you hear choirs singing the jewels of the Church's treasury of Sacred Music. You are witness to a great moment. Culture is being changed, and starved souls are being filled with God.

Victor Hugo once remarked that a man has the power to make of his soul a sewer or a sanctuary. Music does too.

Beware.

WHITHER OUR CATHOLIC CHURCHES?

I f grace is the Church's heart, and truth the Church's soul, then art would have to be her face. And faces reveal the soul, whether a man's soul would be intact even though some calamity deprived him of his face, the soul would become mute. It would possess nothing through which to speak. Yes, there might be the voice through which words come. But without a face, a vitally evocative aspect of communication would be gone. Think of Hamlet on the written page, then Hamlet on the lips of Olivier. Same Hamlet, but such a different Hamlet.

If the art of the Church were suddenly to be sabotaged, the unchanging truths she teaches might undergo a slight, then ultimately a grave, distortion. Not that her teachings would change, but her art, their most potent human communication, would have damaged their understanding. That would spell a crisis. Precisely that kind of crisis occurred in the eighth and ninth centuries, all of it over art. Or, in this case, the absence of it. The crisis developed into a heresy, Iconoclasm. It maintained that the veneration of any images of Our Lord, His Mother, the saints or angels, was a blasphemous act: the worship of idols. For almost 100 years this heresy sundered the Church.

Roving bands of Iconoclasts destroyed art, and the churches that held them, with fanatical fervor. Eventually, the Church resolved the crisis, not only to save her churches, but to save the Faith itself. But why did the Church so closely ally art and Faith? Art is part of the Incarnation. As the Word shone splendidly through the flesh of Christ's manhood, so the Church's truths are given splendor through art. In 870 the Church closed the chapter on the Iconoclastic frenzy by convening the Second Council of Nicea. There she solemnly taught: "For, as through the language of words contained in this book all can reach salvation, so due to the action which these images exercise by their colors, all, wise and simple alike, can derive profit from them. For what speech conveys in words, pictures announce and bring out in colors." This same Council applauded the work of St. John Damascene's

Treatises in Defense of Holy Icons. He argued that rejecting art is tantamount to a rejection of the Incarnation:

> But when you see Him Who has no body become man for you, then you will make representations of his human aspect. When the Invisible, having clothed Himself in the flesh, becomes visible, then represent the likeness of Him Who has appeared... When he Who, having been the Consubstantial image of the Father; emptied Himself by taking the form of a servant (Phil. 2:6-7), thus becoming bound in quantity and quality; having taken on the carnal image, then paint and make visible to everyone Him Who desired to become visible.

Ringing confirmation of this marriage of art and the Incarnation comes in the words of Leonid Ouspensky in *The Theology of the Icon*: "The Church declares that the Christian image is an extension of the divine Incarnation, that it is based on the Incarnation and that, therefore, it is of the very essence of Christianity, from which it is inseparable."

To those who might think either the Church's concern for art obsessive or trivial, there is also Chesterton in *Orthodoxy*, where he gives his customary penetrating insight into the relationship between the Church's dogmas and her art:

> Last and most important, it is exactly this which explains what is inexplicable to all the modern critics of the history of Christianity. I mean the monstrous wars about small points of theology, the earthquakes of emotion about a gesture or a word. It was only a matter of an inch; but an inch is everything when you are balancing. The Church could not afford to swerve a hair's breadth on some things if she was to continue her great and daring experiment of the irregular equilibrium. Once let one idea become less powerful and some other idea would become too powerful. It was no flock of sheep the Christian shepherd was leading, but a heard of bulls and tigers, of terrible ideas and devouring doctrines, each of them strong enough to turn to a false religion and lay waste the world. Remember, the Church went in specifically for dangerous ideas: she was the lion tamer...
>
> Here it is enough to notice that if some small mistake were made in doctrine, huge blunders might be made in human happiness. A sentence phrased wrong about the nature of symbolism would have broken all the best statues in Europe, a slip in the definitions might stall the

dances; might whither all the Christmas trees or break all the Easter eggs. Doctrines had to be defined within the strict limits, even in order that man might enjoy general human liberties. The Church had to be careful if only that the world might be careless.

But what of that careless and vapid new church art, to say nothing of plundered churches themselves? Would that the Church's art of the last third of the last century be called merely careless, implying something done without due thought. The New Churches came packed with a full agenda. Those who produced it traveled closely with the Dissenting (and governing) Class who were slightly uncomfortable with the too tightly fitting Ancient Faith. Nothing irked them more than those old churches, old paintings, old vestments, old everything.

That dazzling, millennial old artistic culture worked too well in stamping upon souls the grandeur of the true Faith. If the Dissenting Class were to reimagine the Faith, the old churches and the art which adorned them had to go. Replacing it had to be New Churches and their New Art. The new ecclesial art and architecture willingly drowns itself beneath the secularist tsunami. They do not tell the truth. Not about man. Not about God. Not about the Catholic Church. They are lies set in stone. In fact, they do not present the Faith; they distort it. They do not help Catholics to see; they make it impossible to see. They dramatically embrace every Modernist assumption about art, which is the mutilation of art. Any Catholic not deeply disturbed by this should be deeply disturbed.

Every Catholic Church is a book. In fact, so is every building made by man. They tell a story. Since only art tells stories with the greatest and most felicitous force, after art is created, it creates. Winston Churchill appositely commented, "After a man shapes a building, the building starts to shape us." Buildings are not like lectures; they are more like songs, or should be. Their beauty pierces man's soul and teaches as no teacher can. They are like poems, not position papers. Each communicates meaning, but a song does it ineffably and indelibly; a position paper does it efficiently but only fleetingly. The old saying goes, "You can write a nation's books, but let me write its songs." Similarly, art stirs, moves, and animates. It tosses man's soul to and fro and makes sure that despite his enervating complacency, he sees things. Men do not march to careful scientific conclusions; they march to songs. Churches make sure we see things, the supernatural. In that glance, a man is never the same. In 886 Prince Vladimir of Rus decided he needed a religion for all the subjects of his empire. He dispatched emissaries to the Western city of Constantinople where they attended Holy Mass at the Hagia Sophia (Church of Holy Wisdom). Upon returning the Prince asked what it was they discovered. The emissaries replied that they entered the Churches and did not know whether they were on earth or in heaven. With that, what is now present-day Russia embraced Christianity. Every Church must be like stepping into heaven, always stretching to mirror the mystical verses of the book of the Apocalypse.

Large or very small, rich or poor, Catholic Churches must possess grandeur, clarity, nobility, and most importantly, the drama of the Faith. Since the Faith is changeless, there are certain architectural details and designs which bespeak that timelessness. Speaking idiomatically, one may call that congenial form traditional, which would be unquestionably correct. Put more precisely, traditional architecture (Romanesque, Gothic, Baroque, and Rococo) possess the architectural features necessary to bear the heavy metaphysical weight of the Faith in their height, breadth, light, shadow, shape, ornamentation, and solidity.

All of this permits the Catholic Church to teach both directly and indirectly, explicitly and implicitly. This double motion only occurs because Holy Church enlists the help of art. For instance, the Tabernacle is observed and understood to house the Body, Blood, Soul, and Divinity of Christ. All true, but cerebral at best. However, when the Tabernacle is seen at the front and center of a splendid sanctuary, radiant in finely sculpted gold, flanked by candlesticks, and standing behind seven hanging lamps, fire blazing, night and day, one not only understands the Mystery, he feels it. He not only nods his assent to the Doctrine, he trembles before its beauty. For beauty is not elitist, it is democratic. If it needs to be explained, we are not in its presence. Beauty strikes with the swiftness of an arrow. Beauty is the swiftness; the arrow is the truth. Plato teaches in the *Symposium* that beauty is "absolute, separate, simple, and everlasting." More telling is the Greek word for beauty, *kalon*, derived from the Greek verb, *kaleo*, meaning to call, summon, or beckon. Isn't that what beauty does? Pope Benedict XVI illuminated the purpose of beauty on November 21,

2009, in his address to artists in the Sistine Chapel organized by the Pontifical Council for Culture:

> "An essential function of genuine beauty... is that it gives man a health shock; it draws him out of himself, wrenches him away from resignation and from being content with the humdrum – it even makes him suffer, piercing him like a dart, but in so doing it reawakens him, opening afresh the eyes of his heart and mind, giving him wings, carrying him aloft." Pope Benedict called this the *via pulchritudinis*. Similarly, he cited the marks of the Church's divinity as "the saints, her architecture, and her art."

This same synergy accompanies all the architectural and artistic depictions of the Faith: the Crucifixion, Our Lady, the Holy Angels, the Saints, the Confessional Boxes, and on and on. Each Church teaches the faith symphonically. Just as a symphony combines diverse instruments and sundry notes to produce the effect of music, so every detail of architecture and Faith joins forces to produce the one single effect of closeness to God. With that proximity comes examination. When dwarfed by the dizzying heights of Chartres's vaulted ceilings and massive columns, a man cannot help but measure all of one's life against the demanding will of God. Moreover, Churches generate contrition. They are unrelentingly existential not merely self-referential. Entering Rheims or St. Peter's in Rome leaves even non-Catholics deeply moved, not only because of their beauty but because it houses our beautiful God against whom we are so often blind. St. Augustine once preached, "If Christ were to come into this room and stand before you, what would you think? Not of Christ, but of yourself." Churches compel that question, too.

There would not have been such a rush to this modernist architecture unless there was first a rush to Modernism. How else to explain the global collapse of authentic Catholic architecture? Notice of this does not require sophisticated theological degrees, only a common humanity. Doesn't Chesterton capture this perfectly: "Do not be proud of the fact that your grandmother was shocked at something which you are accustomed to seeing or hearing without being shocked – it may be that your grandmother was an extremely lively and vital animal, and that you are a paralytic."

Even an untrained eye sees that the architectural details of New Churches and their art are designed to disorient: vastness as emptiness, bareness as blindness, simplicity as vapidity. Almost every element is a tribute to transgressive non-conformity. Even the scarce Catholic images which manage an appearance are so attenuated as to create wondrous confusion, not wondrous awe. Devotion has always been an embarrassment to the Modernist, and the New Churches will always be a shameful testimony to that. They will always stand as relics of a gutted Catholicism. Unquestionable evidence of an experiment gone terribly wrong, a doctrinal meltdown.

Three characteristics mark Modernist architecture's Long March into the Gnostic demimonde. First, it must be nondidactic: the new art must always appear obscure, ambiguous, and undefined, eschewing any expression of classic Catholic truths or piety; secondly, it had to be nontraditional: it could never be redolent of any former periods of the Church's history, on the unspoken assumption that 1965 was to be considered the New Year One of a refashioned Church; finally, and most crucially, it must be non-Roman: all art (statues, chalices, vestments) must never convey the formality or splendor of the Church's self-understanding as the true Church but rather appear indigenous and ardently preliterate. An occasional Byzantine icon would be tolerated only because at least it was non-Roman.

An old saying warns never to judge a book by its cover. But when it comes to Catholics and their art, that yarn has no relevance. Rather, the rule is to always judge a Catholic by his art. It might not tell everything, but it will tell you most things. Like the smile on someone's face.

WHAT IN THE WORLD IS A "WORSHIP SPACE"?

Euphemisms are *de rigeur* for revolutionaries. Communist states call themselves people's republics. When they instigate conflicts, they are called wars of liberation. Abortionists call their abattoirs pregnancy centers and their executions terminations. Most currently, surgeons call sexual mutilation gender reassignment. All of this is a clever strategy to stave off natural human revulsion so that after a sufficient passage of time the moral sense is deadened. And it works. George Orwell dramatized it in *1984* when he minted the word newspeak to name the manipulative devices of the Ubiquitous State and that very brutalizing State itself the anodyne big brother. Orwell was only dramatizing a parlous trend in Western culture, namely, plying junk sentimentality masquerading as Progress. It served to clog human language, prompting Graham Greene to quip: "When I hear about the brotherhood of man, I think of Cain and Abel."

A deeper intellectual rot goes beyond euphemism to neologisms. Such novel constructions are yanked from the ether of a dreamy Gnostic redesign. These odd-sounding constructions are the bricks of a kind of Magic Kingdom far removed from the world of ordinary men. They are Gnostic because they leap from the inventive imaginations of intellectuals frustrated by the humdrum landscape of reality. T. S. Eliot wrote well in *Burnt Norton*: "Human kind/ cannot bear very much reality." The twentieth century boasted of many intellectual tribes who excelled in the manufacture of neologisms, not least in the Catholic Church. One of her tribes was called the New Theology (*Nouvelle Théologie*). Spawned in the ferment of early twentieth-century Modernism, its members devotedly went about the business of refashioning the Catholic Church. Once they had finished their labors of reimagining the doctrinal pillars of Catholicism, they turned their attention to the principal engine used to propagate the Church's dogmatic teaching: the Sacred Liturgy.

These Imaginers of New Things left no stone unturned. One ironclad rule controlled their thinking: all that existed before 1970 must be held in the highest suspicion. In this regard, they were absolutists of the highest order. To these theological pioneers the Sacred Liturgy was to be their private *tabula rasa*. Untethered from ancient liturgical tradition, their creativity knew no limits. For each jarring novelty, an even more jarring neologism appeared. One of them was the idiosyncratic worship space. It suggested a protean world of insertions and subtractions wide enough to accommodate the most fanciful ideas of man and God. It was sufficiently ambiguous, amorphous, and malleable – like a soft clay – into which a New Theologian could knead any theological whim.

Simple Catholics treated such open-ended argot like nails scratching on a black board – or should have. All of it poured out from that bottomless cornucopia: The spirit of Vatican II. As G. K. Chesterton warned: "Beware of those who speak of the 'spirit of Christianity'; they mean the 'ghost of Christianity.'" Apply the same logic to those who utilize the capacious spirit of Vatican II; it means in translation: "be anything you want to be." In other words, Gnosticism.

Theologians anchored in the normative tradition of the Church speak of "sanctuary," "nave," "clerestory," "narthex," transept," and "altar." Unmoored from this criterion, whimsical interpretations such as "worship space" suddenly materialize. Under this unforgiving regime, Catholics have suffered architectural and artistic anomalies that strain credulity.

Without wasting a moment, the New Theologians rolled out edict after edict, all treated as solemnly as the Nicene Creed. One of their diktats was that every church in Christendom required retooling. Never has such a fashionable lie taken such firm hold of the global population of Roman Catholics. Truth to be told, there has never existed a duty to renovate any Church. Similarly, no mandate has ever been issued by the Holy See commanding the appalling designs of not a few newly constructed churches. Just as the Supreme Court discovered a right to privacy in the Constitution and called it a penumbra, i.e., a shadow, so The New Theological Knowledge class did the same.

To them, the penumbrae were the parts of text that might remotely suggest a meaning compatible with a highly specific (usually anti-traditional) agenda. No one can divine these penumbrae except the elite group that displays the proper academic credentials. Philosophers call this privileged meaning. Sound strange? It is. Stranger still are the vast numbers of people who eagerly swallowed this fantasy whole. Since these liturgists obsessively invoke the Second Vatican Council, intelligent Catholics should know what this 1962-1965 ecumenical council taught. Vatican II devoted exactly nine paragraphs to the topic of Sacred Art and Sacred Furnishings.[2] From the universal sacking of churches accomplished in its name, it might be assumed that it was volumes.

Under the umbrella of worship space, they stretched terms used by the Church beyond comprehension. Take simplicity, for instance. Of all the terms that have served these liturgists best, "simplicity" holds pride of place. They splashed thousands of gallons of white paint over sacred images and precious ornamentation under the banner of simplicity. Many a trash dumpster was stuffed with magnificent vestments while modernist vandals intoned simplicity. A former age called this Iconoclasm. Tabernacles, ciboria, chalices and candelabra found their way into display windows of antique shops, and other odd places, for not conforming to the new sacred norm of simplicity. And where is the justification for this term and its scorched-earth policy? Paragraph 124 of *Sacrosanctum Concilium*: "Ordinaries are to take care that in encouraging and favoring truly sacred art, they should seek for noble beauty rather than sumptuous display. This same principle applies also to sacred vestments and ornaments."

Not even the most fevered imagination could find in that paragraph a justification for simplicity and its trail of unrelieved chaos. Noble beauty is what every Church has striven after these 2,000 years. The Council changed nothing. It called for more of what former centuries have shown will elevate the faithful. What it did caution the bishops against is precisely what has befallen our churches today: "Bishops should be careful to ensure that works of art which are repugnant to faith, morals, and Christian piety and which offend true religious sense... be removed." How many penumbrae can survive those words?

There is a bible of liturgical penumbrae, issued by the USCCB in 1978, entitled *Environment and Art in Catholic Worship* (its

---

[2] *Sacrosanctum Concilium*, December 4, 1963, nos. 122-30.

successor is the 2000 document *Built of Living Stones: Art, Architecture and Worship*). Read it and stare down the circles of liturgical hell. Every conceivable distortion that has appeared in churches is given theological justification there, and it is chockfull of Gnostic neologisms. Chancery offices have quoted it as reverently and (probably) more frequently than Matthew, Mark, Luke, and John. But they are hiding a dirty little secret—though never admitted: *Environment and Art in Catholic Worship* enjoys absolutely no binding force. Never underestimate the legerdemain of a liturgist. Whatever logic these Imaginers followed, it is not a logic flowing from the perennial teaching of the Catholic Church.

Catholics irked by the din of theological newspeak ought not feel disenfranchised. While many a Catholic has come to feel right at home with the *nouveau* jargon, Catholics of the Old Faith must endure in the world of Catholic reality. Boycott all such newspeak. Again, Orwell writes: "We have now sunk to a depth at which the restatement of the obvious is the first duty of intelligent men." Let Catholics be about the task of restating obvious things. In God's good time, the claws of the Gnostic netherworld will loosen.

MODERNIST CHURCHES: LIES SET IN STONE

Like pouring gasoline on a raging fire, France's National Heritage and Architecture Commission has given the green light to the Archdiocese of Paris's proposition to modernize Notre Dame Cathedral. With astonishing blindness to the March of Death of the Faith that the French hierarchy has launched in the past half century, they are redoubling their efforts to deepen the ruins. It seems they will not rest until only embers remain of the once glorious Faith of the Eldest Daughter of the Church. Their proposal for Notre Dame? Removing religious statues and confessionals and replacing them with emotional spaces and a discovery tour with a strong environmental emphasis. The justification by the Archdiocese is that these changes would make the cathedral's religious meaning more accessible. Even the Commission denied some of the Archdiocese's requests in an open letter titled *Notre Dame de Paris: What the fire spread, the diocese wants to destroy*. It has come to this. Agnostic aesthetes must teach obvious lessons of religion to Catholicism's religious leaders. Such absurdities would escape even the absurdist pen of Kafka.

This screeching anomaly was reprised in Our Lady of the Angels Cathedral in Los Angeles, a zany liturgical dreamer's paradise. That monstrous insult to holy religion was the brainchild of now retired Cardinal Roger Mahoney. In 1997 he proclaimed that he was attempting to de-Europeanize the sacred liturgy. That is liturgical mumbo-jumbo for further loosening the liturgy from the bonds of Roman tradition. Europeanisations include things such as kneeling, genuflections, and, of course, Latin. More generally, they mean gestures, words, and hymns that conventionally suggest reverence for the Divine. Quite a plan. These secularist henchmen recognize that Catholics receive most of the formation in the Faith from the Sacred Liturgy. Refashion that and one successfully refashions the Faith, and Our Lord Jesus Christ Himself! Hence, *lex orandi, lex credendi*. What is at stake in the spanking new Los

Angeles Cathedral is that it doesn't tell the truth. Not about God. Not about man. Not about the Catholic Church. It is a lie set in stone. Any Catholic not deeply disturbed by it should be deeply disturbed. Once more Chesterton had it exactly right when he wrote: "The new theologians do not worship the sun or moon; they worship the clock... They put first things last."

From time immemorial, the traditional Roman form of the Mass has been under attack. For the Gnostics, it was too purely physical. For the Jansenists it was not pure enough. Our own century has produced a number of liturgical iconoclasts. Having suckedl on the antinomianism of the '60s, they now decide that rubrics and ritual laws hamper man's unbounded elan. The externals of religion in general and liturgy in particular cramp their style. What's inside is what's important, they squeal. True enough, but that's not the whole story. The interior state of one's soul is indeed an interest that towers above all others. It is standard Catholic dogma that external practices can never substitute for interior grace. Interior grace, on the other hand, doesn't flourish without external actions. Our Lord, in fact, designed the sacraments to be external signs of the granting of invisible graces.

Those primordial sacramental signs have a mighty ripple effect. Every part of Catholic life imitates their divine pattern. Catholicism is never more itself than when it enlists physical things to manifest its invisible mystery. Thus, the ancient dogmatic principle applies: The invisible is seen in the visible through the physical. That's why Baroque churches served her purposes so well. Their sumptuous complexity inebriates the senses and impresses upon the mind the supernal truth of Christ's conquest over sin and His Kingly reign of grace. Angels do not require the heady lessons of the Baroque. Men do. Their body/ soul nature craves grace's fleshly epiphanies. Catholics should never be squeamish when the Faith announces itself to the world in lavish physical forms. After all, we daily bend our knees at the Angelus *et Verbum caro factum est* because the Son of God chose to save us through the visibility of human flesh. No Catholic ought to be sheepish with that divine logic. The incarnation demands that the church utilize splendid things for splendid truths.

To de-Europeanize the Mass is to replace magnificent forms with banal ones, even ones that de-Christianize Christianity. Though the Faith might remain intact, when its forms do not measure

Modernist Churches: Lies Set in Stone 297

up to its glory, the Faith becomes a shadow. Cardinal Newman preached to this in his *Plain and Parochial Sermons:*

> No one can really respect religion and insult its forms. Granted that forms are not immediately from God, still long usage has made them divine to us: for the spirit of religion has so penetrated and quickened them, that to destroy them is, in respect to the multitude of men, to unsettle and dislodge the religious principle itself. In most minds usage has so identified them with the notion of religion, that one cannot bear transplanting... Precious doctrines are strong like jewels upon slender thread.

Chesterton once remarked that the shimmering of Cardinal Manning's scarlet robes struck his imagination as the *Arabian Nights* did, as signs of a glory beyond imagining. Yes, interior things only flourish in the soil of external things. That is why a nun in full habit is replete with interior invitations of grace without uttering a single word. A priest in a Roman cassock pierces the soul more deeply than ten brilliant sermons. So does the Pope in jeweled tiara or a cardinal in scarlet *cappa magna*. All signs of a glory beyond imagining.

As I said in "Whither Our Catholic Churches?," every Catholic church is a book; every one tells a story. A church well made tells us what we ought to see, how we ought to live; it is a stepping stone to the heavenly Jerusalem, the mother and model of every temple. The Church rightly insists on teaching through her fine arts—but she must teach the truth, and not a deception. The truth is beautiful, and the only true beauty is truth manifested.

Sadly, very sadly, the new Notre Dame or Los Angeles Cathedral of Our Lady of the Angels accomplishes none of these things for Catholics. In fact, it does not present the Faith; it distorts it. It doesn't help Catholics to see; it makes it impossible to see. It excitedly embraces every modernist assumption about art, which is the mutilation of art.

But as they say, where there's smoke, there's fire. There would not have been such a rush to this modernist architecture unless there was first a rush to modernism. How else to explain the new church's absence of any traditional sign of Catholicism? Even the architectural details are designed to disorient: vastness as emptiness, light as blindness, sterile non-description as a deconstructionist nod to transgressive non-conformity. Even the scarce

Catholic images which might manage a slight appearance are so attenuated as to create nonplussed confusion, not wondrous awe. It is axiomatic that devotion is an enemy of modernism; Notre Dame and Our Lady of the Angels will be a centuries-long confirmation of that. It is gutted Catholicism, nothing less than doctrinal meltdown.

Yet someday, perhaps in fifty years, a Sovereign Pontiff will send a new Bishop to the Sees of Paris and Los Angeles. He will be a Bishop after the heart of Borromeo and Bellarmine, Pius X and Leo the Great. After setting his eyes on Our Lady of the Angels Cathedral of 2002 he will quickly come to a decision. It must be torn down. And all the children of those benighted Catholics whose parents donated the $193 million dollars to construct this mistake will raise no fuss.

For a time of renewed common sense will have returned. God's honor will be foremost, not man's folly.

WHY THE WALLS OF NOTRE-DAME ARE GROANING

Some things are worse than a devastating fire. Notre-Dame de Paris proves the point. While its façade, walls, and roof have been restored to a pristine perfection, its interior liturgical appointments tell another story.

- The altar has become a bathtub
- The pulpit, a highway barrier
- The sedilia a *Star Wars* prop
- And the reliquary for the Crown of Thorns, detritus from a wasteyard landfill

But the vestments! The vestments were the *pièce de résistance*. They were worn by the Archbishop of Paris and his attendants. Any man of taste (to say nothing of commonsense Catholics) cringed. They seem to be borrowed from a troupe of clowns at some local circus.

In 2025 Duncan Stroik reported in *Sacred Architecture*:

> On July 11th, France's National Heritage and Architecture Commission unanimously rejected president Emmanuel Macron's proposal to replace nineteenth-century stained glass windows designed by Eugene Viollet-le-Duc with contemporary designs. The proposal and subsequent design competition sparked controversy and a petition of over 140,000 signatures against the removal of the historic windows and six of the side chapels. The Commission ruled that Macron's proposal, which Archbishop Laurent Ulrich supported, would be a violation of the Venice Charter, a set of international guidelines for the conservation and restoration of historic sites and buildings. Since the windows were undamaged by the fire, their removal from the historic cathedral was deemed unjustifiable. Despite the commission's ruling, the proposal could still be implemented.

All this, quite deliberate. You are witness to the grand struggle between the Revisionist Faith and the Ancient Faith. In this makeover, Notre-Dame becomes ground zero in the mortal struggle between the World and Christ.

The Modernist crusade has been nothing less than the successful burial of God beneath the debris of Modernity.

Overwrought, you complain? Ponder the words of Bishop Franz-Josef Overbeck of Essen (Germany): "We must not evangelize the whole world. God will find a way to guide non-believers. Many do not need religion, faith or, of course, any church."

This, dear Catholic readers, is a burial.

Of course, many, at every level of the Church, pooh-pooh remarks such as this as quaint and untroubling, treating it like the use of the improper silverware at a dinner party. They prefer to take a more positive approach. Such head-in-the sand cowardice has greased the skids of the present calamity.

While the preferred battlefield for the Modernists has been the rarified walls of seminaries, universities, graduate schools, and learned societies, they appreciate that their most potent weapons lie in the vocabulary of symbol, art, and architecture. These are the lexicon of the human heart. They are the privileged places where man's life is anchored and changed. Manipulate them and you change the world.

Such is simple to prove. For instance, read St. Thomas's doctrinal masterpiece on the Holy Eucharist. Your mind is instructed and convinced. Then, listen to Mozart's *Ave Verum Corpus* or the familiar (once standard) Catholic hymn *Let All Mortal Flesh Keep Silence.* Your heart swoons and your feet want to gallop to Heaven.

This ironclad law of human nature applies to darker things. Study the paragraphs of *Mein Kampf,* and you touch the roots of hate. Then, look at a swastika, and you break into a cold sweat. Hence, the commanding vocabulary of symbol and art. It is in this field of combat where hearts and minds are won.

The theological grandees understood this well. After their tomes were carefully written, they well grasped that what would win hearts and minds was their iconoclasm. Sacrosanct rules that guided the architecture of churches for millennia were overturned with a rage verging on the fanatical. Sacred vestments, always resembling the canvasses of Rubens and van Eyck, were systematically gathered and destroyed. Sanctuaries that once evoked pages of the Book of the Apocalypse were leveled. Sacred vessels, always meticulously crafted with gold and jewels bespeaking awe of the sacred wealth which they contained, were cast aside with a malign devotion bordering on the maniacal.

All the while, Catholics were reassured that this liturgical carnage was the wish of the Church's new conciliar spirit of simplicity. It was not. In typical fashion, this was the Modernist's favored term to palliate the unwashed masses. With brutal consistency, the effects of *lex orandi, lex credendi* set in. Doctrines such as the Real Presence, the Mass as sacrifice, the reality of sin, the cult of the saints and angels, and the very notion of piety and devotion were blurred, if not swept away like flotsam in a tidal wave.

Beauty in the Sacred Liturgy is as critical to its integrity as flesh to a man's body. Actually, more important. In the language of St. Thomas, it is the resplendent grandeur of form (i.e., that which makes a thing be what it is). Beauty is the irresistible attraction of truth. The Ancient Greeks understood that it possessed the power to shape or misshape the souls of its people. Churchill was probably echoing this insight when he once wrote, "After man makes his buildings, his buildings make him."

St. John Damascene came to the rescue of beauty in the 8th century when the Iconoclastic controversy threatened the Church. The heretics believed that beautiful art distorted the truth of the spiritual. They conducted a campaign to destroy it all and would have done so if not for the intervention of the Second Council of Nicaea in 787, whose principal inspiration was St. John Damascene.

Basing his arguments for sacred art upon the Incarnation, he argued that Christ deigned to assume ordinary visible flesh so men would see the Word made Flesh. If God Himself set forth this example, no man should dare prohibit the visible renderings of heavenly persons. With lyric persuasion, Damascene wrote:

> The whole earth is a living icon of the face of God... I do not worship matter. I worship the Creator of matter who became matter for my sake, who willed to take His abode in matter, who worked out my salvation through matter. Never will I cease honoring the matter which wrought my salvation! I honor it, but not as God. Because of this I salute all remaining matter with reverence, because God has filled it with his grace and power. Through it my salvation has come to me.

Damascene's arguments are germane to the discussion of the role of beauty in the Church. Before the Second Person became flesh in the womb of the Immaculate Virgin, He was the *Verbum* in the bosom of the Trinity. His other name was Σοφία (Sophia-Wisdom), through Him all things were made (Nicene Creed). There is order in the cosmos because of the work of Holy Wisdom. So it is that order is of the very essence of beauty (hence, St. Thomas and the three features of beauty: integrity, proportion, and radiance).

Thus, we learn from the Angelic Doctor, as well as the Greeks and the entire tradition of Western art, that beauty is not subjective but stunningly objective, mirroring the order and beauty of nature, which radiates the Beauty of Christ, who is Beauty itself.

Modernity has utterly discarded the classical understanding of beauty, debasing art to a mere voyage into the shallows of subjectivism. Modernism has followed the lead of Modernity with slavish obedience. The purpose of modern art is to create a metaphysical disequilibrium. No points of reference, no fixed notes of observation, no objective index of evaluation. Its slogan is well known to all who inhabit the disorienting universe of Modernity: beauty is in the eye of the beholder.

No, it is not. Beauty is in what the eye beholds. Therein lies a world of difference. As with reality, man bows humbly before it. For the Modernist, reality bows obsequiously before man.

Listen carefully and you can hear echoes of *non serviam*. Yes, that primordial First Re-Designer of Reality routed by St. Michael.

Pope Benedict once remarked,

> If the church is to continue to transform and humanize the world, how can she dispense with beauty in her liturgies, that beauty which is so closely linked with love and with the radiance of the resurrection. Without this the world will become the first circle of hell.

More famously, he wrote, "The only real effective apology for Christianity comes down to two arguments, namely the Saints the church has produced and the art which has grown in her womb."

The new Notre-Dame de Paris would shock the saints and holy doctors who prayed within its hallowed columns and vaulted ceiling. But today its walls moan as they are compelled to embrace the hellscape of liturgical innovation.

It might not be the first circle of Hell. But it comes pretty close.

AWAKE IN PARADISE

No motion picture script could match this derring-do plot. Picture an Achilles-like warrior marching out to battle for his kingdom, subduing a menacing foe, and freeing his suffering subjects. Now imagine, not a script, but reality. The Second Person of the Blessed Trinity marched forth from His eternal abode of glory in the bosom of the Trinity, to do battle for His kingdom. This kingdom was once populated by men and women made in His image and likeness, properly his subjects, destined for glory unending. But one day, a cataclysm erupted in a Garden and all were taken into a pitiless captivity by a foreign potentate whom that helmeted Word Incarnate named the Prince of this world (Jn 12:31). Once created for eternal bliss; now, citizens of the empire of sin.

The story continues. In a cosmic battle the Son of God heroically steps upon the battlefield, Calvary, and slays the Infernal Serpent with only five blows, the wounds He carried on Golgotha. Before taking His last breath he proclaims to heaven and earth His victory, "It is finished" (Jn 19:30). The Son's assignment was complete. Fittingly, He wore a King's crown, not of laurels, but of thorns, announcing to world that this was not an ordinary human triumph, but a divine one. As lasting proof of the valiant victory, the Divine Captain rose from the dead, generating tremors shaking the very depths of Hell. The first visitation of this Divine Warrior was, of course, to His Virgin Mother, then, to the pillars of His Catholic Church, the apostles. For forty days he instructed them on the mysteries of His triumph, and tutored them on the application of those fruits to mankind through His Holy Catholic Church.

When that fortieth day dawned, the Savior knew that He must return to His natural home where He would reign forever with His Father and Holy Spirit, and ascends before the eyes of His apostles. Seated at the right hand of His Father, He reigns with a double majesty: not only as Eternally Begotten Son, but as Divine Redeemer, dazzling in the raiment of his Sacred Humanity. That splendor, that grandeur, is captured in the moving images of the book of the Apocalypse. Artists have strained to depict this royal chamber, no one more famously than Jan van Eyck in his Ghent altarpiece: *The Supper of the Lamb*. Gazing upon it we see the New Jerusalem, replacing the Old Jerusalem. Now, all the promises made to Patriarchs and Prophets are fulfilled beyond imagination, not only of those ancients, but of any man. "Eye hath not seen, nor ear heard, neither have entered into the heart of man, the things which God has prepared for them that love him" (1 Cor 2:9).

From the dogma of Christ's Ascension, Holy Church learns the manner in which to house the Savior. Each church should mirror the splendor and majesty of Our Lord's abode in Heaven, limned so stunningly in the book of the Apocalypse. Every Catholic Church is the New Jerusalem, reflecting the words of Our Savior in that inspired book, "Behold I make all things new" (Rev 21:5). Make no mistake, this newness is not novelty. Novelty is arsenic to the Mystical Body of Christ. The newness is the new standards of glory which now apply for a Reality hitherto never seen by angels or men: Christ with us in the Most Blessed Eucharist. And the blueprints are found in the *Book of the Apocalypse*. Sample some of them: "Merchandise of gold, and silver, and precious stones, and of pearls, and fine linen, and purple, and silk, and scarlet, and all thyine wood, and all manner vessels of ivory, and all manner vessels of most precious woods, and brass, and iron, and marble" (Rev 18:12); "And saying, Alas, alas, that great city, that was clothed in fine linen, and purple, and scarlet, and decked with gold and precious stones, and pearls!" (Rev 18:16); "And the twelve gates were twelve pearls; every several gate was of one pearl, and the street of the city was pure gold, as it were transparent glass" (Rev 21:21). These lines should leave no doubt at how every Catholic Church as the Palace of the King should appear. In fact, St. John Henry Cardinal Newman delivered one his most impassioned sermons (sermon 19) commenting on Psalm 78, "He Built His sanctuary like high palaces, like the earth which He established forever." So rich, it deserves to be cited at length:

> Religious edifices are a Christian ordinance, though so very little is said about them in Scripture will also show that it is right and pious to make them enduring, and stately and magnificent, and ornamental: so that Our Savior's declaration, when He foretold the destruction of

the Temple at Jerusalem, was not that there should not be any other house built in His honor, but rather that there should be many houses; they should be built, not merely at Jerusalem, or at Gerizim, but everywhere... The glory of the Gospel is not the abolition of rites, but their dissemination; not their absence, but their living and efficacious presence through the grace of Christ... Rich and "exceedingly magnificent" was Solomon's Temple... it is not presumptuous surely to say that Catholic Temples should as far surpass it in size, beauty and costliness... Stability and permanence are, perhaps, the especial ideas which a Catholic Church brings before the mind. It represents, indeed, the beauty, the loftiness, the calmness, the mystery and the sanctity of religion also, and that in many ways; still, I will say, more than all these, it represents to us eternity. It is the witness of Him Who is the beginning and the ending, the first and the last; it is the token and emblem of Jesus Christ, the same yesterday, today, and forever!; it is the pledge of One, who said, "I will never leave thee or forsake thee, but even to your old age I am He, and even to hoar hairs I will carry you"... Thus the Palaces of God are withal the mountains of His saints... Their simplicity, grandeur, solidity, elevation, grace, and exuberance of ornament, do but bring to remembrance the patience and purity, the courage, meekness and great charity, the heavenly affections, the activity in well-doing, the faith and resignation of men who did but worship their King.

At length as well, should be cited the famous words of Abbot Suger, the 12th century abbot of St. Denis, in *On His Abbatial Administration*:

> As for me... I confess that I took great pleasure in devoting all the costliest and most precious things I could find to the service and administration of the Most Holy Eucharist. If to fulfill an order from God manifested from the mouth of the prophets, golden chalices, vases and cups were used to receive the blood of goats, calves and the red cow of the expiation, how greater is our obligation to use, in order to receive the Blood of Jesus Christ, in perpetual service and with utmost devotion, vases of gold, gems and everything that is considered most precious. Surely not we or our worldly goods can suffice to serve such great mysteries. Even, in a new creation, our substances were changed into that of Cherubim and Seraphim, it would still be unworthy to serve the Ineffable Host... Some,

no doubt, would in contradiction, tell us that all that is necessary is to bring to the cult a pure heart, a holy soul and true intentions; we also think that these conditions are a prime necessity and have a very special importance. But we likewise affirm that the ornamentation of the sacred vessels used for the Holy Sacrifice should possess an outer magnificence, which, as far as possible, equals our inward purity.

All of these great writers and saints were inspired by the words of Genesis: "Terrible is this place; it is the house of God and the gate of heaven; and it shall be called the court of God" (Gen 28:17). Similarly, "We are lost in wonder at all that you have done for us, mighty God" (Rev 15:3).

Each time someone enters a Catholic Church it should seem strange because its splendor and majesty is unlike any other thing in the world. Familiarity collapses here; only awe remains.

So transfixed were the apostles at the sight of Our Lord ascending in ineffable majesty that an angel was sent to reprove them, "Ye men of Galilee, why stand you looking up to heaven?" As much as our Churches should leave us dumbfounded by their glory, it is not meant for us to remain staring, like immobilized spectators. The rapturous staring upon Mystery is granted by God as a privilege of grace, so that we may march into the world and accomplish the work of God in our families, our workplace, at our recreation, among our friends. Our Churches are glimpses of paradise, glances into the throne room of the King. But the last words of that King are the ones that should concern us, "...you shall be my witnesses...even to the uttermost parts of the earth." Our King commands us to change the world, but first by changing ourselves. My friends, no hesitation! Our Lord waits.

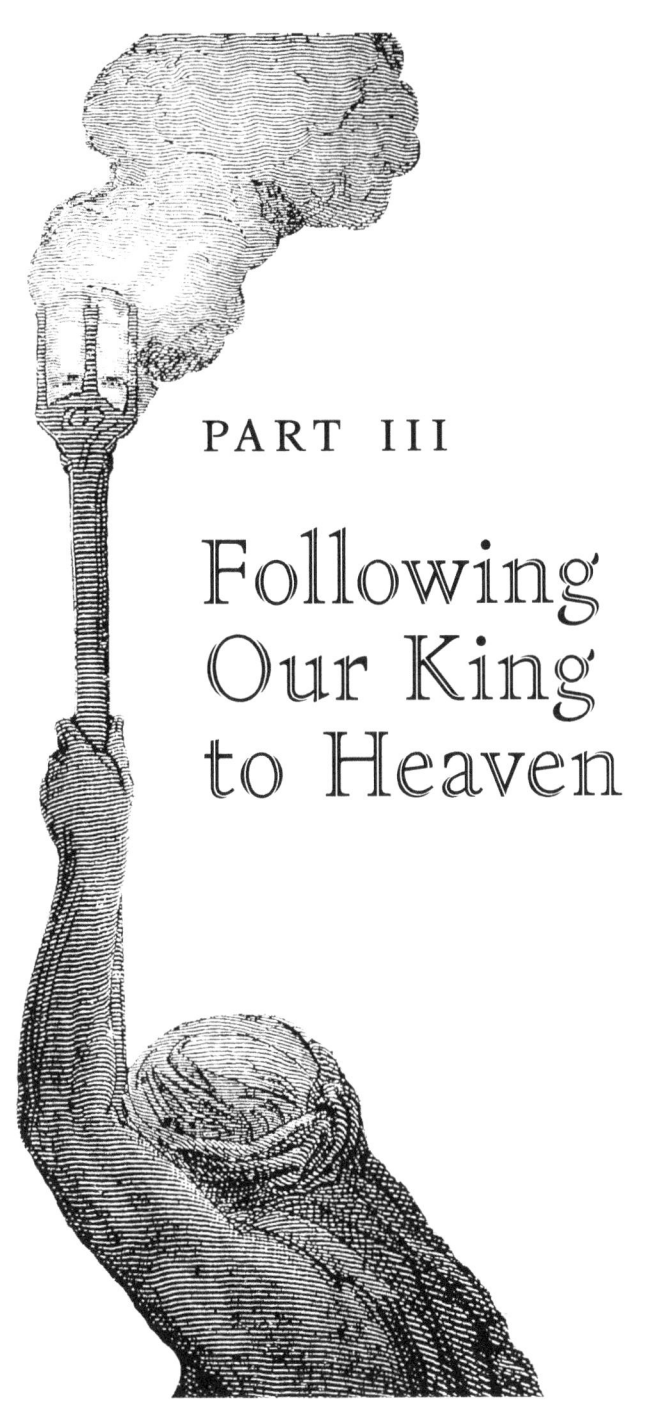

PART III

Following Our King to Heaven

8
Death and Resurrection

WHATEVER HAPPENED TO LENT?

O *America!* No, not the nation, the Jesuit monthly. It never fails to disappoint. That is, if you are a secularized, self-loathing Catholic.

Actually, that was not always its audience. When it began in 1909, it was a robustly intellectual journal of Catholic writing rivaling the tony liberal periodicals of the early 20th century. This was the heyday of liberal hegemony in American thought, with such names as John Dewey, Henry James, Woodrow Wilson, and Oliver Wendell Holmes shaping American thinking. The titanic Jesuits of that time would have none of this. They founded *America* with the intention of toppling the reigning liberal gods of the time. Issue after issue defended the Church's immemorial teaching with deep intellectual precision coupled with a dash of delectable panache.

The Society of Jesus, in 1909, did not suffer fools gladly. They were trained in an intellectual hand-to-hand combat, and they performed it with relish. Their pens were like javelins thrust at the throat of every liberal idea from law and education to the arts and public morals. *America* magazine (then a weekly) was a deliberate red flag in the face of the leftist bulls charging at the Church and the conservative pillars of the American ethos.

Today, we have a new *America* magazine. It leads the way in accommodation with the woke culture. Its *raison d'être* since 1968 (or thereabouts) was the attenuation of Catholic doctrine – and, at times, its outright denial – and a belittling of Catholic tradition. To read *America* today is to be lost in a fog of intellectual doubletalk and a chic acceptance of the zeitgeist. They work diligently to make doctrinal Catholicism appear like a fly trapped in amber.

Take Fr. Massingale who, in a March 2024 issue of the magazine, explains how he eagerly embraced the Ramadan fast:

> In the spring of 2019, after a series of high-profile attacks on Muslim people in New York City and a reported rise in Islamophobia, I felt compelled to act in tangible solidarity with this vulnerable and targeted community. It just so happened that Ramadan was starting the next day.

I decided I would observe its discipline of fasting as a way of accompaniment and solidarity.

I knew this sacred time in the Islamic tradition meant abstaining from eating and drinking from sunrise to sunset, but I discovered it was even more rigorous. You fast from dawn – that is, even before the sun rises – until sunset…

That's the gift of fasting; it attunes us with a deeper level of reality. The discipline of fasting helps me to see the world as God sees it. Fasting has helped me to look at the world around me in a new way: We are all vulnerable, but we are not all vulnerable in the same way or to the same degree.

Observe the sly legerdemain being played here. How could one not pity the poor? The disadvantaged? A closer look would discover that otherwise noble sentiment conceals one enormous fact: the disappearance of the supernatural. Where in *America's* pages can you find a horror for violating the commandments? Atonement for sin? A dwelling upon the sufferings of the Savior? Even a slight nod to the entire Catholic tradition of joining oneself to Christ Crucified through prayer and mortification.

Look as you may. You will find none of these.

But, all the blame should not be laid at the doorstep of *America*. This New Idea of Lent has invaded the entire Church. A gauzy altruism has taken the place of a rigorous program of penance and prayer.

Even more tragic is an almost complete disappearance of the Passion. Its absence is easily evident by simply glancing at the typical modern Catholic Church. In its struggle to create a welcoming space, it duplicates the sterile décor of a Ramada Inn. The iconography of the Passion has disappeared. Or, if still present at all, its modernist disfigurement is alienating. The whole project is meant to produce a metaphysical disequilibrium. Put another way, it is like a Rorschach test, making it possible to read into the formerly stolid Faith anything one wishes.

The traditional disciplines of Lent in no way ignored the primacy of holy charity – or as the ancient formulation had it, almsgiving. In fact, for two thousand years, Mother Church has consistently taught that the holy season of Lent stands upon three legs: penance, prayer, and almsgiving.

But the order is crucial.

Only by emptying ourselves through mortification and prayer can we begin to have a heart for others. That is, a heart like the Sacred Heart of Christ, not a political toady.

An example would clarify. In the days of the Old Lent, children in Catholic grammar schools were handed something called a mite box, after the widow's mite so praised by Christ, for she gave out of her want. The box was only about five inches in diameter, and the children were instructed to deposit in the box the nickels and dimes they would otherwise spend on candy and such. These mite boxes taught a profound theological lesson, all due to the image on its surface: Christ in the Garden of Gethsemane kneeling in agony.

The children instantly grasped that every sacrifice they made of their small change would be a sacrifice joined to the sacrifice of Christ. Imagine. Such mystical lessons communicated by a mere small metal box. Even a nickel took upon itself a weighty doctrinal lesson of expiation.

In the Old Lent, no action escaped the supernatural embrace of Christ, and every action was done for that transcendent purpose.

Today, those mite boxes have been replaced by some new contraption called rice bowls. The lesson is identification with the poor. Even a Marxist can be comfortable with that.

Where is the supernatural dimension? Where is the identification with Christ Crucified? The entire trajectory of the mite box was the Cross. One acts charitably because Christ demands this as union with Him. St. Paul's words ring out: "Amor Christi urget nos!" ("The Love of Christ compels us!").

The difference here is dramatic. The mite box hurls us into a domain of grace, and that is world changing. The rice bowl produces a transient titillation.

The New Lent swims in the waters of a vapid Catholicism which sees no difference in religions, miniaturizes doctrine, flattens the saintly pinnacles of perfection, and casts an embarrassing shrug at the erstwhile harsh disciplines of the Old Lent. For these belonged to a pre-1965 navel-gazing Church.

Add to this denuded Lent the tone-deaf prelates who delight in the sandbox pieties of a deracinated culture. Examples abound. Just a few days ago, one of our more prominent shepherds uttered this inanity sans embarrassment: "Blessings and graces to our Islamic brothers and sisters, because their holy season of Ramadan begins today! They're a good example to us on our Lenten journey."

Well, has it escaped this prestigious cleric that the Roman Church might have a few instances of good example over 2,000 years to make our Lenten journey more fruitful? Can he not find any more becoming way of expressing kindness to men of disparate religions other than embarrassing and slavish groveling?

But there is more to this collapse of Old Lent. In more parishes than one would care to mention, there has grown the practice of emptying holy water fonts and replacing them with gravel. This is supposed to replicate the desert experience, you see. Of course, these are the props of cheap vaudeville – nothing less than the replacement of Calvary with high-kicking Rockettes.

There is a direct correlation between the demise of Old Lent and the descent of the Church into a comic sideshow.

As the Church goes, so goes civilization. When the Church steps away from its salvific mission, the Gates of Hell march forward. When Gethsemane gives way to soap opera, man finds himself disappearing. When Catholic officialdom persist in making the Holy Faith more user friendly, then the Man Come of Age whom they seem so eager to serve and mimic will find that the Age smothers them.

Bring back the Old Lent. Before it is too late.

UNION WITH GOD OR UNION WITH THE WORLD

It would seem so, if some of the higher prelates have anything to do with it. More than a few of them, at the beginning of Lent, urged us to imitate our Muslim brothers as they undergo their Ramadan fasts.

Us imitate them? The Catholic Church had been exercising the rigorous disciplines of Lent for 500 years before Muhammad arose from the sands of Arabia. Have these good prelates forgotten the fasts of the apostles? Or the emergence of Christian men and women braving the wildernesses of Arabia and Egypt to give birth to the great eremitical and coenobitic Orders? Have St. Anthony, the Desert Fathers, or St. Simeon Stylites slipped their minds? Monasticism as it is known emerged from those centuries with the great stress upon taming the beast in man so that he becomes even more than angel.

Perhaps their lapse in memory is due to their predecessors' devaluation of the whole apparatus of atonement for sin, reparation for past offenses, and the singular value of mortification and fast? Pope Montini, after all, was driven by the need to soften the signature self-abnegations of the Church's millennial tradition as empty exercises of a benighted past. Thus, the obligatory Friday abstinence, the three-hour fast before the reception of Holy Communion, and many other worthy disciplines that had been emblematic of a robust Catholic existence were cast aside.

Whether Pope Paul VI intended it or not, the approved theological cognoscenti of the time were allowed to spin all kinds of romanticized tales to buttress this fatal mistake. One of them touted a Promethean trope, man come of age. Recognize that these ranks of enlightened thinkers were willing avatars of the decadent '60s, drinking deeply at the poisoned springs of that antinomian age. Ringing in their callow ears was that ubiquitous refrain, the age of Aquarius, so beloved by that deluded generation. For those blessed not to live through those chimerical times, it was that zodiac figure, Aquarius, who embodied a trancelike abandonment to a fanciful life of wanton self-absorption and unchecked sybaritic pursuit.

All too willing, theologians readily surrendered to this siren call, more sophomoric than theological. They traveled hither and yon preaching the message of a liberated self, pursuing the spirit of satiety. All past codes, traditions, and ordered disciplines of the Church's tradition were mocked, then proscribed as shackling the movements of the spirit. Convents emptied, seminaries were drained (or transformed), and priests abandoned their sacred vocation pleading obedience to a higher call of fidelity to self.

Most bishops of that time surrendered; others, who recognized The Lie, surrendered, mistakenly concluding that resistance was futile, rather like a flea struggling to halt a hurricane. And the sacred walls of Mother Church suffered fatal cracks.

Then there was the conceit man come of age. This emerged from the decomposing carcass of modern philosophy. The Modern Man of the '60s had long outgrown the strictures and moral code that were the narcotic of past ages. A New Illumination had arrived, and the Catholic *bien pensant* treated it like catnip.

Montini had opened the door, and it was now the obligation of these New Catholic Thinkers to remove the hinges. They screeched that the Church before 1965 (hmmm, what infallible marker could that be?), treated its members like children, with imperatives like obedience to moral law, ancient penances, and even time-honored forms of piety.

Abandoning them all was the law of the day. Beneath that mushroom cloud was Old Lent. With the firm hand of their newly won position, they displayed an unrelenting exercise of embarrassing masochism.

Pondering the wounds of the Savior? Nothing more than an unhealthy fixation.

Take note of the *au courant* Lenten symbol in most parishes and Catholic institutions: a cross without the corpus of the Savior, a purple cloth draping it. Of course, a Cross without its Corpus is a mere release from the obligation of self-conquest. Its message is a liberating move on. Would a Catholic staring at the sterile symbol comprehend the affecting words of that time honored prayer, the *Anima Christi*?

Soul of Christ, sanctify me.
Body of Christ, save me.
Blood of Christ, inebriate me.
Water from the side of Christ, wash me.
O good Jesus, hear me.
Within Thy wounds hide me.
Suffer me never to be separated from Thee.
From the malicious enemy defend me.
And at the hour of my death, call me.
And bid me come to Thee, so that
I may be joined with all the angels and saints forever.
Amen.

Lent has had its innards torn out. It emerged as a mere ghost of its former self. Is it possible for any Catholic flattened by the inanities of the kinder and gentler Lent to have their hearts moved by the Mass Propers of the Traditional Missal:

> Grant, Almighty God, we beseech Thee, that these fasts which chasten may also fill us with holy joy; so that, with our earthly affections weakening, we may more easily lay firm hold on the things of Heaven.

In those majestic words there lies concealed priceless treasures of theological precision and sound philosophical wisdom. To think, all that spiritual richness traded for a fast-food version of the Heavenly Banquet. Without the regal trappings of the Old Lent, the spine-tingling Easter Alleluias become Muzak ditties.

Or can the user-friendly New Lent register the least understanding of the grave summons of the prophet Joel still used by Mother Church to awaken the souls of her children on Ash Wednesday:

> Return to me with your whole heart,
> With fasting, and weeping, and mourning.
> Rend your hearts, not your garments,
> And return to the Lord, your God.
> For gracious and merciful is He,
> Slow to anger, rich in kindness,
> And relenting in punishment.
> (Joel 2:12-13)

This language of the Holy Spirit in the prophet sounds so strange and unwelcoming to most Catholics today. Its dramatic decree to self-divestiture is disturbing and flies in the face of man come of age. It smacks of a negativity out of place in the new positive mood set in place by our Betters from a more enlightened time.

Against this denuded Lent, perhaps higher prelates should not be blamed for invoking Ramadan. For what is there to invoke in the New and Improved Lent, shorn of all its former spiritual *gravitas*?

Pity, that some priests feel compelled to invoke the penances of a false religion (oops, terribly retrograde of me) for Catholic example.

Even more of a pity that some Catholics may remark, "O my, penance. What a novel idea."

No, Ramadan ought not to replace Lent. Not even the New Lent. Let's have the Real Lent back.

HAUNTED BY PASSIONTIDE

Every one of our lives is a drama – a story involving powerful antagonists in pitched struggle. The antagonists are sin and grace; Christ and Satan; self-love and self-oblation. These dramatis personae are further complicated by the singular dispositions, personality, background, and place of each man compounding the conflict. All of which is the *proscenium* for the staging of a man's salvation. But there is a drama surpassing all of these: the Holy Sacrifice of the Mass where Christ appears upon the battlefield of Golgotha to slay Lucifer. That Divine Victory is re-presented each time a priest ascends the steps of the altar to offer the Holy Sacrifice.

The historical antecedents for this Grand Triumph are set forth before our eyes in Passiontide. They leap before us in the ancient liturgy of the Church, where she unveils the accumulated liturgical symbols that the centuries have fashioned, leaving us in thrall. This is a drama of such magnitude that the very word drama itself takes its name. Beginning on this Passion Sunday, Mother Church surfeits our senses and rouses our souls to a pitch no human drama can match. From now until Easter Sunday she deploys the most striking symbols in her sacred arsenal.

Today man understands how symbols seize the soul without a word being uttered. Upon entering the Church we are seemingly accosted as we notice every image draped in purple shrouds. An eerie sense of foreboding envelopes us. A deafening absence leaves us unsettled. Each veiled statue seem to be covering itself against the impending horror of the Savior's Passion. Beholding the scene leaves the soul on the edge of shrieking, almost too much to bear.

Indeed, there is much bearing. Emotions swirl as the sublimity of the symbols sink deeper into the soul. A sense of isolation permeates, a disturbing sense of being left completely alone. The sharp drama of shrouds reminds of our sins which also cover our souls in darkness. Too often we have preferred that darkness to the blazing light of Christ's grace. More dreadful is the reality that the darkness is always my choice. Those calculated separations from Christ are calculated decisions to love sin more than the Redeemer. The icy state of sin is traded for the sweet warmth of Christ's grace. The shocked soul wonders how such lunacy could invade his soul. The purpled images relentlessly speak this unrelenting truth like pincers jabbing the flesh.

Isolation is followed by a crushing loneliness. For every Catholic there is a great sweetness to know that we are crowded by the Communion of Saints, each one of them available to us at the instant of a whispered prayer. These are men and women in full, and their fullness is always at our fingertips. This cloud of witnesses spurs us to imitate their heroic love, their grand sacrifices, their daunting Charity. Today, Mother Church hides them from us. It is almost as if she needs to heighten the wages of sin, showing the excruciating solitude it brings in its trail. Heaven seems almost to be taken aback at the approaching Divine Holocaust. It seems as though she shivers in shock.

Peering at the muted statues calls to mind the haunting words of St. John of the Cross in his *Spiritual Canticle*: "Outside of God, everything is narrow."

Indeed. And the hushed statues bespeak that sense of disturbing narrowness. We are forced to consider how our sins lead us down a black hole breathing the fetid air of our own self-interest. It is darkness having no room for any other—a loneliness of aching proportions. Such wisdom in the church's ensemble of sacred symbols. With typical Roman restraint, spare symbols, such as a purple drape covering the once spirited voice of those images, leaves the soul prone. The symbols speak in slight whispers, yet leave the soul deafened by its truth. The loneliness? Because sin creates a kind of entombment, a walled city of our own making.

Finally, each shrouded statue leads us to sorrow. Like the unrelenting ticking of a clock, we count the many follies of sin. Clinging to the old habits and attachments that are the wellsprings of sin. We ignore them, but ignore them at our eternal peril. All the neglect we have accumulated at the invitation of grace sent to us from the hand of a Merciful Redeemer. Cardinal Newman's words in his sermon *The Calls of Grace* indict us,

> God's opportunities do not wait; they come and they go. The word of life waits not—if it is not appropriated by you, the devil will appropriate it. He delays not, but has

his eyes wide always and is ready to pounce down and carry off the gift which you delay to use.

And then, Father Garrigou-Lagrange: "The daily resistance to grace in small points is as harmful as hail on a tree in bloom which promised much fruit; the flowers are destroyed and the fruit will not form."

To all this there is added all the hesitations, excuses, and broken resolutions to change, with no change.

Each purple shroud is an accusing finger that what is approaching for the Savior is my doing. And the silence of those shrouded images is only broken by the solemn words of the *Improperia*:

"My people, my people, how have I offended thee. Answer me. I led you out of the land of Egypt, and you have led me to the gibbet of the Cross."

THE ECSTASY AND TERROR OF HOLY THURSDAY

And it was night.
John 13:30

If you are not paying close attention, you might miss it: two small omissions in the canon of the Holy Thursday Mass. While these occur only in the Extraordinary Form, their observation and consideration unleash the chilling power of Holy Thursday for every Catholic. They produce in the soul a kind of thunderclap. As with everything in the Roman Rite, their appearance is understated and demure, which is its genius and majesty.

Both of those omissions appear in the body of the Canon. The first comes in the last invocation of the *Agnus Dei*. Ordinarily, the plea is *dona nobis pacem*. But on Holy Thursday, that cry for peace is replaced by a third *miserere nobis*. The second alteration occurs at those three prayers that the priest prays directly before his personal Holy Communion. In the first of those prayers, the initial sentence reads, *Domine, qui dixisti, pacem relinquo nobis*... (O Lord, Who said, my peace I leave you...). The prayer includes several more sentences, but the prayer in its entirety is censured.

Why both changes? Because each is invoking peace. On this Holy Thursday night there can be no peace. For a treachery of cosmic magnitude has been perpetrated. The Son of Man has been betrayed with a kiss. Where there is sin, peace becomes a stranger.

But Holy Thursday night possesses a complex duality. On the one hand, there is a burst of joy at the outset. Not only is the priest clothed in raiment of radiant white, but bells peal at the intonation of the *Gloria*. This crescendo of jubilation celebrates two of the most central mysteries of the Catholic Faith: the institution of the Priesthood and of the Holy Eucharist, instituted together by the Savior because they are inextricably linked. Both are the infallible guarantees that Christ dwells among us, even as He reigns at the right hand of His Father in Heaven.

In fact, in the Holy Eucharist, we possess Heaven and the way to Heaven. Some of the most glorious structures known to man have been built to house this wondrous mystery. All that touches this Mystery is draped in a beauty that astonishes and leaves men spellbound. Indeed, the artistic imagination so stretches itself to bespeak this Blessed Sacrament that it seems to exhaust itself in extravagant virtuosity. Whether it be sculpture, painting, vestments, sacred vessels, architecture, or music, all conspire to touch the edges of Paradise.

No one gives more eloquent testimony to this than the twelfth-century Abbot Suger of Paris in *On His Abbatial Administration:*

> As for me, I confess that I took great pleasure in devoting all the costliest and most precious things I could find to the service and administration of the Most Holy Eucharist. If, to fulfill an order from God manifested from the mouth of the Prophets, golden chalices, vases and cups were used to receive the blood of goats...how much greater is our obligation to use, in order to receive the Blood of Jesus Christ, in perpetual service with and with the utmost devotion, vases of gold, gems and everything that is considered most precious. Surely neither we nor our worldly goods can suffice to serve such great mysteries. Even if, in a new creation, our substance were changed into that of Seraphim and Cherubim, it would still be unworthy to serve the ineffable Host.

This great mystery of the Holy Eucharist would disappear from our midst without the priest. In the sacrament of Holy Orders, a man's soul is reconfigured to be *alter Christus*, another Christ. His entire identity is changed. He is no longer himself but the minister of the Absolute. His voice is Christ's voice; his hands become Christ's hands. He wears the black Roman cassock as a sign to humanity that though he is made like other men, he is no longer like other men. He exists to make Christ's presence real to a sinful and crippled world.

Yes, no man is worthy of such privilege. But Christ's divine power shines through his unworthiness, and even sin, so men may not be left orphans. St. Norbert gives a kind of rhapsodic inflection to the great mystery of the Priesthood:

> O Priest! Thou are not thou, for thou art God;
> Thou dost not belong to thyself,
> For thou art the servant and minister of Christ;
> Thou are not thine own, for thou art the Spouse of the Church;

Thou are not for thyself, for thou art the Mediator
between God and man;
Thou art not of thyself, for thou art nothing.
Who art thou then, O Priest? Nothing and everything.
O Priest, beware lest what was said of Christ in His Passion, be said of thee:
"He saved others, himself he cannot save."

Amidst this clamorous joy, an abrupt, indeed dramatic, shift occurs. The dull thud of wood clappers replaces silver bells. A dark curtain seems to descend, wresting us from elation, leaving the faithful with only bleak sorrow. A kind of dread at imminent horror. Recall St. John's words at the exit of Judas from the Last Supper, "And it was night." These words of great foreboding fall heavily upon our souls at the conclusion of the Holy Thursday Mass.

Our Lord is carried from His throne of majesty at the altar and is mournfully borne through the Church in solemn procession. This is a liturgical re-enactment of that procession of Christ from the Garden of Gethsemane. Those heart-searing words of the Savior to Judas burn themselves into our souls, "O Judas, wouldst thou betray the Son of Man with a kiss?"

The human heart sinks at the memory of the many times it has betrayed the Savior with a kiss: heart in love with the Savior, concealing a heart in love with myself. In return for all His lavish graces, ever-faithful friendship, and undeserved mercies, we reciprocate with small betrayals. Over and over, in return for Love, treason.

Such duplicity governs our souls: one day fervor, another, tepidity; one moment willingness to conquer sin, another surrender; sometimes, sincerity, other times, dissimulation; once resolution, then dissipation; sometimes courage, most times cowardice; at times truth, other times, rationalization. Indeed, for us, it is night. It is a night which seems always to overstretch us. Indeed, a night in which we often take comfort, even refuge. *Miserere, Dominus!*

All that is left is departure. The sacred rites are finished. But our parting steps are heavy. For we know all that faces the Innocent Lamb of God. Each Catholic can only exclaim: what have I done? The words of the ancient *Improperia*, chanted on Good Friday, capture this mystery. They literally plunder our hearts: "My people, my people, what have I done to Thee? How have I offended thee? Answer me."

GOOD FRIDAY:
THE START OF A NEW BEGINNING

To the sophisticated Romans of the ancient world crucifixions were a hum-drum affair. They were as routine as writing a traffic ticket. For instance, in 71 B.C. seven thousand slaves led by Spartacus revolted. After they were captured, each one was crucified. Suetonius tells us that the line of the crucifixions extended for 240 miles, from Naples to the borders of Rome. So common were crucifixions that the hill of Calvary became a Roman nickname for the place's Hebrew name, Golgotha. Usually the crucified were left hanging on their crosses for days, leaving their bodies to decay, with rotting flesh devoured by wild dogs, only skeletons remaining. The Latin term for skull is *calvus*. Since skulls on Golgotha were scattered about like shells on a seashore, why not call the hill Place of Skulls?

Though commonplace, crucifixions were not left to common soldiers. Refined skills were required for the grisly occupation. For this there was Roman legion's elite death squad – the *Quaternion*. As the name suggests it comprised four soldiers. One to tie the crucified, a second to nail him, a third to hoist him upon the beam, and the fourth was the most important. He was called the *Exactor Mortuis*, a foreman of sorts, who not only certified death, but also closely inspected every phase of torture and execution. His was the crucial task of guaranteeing maximum agony with an eye to the careful postponement of death. Not surprisingly, the Gestapo modeled much of their business upon the *Quaternion*.

Amidst the whole ensemble of crucifixion, scourging summoned the most well-practiced artistry. Singular brutality was required of the executioner as he wielded the whip with the precision of an artist's brush to his canvas. Each whip consisted of three four-foot leather cords; to whose end was attached a mature goat's sharpened tooth. The challenge was to land the whip deeply enough into the flesh, slightly twist, then rip out as much flesh as possible. Both front and back of the crucified was lacerated. With the *Exactor Mortius* keeping as close a watch as a surgeon does to his patient, soldiers were observed for either leniency or excessive sadism. Scourgings must be just right; a perverse nod to the Greek standard *in media stat virtu*. So gruesome was this feature of Roman efficiency that it called forth commentary by the fourth century Church historian, Eusebius:

> Bystanders were struck with amazement when they saw the crucified lacerated with scourges, even to the innermost veins and arteries, so that the inward parts of the body, both their bowels and their members, were exposed to view.

But on this Good Friday, the crucifixion was different. Christ was not dying for a sin committed, but for sinners. His shedding of blood was not an act of justice; it was an act of redemption. This was not a paroxysm of howling despair but a veritable feast of ravishing love. He was dying out of love for sinners, though so many of those would never love him – or never as much.

Here we are face to face with the Crucified Savior, but just as vividly, ourselves. Though we see what our sins have wrought, we are confronted with the inexplicable fact that we persist in sinning. We watch as Christ bears in his withered body every single wound of our defiance, and yet there is the incomprehensible: we persist in our defiance. We are riveted by the crown that sits securely upon his head, tethered by the rough thorns that act like fingers digging deeply into his skull. This ironic crown proclaims his majesty while simultaneously delivering to us a writ of guilt. Guilt for all our hesitation in coming to his defense when the world mocks him. Those innumerable times when his Church's teachings are vilified, and we keep comfortable distance lest we be thought unacceptable by the cultured despisers. Yet even with this bitter sight of God "as a worm and not a man" before us, we persist in our hesitation.

More importantly than these stinging indictments, we are face to face with the Savior's love for us. This Divine spectacle of love upends us even more than the price of our sins. Two of the three times that Christ weeps it is because of his broken heart. Just the day before the Last Supper, Our Lord is on a premonitory overlooking his beloved Jerusalem exclaiming, "O Jerusalem, Jerusalem, that killest the prophets, and stonest them that are sent to thee, how often would I have gathered thy children as the bird doth her brood under her wings, and wouldst not" (Lk 13:34). Jerusalem is you and me. We are the ones he desired "to gather." We are the ones who "wouldst not." Then Gethsemane, "In his anguish he prayed more earnestly and his sweat became like great drops of blood" (Lk 22:43). He longs to have us come to him, seeking the slightest gesture of love so that he can squander upon us the riches of heaven's joys. The Good Thief merely asked that Our Lord remember him in his kingdom, and for that modest plea, the Savior pours upon him mercies beyond imagination. The same awaits us. Why do we tarry?

It is 3:00 pm. Our Savior has breathed his last. Now, with a Thief following him like a loyal attendant, he descends into Hell. Not the dominion of Satan, but the Hell of the Fathers, the place where those who were faithful to Christ without knowing it wait. All from Adam to his foster father, St. Joseph, his Grandmother St. Ann and his precursor, St. John the Baptist. After he shatters the ancient rusted gates, he leads them all on a victory march. Like prisoners fleeing their gates, they must have been so delirious with joy that they stumble like drunkards. Indeed, one of the Fathers remarked that as Christ declared victory, "Adam danced." And all of Hell trembled.

We leave this Good Friday afternoon marked by the Savior's blood.

Unafraid to show the world our passion for the Faith, which alone, as St. Catherine of Sienna writes, claims "the keys of the blood."

Unafraid to tell men we belong to Christ and his Holy Bride, the Church, even as some of her very own work conscientiously to dull her bright marks.

Unafraid to obey what only pleases him, even as our enveloping culture preaches the gospel of the Almighty Man.

Unafraid to be faithful to his shed blood, even when most men enshrine the comforts of the sated self.

Unafraid to be different, even though so many struggle to fit in.

Unafraid to recognize that the mark of that shed blood demands that we change, even as the world insist that Christ change.

Unafraid that that change will demand our blood as well.

Good Friday is the start of a new beginning. It's about time the world knew that. And they will. All they should have to do is look at us.

A FRIDAY UNLIKE ANY OTHER

One might find it surprising, but it is impossible to find an image of the crucifix existing before the sixth century. Even then, the only one that can be found is carved on the massive bronze doors of the cathedral in Ravenna. It sits as a mere panel among a number of other panels, and with that, tucked away in the upper left-hand corner, easily missed by the casual observer.

This seemingly strange circumstance is easily understood by putting ourselves in the mindset of the ancient Roman world, albeit drawing its last breath. Crucifixion was one of the most humiliating sentences devised by the Roman Imperium, imposed for the most shameful crimes, involving one of the most excruciating deaths. Understandably, crucifixion was not a matter of boasting. One would want it kept hidden, like a relative who suffered execution by a firing squad. Even though suffered by a loved one, it would never be spoken of except in embarrassed whispers.

Seen that way, it is no wonder the early Church kept Our Lord's crucifixion locked away in the silence of red-faced shame. If a cross did appear, it was encrusted with jewels as a boisterous reminder of Our Lord's glorious resurrection. After all, who would not want to forget the hours of that awful Friday when the world turned dark, the earth shook and temple curtains were mysteriously torn from top to bottom. And those grisly details. Roman soldiers pounding the plated crown of thorns deep into the skull of the Savior. The blows of the hammer that spiked His hands and feet to the cross. Then, the outsized clumsy rusted nails that broiled Our Lord's open nerves whenever he tried to lift His body even a little, to relieve the strain on His hands, or to take a small breath into His drowning lungs. This was an ordeal that anyone would want forever forgotten.

Even us. Even today. It is understandable why the World turns away from the crucifixion. It sees only senseless death. Nothing else. It is exactly as the look at their lives in this world – senseless, and then they die. When John Maynard Keynes was asked about deficit spending, and the numbing legacy of debt left to our children, he quipped insouciantly, "Oh please, in the end we're all dead anyway." Spoken as a true man of the Modern World. Even worse, a certain slice of modernity sees faith in Christ as a failure to grow up: a bad case of thumb sucking into adulthood. The late Elizabeth Fox Genovese expressed the attitude perfectly. This pre-eminent professor of history and women studies at Emory University converted from the chic atheism of the University to the Catholic Faith. She later wrote of the price she paid,

> Thus when, in December 1995, I was received into the Catholic Church, my non-believing colleagues tactfully refrained from comment, primarily, I suspect, because they literally did not know what to say. more likely than not, many assumed that, having lived through some difficult years, I was turning to faith for some form of irrational consolation, consequently from their prospective, to acknowledge my conversion would, implicitly, have been to acknowledge my vulnerability... From their perspective, I had exiled myself from acceptable conversation of any kind.

But why do Catholics look away? Why has it become a seeming commandment in many Catholic churches to depose crucifixes from their sanctuaries? Why have even more replaced the crucified Savior with an epicene resurrected One? Differing theological emphasizes? Oh, no. Perhaps changing artistic tastes? Most definitely not. Something graver is afoot here. Displacement of the crucifix is always a demand for an easy Catholicism – Catholicism lite; a protest in favor of cheap grace. Hiding the crucifix is a march for a religion of short cuts, rather than the steep road; the reward of heaven without exertion; a religion without cost and redemption without sacrifice. A stretch, you say. But, the evidence abounds.

Where are the millions of Catholics boldly protesting the incursions of a crusading secularism against our Holy Religion? Most preferred the easier path of keeping quiet. Where are the large Catholic families that were the shining jewels of Christ's Holy Church? Catholics now prefer to hide from the cross and its sacrifices – electing to mimic Modern Man with his carefully planned boutique family of one and a half children. Never realizing that such chicly modern families are the very nooses from which society will hang in its unwitting suicide.

The Holy Gospel tells us that Peter kept a distance when Christ was taken in Gethsemane to face Pilate. Like Peter, we too keep our distance from Christ. We dread not fitting in. We fear the sacrifices of fidelity. We don't want to commit the faux pas of appearing too closely associated with a Church so clearly out of step with the times. In our desperation to go along with the rest, we forget Chesterton's warning that only dead things go along with the current, living things swim against it. In keeping our distance from Christ, our souls become mummified. We think we're alive – but we are the walking dead. Such a heavy price to pay for getting on with the World. Can't you hear the haunting words of the Savior, "For what shall it profit a man, if he gain the whole world, and suffer the loss of his soul?" (Mk 8:36)

When the fifth century chieftain Clovis, pagan king of the Franks, first heard the story of Our Lord's crucifixion, he shouted, "If only I had been there with my Franks!" Charming. But charmingly naïve.

We must realize that the Jews did not perpetrate this atrocity against God.

The Romans cannot be blamed.

This crucifixion is our doing.

Each time we find excuses to hide from the Cross, Good Friday stays and stays.

And Easter never comes.

LIFT HIGH THE CROSS

Strange wars are waged these days. Take the blood being spilt on most Catholic College campuses. No, no, I don't mean the red blood pouring from the knife wound on someone's flesh. I mean the more serious bloodletting – the wounds to men's souls when inalienable truths are yanked from their hearts.

That is exactly what happened so many years ago when administrators at nominally Catholic colleges decided to remove crucifixes from their classrooms. That's right. Up until only a few decades ago every Catholic student, from first graders to doctoral candidates, sat in Catholic school classrooms with a crucifix front and center. Like the incessant roar of the ocean surf whose pounding quickly becomes soothing music, so the crucifix was the ever-present reminder of He Who alone is The Teacher. Even as the professor engrossed his students with the truths of his science, the crucifix enchanted them still more with He Who is the Way, the Truth, and the Life. No one knew better than Holy Church that any classroom without a crucifix risked producing students who possessed facts but no wisdom, having it all but never knowing what any of it was for. Could Chesterton have had this in mind when he wrote of the sad state of the scientist/professor, "Who understands everything and everything does not seem worth understanding"? Those classroom crucifixes guaranteed that knowledge would be a crown upon a student's head and not a dagger in his soul.

That, unfortunately, was then. Let me tell you about how it is now. Last spring a prominent Catholic university in the Northeast planned to erect a heroic-sized crucifix in the middle of its campus. It was to be a memorial to some deceased students. Overnight the tranquil campus turned into the Gaza Strip. On one side, a group of laity and priests defending the erection of the crucifix. On the other, a group of priests fiercely opposed. Yes, opposed. Odd to find priests warring against a crucifix – somewhat like English professors lobbying for the abolition of the alphabet.

Unfortunately, this case is not isolated. It is repeated over and over again. At Georgetown, once a premier college of human learning and chest-thumping Catholicism, the administration remade itself into a proudly secularized college with a patina of chic anti-Catholicism to recommend it to the new knowledge class. At the very beginning of its evolution away from the Faith, it stripped every classroom of its crucifixes. Georgetown was rather settled in its long won secularism until a guerilla insurrection in 1998. To the dismay of Jesuit administrators, a group of Catholic students demanded the return of the crucifixes. Campus ministers (formerly, chaplains) were particularly horrified at such atavism and were eager to wield whatever weapons necessary to address it. The Catholic students would have been alone if not for the support of some faculty – Muslims. These Islamic professors suggested that it might be fitting to hang a symbol of Christian belief in a Catholic college classroom. This idea failed to intrigue the Georgetown clerisy; ministers hissed and Jesuit bosses scolded the students about their lack of fidelity – to the prevailing zeitgeist. These Catholic kids, unperturbed, dug in their heels and, in the end, prevailed against their ideologized elders. Crucifixes went back up. As far as we know, the classrooms still have them. Looks like the future belongs to Christ crucified.

More people than Catholic college administrators need to be told this story, such as the folks designing/renovating Catholic churches without crucifixes or with deconstructed ones. Some good Catholics should read them St. Paul ("But God forbid that I should glory, save in the cross of Our Lord Jesus Christ: by whom the world is crucified to me, and I to the world," Gal 6:14), or Pius XII ("one would be straying from the straight path were he to forbid the use of sacred images in Church... or order the crucifix so designed that the Divine Redeemer's Body shows no trace of His cruel sufferings," *Mediator Dei*, no. 62). Perhaps we can find a few good Catholic young people to sit down and talk with all those obdurate priests who flinch from the display of a crucifix on the altar where they offer the Holy Sacrifice of the Mass (and never mind both the 1975 and the 2000 *General Instruction of the Roman Missal* which specifically direct there to be "a crucifix, clearly visible to the congregation, either on the altar or near it" (no. 270). If those priests will not heed the terse commands of the Church, perhaps they will listen to the silken theological wisdom of Cardinal Ratzinger:

Lift High the Cross

>Where a direct common turning towards the East is not possible, the cross can serve as the interior "east" of faith. It should stand in the middle of the altar and be the common point of focus for both priest and praying community... Moving the altar cross to the side to give an uninterrupted view of the priest is something I regard as one of the truly absurd phenomena of recent decades [italics added]. Is the cross disruptive during Mass? Is the priest more important than Our Lord?[1]

So the strange wars go on. Stranger still are the victors. It is children holding crosses high, kids who are shaming their priests not in disrespect but for the sake of God. More than their elders they vividly appreciate man's role on earth as expressed so simply by Chesterton: "All human beings without exception whatever, were specially made, were shaped and pointed like shining arrows, for the end of hitting the mark of Beatitude." You can't stop people, not even kids, from standing above their time and wanting to be saints. Not even when others are trying mightily to bury them under the debris of the secular rot of their times.

But why must it be children who lead us? What happened to so many of those consecrated with the grace of Holy Orders? Indeed. But it serves no purpose here to explore the reasons for their shocking reversal of loyal ties. That only takes away from the thrill of seeing Catholic children taking up the cross again.

So what if it takes children to lead us. There is plenty of Divine precedent for that.

---

[1] *The Spirit of the Liturgy*, p. 83.

ESCAPING THE CROSS: THE UGLIEST TEMPTATION

Hundreds of thousands, if not millions, of Protestants are spending their Sunday mornings in football size stadiums. Not for sports, but to listen to their ministers preach the Gospel of Success. This new twist on the Holy Gospels renders the revelation of Our Lord as a guarantee of prosperity, good fortune and freedom from pain and suffering. Quite attractive, no doubt. But quite wrong. Without doubting the sincerity or good will of these likely fervent believers, this so-called Gospel of Success is as far from the truth of the Gospels as astrology is from astronomy. Our Lord did not walk among us and then die on Calvary to save us from suffering, but to save us from sin. No doubt Christ wills the relief of suffering, His miracles attest to that. But those are effusions of His pity, quite accidental to the utterly consuming point of His Divine Mission to redeem us from our sins. Why else would He scold, "A wicked and adulterous generation seeketh after a sign" (Mt 16:4)? Christ's Gospel is exquisitely expressed when He cries out, alluding to His being mounted on the hill of Calvary, "And I, if I be lifted from the earth, will draw all things to myself" (Jn 12:32). Hardly a Gospel of the Fortune 500.

A gripping lesson is to be learned from the *Domine Quo Vadis* Church on the Via Appia just outside of Rome. According to tradition this church is built on or near the place where St. Peter had a brief encounter with Our Lord. St. Peter was fleeing the great persecution of Christians which had been ordered by Nero. As he hurried from the perils of the slaughter, he saw Our Lord walking toward Rome. St. Peter queried the Savior, "*Domine, quo vadis?* (O Lord, where are you going?)", to which Our Savior replied, "I am returning to Rome to be crucified again." With bitter recollections of his first betrayal, he suddenly appreciated what he was about to do a second time. He turned on his heel and returned to Rome. Soon he suffered his own crucifixion, but only after begging executioners that his cross be planted upside down. He understood his unworthiness to die in the position of His Redeemer.

Escape from the cross runs deeply within the spiritual bones of each of us. Even the best of us. Our life is such that at every turn we find the sacrifice of the Cross, confronting us with the choice of embracing it or not. Struggle against our sins, there we face the wood of the Cross. Honestly addressing our weaknesses and defects without excuse, again, the sacrifice of the Cross. Fulfilling the duties to our state in life with fidelity and love is always a matter of the Cross. Exercising Holy Charity, especially to those who show us none, sorely try our patience or treat us disgracefully, most certainly entails the heroic sacrifices of the Cross. Weariness and complacency invades the souls of all of us, and each time, in each instance, the Cross summons us. Man is capable of devising the most ingenuous strategies to escape the Cross. A simple examination of conscience makes that crystal clear. But escaping the Cross is always escaping Christ.

We take all consolation from the mercy of Christ. To this Divine Mercy we all rush. Nothing less than doom awaits us without our Savior's mercy. But His mercy *is* the Cross. Some speak of mercy of Christ as though it is a detour around the Cross. Some kind of supernatural exemption from the agony of having to change our lives and conform to the Holy Will of God. This is a caricature of the Savior's mercy, robbing it of its infinite richness and depth. Our Lord's mercy is offered to us as the firm assurance that we need not fear approaching Him. Yes, covered in our sins, sometimes even with a lingering affection for them. Still, Our Lord's arms are outstretched, as if begging. All that is necessary is "O my God, I am heartily sorry for having offended Thee" on our lips, knees bent in contrition before the priest, and a heart filled with purpose of amendment. Instantly, Christ's mercy covers us like a summer shower, drenching us with the confidence that we can become saints for "nothing is impossible with God" (Lk 1:38). After all, if a thief could steal Heaven, why can't we?

For the Romans, so expert in the art of grotesque executions, the Cross was the end. For Christ, and for us, it is a beginning. We do not bear its suffering for their own sake, but for the sake of winning a happiness "That eye has not seen, nor ear heard, neither has it entered into the heart of man, what things God has prepared for them that love Him" (1 Cor 2:9). God does not will suffering for us, but eternal bliss. But for us poor children of Eve, burdened by the effects of Original Sin, bliss can only come through the wood of the Cross. *Ave Crux, unica spes,* Hail the Cross, our only hope!, as the ancient prayer of the Church declares.

Yes, we must always be wary of the ugliest temptation: wanting heaven on earth. Happiness without a price. Christ without the Cross. In 2018 a prominent Catholic congratulated a celebrity athlete on his public admission of a profound moral disorder. However noble his intention, it left the impression that it is possible to be good without being good. Oh my, Christ without a Cross. How often political systems have tried state programs that would guarantee heaven on earth: happiness without paying the price. Shades of Christ without the Cross. St. Thomas More once wrote a political treatise on a country where everyone was always happy. He titled it *Utopia,* which is the Greek work for nowhere. Few have grasped the irony. Commenting upon the political temptation to creating a state where everyone earns the same, enjoys the equal amounts of happiness, and no one ever has to work too hard, the political philosopher Donoso Cortes remarked, "Imagined utopias always become real hells."

Catholics must ever by wary of the ugliest temptation. Christ cannot be loved without the Cross. We must never try to find heaven in this world of ours, the vale of tears. The only place we will ever find Heaven is in Heaven.

O DEATH, WHERE IS THY...TICKLE?

Death just isn't what it used to be. That is, if the conversation I heard the other day was any indication. It was at a modest restaurant where a number of joined tables were accommodating a rather large family. My ears shot up when I heard the odd phrase 'bereavement team.' Odder still was the seventyish, Italian woman saying it. Trendy phrases like that are expected from soccer moms or deracinated chancery bureaucrats, not from an affection-oozing lady who could easily be pictured over an outsized, dented, aluminum pot stirring tomato sauce.

That wasn't all. This large ethnic woman, perfectly imagined praying at a Sacred Heart novena, began comfortably gabbing about a questionnaire required by the Liturgy Committee for Grandpa Tony's Mass of the Resurrection. Incongruities were flying. It was as if Jimmy Durante had been delivering a lecture on Deconstructionist epistemology. What was happening here? Who turned that good Italian lady's soul inside out?

As complex as Churchill's definition of the Soviet Union – "A riddle wrapped in a mystery inside an enigma" – is the villain of that Italian lady's anomaly. It is a Modernism wrapped in secularism inside sentimentality. This numbing error has taken not only holy doctrine hostage but has done the same to the God-given web of noble emotions accompanying those truths. After modernity impaled religion, it knew its work had only begun. It now had to reconfigure man himself. He could no longer weep over Old Things like death or sin or disloyalty. Man had become the New Man, or in a construal more suited to readers of a certain age, man had come of age.

Those New Men now weep over new things like intolerance or being judgmental or indifference to difference. At one time, the Church's impregnable battlements protected us from such New Men. No longer. Those thick walls have been breached. Our Italian lady is proof enough of the fissure. It's the old Italian woman on the outside, but it's the New Man on the inside.

Only two generations ago, men faced death as the Church did—with her ancient liturgy replete with glorious paradox, that eye-popping device that Chesterton explained as "Truth standing on its head to attract notice." Men once sat close to their humanity, relishing all its mysteries, even ghoulish ones like death. Glance again at Homer in the *Iliad* or Leonidas and his 300 at Thermopylae. See what I mean.

But what were those paradoxical truths which Mother Church pointed to with her wise finger? There were two: death's terror and Christ's conquest. Denying either is to be left with neither. The Church began with the inescapable natural truth of death's shattering tragedy: one which was only an echo of the more primordial catastrophe of Adam's Original Sin. Death was part of the slime heaving from the festering swamp of Original Sin: unnatural, painful, and utterly punishing because it was decreed by God to be a punishment.

For all of its fearfulness, the Church never cheated her children of death's sublime, albeit mournful, reality. As a Catholic brought his beloved into the arms of Mother Church for the final supernatural farewells of her Requiem Mass (properly called "Requiem" because of the then, and even now, first words of the Introit prayer, *Requiem aeternam dona eis, Domine...*, "Eternal rest grant unto them, O Lord..."), she looked for every opportunity to lecture about sin and its harrowing consequences.

For instance, after the Epistle, the choir would moan the piercing stanzas of the Requiem sequence *Dies Irae*, "Dies irae, dies illa/Solvet saeclum in favilla/Teste David cum Sibylla" ("Day of wrath and terror looming/Heaven and earth to ash consuming/Seer's and Psalmist's true foredooming"). This is certainly light years apart from the treacly, therapeutic Muzak familiar to most Catholics today (I suppose some things are worse than death). Excising the grim stuff of death only results in producing papier-mâché men, able to speak only of lifestyle and never of life. But bid man gaze at truth's depths and you will find truthful men of great depth.

If Samuel Johnson was right in saying that nothing concentrates a man's mind more than hanging, the Church knew it first. She understands that nothing rouses our souls to existential clarity and fervent prayer more than death. Everything in the old Requiem Mass forced us to consider death and God's judgment, Christ's mercy and our complacency. Enveloped in that Requiem's splendor, what man does not fall to his knees to pray both for himself and the deceased, now standing naked before Christ's eyes? The smarmy stanzas of On Eagle's Wings simply shatter beneath this theological weight.

In the past, every distraction from those grand truths was chased away by the majesty of her Requiem. All the senses of a Catholic were tutored by the mystery: he sat spellbound as he listened to the haunting Gregorian chant; stared uneasily at the eerie, unbleached, yellow funeral candles flanking the coffin; then was strangely consoled by the brooding black priestly vestments which gave fitting salute to the realities of man's fallen condition. Every symbol conspired in a profound wonder that acknowledged searing sorrow even as they refused to be conquered by it.

Yet, through all that grim reality of death, the other side of the paradox revealed itself. Christ shone through like some blazing horizon, glowing all the more brightly because of the liturgy's carefully articulated dread. Anything less airbrushes death's terror and miniaturizes Christ's victory. The old Requiem palliated none of the stark edges. Rather, it armed us with the grace to stand erect and carry their awful weight manfully.

Pity those who rob death of its metaphysical punch by dressing it in the epicene white folds of unctuous sweetness and light. For them, there is Flannery O'Connor's stinging rebuke in her introduction to *A Memoir of Mary Ann*:

> In the absence of the Faith now, we govern by tenderness. It is a tenderness which, long since cut off from the person of Christ, is wrapped in theory. When tenderness is detached from the Source of tenderness its logical outcome is terror. It ends in forced labor camps and the fumes of gas chambers.

Slightly overwrought, you say? Look at Lewis's *That Hideous Strength*, with the inhuman atrocities of the futuristic committee acronymed N.I.C.E. Or Huxley's *Brave New World*, with its mummified humanity suckled at the teats of the Master State. But leave fiction aside, just glance at what modern culture nonchalantly tolerates in the name of compassion. Overwrought? Hardly.

Even when we rightly pray to St. Joseph for that much desired happy death, there is still the paralyzing horror of separation.

Nothing can soften that agony, as St. Bernard of Clairvaux testifies when he weeps at the news of the death of Gerard, his first companion in religion and a close collaborator in his work. He declares,

> You tell me not to weep? My bowels are torn out; shall I have no feeling? Nay, if I suffer, I do so with my whole being. I am not made of stone; my heart is not a heart of bronze. I confess my woe. It is carnal, you say? I know that well for I know that I am a creature of flesh and blood, sold under sin, delivered unto death and subject to suffering. What would you? I am not insensible to grief; I have a horror of death, both for myself, and for my own. Gerard has left me, and I am in pain; I am wounded unto death.

Alas, paradox again. Hope in Our Lord's mercy is sharpened even as death's lessons are made more graphic. Is this what Dorothy Sayers was trying to tell us when she wrote in *Creed or Chaos?*: "It is hopeless to offer Christianity as a vaguely idealistic aspiration of a simple and consoling kind; it is, on the contrary, a hard, tough, exacting and complex doctrine, steeped in a drastic and uncompromising realism." Tell that to the sunny priest giddily dispatching his bereavement teams, or commanding you to be happy at the next Mass of the Resurrection you attend.

Better yet, quote him St. John Henry Cardinal Newman:

> We like to abandon ourselves to the satisfactions of religion; we do not like to hear of its severities. The age, whatever its peculiar excellences, has this serious defect: it loves an exclusively cheerful religion. It is determined to make religion bright, sunny and joyous.

Or, when he hollers about not being in the spirit of the new liturgy, show him Our Lord weeping over his friend Lazarus. The spirit of the new liturgy must have passed Him by too.

When St. Paul thunders, "O Death, where is thy sting?" (1 Cor 15:55), he admitted that it was a *sting* that death inflicts. Modernity turns it into a tickle. Bereavement teams and Liturgy Committees make what was once the solemn committal unto God's throne of Judgment into a piece of Disney kitsch. Lay people undoubtedly labor on these things with the very best intentions. Little do they know that they are being used as props in the dehumanization of man, to say nothing of the trivialization of God.

But what of the old Italian lady? How can she prefer the

grave assurances of the solitary priest to the gauzy hugs and smiles of a team? Wouldn't she quickly surrender the liturgist's slickly bureaucratized questionnaire for a simple Rosary with Fr. Brown? Of course, she would. If only she could be left alone to be herself. But modernity and Modernism won't let her.

No surprise. If they won't leave death alone, how can old ladies stand a chance?

PURGATORY

In Dante's *Purgatory* each of the souls struggling their way to Paradise have seven marks engraved upon their heads. Each one is the letter "p" – "p" for *peccatum*, the Latin word for sin. As the souls makes their way higher and higher to Heaven, one by one the p's disappear, until the soul enters the vestibule of heaven, and the p's are gone altogether. Poetic insight joins here with theological precision.

Seven p's upon the soul's forehead represents the seven capital sins to which all men are prone. Their gradual disappearance is the result of the comforting purifications of purgatory.

Purgatory comforting? So teaches Holy Church. Souls confined there are called holy for this reason. Their souls are being washed clean in the burning fires of God's love. Certainly there is pain. But the knowledge that a necessary purgation is occurring as prerequisite into heaven is reason enough to sustain the pain with elation. Other reasons for joy exist for the Holy Souls: no temptation to sin taunts them any longer; they have no fear of Satan's lurking presence; their waiting will conclude in the perfect splendor of heaven.

No understatement should be made of the soul's torments in purgatory. They are quite real. So it is that they are called poor. Actually the first and primary reason for this attribution is their ontological state: with death they are no longer to elicit any free acts. Only life on earth affords that blessing. Souls in purgatory are left only to the consequences of the acts they performed when alive. They can pray for us; they cannot pray for themselves. Their time in purgatory shall not be lessened until the purification set by God is complete. Only one thing can shorten their purgation: your Masses, prayers and sacrifices.

How do the poor souls suffer? First, they know acutely the absence of God and know even better how much they want Him. This suffering is indescribable.

Have you ever felt the separation of a loved one? Their betrayal? Abandoned inexplicably by an intimate friend? That is a gnawing and implacable pain. Multiply these by factors of one hundred and you will know the torment of the Poor Souls.

Moreover, they no longer enjoy the luxury of distraction. Distraction is a blessing that occasionally set us free from our miseries. In purgatory there are none. Souls train their attention only on God and being with Him. Time seems to stand still.

Ever watch a pot boil? You get the idea. Apart from all that the soul is plagued by the constant regrets over its sins. Not only that they were committed, but also that they are the reason for their long separation from God in heaven.

Much to think about in November.

RESISTING A COUNTERFEIT EASTER

To celebrate Easter properly, we should probably recall Luca Signorelli's 1499 masterpiece *The Sermon and Deeds of the Anti-Christ*. It now hangs in the Chapel of San Brizio in Orvieto. Upon first glance, it appears that Christ stands in the foreground. Then the observer realizes that it is not Christ at all. It is an imposter. More than that, it is the anti-Christ, indeed Satan. But how is this discovered? Only an informed Catholic eye could know.

The devil points to his heart. But isn't this a common gesture of the Savior since the marvelous revelations of the Sacred Heart to St. Margaret Mary Alacoque? Yes, but something is conspicuously absent: no wounds on the body of Christ. In the many counterfeits of Christ through the centuries the dead giveaway of a false Savior is a smooth skin unburdened by the wounds of Golgotha. Those wounds alone mark the presence of the true Redeemer; the other, a counterfeit one.

Counterfeit Christianity always delights in showing the heart of Christ, but not His pierced heart. From that seemingly harmless symbolism tumbles the inverted creed of Counterfeit Christianity. It centers not on sacrificial love but on sentimental luv, a perennial temptation for all the fallen children of Adam and Eve. Even the thoroughgoing existentialist Albert Camus echoed this truth when he wrote, "Future generations will be able to summarize our culture in two propositions: they fornicated and read the newspapers." This faux Christianity turns the Gospel's truth inside out by dictating bonhomie as its ironclad imperative.

This comic reversal of the Cross's grandeur provoked the disgust of Graham Green, causing him to impatiently reply with delicious contempt, "When I hear the summons to brotherly love, I think of Cain and Abel." Instead of Christ Crucified they sententiously preach the approved jargon of their decaying culture blended with cliches which choke rather than chasten. Their hollowness is captured by T. S. Eliot in *The Love Song of J. Alfred Prufrock* with pitch perfect scorn: "I have measured out my life in coffee spoons."

Resisting a Counterfeit Easter

The ultimate fate of those wedded to this Counterfeit Christianity is to sink ever more securely into the morass of self-satisfaction.

This is a rank betrayal of Easter. It is God's greatest triumph because it is the victory of the Cross. Therein lies the soaring joy of the Third Day, and it will sound through the corridors of eternity. No separation is possible: The Crucified One *is* the Risen One.

During the time of the Great Terror, that immediate aftermath of the closing of the Second Vatican Council, a great effort was mounted to erase much of historic Christianity. Sterile catch phrases replaced immemorial teaching. One of the more insipid was a newly coined attribution for Catholics: an Easter People. Sophomoric as it was vacuous, it fully captured Counterfeit Christianity: a religious identity without Calvary. The barren phrase has mercifully disappeared, but its spirit has not. It hangs over many a church and sacred liturgy like dripping tar. Sadly, it enters into the soul slowly, albeit surely, with corrupting effect.

Page after page of the Holy Gospels give the lie to this fraud. When Christ stands at the empty tomb, He stands wearing the wounds of His crucifixion like so many trophies. For His Risen Body *is* His Crucified Body; the Risen Victory *is* the proclamation of the Golgotha triumph. In the upper room, Our Lord encounters the doubting Thomas like a victorious general returning from battle. Recall what the Savior does: He sets the apostle's hands in the holes where the spear pierced and the nails sat. Note that as soon as the Savior bids the Apostles "peace," He shows them His wounds. Such a gesture is a resounding blow to those who would effeminize Christ and neuter His bracing summons to take up our cross and follow Him.

Treacly smiles, language of inclusion, and cheery ditties will simply not do. They disappear like pieces of dust in a conflagration. Even now, Christ stands at the right hand of His Father in Heaven in His glorified body made all the more beautiful by the Calvary ribbons. Of these sacred wounds, St. Thomas teaches "They illuminate the precincts of heaven like rubies and sapphires."

Venerable Fulton Sheen once wrote that the *Via Pacis* is the *Via Crucis*. This is his variation on the ancient ejaculation, *Ave Crux, spes unica*. Without the Cross, life is bereft of joy, hope, and peace. Here the paradox of Christianity hits modern man like a racing comet, leaving him dazed. The great Bishop continues with words that easily cut against the grain of Counterfeit Christianity: "God hates peace in those who are destined for war." The secularized Catholic finds this a bridge too far. They shriek, "We are a religion of peace." But for that kind of inanity, they must take up their case with God Himself: "Think not that I am come to send peace on earth: I came not to send peace, but a sword" (Mt 10:34). What war? What sword? The only true one: the war against sin; against error and the world's lies; against our weakness and compromises; our complacencies and indulgences. These are the only wars worth fighting. Victory in these wars brings peace.

Let good Catholics revel in the joys of the Risen Christ. Let us not tire of repeating the ancient antiphon: Christ is Risen; He is truly Risen. Let us bask in the mystery of the empty tomb. But let us not forget whence this perfect divine victory comes—only from the resounding defeat against Satan and his Hellish Kingdom. And that, by the weapon of Christ's invincible Cross. Beware the Counterfeit Christ. He will woo the unsuspecting with messages that rest comfortably on the fallen nature of man. He will speak a language of rapprochement with the spirit of the world. And it will sound oh so reasonable, oh so sweet.

Settle only for the real Risen Christ, the One Who invites us to rest in His wounds. Insist only on God.

EASTER: LAUNCHING THE REVOLUTION OF THE CROSS

In the year AD 132, Emperor Hadrian punished a Jewish insurrection by leveling all of Jerusalem. His engineers selected Calvary as the site of the Forum and capital of the new city *Aelia Capitolina*. He erected a statue of Jupiter over the Holy Sepulcher, and of Venus over the spot where Christ was crucified. In Bethlehem, Hadrian built a temple to Adonis over the site of the Manger.

There will always be something in man eager to bury Christ's victory over Satan. Whether it be Roman emperors building cities over Calvary. Or, Jacobin fanatics enthroning the Goddess Reason on the high altar of Paris's Notre Dame Cathedral. Or, Joseph Stalin exploding 72,884 churches in Russia.

It must not be thought that this fever is restricted to the more obvious enemies of the Church. They are too easily recognizable, leaving us to a deceptive somnolence.

The most formidable enemies of Christ are the ones who bear His title and anointed privileges.

Their betrayals are far more lethal, for they are more unexpected. Invested with trust by God's little ones, they are more easily led away to bury Christ's victory. Their naivete serves the aims of the *trahison de clercs*.

No Roman emperor could bury Christ more effectively than one cleric who preaches a Christ without the Cross or a religion of sentimentality, rather than redemption. Outrages against Christ don't come principally from blowing up churches but refashioning the exacting moral teaching of Christ. Can anything more securely bury Christ's victory than this proposition of the German Synodal Way, winning their bishop's vote by a majority 176 to 14: "(we call for) the blessing of same-sex couples on the basis of a reevaluation of homosexuality as a norm variant of human sexuality."

Christian-loathing Roman emperors could never outdo this.

Permitting divorced and re-married to Holy Communion is more insulting to Christ than a hundred persecutions from Communist governments. Theatricalizing Holy Mass delivers more

Catholics into the jaws of a sterile faith than all of Stalin's gulags. Trading the stringent balm of Christ in the holy sacrament of Confession for the therapeutic babble of accompaniment is to become the friends of sin, not the "friends of sinners" (Mt 11:19).

When Successors of the Apostles maintain a safe silence in the face of LGBTQ+ propaganda, they are burying the victory of Christ more effectively than Hadrian burying the Holy Sepulcher under the statue of Jupiter. Permitting pro-abortion Catholic politicians to receive Holy Communion is far more malicious to Christ than building a pagan temple to Adonis over the manger at Bethlehem. Of course, decades of dissimulating theological debate over the issue only aggravates the offense. Aren't clerics such as these terrified by Hebrews 10:19–39?

> If we sin deliberately after receiving knowledge of the truth, there is no longer remains sacrificed for sins but a fearful prospect of judgment and a flaming fire that is going to consume the adversaries. Anyone who rejects the law of Moses is put to death without pity on the testimony of two or three witnesses. Do you not think that a much worse punishment is due the one who has contempt for the son of God, considers unclean the covenant-blood by which he was consecrated, and insults the spirit of grace? We know the one who said: "Vengeance is mine: I will repay," and again: "The Lord will judge his people." It is a fearful thing to fall into the hands of the living God.

St. Columbanus of the fifth century swept down from Holy Ireland into the darkness of Western Europe identifying himself and his towering, ruddy and fearsome monks, Revolutionaries of the Cross. They were fearless in challenging the regnant paganism, not announcing a détente with it. They happily destroyed pagan temples and sacred pagan totems so that the bright fires of the Cross's Revolution could blaze for all the world to marvel.

These herculean priests traveled pagan Europe with the Revolution of the Cross which would never leave men's souls the same again. Their apostolic work calls to mind the laments of an Anglican cleric in the nineteenth century, who groaned, "When St. Paul entered into towns, there were riots. When I come into a town, they invite me to tea."

Easter is the unleashing of the Revolution of the Cross. It should be unsettling, like an earthquake. Wondrous, as the explosion of galaxies. Penetrating, as the sound of a thousand marching armies.

Easter: Launching the Revolution of the Cross

Under the deadening hand of secularism, Easter has become a genteel rapprochement with the world; a time to go-along to get-along. Easter's raw and transformative divine power has undergone a vicious *reductio ad absurdam*. It is now a mincing wide-eyed bonhomie. For all intents and purposes, Easter has been reconfigured to mean the nullification of the Passion. Useless is the Cross. In the anthem drone heard in most parishes and pasted on cheap felt banners: We are an Easter People.

Nowhere is this more painfully obvious than in the theatrical burlesque now being passed off as the Mass of Christian Burial. Through this disfigured funeral rite, most Catholics have been bullied into believing that everyone who dies has already won the palm of heaven's victory. Consequence? No prayers and suffrages required for the deceased, severing one of the bulwarks of Catholic piety and soteriology. Any wonder why the offering of Mass cards for a happy repose is a thing of the past? Look no further than here.

This re-booting of the Easter Mystery camouflages its blinding grandeur in a shroud of lifeless grey. It renders its majestic impact a mere cartoon: All are saved by the fact of merely being human. Or, in the argot of the day, being a good person. Calvary is rendered a fussy historical curiosity. For man now lives his life without God. This is full-court Pelagianism. Detestable in the time of St. Augustine; even more detestable now.

The ancient aspiration proclaims *Ave Crux, Spes Unica* – Hail the Cross, Our Only Hope! How much that aspiration makes reimagined Catholics squirm.

But the Resurrection confirms this! No merit accrues from the Resurrection; only the Crucifixion saves us from our shipwreck.

Easter makes of us all the Revolutionaries of the Cross. Without that sweet Revolution, other dark, very dark, revolutions will triumph.

And they already are.

HEAVEN IS ONLY IN HEAVEN

No morning passes these days when a Catholic does not wake up to the unsettling presence of that two-headed beast that roams about our society: secularism. One of its heads is atheism—modern man's passion to be god, and the other is utopianism—man's other obsession to turn this world into some kind of heaven. These are twin evils, feeding off one another. Seldom can a culture survive their terrors. Christ's grace alone can slay them.

Christ's grace alone lets us even see them, for their greatest triumph is to convince men that they are his greatest triumph. Thus, Walt Whitman in *Leaves of Grass*: "Nothing, not God, /Is greater to one/Than one's self is." Percy Bysshe Shelley is even more chilling in *Prometheus Unbound*, when he shrieks at an image of Christ Crucified, "O Horrible! Thy name/I will not speak/ it has become a curse." Indeed, this is nothing less than a beast in our midst.

Today, atheism appears with two faces. More familiar is the face of man emancipating himself from all manner of authority save the authority of the Self. Whittaker Chambers called this the cult of Almighty Man. Not only does God fall before Almighty Man, but morality, religion, law, the family, and even gender itself. The second face of atheism is more insidious, as it is camouflaged in the smarmy vanities so beloved to secular man.

This species of atheism does not toss out God but merely relocates Him. The Old God was purely God; the New God is now Me. An eminently convenient switch: for God is now being me at my best. With his usual trenchancy, G. K. Chesterton saw this new God (actually atheism for the fainthearted) for the fraud it truly is: "Of all the horrible religions the most horrible of all is the religion of the God Within. For when Mr. Jones is speaking to the God within, Mr. Jones is only speaking to Mr. Jones."

Secularism's other side is utopianism, the idea that man can create a perfect world here and now. It is a relentless ideology that brooks no opposition as it strives for a designer universe, made in the image and likeness of one fanatic, or, more likely today, a faceless team of experts at a drawing board. Sometimes it is a Marx, most times it is a seemingly anodyne bureaucracy that promises everything and leaves man with nothing. Bloated assurances of a risk-free existence are touted with one obligatory mandate: that eyes be closed to the means for obtaining them.

Things that once were horrifying are today viewed as the price of progress. Who protests now that the wombs of women have been turned into killing fields in the breathless quest for the perfectly timed, perfectly healthy, perfectly wanted, and perfectly formed child?

Perverse ideas of equality are commonplace where all must have the same thing, by everyone coerced into surrendering everything. Add to these the terribly modern aspiration for a world without physical or emotional pain or slightest inconvenience. All of this is purchased at a very high price, the sacrifice of our very humanity. Yet, before this ruthless cost, modern man raises nary a whisper of protest.

Before such formidable foes, mankind's only defense is the Ascended Christ. Deeply woven in the ineffable folds of this feast's mysteries are the instruments of our victory. Christ leaves this world, a world affectionately crafted by His loving hand, to take the majesty of His Sacred Humanity to the world of Heaven. He often taught us that "my Kingdom is not of this world" (Jn 18:36). Our imaginations stumble before this mystery. It becomes easier to comprehend if we consider that if the Savior created this world with such dazzling loveliness, what possibly awaits us in this Kingdom to which He ascends. Truly, we would be the dullest of men to treat this world as any kind of proxy for the Kingdom where He now reigns at the right hand of His Father.

Our Savior instructs us that He leaves this world only "to prepare a place for you" (Jn 14:3). It is foolhardy to settle for a home here when God announces that He is waiting for us in a home that sates every desire without limit. Dr. Johnson remarked once, "Man's entire endeavor is to be happy at home." In that sage insight, he was reminding us that joy is not to be found in grand projects, cerebral philosophies, or accumulated wealth, but in the profound delights of family and the very simple things that surround them.

Heaven is the enlargement of those joys beyond what any man could fathom. Trying to fit Heaven into the meager vessel of this world results in shattering both—with devilish consequences. Gulags and concentration camps were attempts at creating a perfect world—a heaven—on earth. Only hell results. Eliseo Vivas expressed it piquantly: "imagined utopias are always the real hells."

Without demeaning the beauty of this world, the Ascended Christ raises our eyes to the perfectly beautiful one. This world is only a proving ground where we deepen the most important possessions of any man—Faith, Hope, and Charity. As these become greater and occupy vaster parts of men's souls, this world is seen for the very small—albeit "very good" (Gen 1:31)—place that it is. As grace expands our souls, we clearly see that expecting Heaven's joys here in this world is like trying to capture a sunset in a thimble, or squeezing Halley's Comet in a bottle. Without demeaning the beauty of this world, the Ascended Christ raises our eyes to the perfectly beautiful one. This world is only a proving ground where we deepen the most important possessions of any man—Faith, Hope, and Charity.

Mother Church is so right to call this world of ours a valley of tears; not that we are perpetually sorrowful, but that we are perpetually disappointed. We desperately crave Heaven, and this world is simply not it. To be sure, Catholics will make of this world what God wants it to be, each one of us carefully honing all the powers with which He has blessed us.

But we shall never expect from this world what we only expect from the next. Grace furnishes us with a supernatural immunity to utopianism. Leo Strauss wrote that modern man is fated to the "joyless pursuit of joy" precisely because he demands from this world what this world cannot give. Catholics know where joy is found, so they possess joy, making their joy the envy of the world.

Even the best of Catholics must be reminded of Our Ascended Savior's blessed truths: that this world is not Heaven; only Heaven is Heaven. Seems to be simple enough; but even the best of us persist in trying to find in this world what Our Lord is saving only for the next.

9
Spiritual Combat

LOVE'S VIOLENCE

But above all things have constant mutual charity among yourselves; for charity covers a multitude of sins.
1 Peter 4:8

Speaking of charity always involves great risk. Especially these days. Modernity run amuck has so bruised the word charity, or love, that its original meaning is barely recognizable. It must first be noted that the very term charity (*caritas*, in Latin; *xaris*, in Greek) is the love that God has for man, and him for God. So demarcated, its privileged status raises it far above the parodies given it by our sensate culture. In the Catholic economy the term has nothing to do with feeling, sentiment, subjective judgment, common friendship or bonhomie. It is as far from those as a candle flame is from the blazing inferno of the sun. Care should be shown in deploying the word love or charity. Both words have suffered defacement. Love has become synonymous with oleaginous feeling or the hegemony of the self. Charity has become attenuated into a thin philanthropy. Good Catholics must avoid this *Scylla* and *Charybdis*. Only the truth of Christ will assist us to sail safely through these imposing hindrances.

All of this helps us understand the enigmatic verse of St. Peter, "Charity covers a multitude of sins." Of course, he was merely echoing the words he had heard from the lips of Christ defending the Magdalene, "Wherefore I say unto thee, her sins which are many, are forgiven; for she loved much" (Lk 7:47). Whom was the Magdalene loving? Clearly, Christ Who is God. Here we peer into the heart of love – which is the love of God, and the love of others out of love for Him. The greatly misused text of St. Augustine comes into proper focus, "Love God, and do what you will." When we love God and burn to do His will, then we choose our every act and thought to please him. So, 1 Corinthians 10:31, "Whether therefore ye eat or drink, or whatsoever ye do, do all to the glory of God." These revealed texts caused St. Thomas to culminate his sublime teachings on love[1] with: "Charity is the

---

[1] *Summa theologiae* II-II, QQ. 23-27.

form of all the virtues." In his rather clinical vernacular, he is teaching a truth of explosive dimensions. Every virtue, cardinal and moral, all have as their end the love of God.

Reflecting St. Thomas, St. John of the Cross, in his last mystical work, *The Living Flame of Love*, memorably writes, "In the twilight of our lives, we shall be judged on love." Wasting no time, twentieth century revisionists twisted this elevated text into mawkish drivel. Their shallowness could never grasp the grave allusions to the Last Judgment when Christ in glory thunders, "Verily, I say unto you, inasmuch as ye did it to one of the least of these, ye have done it unto me" (Mt 25:40). Of course, the most perfect demonstration of love is Christ hanging upon the Cross. In fact, it becomes the paradigm and model of all love. This is the gift of oblation where one ceases to pause for comfort, self-interest, ease or convenience. Its only joy is the joy of the other. Indeed, charity "covers a multitude of sins."

Henri Daniel Rops calls this the "Revolution of the Cross." The estimable church historian traces the human race's quest for God in religion and notes the conspicuous absence of love. These ancient religions certainly displayed fear of the gods, propitiation to the gods, punishment for disbelief in the gods, exquisite temples for their gods. But never a mention of love. Though Judaism was the preparation for Christianity, it still failed to manifest the primacy of love. Daniel-Rops elucidates:

> While Judaism...on several major points gave the religious hearts- searchings of the world answers which were perfectly correct ones, (it) could not assume the decisive role which Christianity was to have, because its abstract monotheism alienated too many mystically inclined souls and because its narrow legalism completely failed to possess the influential force of the doctrine of love.

To the surprise of many, Aristotle and the Greek masters never speak of love. In the *Nicomachean Ethics* Aristotle praises the virtue of magnificence, the creation of grand physical works for the polis, but even that is done for purposes of self-aggrandizement. One would imagine the Stagirite's profound teaching on friendship (canonical texts for Aquinas) might finally utter the name of love. But it does not. Appreciating these gaping lacunae, St. Augustine, in his *City of God*, admits that scars mar his beloved Roman Empire. He confesses that even its apparent virtues are contaminated by self-love, and damningly calls them glorious vices. Against this barren civilizational backdrop, the earth shook at the sound of Our Lord's doctrine on the primacy of love. It was like springtime after a long and bitter winter. No man had heard or seen such a thing. It was truly a Revolution, with the vast ancient Roman Imperium as its first conquest. Even the brief attempt of Julian the Apostate in the mid fourth century to revive the cult of the pagan gods comes to naught. As if in final surrender, the dying emperor crying out at the A.D 363 Battle of Marianga against the Persians, "You have won, O Galilean!"

We are finally left with St. Peter's command, "Have mutual charity among yourselves." The injunction demands heroism. Thus, Richard of St. Victor in the twelfth century writes his challenging work, *On the Four Degrees of the Violence of Love*. Seems counterintuitive, doesn't it? Violence in the same breath as love. But it dramatically captures the essence of charity. The divine virtue does violence to our self-love, vanity and pride. How deeply the precept of charity plunges its sharp dagger. Think of Bernini's spectacular *Ecstasy of St. Teresa* in the Cornaro Chapel of Santa Maria della Vittoria in Rome. It is considered one of the cultural masterpieces of the High Roman Baroque. The eye is drawn to two details. First, the saint's posture of total surrender to Christ. Her mouth ajar reminds the observer of St. Augustine's piercing lines in the *Confessions*:

> Thou didst call and cry aloud and didst force open my deafness. Thou dost gleam and shine, and didst chase away my blindness. Thou didst breathe fragrant odors and I drew in my breath; and now I pant for Thee. I tasted, and now I hunger and thirst. Thou didst touch me, and I burned for Thy peace.

Then there is the arrow. This strange detail unveils the mystery. An angel hovers above the Saint and is prepared to thrust an arrow into her St Teresa's heart. Alas, the violence of love: indescribably sweet while simultaneously agonizing. Thus, the angel discharges this task with a smile. No little amount of pain is entailed in laying aside grudges and emotional wounds, slights and injustices, unfair injury and insult, ruffled feelings and shattered expectations. To conquer these cherished imperfections, clutched so tightly to our breast, is a violence: a pain beyond any physical suffering.

This crucial pursuit of the love of God has been undermined in the Church for the past half-century. Longing for perfection has given way to something called spirituality. Clearly the term has possessed a legitimate meaning in the history of the Church, an exploration of the varied ways that saints have adopted in the attainment of that precious goal of sanctification, viz., Dominican spirituality, Franciscan spirituality, Benedictine spirituality. Each one of these holding to the doctrinal lineaments of sanctification, but each with a slightly different emphasis, resulting in a lovely new key of interior orchestration. Their reliability stamped by Catholic tradition and the Church's stamp of approval. But this once venerable theological term has borne the same blows as charity and love. The new 'spirituality' is merely a sterile exploration into the wonders of the Inner Me—a witch's brew of Freudian *cul de sacs* and Buddhistic nihilism topped with a veneer of occasional Christian wording. It leads not to the Cross but to the raising of the Imperial Self.

This Revolution of the Cross must pass through each of our souls. But violence will come. If it doesn't, we languish in the land of the Unconquered. A land far from Christ.

CATHOLICS AS "STRANGERS"

More than a few passages in the Bible can cause Catholics a bit of a shiver. Take, for instance, "When the Son of Man cometh, shall he find faith on the earth" (Lk 18:8). Or, "Think not that I am come to send peace on earth; I came not to send peace, but a sword" (Mt 10:34). Then there is this, "And if thy right hand offend thee, cut it off, and cast it far from thee" (Mt 5:30). Amongst all these, one perplexes more than the rest, "I beseech you, as strangers and pilgrims" (1 Pet 2). Of course, faux biblical experts will take their scythes of Higher Criticism and reduce these divine passages to a mound of husks. These *bien pensant* render the pages of Holy Writ a theological dust bowl. True devotion to the Word of God first proclaims that it is true. Then seeks its meaning from the Church: the millennial Tradition of the Church Fathers and Doctors, as well as her Sacred Liturgy. These are wellsprings that yield riches truly Divine, refreshing and enlivening the souls of men.

Perhaps the epistle of St. Peter should occupy our attention for a moment. His salutation gives many modern Catholics pause.

He addresses us as "strangers"? Strangers? The first Pope's description of us is stamped with the fire of the Holy Spirit, and there can be no doubt as to its veracity. It can only be understood by properly grasping the world in which we find ourselves. That world ought to be strange to us, not strange in the sense of wicked, but strange in the sense of foreign, unfamiliar, far beneath our aspirations. Indeed, this world, as lovely as our good God has created it, is not our home, not where we should be, not where we belong. Each of us has been created for joys far deeper, far higher, far more infinite. Chesterton expressed it perfectly: "For the Catholic, it is a fundamental dogma of the Faith, that all human beings without exception whatever, were especially made, were shaped and pointed like shining arrows, for the end of hitting the mark of Beatific bliss." Though we accept our fate as dwelling in this valley of tears, it is not the state for which we created. It is ectopic, a disjunction of Original sin.

It is within this ontological strangeness that innocence finds its home. It stands as a principal trait of the Catholic striving for sanctity. It would be a betrayal of its nobility if it were misunderstood as a callow naiveté. Innocence is not a shrinking embarrassment before evil, nor a childish ignorance of all things wicked. It is not a cartoon; it is a heroic canvas. Its splendor lies in its all-consuming love of the good, making sin something uninteresting, unworthy of attention. O yes, innocence knows wickedness well, but loves goodness more. It avoids sin not out of Puritanical stiffness, but from an extravagance born of having seen the face of the Crucified Savior. It feels strange in the presence of sin because it is something so alien to the longings of its heart.

Yes, for Catholics this world is indeed strange, or should be. It is this mystery to which St. Augustine gives the memorable words on the very first page of the *Confessions*: "Thou has made our hearts, O God, and our hearts shall not rest till they rest in Thee." Every good and blessed delight that God showers upon us in this life is only a morsel of what awaits us in the ecstasies of Heaven. C. S. Lewis's words, like a golden key, unlocks the mystery:

> The books or the music in which we thought the beauty was located will betray us if we trust them; it is not in them, but only comes through them. And what comes through them is longing. These things – the beauty, the memory of the past, are good images of what we what we really desire, but if they are mistaken for the thing itself, they turn into dumb idols, breaking the hearts of their worshippers. For they are not the thing itself: They are only the scent of the flower we have not found, news from a country we have never yet visited.

So it is that Holy Church begs her children to acts of mortification. To keep our eyes on that which befits our dignity, not on the fleeting flashes of this world's delights. Not that we should not love these created things, but we love them with an ordered love, all ordered to God. No one illustrates this more than St. Francis of Assisi, whom Chesterton said, "Taught (the world) how to enjoy enjoyment." If not for consistent bodily penance man will fall in love with shadows, leaving the glorious Reality behind. So stands the plight of Modern Man – to become infatuated with shadows, which is madness. Chesterton once more: "Catholicism is sanity preached to a planet of lunatics."

The "pilgrim" is an appellation less opaque. We poor banished children of Eve suffer an exile from which we desire relief, always searching for the place where we truly belong. How else to describe our mission in this world? We are on an adventurous search for a perfect happiness not be found here. We are nomads desperately hunting for the pearl of great price. Pilgrims are on their way to a prized destination. We rest occasionally, but only as a pause as we necessarily make our way forward. St. Thomas rightly defines man as *homo viator* (man on the way). The journey may be strewn with obstacles, but the pilgrim tackles them, then, moves steadily forward. In W. H. Auden's poetry, "stumbling forward, rejoicing." No room for sentimentality here, only the blazing truth of the Church. Urgency beckons. There is a place where we must be; no tarrying; no self-pity at setbacks; no falling back due the severities of the climb. Only joy that we are on our way, that God has marked out for us the way, and that His graces guarantee our final arrival home. Herein lies the reversal of Leo Strauss's melancholic description of modern man's dilemma: "the joyless pursuit of joy."

Modern Man has made the world, not the place through which we pass, but the place beyond which there is nothing to pass towards. He has buried himself in a tomb of his own doing, and makes merry of his entombment. This devoted immanentism of Modern Man has even breached the walls of Holy Church. Rare is the mandate from her pulpits of saving one's soul, but to saving the environment. Such sacerdotal myopia does not grasp that the environment is indeed sinfully wasted, but only because man has first wasted his soul. Unusual are the sermons enjoining us to the love of the Cross, instead, the cheery duty of assisting others to be at ease with their sins. The Savior bequeathed to His Holy Church only one mission, to carry us to heaven. It is salvific, not sociological. All other temporal concerns, *sub aeternitatis*, are only mirages fashioned in the laboratories of Hell.

Lamentably, not a few voices in the Church preach this humanitarian message, rather than a redemptive one. Lacking the sparks of transcendence, their message cheats man and makes him a spiritual dwarf. He is consigned to the sentence of never knowing the thrice Holy God, and, and therefore, never knowing himself. These deracinated members of the First Estate would miniaturize Christ to fit the demands of the zeitgeist. They are pleased to ban the crystalline teachings of the Faith for a gruel of Neo- Marxist analysis and post-Modern rubbish. Isn't this feeding the flock scorpions when they crave bread?

Aurel Kolnai, distinguished Hungarian political philosopher, dramatically diagnosed this malady when he wrote: "The worshipers of Baal professed a more genuine religion than many present adherents of a vague and threadbare religion soaked in humanitarianism." Even in places where Catholics enjoy the blessing of spotty Catholic truth, it is still bedeviled by blinkered clerics who fervently kneel before the world, in the evocative phrase of Jacques Maritain. With toothy good cheer they proffer a happy talk Catholicism. No scorpions, perhaps, but certainly bubble gum instead of bread. Where is the majestic Catholicism that meets the challenge of Victor Hugo, who, with great *gravitas*, rightly told of man able to make of his soul a sewer or a sanctuary. Where is the summoning "Athanasius contra mundum!"?

Peter's salutation to all of us as "strangers and pilgrims" perfectly embraces our vocation on earth. Unless we work each day to make of ourselves strangers in this strange exile, then we shall ever be strangers to Heaven.

AN EMBARRASSING FEAST FOR A "REIMAGINED CHURCH"

S light squeamishness settles about the minds of a certain kind of Catholic one Sunday a year. Reimagined Catholics, that is: Catholics more at home with *America* magazine and the *National Catholic Reporter* than *The Baltimore Catechism* and the unredacted *Lives of the Saints*. You know, those Catholics quite comfortable with Mr. Biden warmly received at our altar rails; or, ones giddy at the prospect of accompanying Catholics in their drift from the millennial doctrines of the Catholic Church. This feast is equally unsettling to the vast majority of Catholics in parishes who have received a steady diet of deracinated Catholicism and welcoming Unitarian liturgies. All of them would rather this feast pass as quickly as possible.

The feast of Christ the King trumpets a robust and sanguine Catholicism that brooks no compromise. It presents Christ as triumphant over the world, sin, and death. It proclaims Christ, Who mandates: "Go ye therefore and teach all nations" (Mt 28:19) and, "So then because thou art lukewarm, and neither cold nor hot, I will spew thee out of my mouth" (Rev 3:16).

It is a feast that does not sit well with dialogue, equivocation, and respecting the process. Or with those who would like to finesse the Faith with more nuance. Even the word triumph makes a certain kind of Catholic bristle. After all, Catholics have been solemnly taught for decades to fit in and embrace a carefully massaged Catholicism that makes no demands except to prescribe (in Maritain's arresting phrase) "Kneeling before the world."

When Pope Pius XI, in 1925, promulgated this feast with his encyclical *Quas Primas*, he wrote:

> The faithful, moreover, by meditating upon these truths, will gain much strength and courage, enabling them to form their lives after the true Christian ideal. If to Christ our Lord is given all power in heaven and on earth; if all men, purchased by his precious blood, are by a new right subjected to his dominion; if this power embraces all men,

it must be clear that not one of our faculties is exempt from his empire. He must reign in our minds, which should assent with perfect submission and firm belief to revealed truths and to the doctrines of Christ. He must reign in our wills, which should obey the laws and precepts of God. He must reign in our hearts, which should spurn natural desires and love God above all things, and cleave to him alone. He must reign in our bodies and in our members, which should serve as instruments for the interior sanctification of our souls, or to use the words of the Apostle Paul, as instruments of justice unto God.[35] If all these truths are presented to the faithful for their consideration, they will prove a powerful incentive to perfection. It is Our fervent desire, Venerable Brethren, that those who are without the fold may seek after and accept the sweet yoke of Christ, and that we, who by the mercy of God are of the household of the faith, may bear that yoke, not as a burden but with joy, with love, with devotion; that having lived our lives in accordance with the laws of God's kingdom, we may receive full measure of good fruit, and counted by Christ good and faithful servants, we may be rendered partakers of eternal bliss and glory with him in his heavenly kingdom. (no. 33)

Observe the tone: apodictic, unequivocal, and resoundingly clear. Not a scintilla of ambiguity; not the slightest hint of accommodation to the zeitgeist; not a hint of softening sharp edges. This feast is unafraid to announce that Christ and His Holy Catholic Church alone are the hope of the world. He has won the triumph; we must cast His victory throughout the whole world.

This kind of certitude creates disquiet in a reimagined church. These attenuated Catholics are left deeply disturbed by that one, true Church talk. Such are sure the Catholic Church does not possess all the answers. She is only a possible answer among a plenitude of answers. This attitude calls to mind the interview of a British journalist interviewing an Anglican clergyman. "Sir," the journalist queried, "Does it alarm you that your churches are nearly empty? What about belief in God?" To which the Anglican replied, "Well sir, we are not opposed to that sort of thing, if some find it desirable."

Many of this species of Catholic have long spurned the supernatural mission of the Church, advancing a political/social agenda more in conformity with a secular model. For these trailblazers, the Church is more akin to an NGO, whose entire charge is seeking equity (whatever that may be) for the masses. If this is redolent of another kind of agenda birthed in the mid-nineteenth century, you would not be mistaken. It is understandable that this feast's dramatic stamp of triumph would lead many Catholics of a certain disposition to embarrassment, if not rage.

There are other aspects of the feast that alarm the reimagined Catholic. It is manifestly clear that Christ our King requires that He be sovereign over every part of our lives, private and public. Not a few Catholics would take umbrage at that blunt summons. Over the past century, there has been introduced a softer and gentler Christ. One who ought not be called a ruler but a chum; one who does not lead, but accompanies. One who does not ruffle old errors, but affirms them. For such as these, Christ is one who seeks adjusted men, not redeemed ones.

Look no further than the manner in which Holy Mass is celebrated in most parishes. It appears more like the annual parish variety show than the unbloody sacrifice of Calvary. Notice how a posture of solemn adoration has been replaced by a casual bonhomie, at best, or a noisy after-hours club, at worst.

Then there is the reception of Holy Communion. Ah, there is the real tale. Typical Communion lines are akin to a stroll with friends, rather than an encounter with the All-holy God, whom the old Catholic Communion hymn proclaimed, "Let all mortal flesh keep silence." Where is the "fear and trembling" of which St. Paul writes? It is not hard to imagine the jump from this to the attitude that everyone is welcome to Holy Communion. After all, who dare deny anyone the opportunity for such a stroll?

This paradigm does not see Holy Communion as a sign of union with the will of the Savior and a hunger for greater surrender to His grace. Rather, the reimagined model is therapeutic, nonjudgmental, and affirming. The mantras of this distortion have become so familiar as to become comical: the "altar rail (as if there were any still left standing) is not a battlefield," or, "We don't want to make the Eucharist political," and on, and on, and on. In the meantime, the doctrine of the Eucharist fades, and souls wither. Doesn't this remind you of Belloc's terrifying lines:

> We sit by and watch the barbarian, we tolerate him. In the long stretches of peace, we are not afraid. We are tickled by his irreverence. His comic inversion of our old

certitudes and fixed creeds refreshes us; we laugh. But as we laugh we are watched by large and awful faces from beyond; and on these faces, there is no smile.

No. True Catholics glory in this feast of Christ the King. For us it is a drum beat summoning us to battle. Battle against our sins, our infidelities, our hesitations and rationalizations. It is the bugle cry rousing us to march against the enemies of Christ and His Holy Church.

A story is told in Thucydides's *History of the Peloponnesian War*. As the Athenians were deciding on a course of action against the Spartans, the elders of the city ordered all the citizens to assemble in the great Amphitheatre where matters could be voted upon. Two of Athens's premier orators were chosen to address the crowd: Asclepius and Demosthenes. After Asclepius delivered his oration, the Athenians all remarked politely, "How well said." After Demosthenes had spoken with his consummate oratorical skill, the Athenians leapt to their feet and shouted, as in one voice, *"Charge!"*

This feast is not for us to sit back comfortably and say, "How lovely."

This feast demands that we stand together and bellow, *Charge!*

CATHOLICISM IS ABOUT SWORDS

It may seem like a lifetime ago, but some may still recall the habited Catholic nun who spoke at the Republican National Convention of August 2020. She held up her Rosary and exclaimed: "This is our most powerful weapon!"

With lightning speed, a post appeared on social media from a priest. He moaned that the good nun's declaration was an unfit statement for Catholics: "Too bellicose," he moaned, "We are a religion of peace."

Such gauzy drivel has been filling the heads of Catholics for some half-century, gaining traction because it pours from the lips of those in authority. It has enfeebled the Church and left the Faithful enervated, susceptible to any stray intellectual virus concocted by the cancel culture. The Jesus-gets-us agitprop Super Bowl commercial and the February 2024 LGBTQ+ desecration of St. Patrick's Cathedral are both graphic examples of its encompassing ooze.

Nothing short of kneeling before the Enemy.

This unchecked malady besetting Mother Church has left our Catholic patrimony dimmed. A Trojan Horse has invaded the walled City of Christ's Bride, looting and plundering the Church's rich inheritance of doctrine, moral law, liturgy, and tradition. And as the enemy rolled out from the horse's belly, they sacked and effaced with singular purpose. Many Catholics found themselves helpless and destitute. Indeed, generations of Catholics watched in horror as the honor of God and His Church were mocked.

By the grace of God, many Catholics have risen from their dazed shock and have seen the Big Lie burying the truth of God. They have recognized that the Faith is not about a fey peace but of manly war. We have been fashioned by the grace of the Holy Spirit to raise not white flags but gleaming swords. Effete surrenders do not mark us, only the dust of war. The dear Father of that epicene remark should read and reread Matthew 10:34 and know that Our Savior means what He says when He thunders, "I have not come to bring peace but the sword." And not a stack of biblical criticism can change that.

Our Faith is about swords, not hand-holding.

Swords first wielded at ourselves, our sins. The first warfare is the interior one where we march into battle declaring war on anything that keeps us away from God. This is the meaning of St. John of the Cross's *nada, nada* as steps leading souls in the Ascent of Mount Carmel. Each level of that mountain is a *nada* (nothing), a stripping of all that magnifies the self and its conceits. In the affecting prose of Fr. Gerald Vann:

> It is so easy to lose vision and love. God gives you an insight into reality, a glimpse of Himself, which would take you deep into His love and far in His service: but the superficialities call to you, the world unlit by vision calls to you, and you may roll a great stone between you and what you saw, and go your way, and the vision is lost. But He rolled the stone: it must always be ourselves, it is never God, who will erect the barrier: the only obstacles are those we make ourselves. God is always pursuing us with His love; it is we who try to escape, to blot out the vision. We blot it out by prolonged, deliberate disobedience; we blot it out by open rebellion, by hatred, to which prolonged disobedience can lead; we blot it out by becoming hardened in indifference, which means indeed a gradual closing of all avenues to the greater world of eternity, a severing of all our roots, a stifling of all the deepest elements in our being, so that in the end, unless we turn back again, desolation inescapably follows, the mover of immovable separateness and loneliness of hell.

This first sword of Catholicism in the past half century has been turned into a welcome mat for the zeitgeist. Theologians eager to spread the gospel of accommodation have reworked the battle against sin into a softer therapeutic of self-affirmation. Calvary is embarrassedly shunned so that spirituality centers could reign. *Mea culpas* are traded for "have a good day," and contrition disappears to make room for accompaniment. True compassion, shown in rescuing those entangled in the web of sin, becomes an exercise in managing the web more effectively. Purveyors of this bogus Catholicism earn the damning words of St. John Henry Newman:

> We like to abandon ourselves to the satisfactions of religion, we do not like to hear of its severities. The age, whatever its peculiar excellencies, has this serious defect, it loves an exclusively cheerful religion, it is determined to make religion bright, sunny, and joyous.

At which point we have no religion but only parlor games.

Only changed men can change the world.

The second sword follows directly from the first. When Catholics become serious about their sanctification, they instantly become equally serious about the activity of conquering evil in the world and in our beloved Church. Every prayer reaches its consummation in action, action to spread Christ's love where it has become suffocated by the lies of the age and the *trahison des clercs*. For every Rosary, there must be the conquest of an enemy of Christ. Our motto must become the one forged by St. Dominic to his friars: "contemplare et aliis tradere contemplate," contemplate and then pass the fruits to others.

This counsel has already been taken to heart by increasing numbers of Catholics. In a twist of Divine Mercy, the very crisis in the Church has galvanized many into warriors, spurring them to heroic action. Growing numbers of the faithful will not stand idly by any longer. They are banding together in small pockets of resistance to stand with the angels, again pealing *Gloria in Excelsis Deo*. Catholics, young and old, bright and ordinary, are steadily recalling the courage of Catholic martyrs who, facing vicious enemies, dauntlessly shouted *Viva Cristo Rey!*

With characteristic Catholic hearts, they do not react harshly to shepherds who sleep. With hearts trained on the heart of their King, they refuse to wag their fingers at guardians who cheered the Trojan Horse while expelling the Savior's faithful little ones. No. They have risen simply to be about the work of restoring the beauty of God's Holy Church. The late Thomistic scholar Dr. Frederick Wilhelmsen voiced all of this with lyric expression:

> Catholicism is...the Mexican Jesuit Father Miguel Pro blessing his Marxist firing squad in Mexico with the stumps of his arms after the barbarians had finished cutting them off. It is Spanish soldiers charging Communist trenches with fixed bayonets and rosaries... Catholicism is about an army marching through history chanting the *Te Deum*. Catholicism is about swords.

It is also about St. Nicholas striking the heretic Arius at the Council of Nicaea for denying the divinity of Christ. It is St. Ambrose denying entrance to Emperor Theodosius into his Milan cathedral for perpetrating the Thessalonian Massacre of 10,000 citizens in 389.

More and more Catholics must enlist in this supernatural struggle. More must raise swords of holiness and truth. Swords against our reservations, hesitancies, and rationalizations to surrender in silence. Swords of doctrine against the mendacity of those who have trimmed our glorious Faith for too long. Bright, glistening swords raised bravely, unafraid of any foes, no matter where they be found, no matter their title, no matter their official attire. More and more Catholics must enlist in this supernatural struggle. More must raise swords of holiness and truth.

In the 1970s, in the teeth of the Great Terror (aka: Spirit of Vatican II), a lone gallant Catholic, Brent Bozell, created an intellectual Catholic journal named *Triumph*. He intentionally gave it that name to tweak the noses of the regnant Catholic Left plunderers. That crowd loathed what they called the Triumphalism of pre-Vatican II Catholics.

By that they meant Christ's Victory over the world through His Catholic Church. Their position? To grovel before the unredeemed world. To imitate it. To become a part of it. To comfortably fit in. To make their agenda the agenda of the Church.

It was a vertiginous time, when every Catholic certitude was mocked. Mr. Bozell decided to stand in defiance of the Great Betrayal. He did this by decisively proclaiming that Catholics do stand for triumph. We are indeed members of a Triumphant Catholic Church, who alone administers the fruits of Christ's Triumph.

Fellow Catholics, join the Triumph.

Stand with Mother Church, who now kneels in her Gethsemane (but not for long).

For faithful Catholics are rallying under the *vexilla regis* – under Christ's banner. And only one thing lies ahead.

Victory.

THE PROPERLY ANGRY CATHOLIC

Of late, anger has fallen on bad times. Especially in the Church, where the consecrated processes of dialogue and toleration have rendered conviction taboo. Since anger is the fusillade aimed at conviction dishonored, it too stands beneath a cloud. In this kind of gauzy world a St. Polycarp would have no place, especially with his memorable remark to Marcion, "You are the first born of Satan!" What of St. John Chrysostom who condemned the Empress Irena for her worldliness from the pulpit of Hagia Sophia? Or, St. Ambrose scolding a kneeling Theodosius for the slaughter of thousands in Thessolonica. Saints like these, and thousands more, would seem like misfits in not a few sophisticated Catholic circles today. Our precious Catholic patrimony has become dimmed by the muting of Catholic indignation. A Trojan Horse invaded the walled City of Christ's Bride. And as the enemies poured out from the horse's belly, they sacked and effaced with singular purpose. Too many Catholics watched helplessly, supinely. Indeed, generations of Catholics looked on as the honor of God and His Church were mocked. Epicene gestures will not do. Only sanguine courage.

The disappearance of anger presages the eclipse of a passionate standing with Christ. It also signals a sickly attenuation of human nature. Men without anger are only half-men: Men who hold very little dear. Anger is a noble human passion to be enlisted in defending the most ennobled natural and supernatural goods. St. Thomas teaches, "The good is never more fittingly defended than when it is defended with passion." Problems with anger come not from becoming angry, but from not becoming angry in the right way, in the right cause. Notice, the Catholic is not enjoined to refrain from anger, for that would be extracting a vital cog in the apparatus of achieving the good and attacking the evil. Anger is essential in the ensemble of human passions that assist man in being himself.[2]

---

[2] See *Summa theologiae*, I-II, Q. 23, art. 4.

The late Thomist scholar, Dr. Frederick Wilhelmsen, expressed this in his typically stirring style, "Catholicism is...the Mexican Jesuit Blessed Miguel Pro blessing his Marxist firing squad in Mexico with the stumps of his arms after the barbarians had finished cutting them off. It is Spanish soldiers charging Communist trenches with fixed bayonets and rosaries... Catholicism is about an army marching through history chanting the *Te Deum*. Catholicism is about swords." Swords that Our Lord commanded us to wield when declaring He had not come to bring peace (Mt 10:34). Swords of holiness and truth. Swords taken up first against our own sins, defects and smelly mediocrities. But also swords of doctrine against our duplistic enemies. Bright swords, raised bravely unafraid of any of Christ's foes.

But how does one of the Seven Capital Sins become a virtue? Why does sanctity itself demand anger? Before we set right reason to clarify this issue, let us turn to the Word Incarnate. In the Gospel of St. Matthew Our Lord is absolutely livid when he reproaches the Pharisees: "Woe to you scribes and Pharisees, hypocrites; because you are like to whited sepulchers which outwardly appear to men beautiful, but within are full of dead men's bones, and of all filthiness... You serpents, generations of vipers, how will you flee from judgement of hell?" (Mt 23:27,33).

Of course, there is the riveting scene of a rare display of Our Savior's pique when he lashes out at the blasé indifference of the Temple moneychangers: "And Jesus went into the temple of God, and cast out all them that sold and bought in the temple, and overthrew the tables of the many money changers, and the chairs of them that sold doves: And he saith to them: It is written, my house shall be called a house of prayer, but you have made it a den of thieves" (Mt 21:12-13). With these divine actions it is certain that anger is not only tolerable, but an integral spoke in the wheel of sanctity. Any lingering doubt is chased by the pungent words of the book of the Apocalypse, words that send shivers down our spine: "But because thou art lukewarm, and neither hot or cold, I will begin to vomit thee out of my mouth" (Apoc 3:16). That same book cities the reason for such timidity, "Thou hast lost thy first love" (Apoc 2:3). Quite simply: no love, no anger.

St. Thomas Aquinas heeds this divine pattern, even as he deepens the theological and philosophical tradition, when he teaches that anger is a part of the cardinal virtue of fortitude. Thus,

> Whereas fortitude... has two acts, namely endurance and aggression, it employs anger, not for the act of endurance, because it is guided by the reason by itself, but for the act of aggression for which it employs anger... since it belongs to anger to strike at the cause of the sorrow, so that it directly cooperates with fortitude in attacking... Hence the Philosopher say (*Ethics* iii, 5): Of all the cases in which fortitude arises from a passion the most natural is when a man is brave through anger, making his choice and acting for a purpose, i.e., for a due end: this is true fortitude."[3]

St. John Chrysostom writes in his *Commentary of Hebrews*: "Anger is often useful because it is by nature designed for waging a war with demons and for struggling with every kind of sin." Our Lord and his great saints are declaring anger holy when it is passion against those things that stand opposed to God's glory. It curdles into sin when its use is twisted by self-interest, precipitousness or toward an elicit end. No man must mistake timidity for meekness. Our Lord's anger shatters such confusion. Fire used properly sustains life; improperly, destroys it. Man's passions are no different. God Himself has embroidered human nature with passions, hence they are good. Used according to right reason, guided by the grace of Christ, these passions accomplish grand things. Similarly, evil is crushed most effectively by incited passions. Look no further that St. Joan of Arc or St. Bernard of Clairvaux in the preaching the First Crusade.

Bravery and anger are inextricably bound. Once we begin to calm our passionate anger against enormities like abortion, same sex marriage, or contraception we gradually fall into a settlement with these evils. Toleration cedes ground to the enemy, and he begins his next assault on higher ground than he did before. Each time we pause, moved by faux mercy, the enemy does not. It is a dangerous naivete that supposes compromise or quiet on issues close to the heart of the enemy will leave the enemy less our enemy. Such weaknesses only feed his appetite. So many in the Church have simply mimicked the entire West in its effete courting of détente with vice. Aleksandr Solzhenitsyn's famous address to the Harvard graduates in 1978 was like a stinging slap across the face of the genteel *bien pensant*. Recall his words:

---

[3] *Summa theologiae* I-II, Q. 123, art. 12, ad 3.

A decline in courage may be the most striking feature which an outside observer notices in the West in our days. The Western world has lost it civil courage both as a whole and separately, in each country, each government, each political party, and, of course, in the United Nations. Such a decline in courage is particularly noticeable among the ruling groups and the intellectual elite, causing an impression of a loss of courage by the entire society. Of course, there are many courageous individuals, but they have no determining influence on public life.

Perhaps Catholics need to remind themselves that theirs is the triumph of the Cross. To be a part of the Church is to inherit triumph. Smiles on the faces of martyrs proves this. Once convinced that we are members of a Church triumphant, it is not long that we realize that we are privileged members of a Church Militant. While this classical ecclesiological term is no longer fashionable, it is one that the gates of hell dread Catholics rediscovering.

Christ was indeed angry at the money changers. He knew that sometimes there is no other way of awakening souls half-dead. Perhaps it is time for more Catholics to imitate the Savior. A Christlike anger is just the thing to reverse all the reversals piled up by those who accommodated sinners and their sinful actions over these many decades with broad smiles.

Try it. You'll be in good company.

THE PLACE OF JOY IN TIMES OF CRISIS

On October 22, 1939, less than two months after England declared war on Germany, C. S. Lewis wrote his memorable essay, *Learning in a Time of War*. It was a brilliant piece explaining how the desire for truth was such an exalted vocation for man, that not even the terrors of war should distract from it. This essay borrows from Lewis's profoundly Christian insight.

First, permit me to bring you back to the mid-1950s.

Alger Hiss, the notorious State Department spy, had just been sent to prison. Not on the charges of espionage (which the House Committee on Unamerican Activities had failed to convict him) but on the charge of perjury.

The star witness who had brought this traitor to the attention of the American people was a former Communist himself, Whittaker Chambers. Brilliant writer and senior editor of *Time* magazine, he had published *Witness*, his odyssey from a Communist agent and atheist to American patriot and Christian. It was a *tour d force*; a gripping tale of Communist tactics and conversion, graced in the elegance of his magical style. These struggles left Chambers resolute, albeit decidedly saturnine.

Fascinated by Chamber's spiritual struggles, the writer and conservative firebrand William F. Buckley lost no time in befriending Chambers. In a now-famous letter to Buckley, Chambers wrote with his characteristic melancholy:

> I never really hoped to do more in the Hiss case then give the children of men a slightly better, only slightly better, chance to fight a battle already largely foredoomed... How odd that most of the world seems to have missed the point in *Witness*; that it seems to suppose that I said: "Destroy Communism and you can go back to business as usual." Of course, what I really said was: "This struggle is universal and mortal and only by means of it, on condition that you are willing to die that your faith may live, can you conceivably recover the greatness which is in the souls of men. When I left Communism, I knew I was leaving the winning side."

Such a brilliant assessment. Yet shot through with a deadening despair.

Catholics can certainly identify with his unsparing account of our present condition, but not with his gloom. Or they shouldn't. Satan's great temptation in these dark days is to strangle our spirit and leave us with nothing but the darkness. And that darkness leads to madness: a madness of irrational conclusions, unreasonable strategies, intemperate actions, and uncareful speech. How pleasing to the Prince of Lies to watch the best and brightest Catholics yield to this chaos rather than joining arms to make war upon it. Our lesson should come from Sarah, Lot's wife. As they fled Sodom and Gomorrah God commanded them to not turn around and look back. Sarah did. And she turned to salt.

It is always a defeat to steadily gaze at the chaos, for gradually our souls turn to salt. Even a doctrinaire Nihilist like Friedrich Nietzsche possessed the genius to recognize the ugly powers of evil, "Do not look long into the abyss, for you will find it looking back."

Clearly, Catholics have the obligation to know perfectly the evil they face, but not to obsess about it. Such rot does not deserve our attention. We look enough so as to conquer. No more; no less.

C. S. Lewis gives compelling and ingenious commentary to this fascination with chaos in his *Screwtape Letters*, shining with uncanny insights. In this passage replace noise with gloom as Screwtape, a senior devil, counsels his beloved nephew, Wormwood:

> Music and silence – how I detest them both! How thankful we should be that ever since our Father entered hell – though longer ago than humans, reckoning in light years could express – no square inch of infernal space and no moment of infernal time has been surrendered to either of those abominable forces, but all has been occupied by Noise – Noise, the grand dynamism, the audible expression of all that is exalted, ruthless, and virile – Noise, which alone defends us from silly qualms, despairing scruples, and impossible desires. We will make the whole universe a noise in the end. We have already made great strides in this direction as regards the Earth. The melodies and silences of Heaven will be shouted down in the end. But I admit we are not yet loud enough, or anything like it. Research is in progress.

Chambers made a fatal turn in declaring that, in abandoning Communism, he left "the winning side." No surprise. He did not enjoy the light of the Catholic Faith. If he did, he would have known that as a Catholic he was on the winning side.

Martyrs embraced their death enveloped in this bright supernatural confidence.

Confessors, like Francis Xavier, traveled the world proclaiming the Holy Faith and planting the Holy Cross in faraway places.

Heroic souls like St. Peter Claver boarded stomach-turning slave ships in Columbia so that he could console and baptize African slaves.

Why? They knew they were on the winning side.

Similarly, ordinary Catholics today take the Faith to non-Catholics despite every effort by not a few clerics to peddle the fraud of universal salvation. They do, because they know they are on the winning side. Special graces inspire them, even as some Shepherds in the commanding heights of the Church impose a ban on what they call proselytizing.

Being on the winning side is accompanied by a singular and unruffled joy. Too often some Catholics forget that the certain sign of God's favor is the presence of the fruits of the Holy Spirit, which may be a result of too much YouTube and too little *Baltimore Catechism*. Recall the first three: charity, joy, and peace. They are the litmus test of God's presence; the sure sign of God's pleasure.

Pause upon joy for a moment. For a Catholic in a state of sanctifying grace and always seeking the will of God, it is a permanent possession.

Impregnable, for it sees all things as part of God's Providential Design: be they sufferings, reversals, contradictions, betrayals, tragedies, or defeats. To this, St. Paul to the Romans: "Who shall separate us from the love of Christ? Shall tribulation, or distress, or persecution, or famine or nakedness, or peril, or sword? Nor height, nor depth, nor any other creature, shall be able to separate us from the love of God, which is in Christ Jesus our Lord." Whose name is Love? The Holy Spirit.

Only the Holy Spirit's divine work can produce such startling results. Recall the old story of Caligula. This demented Roman emperor would delight in the games of the Coliseum, especially when Christians were exposed to ghoulish tortures and death. It is told that after the spectacle he would order his Praetorian Guard to escort him to the arena to take sadistic pleasure at the corpses, imagining he would see the faces of the martyrs twisted

in torment. After inspecting body after body, in a fit of madness, he roared; "but why do all have smiles on their faces?!"
Why indeed.

It is important not to confuse joy with giddiness or hilarity. The latter are the mere reflections of sentimentality or feelings. They are fleeting, followed by instant dissipation. Their origins are purely human and disordered, preambles to compromised souls.

Joy of the Holy Spirit saturates man to his metaphysical depths, with as indelible a possession as his own name. For it is not of human making, or it would be as fragile as human life. The Third Person's fruit of joy bears the mark of Heaven, hence invincible. This fruit is not contrived or invented; not produced in a laboratory, or conjured in a therapy session.

Neither can it be roused by the fabricated pseudo-liturgies whose number is legion. Nor the Pelagian antics of some prayer groups, where hysteria parades as piety. All of this is what St. Paul meant when he wrote to the Ephesians: "And grieve not the Holy Spirit of God, whereby ye are sealed unto the day of redemption."

Yet this fruit of joy does not injure the ontological nature of man: It repairs, complements, and elevates it. Tears will still be shed at heartbreaks, tragedies, and catastrophe, but always commingled with joy. Joy does not camouflage these inevitable woes indigenous to this valley of tears. Quite marvelously, joy is the result of a supernatural vantage point that leaves a tormented soul still seeing grand divine truths writ large.

Jean Paul Sartre's dilemma was that he only saw the wrenching coils of human suffering and cursed it as absurdity. Without seeing through God's eyes, who wouldn't? Never ought we to hide from the reality of suffering and the chaos of this world; neither should we be fixated upon it. But when we look at it through the eyes of Faith, anguish becomes redemptive, releasing us from its brutalizing clutches to enjoy the "glorious liberty of the sons of God" (Rom 8:21).

Joy proceeds from one more source: the supernatural virtue of Hope. Because this virtue is supernatural (theological, that is, caused by God alone), it is never to be confused with optimism. Optimism is its pale stepchild. It is born of the natural calculations of men, and therefore stands upon the shifting sands of human naivete. It is unreliable, untrustworthy, and often a traitor, as are all human creations. Supernatural Hope is the granite-like confidence that with God's grace all things are possible and no obstacle insuperable. It is the thick bedrock upon which our efforts stand. Yes, it shocks the world, for the men of this world see only dread and impossible escape. Hope shouts into the deepest parts of our souls, "With God all things are possible" (Mk 10:27). W. H. Auden's poetry captures this chiaroscuro mystery, "stumbling forward, rejoicing."

In these days Catholics are not made to crouch in hiding, or to wring our hands in self-pity. We are made of better stuff. Grace is knitted into our souls. Joy too.

We are on the winning side. It's time to act like it.

THE BASHFULNESS OF SIN

B eware the disguises of sin. Its guise of choice is the brash and loud ugliness, atrocity, wantonness and ruin that makes our skin crawl. While this serves as splashy spectacle, it captures few. Its most effective tactics are never so meretricious. Sin is normally a shy and bashful thing. It operates with consummate legerdemain, more in keeping with its inventor's angelic skills. The Prince of Darkness dwells where he is barely noticed, better suited to his designs. His primordial depictions as a snake perfectly reflect his stratagems: slithering speedily, without fanfare, attacking before any defense can be mounted. Anything less would be an affront to his preternatural intelligence. Gaudy displays are not his métier, except as distractions from his proven modus operandi. Hannah Arendt famously named this the "banality of evil."

Sin hides itself in the folds of character. Proof of this is the sinner's refrain, "That's just the way I am," when confronted with the incursions of sin. We sinners are heavily armored against the sorties of grace, prompting St. John Henry Newman to call the mandate of contrition "The laying down of arms." Sin camouflages itself among the idiosyncrasies of personal disposition. It insinuates itself in what the medievals called the four temperaments: sanguine, choleric, melancholic and phlegmatic. Those are indeed the legitimate molds into which each man is fitted, and through which he meets the world and works out his sanctification. Thus St. Paul, "By the grace of God I am what I am" (1 Cor 15:10).

Sin cleverly takes what is good and sows within it the seeds of corruption, making it more difficult to distinguish one from the other. Sin remains invisible as it works itself into the manifold struggles of ordinary life, cleverly deflecting attention from the quiet work of vice. With indefatigable tenacity it burrows deeply into the soul, until the sinner thinks the sin is as much a part of him as his own name.

Sin is bashful as it stoops behind a hundred excuses. The Tempter first employed this weapon to great profit in Eden when

Adam insisted that his wife was to blame for his infraction, "And the man said, the woman whom thou gavest to be with me, she gave me of the tree, and I did eat" (Gen 3:13). Adam's readiness to make excuse for his sin becomes part of the hard inner core of concupiscence as it hurtles through the millennia. From showing itself as a Manicheanism, blaming the rancid physical world for man's sin, or, its modern variant, accusing the rise in crime on guns. Excuses reign in the kingdom of sin. It peeks from beneath the quick justifications that spill so comfortably from our lips. Our age excels in this subterfuge. The hoi-polloi use it when it protests that love wins or love is love to license promiscuity or the clerisy invoke it when they speak of life's ambiguity to refashion Christ's teachings. St. Thomas teaches "The greatest violation of reason is to use reason against reason." Sin lurks where there is pretense, mediocrity, compromise and sentimentality.

Fr. Frederick Faber, contemporary and Oratory fellow traveler of Cardinal Newman, wrote perceptibly of sin's wiles under cover of self-deceit:

> Self-deceit is most aggravating; it is so elastic, who can punish it? To try to do so is like whipping the air. It is such a confounded optimist – who has ever humbled it? It is almost embarrassed by its own success... repeated victories over it seem to give us no habit of victory. No amount of mortification seems to cow it. Then we must note its ability to put on the appearance of good, its ability to assume the disguise of virtue. For this it always wears. It is its normal state, its law of gravitation, something essential to it. Self-deceit is that which makes us do the devil's work, believing, though not always with an entirely honest faith, that it is God's. The co-existence of self-deceit with so much good is another of its characteristics. It has a genius for alliances. And it tends especially to ally itself with good. It abides in the neighborhood of good in order to be fostered and kept warm. Thus we have always to regard the amount of our grace as some index to the amount of our self-deceit, and akin to this we must notice its quiet partnership with the sacraments... into which self-deceit intrudes itself. It increases with age.

Sin is like the accumulating layers of a cataract acting over years as it seals off the eye to vision. Its stealth progress proceeds so slyly that a world stripped of its sharpness seems to be the world as it is. This is sin's greatest triumph: to make itself disappear.

So it is that Advent is a waking from sleep. This is Advent's leitmotif: shaking man from his metaphysical sleep; his amnesia from being truly human; a forgetfulness of what man should be; a slipping away the stern demands of being made in the image and likeness of God or a hesitancy in mounting the steep heights of sanctifying grace. "Brethren, knowing the time, that it is now the hour for us to rise from sleep" (Rom 13:11). The Collect of the First Sunday of Advent trumpets, "Stir up Thy power, we beseech Thee, o Lord, and come: that from the threatening dangers of our sins we may be rescued..." A sobering prayer. It teaches us the insidious wiles of sin. So insidious that only God's power can thwart it. The heroic Jesuit martyr Fr. Alfred Delp digs deeply into the marrow of Advent's urgency:

> Advent is the time for rousing. Humanity is shaken to the very depths, so that we may wake up to the truth of ourselves. The primary condition for a fruitful and rewarding Advent is renunciation, surrender. Humans must let go of all their mistaken dreams, their conceited poses and arrogant gestures, all the pretenses with which they hope to deceive themselves and others. If they fail to do this, stark reality may take hold of them and rouse them forcibly in a way that will entail both anxiety and suffering.

Advent's premier saint is John the Baptist. Mother Church sets this stark and dramatic figure before us as the model of Christian purity of purpose. There he is in penitential rags, amongst the rocks of the unforgiving Sinai desert, subsisting on locusts and honey and clothed in unsparing humility. The Baptist is our indictment.

Advent is indeed our time to wake from our deepest illusions. The ones that have kept us under lock and key. And the deadliest illusion is that I am quite good just the way I am.

MERCY ON THE CHEAP

Ah, Mercy! To the fallen children of Adam and Eve it is sheer music to our ears. Only mercy moved God to rush to the assistance of men who believe they have no need of His attention. In the old rite of admission for Trappists the prior asks of the candidate, "Why do you come here?" to which he responds, "For the mercy of God." Of its very nature, mercy assumes in the recipient a depth of need, almost a gulf, which separates him from Him Who bestows the mercy. Thus mercy requires both truth and humility in the recipient. Truth in recognizing the defect which begs for mercy, and humility which compels the recipient to plead for a gift he neither deserves or can possibly earn for himself. Mercy is at the heart of our holy religion because in God's infinite love He sends His Only Begotten Son to salvage man from his miserable condition. Such a Divine Condescension is utterly undeserved, and hence all the sweeter. So it is that Mother Church exclaims in the *Exsultet* on Easter Vigil, "*O Felix Culpa*" (O Happy Fault!) It is man's awful sin that has moved the pity of God not merely to aid sinful men, but to bring pallid aid to the heights of dizzying extravagance.

The Savior exhibits this lavish mercy in every corner of the Holy Scriptures. He has pity on the multitude for He saw they were hungry (Mt 9:36). He leaves the ninety-nine sheep in search of the one who is lost (Lk 15:4). The Good Samaritan pities the wounded man and supplies all that is necessary for his recovery (Lk 10:33). The Father rejoices in his prodigal son "who was lost, and now is found" (Lk 15:32). Each time we read any of these passages we are startled. The extremes of such love are unsettling, defy comprehension, and invite incredulity. So Graham Greene rightly speaks of God's mercy as strange. Only because it upends the conventional categories of human measurement. Divine Mercy stretches ordinary reason beyond its ability for sober assessment. Isn't it this which provokes the Magdalene to "wash Christ's feet with her tears"? (Lk 7:38). God's mercy shocks. It leaves sinful man flummoxed. His normal steps are thrown off, and all the old certainties collapse before the stunning mercy of God.

Elation at the Divine Mercy warrants some caution. It should not lead to swoons but to steadiness. It shouldn't sweep us off our feet, but place our feet more securely on firm ground. It would be a serious affront to Divine Goodness to think that His mercy is a no-fault proposition: God gives, man merely takes. Unfortunately the secular mood of our times has forced such thinking into the retail consumption of more than a few. Without the presence of both truth and humility, mercy curdles. It becomes trafficking, for trafficking is the callous indifference to the worth of the person for the sake of mercenary profit. It cheapens a glimmer of the Divine Beauty into a worthless knockoff. It becomes a replay of the Israelite worship of the Golden Calf: Impatience with the efforts necessary to win the Divine outpouring threw the Jews into a frenzy of bloated self-indulgence, all the while calling it religion.

God extends His mercy to sinners only after there is evidence of a turning of the will. Truth is necessary in this terrible encounter of man and God. For this reception of Divine Mercy, God expects human conformity to His will. Or at least its sincere beginnings. All that is necessary for the Father of the Prodigal Son is to see his son running toward him from afar. It must not be presumed that the Prodigal Son changed overnight. No sinner does. God does not expect that. Overnight conversions are always highly suspect. Just as natural things grow ever so slowly, making changes imperceptible step by imperceptible step, similarly with man. God knows this, because He designed us that way. All natural things operate according to the laws of nature. Trouble surfaces when thinking ourselves above these laws of our nature.

Even with the assistance of Divine Grace, the changes are glacially slow. Grace is not amazing, despite what many Catholics these days shout from the top of their lungs (even, I fear, in the very presence of the Divinity). Grace is supernatural. As St. Thomas teaches us, *gratia perfecit naturam* (grace builds upon nature); it neither destroys it, replaces it, or transcends it. Grace moves us according to the nature of the thing being moved. Just as the sun remains the same even as it produces different results in different things: scorches the earth, softens the flowers, and evinces green in the leaf, so it is with grace. Even though God is infinitely superior to any natural thing, God still respects the nature of natural things.

God's mercy waits for the slightest nod from the sinner. But there must be the nod. When that nod comes, the floodgates of the Divine Heart open, and mercy rushes in upon the soul. The nod is a recognition of sin; a desire to rectify the offense. Divine Mercy is not promiscuous, given without truthfulness. Such would make God a simpleton. God will not be tempted, as the Old Testament warns. Tempting God is assuming God gives of His bounty without man having to return a thing.

If our age wants any part of God, it is this kind of God it wants. It heaps scorn upon the Holy Catholic Church because she will not second its self-serving logic. The world becomes delirious at leaders in the Church who speak as the worldly do. Thunderous applause awaits any voice which will squeeze the church into the culture's puny prejudices. The culture is patient. Even if the Church announces no denial of past moral doctrines, as long as there is a discrete silence, the world is satisfied. Great rejoicing ensued when a prominent European cardinal advanced a preposterous separation between the unchangeable doctrine of the Church and the ever-accommodating obligations of his compassion. Translation: Christ commands one thing, but His mercy allows me to do quite another. With that, a certain kind of Catholic joined with the culture in a boisterous roar of approval. Finally, in the words of Flannery O'Connor, a church of Christ without Christ.

Yes, mercy. To find it look at it practices by a St. Vincent de Paul, a St. Katherine Drexel, or a St. Peter Claver, along with the countless army of other saints. Their exercise of mercy changed the face of the earth because it was a mercy imitating the Divine Mercy. Adoration of the merciful Heart of Christ allows them to bring mercy to the world. Every saint lights fires in a dark world because everything they do they do out of love for God.

As St. Thomas teaches, "The sum total of the Christian religion consists in mercy, as regards external works; but the inward love of charity, whereby we are united to God, preponderates over both love and mercy for our neighbor."[4] Tell that to those who chatter endlessly about love of the poor. Only the truth about God and His mercy will relieve the plight of the poor. Oh yes, they want

---

[4] *Summa theologiae*, II-II, Q. 30, art. 4, ad 2.

bread, but their hearts crave the Bread of Angels more. Yes, they desire justice. Don't we all? But the justice they covet most of all is the right to know how to love God. "What does it profit a man to gain the whole world and lose his soul" (Mk 8:36). Outside of this luminous Divine Truth, all mercy talk is just cheap talk.

It might be time to stop kicking around mercy. Otherwise it won't be long before mercy becomes unrecognizable and ultimately fades from our midst.

If that happens we shall rue the day, because the consequences for man will be merciless.

DOES JESUS LOVE YOU JUST THE WAY YOU ARE?

No. Against such absurd claims, only sharp replies will do. Like ice water splashed onto the face of a hallucinating man, the sharp reply brings a man back to his senses. Indeed, such ubiquitous sloganeering is built upon decades of theological dissent, very much the way landfill, when accumulated, creates mountains. The mountains sometimes rise very high, but what makes them seemingly mountainous is – garbage.

Sadly, such follies have settled so deeply into the Catholic soul that dislodging them is something almost Herculean. All of it due to the assiduous efforts of a complicit theological elite who has controlled the levers of both universities and colleges for over half a century. They have left most Catholics with a throw-away religion, rendering them blind – not seeing what their eyes see.

Evidence abounds. In 2023, press accounts have shown photos of Catholic churches in Europe being redesigned into tony hotels (this occurring on every continent). Where once stood tabernacles, saints and angels, there now stands boudoirs. And no one grieves. Notre Dame's Cathedral's post-fire interior now resembles a Jackson Pollack canvas rather than one of the mightiest Cathedrals in Christendom, whose sanctuary and furnishings made Catholics tremble in awe. And no one grieves.

You see, Jesus does not love us just the way we are. He pities the way we are. Such Divine pity caused the Son of God to take flesh in the womb of His Virgin Mother. All these motions proceeding from the Divine Mercy. Under the weight of Original Sin, and its concupiscible effects, man has been left, in St. Augustine's disturbing phrase, a *massa damnata*, a damnable assemblage. Our lot is to cast about under the weight of this Original catastrophe. It is against this forbidding fate that we properly appreciate the Divine Mercy and capture the vacuity of the statement that 'Jesus loves us just the way we are'.

In Psalm 24:10 we read, "All the ways of the Lord are mercy and truth (justice)." St James adds, "Mercy exalteth herself above judgment (justice)" (Jas 2:13). On these two passages, St. Thomas comments:

> In this sense, that every work of justice presupposes and is founded upon a work of mercy, a work of pure loving kindness, wholly gratuitous. If, in fact, there is anything due from God to the creature, it is in virtue of some gift that has preceded it... If he owes it to Himself to grant us grace necessary for salvation, it is because He has first given us the grace with which to merit. Mercy, or pure goodness, is thus, as it were, the root and source of all the works of God; Its virtue pervades, dominates them all. As the ultimate founder of every gift, it exercises the more powerful influence, and for this reason it transcends justice, which follows upon mercy and continues to be subordinate to it.[5]

In the light of this teaching of the Angelic Doctor, such sandbox assertions as 'Jesus loves us just the way we are' are shown in all their embarrassing shallowness.

Fr. Garrgou-Lagrange expounds further on St. Thomas's teaching in his rich masterpiece, *Providence*:

> If in this present life divine justice gives to each of us whatever is required for us to live rightly and so attain our end, mercy, on the other hand, gives far beyond what is strictly necessary, and it is in this sense that it surpasses justice... Out of pure goodness from the very day of creation He has granted us to participate supernaturally in His intimate life by bestowing on us sanctifying grace, the principle of our supernatural merits.
>
> Again, after the fall, he might have left us in our fallen condition so far as justice is concerned. Or he might have raised us up from sin by a simple act of forgiveness conveyed to the mouth of a prophet after we had fulfilled certain conditions. But He has done something infinitely greater than this: out of pure mercy he gave us his only Son as a redeeming victim, and it is possible for us at all times to appeal to the infinite merits of the savior. Justice loses none of its rights, but it is mercy that prevails.

Properly exalting mercy should not leave us victim to those who have neutered mercy. Mercy has undergone a makeover at their hands. In the past decade or so it has come to take on a no-fault coloration, perpetrated by some of the most highly placed

---

[5] *Summa theologiae* I, Q. 21, art. 4.

prelates in the Catholic Church. They have drained mercy of its true meaning. To them mercy comes from a God happy with man and all his sins. This is a mercy turned into a lie, a cruel parody of divine truth.

Mercy is offered to those who crave forgiveness; those who express profound contrition; those who possess a deep horror of sin. When the hands of a sinner are held out with all these dispositions, Divine mercy rushes in like a tidal wave.

The Divine Mercy is not a promiscuous thing. It is always searching, always on the watch for the smallest regret for sin, not excuses for sin. Nowhere is this expressed more poetically than in G. K. Chesterton's *The Innocence of Fr. Brown*. Fr. Brown is explaining to the Inspector how he apprehended the thief:

> Father Brown looked him full in his frowning face. "Yes," he said, "I caught him, with an unseen hook and an invisible line which is long enough to let him wander to the ends of the world, and still to bring him back with a twitch upon the thread."

That twitch upon the thread is the always roaming eye of God Whose mercy seeks the least bit of contrition to lavish His mercy. Quite different than the cartoon version of mercy on offer from the clerics of 'Jesus loves you just the way you are.' This is a mercy which rewards bare-knuckled struggle for fidelity to Christ. His is a mercy that looks for the tears of the Magdalene or the sobbing of an Augustine.

The clerics who persist in the bilge of 'Jesus loves us just the way we are,' are twisting the Catholic faithful into religious stooges. Beneath the weight of such kitsch, it doesn't take long to recognize there is no need of a Savior, or His Church, of Redemption, or of the Sacraments. Religion becomes but the moment of supreme togetherness and self-realization. Religion becomes a mutual admiration society; Jesus admires me; I admire Jesus.

Assisted by the lounge music which accompanies most parish Masses, the circle is complete. No surprise that Catholics have made their own the propaganda of the Woke culture. The doctrinal vacuum created by the spirit-of-Vatican-II cognoscenti leaves them no choice. Much of Catholic America has become its rear guard. And armed with unvarnished stupidity such as 'Jesus loves you just the way you are', there is no relief in sight.

Take a moment and observe the Synod on Synodality and watch Catholicism melt before your very eyes.

Truth to be told, this is just the way we are: prisoners of sin. Even when we have been bathed in the graces of Confession, we are hostages to the wages of concupiscence. So it is that Mother Church calls us by our proper name, "poor sinners", or "poor banished children of Eve." Our whole existence on earth is, in the trenchant title of Dom Scupoli's classic, *The Spiritual Combat*.

The Savior is called precisely that because He comes to rescues us from our wretched fate. That is the way we are. He pities us because we are the way we are. What is the meaning of His summoning words, "Come to me all you who labor and are burdened..." except to relieve us of the affliction of existing the way we are. The lie that falls so easily from the lips of Catholics today implies that the Savior is happy with the way we are. He isn't. But because He loves us, He shows us pity, and then mercy. And then He shows us the way forward, so different than the way we were on before.

The soul of man was made for the infinite grandeur of God. In St. Augustine's memorable words, "Thou dost excite him that to praise Thee is his joy. For Thou has made us for Thyself and our hearts are restless till they rest in Thee." This is man's most noble patrimony: to seek God in His majesty with only the poor gift of our contrition. That, my dear reader, is sadness at not being the way I should be.

That overpowering reality clothes man with a kind of royal identity. Recall the father of the Prodigal Son upon his son's return: "Bring forth the best robe, and put it on him; and put a ring on his hand, and shoes on his feet; and bring hither the fatted calf and kill it and let us eat and be merry" (Lk 15:22). Exchanging this for the low lie of Jesus loves you just the way you are reduces man to rags. It abandons the Prodigal Son to feasting on the husks of pigs. This is prizing graffiti to Fra Angelico.

No. Jesus does not love you just the way you are.

For God does not play such dirty tricks.

"BLESS ME, FATHER, FOR I HAVE SINNED"

Vainly do men of our time seek remedies for the cultural maladies affecting us. Each exertion of the political elite or the bien pensant only seem to deepen their woes. Faced with such existential crisis modern men seek corrupting escapes or the violence of bankrupt political extremism. Indeed, these things assume the kind of devotion once reserved to religion. Andrew Sullivan is hardly a credible source for the hearty Catholics who read these pages, carrying all the *bona fides* of the secularist Left. However, a 2018 piece of his presented a compelling taxonomy of our circumstance through the lens of the opioid crisis:

> It is a story of pain and the search for an end to it. It is a story of how the most ancient painkiller known to humanity has emerged to numb the agonies of the world's most highly evolved liberal democracy. Just as LSD helps to explain the 1960s, cocaine the 1980s, and crack the 1990s, so opium defines this new era. I say era, because the trend will, in all probability, last a very long time. The scale and darkness of this phenomenon is a sign of a civilization in a more acute crisis than we knew, a nation overwhelmed by a warp-speed, post-industrial world, a culture yearning to give up, indifferent to life and death, enraptured by withdrawal and nothingness. America, having pioneered the modern way of life, is now in the midst of trying to escape it.

Those volcanic lines could very well have come from the pen of C. S. Lewis or Rod Dreher. But the crisis of modernity has reached such critical mass that even some of its most ardent fans are having buyer's remorse. Having exhausted every recourse, Sullivan and his tribe have nowhere to go. The abyss stares at them, and they tremble. In a former time, they would have found refuge in the arms of the Catholic Church. Long gone are the days that Joseph Epstein, esteemed scholar of the University of Chicago, wrote about his reminiscence about his native Chicago:

The Chicago of my boyhood was an intensely Catholic city. Ask someone where he lived and he was likely to answer with the name of his parish (St. Nicholas of Tolentine, St. Gregory's). Catholic culture was everywhere... So Catholic did the place seem – with priests in cassock, nuns in habit everywhere part of the city scape – that as a young Jewish boy I took Catholicism and Christianity to be coterminous.

But these days the Bride of Christ, wounded so badly after decades of slashing, can scarcely give these souls succor. Too many of her leaders rush to "kneel before the world," as Maritain lamented in his mournful *The Peasant of the Garrone*. If they look to the Western European Catholic Church, they only find it happily impaling itself on the bayonets of the Sexual Revolution, shamefully dissembling as they call their mass suicide "accompaniment." Such hypocrisy would make Nietzsche howl. If these lost secularist souls look to Catholicism in North America, they find not a few Catholic leaders playing in the sandbox of therapeutic religion. The Catholic Church in South America? No comfort there, as it still marches to the discredited platitudes of the hammer and sickle-lite.

Where does the scarred man of modernity turn? To the true Catholic faith, of course. Once there they will find in her churches a dimly lit box: The Confessional. Well, not all of them. In a mad rush to catch up with the world, many of those churches dismantled those blessed boxes. Other places sanitized them into cheery, well-lit clinics where self-affirmation reigns, and nary a bad word of sorrow for sin can be heard. But with perseverance they will find that sacramental oasis.

Sad, isn't it, that such an enchanted place of God's regenerative grace has become a *terra incognita* to so many Catholics. Even otherwise fervent Catholics are not exempt from an alienation from that precious bath of Christ's redemptive Blood. But absence from that encounter with the drama of Calvary carries a heavy price. One that resembles those silent killers modern medicine warns us about: killing without warning, after a silent and unnoticed march through the human body. Neglect of Confession is a silent spiritual killer. Like a pillow pressed over someone's face, it deprives the soul of the sacramental graces proper to the health and perfection of the soul. Consequently, a man's soul suffers a slow asphyxiation: gradual and unnoticed. As it suffocates it experiences a kind of spiritual delirium.

That delirium is marked by six symptoms. The first is complacency, leading the soul to adopt a coziness with the status quo. It readily subscribes to the ubiquitous slogan of being a good person, the paralyzing narcotic for those who desire nothing more than to abide by the standards of the world, rather than the standards of God. As with every prescription from the secularist shelf, it reeks of solipsistic reverie. You know the refrain: "Confession: Oh, not me. I'm a good..."

The second symptom manifests itself in the inability to see sin for what it is. Invariably, the afflicted soul finds itself relabeling sins, shaving away their sharper edges and producing construals more anodyne. Increasingly, it finds itself passionately committed to causes: social justice replaces sanctity. Little by little, the works of mercy become detached from their supernatural roots, and flatten into hollow philanthropy. These men eagerly feed the poor, and just as eagerly let their souls rot. They ignore Our Lord: "Seek ye first the Kingdom of God, and his righteousness; and all these things shall be added unto you" (Mt 6:33).

Third, the soul becomes expert at manufacturing excuses for the sins it commits. Conscience is muffled, so that the soul finds itself able to displease God with impunity, even claiming that its very sin *is* the will of God. The German bishops come to mind (and many others as well) as they solemnly preach their new paradigm, which is only Newspeak for letting my sin be God's will.

Fourthly, since most defenses erected by grace have been breached, the soul finds itself flirting more easily with mortal sin. Vices that once were clearly forbidden, appear more approachable, less ominous.

The fifth symptom is tepidity. The medieval term was *acedia*, or sloth. It is a sluggishness in carrying out the Holy Will of God, an increasing reluctance for acts of piety, and eventually the execution of duties to one's state become onerous.

The final symptom is the clearest sign of the soul's death rattle. The Faith itself becomes merely ceremonial, the redoubt of the aesthete. And its Truths no longer breathe life into the soul, but are seen as only attractive intellectual abstractions, like some elegant Euclidean demonstration. For some it is more deadly, the articles of the Creed become meaningless.

Lent is a time to gaze upon the face of the Crucified One and indict ourselves for his suffering. But a good Lent is not only seeing those sins, but begging pardon for them. Being finally rid of them in the cleansing fires of Confession.

In 1979 John Paul II addressed a crowd of two hundred and fifty thousand Catholics at Victory Square in Warsaw. During his remarks he was frequently interrupted by those heroic Catholic Poles, shouting, "We want God." Within a decade of that earth shaking event, the Western Communist behemoth crumbled. Its collapse was not due to tanks and missiles; not parliaments and Congresses; certainly not ivory towered academics or their learned journals. Catholicism slayed the monster. The Holy Catholic Faith won the triumph. Simple Catholics, over decades of brutality, kneeling in dimly lit Confessional boxes, begging the purple-stoled priest: "Bless me Father, for I have sinned."

Wandering secularists, do you want to change the world? Despairing moderns, do you want respite from your grinding emptiness? Come to those earth-moving words: "Bless me Father, for I have sinned."

CHRISTMAS AND NIETZSCHE'S ABYSS

Nietzsche portentously remarked in *Beyond Good and Evil*, "When you gaze into the abyss, the abyss gazes back." The German nihilist fully appreciated where a world without God was gamboling. For him, no airbrushing the Brave New World. If only his scions were as brutally frank. Bereft of his Teutonic steel, they soak secularism in treacly sentiment. To which honest men shudder. Or should. Which brings us to the luminous genius of Caravaggio, who knew not bottomless abysses but only blazing supernatural horizons.

In 1609 the last great altarpiece was painted in Sicily. Its artist was the Renaissance genius, Michelangelo Merisi da Caravaggio, known to the generations simply as Caravaggio. The title of the masterpiece is the *Adoration of the Shepherds*. It is a strange painting, insomuch as it depicts the familiar Christmas scene with no angels, no trumpets, no human tributes and no celestial light. All the spectator sees is the Blessed Virgin Mary, as a refugee mother owning nothing but the clothes on her back. She clutches the Infant Jesus, who is barely covered by some tattered rags. The Virgin stares blankly into an uncertain future, exhausted in the semi darkness. Her weariness is propped up by an animals' feeding trough, anchored firmly in the beaten earth of the windswept stable. The adoring shepherds are three baffled workmen not knowing quite what to make of the supernatural episode unfolding before them. Finally, there is St. Joseph, the Virgin's elderly husband, beholding the entire event with restrained fear.

This Caravaggio Christmas scene is brutally bleak and hard. Aptly so. For Christ breaks forth into a world which has been made brutally bleak and hard by man's sins. A world wizened by the exhaustions of self-love.

But the master strokes of Caravaggio's brush place the Christ child at the center of his canvas, announcing to every man and woman, to ever set their admiring eyes upon this painting, that the world's only hope is Christ, the Infant King, born in Bethlehem. Without him there man suffers only an aching hunger, but never any bread; maddening questions, but never the comfort of answers; wrenching anxiety, but never a blessed peace; a brittle vanity upon vanity, without even a whisper of truth.

When Bethlehem fades from the heart and souls of men, then their starved souls escape to a dead-end transcendence. Look at our culture without Christ. Its men and women, especially its young, seek to step beyond their flattened world by absorption with ghosts, and zombies; with end of the world obsessions and cartoon superheroes. In Eliot's arresting lines from *Burnt Norton*, they "distract themselves from distractions by distractions." A thousand pities—for the true Hero is so close—awaiting them in the unintimidating face of a Divine Child.

Christmas imposes upon every Catholic a solemn obligation: to tell the world that our joy, our answer, our peace and our rescue lay in the humility of Bethlehem. We must tell them that looking anywhere else is staring into the abyss.

ABANDON ALL PRIDE THOSE WHO SEEK THE KINGDOM

At the very end of Evelyn Waugh's novel on the finding of the True Cross, *Helena*, he writes a paean to the Magi in the form of a prayer:

> You are especial patrons, and patrons of all latecomers, of all who have a tedious journey to make to the truth, of all who are confused with knowledge and speculation, of all who stand in danger by reason of their talents... Dear cousins pray for me. Pray for the great, lest they perish utterly... For His sake who did not reject your curious gifts, pray for the learned, the oblique, the delicate. Let them not be quite forgotten at the Throne of God when the simple come into their kingdom.

Of course, Waugh was praying here for himself and all his jaded fellow travelers in the tony upper classes of England. He knew their insouciance, their condescension's, their stiff unbending pride. Before his conversion to the One, True Church, he was one of them. In fact, even after his conversion much of those entrenched flaws plagued him. Though this prayer to the Magi is Waugh's *cri de coeur*, it is the tearful pleading of all of us.

Whether cradle Catholics or converts, all of us are latecomers to Our Lord, for all of us tarry in surrendering all to God. He desires our hearts now, and we delay. We want so much for ourselves, making bargains with Christ that we will love him here, but not there. Some parts of our life we love too much to surrender right now: our petty grudges, our cherished way of doing things, our fixed perceptions of others, our stubborn resistance to the purifying fires of charity. Though we truly love Christ, still we do not love him in so many details of our life. Rightly, with St. Augustine, we passionately confess, "How late have I loved Thee."

Then there is in us all "the danger by reason of our talents." This is the peril of our age, those who think their considerable accomplishments in the arts, science or higher learning have placed them slightly above the eternal, unchanging truths of Christ and his Church. The age prides itself on hitherto undiscovered intuitions into the human condition. Such entitle them to modify the teachings of the Savior. In the words of a prominent American Jesuit, Fr. Thomas Reese, "Like the Second Vatican Council, the 2018 synod on the family achieved consensus through ambiguity." It takes a certain kind of talent to replace the teachings of God with a *novum* like ambiguity. But this flaw of talent does not reside only with the gifted, but with all of us. It is that flaw which tempts us to place our most impressive abilities, the ones that make us feel quite special and unique, above the will of God.

What of the "learned, opaque, the delicate"? Each one of these describe our civilization, and therefore, you and me. We know we are part of one of the most highly sophisticated cultures the human race has ever known. With such genius the Man of the West finds himself climbing to ever new heights, dazzling in their reach. Who has need of God? Or religion? Rudolph Bultman was the German Lutheran theologian who bleached the Bible of the supernatural and made secularism the New Creed. He famously remarked: "Now that modern man can illuminate a room with the flick of a switch, how can he ever believe in miracles?" Or God.

As we come more acclimated to ease, convenience, instantaneous satisfactions and fulfillment as the *summum bonum*, sacrifice stands alien to us. We become the delicate. The ancient disciplines of the Church designed to tame the self are rejected for that very reason. To modern man they are oppressive and insulting, if not harmful and demeaning. The sociologist Christian Smith names this "Moralistic therapeutic deism": Acceptance of a God who solely massages the self and leaves us satisfied in caring for more pressing matters comfortably distant to the soul, viz., the environment, good health, safe sex and climate change. With these as the new *idée fixe*, our wayward souls remain our own business. After all, it is easier to worry about climate change or world peace than about fidelity to Christ. While the Lutheran theologian H. Reinhold Niebuhr subscribed to this new secularist creed, he did have a pang of conscience when he wrote that it was merely proffering "a God without wrath, brought men without sin, into a kingdom without judgment, through the ministrations of Christ without a cross." One of the most eloquent voices warning of this metaphysical inversion was the estimable Philip Reiff in his 1966 book, *The Triumph of the Therapeutic* where he presciently wrote, "That all communications of ideals come under permanent and easy suspicion." W. H. Auden lamented this decline of the Übermensch West,

> Instead of Gnostics, we have Existentialists and God-is-Dead theologians; instead of Neo-Platonists, devotees of Zen; instead of desert hermits, heroin addicts and Beats; instead of mortification of the flesh, sado-masochistic pornography; as for our public entertainments, the fare offered by television is still a shade less brutal than that provided by the Amphitheater, but only a shade, and may not be for so long.

Delicate, indeed.

We can almost feel Auden's pen trembling when he writes the last lines of the prayer. With a reverent foreboding, the great English writer reminds us that only the simple come into the kingdom. He is terrified that the rest of us self-satisfied, priggish men risk being "forgotten at the Throne of God." With these harrowing words the prayer ends, and our hearts are left raw, but strangely consoled. Though we stand indicted, we see ourselves as we truly are. There is peace in that. This is the glory of our Holy Faith. That, my Catholic friends, is the bliss of Bethlehem. No airbrushed platitudes: Just Christ. Only Christ. Fearlessly, Christ.

With the Three Kings let us kneel – no, prostrate – before the divine King of Bethlehem. For unless we surrender the heights of the parapets of our pride from which we reign, we shall never enjoy the reign of Christ.

THE HOLY SPIRIT MAKES MEN OF STEEL

Upon entering St. Peter's Basilica, facing the visitor, like some sunburst, is the Great Altar. It is spaced majestically beneath Bernini's massive baldachin, held up by four thick, twisted columns, identical to the ones in Solomon's Temple – clearly a sign that the typological figures of the Old Testament had come to fulfillment in the immolation of the Lamb upon the altars of Christendom.

When the eye of the visitor wanders further down beyond the baldachin, it arrives at the resplendent Altar of the Chair, above it a heroic-sized bronze and gold throne which seems to float in thin air. Sealed within it is the actual chair of St. Peter from which he ruled the primatial see of Rome. It is quite mystical in its aura, bespeaking the supernatural authority of the Roman Catholic Church. As the eye moves upward from the Chair, it sets itself upon the alabaster stained-glass window of the Holy Spirit. That window announces to the world the great privilege of the Roman Church to enjoy the guidance of that Third Person, guaranteeing the privilege of infallible security in the Truth.

Stained glass windows are an apt lesson for us on this feast of Pentecost. As with all stained-glass windows, without external light pouring through them, they appear black and opaque. Light discloses their beauty, colors explode, miraculous persons emerge and an ethereal atmosphere bathes the Church in lessons the tongue cannot express. Such is the magic of light.

The work of the Holy Spirit is akin to that light. Not magical, by any means, but rather, quite real, transcendent, and supernatural. As the soul's Divine Guest,[6] it is flooded with His light through sanctifying grace, unveiling beauty hidden without His light. Light alone, however, does not exhaust the plenitude of His presence. The Acts of the Apostles describes a scene of near terror, when the room where the Apostles gathered shook violently, as if

---

[6] See *Summa theologiae* I, Q. 38, art. 1.

by earthquake. Then, a great fire descended from Heaven setting upon each of them a crown of flames.

The Third Person is not only the blessed sweetness of light but also the arm of heavenly power. His indwelling is transformative. Before His arrival, the Apostles are rent with fear, uncertainty, ambivalence, confusion, hesitancy, and abandonment. After He comes, all that melts away. Before Pentecost, the eleven were simpering fishermen; after Pentecost, they are Apostolic giants.

These heavenly tremors erupting in the soul are not a gift reserved to the Apostles, they are the inheritance of every soul clothed with sanctifying grace. They are yours and mine. It is these supernal wonders that caused St. Basil the Great to write in his treatise, *On the Holy Spirit*, words that verge on delirium:

> Even as bright shining bodies, once touched by a ray of light falling on them, become even more glorious and themselves cast another light, so too souls that carry the Holy Spirit, and are enlightened by Him, become spiritual themselves and send forth grace upon others. This grace enables them to foresee the future, to understand mysteries, to grasp hidden things, to receive spiritual blessings, to have their thoughts fixed on heavenly things, and to dance with the angels.

The Holy Spirit illuminates all things because He is the Truth. Our lives, like stained glass without light, become opaque and lose their meaning over time. Sin does this, as well as the complacency and inertia accumulating over a life of living only for ourselves. Years accumulate and we see ourselves finding only misery and contradiction in life. Notice the many men and women, and not a few Catholics, who endured this COVID-19 crisis. They obsessed over the damage of this microbe rather than upon the mercy of God, Who allowed it for His loving purposes and our perfection.

When we give permission for the Holy Spirit to take up residence in our souls, by our free cooperation with His Gifts, we find ourselves changed. We see the purposes of God's mysterious designs, and we can only be seized by wonder. In the fourth century, St. Cyril of Jerusalem, gave moving expression to these marvels of the Holy Spirit:

> As light strikes the eyes of a man who comes out of darkness into the sunshine and enables him to see clearly things he could not discern before, so light floods the

soul of the man counted worthy of receiving the Holy Spirit and enables him to see things beyond the range of human vision, things hitherto undreamed of.

Moreover, the Holy Spirit infuses souls with a daring they find quite inexplicable, except through His power. How else do martyrs face some of the grisliest torments known to man? How else do mothers and fathers carry the sacrifices of having their eighth or ninth child? How else can one explain how young men and women surrender their liberty and the beauties of married love to serve Christ's perfect beauty in the priesthood or religious life? What of the heroism that must be exercised by unmarried men and women, especially the young, to maintain the virtue of perfect purity?

Nothing earthly or natural can account for all this. Only the mystery of the grace of the Holy Spirit. Listen to the words of a contemporary of St. Cyril of Jerusalem, St. Cyril of Alexandria, the great hero of Ephesus, the defending champion of the *Theotokos*, the God-bearer:

> With the Holy Spirit within us, it is quite natural for people who had been absorbed by the things of this world to become entirely otherworldly in outlook, and for cowards to become people of great courage.

Surpassing all these, the greatest manifestation of the Holy Spirit's power is charity: love for Christ and for the neighbor. His is not a sentimental love, dependent on feelings. Nor is it a love driven by self-interest. His is a love, in Chesterton's evocative phrase, "of goodness gone wild." His is the love that makes the world stand up and take notice. It is also a love which confounds all the safe and self-serving standards of the world.

The motions of the Holy Spirit's love in souls bewilders the conventions of the world, and even Catholics who have capitulated to them. The past fifty years have shown some Catholic thinkers suppressing the divinity of the Holy Spirit only to replace it with the spirit of their inner voice. Cringe when you hear talk about following the spirit. It is as far from the doctrine of the Church as astronomy is from astrology. The drama of the Holy Spirit's grace of charity is explained by Chesterton:

> Rationalists will find things like the Stigmata of St. Francis a stumbling-block because to them religion is a philosophy. But a man will not roll in the snow to preserve his purity, as St. Francis did, for a stream of tendency

by which all things fulfill the law of their being. He will not go without food in the name of something, not ourselves, that makes for righteousness. He will do things like this... under quite a different impulse. He will do these things when he is in love... Tell it as the tale of one of the troubadours, and the wild things he would do for his lady, and the whole of the modern puzzle disappears.

Yet another counterfeit of the Holy Spirit is peddled today: the proselytization of novelty. The true sign of the Holy Spirit is a growing and passionate firmness in the unchanging teachings of Holy Church and her immemorial traditions. Allied to this is an equally parlous fraud: the regime of emotion. For quite a time (interestingly parallel to the vacuum of doctrine the Church has suffered) there has been the association of the work of the Holy Spirit with spasms of emotion. This meretricious display has degraded the classical virtue of piety, with its admirable humility guarded by the proper bonds of ordered restraint. Exceptions to this litter the millennial landscape of the Church's history, all epiphenomena of heresy. Evidence of these baneful moments are meticulously chronicled in Msgr. Ronald Knox's magisterial work, *Enthusiasm*.

Refutation of this unseemly trend is the example of the Virgin Mother of God. Of all human persons, she is the vessel of the Holy Spirit *par excellence*, indeed His spouse. Where are her fits of emotion? Or the Saints. Where do we find them luxuriating in carnival transports?

Catholics must be immoveable in the solid teaching of the Church: The most secure and decisive sign of the presence of the Holy Spirit is the love of the Cross and heroic love of neighbor; men and women on their knees adoring the Holy Eucharist or in reverential awe at Holy Mass; and passionately defending the unchangeable doctrines of the Church. These are the Catholics filled with the Spirit.

It is time to get the Holy Spirit right. He is not a rubber stamp of the *Zeitgeist*. He is the Visitor from Heaven who renews the face of the earth. Catholics must resist His enfeeblement.

The Holy Spirit makes giants of us Catholics. Isn't it time we start acting like them?

NEVER LET A CRISIS GO TO WASTE

In the Greek tongue, the word for decision or opportunity is *krine* from which our English word crisis is derived. As it is so often, the ancient Greek masters of this supple language possessed a natural wisdom which enjoyed an unusual concurrence with the reveled truths of the Catholic Faith. Such consonance caused amazement amongst the ancient Church Fathers, prompting them to anoint many Greek thinkers, viz., Socrates, Plato and Aristotle, as proto-Christians. So it is that Dante takes Virgil as his navigator in the exploration of both the Inferno and Purgatorio. The Italian poet names Virgil a virtuous pagan, and along with many other virtuous pagans, dwell in the regions of Limbo, spared the punishments of Hell. It might also be remarked, that the founding editor of this prestigious journal, Ralph McInerney, took its title from this ancient Greek usage.

Similarly, the corona virus crisis brought into relief several teachings of the Church, fulfilling its classical Greek meaning of seizing an opportunity. The obvious one is the doctrine of Divine Providence. Nothing that happens to us in this life is not without God's concurrence, and ultimately permitted for our ultimate good. Even evil, physical and moral. God, of course, does not will evil, which is opposed to His perfect nature, but in His Wisdom He permits it, so that greater goods may occur. Sometimes these greater goods are hidden are from eyes, but not from the eyes of supernatural Faith. God knows His wayward fallen children of Adam and Eve, and appreciates that the hardened carapace of sin often dims their understanding, if not blinding them entirely.

Being a Provident Father, He applies a remedy that seem *prima face* painful, but necessary for our happiness. Oftentimes suffering is obligatory to shatter the walls of our own making. Too much ease, convenience and pleasure settles onto the soul like a narcotic, numbing the soul to the exertions of spiritual warfare. Cardinal Newman thus warns: "Health of mind and body is a good thing, if you can endure it." From our most bitter afflictions God's power triumphs. So Aquinas: "The greatest manifestation of God's power is to bring goodness out of evil." In a few weeks we shall be praising this power of God as the Exultet rings out in the darkness of Easter Vigil, "O felix culpa!" Imagine, Holy Church praises a sin! "O happy fault! O necessary sin of Adam!" For from it the Savior was moved from His place at the right hand of His Father, to stand by the side of the likes of you and me. This same beneficent Divine Providence stands as a conundrum to those without supernatural Faith. Remember Mephistopheles's despairing howl in Goethe's *Dr. Faustus*, "I desire only evil, and produce only good!"

A second doctrine comes to mind. Pause and consider the Church's teaching that all men are made unto the *imago et similitudo Dei*, the image and likeness of God. This image encompasses two critical powers that comprise the nature of man: his intellect and will. God does not grant powers in vain. They are meant to be used, used well, and used unto our perfection. If not, we come under the dire obloquies of the Savior. Reread the parable of the talents in Mt 25 16. God will not do for us, what we can do for ourselves. Such a slothful attitude tips over onto the heresy of presumption: assuming that God will always compensate for what I refuse to do myself. The Church has also identified this sin with the rather spine-tingling name of 'Tempting the Holy Spirit.' Frightening indeed, for its an affront against the Third Person whose identity is the Truth.

Playing games with the gifts God has given us is a prospect that should make our skins crawl. No voice has been more insistent in using the intellect *ad maiorem Dei gloriam* than the Church. To face this crisis, we rely upon the finest minds at our disposal, carefully implement their cautions and always take due consideration of the common good. It is the *modus Catholicus*, par excellence. For good reason, Etienne Gilson named the final chapter of his 1939 classic *Christianity and Philosophy*, *The Intellect in the Service of Christ the King*. But this lofty teaching was expressed to us as we sat on our mother's knee, "God helps those who help themselves."

The next teaching is summarized in the pithy phrase of St. Ignatius Loyola: "Work as if everything depended upon you; and pray as if everything depended upon God." In the final analysis everything depends upon God's grace, and pleading for it—like beggars. Before, during and after our work we are on our knees, paupers at the throne of God. Yes, we enjoy all the powers that

God has given us, but they remain stillborn or misdirected without God's grace. After we have exhausted all that we can do, we leave the rest in the hands of God. As the ancient *Allocutio* before Marriage so elegantly put it: "Nor will God be wanting to our needs." The lurking heresy here is Quietism, the seventeenth century error that riddled the Church. It possessed a siren appeal because it took a little bit of the Truth and exaggerated it, which is the trademark of all heresies. In the case of Quietism, it acknowledged the necessity of prayer and grace, then stopped there. No human action was necessary. God will take care of everything as long as we pray. Notice the snare. God can do all things, true enough. Man need do nothing except pray, there the heresy.

Its contagion is so subtle that its lie captures the best of Catholics even today. When you hear prominent Catholic voices in the face of the gaping crisis facing he Church simply prescribe, "Stay positive and pray", know you staring into the maw of Quietism. These voices are the Shirley Temples of Catholicism today, when what we need are St. Athanasius's. Adopt the classical prayer that avoids the Scylla and Charybdis of both Quietism and Activism: "Direct, O Lord, we ask Thee, all our actions by Thy holy inspiration and carry them on by Thy assistance, that every prayer and works or ours may begin from Thee, and through Thee be brought to completion." A perfect plea before God: a perfect expression of Catholic doctrine.

After all this we are obliged by the command of God to be of good cheer, and have supernatural hope in God's care. This past Sunday was called Laetare and we began Holy Mass with the exclamation from Isaiah 66: "Laetare Jerusalem" (Rejoice Jerusalem!). Since we are in the hands of a Provident God who loves and cares for us without measure, gloom and worry has no part. Lest God think we do not trust Him.

In the administration of the last president (Obama), his chief of staff once cynically remarked, "Never let a crisis go to waste." That epitomizes modernity's shrill, cold and scheming designs. True crises belong to Catholics, and to saints. For through them we can see God's wondrous designs.

10
Lessons from the Saints

OUR LEPANTO MOMENT

The year 1571 was a year that sent shivers down the spines of Catholics. Each one was staring down the tip of a spear. Islam's spear. Like a salivating beast, Islam was devouring nation after nation, and now, Catholic Europe was in their sights. The political establishment was paralyzed before such a fanatical foe, and every corner of Europe looked to the only world leader with fortitude to face such a brutal enemy: the Successor of the Apostles, Pope St. Pius V.

This Dominican saint ascended the throne of St. Peter in 1566 and immediately launched a vigorous implementation of Trent's reforms. Those who mistook his great humility for timidity were quickly disabused as he wielded his pontifical power like a gleaming saber. Hanging in the Renaissance air was the strong scent of pluralism. It had especially invaded the sacred precincts of the Divine Liturgy where the celebration of Mass from place to place was a disunified patch quilt, Mass having become a palette of individual and personal self-expression. Pius rooted out this excrescence of cultural decadence, mandating strict regularization of liturgy codified in the spirit of Trent. But his reforming eye did not stop at the Liturgy. When seven bishops were accused of favoring Protestantism he wasted no time in dismissing them. He took seriously St. Paul's injunction, "For if the trumpet give an uncertain sound, who shall prepare himself to the battle" (1 Cor 14:18).

No challenge tested his mettle more than the fall of Cyprus to the Ottoman Turks in 1570. Islam's maw was opening wider and wider, threatening to swallow the Europe of the Holy Apostles. Pius rushed to assemble the Holy League, composed of the Papal States, Spain, Naples, Sicily, Venice, Genoa, Tuscany, Savoy, Parma, Urbino, and the Knights of Malta. In 1571 its fleet confronted the superior Islamic warships. Defeat seemed all but certain, until Pius summoned the most powerful weapon he knew, the Holy Rosary. He pleaded that every Catholic join together in the recitation of the Holy Rosary for the intention of soundly vanquishing the Islamic hordes.

Churches swelled with Catholics fervently praying the Rosary; families collected in their homes, guildsmen in their stores, shepherds in their fields, soldiers in their barracks, professors in their universities, students in their campus halls, tradesmen in their stalls. All lifting their hearts and voices to the Mother of God. Then, Lepanto. Then, 1571. The Holy League routed the Islamic Turks and their impressive fleets. Catholic Europe was rescued, yes, by Don Juan's brave soldiers, but even they knew that their true captain was the Mother of God. She was the Victor. Pope St. Pius immediately established a feast for the Universal Church on October 7, honoring the Blessed Virgin Mary as Our Lady of the Holy Rosary. It should dismiss in the minds of every Catholic any doubt as to the efficacy of the Holy Rosary, especially when many Catholic voices are joined as one.

The saintly Dominican pope recognized that a certain potency attaches when Catholics unite their voices in prayers to the Queen of Heaven. Our Lady noticed that such joint acts are inspired by the intensity of the petition and listens with greater eagerness. One need only look at Cana. More than a few importuned her at once, and her maternal heart was moved. How could it not be? She is the perfect mother, always seeking to give her children whatever they require. It was her Son, after all, Who taught, "For where two or three are gathered in my name, there am I in the midst of them" (Mt 18:20).

More than a few Catholics probably recall Catholicism's Golden Age in America. During that time, each year the pilgrim statue of Our Lady of Fatima would travel from parish to parish. Families would enroll in hosting the statue, inviting their friends and extended family to join them kneeling before the statue as they begged Our Lady for peace in the world. Was it not those impassions rosaries, recited by family and friends, that averted the Cuban Missile Crisis in 1962? Can we not name those family rosaries as the cause of the events that led to the collapse of the Iron Curtain in 1989 and the crumbling of the Soviet Union in 1991? It is no accident that the seemingly invincible Soviet Empire, with its thickly knotted tentacles enveloping the world, imploded during the reign of John Paul II whose pontifical coat of arms bore the inscription *Totus Tuus* – all thine, O Virgin Mary.

The 1950s also boasted a priest second only in popularity to Bishop Fulton Sheen, Father Patrick Peyton. He made it his priestly mission to propagate, not merely the recitation of the Rosary, but the common praying of the Rosary by families. On account of Father Peyton the phrase, "The family that prays together, stays together" was on the lips of score of Americans, Catholic and non-Catholic alike. Father Peyton cast an amazingly wide net, reaching even the Hollywood glitterati, who frequently supported him with their generous donations to guarantee that as many as possible would hear the message of the Family Rosary. Only Heaven knows how many crises were averted because of fathers and mothers, sons and daughters raising their voices together to the Queen of Heaven.

Our straitened circumstances beg for a return to the Rosary prayed by Catholics in common. A group of men, young and old, decided to pray the Rosary together as they strolled through the streets and parks of a major city. They prayed *sotto voce*, but were not afraid to let their rosaries drape at their sides in view of all the passerby. The impact was palpable. These Catholic men saw the expressions on the faces of sophisticated and urbane city dwellers as these equally sophisticated Catholic men quietly prayed, with their rosaries swaying at their sides. Who knows how many Iron Curtains fell during that blessed walk? Iron Curtains of imbedded sin, encrusted anti-Catholic resentments, Olympian hubris, blind devotion to passion, and boastful emancipation from God. If not a complete fall, perhaps those rosaries created a hundred cracks in their Iron Curtains: cracks in their dogmatic hatred of religion, their hermetically sealed confident in materialism, their contempt of Christianity.

Walls of darkness seem to be closing in upon us. The air of common sense is being sucked from the corridors of our daily life. Enemies of Christ seem to be appearing in places that shock us. Catholics knew what to do in 1571. Catholics have no reason not to know what to do today.

CATHOLICISM, THE WORLD, AND A WARRIOR ANGEL

Until 2017, the word snowflake enjoyed only one meaning: frozen rain in winter. But in the last year or so the word assumed a secondary meaning: students in elite college campuses who fall to pieces at the least offense or contrary opinion to their own. This new youthful brittleness makes perfect sense in the context of the secular culture that weaned them. It pampers its entitled members into a self-absorbed nirvana producing men and women, risk averse, committed to ease and instant pleasure and concerned only with Me as #1.

With this as a backdrop the figure of St. Michael the Archangel is not likely to meet a happy welcome. His image in Catholic iconography is well known, probably the Guido Reni painting comes to mind: a daunting Roman soldier, poised for battle, covered by impressive breastplate, holding a spear as he thrusts it down the throat of a demon. Not exactly the irenic, self-affirming pose so beloved by our culture. St. Michael's stirring image probably inspired the words of the late Thomist scholar, Frederick Wilhelmsen: "Catholicism is ... the Mexican Jesuit Father Miguel Pro blessing his Marxist firing squad in Mexico with the stumps of his arms after the barbarians had finished cutting them off. It is Spanish soldiers charging Communist trenches with fixed bayonets and rosaries... Catholicism is about an army marching through history chanting the *Te Deum*. Catholicism is about swords."

St. Michael the Archangel is precisely the perfect model for our sagging civilization. He is just the right antidote to the petite Christ that many have preferred to the Crucified One. He is a warning against the "no strings attached" mercy that competes with the severe mercy announced by the Lamb of God. St. Michael is a rebuke to those who would tame the force of the Gospel's furiously extravagant demands which so embarrasses not a few Catholics who have long wedded themselves to the world.

This formidable saint who conquered Satan and his minions in that great primordial battle, fittingly earns the title Protector of the Church. For this reason, Pope Benedict XVI erected a heroic size bronze statue of St. Michael in the Vatican Gardens, suggesting that these wrenching times besieging the Church require his assistance more than any other in the Church's long history.

One of the lines of St. Michael's prayer beg that "he defend us in battle." The "battle" is more than the clash of tanks and bullets, it is the battle that each man wages on the planes of his soul. This is the arena where each soul encounters Satan face to face, every day. It is the arena where we meet alluring temptation, enticing rationalizations, cozy complacency and surrender to mediocrity. Life is a daily battle against sin and sin's patron, Satan. Neglect of this principal war leaves the soul prey to a creeping blindness. Satan, the father of lies, creates illusion about the soul as a spider spins the near invisible strands of his web.

For some time now many in the Church have made a settlement with vice. Therapeutic wellness has taken the place of the spiritual combat, leaving once long confessional lines a mere trickle. The very phrase of saving one's soul, the *raison d'etre* of Catholicism, has become as foreign to Catholics as a line from the Upanishads. This dealt a dagger to the heart of the Church, rocking her to her very foundations. The fallout was half a century of social activism displacing religion itself, leaving the priesthood prostrate and scarred, religious orders eviscerated and the Faithful rudderless. St. Michael breaks the spell of the cultural blather which beckons, "Be all you can be," and returns us to the Catholic sanity of "Be all God wants you to be."

Recall the St. Michael prayer for a moment:

> St. Michael the Archangel, defend us in battle, be our defense against the wickedness and snares of the devil. May God rebuke him we humbly pray, and do thou, O Prince of the Heavenly Host, by the power of God, cast into Hell Satan and all the other evil spirits who roam about the world seeking the ruin of souls. Amen.

It was composed by Pope Leo XIII on October 13, 1884, thirty-three years to the day prior to the final apparition of our Lady at Fatima, and the Miracle of the Sun. But the circumstance of the composition is interesting. On that day Pope Leo had completed offering Mass in his private chapel with several cardinals and his household in attendance. After descending the altar, he was about to genuflect and make his exit. But the pontiff froze in place. He remained staring at the tabernacle for several minutes, a long enough time for those in the chapel to be concerned. Finally, he made the genuflection, and proceeded to the sacristy to unvest. Upon doing so, he repaired immediately to his study and wrote the prayer. At breakfast one of the cardinals inquired about the unusual pause. The pope explained that he was listening to a conversation at the tabernacle. One of the speakers had a voice harsh and guttural, the other, one soft and comforting. The guttural voice was Satan, the other, Christ:

Satan: You know that I can destroy your Church.

Christ: Is that so? Then do it.

Satan: I would need more time and power.

Christ: How much time and power?

Satan: 75 to 100 years, and power over those in the Church whom I would enlist in my service.

Christ: Done. Do what you will.

Within days of that chilling supernatural conversation, Pope Leo mandated that his composed prayer to St. Michael the Archangel be recited after every Mass, in every Catholic church and chapel throughout the world. And it was. Up until 1966, when it was abolished by prelates convinced that the Church had entered upon a new maturity which demanded a new détente with the World.

Could that détente have been another trick in the bag of the Prince of Darkness? We wonder.

"RE-ENCHANTING" THE WORLD

Just as the Catholic Church forgot about angels, the world became obsessed with them. Of course, not in the doctrinal manner of the Church, but in their own fashion. Angels became extensions of the Self. All part of the Gnostic craze enveloping the decadent West. In Dr. Frederick Wilhelmsen's witty, albeit premonitory, characterization,

> Today angels have suddenly erupted into vogue, and they seem to be everywhere: charming, chubby, cheerful cherubs, dancing from little pins pinned to the blouses of young women; becoming heroes of a television programs; emerging on the screen disguised as serious fellows in three-piece suits; swooping down from heaven and saving the day for people implicated in seemingly inextricable difficulties. They even win football games by their ghostly appearance on the field. They threatened to displace Santa Claus in the hearts of children at Christmas. We seem to be suffocated in their wings and it is time that Christians ask themselves seriously what is it that we really believe about angels.

It is part of the Modernist project to render every belief of Catholicism obsolete. Angels and saints are at the top of their list. Since angels trumpet the air of the supernatural they become insulting to Man Come of Age. The New Man recognizes a god within him, thus an erasure of the supernatural. Since man cannot suffer such an arid existence, he conjures proxies for the supernatural. Hence, the current obsession with the spirit world. Secularized audiences crave diabolical possession, zombies, strange life on other worlds, witches and covens. It is *cri di coeur* for God and His real hierarchical world of spirits. Dr. Wilhelmsen again, "... angels have returned with a vengeance in popular folklore. But Christians have not brought them back. Pagans have."

The Modernist mind is content to live in the claustrophobic world of secularized dogmas, viz. transgenderism, diversity, equity, inclusion and doctrinal environmentalism. All counterfeits for God and the world of the supernatural. But only God and his spiritual firmament can bring man peace and liberty. Faux Modernist dogmas slowly choke and kill. Sad that so many in the Church propagate this with impunity. Sadder still that such large numbers of Catholics embrace this like a New Gospel, thinking it better fitted to modern man than the Old One preached by Incarnate God.

Max Weber, renowned sociologist/philosopher wrote in his now famous lecture at Munchen in 1917, "The fate of our time is characterized by rationalization and intellectualization and, above all, the disenchantment of the world."

The Church today seems to be the fulfillment of this atheist Weber's prediction. His patronizing use of the term 'enchantment' referred to supernatural religion, in general, and Roman Catholicism, in particular. While casting a disapproving eye on both, he credits them with giving pre-modern man meaning, albeit an ephemeral and puerile one. The New Man must now set aside such infantile 'enchantment'. It is his obligation to now bravely accept the new vistas of man without God. Weber's was the 'disenchantment' that modern science world deliver.

The Modernist Project has introduced a new enchantment: the magical world of the Self. From this demimonde it spins its new dogmas. Or in Milton's words in *Paradise Lost*,

> The mind is its own place, and in itself
> Can make a Heav'n of Hell, a Hell of Heaven.

This is the locus of the Gnostic Man. Dr. Philip Reiff has named him the Psychological Man. Of this new creature, he wrote pungently: "Religious man wants to be saved; psychological man wants only to be pleased."

Isn't this the thrust of the upcoming Synod on Synodality? It applauds the agenda of the World and shuns the demands of Christ's Holy Church. It eschews the Divine constitution of the Savior for His Mystical Body and adopts a latitudinarian model where the *vox populi* replaces the *vox Dei*.

Critical to the enterprise of restoring the True Faith, is a reintroduction of a devotion to the angels, particularly our Guardian Angels. It reasserts the prominence of the supernatural in our Holy Religion, an aspect quite embarrassing to the Modernist elite.

Witness the manner in which the Sacred Liturgy is conducted in a majority of parishes throughout the world. Do we find the electrifying presence of God? Is it an irruption of the astonishing presence of the Immolated Lamb of God? Does it evoke in those present a deep sorrow of sin as it touches the hem of the Divine mercy?

Lisbon's World Youth Day was shocking evidence of quite the opposite. There were bishops looking on approvingly at Holy Mass while a priest manipulated a synthesizer as though he were a DJ at a New York City nightclub. Isn't this enough to convince any skeptic of the depths to which liturgy has fallen. Naïve Pollyanna's can no longer defend this as ectopic. It was performed at a papally approved event with bishops giving their nod of assent. Catholics who boast of a sensible conservatism have much to answer for as their 'see-no-evil; hear-no-evil; say-no-evil' strategy leads to a seemingly irreversible metastasis of heterodoxy. Remember, as the Liturgy goes, so goes the Catholic soul, viz., *lex orandi, lex credendi*.

Every Catholic has a part in a return to the supernatural as the essence of our Holy Religion. Devotion to the Guardian Angels is an important first step. Any number of reasons can be adduced for the critical importance of devotion to the angels in these straitened times.

One is metaphysical. God is omnipotent, and yet he takes great joy in channeling His power through others. It further manifests His glory and goodness. St. Thomas calls this 'secondary causality'. Take a good parent who has labored to instill in their children a solid Catholic character. When others praise the child for their admirable conduct, they are praising the parents who bestowed it. The child is the secondary cause of his character, because the primary cause is his parents. He would not enjoy that quality, if not for his parents. God exercises His power similarly. Though He grants us all we require to execute good actions, such actions would not be possible without His primary causality. The Angelic Doctor explains more fully in several places,

> It is a greater perfection for a thing to be good in itself and also the cause of goodness in others, then only to be good in itself. Therefore, God so governs things that he makes some of them to be causes of others in government, as a master who not only imparts knowledge to his pupils but also gives the faculty of teaching others. If God governed alone, things would be deprived of the perfection of causality.[1]

---

[1] *Summa theologiae* I, Q. 103, art. 6.

> There are certain intermediaries of God's Providence; for He governs things inferior by superior, not on account of any defect in His power, but by reason of the abundance of his goodness: so that the dignity of causality is imparted even to creatures.[2]
>
> It is not on account of any defect in God's power that He works by means of secondary causes, but it is for the perfection of the order of the universe, and the more manifold outpouring of His goodness on things, through His bestowing on them not only the goodness which is proper to them but also the faculty of causing goodness in others.[3]

God bestows upon the angels an invaluable secondary causality. Through them he governs the created order. This includes a stunning complexity of beauty, which is a pale refraction of the staggering beauty of the Blessed Trinity. Not to be overlooked is the genuine agency of secondary causes, amplifying the infinite dimensions of Divine Providence: each producing genuine causality, but in their ordered manner. All of this unfolding in a hierarchical order that delivers satisfaction to the intellect and peace to the human soul. Thus, Our Blessed Mother is *Mediatrix* of All Graces. Even Dante in the Divine Comedy has the Virgin Mary summon St. Lucy who, in her turn, selects Beatrice to speak to Dante.

Reflect on the *Nine Choirs of Angels*. The First Hierarchy forms God's immediate court and receives its justice, splendor and burning love by direct communication from Our Lord:

- *The Seraphim*, uniquely united to the very love of God
- *The Cherubim*, united to God by their profound knowledge of the mysteries of God
- *The Thrones*, united to God by contemplation and serve Him in an ineffable fashion

The Second Hierarchy was created by God to govern the world, both spiritual and material in the name of Him, whose inheritance it is, the Man-God, and King of Glory, Jesus Christ.

- *The Dominations* preside over the government of the universe, from the steps of God's throne
- *The Virtues* watch over the course of nature's laws, the preservation of species, and the movement of the heavens
- *The Powers* hold the spirits of wickedness in subjection under the command of Our Lady, Virgin Most-Powerful

---

[2] *Summa theologiae* I, Q. 22, art. 3.
[3] *Summa theologiae Supplementum*, Q. 72, art. 2, ad 1.

The Third Hierarchy executes the Divine decrees, both for angels and men. Heaven's messengers, ambassadors and overseers, they are the ministers of salvation wrought on earth by Jesus, the Heavenly High-Priest.

- *The Principalities* preside over the whole human race in general and great social bodies, such as nations and churches, in particular
- *The Archangels* rule the Angels and transmit to them the commands of God together with the love and light which comes down to us from the highest hierarchy. They preside over smaller communities, such as religious Orders and families
- *The Angels*, the messengers of God, also deputed with the guardianship of man. From their numbers come the Guardian Angels

The Guardian Angels are the closest collaborators with the Blessed Trinity on our behalf. Their entire existence is consumed with caring for our existence – both spiritual and physical. Of course, their mediation follows that of Our Lady. Nonetheless, they are deputed in a singular fashion to bring us to heaven. It is their role to inspire our intellect with contrition and works of virtues (especially Holy Charity) as well as assisting us to comprehend matters of great complexity. They fortify our will, so that we not falter before great temptations or crosses that it pleases Our Savior to send us. They are present to protect us from physical dangers, and simply to answer our pleadings for the most pedestrian needs.

While protecting us, they are teaching us humility. We come to the realization that without God's help coming through the angels and grace, we could do nothing that is good. Our friendship with our Guardian Angels ought to be cultivated daily. Gradually we develop a dependence upon them, which slowly becomes a profound affection.

We must imitate the saints who would frequently commissioned their angels to rush to the assistance of others. Before preaching, St. Vincent Ferrer would plead with his Guardian Angel to visit all those who would be listening and open their hearts.

Perhaps returning to the old Prayer to the Guardian Angels would be a good first step:

> Angel of God, my Guardian dear,
> To whom God's love commits me here,
> Ever this day be at my side,
> To light and guard, to rule and guide. Amen.

Too saccharine, you say? That would be the complaint of the Catholic who thinks he has grown up, but actually grown out of the Faith. The Faith bestows a childlikeness that is never childish. It is gilded by the protection of humility. Any Catholic who sneers at the quality of this prayer is not too far from the apostle who protested, "Why was this ointment not sold for three hundred pence and given to the poor?" (Jn 12:5). Here is where cynicism usurps innocence.

While Modernist clerics mock devotion to the Guardian Angels (along with any trace of supernatural religion) we must remember one thing. Good Catholics fighting for the True Faith will win in this greatest of contests facing Mother Church in two thousand years.

For we have the armies of Heaven fighting with us through our prayers and sacrifices.

Modernists do not. How could they? For them the armies of Heaven are a fantasy.

ST. MARY MAGDALENE

Every painting of St. Mary Magdalene depicts her seated sorrowfully in a darkened cave. But that is not the detail that captures the observer: the human skull is. With eyes filled with tears, the Magdalene stares at the skull as though she was reading a book or listening to a message. She was. Not a morbid one, but a profoundly Catholic one, driven through with realism about the human condition.

In Catholic iconography the human skull is an arresting symbol of this passing world, as in 1 Peter 1:1, "I beseech you as strangers and pilgrims." Or Hebrews 13:14, "For here we have no abiding city." Under the power of the Faith, an otherwise ghoulish object translates into a luminous sign of the transient pleasures of human existence which titillate but never satisfy. Pleasures which, in T. S. Eliot's sobering rendering in the *Four Quartets*, are like a "distraction from distraction by distraction." In the end, all that the world offers becomes old, heavy with ennui. Except Christ.

When we consider the Magdalene our minds turn to that dramatic scene when she washes the Savior's feet with her tears. Finished, she breaks an expensive bottle of perfume, one of the many gifts she had received for her rendered carnal services, and anoints His feet, wiping them with her hair. Ah, that silken hair, whose beauty had once been a summons to her many suitors, becomes a token of adoration for the Redeemer. Judas wastes no time in protesting that the poor had been cheated. The traitor becomes the model of those who shout social justice, rather than *Viva Cristo Rey!* Iscariot is the paradigm of those who put chic causes above the Savior's Divine Mission. For Judas, religion is no longer serving Christ through serving others, but *merely* serving others. Such a striking contrast: Magdalene, swept in the perfect love of God; Judas, scheming self-interest under the veneer of generosity. This temptation will harass our Holy Religion till the end of time. It is the solvent of religion; the dominant heresy of our time.

After Judas's demurral, a mild scold falls from the lips of the Savior, "She has done something beautiful for me" (Mt 26:10). Love always expresses itself with beauty. Thus Pope Benedict XVI: "I have often affirmed my conviction that the true apology of Christian Faith, the most convincing demonstration of its truth... are the saints and the beauty that the Faith generates." And again:

> Yet, the beauty of Christian life is even more effective than art and imagery in the communication of the Gospel message. In the end, love alone is worthy of faith, and proves credible. The lives of the saints and martyrs demonstrate a singular beauty which fascinates and attracts, because a Christian life lived in fullness speaks without words. We need men and women whose lives are eloquent, and who know how to proclaim the Gospel with clarity and courage, with transparency of action, and with the joyful passion of charity.

So it is that the Church constructs grand churches, never counting the cost. She clothes her priest with sumptuous vestments, and festoons the vessels that carry the Body and Blood of Christ with precious jewels. Priests routinely wear a simple black cassock as a sign of his death to the world and his poverty without Christ. At the altar all is transformed. There, the priest is *alter Christus*, and dazzles the faithful with splendid vestments. Here the priest represents Christ, the King of Kings, who fills us with His divine riches.

First among those riches is His mercy, as the Magdalene had known so well. The Magdalene's contrition (prompting the Savior's amazing words, "Wheresoever this gospel shall be preached in the whole world, there shall also this, that the woman hath done, be told for a memorial of her," Mt 26:13) made her a special object of His election. She accompanies Our Lady and the Beloved Disciple at the foot of the Cross; she is chosen to be the first herald of Our Lord's Resurrection; she is the first to have a conversation with the Risen Savior. Why this lavish favor from the Redeemer? For she has "loved much." At the heart of love is the sorrow of love, or contrition. The Magdalene is the model of contrition. She knows her sin and refuses to call it anything but sin. She promises to change, or the purpose of amendment. She doesn't ask for accommodation, compromise or to be accompanied in her sin. She desires only to be perfectly united with her

Savior; for that, truth alone suffices. Upon such contrition and amendment, Christ pours forth His mercy. Nothing less. Divine mercy is not a cover-up for sin; it is the reward for struggling to sin no more.

All Catholics, especially those who have strayed into a caricature of mercy, should imitate St. Mary Magdalene. Otherwise, they will never know how guileless love meets Incarnate Love. The way the impure meets the All-Pure. Unless Catholics learn to see through her wetted eyes, they shall never know how the merciful eyes of Christ can ever meet their own.

A MEDIEVAL REMEDY
FOR MODERNITY'S ILLS

Show me a Catholic not troubled by the circumstances of these days, and I will show you a Catholic asleep. Society's woes rock his soul, but the historic perils facing Holy Church do so even more. Not only from outside her walls, but more frighteningly, from within. How are we to keep our spirits from sagging? How do we keep at bay critical spirit, one of those acids which eats away at the soul? Clearly, the obvious answer is increased prayer and mortification. Added to this, however, is a consistent return to the lives of the saints. We often hear that puerile retort: "What would Jesus do?" The question is as vain as asking the way I can fill the oceans in a thimble. Our Lord's divine teachings can only be applied by attention to the teachings of his Holy Catholic Church: He is the Light, she the prism. Also studying closely the manner in which the saints lived divine instructions in their simple human lives, gives us clues to our own.

Fr. Gerard Manly Hopkins gives this truth poetic expression when he writes: "For Christ plays in ten thousand places, / Lovely in limbs and lovely in eyes not His / To the Father through the features of men's eyes." The clever quip, "What would Jesus do?" is merely a penumbra of Protestantism's *sola fides*. It assumes a direct contact with the Wisdom Incarnate, without the mediation of the Church, her doctors and saints. This is presumption run amok. A more thoroughly Catholic approach is articulated by John Henry Cardinal Newman in his *Grammar of Assent*:

> One ordinarily arrives at the heart... by way of the imagination, through direct impressions, testimonies to facts and events, through history, through description. People influence us, voices move us, gazes strike us deeply, needs kindle us. Men will live and die for a dogma; no one will endure martyrdom for a conclusion.

To this end, a look at the life of St. Bernard of Clairvaux is instructive. He so dominated the twelfth century that church historians call that century his, for there is no corner of it that does not live beneath his shadow. Mother Church seemed hard put to find enough encomia to bestow upon him. Not only does she bestow the honorific doctor but Pius XII, in the encyclical written on the eighth centenary of his death, *Doctor Mellifluus*, does not hesitate in the first lines to repeat another title, *Last of the Fathers*. This appellation soars above the rest. Though Bernard is separated from the last Father of the Church by 400 years, Mother Church shows no hesitation in setting upon his head this singular title. Infrequently does the Church add to the already splendid attribution, doctor, anything further. But in the case of a rare few she does. Thus, St. Thomas Aquinas boasts two, the *Common Doctor*, and *Angelic Doctor;* St. Bonaventure, the *Seraphic Doctor.* St. Bernard stands in this august select company when the Church crowns him with the title, *Mellifluous Doctor*: Literally, honey filled. Strange sounding as it may be, it is an apt reference to the magnetic sweetness of his preaching and writing, adumbrating the style of the ancient Fathers. His preaching and writing, as theirs, was direct, affecting, summoning, enchanting and allusive in its poetic cadences.

Caution is in order here. Great care must be given to calling his writing sweet. No one should think that St. Bernard's style mimics the nineteenth century's soggy romanticism. Perish the thought. Thomas Merton explains it perfectly in his 1954 work, *The Last of the Fathers*, a commentary on the 1953 encyclical of Pius XII:

> The encyclical brings out quite clearly that the 'honey' in the doctrine of St. Bernard is not the cloying sweetness of a soul enclosed within itself, but the clean, fresh sweetness of the fields and the forest. It is the breath of true life, of divine life, of supernatural charity, and of the Holy Spirit. It is the happy vitality of a soul made alive by self-sacrifice, and the joy of a heart that lives no longer for itself but for others, and above all for God... Sentimentality is, after all, only a fake. It is a meretricious pretense of emotion, and has nothing to do with genuine human feeling, except that it sometimes gets itself accepted as a passable imitation... The preaching of St. Bernard of Clairvaux does have emotional repercussions. Let us not be so foolish as to deny the emotions, as part either of our life or our religion. But for Bernard emotion is never the end in view... The sweetness of Bernard remains clean because he seldom stops to think subjectively about sweetness. It is not at all self-conscious. It

does not even spring up from any source within Bernard himself. It is an overflow from the goodness and mercy and charity of God.

By 1109, at the age of nineteen, St. Bernard possesses certainty that God is calling him to the priesthood as a Cistercian monk. He enters the monastery at Citeaux in France. It was not long that his superiors recognize the superlative qualities of sanctity and intellectual prowess and send him to establish another foundation at Claire Vallee, which finally was abbreviated to the familiar, Clairvaux.

The twelfth century was no stranger to heresy, and St. Bernard's love of the Cistercian silence was never an obstacle to heeding the call of the Church to do battle with it. With his quicksilver intellect he engaged hard-bitten heretics like Peter Abelard and the Cathars with impressive success. The Saint of Clairvaux full well knew that right Catholic living was intimately bound to right Doctrine. Doctrine is the flesh and bones of Christ himself. Thinking it unimportant is settling for an *ad hoc* Christ, designed according to the whims of the self, or the passing enthusiasm of the age.

Admiration followed Bernard everywhere. Not only did popes, bishops and kings seek his counsel, but the saints' humility prompted him to remonstrate those very notables when he observed them failing the duties of their high office. Well did the Saint make his own the words of St. Gregory the Great in his *Pastoral Guide*:

> Pastors who lack foresight hesitate to say openly what is right because they fear losing the favor of men... The Lord reproach's them through the prophet: 'They are dumb dogs that cannot bark'... To advance against the foe involves a bold resistance to the powers of this world in defense of the flock. To stand fast in battle on the day of the Lord means to oppose the wicked enemy out of love for what is right.

Even though he reproved popes, no Catholic must think St. Bernard a disloyal son of the Church. Fidelity to Christ is fidelity to the unchanging Magisterial teachings that steel Roman Catholics against the gates of Hell. High office does not exempt from absolute fidelity. Never did Bernard place himself either above those sacred teachings or those anointed with those sacred offices. Paths to hell are paved with the souls of those who immodestly think themselves teachers of the Church. Listen to Bernard's warning to Pope Eugenius III written in five noble letters that now form his celebrated treatise *De Consideratione*:

> You are the bishop of bishops; the Apostles, your forbears, were instructed to lay the world at the feet of Jesus Christ. You have inherited that duty; the whole world is your legacy. Pastor of all the sheep, Pastor of all their pastors! In case of necessity, and if the fault deserves, you can bar Heaven to a bishop, depose him, cast him out to Satan. You are in very truth the Vicar of Christ. What is this your power? A burden to take up. Be not proud on Peter's throne; it is but an observation post, a high place from which, like a sentry, you may cast your glance over the world beneath. You are not the owner of that world; you are no more than trustee. The world belongs to Christ... There is not iron or poison that I fear so much for you as I fear the pride of power.

In 1146 St. Bernard was called to preach the Second Crusade. Catholics were understandably hesitant to comply with this invitation, entailing as it did considerable sacrifices. A prospective Crusader had to weigh leaving family and friends; the risk of losing property and fortunes; being captured and sold into slavery, or, ultimately the likelihood of losing his life. So much for the centuries old bigotry of Crusading Catholics' lustful appetite for the massacre of Muslims. Putting behind them all these fears, tens of thousands marched forward with heroic courage. Likely, these spirited words of St. Bernard inflamed them:

> O ye who listen to me! Hasten to appease the anger of Heaven, but no longer implore its goodness by vain complaints. Clothe yourselves in sackcloth, but also cover yourselves with your impenetrable bucklers. The din of arms, the danger, the labors, the fatigues of war, are the penances that God now imposes upon you. Hasten then to expiate your sins by victories over the infidels, and let the deliverance of the Holy Places be the reward of your repentance. Cursed be he who does not stain his sword with blood.

No ambiguity here. Only full-throated Roman Catholicism unfettered by the modern addiction to sentimentality parading as compassion. Bernard was confident in the Church's crisply stated teaching on the use of force in war. Not only is it morally permissible, but, when in the pursuit of the common good of the nation, force becomes morally obligatory. Of late, Catholics have become squeamish about such unvarnished language. But it is the language of Christ, because it is the immutable doctrine of his Church.

In 2017 the world again watched with horror the gratuitous savagery of Islamic terrorism in Barcelona. Similar shock should have been experienced several days later when Barcelonans marched in the tens of thousands. Why? Weren't they demanding justice for the death of innocents? No, their demand was—love and toleration. Don't mistake this myopia for Christian love. Nothing smacks so little of Christian love than such exhibitions of a desiccated humanity. It is nothing less than the exhaustion of the Secularist Project on full display. Modernity is no longer capable of even the most primordial human responses: loathing, pity, revulsion and retributive justice. Forgetfulness of eternal verities is the mark of modern man's hollow soul. Our present condition reminds us of C. S. Lewis's chilling words in a little-known essay, *Modern Man and His Categories of Thought*:

> The original hearers of the message of the Gospel had—in common with the Church—a belief in the supernatural, a fear of divine judgment, and an awareness that the world had once been better than it is now. The Jewish doctrine of the Fall, the Stoic conception of the Golden Age, and the common Pagan reverence for heroes, ancestors and ancient lawgivers, were in this respect more or less agreed... I sometimes wonder whether we shall not have to reconvert men to real paganism as a preliminary to converting them to Christianity. If they were Stoics, Orthics, Mithraists, or (better still) peasants worshipping the Earth, our task might be easier.

Future Barcelonan holocausts will be thwarted only by applying the astringency of Catholic teaching, which simply states common sense. Muscular military might must be exercised in thoroughly destroying the enemy who wish to destroy us. Anything less is a strategy of sentimentality: An effete luxury upon which the Jihadist enemy thrives. Only one thing is a worse blow to the Catholic Church and society than heresy; that is sentimentality.

By the end of St. Bernard's life Cistercian monasteries had multiplied from 161 to 343. So revered was the Mellifluous Doctor that Dante had St. Bernard take the place of Beatrice as he entered the Empyrean of Paradise leading to the unfolding White Rose of the Virgin Mother of God to whom he had such deep affection, evidenced by his composition of one of the most cherished prayers in the Church's treasury – the *Memorare*.

So magnetic was the preaching of St. Bernard that it is told that when the Saint approached French villages, mothers would take their boys and cover their ears, certain were they that his words would so enchant them that they would leave everything and follow him.

God didn't stop calling young men to be like St. Bernard in the twelfth century. He is calling young men to be like Bernard today.

Are they listening?

BLACK LIVES REALLY MATTERED TO ST. PETER CLAVER

Hollywood award shows used to be *de rigeur* viewing for most Americans. No more. Perhaps because a kind of collective delirium has set upon the artist class. Take the Emmy's this past Sunday, for instance. One of the celebrity winners, Donald Glover – a black man – snidely remarked, "I want to thank Trump for making black people number one on the most oppressed list." Not only was the remark counterfactual, it was sheer madness.

No wonder Americans are fleeing from award shows. Americans prefer listening to sane voices like Shelby Steele, the black intellectual, who in 2017 analyzed this circumstance in the Wall Street Journal, "Today Americans know that active racism is no longer the greatest barrier to black and minority advancement." Steele rightly pointed out that "White racism did not shoot more than 4,000 people last year in Chicago.

Jason Riley, also a black man writing in the Journal, echoed Steele: "Between 1890 and 1940, for example, black marriages rates in the U.S. were higher than white marriage rates. In the 1940s and '50s, black labor participation rates exceeded those of whites; black incomes grew much faster than white incomes; and the black poverty rate fell by 40 percentage points."

So much for blacks occupying "the most oppressed list." Facts are inconvenient things, the bane of fevered zealots. But what might a true champion of the black people look like? Well, he'd look like St. Peter Claver, who cared less for zealotry, and more for charity.

While Claver was born in Verdu, Spain in 1580, he was ordained a priest in Cartagena, Colombia in 1616. Deeply impressed by the mistreatment of African slaves he requested his Jesuit superiors that he be assigned to them to teach the Faith and administer the sacraments.

For some 100 years prior to St. Peter's arrival in Colombia the Spanish government had dealt in the inhuman and barbaric slave trade. By the early seventeenth century Spanish entrepreneurs were importing over 10,000 slaves to Colombia every month. All in open defiance of the condemnations of both Pope Paul III and Urban VIII, culminating in Blessed Pius IX's declaration that slavery was a supreme villainy.

With an impassioned priestly soul St. Peter would daily find a spot at the Cartagena's bustling harbor to await the tortured human cargo. Impatient with the docking protocols, the saint would convince sailors to procure a small boat to take him to the anchored ships. Climbing aboard he hurriedly made his way down into the bowels of the ship where the slaves were packed like cattle, mere inches separating one from another. Within such suffocating confinement the slaves ate, drank and evacuated themselves. During the long transatlantic voyage, the men had hands and legs shackled, causing excruciating open ulcerations. Along with the ravages of dysentery, the floors of the deck were coated with mucous and blood. The stench was so overpowering that not even seasoned sailors could bear it for more than several minutes at a time. This was Hell. Until St. Peter Claver arrived.

Without a slightest hesitation, the saint rushed to the chained slaves as though they were long lost friends. Their captors treated these slaves like animals; Claver handled them like rare jewels. Shocked surprise shone on their faces as St. Peter fed them, washed their wounds, carried those too weak to walk. But then the saint did something that went beyond food or drink or relief from suffering. He kissed them. Only an ordinary kiss, but far beyond ordinary to these prisoners. It swept these unfortunates into a different world, one shimmering with a transcendence few men ever know.

On land, St. Peter followed the slaves to their new places of bondage. There he instructed them in the Catechism, baptized them, administered Holy Communion, and heard their Confessions. In his preaching, the saint would show them a large gold medal, with the images of Jesus and Mary, then spend hours standing as the slaves queued to kiss the holy medal. The saint set up his humble quarters near where most of the slaves were housed. Some suffered wounds from their labors, and for lack of treatment, became infected, producing a nauseating odor. Other slaves would refuse to live near them. St. Peter would take the infected slaves and give them his quarters, while he slept on the floor.

By the time the saint died, he had spent 33 years among the Colombian slaves, having baptized 300,000 of them.

To a modern world weary of religion, but boasting a fashionable sensitivity to the plight of the suffering, St. Peter teaches the only answer to human misery is supernatural love. He never turned to political solutions, cries of injustice or rebellious demonstrations, he gave them only the consolations of the sacrament of Penance, and the nourishments of Christ's Body in the Holy Mass. Claver never removed his simple black cassock, even as he endured the heavy labors of caring for the souls of his charges. He would have found strange the modern excuse that the cassock separates the priest from his people. On the contrary, he knew that the cassock unites the priest to his people. Like glue. Clothed in the cassock, the people don't see the man, but Christ. But perhaps therein lies the contemporary neuralgia to the classic habit of the priest.

St. Peter Claver can never be called a humanitarian. Humanitarians are moved by their feelings; saints are moved by their love of Christ. Humanitarians see only victims, saints see souls for whom Christ shed his Precious Blood. Outside the orbit of Christ's Cross, men become mere pawns on a chess board or props to score political points. The current vogue for Third World adoptions is perfect illustration. Most of it is grandstanding for political effect, whilst simultaneously telegraphing their loathing for all things redolent of Western Civilization.

Humanitarians would never do what Peter Claver did, only saints could.

Debilitating sickness riddled the body of the saint in his waning years. An African slave was assigned to care for him, in fact, one of those who had been the recipient of Claver's transformative priestly ministrations. For the remaining months of the saint's life, Claver's caretaker mistreated him, often refusing to feed him, frequently even beating him. Claver finally died alone, not one of the 300,000 near him to bring some sweetness as he lay taking his last breaths. His solitary accompaniments were the ungrateful brutalities of one whom Claver had poured the goodness of his priestly heart. Never did the saint utter a word of complaint, excusable considering the context and circumstance. But a saint sees all as possibilities of merciful closeness with the Crucified.

St. Peter Claver never restricted his priestly attention to only the African slaves. He was available to every soul in need of Christ's salvific power. Once he ministered to a wealthy Spanish official who was in prison, awaiting execution for a capital crime. St. Peter found his way to the high-ranking Spaniard, and gave him a prayer book, encouraging him to pray from it every day. He did. Every day until his death, and before his execution he received Last Rites from the saint. When his family recovered his belongings, they were surprised to find a prayer book among this bon vivant's possessions. Upon opening it, they found an inscription written in the hand of the deceased, "This book was owned by the happiest man in the world."

Only one thing would make a man happier than being cared for by a saint. Becoming a saint himself.

THE PARADOXES OF AUSCHWITZ: BARBARITY AND BEATITUDE

Shivers of horror still travel down the backs of the sturdiest of men at the mention of Auschwitz. It is a place forever synonymous with satanic evil. Yet, Catholics know differently: not a denial of Auschwitz's inhuman terrors, but its standing as a crucible of holiness.

Its barbarity created two canonized saints: Maximilian Kolbe and Teresa Benedicta of the Cross. And they are only the acknowledged ones. Who is to say how many countless souls united themselves to Christ's cross in that unremitting hell of grisly death, gaining swift entry into paradise?

To the world, this is a troubling sign of a pathology of masochism, the ressentiment of Nietzsche's anti-Christian rages. To the Catholic, it is the exquisite paradox of the Cross: acceptance of suffering as the stuff of triumph. Moreover, it is ringing proof of St. Paul's stirring words that "To them that love God, all things work together unto good" (Rom 8:28). It is Milton's Satan in *Paradise Lost* who shrieks in maddening frustration, "I will only evil, and accomplish only good."

Souls famished for God can only reach Him through Christ's Cross. Otherwise, man's heavy pride weighs him down like a giant concrete slab, sinking him ever more deeply into the dark abyss of the self. Too many rivals of Catholicism within Catholicism itself have worked earnestly to erase this inconvenient mystery.

They are the objects of St. John Henry Newman when he wrote in his *Sermons Bearing on Subjects of the Day*:

> We are cherishing a cheerful religion, a hollow religion, which will not profit us in the day of trouble. This age loves an exclusively cheerful religion. It is determined to make religion bright and sunny and joyous... we take what is beautiful and attractive, and shrink from what is stern and painful.

This cheery religion fixation has been propagated in ways painfully familiar to Catholics of the past half-century. It is no accident

The Paradoxes of Auschwitz: Barbarity and Beatitude 435

that crucifixes have been removed from sanctuaries and solemn hymns lyricizing the dogmas of the Faith have been replaced by puerile jingles celebrating our specialness. This same mindset has turned the grave divine summons to contrition into the soft tones of therapeutic chic. Michelangelo's *Christ in Judgment* leaves these folks unsettled; their Christ is more a fusion of the Buddha with a dash of Gandhi.

Chesterton put his finger on the problem when he wrote,

> There is more logical consistency in reacting to Jesus by rending one's robes with a cry of blasphemy and in trying to seize Him as a maniac, than in calmly saying with contemporary rationalists that Jesus was a wise and holy man.

A direct line connects this cheery religion with current attempts to accommodate Christ's sublime teachings. The indissolubility of matrimony, for instance, is redesigned with cheap compromises oozing from the sterile wasteland called post-modern culture. That same line connects the mushrooming acceptance of same-sex marriage and the scandalous reticence of so many Catholics. Today's version of Judas's kiss.

This cheery religion would have drained Auschwitz of its power to forge men into saints. St. Teresa Benedicta of the Cross chose that name at her profession as a Carmelite because she knew well the Cross as the exclusive gate to redemption. In fact, she knew that all joy found its source in the Cross. Armed with that confidence, she greeted the Gestapo when they came banging on the convent door at Echt, Holland, in 1942.

No doubt shaken, the saint was not surprised. After all, the Dutch bishops had breached the prudent reserve of Pius XII to the maniacal Reich by promulgating an official condemnation of their treatment of the Jews. Ironically, it put more innocent Jews at risk, a result Pacelli strained so mightily to avoid. The Gestapo would now hunt down even Jews converted to the Catholic Faith.

Sr. Teresa Benedicta of the Cross made a delicious target. Loaded into a paddy wagon, she soon found herself at Auschwitz. Only seven days from her arrest she was gassed and incinerated. Eyewitnesses tell us that as she was marched to the gas chambers with thousands of others, she was in her Carmelite habit. Little boys and girls covered their faces in the folds of that blessed garment of the Mother of God as they watched their mothers descend into madness.

St. Teresa Benedicta's final walk to her Calvary at Auschwitz was preceded by a life at once illustrious and melancholic. Edith Stein had been born into a strict German Jewish family in 1891. However, by the age of 14, this gifted prodigy proudly declared herself an atheist.

Her remarkable intellectual gifts won her speedy entrance into the University of Göttingen; and even more remarkably, she received her doctorate in philosophy at age 29, under the demanding mentorship of the celebrated phenomenologist Edmund Husserl. Edith was quickly feted as one of Europe's premier philosophers, with a secure academic teaching position at the University of Freiburg, when this meteoric rise came to a dramatic halt.

In fact, the exact moment can be pinpointed. Edith Stein had been invited to the country home of one of her colleagues at the University for a restful weekend. After her hosts had retired, Edith's restless intellect found its way to the professor's library. She quickly scanned the shelves and paused at a title which piqued her curiosity, *The Autobiography of St. Teresa of Avila*.

Lifting it off the shelf, she sat in an easy chair and devoured every word. So absorbed was she that Edith lost all track of time. As she turned the final pages, she noticed the rising sun spilling through the library windows. As she closed the book, she murmured to herself, "This is the truth!"

Soon after that providential evening, she made the shocking decision to convert to the Catholic Church. She was baptized on January 1, 1922.

Her conversion was shocking for two reasons. It shook the academic firmament of Europe's toniest Universities. Think of the reaction if Laurence Tribe or Elena Kagan announced their conversion to the Church and then entered a cloistered Carmelite enclosure. Exactly. More personally for Edith were the effects on her pious Jewish family, especially her mother. She wept bitterly upon hearing her daughter's decision to be baptized. So did Edith.

Ten years later she disclosed to her mother that she would enter the Carmel. This was Mrs. Steins's breaking point, and she cried out that Edith was dead to her. These were the first shadows of the crosses that would follow Edith. Heroically, she embraced them all.

Lovers of a cheery religion would flee from such circumstances.

Easier to worry about the environment or low wages than to disappear into the arms of the Crucified. Ah, "for what does it profit a man, if he gain the whole world and suffer the loss of his own soul" (Mt 16:26).

We are told that Edmund Husserl, along with other professorial luminaries, attended the new Sr. Teresa Benedicta of the Cross's profession in April 1934. We are further told that these bright academic lights wept. The severe majesty of the Faith always vanquishes hearts. It compels man to look at the poverty of his life compared with the riches of Christ and His Holy Church. Any honest man knows what it is that he must do.

Slowly but surely, our age is being covered by the darkness of Auschwitz.

Obviously, there are no gas chambers; but there are souls choked by the casual acceptance of vices which would make men of another generation wince. Clearly, no emaciated and skeletal bodies are piled neatly on successive small hills; but there are emaciated souls who consider God an embarrassment and Catholics a dangerous obstacle to human freedom and progress. There is no Gestapo; but there is a government which has begun a furtive persecution of the Catholic Church and an intellectual elite that is increasingly successful at painting Catholics as misfits.

All of this would probably make even a Dr. Goebbels grin.

Only an army of Edith Steins can confront the looming darkness.

But cheery religion can't produce Edith Steins. Only the Old Faith (to borrow the phrase of the sixteenth-century English recusant Catholics) can do that. The Old Faith, unafraid of the Cross. Unafraid of those who are.

ST. MOTHER TERESA: LOVING THE POOR CATHOLIC STYLE

Much before Pope Francis declared Mother Teresa a saint, the world had already canonized her. But they did not see Mother Teresa, they saw what they wanted to see. Like a Rorschach test, they read onto the saint their own slanted ideas of society, the good and justice itself. The world saw her heroic work but not the reason why she did it. What resulted was seeing a cartoon Mother Teresa, not the real one; they admired half of Mother Teresa, not the whole saint. They gazed at Mother Teresa through their unacknowledged prejudices, not through the lens of truth. Seeing Mother Teresa as she really was would be intolerable to the Secularized West. Call to mind the squirming of the members of the United Nations when she addressed them on Oct. 26th, 1985. She bravely declared to those assembled notables that the unborn are the poorest of the poor. It sounded to them like fingernails scratching a blackboard. One recalls a similar reception that Aleksander Solzhenitsyn received when he spoke to Harvard on June 8th, 1978. Those effete elites believed they would hear a Che Guevara stand-in going on an agitprop rant, in what Tom Wolfe dubbed *radical chic*. Instead he passionately reproved the West for its decadence, while pointing out with dripping irony a school which still retained its motto *veritas*, while long finding its very alleged existence amusing.

While St. Mother Teresa walked in the same world that we do, her soul dwelt in entirely different one: the supernatural world. All she did was in obedience to the Divine command: "Whatsoever you do the least of my brethren, you do unto me." No chorus of social justice here, only submission to the Divine Will. She did not love the poor because they were poor, she loved the poor because she first loved Christ. When man loves others on account of his own reasons, his love becomes a more noble form of mere self-love. In his *City of God* St. Augustine similarly indicts the ancient Roman Empire for this very reason, calling even their virtues, vices. Such human love is bound by the limits that man places upon it.

St. Mother Teresa: Loving the Poor Catholic Style 439

Saints love without limit, because their love is bound only by the limits of God, Whose love knows no limit. Moreover, purely human love is fashioned according to the rules that man makes, which are as flawed as he is. Saints love with a perfect love, for its direction is always charted by God. Love of man that is not done out of love for God collapses into an epicene philanthropy, at best, or Marxist exertions, at worst. St. Mother Teresa would have none of this, earning her the epithet of the prominent Indian physician, Dr. Araupe Chatterzu of "propagating a cult of suffering." Isn't it just like the world to see suffering as some kind of Sartrean no-exit? No wonder it must expel suffering through the ghoulish rationale of euthanasia. Irony is stretched to its limits when this killing is called mercy. Interesting how porous secularism has made mercy. Tragic how some Catholics excitedly try to play catch-up with this secularist Brave New World. Saints desire only to ease the pain of the suffering man in front of them, rather than organizing a rent-a-mob to protest that men are suffering.

Every act of this saint was first an act of the love of God. St. Camillus de Lellis would kneel before the hospital bed of the suffering to whom he tended and called them, "My Christs." Such supernatural motivation unleashes heroic acts that shock the world, leaving its self-absorption under indictment. Apart from the most callous secularist, the remark of Mother Teresa that she would "take men who lived liked animals, and have them die like angels" causes earthquakes in the souls of men. To liberal elites who only see the poor as a political category she was anathema. She did not exhaust her life among the poor because they were hungry but because they were made in the image and likeness of God. As her religious order flourished beneath the banner of this supernatural impulse, other religious Orders were withering under the metastasis of their secularity.

It was so easy to see. Where St. Mother Teresa hands were wiping the sweat off the brow of a dying AIDS victim, more than a few Religious Orders had their hands raised in a clenched fist against patriarchy. While the Saint held little babies in her hands, other Religious joined their hands with their pro-choice Sisterhood. Many other Religious marched solemnly for the empowerment of the poor, all that St. Mother Teresa did was feed the poor. When certain other Religious traveled to foreign lands to join Communists in the Struggle, the Saint struggled to please her Savior by quenching the thirst of a small child. Some of those religious were called martyrs for dying for the People's cause; but anyone of the most basic common sense knew the true martyr was St. Mother Teresa, who gave her entire life for the poor for the love of God.

Most importantly, the Saint wanted always to be known and seen as a faithful Daughter of the Church. Neither she nor any of the sisters in her Order were ever seen outside of their religious habit. Religious habit? Why such emphasis on a mere incidental, at best, an outdated impediment, at worst? Because it is not an incidental. It is a sign integral to the mystery of consecration. Man's deepest truths beg for expression; they demand dramatic visibility lest they recede from proper attention. Signs are humankind's trumpets, and man's most sublime verities mandate trumpet blasts. Of sublime verities, consecration to God stands loftily above all others. It deserves nothing less than the silverest trumpets: the habit, the cassock.

St. Mother Teresa's nuns radiate a joy embedded in an absolute obedience to the Church. The PC jargon of the world is alien to them as rap is to a Bach concert. They know only the eloquence of the teachings of Christ and His Holy Church. Inscribed on their hearts is the saint's famous dictum: "God does not want success, but fidelity." To the Saint, the world's logic is a deafening din; the Church's voice, operatic.

The saint's audiences often heard her plead that they must all go out and do something beautiful for God. For her it was care of the poor, for me and you, something entirely different; for God created all of us differently. Make no mistake, the most beautiful thing on earth is man's sanctity.

Catholics cannot afford hesitation in doing something beautiful for God. How else will the world become beautiful again?

ON NOT KEEPING THE POOR POOR

No war has been lost so miserably than America's War on Poverty. Launched 50 years ago by LBJ, a president not usually given to the swoons of political naiveté, was a headfirst slam into the brick wall of common sense. With Wilsonian contempt for the delicate rhythms of human liberty and the humble acknowledgement of human imperfectability, he initiated one of the most egregious redistribution programs in human history. What did it accomplish? A taxpayer bill of 13 trillion dollars, and, as of today, a decrease in American poverty from 15% in 1964, to 13% today. The perverse consequences of such an ivory academic tower blunder has been the creation of a permanent underclass of Americans who no longer believe in themselves, but only in government. The War on Poverty was really a War on Human Dignity because it neutered countless tens of millions of men and women.

This War rendered sterile the natural aspiration of every human person to *be* more. They truly became the wretched of the earth, or in Eliot's evocative phrase, Hollow Men. Once grand American cities became wastelands of violence and ruin, monuments to the scourges of secular hubris. This War instilled in this underclass a breathtaking indifference to most crucial institutions upon which civility and happiness are built: religion, family, law and authority itself. Atom bombs falling on cities could not have accomplished such devastation. Concentration camps could never have so completely stripped man of his dignity. Torture chamber could not have executed such barbarity. So goes the cost of ignoring human nature, and nature's God.

Even with a half century of such bruising human folly, that same folly still sits at our doorstep. Instead of the choruses of the War on Poverty, we have the atonal refrains of something called Income Inequality. Different names; same programs. Different century; same dangerous naiveté. What bewilders is not so much that these tropes of Income Inequality are being chanted in the power corridors of Washington, D.C., but that they have even reached the sacred precincts of the Vatican. Strange, given the fact that the vast riches of the Church's teachings prevent man from such folly. The Church immunizes us from such retreats from reason, because she alone protects reason from its enemies. Reason stretches to its highest peaks under the protection of the Church's Magisterium.

In the Church's theological lexicon the poor is not a political or demographic category, but a theological one. Moreover, nary a whisper can be found in any of the Holy Gospels of a scolding of any class (except the Pharisees), certainly not the so-called rich. In fact, when Our Lord warns that "It easier for a camel to pass through the eye of needle than for a rich man to enter the kingdom of Heaven" (Mt 19:24), He is not condemning riches but attachment to riches. Many a rich man and centurion were friends of Our Savior; St. Matthew himself, a tax collector, was likely a rich man. Confirming this point, Our Lord is well known as "a friend of tax collectors and sinners" (Mt 11:19).

The Savior doesn't pity the poor, for he doesn't address categories. He speaks to persons. Amazed by the poor widow, Christ singles her out not because she is poor, but because, in spite of her poverty, she is generous, "And calling His disciples together, he saith to them: Amen I say to you, this poor widow hath cast in more than all they who have cast into the treasury. For they did cast in of their abundance; but she of her want cast in all she had, even her whole living" (Mk 12:43-44). Generosity creates happiness, and with happiness poverty is forgotten. Ronald Reagan once remarked that he grew up poor, but never knew it. Just as Aristotle teaches in the Ethics that where there is love, justice is not necessary, so it is with generosity: when present, misery becomes invisible.

St. Matthew's widow is so praised not because she is poor, but because she is poor of heart, following Our Lord's counsel, "Blessed are the poor in spirit; for theirs is the Kingdom of Heaven" (Mt 5:3). Throughout the entire Bible, the poor are the poor in spirit. What they are without is pride and vanity; empty of any desire that would not lead them to God. Thus the paradox: those truly poor are the truly rich. It is this mystery that Our Lady proclaims in her Magnificat, "He hath filled the hungry with good things, and the rich he sent empty away" (Lk 1:53). Here is the Mother of God's aria to humility: The poor are those whose only deprivation is the self, and the rich, those who hearts are heavy with interest *only* in self. When we read in Revelation, "Behold I stand at the door and knock" (Rev 3:20), Our Lord waits for the soul to become poor: to love Him more than all else.

Of course, when the soul becomes poor, it seeks what God seeks. Above all it seeks the good of all for whom Christ shed His Blood. As Our Lord pitied the suffering of the soul buried in his sins, with equal compassion he pitied their physical suffering. For both afflictions there is mercy, but the deeper and more divine compassion is for the burden of sin. Notice that Christ does not release the Good Thief from his agonies, but He accepts his contrition, and then welcomes him to Heaven. While He feeds the hungry and alleviates the lot of the poor, he never fills any man's pockets with lucre. Undoubtedly there was income inequality in the Roman Empire, but not once did Our Lord mention it. Rather, he called men to the treasures laid up in heaven, and challenges them to tap the natural riches He has given man.

Wasn't He teaching the human race about using their natural gifts in the miracle of the multiplication of the loaves and fishes? Our Lord has compassion on the multitudes and remarks to the apostles that He will not send them away fainting from hunger. When the apostles complain that they do not have enough to feed so many, Our Lord replies, "How many loaves have you?" (Mt 15:34). A small detail with a profound divine lesson. Our Lord expects us to begin by finding in ourselves what is necessary to the task. After our best work has been done, He does the rest. Thus St. Augustine when he writes, "The God Who creates us without us, does not save us without us."

Clarity shines here. 'Tis a thousand pities this divine design has been lost upon so many, even in the Church. An embarrassment seems to distract the conscience of many Catholics today. Unless they mimic the solutions of the political left, they fear they will be seen without the bona fides of a properly enlightened man. It is a well-known joke that the Episcopalian Church is the Republican Party at prayer. That could very well be rephrased to read that much of Catholic leadership these days is the political left at prayer.

For good Catholics the plight of the poor demands our compassionate concern, or else the dynamism of the Saints is inexplicable. But that concern must be imbued with Catholic nerve and bear the imprint of Christ. Our greatest charity is to guarantee that the poor will not stay poor. A poor man's dignity is not honored by throwing him a dollar each day, but by helping him earn his own dollar each day. To suffer poverty is not a virtue – to be poor of heart is. Trends in some Catholic theological circles see poverty as a permanent mark of status. Perhaps this explains Samuel Huntington's 2004 book, *Who Are We?* The Challenges to America's National Identity. The distinguished Harvard professor writes, "Hispanic traits... that hold Latino's back: mistrust of people outside the family; lack of initiative, self-reliance, and ambition; low priority for education and acceptance of poverty as a virtue necessary for entrance into heaven." The last sentence is deeply disturbing. If it is true, it reveals a parlous misreading of Our Lord's own teachings. Unfortunately, this is the prevailing attitude in the Church of the Southern Americas. Aside from a clear distortion of the Gospel, it leads to a slow strangulation of the human spirit made in the image and likeness of God. Beneath its deception, man is left a husk, drained of dignity and striving.

An allied corollary is the peculiar notion that men are poor because some men are rich. It is the old Marxist cliché of haves and have-nots: you *have* only because I *have not*. The real truth lies in the fact that men are different because they are free. So will their outcomes. Right reason has always seen the disparity as a tribute to human liberty; but now the Left view it as a treacherous breach of fairness. Only the imagination of great artists can express the absurdity of such blatant anomalies. George Orwell answered that call in *Animal Farm*.

A remedy to this inversion is the lives of the Saints, especially those renowned for their works of charity and holy poverty. St. Francis of Assisi, for instance. He wed Lady Poverty. While he remained faithful to her all his life, never once did he decry those who did not. His preaching was the authentic doctrine of Christ. All are to be poor in spirit – rich and poor alike. Men are called to be saints. Not all in the same way. Some will be saints through becoming poor; most will become saints by keeping their possessions, but being sure that they are never possessed *by* them. In the end, becoming a saint is all that matters.

Not a few clerics these days would be utterly bemused at St. Francis's balance, of embracing poverty for himself, but not presuming it for others. But it was merely a reflection of the balanced teachings of the Church he loved. In St. Thomas's *Treatise on*

Law he articulates the *raison d'etre* of human and divine law. In this context he also supplies us with a masterful analysis of that admirable balance of Catholic teaching, which does not command the same things for everyone: "Wherefore it (law) does not lay upon the multitude of imperfect men the burdens of those who are already virtuous... Otherwise these imperfect ones, being unable to bear such precepts, would break out into greater evils." Those same clerics might be terribly embarrassed by St. Francis's intransigent attitudes toward the Sacred Liturgy. He insisted that his friars find the most precious vestments, vessels and ornaments for the celebration of that Sacred Liturgy. St. Francis himself certainly did when he assisted at Mass as deacon. These same clerics would be met with even more confusion when they peruse some of Francis letters. Like a broken record, he enjoined his friars to be sure that Churches be appointed lavishly, especially all that touched upon the Holy Sacrifice of the Mass. Yes, this is *Il Povarello* who speaks.

Why should this confuse anyone? St. Francis imitated Christ down to the stigmata he bore upon his body. Balance is a divine thing because it proceeds from order: it means that even good things done to excess become bad things. Few saints embraced poverty more perfectly than St. Francis. Yet he would never dare think that the Churches that held the Divine Word Incarnate should look like the cell he prayed in. Chesterton makes the point forcefully: "Becket wore a hair shirt under his gold and crimson, and there is much to be said for the combination; for Becket got the benefit of the hair shirt while the people in the street got the benefit of the crimson and gold."

Odd that some might want to sport the hair shirt outside, and spurn the crimson and gold. As far as balance is concerned, nothing comes close to one of Chesterton's most memorable tour de forces in *Orthodoxy*:

> This is the thrilling romance of orthodoxy. People have fallen into the foolish habit of speaking of orthodoxy as something heavy, humdrum and safe. There was never anything so perilous or so exciting as orthodoxy... The Church swerved to left and right, so as exactly to avoid enormous obstacles. She left on one hand the huge bulk of Arianism, buttressed by all the worldly powers to make Christianity too worldly. The next instant she was swerving to avoid an orientalism, which would have it too

unworldly... Here it is enough to notice that if one small mistake were made in doctrine, huge blunders might be made in human happiness. A sentence phrased wrong about the nature of symbolism would have broken all the best statues in Europe. A slip in the definitions might stop all the dances; might wither all the Christmas trees or break all the Easter eggs. Doctrines had to be defined within strict limits, even that man might enjoy general human liberties. The Church had to be careful, if only that the world might be careless... To have fallen into any one of the fads from Gnosticism to Christian Science would indeed have been obvious and tame. But to have avoided them all has been one whirling adventure; and in my vision the heavenly chariot flies thundering through the ages, the dull heresies sprawling and prostrate, the wild truth reeling but erect.

Always in the Church's quiver has been the most formidable weapon in the War on Poverty: the Catholic School. Behold its arsenal: systematic immersion in Catholic doctrine, its pervasive cultivation of Catholic piety, its inculcation of the human virtues of self-control, discipline, hard work, respect for others, fair play, rigor, civility, good manners, honesty and the constant training in the permanent truths through a classical education. Like a divine alchemy, self-absorbed boys and girls were transformed into generous men and women. Men and women prepared to make sacrifices necessary to pass that legacy to the next generation. Men and women who become their nation's finest citizens.

Rich men are the ones with full souls. They are to be found in the barrios as well as on Rodeo Drive. Happiness is not a matter of erasing income inequality. It is a matter of souls becoming rich, with a spiritual wealth available to every man whether he lives in a Detroit ghetto or in a Beverly Hills chateau.

But if we keep speaking of income inequality, everyone will certainly remain poor.

11
Marriage and the Family

FATHERS, RISE TO YOUR GREATNESS

First, a bit of digging. As with every mystery of our Catholic Faith, the Holy Trinity is called a mystery not because it is like a riddle but because it is like an ocean. Divine mysteries are as incomprehensible as trying to count all the stars of the universe, or the sands on earth. They are beyond our ken because their beauty, truth, and wonder are infinite, exceeding reason's grasp.

Even in the Beatific Vision the mysteries of the Faith will never be entirely comprehended by men or angels because our intellects are created, and therefore limited. All of eternity for the Blessed will be a series of new adventures into the bowels of Love, one never like another. Each one fuller, deeper, and bursting with an ecstatic joy far grander than the one before.

One of the ways to begin climbing near the edges of the mystery of the Holy Trinity is to look at human fathers. They are faint echoes of the Trinity; traces of Their ineffable beauty. St. Thomas teaches: *bonum est diffusivum sui* (good, of its very nature, pours itself out). Since the Trinity is the Good Itself, Its very nature is always pouring out Itself in love. Father eternally begets (pours out Itself) the Son, and their infinite love spirates (pours out) the Holy Spirit. Yet this divine diffusion could not end there. *Per impossibile*, or else God's Divine Nature would be violated. So God then pours Himself out of Himself, resulting in creation.

In the words of Fr. Edouard Hugon, O. P., the great Thomist and tutor of Fr. Garrigou-Lagrange, O. P.: "The world (creation) is the first revelation of God, the first book where His eternal ideas are printed, the first vestiges of His attributes, the image of His beauty, the first echo of His voice." The apex of God's material creation is man, but not man alone. Man is truly man only *with* and *in* another in love ("It is not good for the man to be alone," Gen 2:18).

The heights of human love are reached in the nuptial union where the spouses pour themselves out to the other resulting in the pouring forth of new life. This kind of motion, intrinsic to the Holy Trinity, imprints Itself in a unique fashion on fathers. As the Father begets the Son in love, so fathers beget children in blessed union with their spouses. Fathers are intrinsically allied to the Heavenly Father in the generation of new children.

This alliance is irreparably betrayed when man uses this generative faculty in any other way than the Father does. Just as the Father's actions are always fecund, so must be every nuptial act of natural fathers. Just as the Father's acts are always overflowing with abundance, so must the marital acts of human fathers result in abundance of children. Our God is not a God of carefully calculated limits, neither should earthly fathers be. If so, he ceases to be a man at all and deforms himself into a caricature of a man.

This splendid mystery is captured in the words of the formidable Thomistic writer of the early 20th century Fr. Gerald Vann, O. P.: "Husbands and wives are the ministers of God's omnipotent power bringing into the world eternal beings." Both cultural nihilism and the unchallenged dissent in the Church have muted the enchanting stanzas of married love, leaving only dimmed grandeur.

No wonder studies reveal Catholic married couples contracepting at a *higher* rate than the general culture. It's not difficult to understand. A quick glance at a routine nuptial ceremony at St. Typical's (to use a felicitous phrase from the pen of my gifted friend Fr. McTeigue) displays a crass secularization burying the glories of this holy Sacrament. This merely verifies the gaseous mess of do-it-yourself liturgies. There is a high price to be paid when *On Eagle's Wings* usurps *Let All Mortal Flesh Keep Silence.*

Natural fathers possess a special duty to uphold and defend the natural order of things. They are guardians of truth. The Trinity bequeaths fathers a singular imitation of Their inner life and expects them to be on the front lines of exhibiting Their riches. Hence, the obligation of nurturing their own families in the truth of God's life.

Today, this is a formidable task. Navigating the heaving swells of secularism demands the courage of a hundred armies and the savvy of a dozen Pattons. As we have seen in the past few years, swarms of militants will not rest until they have shredded every fabric of civility, morality, and Western civilization. They must be met and scattered.

First, by fathers.

This is a part of their principal vocation. Yes, they must furnish food, shelter, and security for their families. However, all of that will be in vain if truth is permitted to die on the vine.

Where were the voices of the millions of good fathers when political leaders, sports idols, Hollywood elites, and the Fortune 500 titans bowed to the Maoist venom of Black Lives Matter, Antifa, and LGBTQ+ agitprop?

Where was the Million-Man-March of good fathers as Stalinists occupied actual sectors of our cities?

Fathers, you are marked with the sign of the Trinity.

Where is your valor? What has become of your thirst for heroism? Before the Holy Trinity, it is your solemn obligation to discover it again.

Fathers, with all that the Trinity has blessed you, you are invested by Them with even more. Threaded into the very fiber of your being is an aching homesickness: a homesickness for Heaven. Never rest in reminding your boys and girls of this homesickness. Even as they admire your success and wealth, warn them that life is not about these, though important in their proper place. Life uses all these things to win Heaven.

Teach them that every hour in the classroom, all the days in the library, all their struggles for good grades are for one purpose: *ad maiorem Dei gloriam*. Remind them of the stirring exhortation of the seventeenth-century bishop Jacques-Benigne Bossuet, who once exclaimed from the pulpit at the court of Louis XIV at Versailles: "Woe to the knowledge that does not turn to loving God!"

Tell your children that Christ Crucified matters above all things. They will not believe you unless they see you acting, day in and day out, with this primacy of purpose. When you become lukewarm, they will become bad. To your horror, they will become the heirs of the children looting stores and tearing down our nation.

On this Father's Day, the Trinity and Holy Church beg you to be true fathers.

Only when you execute that role will our lost world find its way back to God. Your virile example will teach other men to be men again and resist the cowardly retreat we have seen on full display these past few years.

Let ring in your minds the warning of Shakespeare in *Julius Caesar*: "Before a coward dies, he dies a thousand deaths." Make your campaign to take captive the debased ideas that have brought our beloved America to her knees, and chain them in cages.

Then drag your conquest to the throne of Christ the King and present it as the booty of your brave war for Him.

Fathers, be the standard-bearers of the Blessed Trinity.

Though you are not that Mystery, you bear the royal mark of that Mystery. Heavy responsibilities lie upon your shoulders. Don't fear them. The Blessed Trinity expects you to make Their echoes heard to every corner of the earth.

We wait to see the mark you make. More importantly, God does.

HOW LONG, O LORD?

Don't blame yourself for never having heard of the Brothers of Charity. Not many American Catholics have. After all, they are a Religious Order an ocean away in Belgium where they operate the largest chain of Catholic psychiatric hospitals in that once Catholic country. However, in the past few months the Brothers of Charity have crowded all the headlines in both Europe and North America. And not for reasons that will comfort Catholics. The Order has decided to permit euthanasia to its nonterminal patients. When queries about the firm opposition of the Church, the board of the Brothers of Charity replied that truly Christian values "should privilege a person's choice of conscience over a strict ethic of rules." Clearly, the good Brothers have forgotten the role of conscience. It does not create its own moral norms, rather it guides absolute moral norms to their proper fulfillment in particular situations. Moreover, dismissively referring to God's commandments as "a strict ethic of rules" is unsettling to a Catholic mind. A fortiori, from a group of Consecrated men.

Such a shocking turn did not appear out of nowhere. Recall that Belgium legalized euthanasia in 2002, the first country with a majority Catholic population to do so. Within two years, more than eighty percent of Catholic health care institutions and nursing homes in Belgium's Dutch speaking Flanders region permitted euthanasia. A seemingly supine clergy offered no resistance, some even cheering the ghoulish development. Take Father Marc Desmet, a palliative care specialist who frequently counsels patients who are considering euthanasia. In 2017 he remarked, "I do not say what they have to decide." Or another Belgian priest, Father Gabriel Ringlet, author of a popular book on spiritual accompaniment to euthanasia, has encouraged people to develop their own unofficial rituals for the practice. It would not have been rash to expect a hailstorm of censures from Church leaders. But, there was–nothing.

All of this is quite apposite on the eve of the forty-fifth anniversary of *Roe v. Wade*. Abortion did not only cheapen the life of the unborn in the womb, but the lives of us all. The tentacles of this debasement reach to the very roots of secular man's self-understanding. The matrix of all his moral decisions lies in the sheer exercise of his will, leaving the voice of truth as some long-discarded tool of oppression. Antecedents begin with Kant's Autonomous Self, emancipated from all external constraints on his freedom, through Rousseau's emancipated self who struggles with the condition "of being born free, and now finding himself everywhere in chains." Mill carries the crusades of the Imperial Self forward with his maximization of freedom, only brought to a climax in Nietzsche's *Übermensch* and Sartre's existential prison. For four hundred years these thinkers waged a philosophical scorched-earth policy, destroying the slightest trace of a properly common sense thinking (viz. natural moral law). Thus allowing to settle upon the culture a cordial mood for the breezy acceptance of the moral enormities we witness today. Even more chilling, reservations about such moral collapse have come to be seen as *déclassé* by the genteel *bien pensant*.

Such a climate places Catholics in an untenable position. Not only are we resented for defending an unpopular position, but now once universally cherished moral laws are successfully construed as bias. The Secular Left has effectively turned reality inside out: the strange and unnatural has become the familiar and normative. Many a good Catholic demurs from the heat of this battle for fear of being branded a bigot, insensitive to The Other. Mission accomplished.

Chesterton's remark must not be forgotten: "When man forgets the supernatural, he does not become natural, he becomes unnatural." His uncanny wisdom makes hm unusually prescient. Most troublesome about today's parade of novel enthusiasms such as LGBT and the transgender fever is the sheer unnaturalness of it all. Once God is abandoned, as Dostoyevsky reminds us, all is permissible. Without God, man becomes a blank canvas waiting for his creative brush. Only God's hand, seen through the fixed designs of His creation, can keep man anchored in the truth. Indeed, it is the only guarantee of man being himself. Anything else is a deception, tumbling down through Alice's Looking Glass.

This forty-fifth anniversary of abortion in the United States is only the latest symptom of disease that had long been growing in the blood stream of Western Civilization. Holy Church alone can stanch the mushrooming plague. But Good Catholics have long charged into the battle over these long fort-five years. The problem is that they often find themselves nearly alone. When they look for their leaders, most are not even leading from behind. Worse still, more than a few seem to give tacit permission, if not explicit license, to those aggressively advancing the disease. Abortion, euthanasia, and an assortment of other moral breaches should have prompted deafening howls of resistance from the First Estate. But not infrequently Catholics hear the timid voice of a bare few. For instance, one major Church leader in the past few months delivered a major address at a prominent venue, calling for Catholics to "Let go of cherished beliefs and long-held biases." What exactly can that mean? Could he have possibly intended what his words actually said? What is the ordinary Catholic to think? Even an adroit finessing from the most dissimulative academic could not blunt the actual intention of such a summons. How else explain the stunning developments throughout the Church Universal except to a calculated silence on the part of its Catholic leaders, if not worse?

On this forty-fifth anniversary, Catholics must be resolved to this New Normal. Providence has placed us in this time, and under these conditions, for His purposes. Of one thing we are certain: He requires us to engage in an unending, thankless battle for His truth. Questions will not fade. Isolation will discourage. Betrayals from those in the highest places will sting. Failures will often outnumber triumphs. Through it all Our Savior calls us to fidelity to the unchanging Truth of His Church, even as some insist it has changed. Isn't that the deepest suffering? Father Sertillanges once warned, "The greatest suffering is not for the Church, or with the Church, but by the Church."

T. S. Elliot wrote in *East Coker*: "For us/ there is only the trying/ The rest is not our business." A perfect expression of man's vocation in this Valley of Tears. We work and toil and labor. Still, with all our long-suffering, there will linger legitimate complaints, insoluble questions, or disturbing contradictions. But those things are not our business.

They are God's.

MOTHERHOOD AND CIVILIZATION

Crowns fall fittingly upon the head of the Virgin during this month of May, but it is also fitting that they fall upon the head of every mother. Mothers possess hearts that act like God's megaphone. It is of the very nature of mothers willy nilly to be God's proxy in a world weary of God. Even when a science gone awry preempts much of mothers' biological prerogative, that ghastly preemption cannot not blunt the lovely music of mothers being mothers. Indeed, those unstoppable stanzas of God's elegant design will be the very chords that ultimately will convince man of his doomed love affair with the brutish promises of science. All the IVF's, surrogate mothers and sundry manufacturing devices created by unmoored science will never replace the beauteous mystery of a single mother and father cooperating with God in bringing us a single precious baby. This is God's script, and any interference brings only the blackest nightmares. Just because some men become used to nightmares, even delight in them, doesn't mean they still are not nightmares.

A mother's heart is the heart of the supernatural. Mothers are *not* supernatural, but they prepare us for the supernatural. In carrying and raising their child, they are never far from suffering. The delivery of their child is not the end of their suffering, only its beginning. Because they desire only the good of their child, suffering is never but slightly behind each and every day. However, it is never looked at that way, because what fills a mother's heart is the selflessness of love. If love is the blossom, suffering is its ever-present stem. Even the Mother of God whose Heart is Immaculate is called the Mother of Sorrows. Richard of St. Victor called this the violence of love. For as it unfetters from the self, it readies the human heart for ecstasy. Recall that ecstasy is derived from the Greek, *exstasis*, meaning to stand outside of oneself. Ecstasy is being so beset by the joy of the beloved that one is taken out of oneself. We are carefully taught by Mother Church that the truest ecstasy is in the Beatific Vision, when man finally becomes himself. That training for future ecstasy begins by looking at mothers. Isn't God a lenient teacher?

Not only does the supernatural radiate from the hearts of mothers, but their hearts are the cradle of the natural world. Every mother teaches us to love the world of nature, or as Edmund Burke expressed it, the unbought grace of life. It is important to notice that there is an order in love of a mother, unlike the disordered loves of modernity. Mothers tutor us to love the world of nature, not to idolize it. The world is not to be worshiped; it leads us to the worship only of God. Every loveliness that the world presents should leave us sighing for God. Thus C. S. Lewis in *The Weight of Glory*:

> The books or the music in which we thought the beauty was located will betray us if we trust them; it is not *in them* but only comes *through them*, and what comes through them is longing. These things – the beauty, the memory of our past – are good images of what we really desire; but if they are mistaken for the thing itself, they turn into dumb idols, breaking the hearts of their worshippers, for they are not the thing itself: They are only the scent of the flower we have not found, news from a country we have never yet visited.

Precisely because this lovely world of nature proceeds from the bounty of God, and bears the imprint of His finger, we cherish and care for it with fastidious attention. All of these lessons are lyrically presented to us by the wombs of mothers. In these mysterious chambers, mothers allow God to stitch together the soul He created with the bodies offered by mothers and fathers. All of this accomplished in blessed silence and dark concealment. Here too is another lesson. Mothers teach us a proper reserve toward the mysteries of God's good world. Some things are so beautiful that they demand veiling; they summon protection; they ought not to be on public display before the vulgar leering of the masses. Mothers teach us proper reticence toward the mysteries of the natural world, especially those touching upon the human person.

The late eminent professor of English at the University of Chicago, Richard Weaver, gives a forceful analysis of this when he wrote in *Ideas Have Consequences* that the withering of this reticence leads inevitably to obscenity. He then proceeds to diagnose societies who adopt openness, which is simply the window to obscenity:

> The failure of the concept of obscenity... makes a virtue of desecration. Propriety, like other old-fashioned anchorages was abandoned because it inhibited something. Proud of its shamelessness (modernity) served up in swaggering style matters which heretofore had been veiled in decent taciturnity... (This) testifies to man's loss of points of reference, to his determination to enjoy the forbidden in the name of freedom. All reserve is being sacrificed to titillation.

The wombs of mothers are one of the most splendid works of nature and nature's God. Without uttering a single word, they instruct men in the foundation of civilization. It is mothers who civilize us.

Finally, mothers' hearts are the heart of wisdom. Wisdom differs from knowledge: knowledge merely teaches us what things are; wisdom teaches us how they lead to happiness. By being themselves, mothers teach us wisdom because they direct us away from the tyranny of the fleeting moment to the wisdom of abiding happiness. Two of those lessons are apposite.

The first: Human bodies are not machines, but temples. No science, no matter how formidable, has the right to manipulate, alter, frustrate or degrade them. Equally forbidden are human appetites that might do the same, no matter how much those desires tug at our heartstrings. Once the truth of the human body yields to the flights of human fancy, the human person disappears, and horrors materialize.

The second, and no less important, is the wisdom mothers teach us about love. A mother's love is absolutely permanent, because true love is. It knows no expiration date. It is contingent upon nothing. It doesn't lapse because of boredom. It knows nothing of temporary commitment, that odd corruption of fidelity so beloved by moderns, always on the lookout for the next better offer. It stands utterly above all transitory things. C.S. Lewis again, "love possesses too much grandeur to be reduced to mere feeling or romance." Love's poetry is made of steel. Its verses defy being bent to man's carnal dissemblings. Contrast this with the hook-up-luv choking modern culture, as it leaves man stranded in the filthy back alleys of secularism. This is a degrading caricature that undermines love and signals its demise. It is wedded only to the ephemera of the present moment. A mother's love, and all true love, will have nothing to do with passing whimsy; hers is an echo of the permanent love of the Blessed Trinity. Man will flourish with nothing less.

Let children happily rest upon their mother's bosom, for they lean on one of the pillars of civilization. Then let those children, especially those grown to adulthood, learn well what mothers teach. And all of it spoken without uttering a single word.

WHY VALENTINE'S DAY IS NAMED AFTER A SAINT

With the bustle associated with Valentine's Day we often forget that February 14th is about love. True love, that is. We also forget that it is the celebration of the martyrdom of a saint who points the way to true love. Yes, Valentinus (anglicized, Valentine) was a priest of the third century Roman empire. Heavy persecution still hung over the head of the Church, forcing her to tiptoe cautiously around possible torture or death at any moment. Valentine was a priest who was particularly devoted to preparing young Roman couples for the sacrament of matrimony. His tender yet firm instructions in the ways of wedded love captured the hearts of young couples, making them even more eager to have him witness their sacred vows.

In the midst of his noble work with newlyweds he won the notice of the Roman Emperor, Claudius Gothicus. Quite surprisingly, a bit of friendship began to grow. Valentine wasted no time in raising the perilous question of conversion. After all, the affections of friendship are usually the ideal occasion for opening profound questions of this sort. So it is that St. John Henry Newman takes the motto on his coat of arms: *Cor ad Cor Loquitur*. The same cardinal wrote:

> The heart is commonly reached, not through the reason, but through the imagination, by means of direct impressions, by the testimony of facts and events, by history, by description. Persons influence us, voices melt us, looks subdue us, deeds inflame us. Many a man will live and die upon a dogma; no man will be a martyr for a conclusion.

For all of that, this friendship was not so deep. A highly insulted Claudius arrested Valentine and sentenced him to death. After the ingenious tortures of the Roman imperium, Valentine succumbed to death on February 14, 269. Veneration quickly arose among the Roman people, and not too long afterwards, St. Valentine was named Patron of Those in Love.

This may sound strange to the Catholic ear—Patron of Those in Love. But it shouldn't be. While our secular culture has vandalized the word love, it is central to our Catholic Faith. Aquinas, remarking on Christ's Passion, teaches the proper doctrinal emphasis: "By suffering out of love and obedience, Christ offered to God more than was necessary to overcome all the sin and evil of humanity. Above all, because of the greatness of the love with which he suffered, the love of perfect charity for the Father and for us sinners."[1] Isn't this clear from the crucifixes we wear? No institution on earth honors the love that joins man and woman more than the Catholic Church. Look at the taunts she endures to protect love from those who would drag it through the mud of mere carnal amusement. Oh no, the Catholic Church practically invented romance. She rescues it from the clutches of those who would pull it down from its pedestal of purity. Only the Catholic Church summons men to see romance as a kind of symphonic overture to the beauties of marriage.

Romance is chaste, not promiscuous, sincere not cynical, and filled with promises of forever, not the lies of a one-night delight. Romance moves happily in the self-control of courtship so that it could flourish in the sweet fidelity of marriage. The Church is not blind to the quotidian snares that threaten the integrity of romance and conjugal love. This high calling can never flourish by itself; only the divine assistance can protect and sustain it. Beset by a purely natural outlook, more than a few voices in the Church recommend capitulation to the zeitgeist. They seem to forget the words of St. Augustine: "God does not order us to do impossible things, but in ordering us he admonishes us to do what we can, and ask his help for whatever is outside our power." That sound theology receives the infallible seal of the Council of Trent.

The vocabulary of love sounds like the arias of a glorious opera: fidelity, purity, restraint, marital privilege, vow, oblation, and promise. No matter how hard secularism tries, it cannot steal the melody from those words. It tries to bury them beneath the sludge of self-absorption, but they cannot be kept buried. Every human heart longs for them, and no secular pantomime of love will do. In fact, it is romance that carries with it still another longing—that for the Perfect Love of God. St. Augustine memorably writes in

---

[1] *Summa theologiae* III, Q. 48, art. 2.

the *Confessions:* "You have made our hearts, O God, and they shall not rest until they rest in you." Yet, we become enchanted with all the beauty that God created for us in this world, especially romantic love. God intends to seduce us with this beauty. C. S. Lewis expresses this truth eloquently in the *Weight of Glory*:

> The books or the music in which we thought the beauty was located will betray us if we trust them; it is not *in* them, but only *through* them, and what comes through them is longing. These things—the beauty, the memory of our past—are good images of what we really desire; but if they are mistaken for the thing itself, they turn into dumb idols, breaking the heart of their worshippers. For they are not the thing itself: they are only the scent of the flower we have not found, news from a country we have not yet visited.

In the end, romance on earth leads to the final Romance of Heaven. It is only right that the world should love to celebrate Valentine's Day.

What is there not to love?

That is, if we remember it is St. Valentine's Day. Otherwise its just another day to bore us. Or worse.

THE HOLY FAMILY AND HOLY FAMILIES

Though not a Catholic, Samuel Johnson once made an eminently Catholic remark when he wrote, "The end of all human activity is to be happy at home." Yes, happy at home; with the family. The juxtaposition seems a little naïve. Subordinating the most noble pursuits of man, his achievements of the highest grandeur, in service to the humble unit of the family seems slightly askew. Isn't it the reverse? Atomized Modern Man thinks so. He suffers an ontological fissure that leaves him marooned in a sea of inert flotsam called human individuals. Family? Home? Such quaint notions can no longer bear the grandiose pretensions of Man Come of Age. His new credo enshrines appetite over fidelity, fulfillment over sacrifice, affirmation over obligation and devotion to self over devotion to God. Family has become an atavistic throwback, unless, of course, it is reconfigured to serve the new purposes of the New Secular Man.

The family and home is where the human race begins. This is the womb where whole and wholesome men and women are created. Man is taught here that there is infinitely more to man than man. More to man than flesh and bones, appetites and longings. All attempts to reduce man to his bodily parts or base passions leaves man without himself. Modern times present man with tantalizing novelties like laboratory grown human beings and rent-a-womb for the affluent needy. If these are not resisted, man finds himself in a Brave New World so perverse that even Huxley would wince. Mary Shelly was prescient when she wrote chillingly about untethered science, that is, untethered from right reason and religion. Recall when the novelist has Dr. Frankenstein stare up at his new creation, the monster stares back down at the hubristic doctor saying, "You are indeed my creator, but now I am your master." Science tyrannizes us when its intoxicating knowledge becomes our god. Chesterton correctly grasped the gravity of the matter with his usual simplicity, "We are learning to do a great many clever things... The next great task will be to learn not to do them." Along with any Catholic, Chesterton had a great respect for science, but science in its rightful place, "Science is a splendid thing; if you tell it where to go."

Of course, only the Church is able to tell science where it must go. But love for the Church is poured into men's hearts through the family. Ordinary families tutor children into the most extraordinary things. And the larger the family the more effective is its children fitted for the protections against pride. It is only within the embrace of the family that man learns the limits of all finite things, and that limitless goodness found only in God. Again, Chesterton, "The human house is a paradox for it is larger inside than out." Though the world proffers its counterfeits, the person formed well by his family spurns them. Aristotle remarks in the Ethics that only the young men from noble (i.e., good) families will be able to take his rightful place in the ruling of society.

All this is true about the family not simply because it has been around for as long as man remembers. That would make the family merely conventional; one way this century, another way the next. The family is not conventional; it is ontological. Its structure reflects and perfects the very nature of man, and divulges what man ought to be. Families have their roots deep in the heart of God Himself. Just as He designed water to be wet, and the wings of birds to fly, so has He ordered man's fulfillment in the bosom of families.

The family is not only man's origin, it is his end. All the highly elevated vocabulary of the Church's theology can be reduced to the vernacular of the family: Mother Church; priest as Father; the Bishop's ring as wedding band marrying him to his diocese; Mother superior; religious brothers; nuns as sister; devotion to the Mother of God; the Father eternally begetting the Son. Family is inescapable—from the Trinity all the way down to us. Thus the Catholic passion for the family, and their equivalent rage at those who would redesign it. Such would be to turn the world inside out, and leave man asunder.

In His omnipotence God could have saved the world in an infinitude of ways staggering the imagination. Which way to did He choose? His only begotten Son incarnate as a man; born of an ordinary woman called His Mother; a foster father he called poppa. An accident? God does not rule or teach by accident. In the family we peek into the mind of God; dazzling in its revelation. The strokes of the Divine Artist show us the father, the one who leads and protects. The mother, the one who nurtures and teaches. The children, the ones who obey and learn.

Vanity and pride has made our world deaf to God and His plans for our happiness. To that deaf world, Catholics alone are left to tell the truth about the family. When Flanner O'Connor was asked why she presented such grotesque characters and sadistic violence in her stories, she replied: "To the hard of hearing you shout, and for the almost blind you draw large and startling figures." O'Connor spoke to that deaf world with the artistry of her stories; the rest of us are left with our fidelity and bold voices. Voices that sharply tell the world what the family truly is. Voices confident in the power of its truth. Elites will be enraged. Often those once thought our friends will harangue us or slither into the safe background of compromise.

Only the brave few can resist the blandishments of being loved, or worse, the approval of the bien-pensant hiding beneath the skirts of smarmy pieties is not the heroism this age demands. Neither is the vain hope that if we say nothing, or very little, some path for dialogue will remain open. Strategies like that serve victories to the enemy on a silver platter. Worse of all is the naivete which simply declares the war over, and a time for positive action has dawned. Such a supine posture invites our enemies to see us as fools. And as they happily escalate their hostilities, we are left routed and dazed. Catholics must summon the courage to tell the world what the family is – even when some may call us obsessed. Only by keeping the family what it is will families be holy.

Only holy families will save the human race. Hyperbole? Look again at how God chose to save us: by sending His Son into a family. Who dares think he can improve on that.

MODERNITY'S NEW DRINK: MARRIAGE ON THE ROCKS

Hell is up to its old tricks again. It has pulled out its tried-and-true strategy of attacking the sacrament of marriage. Not that it is a drink that hasn't worked before, but it seems to be enjoying unparalleled success in the past 50 years. It doesn't take a genius to know that marriage and families collapse once you release the unfettered sexual appetite to rule as a god. But seeing how effective that has been, hell's tacticians have taken their strategy one step further. It has successfully created a cancel culture giddy to neuter the identities of man and woman itself. This androgynous dream has taken hell's hopes of success beyond their wildest expectations. Never could it have it expected such frenzied embrace from modernity. Yes, its elites; but its ordinary masses as well. But let us linger a moment on the glories of marriage, one of God's most exquisite natural gifts. Hell knows well the old scholastic adage, *corruptio optimi pessima* (the corruption of the best is the worst).

Countless millions of tourists visit the great capitals of Europe each year delighting in places such as Paris, Rome, London, Prague and Madrid. They marvel at how great cities were built and adorned in such splendor. But the greatest builders are not the ones whom history records as architects of cities or heroic monuments. The greatest builders are mothers and fathers. The cities they build are families, and these cities dwarf the glories of Paris and Rome. For while the Coliseum and Buckingham Palace are worthy of tourists' admiration, their inert grandeur cannot match home and hearth, the lively songs of children and the tender embraces of their parents. Therein lies a different kind of grandeur, a grandeur more essential to the grandeur of man. As Samuel Johnson remarked, "The whole purpose of life is to be happy at home."

The nuptial bond solemnly joins man and woman in a pact fashioned in paradise. But the transformation of man and woman into husband and wife is only the beginning, like the rosebud before it is a rose. The full flowering of marriage's purpose is not seen till husband and wife become father and mother. This is when contract bursts into melody, a page of musical notes become symphonic sounds, a palette's paints are put to canvas and, *voila*, an artist's masterpiece. Each newly minted married couple receive an august commission from Almighty God in the holy sacrament of Matrimony. In the words of Fr. Gerald Vann, "They become ministers of God's omnipotence in making immortal beings." This startling mandate shimmers with grave obligations which God lays upon a couple's shoulders, promising the divine assistance of grace making their fulfillment possible.

Besides the already heavy weight of wedded love there is the burden of the world's provocative deceptions. They entice with the hoary lies once offered in the Garden of Eden. Rather than rest in the designs of Almighty God, husband and wife are lured with the tantalizing offer, "Ye shall be as gods." In the memorable words of Whittaker Chambers, they would trade Almighty God to become Almighty Man. Rather than increase and multiply, the world preaches be yourself. Beneath this propaganda large sprawling families sink into secularity's proper 1.2 children boutique units. No sooner is this fateful bargain sealed than a cascade of lies floods the mind. Like Pandora's Box a series of cruel demons fly out. Unlike Pandora's Box nothing is left but more lies. Wickedness possesses its ineluctable logic.

The first fatality is love itself... The world whispers the tall tale that marriage is after all for *luv*. But bubbling beneath the surface of this lie is love's counterfeit. It is drained of the sacrifice which defines its nobility and descends into fakery. It is matter of a small step to miss that God is the author love's first enchantments, intimations of a grander adventure to follow. Every Sacrament is a sharing in the cosmos-shaking love of Calvary. Marriage is no different. The initial swoons of courtship are only preparations for the formidable tasks of Holy Matrimony. All the movements of romance are to be placed in the service of marriage's highest purpose – the procreation of the human race. Only here can be found marriage's towering beauty. Love of two placed at the service of One who alone is Love. When this logic of heaven becomes the daily motions of married love then husband and wife find themselves, in the words of the seventeenth century Metaphysical poet, Thomas Traherne, "Awake in heaven."

The sacrifices will be aplenty, but the joys will outnumber them. Within the folds of those graces and their corresponding crosses, the married couple come face to face with one of the world's other titillating lies: the cult of the self. This idol has not only strangled marriage and the family but has left culture a tomb for the carcasses of man totally devoted to Man. Since marriage demands the selfless oblation to the other, the looming divinized Self always lurks as a foil. It dares replace "Till death do us part" with "Until the feeling is gone." Marriage must stand as a heroic standard against this flattened caricature of love. It bids husband and wife leave the isolation of the sovereign Self so that the "Two become one flesh." All the joys of the one is now the joys of both. Nothing is any longer mine or yours, but *ours*. All the while a distinction of roles remain, just as does the distinction of sexes. In the words of Pius XI in his ode to marriage, *Casti Connubii*, "God did not take Eve from Adam's head that she might be his master, nor did he take him from his heel, that she might be his slave. He takes her from his side, beneath his heart, that she be his partner." The wife exercises the leadership of love, always softening her husband's tendency to brute virility. Husbands, in their turn, exercise the leadership of strength stealing tenderness when necessary, curbing sentimentality when needed.

The graces of marriage must weather the tempests of immanentism: that conviction of modernity that the whole of life is bound by the walls of this physical world and its chronological time. It is impervious to the truth that man bears the weight of eternity upon his shoulders. No reminder of that rings more loudly than in the graces of marriage. Eternity is always tapping at the door of the souls of husbands and wives as the words of the priest rings ever in their ears, Till death do ye part. It raises the couples love out of the frictions and tribulations of the trifling moment. Their eternal pledge miniaturizes their woes for they see all of them *sub aeternitatis*. God's perspective becomes their own.

With each new child comes an opportunity to share in the abundance of God. Modernity has fallen in love with carefully calculated limits, shrinking the human person and leaving him without the dignity God intended. With each settlement for less, man finds himself less a man. In the words of St. John of the

Cross, "Outside of God, everything is small." Could this be the point of Johnathan Swift's parable, *Gulliver's Travels*? This hail and tall-standing man is immobilized by hundreds of little men restraining him with a thousand strings. Alas, the plight of Modern Man, held captive by the thousand strings of serial arousals and endless superficialities. The Sacrament of Matrimony confronts stunted Modern Man with the vision of the soaring Christian Man, the man made in the *imago et similtudo Dei*.

Every Catholic sanctuary should be a fortress against modernity's mendacities. Not so any longer. With great enthusiasm not a few priests have permitted marriage's solemnity to be debased into a billboard for modernity's beguilements. Absent is the ancient Catholic marriage ritual's *exhortatio*, "You are about to enter into a union which is most sacred and most serious, a union which was established by God Himself." After this first sentence, the *exhortatio* goes on to declare at three other times that their union is most serious. No doubt can remain in even the most dimwitted. Yet, even if the priest struggles to articulate such *gravitas*, it is belied by the couple's choice of non-sacral music injecting a sinking frivolity. Usually the music wins out. This burial of the marriage ceremony in sentimental ooze only serves to raise the white flag of surrender to the zeitgeist's sterility.

Each man must face God in final judgment. To husbands and wives, He will ask them to show Him the cities they have built. The cities of their families teeming with children bathed in the light of mothers and fathers who lit those cities with their sacrificial love. Only then will Christ smile, and say to them, now enter into the eternal City of Paradise.

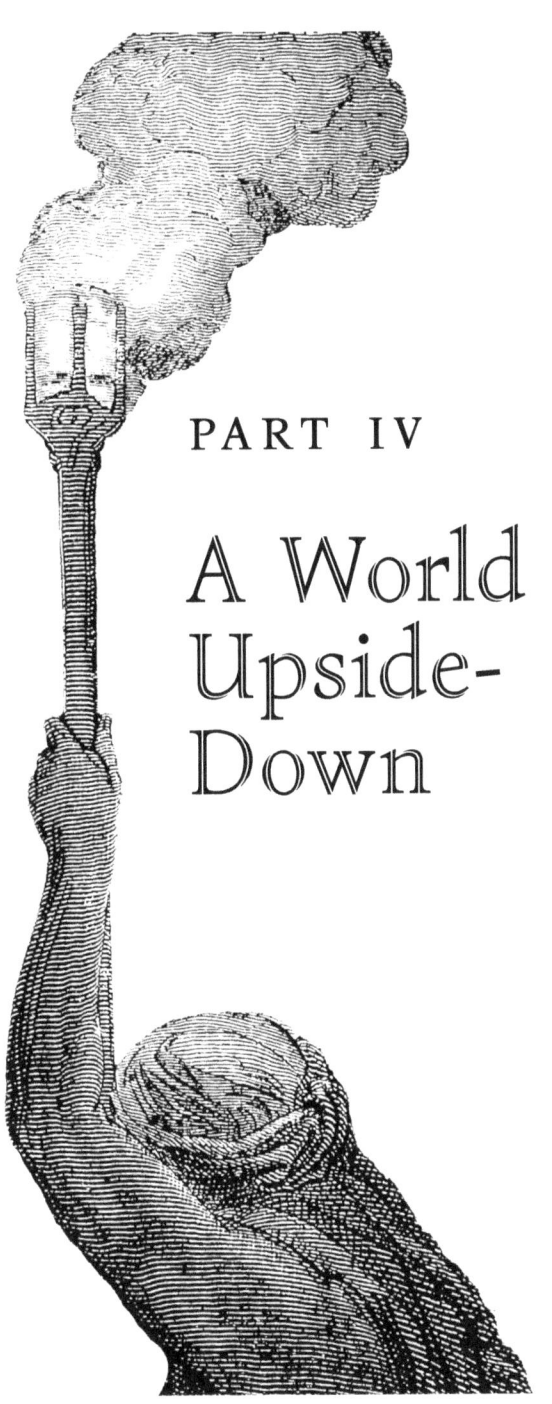

PART IV
A World Upside-Down

12
Our Fraying Culture

GOD BLESS AMERICA?

To Catholics of a certain frame of mind, Pope Leo XIII's 1895 apostolic letter to the American bishops, *Longinquo*, might come as quite unwelcome. The great Pontiff bestowed unqualified praise upon America's founding principles. But, America? Land of wholesale abortion and creeping infanticide? America? Where sea to shining sea embraces same-sex marriage and transgender militancy? Could it be that the very idea of America was always inhospitable to the Faith from its beginnings? No wonder not a few faithful Catholics reached their breaking point and began to conclude that the decline was the inevitable trajectory of principles adopted by Deistic Founding Fathers.[1] While it is not difficult to sympathize with such a leap, it does demonstrate a flawed logic (*post hoc ergo propter hoc*), Pope Leo's letter serves as a corrective. He writes:

> All intelligent men are agreed, and We ourselves have with pleasure intimated it...that America seems destined for greater things. Now, it is Our wish that the Catholic Church should not only share in, but help to bring about, this prospective greatness. We deem it right and proper that she should, by availing herself of the opportunities daily presented to her, keep equal step with the republic in the march of improvement, at the same time striving to the utmost, by her virtue and her institutions, to aid in the rapid growth for the States.

This Leonine letter continues with unmistakable confirmation of America's beneficent singularity:

> Nor, perchance did the fact which we now recall take place without some design of Divine providence. Precisely at the epoch when the American colonies, having with Catholic aid, achieved liberty and independence, coalesced into a constitutional Republic the ecclesiastical hierarchy was happily established among you; and at the very time when the popular suffrage placed the great Washington at the helm of the Republic, the first bishop was set

---
[1] See Patrick Deneen, *Why Liberalism Failed*.

by apostolic authority over the American Church. The well-known friendship and familiar intercourse which subsisted between these two men seems to be an evidence that the United States ought to be conjoined in concord and amity with the Catholic Church.

Doesn't Leo echo the words of George Washington *Farewell Address*?

> Of all the dispositions and habits, which lead to political prosperity, religion and morality are indispensable supports. Whatever may be conceded to the influence of refined education on minds of peculiar structure, reason and experience both forbid us to expect that national morality can prevail in exclusion of religious principle.

John Adams's 1813 letter to Thomas Jefferson underscores this primacy of religion: "The general Principles on which the Fathers Achieved Independence, were...the general Principles of Christianity...and the general Principles of English and American liberty." Tocqueville saw the very same fusion in the American experiment and identified its "intimate union of the spirit of religion with the spirit of liberty" an essential feature of America's genius. Paul R. DeHart completes the circle with an impressive analysis in the *Social Science Review*:

> The founders and framers affirmed the necessity of consent for political authority and obligation. But they also situated the necessity of consent in the context of a morally and metaphysically realist natural law, maintained that an objective good of the whole constitutes the final end of political association, and described liberty as subjection to the law of nature and the government of God.

Clearly, this nineteenth century Pope enjoyed a decided affinity toward professed Catholic states. Moreover, there was the Church's justifiably deep suspicion of Republicanism, which the French Revolution's *laïcité* had strangled the Church in so many places. Against this backdrop, the endorsements of *Longinquo* might seem puzzling. But only puzzling for those who see with dimmed Catholic eyes.

No such myopia for this great Pope. Leo recognized that the founding of the American republic rested upon the perennial principles of the Natural Moral Law, and for that, acknowledged gratitude was due. The cornerstone of that Law (which is, according to

Aquinas, "A participation in the Divine reason"), is the sacredness of the human person. That singular dignity bestowed only by God makes man into the *imago et simulitudo* Dei. An abundance of riches follows upon this Divine inheritance, whose fountainhead are man's powers of intellect and will. The former makes man's knowing intrinsically ordered to the truth, and the latter grants man his own agency by making him free.

Experience confirms that both Divine endowments can be manipulated to ends not ontologically theirs by nature. For instance, man can employ intellect against the natural end of the intellect, i.e., truth. As Aristotle teaches in the *Nicomachean Ethics*: "One can act for a reason, while acting against reason." A man can cleverly plot a foolproof embezzling scheme. His plot is clearly an act of reason, but an act of reason that undermines reason because it aims at wickedness. Similarly, the will enthrones man as a free person. While freedom is necessary to make an act fully human, its mere presence does not guarantee that the act morally good. Freedom is merely the means by which man achieves the true good; it is corrupted when used to achieve anything that seems good, but not truly good. Chesterton wrote, "Freedom is the capacity of a man to be himself." Chesterton is not to be understood licentiously, but ontologically. For man to be himself is quite simply, to be a saint, not a degenerate. So Leo fittingly lauds the Declaration when it boldly proclaims: "All men are endowed by their Creator with certain unalienable rights, that among these are life, liberty and the pursuit of happiness."

As easily as those words fall from our tongues, not so their gravity. Their brevity betrays their monumental importance. Rights are not granted by a Parliament, as they are in England. Nor are they bestowed by a majority, as in France. Nor are they the gracious gift of a despot, as in most parts of the world. God alone grants them. For that reason, no power on earth can abridge or abolish them. The rightly ordered state can only protect them. Blessed Fulton Sheen gives a certain lyric logic to this fundamental truth: "If we wish to have the light, we must have the sun; If we wish to have forests, we must have the trees; if we wish to have perfume, we must have the flowers; If we wish to keep rights, we must have God." Chesterton puts it another way: "When a nation no longer has room for God, it soon will have no room for man."

Preserving rights requires properly understanding rights. This is an urgent task especially in light of the corruption they have suffered since the time of Locke and Hobbes. Rights correctly appears only in the web of obligations. The very word right is derived from the Latin, ius, the etymological root of the English word, justice. Justice is that which is owed to another. Ultimately obligations are those kinds of acts which are owed to the truth, and ultimately to God, the First Truth. Therefore, rights are that which is owed to man in order to fulfill his obligations. Man has only the right to be good. Rights construed in any other way are simply a caricature, and invariably lead to Dachas, Soviet gulags, and Harvard's Committee on Diversity.

Only faithful Catholics can make America great again, because our greatness lies in being "One nation under God." Once again, Sheen: "It is well to remind ourselves that in a crisis like ours, devotion to the stars and stripes is not enough to save us. We must look beyond them to other stars and stripes, namely the stars and stripes of Christ, by whose stars we are illuminated, and by whose stripes we are healed."

"RENDER UNTO CAESAR...":
TO VOTE OR NOT TO VOTE

"Render unto Caesar..." may cause some alarm. God Incarnate seems to be lauding Caesar, yet Caesar hardly seems laudable.

The Caesars were a rather disreputable bunch, given their depraved lives. Let us recall that after the worthy life of Augustus, there were Tiberius, Caligula, and Nero. Hardly Catholic role models.

All the Roman emperors, whether of the Julio-Claudian line, the Flavian, or the Antonine, were devout votaries of pagan gods, whose tribute they exacted from the early Christians. Refusal resulted in over two hundred years of sadistic persecution.

Let us not forget the conduct of Caesar's armies in the conquest of nations. Not only was it barbaric, but to their vanquished enemies they meted pitiless punishment. So staggering was their legendary, totalizing cruelty that it caused Tacitus to write in his A.D. 98 *De Vita et Moribus Lulii Agricolae*, "They create a desert, and call it peace."

How could the Savior recommend homage to Caesar?

Clearly, He does not.

It was not the Caesars to whom he was recommending tribute but to what they represented: the legitimate state and the proper order it established. That order possessed laws and a way of life which afforded citizens to follow their own proper end as their beliefs dictated.

In the Matthean injunction, Our Lord was teaching that we must live in two worlds: the natural/ physical one—namely, the state—and the supernatural world of grace—the Holy Roman Church. Both those worlds have their rights, as well as their limitations. Both are necessary for Catholics. Both are the roads that lead to heaven. The A.D. 130 *Letter to Diognetus* gives eloquent witness to this striking doctrine of the Church:

> Christians are not distinguished from other men by country, language, nor by the customs which they observe.

They do not inhabit cities of their own, use a particular way of speaking, nor lead a life marked out by any curiosity. The course of conduct they follow has not been devised by the speculation and deliberation of inquisitive men. They do not, like some, proclaim themselves the advocates of merely human doctrines.

Instead, they inhabit both Greek and barbarian cities, however things have fallen to each of them. And it is while following the customs of the natives in clothing, food, and the rest of ordinary life that they display to us their wonderful and admittedly striking way of life. They live in their own countries, but they do so as those who are just passing through.

As citizens they participate in everything with others, yet they endure everything as if they were foreigners. Every foreign land is like their homeland to them, and every land of their birth is like a land of strangers. They marry, like everyone else, and they have children, but they do not destroy their offspring. They share a common table, but not a common bed. They exist in the flesh, but they do not live by the flesh. They pass their days on earth, but they are citizens of heaven.

They obey the prescribed laws, all the while surpassing the laws by their lives. They love all men and are persecuted by all. They are unknown and condemned. They are put to death and restored to life. They are poor, yet make many rich. They lack everything, yet they overflow in everything. They are dishonored, and yet in their very dishonor they are glorified; they are spoken ill of and yet are justified; they are reviled but bless; they are insulted and repay the insult with honor; they do good, yet are punished as evildoers; when punished, they rejoice as if raised from the dead. They are assailed by the Jews as barbarians; they are persecuted by the Greeks; yet those who hate them are unable to give any reason for their hatred.

This teaching flows directly from the mandates of the Fourth Commandment. Under the general rubric of Honoring Thy Father and Thy Mother is included the divine requirement to honor all those who sit in rightful authority. Our Savior is echoing this in St. Matthew's Gospel: "The Scribes and Pharisees sit in Moses's seat: All therefore whatsoever they bid you observe that they observe and do; but do not ye after their works; for they do not" (Mt 23:2).

The Fourth Commandment further binds us to observe the legitimate laws of one's country (those in conformity with the natural moral law; without that conformity, they are not laws at all). Moreover, one is required to actively participate in the maintenance of that country's good as well as its flourishing.

To that end, voting is among those serious obligations.

Finally, the commandment flowers into nothing less than the obligation to love one's country. Of course, this goes by the name of patriotism, which St. Thomas includes under the virtue of justice. Sometimes that love includes laying down one's life for the country he loves.

All of this was given a certain dramatic thrust by John Paul II. Each time he visited a foreign country, he was seen to disembark from his plane and then kneel on the tarmac and kiss the ground. This was a riveting symbol of the love that a Catholic should possess for his country. For it is out of the bowels of God's mercy that the men of every nation enjoy the fruits of a good life.

It is, therefore, no surprise that Catholics make the best citizens of any country. For the rule of Faith directs them toward a properly ordered love of their country, with its attendant duties and obligations.

Because God alone is perfect (as well as the infallible teachings of His Holy Catholic Church), a Catholic appreciates that no country is perfect. But it is his vote which holds the power to redress the slippage. Catholic realism teaches that when one vote does not effect the desired change, then maybe another will. And if not that one, perhaps the one after that. Because God alone is perfect (as well as the infallible teachings of His Holy Catholic Church), a Catholic appreciates that no country is perfect. But it is his vote which holds the power to redress the slippage.

No Catholic is permitted to surrender the duty of his citizenship to a sullen despair, exaggerated analyses of decline, idiosyncratic critiques of democracy, or a cynical secession from his duties. If defeat ensues upon his vote, then he must plan and strategize so that the next outcome will be better.

For good Catholics, defeats do not justify throwing up our hands in despair but, instead, throwing up our hands in prayer.

The prayer that God may grant is the light to see more clearly the path to victory next time. In the classic words of T. S. Eliot in his *Notes Towards the Definition of Culture*: "There are never any permanent defeats; nor are there any permanent victories." Well put. Our life here on earth is the lot of poor sinners in a valley of tears. The only permanent victory is praising the Blessed Trinity in Heaven.

The time for voting is almost upon us. Catholics will fulfill their obligations to the Fourth Commandment, walk to the polls, and cast their vote. Or they should. As they do, they will be showing God that they have accomplished all in their power to insure the good of their country with which God has blessed them. Even with all their doubts, they vote. And leave the rest in the hands of God.

As Catholics vote, they must bear in mind that no candidate (as with any country) is ever perfect. Never forget Psalm 146: "Put not your trust in princes." Sometimes the only choice a Catholic enjoys is to vote for the candidate who will do the least harm to God's moral law and the rights of His Holy Catholic Church. Seems like a meager morsel of bread, but a morsel nonetheless.

Keep in mind, as well, that old philosophical axiom: good is not the enemy of best.

THE TIGHTENING NOOSE
OF DIVERSITY IDEOLOGY

Attention to one's duties to state in life prevents normal Catholics from keeping track of the latest depredations of cancel culture. That is as it should be. Staring at the societal collapse only leaves one's soul depleted, while engendering a sterile rage. Reliable sources such as this one should be sufficient in fulfilling one's obligation to be informed, preventing either a surfeit of grim news or a dangerous naiveté, unbecoming of the Catholic citizen.

For those with their mind on better things, a small incident might have escaped them. In a 2021 hearing in the United States Senate on the vote of some of Mr. Biden's nominees, Senators Tammy Duckworth (D., Illinois.) and Mazie Hirono (D., Hawaii) threatened to hold them up. They would vote only "diversity candidates." They were disconcerted by the paucity of Asian Americans on Mr. Biden's list. After assurances that more officials of the desired background would be coming, they withdrew their threat. In the words of a prominent political journal, "In other words, the senators said they were prepared to engage in racial (and other forms of) discrimination in order to extort more discrimination." Exactly.

America has become a willing hostage to a new despotism: diversity parading as equality. It strangles society because it not only erases equality but undermines true diversity. Equality assumes that each member of society is allowed to rise to the level of their own excellence, a potential deeply knit into man made in *imago et similitudo Dei*. Diversity is the blessed result, a multi-textured loveliness which results when equality moves as it should. Let a polity surrender equality for cruel facsimiles, then despotism reigns, excellence dies, diversity is discarded, and unity crumbles under the jackboot of injustice.

> *Despotism*, because when man is deprived of his freedom to prosper according to God's designs, then he must submit to other men in place of God. Man's usurpation of God is always hellish

Excellence dies, the outcome when man turns his gaze away from the interior springs of his own worth and makes exterior characteristics his *summum bonum*

True diversity is discarded, when man is driven to obsess on superficial traits rather than the richness lying in the metaphysical endowments of human nature

Unity crumbles, for it can only flourish where truth reigns, making itself visible in man's natural potencies. Impeding these is the most savage injustice

Consequences of this unraveling of civic order is a daily spectacle of Ideological Diversity. America has witnessed this as every one of its once-reliable institutions fall like dominoes to the reigning ideology of diversity: The *Fortune* 500, entertainment, journalism, education, government, law, and even the field of sports. Decent Americans cannot but feel as though the walls of ideology are closing in, leaving them gasping for the pure air of right reason. *The Wall Street Journal* of December 2, 2020 reported:

> Nasdaq Inc. is pushing to require the thousands of companies listed on its stock exchange to include women, racial minorities and LGBTQ+ individuals on their boards, in what would be one of the most forceful moves yet to bring diversity to US corporations... requiring listed companies to have at least one woman on their boards, in addition to a director who is a racial minority or one who self-identifies as lesbian, gay, bisexual, transgender or queer.

Huxley could not have done better. His *Brave New World* was tame compared to this surreal wonderland.

Aside from the corrosive presence of Diversity Ideology in Nasdaq's decision, something more disturbing shows itself. Notice the nonchalant omission of even a passing nod to any objective moral norms. An acknowledged howl of rage at moral norms would be welcome, rather than smug indifference. A point has been reached where even attacks upon moral norms are unnecessary, since they have faded into the ether of irrelevance.

We seem to be seeing an unprecedented unraveling of human nature itself. In a little-known 1946 essay by C. S. Lewis, *Modern Man and His Categories of Thought,* he notes that the original hearers of the message of the Gospel had—in common with the Church—a belief of the supernatural, a fear of divine judgment and an awareness "That the world had once been better than it now was. The Jewish doctrine of the Fall, the Stoic conception of the Golden

Age, and the common Pagan reverence for heroes, ancestors, and ancient lawgivers, were in this respect more or less agreed."

Such common assumptions are no longer in place, and so Lewis believed that the Christian apologist met more resistance from modern man and woman than did the apostles from their audience. Lewis concludes with typical bravura, "I sometimes wonder whether we shall not have to re-convert men to real Paganism as a preliminary to converting them to Christianity. If they were Stoics, Orphics, Mithraists, or (better still) peasants worshipping the Earth, our task might be easier." Now you can understand Nasdaq. And the unquenchable thirst for diversity.

A modicum of allowance can be made for secular society. After all, they know no better. But such allowance cannot be made for those in the Church who should. Many of them giddily spread the gospel of Diversity Ideology. They are even undeserving of Lenin's obloquy, useful idiots. Perhaps Churchill's stinging rebuke fits them better, sheep in sheep's clothing. Only a few months ago, a prominent American prelate returning from a Roman visit was asked by a reporter about the agenda for his Archdiocese. He excitedly replied, *To promote diversity*. Wouldn't Lenin be pleased? And Churchill would howl. The Church should be in the forefront of protecting human dignity, not degrading it. George Orwell was correct when he wrote, "We have now sunk to a depth at which restatement of the obvious is the first duty of intelligent men."

What is the obvious? Human dignity is only achieved when man is allowed to reach for the highest excellence that conforms to God's plan. Permitting every man that opportunity is the mark of the just society. Since excellences will vary upon native born abilities, there will be differences of accomplishment and reward. The natural placements in society result from that free pursuit of excellence. This is the definition of true diversity. Since a decent people will not resent excellence rising to the fore, they will exalt in another's just accomplishments.

This is what Cicero meant in his *De Offciis*. Though he employs the word property, he was referring to the deeper endowment of the achievements of human persons in their freedom to pursue excellence: "The chief purpose of the establishment of states and constitutional orders was that individual property rights might be secured... For as I said above, it is the peculiar function of state and city to guarantee to every man the free and undisturbed control of his own property." Introduction of any other standard but excellence is the belittling of the human person, whether that be race, religion, age, gender, or disability.

Out of this agreeable true diversity emerges a marvelous unity, *e pluribus unum*. It is not racial or sexual identity that represents diversity, it is the invitation to every human person to excel. Ideological Diversity is the demise of true diversity. Since it is ideology and not truth, it sows disunity, resentment, and implacable hatreds. Obvious to every American eye today are the consequences of Diversity Ideology: distortions of justice and law, a massive corruption of education, and a descent into tribalism, reducing men into a primitive lust for power, filling the vacuum left by the disinterest with truth. Seething resentments bubble over into violence, irreparable divisions, interpersonal strife, and the death of friendship. As Aristotle clearly reminds us in the *Politics*, it is φιλία (friendship or friendliness) which is the glue of the state.

But ultimately all of these lessons can only be learned from the Church because they are supernatural truths perfecting natural reason. 'Tis a thousand pities that many of the Church's leaders look to secular ideology rather than sacred truths. The Catholic people beg for bread and receive only the stones of political platitudes. As Robert Reilly wrote, "Politics cannot meet the demands of the human soul, for it cannot achieve perfect justice...one must look beyond politics for the spiritual fulfillment for which man hungers... Socrates showed that any attempt to fulfill the soul's ultimate desire through politics – by trying to achieve perfect justice here – would transform the state into a totalitarian enterprise."

Woke diversity is like the creeping overgrowth of a jungle, and the jungle is Hobbes's "war of all against all." Decent men must see how it threatens Judeo-Christian civilization as we have known it, to say nothing of our beloved Republic. Tarrying in confronting it is simply not an option.

In Shakespeare's words, "The readiness is all."

RIP, DEI:
THE END OF OUR CAPTIVITY

The reign of DEI was a captivity, in which normal folks were terrified to speak openly, lest they be overheard and dismissed from employment, or worse.

Yes, a captivity. Diversity, Equity, and Inclusion (hereafter, DEI) can properly be called a captivity. Americans were held hostage by this alien ideology born in the claustrophobic classrooms of the Marxist credo for decades. Its noose has finally loosened.

So enveloping was this agitprop that the commanding heights of academe and conventional intelligentsia cast aside outdated things like free speech and launched a campaign of cancel culture, the flip side of Nazi book burning. For years, average Americans crouched in fear at the ubiquity of this Enemy.

No wonder you found yourself rubbing your eyes when *The Wall Street Journal* in 2025 reported:

> Universities are suspending research projects, canceling conferences and closing offices in response to a volley of orders from President Trump banning "diversity, equity and inclusion" across the United States government. The directives threaten vital federal funding and have thrown university leaders into disarray. To avoid running afoul of the orders, which include "the termination of all discriminatory programs", some school leaders have assumed a defensive posture on anything associated with DEI.

It seemed as though we were awaking from a nightmare. We had to pinch ourselves. Was its stranglehold abating?

But as the president severed its tentacles, the only thing he was doing was restoring simple common sense. But in the thick fog of Leftist disinformation, simple common sense begins to become uncommon. So uncommon that it soon becomes simply dangerous. Indeed, cause for arrest, as many pro-life folks discovered. Chesterton, as usual, was eerily correct when he wrote in *Heretics*:

> The great March of destruction will go on. Everything will be denied. Everything will become a creed. It is a

reasonable position to deny the stones in the street: it will be a religious dogma to assert them. It is a rational thesis that we are all in a dream: it will be a mystical sanity to say that we are all awake. Fires will be kindled to testify that two and two make four. Swords will be drawn to prove that leaves are green in summer.

Pause for a moment and savor the depth to which we have fallen. The Leader of the Free World compelled to promulgate a formal document declaring that only two sexes exist—male and female. Mr. Chesterton, how prescient you were!

Not to appear melodramatic, but we did seem to feel the exhilaration of prisoners of Auschwitz as they were freed by the American GIs. Recall the slogan over the gates of that death camp: *Arbeit macht frei* (work makes you free). And inmates heeded The Lie until they were incinerated as a reward.

Similarly, the American people over the long stretch of their captivity. Over and over, the incessant message was drummed into our ears: Diversity, Equity, and Inclusion. Its invocation was inescapable: in workplaces, government, kindergarten classrooms, Army and Navy, Fortune 500 boardrooms, universities and high schools, legacy media, and newspapers. This perverse ideology blanketed the nation like some toxic slime, leaving the conscience and right reason of Americans teetering.

Normal folks were terrified to speak openly, lest they be overheard and dismissed from employment, or worse. Without exaggeration, conditions in America approached the days of the Stalinist Soviet Union when one out of every two citizens worked for the KGB and children routinely reported anti-party speech of their parents to its agents.

When this tale is told to your grandchildren it will beggar belief. Since most rational men will be incredulous, let us rehearse just a few of the more bizarre tenets of this corrupt and corrupting ideology:

- A guide at the University of California, Irvine, became notorious for its discouragement of the idiom "Kill two birds with one stone." The problem for UCI was not that this hoary phrase is a worn-out cliché, but rather that it employed violent language. They replaced it with the bad rhyme "Feed two birds with one scone."
- Jacinda Ardern, former prime minister of New Zealand, during the pandemic sanctimoniously announced, "We

continue to be your single guardians of truth. Unless you hear it from us, it is not the truth."
- The mantra "disparate impact on black criminals" became the excuse to allow crime to run rampant. The blatant madness of the claim went unchallenged, unleashing eruptions of violence. But the irrationality of this nostrum was inescapable. For instance, if more college graduates were jailed for white-collar crime, should we cease arresting them because of disparate impact? If certain segments of a population are clearly seen to be committing crimes, it is not disparate impact to arrest them even though they represent a preponderance of a certain population.

George Orwell identified this agenda better than anybody before or since, first in essays in the 1940s and then in his novel 1984 which introduced Newspeak, a satiric *lingua franca* that showed how totalitarians impoverished language to crush freedom. "Don't you see that the whole aim of Newspeak is to narrow the range of thought?" says a character at the lie-infested Ministry of Truth. "In the end we shall make thought crime literally impossible, because there will be no words in which to express it."

This beloved America of ours came close to becoming Amerika, a client wing of the Davos Global State. Then, Trump. Like Hercules draining the Augean stables, he unleashed the full force of his presidency to allow common sense to reign again. Some may grouse that this is too much credit given to an imperfect instrument. But properly trained Catholics (a dwindling tribe) well understand that God always deploys imperfect instruments. Look at me and you.

Goethe was right in *Faust* when he placed upon the lips of Mephistopheles, "I desire only evil, and accomplish only good." In the mysterious designs of Divine Providence, this is often the way. The imitable Dom Anscar Vonier writes with the crystal clarity of the splendid Catholic modus operandi:

> Goodness itself, sanctity itself, is fostered by the proximity of evil. As St. Augustine puts it so well: it pleased God to make good come out of evil rather than to abolish all evil. God could have abolished all evil in his omnipotence; he did not; he did the better thing; he made good come out of evil, he makes sanctity come out of it; makes martyrs through the cruelty of man and gives his church the most glorious traditions of fortitude and courage through the very presence of enemies in her midst and around her

walls. When the great day of harvest comes sanctity will be found to be so great and so high by very reason of the wickedness that encompassed it.

Sincere questions may come to mind. DEI seem like perfectly noble Catholic ideals. Diversity is, after all, an opportunity for all. Equity, simple application of justice. And, Inclusion, fair play. As with all ideologies, these otherwise honorable sentiments are twisted into new meanings. Under cover of their Old Meanings, they smuggle the malign ideology. Think carefully. Is the People's Republic of North Korea truly a "people's republic"? It is as much a people's republic as Sing Sing. The key to victory for the ideologue is the manipulation of language. Trumpet the Old Words but mean the New Things. Under this clever ruse, Victor Hugo's warning is chilling: "Invading armies can be resisted. Invading ideas cannot."

DEI's Diversity is a violation of human dignity. It replaces the striving essential to the human person for physical traits or skin color. Diversity accomplishes nothing less than choking off the source of human dignity, which is the cultivation of intellectual or physical aptitude. Only this permits a man to take pride in his worth because the work is his own, a fruit of a struggle for excellence. Diversity eviscerates that. In doing so, it leaves the human person impoverished and stunted. Granted, circumstances will sometimes be less than ideal for many. But man is not his circumstance. Man's dignity rises above circumstance. Circumstance is the forge by which he becomes himself. In that achievement, he attains happiness and peace. The ancient Roman adage is apposite: *Ad astra per aspera* (To the stars through hard sacrifice).

DEI's Equity is a violation of justice. Men of common sense recognize that every society will always be marked by inequality. All human work is compensated unevenly, depending upon the nature of the work. This is the nature of justice. The bricklayer's profession is no less worthy than a neurosurgeon. That fact is not compromised by the fact that compensation for them is unequal. Equality is not measured in outcomes but by opportunity. Aristotle once remarked that the greatest inequality is to treat unequal things equally. In a truly just society, the bricklayer understands that true justice lies in the greater compensation for the neurosurgeon. In fact, he would have it no other way. You see, he is grounded in reality. Inequality is not remedied by more inequality.

DEI's Inclusion is a corruption of charity. Discrimination entails arbitrary exclusion, a vicious expulsion of some by virtue of some physical trait or disposition. But discrimination grounded upon the exigencies of the task at hand is obligatory. If an individual cannot meet with distinction the expectations required of him, charity requires he be bypassed by one who can. T. S Eliot wrote in "Ash Wednesday": "Teach us to care, and not to care." Puzzling at first glance. But his poetry expresses the rich teaching of Mother Church given unexpected currency by Vice President Vance.

In citing the *ordo amoris*, he reintroduced the remarkable textures of love. It is not an undifferentiated thing, like a plain white wall. It is more like a kaleidoscope of rich colors. If those textures are not respected, love becomes a caricature. Gross violations of charity arise if an individual is admitted into a position without proper qualification. Not only is the profession harmed but those better qualified become this victim of lack of charity.

Yes, a Catholic must care for the stranger. But caring for the stranger becomes a vice if it entails not first caring for one's family, or the common good of one's nation.

"Teach us to care, and not to care," indeed.

We well deserve to rejoice at the beginning of the end of our captivity.

But if we are not vigilant, the captivity will return. And with a vengeance.

CHRIST WAS A BROWN JEW

Fame came quite suddenly for Desi Arnaz Giles. Slated in 1997 to portray Christ in a local New Jersey Passion play, bigots had a field day with black Mr. Giles portraying the Mediterranean Semite, Jesus of Nazareth. Our friends in the media, who are quick to sniff the slightest racism and quicker still to smack Christianity, got a two-fer by giddily reporting that Mr. Giles was inundated with death threats from the local Christian gentry. Catholic Churchmen stood with Mr. Giles and against hatred. Bravo.

But this is not the whole story. As usual the whole story goes unreported.

First some disclaimers. It is perfectly acceptable for a black man to portray Christ in a Passion play. It is also acceptable for an Asian. It is even acceptable for a Caucasian. If this were not so, then it would be impossible to present the Passion play anywhere but in Israel and certain parts of the Jewish Diaspora. Moreover, it is even legitimate that Christ be depicted in art as members of these groups. If this were not so, then all the blond-haired, blue-eyed Christs on all the walls in America would have to come down.

But there is a crucial difference that must be elucidated because, for all the hundreds of years that Christ has been depicted on stage and screen and in the painted image as blond-haired and blue-eyed, no one has ever developed a theology claiming that He came from the little town of Copenhagen. Yet the Afro centrists not only demand a black Jesus on stage, they demand one in history, because now they claim that the historical Christ was a black man from Africa.

At issue is not the portrayal of a black Christ, but the creation of an elastic God, one that is stretched deftly to accommodate bold new ideas. Have a multicultural agenda? Morph Christ into a different race. Need a feminine slant? Stress that gender is superfluous to divinity and have ICEL inclusivize the Bible. And so it goes. Yet no matter how hard some people wish God to have been something else, He stubbornly remains what He is.

Men begin lying about God only after they have been lying about themselves. And none is a greater lie than the one that claims man cannot know the truth. Truth is the nature of a thing or an action and is available to everyone regardless of where they are from, when they have lived or what they look like. Denying man this rich capacity to know the truth is to clip his metaphysical wings, and deny him the lofty heights of understanding. He is left like an animal, knowing only his immediate experience and refusing validity to anything else.

Truth frees man from his own rigid conditions and in this radiance he achieves an intimacy with all things—"You shall know the truth, and the truth shall make you free" (Jn 8:32). Poor modern man. In emancipating himself from truth he thought he would become boundless. All he found was a hundred knots binding him like a trapped beast. Slave to the rigid categories of experience alone, he must cast the whole wide world into chose cramped quarters, even his God. Only rigid men demand a flexible God, and their calcified ideas can tolerate no God except one in their own exact and puny image.

This neuralgia to truth extends everywhere. The Catholic politician retreats from duty by refusing to impose his moral opinion on anyone, not even himself. The ordinary citizen dreads speaking in absolute moral categories lest he appear judgmental. Even the Holy Mass is under the whip of liturgy committees who cut and paste to suit fickle trends. Just call this world Babel.

So a Passion play with a black Christ is just an innocent variation—until it is tied to pernicious ideology. Mr. Giles probably wanted only a stab at doing what he loved, acting. Sadly he became a shill in the hands of remote hustlers, but isn't that what many of us have become? Certainly it is and will remain, until we start acting like men and demand that things are what they are. Up is up, and Christ was a brown Jew.

THE OBSOLETE HUMAN

I have a sad announcement to make. I shall not be with you much longer. Very likely, along with many other priests I shall be in jail. After the Unites States Supreme Court decision, *Obergefell et al v. Hodges*, making same-sex marriage a constitutional right in all fifty states of the United States of America, all of us are in peril, especially priests. For when a test same-sex couple comes to a rectory, mine or any other, and asks to be married, I must refuse. This will instantly place me in violation of their civil rights under the United States Constitution: tantamount to an Asian couple coming to me for marriage and I refuse them because of their race. That denial would unleash the Left's formidable legal machinery. All their high-powered, fatly financed phalanx of attorneys would descend upon me. Having paltry funds, I would hire a well-intentioned Catholic attorney, whom the same-sex couple's sophisticated battery of lawyers would crush without breaking a sweat. Imprisonment would be next. And this goes for all other faithful priests as well. Those who think this preposterous are the very same ones who said the same thing about same-sex marriage ten years ago

The Obergefell decision on June 26, 2015 is a far greater calamity than *Roe v Wade* in 1973. As much as Roe sparked a tidal wave of children's blood upon the nation, society was able to still go on, albeit, limping. With Obergefell, a dagger has been plunged into the heart of human society – marriage and the natural family. No society can survive such a blow. After Roe good mothers and fathers could continue to have children and families. There could be families. After Obergefell mothers and fathers will gradually disappear, because marriage will. Kill people, and society can still pull itself together. Kill a vital institution, and society withers. Overreacting? Hardly. Definitions mirror reality. Change definitions and reality changes. Not all at once, but eventually. Inevitably. Thus Edmund Burke, that intrepid guardian of good sense and political order, claims: "It is absolutely necessary not to change, unless change is absolutely necessary." Societies are fragile things, dependent upon their members adhering strictly to Permanent Truths. Once those truths are seen as debatable, and ultimately expendable, the society implodes. There exists evidence aplenty. Since the French Revolution societies have been slashed by a thousand cuts, from Nazism to Marxism / Leninist Communism. Nations made bold in jiggling with all kinds of definitions: the person, dignity, rights, and freedom. The results were hellish: from gulags to gas chambers. James Kalb diagnoses this cultural body blow with philosophical gimlet eye:

> This project's goal is best understood as eschatological, or perhaps counter-eschatological: a social world that recognizes no transcendent authority above it, no history behind it except the history of its own coming into being, and no nature of things beneath it that cannot be transformed technologically into what we choose. It is secular saecula saeculorum, a world unlimited by the Divine, by the past, or by nature's laws – including the biological principle distinguishing male from female.

The partisans of same-sex marriage fully understand the power of their accomplishment. Listen to Jonathan Chait, writing in a popular go-to magazine of the zeitgeist, New York, "...a great deal has happened in a very short time... Social autonomy has sprung forward on almost every front... The country as it existed in previous decades is receding permanently into the mists of time." Finally. The mask has fallen, and the Left proudly trumpet their true intentions. Their highly effective tissue of lies, half-truths, and legerdemain has triumphed. Where are the accommodationists now? They dialogued, compromised, diversified, were properly inclusive and bent over backwards to meet the Left halfway. And as the accommodationists showed their toothy smiles, the Left used all of that adolescent naiveté as the rope to hang them.

Often the Left proffers the bromide that Obergefell is nothing to worry about. Straights will marry, and so will gays. Everyone is a winner. You've heard their chants: Love wins. Equality for all. Not so fast. Consider the importance of definitions and reality. The Left does. If asked to define a telephone one would say something like "An electronic device that makes possible conversation between two people over long distances." Let us say that a group lobbied to change that definition. They insisted that a telephone should be redefined as "two people speaking to one another." In that case anyone of common sense would realize that we are no longer speaking about a telephone. But the architects of the new definition would plead that speaking to one another is, after all, the essence of the telephone. That person of common sense would then protest. Yes, speaking to one another is important. But that is not the nature of a telephone. You can't have a telephone if you insist its meaning is merely conversation between two people. Under the weight of the new definition, telephones would disappear.

Similarly with marriage. Its definition is the permanent union of a man and a woman who place their considerable love to the duty of the natural procreation of children. Claiming that marriage is only about love vitiates marriage. Yes, marriage is indeed about love, but so much more. It is love placed in the sacrificial oblation of bringing children naturally into the world. You and I and the human race are given to loving many people; indeed, any one we wish to love. We do not marry them. Why? Because, in most cases, we are not suited to place our love in the begetting of children. Love is necessary, not sufficient for marriage. If marriage is only about love, marriage meets its demise. Its purpose disappears. Of course, other unintended consequences come tumbling forth, like Pandora's Box. Some of those consequences are too unsettling to mention to this whole-some audience. One of the more benign is polygamy. Dancer and writer Brandon Ambrosino tackled this subject with alarming candor in the *New Republic* in January 2014:

> It's time for the LGBT (translation: Lesbian, Gay, Bisexual, Transgender) community to start moving beyond genetic predisposition as a tool for gaining mainstream acceptance of gay rights... For decades now, it been the powerful argument in the LGBT arsenal: that we were 'born this way'... Still, as compelling as these arguments are, they may have outgrown their usefulness. With most Americans now in favor of gay marriage, it's time for the argument to shift to one where genetics don't matter. The genetic argument has boxed us into a corner.

Bold, don't you think? But wait. Here's gay activist Jay Michaelson last year in the *Daily Beast*:

> Moderates and liberals have argued that same-sex marriage is No Big Deal – is the Same Love, after all, and gays

just want the same lives as everyone else. But further right and further left, things get a lot more interesting. What if gay marriage will really change the institution of marriage, shifting conceptions around monogamy and intimacy?... And what about those post-racial and post-gender Millennials? What happens when a queer-identified, mostly heterosexual woman with plenty of LGBT friends gets married. Do we really think that... she will be interested in a heteronormative, sex-negative, patriarchal system of partnership?... Radicals point out that gay liberation in the 1970s was, as the name implies, a liberation movement. It was about being free, questioning authority, rebellion. "2-4-6-8, smash the church and smash the state," people shouted.

Add to this the June 22, 2015 issue of *Weekly Standard*. There Jonathan Last wrote with chilling warnings. As you read, notice the strange new vernacular. Strange words to usher in a Strange New World. Redefinition and novelty are the advance guard in societal upheaval. Reread your Orwell, Huxley, and Olinsky. Now, Mr. Last:

> Changing marriage beyond recognition has been a stated goal of the organization Beyond Marriage, which is a collection of several hundred gay-rights lawyers, law professors, and activists. They argue that same-sex marriage is merely the first step on the path to redefining the family itself. Ultimately, they want legal protection for a host of other relationships, including, as they delicately put it, "Queer couples who decide to create and raise a child with another queer person or couple, in two households" and "committed, loving households in which there is more than one conjugal partner." This group is not a collection of cranks: It includes professors from Georgetown, Harvard, Emory, Columbia, and Yale."

So much for unfounded fears. Within five years the most hard-bitten among us will shudder at what the votaries of Obergefell have planned. It will make Caligula's household look like *Rebecca of Sunnybrook Farm*.

Lastly, we must turn briefly to the matter of rights. The Left has used this word as a cudgel since the time of John Locke and Thomas Hobbes. Its new modern usage casts a hypnotic effect over cultures, leaving them in supine surrender. In the classical tradition, rights bear a muscularity which generates all the virtues that ennoble man. Equal rights simply mean that all men are to be treated according to the dignity attendant upon our shared humanity. Indeed all men and women have the right to marriage, but they only enjoy the rights fitting to their nature. A right is not the license to do what one wants, but the inviolable capacity to do what one ought. While man has the freedom to do anything, he does not have the right to do anything. In fact, man has only the right to be good. Using freedom to be wicked is misusing freedom. Equal rights, properly understood, is the right that every man and woman enjoys to pursue the goods of human nature. A man can be anything he wants to be, as long as it is consistent with the truth of his humanity. Otherwise his nature is twisted out of shape; in other words, he becomes a monster. Aristotle called our human nature a bondage. We are restrained by it; loosing ourselves from it is a literal metaphysical suicide. We cease being what we are. No surprise that contemporary philosophical and political conversation has banished the word 'nature' from their vocabulary. Too constrictive.

Back to my departure. I will willingly go to jail. For the honor and glory of God. For the institution of marriage. For love of the Catholic people. This is the reason why I am called Father, to protect and defend the Truths that win man salvation and happiness. Even with my life. But Catholics cannot think that now they must retreat to their safe enclaves. They must not think that ignoring the looming darkness will save the Light. For the people who are cheering Obergefell never sleep. Their eyes are trained upon all of us. They are not finished.

THE TRAGEDY OF LEGAL POSITIVISM

Summertime's most serious tragedy was not a plane falling from the sky off the coast of Martha's Vineyard, but moral sanity falling on its face in Trenton, New Jersey. On August 4th, 1999, the New Jersey Supreme Court ruled that the Boy Scouts of America must admit professed homosexuals to their number. To add salt to the wound, it screeched its decision with a stinging 7-0 unanimous opinion.

Why worry about a decision from a New Jersey Court? Because it represents the unrelenting pressure being applied by a highly sophisticated, well-funded clique of secularist cultural elites. After all, this is the second attempt to bring such a case before a state court. The California Supreme Court heard a similar plea. Reason somehow prevailed there and that Court declared in March 1998 that the Boy Scouts were a private organization and had constitutional rights of freedom of association and freedom of expression to expel homosexuals. Picture perfect legal reasoning.

But the cultural elite does not suffer such blows easily. They have dragged their case to New Jersey's hyper-liberal Supreme Court. To paraphrase Winston Churchill, never have so few done so much to so many. In the name of rights, the left dismantles brick by brick the natural law ethic that has informed this republic. For that enormity, we muse name this a tragedy whose importance cannot be exaggerated.

Looking at the decision furnishes us with a reconnaissance photo of the battle formations of the secular Left. Chief Justice Deborah T. Poritz wrote that the plaintiff, James Dale, was dismissed from the Boy Scouts on the basis of little more than prejudice. Justice Poritz went on with emblematic blather, "The sad truth is that excluded groups and individuals have been prevented from full participation in the social, economic, and political life of this country. The human price of this bigotry has been enormous. At a most fundamental level, adherence to the principle of equality demands that our legal system protect the victim of invidious discrimination."

Aside from the boilerplate, a characteristic motif emerges here. With deft legerdemain, Justice Poritz switches the equality of persons, which is taught by the Catholic Church, with the equality of actions, which she parrots from secular modernity. The Boy Scouts of America did not ban Mr. Dale because it hates homosexuals, but because Mr. Dale publicly embraces homosexuality. Of course, Mr. Dale enjoys rights and respect. Homosexuality absolutely does not. Love of goodness demands that we discriminate against this vice – and every other. Justice Poritz calls this a prejudice – i.e., an opinion without foundation. Most men call it moral common sense.

Before the surreal lens of modernity distorted life's landscape, most men understood that with unblinking certitude. It rested on the self-evident principle that actions make the man. For instance, we call a man good because he does good things and vice versa. No one would dare say "Just because he risked his life to save three children doesn't make him a good person." Why? Because the principle that actions make the man is utterly axiomatic. Yet how quickly this norm is ignored with vice. How often do we hear, "Just because he is an adulterer doesn't make him a bad person." The contradiction practically moans for redress. Yet the Left conveniently ignores it, while they continue to apply the principle only when it suits their agenda.

Imagine Justice Poritz remarking on other kinds of cases. She would be the first to judge a young tough as evil for beating up a homosexual, or the Ku Klux Klan wicked for lynching a black man, or a corporation boss vile for promoting a young secretary in exchange for sexual favors. Oh no, Justice Poritz fully accepts the principle which is why she would be the first to ban a Klansman from membership in the NAACP. What she doesn't want to accept are the full imperatives of natural law. The quite deliberate refashioning of morality and man's nature leaves no choice but the kind of rigged, tendentious reasoning which riddles Poritz's decision. She understands that society has the obligation to discriminate against vice, especially when it crawls into the public forum. But what is vice? Have no fear, Justice Poritz will tell us. And it will be so new that you will hardly recognize it. That is because the Left sees law without the natural law, and that disconnection leads the administrators of justice to all kinds of injustice. For it is no longer truth they serve but ideology.

The Tragedy of Legal Positivism

This is pure legal positivism. Legal positivists are all alike, they want to look at the law alone, only to find themselves seeing everything but the law. In 2000, Berlin's daily, *Die Welt*, excerpted the published prison diary of Holocaust architect Adolf Eichmann. On one of the diary's 1,300 pages, he writes something apposite to the issue at hand: "The orders (from Hitler) were, for me the highest thing in my life and I had to obey them without question." Whether it is a human law or a superior's orders, without their reference to God's natural law they all lead to the same place – hell on earth. Chesterton had it right, "Merely human law has a great tendency to become merely inhuman law." Bending over backwards to see rights without morality, the Left robs us of the right to be moral.

Try finding a greater tragedy than that.

THREE CHEERS FOR INEQUALITY

It's springtime, and fairness is in the air. And we're choking on it. Everywhere we turn, fairness. Wherever so-called microaggressions and cultural appropriation are condemned or when the University of California bans phrases like 'land of opportunity', it is done in the name of fairness. #LoveWins or #MeToo – fairness. Open borders – fairness. Like a thirsty man at sea trying to slake his thirst with salt water, the more they screech fairness, the less they know what fairness means. Actually, their brand of fairness has as much to do with true fairness as a fire has to do with a firefly. Be careful how you define words. While some may be using the same words, they may be saying totally opposite things. Beating up words is bad enough; but beating up reality is unforgiveable.

If we don't get fairness right, no one will be treated fairly. For all the agitprop of the Left, this is the final result of their fitful rantings. Fairness in their lexicon is, very simply, unfair. Take income inequality, for instance. Some howl that it is unfair that 1 percent owns inordinately more than the 99 percent. As with many simplicities, this is designed only for simpletons. The reason why the so-called rich own so much is because they have worked so much. Whether the work be the heavy lifting of creativity, imagination, sheer intellectual firepower, or the long hours of physical exertion and sheer thrift – it is the reward of hard work. Calling that unfair is bizarre. And suspicious.

Lurking underneath the Left's complaints is a fundamental odium toward the rich themselves. Scratch the surface of their moaning and one finds the odd principle that the reason why there are people who are poor is because there are some people who are rich. In their lopsided calculus, wealth is a zero-sum game: when I gain something, you must lose something. Wealth is seen a finite commodity, so the only way I can enjoy greater wealth is by depriving you of yours. This construal turns the rich into thieves, and the poor into victims. The poor become truncated human beings, not so much underprivileged as handicapped. Not as good as you and me, the poor must be always cared for, like pets.

Few bigotries carry the stench of this one. Fr. Schall punctured this mythology when he once wrote,

> The reason the poor are poor is not because the rich are rich. The only way the poor can be helped on a massive scale is for them to learn from those who know how wealth is produced... We want most people, most of the time, to take care of themselves... if we took the wealth of the world and simply redistributed it equally, we would undermine economic incentives and capital concentration. What would happen is that all would be poorer because the growth dynamism for all would be undermined.

The Left's debasement of the poor creates a static and rigid world bereft of the marvelous expansiveness that man's nature guarantees. Our human nature consists of having a mind and being able to use it freely. Of course, fidelity to our nature will always entail sacrifice; for though we are blessed with freedom, nothing is ever free. This truth hurts the ears of most men. Thus, de Tocqueville wrote in *Democracy in America*: "There exists also in the human heart a depraved taste for equality, which reduces men to prefer equality in slavery to inequality with freedom." How else to make sense of Wordsworth's paean to the prospect of the French Revolution, "Bliss was it in that dawn to be alive/ But to be young was very heaven."

Inequality will always be the flip side of freedom. Einstein, Mozart, and Da Vinci had far more gifts than the rest of us. Where is the rage at such inequality? Patton, Churchill, and Aristotle enjoyed natural endowments towering over most of humanity. Where is the protest for just redress? You received an A in geometry, and your friend failed. Must you insist that fairness demand you receive the same grade? When put that plainly the problem comes into proper relief. Equality is not sameness, and fairness does not erase the sharp difference in the rewards attendant upon achievement. It demands them. Both students have an equal opportunity to learn but also an equal opportunity to fail. Freedom makes unequal outcomes possible because human beings are not the same in ability or motivation. Unequal outcomes are fair as long as there are no artificial impediments to achievement. Aristotle established the perfect principle in the *Nicomachean Ethics*, "The greatest inequality is to treat unequal things equally." Fr. Schall again caps this all very nicely,

That some will always be richer than others is not itself a
sign that anything is wrong with the world... Rich men,
poor men, men in the middle, all [have] their places. All
can save their souls. Each could be concerned with one
another, each could fail... When Christ talked about
the lilies of the field. He told us to see how they grow.
He noted that the Heavenly Father took care of them as
lilies, with the implication that He would take care of
us as men, that is after the fashion of men. The fashion
of men is to learn to do things, to know what produces
wealth, and what does not, and to learn what is good for
us, and what is not. The corruption of our culture is not
in its wealth but in some of its principles.

Notice that we are not trespassing upon the foundational truth that "All men are created equal, and are endowed by their Creator with certain unalienable rights." That is the sterling cornerstone of Catholic anthropology, proceeding from the dogmatic tenet that all men are made *imago et similitudo Dei*. But while all men are to be treated equally, justice demands that their actions *not* be treated equally. Otherwise we have the current predicament of Western culture. Instead of *America the Beautiful*, we are *Alice in Wonderland*.

Our culture must return to the truth of things. Until that happens, those treated unfairly will never know fairness, and those suffering inequality will never enjoy authentic equality. Above all, the most precious lesson is that man's crown is his ability to grasp truth, and act upon it with his glorious freedom. From that there will come a world filled with wild inequalities.

I guess fairness has its price.

THREE CHEERS FOR SMOKERS

Isn't it about time someone gave three cheers for smokers? After all, they are one of the scapegoats in the most recent Liberal Distraction.

First, let it be clear that I am firmly opposed to ill health, cancer, suffering, bad habits, respiratory disease, long lingering death, and of course, (need it even be said), secondhand smoke. That said, these aren't the real issues. Though the stigmatization of cigarette smokers has passed beyond its shelf life, it still remains a helpful metaphor into the current Reign of Woke Terror under which we groan. It signals the Leftist lunacy of passionate focus upon trivialities while entirely oblivious to matters of titanic moral consequence.

Note how they take captive once noble terms and redesign them to suit their transgressive purposes: virtue-signaling, for instance. Verbal engineering always precedes social engineering. Thus, George Orwell, in his influential essay *Politics and the English Language*:

> Most people who bother with the matter at all would admit that the English language is in a bad way, but it is generally assumed that we cannot by conscious action do anything about it. Our civilization is decadent and our language – so the argument runs – must inevitably share in the general collapse. It follows that any struggle against the abuse of language is a sentimental archaism, like preferring candles to electric light or hansom cabs to aeroplanes. Underneath this lies the half-conscious belief that language is a natural growth and not an instrument which we shape for our own purposes.
>
> Now, it is clear that the decline of a language must ultimately have political and economic causes: it is not due simply to the bad influence of this or that individual writer. But an effect can become a cause, reinforcing the original cause and producing the same effect in an intensified form, and so on indefinitely. A man may take to drink because he feels himself to be a failure, and then fail all the more completely because he drinks. It is rather

the same thing that is happening to the English language. It becomes ugly and inaccurate because our thoughts are foolish, but the slovenliness of our language makes it easier for us to have foolish thoughts.

Defending smokers is imperative for even graver reasons having to do with the survival of civilization itself. Overreach you say? Not exactly, only because the symbolism reaches so profoundly. Orwell would agree. With our culture cobbling a New Moral Code to replace the Old one, new virtues and new sins are being created. It used to be that we stigmatized adulterers, now we shun smokers. Once upon a time, society showed disgust for pornography, now disgust is reserved for those who refuse to recycle. As you watch poor smokers huddling in their corners to do the dastardly act, we readily see how the new sins are shunned as effectively as the old ones.

Left unaddressed, these outlier stupidities soon become mainstream strangleholds. Take Critical Race Theory. It gestated in the petri dishes of classrooms of higher academe and now is as common as the ABCs in our children's classrooms.

A public school in Cupertino, California, actually required third graders—in math class—to deconstruct their racial identities and rank themselves according to their power privilege. A public school in Philadelphia made fifth graders march across an auditorium stage bearing signs that read Jail Trump and Black Power Matters in a rally for Black Communism. And a Buffalo school district adopted an emancipatory curriculum instructing students through its pedagogy of liberation that "All white people play a part in perpetuating systemic racism." Now you see, don't you, why we must all shout: *Three cheers for smokers.*

This kind of Woke Maoism possesses an etiology not difficult to trace. It is embedded deeply in the ontological nature of man. He cannot live too long without heeding that persistent voice of the natural law enjoining him to do good and avoid evil—any kind of good, and any kind of evil.

Even though he might campaign for an existence without standards, the steady interior voice demands some calculus of absolute evil and absolute good. And if man won't let God declare what they are, then man will. When he does, despotism reigns. If truth and God no longer govern a man's life, darker forces do, and man's desire for absolutes descends into absolute terror. You see, as Chesterton once put it, "The atheist is not one who believes in no god, he is one who believes in any god."

Not surprisingly, this moral reinvention proceeds deceptively. Glimmers of hope soon become layers of more darkness. For instance, there is Columbia University's Professor Delbanco's 1995 book, *The Death of Satan: How Americans Have Lost the Sense of Evil*. Initially, one is encouraged at such a promising title; from a certified member of the *bien pensant* no less. Could it be a breach in the seemingly impregnable armor of the Liberal Behemoth?

Then, page 3: "A gulf has opened in our culture between the visibility of evil and the intellectual resources available for coping with it." What is that evil? Delbanco tells us: "deforestation, erosion, siltation, exhaustion, pollution, extermination, cruelty, destruction and despoliation." Doesn't this remind you of the quip made by Forrest Davis, adviser to the imitable Senator Taft: "The Liberal has looked upon the face of evil and found it half-good."

The seven old capital sins are now replaced by nine new ones. Alas, Academe nudges out Sinai, and Almighty Man one-ups Almighty God. Can't the fanatical devotion to abortion and the LGBTQ+ agenda be described as a religion with devotion twisted into zealotry. No keen eye is necessary to see how the unwavering dedication once reserved to the dogmas of Christianity have now shifted to the hallowed dogmas of Liberalism. The difference is that the former are rational, the latter are not.

This new moral project is not reserved to agnostic academics. Fr. Theodore Hesburgh, late president of Notre Dame (and designer of the new anti-Catholic Catholic University), was once interviewed at age 81. He confessed that his priestly mission never ends: "My constant pressure is to get students caught up with moral issues – civil rights, human rights, world development and getting rid of the nukes." With such moral men all around us, why do we not feel consoled?

These new *pronunciamentos* reflect not the grand exigencies of human nature but the petrifying posturing of men mimicking God. As a result, true morality is miniaturized, concerned less with issues of man's potential greatness through virtue and sanctity and more with issues of his supremacy. Aristotle's world argued incessantly about the nature of virtue and truth, justice and God, fortitude and the good. The Christian world perfected this natural wisdom with calls to sacrifice and heroism, grace and revelation, beauty and holiness. A post-Christian world offers either a smarmy version of brotherly love, or, more often, thinks, argues, and fights only about "me."

Post-Christian man now finds these former things reeking of an ancient naive objectivity. He rejects them, after brief reflection, in favor of the current vogue solipsism because the new Geist forbids consensus on things like the nature of things: man, good, and evil. It settles on a new and smaller, much smaller, list of absolutes such as saving the earth, banning smokers, the twin hydra of diversity/inclusivity, tribal purity, or the simply desiccated anthem, "being yourself."

This is the grotesque logic which leads to children being hunted down in schools because they are saying their prayers but given gold stars for promoting safe sex; or promoting marches that celebrate anarchy and hatred of police while gagging ordinary Americans for expressing a desire to love God and speak freely.

No hesitation, please: *Three cheers for smokers!*

CENSORSHIP

Smack in the middle of New York City's pollution, there is a place where you can breathe pure air. It is Columbia University, and we are talking about the purest air of all, academic freedom. That fabled Morningside campus indulges their students with the ivy league privilege of consuming ideas pinned with the professors' academic Good Housekeeping seal of approval. Ah, if only everyone could enjoy that cozy protection of academics who know what is good for us.

But Columbia's vaunted academic freedom has started to show a bit of wear lately. It seems that *Accuracy in Academia* sponsored a conference in mid-November at Columbia's campus. Launching the conference was a gala dinner featuring Ward Connerly, the Black businessman who sparked the movement to end affirmative action in the states of California and Washington. War immediately broke out and Columbia's quiescent pursuit of approved ideas exploded. Hundreds of student protesters screamed their opposition to Connerly's uncanonical speech. Columbia responded by informing *Accuracy in Academia* that the balance of the conference could only be attended by officially identified students. In effect, this banned the conference entirely. Yes, you read correctly: banned. As in censorship. Can it be so? Could the Ivy League's coveted academic freedom been all the while a fig leaf, concealing the censorious fascism they so loudly detest? Seems so.

Stack Columbia right alongside all the ocher deceptions of this dark waning century – the People's Republic of China, Cuba, North Korea, Women's Choice, Animal Rights, Private Morality, Consenting Adults, Toleration, and Adult Entertainment. Censorship rightly stands far from that list. While partisans of modernity decry it, men of right thinking do not. Some things are justly banned in a good society. But those things are only recognized by men who are good, or who at least know what goodness is. Fewer and fewer of those kinds of men exist today.

Goodness is not determined by majority vote. The former New York state Attorney General Bob Abrams remarked that our most hard-fought freedoms could be lost if women's right to abort is not protected. With the commonweal populated by this kind of poisoned thinking, things will indeed be censored, but not the right things. Societies with a healthy moral compass have always vigorously proscribed actions that injure the common good. Censorship is critical in a well-ordered society. Liberalism's hypocrisy is railing against it, then slipping it back in while no one is looking.

Secular society is not alone in this stifling reverse-censorship. It has seeped into the society of the Catholic Church. *Aggiornamento's* bright promises have turned into nightmares. 1965 saw maverick theologians come marching into the church proclaiming freedom, dialogue, and openness. To many Catholics it was a sweet melody, like Robespierre's *'liberté, égalité at fraternité'* must have sounded to the witless French masses.

But beneath those words there was aborning a bitter revolution. Out went the *Index of Forbidden Books* (the benign gesture of a Church which respected both the power of the written word and the nobility of man's intellect) and Roman Centralization (read Primacy of Peter and assorted miscellany such as dogma, defined truth and standardization of Roman Liturgy). Similarly jettisoned was the Holy Office, which is rightly the Church's attempt to take seriously Our Lord in Matthew 7:15, "Beware of false prophets, who come to you in the clothing of sheep, but inwardly they arc ravening wolves", and St. Paul in 1 Timothy 6:20, "O Timothy, keep that which is committed to thy trust."

Gradually things changed. The censorship so despised by the left quickly became the cornerstone of the Catholic Left. But theirs was a censorship unmediated by virtue and not in the service of revealed Truth. It is censorship gone awry, and that spells tyranny. Many dioceses began to operate like small gulags. Their seminaries imposed microscopic scrutiny to candidates lest an adherent to the Magisterium slip through. Seminary classrooms often resembled old Soviet style schools—no discussion save praise of the regnant ideology. Offices of Religious Education employed bloated bureaucracies who sniffed out the faintest scent of orthodox teaching. All the while exacting a numbing conformity to a vacuous catechesis which has produced three generations of Catholic ciphers, causing the very bishops who created this state of religious illiteracy to establish committees to study the phenomenon of religious illiteracy. Reverse-censorship's list goes on and on—Catholic Universities who refuse to hire and routinely expel fundamentalist Catholics; and Catholic newspapers and periodicals which not only reject articles of an 'unnuanced Catholicism' but even advertisements which suggest an alternative to the Leftist hegemony.

Can't the liberal heart at least find room to give our small minority a chance to coexist?

After all, even orthodox Catholics have rights.

OUR BRAVE NEW (WOKE) WORLD

Have you heard? A Chief Purpose Officer earns a six-figure salary in a Fortune 500 company. His job profile is to supply meaning to corporate moneygrubbing. Not any meaning, but the approved meaning as handed down with Solomonic *gravitas* by the Woke cognoscenti. "In today's climate," reports Forbes (Feb. 14), "Companies are expected to take a stand on a multitude of societal issues... That's where purpose comes in." In a fit of Orwellian newspeak, Forbes informs us that "The role of a chief purpose officer can supercharge a company's efforts to be truly purposeful."

Working alongside the Chief Purpose Office is another handsomely rewarded executive, the Chief Ethics Officer. If any action, glance, raised eyebrow, inflection, choice of words or absence of words (especially pronouns) smacks of heteronormativity, patriarchy, cultural appropriation, white supremacy, etc. (the full list of crimes is longer than Leviticus's dietary regulations), the Chief Ethics Officer is off and running, and termination lies on the horizon.

If this sounds bizarre, you haven't lost your mind. What should trouble your mind, however, is that these business titans, whose bottom-line mentality once immunized them to such vacuous academic bilge, now slavishly bow down to it. The madness is propagating like some deadly green algae, smothering common sense in its path.

Have you heard of the Harassment Specialist? Still another plump position populating not only the Fortune 500's but the whole of academia. This too is a cutting-edge profession for a culture on the skids. Its principal focus is pious devotion to microexamination of the growing problem of person-on-person sexual harassment, the secular sin *du jour*.

Harassment Specialists in grammar schools, for example, hunt down the abominations ten to twelve-year-olds inflict on one another. You know, things such as (be sure children are out of range) name-calling, spreading salacious rumors, intercepting personal notes, unwanted touching, inappropriate gestures, and the sharing of offensive jokes or cartoons. In other words, all the things average boys and girls of imperfect virtue do when they are ten, the things you and I did at that age.

While the Harassment Specialist is now *de rigueur*, it does have antecedents in our cultural meltdown. In the mid-1990s, Angela Davis, the mother of a ten-year-old Georgia schoolgirl, brought a lawsuit against the Monroe County Board of Education. She was convinced that her daughter suffered grave psychological damage because a twelve-year-old male schoolmate was pulling her hair—or something to that effect. All this was treated with the solemnity once reserved to the defense of God. Not surprising, as this is exactly what occurs when society has replaced holy religion with secularist boilerplate.

Of course, this brouhaha was raging while school nurses blithely distributed contraceptives to conscientious students striving to please their elders by exercising the new virtue of protection.

Consenting copulating teenagers? A laudatory matter of choice. Unwelcome glances at the opposite sex? Jail. Welcome to the ever faster spinning merry-go-round of post-virtue virtue.

As Sophocles once taught, "Whom the gods would destroy they first make mad." How true. How everlastingly true.

With the zealotry of virtue placed at the service of ideology, Ms. Davis drove her case to the U.S. Supreme Court, where Justice Sandra Day O'Connor (along with four other justices) was happy to oblige her pique. "Student-on-student sex harassment could be a deeply serious matter affecting a child's ability to learn," Justice O'Connor wrote for the majority, "and school officials ignoring it could be sued under Title IX of the Federal law prohibiting sex discrimination in educational institutions." One can almost hear judicial activism hammering another nail into the permanent fortress of the secularist state.

Some sanity prevailed when Justice Anthony Kennedy wrote for the minority, "After today, Johnny will find that the routine problems of adolescence ought to be resolved by invoking a federal right to demand assignment to a desk two rows away."

As absurd as Kennedy rightly depicted the decision, it is ironic that it was he who said it. It was Kennedy, after all, who had written, a few years earlier, that "At the heart of liberty, there lies the right of every man to choose his own concept of existence, of freedom, of happiness and the mystery of human existence" (*Planned Parenthood v. Casey*). Since that decision pulled the metaphysical rug out from under us, who was to stop Justice O'Connor from supporting Ms. Davis in building a house of strange new virtues and vices?

Take tolerance. That once-noble part of charity has been turned into the secularist hangman's noose. In saner times, under the aegis of charity, tolerance taught us to bear with people whose virtue is not quite perfect, because ours isn't either. Torn from the side of charity (and religion), tolerance has mutated into indifference to vice and truth. This is the tolerance of which G. K. Chesterton spoke when he declared it to be "The virtue of men who no longer believe in anything." He was even more sanguine in *Orthodoxy* when he remarked:

> The modern world is full of the old Christian virtues gone mad. The virtues have gone mad because they have been isolated from each other and are wandering alone. Thus some scientists care for truth; and their truth is pitiless. Thus some humanitarians only care for pity; and their pity (I am sorry to say) is often untruthful.

Dorothy L. Sayers takes Chesterton further in describing tolerance run amok. Toleration is "the accomplice of other sins, and their worst punishment," she wrote in *Letters to a Diminished Church*. "It is the sin which believes in nothing, cares for nothing, seeks to know nothing, interferes with nothing, enjoys nothing, loves nothing, hates nothing, finds purpose in nothing, lives for nothing, and only remains alive because there is nothing it would die for."

Such a dismal state of affairs was seen with crystalline clarity by Gerald Vann, O. P. "The humanist world is a shallow world, a world of false and facile optimism, inasmuch as it forgets the fact of sin, or tries to ignore it," he wrote presciently in 1946.

> But you cannot ignore the underworld of life with impunity. Either you must go down into it, suffer it, understand it, and overcome it; or you can try to forget it for a time, and then, sooner or later, it will rise up against you and destroy you. And when a whole civilization tries thus to forget the sense of depth, it may well live very placidly on the surface for a while; it may make immense progress, but still on the surface; and then its nemesis

will come up on it and it will find itself driven back to the darkness of the caves.

Pretty serious stuff. But so are Harassment Specialists, Chief Ethics Officers, and Chief Purpose Officers. What makes it even more serious is finding that ordinary folks like your son, your wife, or your grandmother agree with them. For then the political is indeed the personal.

THANK GOD, GOVERNOR CUOMO

Upon hearing the puerile remarks of Governor Cuomo last week, Chesterton came to mind. The lapsed Catholic governor is usually prone to inanity and offense, but this reached new heights: "We have turned the corner on the Coronavirus plague. It was not faith or prayers that did it. Only hard work and science." To such blather, Chesterton: "The madman is the one who has one idea completely right, but one does not know where it fits into the whole of things."

Indeed, as with so many of the Men of Modernity, the governor is a madman. Yet he does have one idea right: essential to man's flourishing is hard work and the pursuit of knowledge. But he does not know "where it fits into the whole of things." The whole is God, which Mr. Cuomo fails to see, and that blindness is as large as a galaxy. Faith and prayer precedes, accompanies and completes every act of man. Denying this is a reprise of the ruinous sin committed in Eden. That Original sin was the emancipation of man from the clutches of God. Pride. The only sin that an angel could commit, and Lucifer did, with his *non serviam*. His was the first act of madness. Cuomo marches in that line.

Pride can infect even the rays of truth. Man is made in the *imago et similtudo Dei*, and bears the obligation to use the gifts of intellect and will for the good. Yet as man deploys those gifts, he knows they are not of his own making. He has received them, they are gifts. To use them without knowing the intended designs of their Maker is to use them to his undoing. Aristotle teaches "The greatest offense against reason is to use reason against reason." Put in Catholic key, to use reason against the designs of God is to leave reason corrupted. Every man in every time stands at the end of this precipice – attempting to use God's gifts without the help of God's grace, or even acknowledging that they are gifts. Isn't this the chilling lesson of Babel? Most of the human race has been bound to this truth, reflexively making religion the cornerstone of culture since the beginning of time. The very word culture traces its derivation to the Latin word *cultus*, or ceremonial rites honoring God. Hence the inescapable union between culture and religion. Only the secular culture of Western civilization since the Enlightenment has exempted itself from this perennial law, with woeful consequences.

If Mr. Cuomo and his fellow travelers so esteem knowledge, they should take note that the Catholic Church alone is its greatest proponent. The very existence of universities is owed to the Church from the earliest medieval Cathedral schools to the founding of the Universities of Bologna (1088), Paris (1150), Oxford (1167), and a score of others. All emerged, in the felicitous phrase of John Paul II, *ex corde ecclesiae*. The Church recognized man's perfection required the progress of knowledge, but that his fullest perfection demanded adoring the sovereignty of God. Otherwise, knowledge repeats the ancient lure of the Serpent, "Ye shall be as gods." Kierkegaard captured this modern inversion when he remarked: "For the Middle Ages, the hero was the saint; for modern man, the hero is the genius." Man without God, or the knowledge he discovers, is a noose from which he hangs. Or worse.

Mary Shelley was writing more than a Gothic horror story when she penned *Frankenstein*. It was a premonitory tale of a modern world without God, where "hard work and science" replace "faith and prayer." In the scene when the monster finally rises from his gurney, he looks down at Dr. Frankenstein and boasts, "You are my creator, but now I am your master." In a world without God, man is no longer his own because he does not first belong to God. St. Thomas teaches that man is *dominus sui* (master of himself). Not master of reality, only master of himself. Man becomes his own master when he first makes God his Master. Through understanding and free will, he lives by God's truth, defying the tug of the unruly passions. This alone is man standing tall. Without God man finds himself becoming smaller, and grotesque. Each man becomes a god unto himself, leaving man only to a Nietzschien triumph of the will.

The twentieth century was the graveyard of these triumphs. Beware. One can easily be distracted by the seeming collapse of most of the totalitarianisms, resulting in a lazy trust of the age. Today, a more genteel totalitarianism has appeared. It is the ideology of the unbridled self. No more gulags, but now, abortion clinics. No more Mengele's experimenting upon children, but now, governors applauding infanticide. No more KGB, but now, an unforgiving thought police patrolling campuses for impermissible conservative speech. No more Dachau's, but now parents happily surrendering their children to gender reassignment or giddily cheering their six-year-olds as they are entertained by drag queens in the local public library. No more of Pol Pot's killing fields, but now the regnant ideology proclaiming biological sex differences as bigotry. No more Stalin's blowing up church after church, but now, the shuttering of religious freedom under the veneer of equal rights. When God is banished, only chaos ensues. Again, Chesterton, "When man ignores the supernatural, he does not become natural, but unnatural."

If this be not madness, what is? Pope Benedict called it the dictatorship of relativism, and it certainly surpasses any dictatorship we have ever seen. It is only the Faith that will save us from madness, only prayer that will win us God's graces. Perhaps much of Governor Cuomo's bravado can be laid at the feet of the Church's silence. Each of his enormities should have been met with lightning bolts of remonstrance. It would have been salutary for his immortal soul, and a purifying clarity to the Catholic people. Listen to the bracing words of St. Catherine of Sienna, in her letter 16, *To a Great Prelate*:

> Let us listen to St. Paul. Let us speak up boldly to profess the Faith without fear of being uncharitable... In these difficult times, everyone should fear to hear God say to him someday these acerbic words by way of reprimand': 'Accursed are you who said nothing'. Ah! Enough silence! Cry out in a thousand tongues. I see that by dint of silence this world has been corrupted, the Bride of Christ is quite pale; she has lost her color, because they are sucking her blood, the blood of Christ which is given by grace... Stop sleeping the sleep of negligence. Do what you can promptly!

Governor Cuomo's madness is not an isolated madness; it permeates the culture. But not all in this culture have succumbed. Scores of good Catholics continue to adhere heroically to the Faith and fall to their knees in prayer. This time of God's trial will only strengthen that fidelity. But we must continue to care for the rest who suffer the delirium of the Imperial Self. Perhaps the graces of this trial will open eyes to the profligate indulgences of modern man. Perchance the isolation will instruct in the old virtues of home and hearth, family and care for loved ones. Maybe even the lessons of human limitation, or more classically, humility, will be learned. In spite of the twenty first century's dazzling technological hubris, still we remain toddlers in God's gracious creation, always vulnerable to the many secrets yet locked in nature. As they are unleashed, for all our brilliance, only a reliance upon God and his graces will bring us peace.

Mr. Cuomo's madness is not the only effective political strategy. Try sanity, Mr. Governor. Try the Catholic Church.

LAWMAKERS DECLARE WAR ON THE CHURCH

Chills ran down the spines of Catholics on January 12th when North Dakota lawmakers announced their intention to amend the state's Century Code relating to mandatory reporting. Under the current law, "a member of the clergy... is not required to report [knowledge or suspicion of child abuse] if the knowledge or suspicion is derived from information received in the capacity of a spiritual advisor," a category that includes sacramental confession. But SB 2180 would delete this exception, making it a failure to report suspected abuse or neglect, even if learned in the confessional, punishable by up to thirty days in prison and/or a fine of $1,500.

Abstract discussions about religious liberty abruptly take on an existential immediacy with news like this. Cancel culture is right on the doorstep of the Catholic Church, and woke America seems to be breathing down our throats. It is a moment redolent of Henry II's drunken lament in 1170 when he moaned to his barons, "Will no one rid me of this troublesome priest?" North Dakota's proposed revocation of the ancient privilege of the seal of the confessional is a second lament, "Will no one rid me of this troublesome Church?"

Libertas ecclesiae was front and center back in the 12th century, and is today as well. *Libertas ecclesiae* is the sovereign right of the Church to exercise her work of saving souls in the ancient fashion of her divine constitution. But the creeping fascism on display in these past several weeks demonstrates how deadly serious the threat to the Church's liberty has become. Mussolini's chilling prescription for the omnipresent State rings in our ears with an eerie shiver: "Everything within the state; nothing against the state; nothing outside the state." Modernity has already reduced the church's bright flame to a fragile flicker. Motions like North Dakota's threaten to blow out the flame entirely.

Only the fire of the Church's presence keeps society whole and honest; her robust presence is the protection of man from himself, and from the grip of the ubiquitous State. The blood of Thomas Becket's martyrdom was the seed that blossomed in the signing of the *Magna Carta* in 1215. The Church's bold resistance in the 12th century created the template for the proper distinction of Church and State.

The Holy Church tutored Western civilization on the proper nature of the State, its rights and prerogatives, as well as those of the Church. When those boundaries are respected, unity is produced and peace prospers. In 1969 the great theologian Cardinal Jean Danielou wrote a landmark book, *Prayer as a Political Problem* – an enigmatic title for a thoroughly unenigmatic masterpiece. He argued that society (politics), without the energetic presence of the Church (prayer), leaves man to a descent into inhumanity:

> A city which does not possess Churches as well as factories, is not fit for men. It is inhuman. The task of politics is to assure men a city in which it will be possible to fulfill themselves completely, to have a full material, fraternal and spiritual life. It is for this reason that we consider prayer as a political problem; for a city that would make prayer impossible would fail to fulfill its role as a city.

If the State's totalism is permitted to grow unchecked, the dignity of the human person becomes imperiled. Is it intemperate to see this moment in our nation's life as following such a trajectory? How else is there to interpret North Dakota's frightful amendment? The Church alone stands between the long reach of the State, and man's inalienable freedom. The heroism of Iron Curtain bishops such as Mindszenty, Stepinac, and countless others stands as proof of this. Each became the solitary shelter of the Catholic people in those slave nations, shielding them from some of the most crushing barbarities of Communism.

Even today, God is raising up similar champions of the Faith such as Cardinal Zen, whose fragile voice marches into battle against the cruel Chinese Communist Party, and even against a Vatican drunk with *Ostpolitick*. These times cause us to return over and over to the words of the late Cardinal George: "I expect to die in bed, my successor will die in prison, and his successor will die a martyr in the public square. His successor will pick up the shards of a ruined society and slowly help rebuild civilization, as the church has done so often in human history." North Dakota's vote to annul the inviolable seal of the confessional makes that fate closer to every Catholic priest.

The seal of the Confessional is the Church's pledge that she is the privileged encounter between man and God, where no other men will ever trespass. So sacred is this protection that the priest is committed to die, rather than divulge secrets told him in the confessional. No place on earth affords such a sublime freedom to man. It is utterly without exception—as is man's dignity—which Mother Church will always safeguard. In fact, man's dignity is given no greater honor than in the confessional, where his deepest disclosures are protected by such a wall of impregnable silence. No utilitarian or political self-serving will gain hearing in these hallowed precincts. The State's insistence on absolute power crumbles here. Audiences around the world had this gleaming jewel of the Church's crown dramatized with artistic force in Alfred Hitchcock's 1953 film *I Confess*. It must have been the director's paean to the great comforts he himself often received in the dark protection of the confessional boxes of his life.

If North Dakota persists in her attempt to breach the citadel of the Church's sacramental exercise, it will meet the fate that all other usurpers have met throughout history. Priests may be flung into prisons in North Dakota, but God will triumph, as He always has. Man's vanity is no match for the power of the Blessed Trinity. Thomas Babington Macaulay, an English protestant Evangelical, wrote an essay on Ranke's *History of the Popes* in the 1840 *Edinburgh Review*. In a now oft quoted passage, he gave a rousing acclaim to the victorious Catholic Church:

> There is not, and never was on this earth, a work of human policy so well deserving of examination as the Roman Catholic Church... No other institution is left standing which carries the mind back to the times when the smoke of sacrifice rose from the Pantheon, and when camelopards and tigers bounded in the Flavian Amphitheatre... The Catholic Church is still sending forth to the farthest ends of the world missionaries as zealous as those who landed in Kent with St. Augustine, and still confronting hostile kings with the same spirit with which she confronted Attila... Not do we see any sign which indicates that the term of her long dominion is approaching. She saw the commencement of all the

governments and of all the ecclesiastical establishments that now exist in the world; and we feel no assurance that she is not destined to see the end of them all. She was great and respected before the Saxon had set foot on Britain, before the Frank had passed the Rhine, when Grecian eloquence still flourished at Antioch, when idols were still worshipped in the temple of Mecca. And she may still exist in undiminished vigor when some traveler from New Zealand shall, in the midst of a vast solitude, take his stand on a broken arch of London Bridge to sketch the ruins of St. Paul's?"

North Dakota, beware.

CHRISTIANITY & ISLAM: MORALLY EQUIVALENT?

In 2015 Barack Obama commented on the current atrocities committed by the Islamic State (ISIS) in light of its barbaric live incineration of a captured Jordanian pilot. In the course of his speech, the U. S. president counseled his audience to get off their "high horse" and recognize that the violence of the type perpetrated by ISIS is "not unique to one group or one religion." He instructed his audience to "remember that during the Crusades and the Inquisition, people committed terrible deeds in the name of Christ." Essentially, Obama was appealing to the received myths that surround distant historical events in order to draw a moral equivalence between Islam and Christianity. Islam has the sadism of ISIS and al-Qaeda, Christianity had its Crusades and Inquisition; what's the difference?

Catholics are rightly outraged by the president's comments. But proper outrage must be based on proper facts.

Christianity's doctrine is found in three sources: the Bible, Tradition, and the authoritative teachings of the Catholic Church. An unbiased and clear inspection will show that Christianity is a religion of peace. Islam, not so much. Christianity offers peace through redemption, freedom through penance, joy through forgiveness, perfection through sanctification, and charity as the crown and driving force of every Christian life. Nowhere does Christianity's Divine Founder counsel violence, mandate war, or promise something sinful as a reward for fidelity. Yet a careful reading of the *Qur'an*, the founding document of Islam, reveals that these three elements are present in its pages. A sampling:

- "Therefore, when ye meet the unbelievers in fight, smite at their necks; at length, when ye have thoroughly subdued them, bind a bond firmly on them; thereafter is the time for either generosity or ransom, until the war lays down its burdens... But those who are slain in the way of Allah, he will never let their deeds be lost" (47:4)
- "May the two hands of Abu Lahab [Muhammad's uncle who betrayed him] perish! May he himself perish! Nothing

shall his wealth and gains avail him. He shall be burnt in a flaming fire, and his wife, laden with faggots [firewood], shall have a rope of fiber around her neck" (111:1-5 sura)
- "Fight those who believe not in Allah nor the Last Day, nor hold that forbidden which hath been forbidden by Allah and his messenger, nor acknowledge the religion of Truth, even if they are of the People of the Book [Jews and Christians], until they pay the jizya with willing submission and feel themselves subdued" (9:29)

The general rule of Islamic ethics is that if Muhammad did or sanctioned something, it's permissible for his followers too: "No blame shall be attached to the prophet for doing what is sanctioned for him by God" (Qur'an 33:38). What might this include? Muhammad married a six-year-old girl and consummated the marriage when she was nine. In violation of Arab moral standards, he married his own daughter-in-law. And Muhammad ordered the beheading of all the men of the captured Banu Qurayza tribe and the enslavement of their women and children. According to various accounts, some eight to nine hundred men and adolescent boys were executed as Muhammad and his child bride looked on.

A moral equivalence between Christianity and Islam? Hardly. That would be like saying a surgeon and Jack the Ripper are no different because both use sharp instruments. Of course, it must be stressed that the majority of Muslims are good, peace-loving, and decent people. But they are good, peaceful, and decent in spite of the *Qur'an*, not because of it. The minority of Muslims who instill terror in the hearts of Westerners do follow, and put into practice, the very violent teachings found in the *Qur'an*. Egyptian President Abdel Fattah al-Sisi, himself a Muslim, delivered a startling address to his nation earlier this year, warning that *Qur'anic* Islam is a problem of global proportions. The wrong ideas that Muslims sacralize, he said, have made "the entire *umma* [Muslim community] a source of concern, danger, killing, and destruction for the whole world."

As for ISIS, the standard rhetoric emanating from the U.S. government paints it as a non-Islamic movement. But Washington is operating on unsupported assumptions, or perhaps willful ignorance. "Centuries have passed since the wars of religion ceased in Europe, and since men stopped dying in large numbers because of arcane theological disputes," writes Graeme Wood in an article in *The Atlantic* (March). "Hence, perhaps, the incredulity and denial with which Westerners have greeted news of the theology and practices of the Islamic State. Many refuse to believe that this group is as devout as it claims to be." The reality, however, is that "the Islamic State is Islamic. Very Islamic... The religion preached by its most ardent followers derives from coherent and even learned interpretations of Islam." ISIS's "officials and supporters," Wood says, "insist that they will not—cannot—waver from governing precepts that were embedded in Islam by the Prophet Muhammad and his earliest followers." Even the lower "ranks of the Islamic State are deeply infused with religious vigor."

How many countless Catholics must be confused at best, and scandalized at worst, when they see consecrated shepherds of the Catholic Church joining hands and praying with Muslim imams? What part of the *Qur'an* are they venerating? What part of Muhammad's life are they honoring?

Back to President Obama's high horse: To be clear, any atrocities committed during the Crusades were not perpetrated by the Catholic Church but by individual Catholics. Pope Urban II, the official head of the Catholic Church, did summon the First Crusade at the Council of Clermont in A.D. 1095. But this was a final act in a drama that had begun four hundred years earlier, as the Holy Land and every bustling Catholic metropolis in the Middle East—Alexandria, Damascus, Baghdad, Tunis, Libya—were being leveled by the Muslims at the edge of a sword, a fact the president conveniently ignores. Moreover, during those centuries, marauding Muslim bandits would viciously attack Christian pilgrimages to the Holy Land, massacring or kidnapping the pilgrims. St. Francis and St. Anthony of Padua originally desired to travel to the Middle East to care for the spiritual needs of abducted Catholics. It's not much of a coincidence that we are witnessing similar acts of Islamic violence and aggression today—a goodly amount directed against Christians.

Four centuries of Muslim mischief had worn down the patience of the Church, and she rightly rallied a response that was too long in coming. True, inexcusable savagery was perpetuated by more than a few crusaders. But this brutality was not commanded by Christ or His vicar, the pope. It was not woven into the very woof and warp of Christianity. Any brutal act of a crusader was his brutal act, not the Church's. The Church teaches that men who commit such acts will be severely judged by God in the afterlife, not given forty virgins for their pleasure, as the *Qur'an* teaches.

But the Inquisition – surely this is a stain on the Catholic Church? Again, no. The Inquisition was established by the Church in the late twelfth century. The southern portion of France, known as Cathar, had seen the rise of a strange and dangerous heretical group called the Albigensians. This group was not satisfied with genteel theological parlor games. They aimed their errors right at the jugular of organized society itself. Aside from denying the Church and her sacraments, the Albigensians rejected the institution of marriage and condemned the procreation of children. They saw created reality as evil, and recommended suicide as the only blissful release from the iron grip of a wicked world. No wonder the civil state considered the Cathars a mortal risk to its survival. The Church agreed. At the request of France's princes, the Church sanctioned the capture and arrest of the Albigensians. In order to stave off overzealous improprieties or breaches of fundamental justice, the Church arrogated to herself the apparatus of adjudication and commissioned panels of scholar-priests to oversee the interrogation of alleged heretics and scrupulously monitor the protection of their rights. This came to be known as the Inquisition. It was, at the time, music to prisoners' ears because they knew the Church was their only protection from the blind vengeance of the princes. In fact, contrary to the revisionist Enlightenment account that sticks like tar to the minds of the *bien pensant* and is still taught to fourth graders the world over, the very staples of Western jurisprudence – rules of evidence, the accused facing his accuser, defense attorneys, impartial judges – arose out of the Inquisition as necessary guarantees of human rights.

Were there wicked inquisitors guilty of cruelty and abuse of power? Undoubtedly. But again, these inquisitors were not acting on the dogma of the Church, even less from the injunctions of our Savior. There were excesses, but the excesses were of individuals, not of the Church, not of Christ.

Catholics can no longer allow these attacks on our faith to go unanswered. But our responses should in no way resemble Muslim ones. No Christian in his right mind would suggest bombing the office of a newspaper that printed a gross caricature of Christ. But respond we must. Historical facts must be set down. Silence will only allow lies to fester and spread and persuade the uninformed that the attacks must be true.

MARIN COUNTY MEETS THE TIBER

Abdul Hamid isn't a name that enrages you, but the name John Walker is. Abdul is Mr. Walker's name in religion, the Islamic religion. It is a religion he embraced not because it was his father's but precisely because it was not his father's. John Walker's father firmly adhered to the dogmas of the late Sixties' liberalism, to which he was so devoted (and according to most 2002 reports, still is) that he named his young son after one of its patron saints, John Lennon. All this may seem somewhat odd, going from sandals-and-beads, give-peace-a-chance Marin County to jihad-obsessed, "Allah be praised" Kandahar. But it isn't. It all has to do with nature hating a vacuum, especially human nature.

John Walker's parents were nursed at the breasts of the antinomian Sixties, a time of shocking intellectual and spiritual malignancies. No one diagnoses this tragic time with greater surgical precision that Roger Kimball in his 2000 jewel, *The Long March*:

> Our culture seems to have suffered some ghastly accident that has left it afloat but rudderless: physically intact, its moral center in shambles. The cause of this disaster... was a protracted and spiritually convulsive detonation – one that trembled with gathering force through North America and Western Europe from the mid 1950s through the early 1970s and tore apart, perhaps irrevocably, the moral and intellectual fabric of our society... The Age of Aquarius did not end when the last electric guitar was unplugged at Woodstock. It lives on in our values and habits, in our tastes, pleasures, and aspirations. It lives on especially in our educational and cultural institutions, and in the degraded pop culture that permeates our lives like a corrosive fog.

Mr. and Mrs. Walker, in the proper fashion of radical chic, encouraged their son John to choose his own spiritual path. One of John's neighbors noted that he grew up intellectually privileged and was enrolled in an alternate school for motivated, self-directed learners who design their own course of study. Mrs. Walker said of her son's Islamic conversion that it is good for a child to find a passion. Picture-perfect liberalism. As Shelby Steele wrote brilliantly in the *Wall Street Journal* (10 December 2001):

> This is a world where learning is self-referential, where adults are only broadly tolerant. There are no external yes's and no's, or rights or wrongs here, just the fashionable relativism that makes places like Marin so cool. But there is another message as well: that traditional American history, culture, and religion are without any special authority. Worse, historic racism and sexism may leave these American offerings with less moral authority that foreign options.

But beneath that thoroughly swallowed radicalism was a deep darkness poised for revenge. Man craves the Absolute and satisfies that craving in absolutes. It cannot be suppressed, even if its expressions are depraved. It wasn't in John Walker, and they were.

One would be mistaken to believe that any institution escaped this antinomian scourge – even the Catholic Church. Coincidental with Vatican Council II came this grinding Sixties nihilism which found its way into the intellectual bloodstream of not a few churchmen. *Aggiornamento*, originally a strategy for sanctification, was retooled as a modernist Taliban. So that now a theological radical chic prevails and becomes the obligatory mark of authenticity. Without it one becomes an ecclesial untouchable, banished from office, advancement, reward, notice, and sometimes, even survival. It is not an exaggeration to say that a kind of Year One was announced in 1962 by the *bien pensant*. All that went before would thereafter be considered an embarrassment – almost taboo. Wounds from this treacherous period are all too fresh to require repeating. Suffice it to say that the likes of John Walker's parents filled the ranks of the Church's intelligentsia and ruling elites. And still do.

Need evidence? Try suggesting to an American Church official the use of the *Baltimore Catechism* in the classroom. Or the exclusive use of priests for administering Holy Communion (or kneeling to receive Holy Communion, for that matter). Or, dare we say it, permission for the Tridentine Mass. Scandalized surprise greets you. A 2002 Gallup poll reported that acceptance of the gay lifestyle was higher amongst students attending Catholic high schools that students in public ones. Need more? At the 2001 October Synod of Bishops in Rome, the loathing of the Roman millennial culture was center stage. Archbishop Sebastian D'Souza, Archbishop of Calcutta, India, moaned "The traditions of a dead language, Latin, which are part of a dead foreign culture, Roman, even if seen as a vehicle for orthodoxy, do not respond in a satisfactory way to the character and lifestyle of Indian life and tribal languages." Not to put too fine a point on it, but Bishop Paul Yoshinao Otuka of Kyoto, Japan, when speaking of a document of the Japanese Conference on Reverence for Life, remarked to the Synod Fathers, "The various themes in the book are not written in a manner that insists that the only correct answer and resolutions for problems comes from a Catholic point of view." Marin County, meet the Tiber.

Let us count our mixed blessings. A John Walker-turned-Islamic-traitor roused outrage in most Americans, thank God. But what of all the John Walkers being turned out by the progressive Catholic Establishment today? Where's the Catholic outrage at them?

ALL OF VIENNA IS GIDDY ABOUT NANYA

All of Vienna is giddy about Nanya. Nanya is that sophisticated city's latest artistic sensation, already monopolizing the attention of the creative illuminati. One leading critic described his work as "Dynamic, expressive and effusive." As much as he is in demand, he will not grant a press conference or interviews.

Another effete snob, you say? No. Nanya is an orangutan. He paints with food colorings, holding the brush between his little monkey teeth. With a century that began by hailing the absurdities of Picasso, then paying millions for the spastic canvases of Pollock, finally standing in solemn awe before the *Piss Christ* of Serrano, could Nanya be far behind? Just more museum antics, you chuckle? But this is no laughing matter because the matter is about us.

Modern art is an act of war. Not against any nation or people, but against man himself, because it forces man to forget what he is. When he makes art, man's soul is on exposition. Crowning his soul's activities is the intelligence, so that when his art is not intelligible it stops being art. Modern art strains to be meaningless. Proudly turning its back on truth, it rejoices in communicating nothing but the personal fancy of the artist. Art was always the cult of the real, but this century has made it the cult of the artist, hence the old cliche, "Beauty is in the eye of the beholder." It isn't. Rather, beauty is in the thing the eye beholds.

Two things are indispensable to creating art, a man who possesses understanding (intellectual virtue) and talent (practical intellect). That mysterious alchemy of truth and talent results in beauty. St. Thomas pithily expresses this by teaching that the beautiful is *id quod visum placet* (that which when seen pleases). Notice, it pleases the observer. Every artist is a servant—he furnishes men with that which pleases. And pleasure only comes from that which is understood. If common men like us must say, "What is it?" it's just not art.

Once man loves the truth, the more grandly he serenades it in his art. St. Thomas calls this accomplishment the "splendor of form." Along with integrity and right proportion, these three create the triple condition of beauty. All things have their forms. Not their physical shapes, but their essence, that which makes them what they are. Even virtues and vices have their forms. Actions have theirs. Great artists see that form and thrust it into full view so that we see it, too, often as if for the first time. How right of the Angelic Doctor to say that beauty pleases, for it make us see reality richly.

There is no tiring in watching the evil of Iago or marveling at Caravaggio's paintings because each conveys a truth that delights man's reason through an execution that grips his emotions. That twin motion demonstrates art's exalted nature. The artist, because he creates, is like God, and the beholder thirsts for God's truth embodied in the artist's creation. True art leaves us spellbound, fakes merely shock.

High talent wedded to perfect truths are the stuff of artistic masters. When they are the supernatural truths of the Catholic faith, art becomes sublime. So Michaelangelo writes,

> Every beauty which is seen here below by persons of perception resembles more than anything else that celestial source from which we come... My eyes longing for beautiful things together with my soul longing for salvation have no other power to ascend to heaven than the contemplation of beautiful things...

Taking seriously the crisis in art is not about idle aestheticism. It's about us. It's about our happiness. It is, most importantly, about God.

THE PARIS OLYMPICS: CALIGULA REDUX

I demur. The Opening Ceremonies of the Paris Olympics last Friday would have been an insult to Caligula. He merely stood for perversity, sadism, and debauchery, while the opening ceremonies at Paris celebrated much, much more. They boldly trumpeted the end of Christianity, in particular, and of Western Civilization, in general. With their Last Supper blasphemy festooned with deviant LGBTQ+ burlesque, they intended nothing less than a battering ram against Christianity and the civilization to which she gave birth.

Aside from a handful of outrages, the general reaction ranged from mild amusement, to "ho-hum pass the salt," to passionate agreement, to muted displeasure.

And therein lies the nightmare.

Not in the debased performance, but rather in the chic acceptance. Even a Caligula would have been embarrassed. His depravity would never have dreamt of mocking the firmament of Roman gods or dislodging the foundations of the Roman Imperium.

More than a few were probably haunted by the premonitory verses of Yeats in his *The Second Coming:*

> Turning and turning in the widening gyre
> The falcon cannot hear the falconer;
> Things fall apart; the centre cannot hold;
> Mere anarchy is loosed upon the world,
> The blood-dimmed tide is loosed, and everywhere
> The ceremony of innocence is drowned;
> The best lack all conviction, while the worst
> Are full of passionate intensity.

The tragedy was not the outrageous blasphemy. It was the absence of howling outrage. No such supine reaction would have met such an attack on Islam. For all its wild aberrations, it does not lack the manliness of instantaneous fury. Not so the once chest-thumping Catholicism of the saints and martyrs. Sixty years ago, that millennial Catholic trademark was thought embarrassing for a Church in a hurry to make friends with the world. Historic Catholic boasts such as the Crusades, the vanquishing of the Old Pagan gods, and the conversion of the nations have been quietly shelved for a more user-friendly Catholicism. Anathemas have been traded for something called dialogical listening and certitude by sensitivity to difference. Some members of the hierarchy have censured proselytism, a slur on bringing men to the Catholic Church.

Catholics are now incessantly drilled on the one and only sin "Crying out to heaven for vengeance": passing judgment. (For you youngsters, there were once four such sins. Look it up.) Of course, that is precisely what the Decalogue is all about. Exactly the reason why religion classes no longer teach them. Well, some of them do. But you can count them on one hand.

This new irenicism-on-steroids is daily reinforced by liturgies eliciting as much fervor and passion for God as the weekly Ladies Auxiliary canasta club. It reminds one of Huxley's *Brave New World's* daily doses of the "feelies" to maintain the proper insensate torpor. This whole dreadful picture is daily propped up by a clergy quite pleased with the standard of a decaying secularity rather than the Standard of Christ the King. Don't believe me? Look at their seminaries-turned-ghost-towns, testament to aggiornamento gone awry. In 2024 an Order of nuns called a festive dinner to celebrate the announcement of their demise.

Yes, you say, but wasn't there the American bishop who registered a gentle reservation? Yes, true enough. But his gray suit and Roman collar seemed to dilute the effect. Call me old fashioned, but a priest in a gray suit does not make hearts race as does the sight of St. Francis Xavier in cassock holding high the cross.

Shall we dare a more provocative question? If the Holy Roman Church were as strong now as it was in the times of the Roman persecutions, the Middle Ages, or in the pontificates of Blessed Pius IX or St. Pius X, would this kind of blasphemy have shown its face? The secular world would not have dared. Yes, those historical periods dealt Mother Church its share of ignominy, but never did they threaten the very cornerstone of her doctrinal patrimony. None would have mocked the very foundations of the moral law, indeed of the divinely established order of sexual difference. And if they had, they would have been met by all the ferocity of her thundering condemnations.

Those manic forces were kept at bay by the might of the Church. And that doctrinal roar bellowed with no uncertainty, and with one universal voice. The World would find no cracks in the solidity of the Church's voice in those sturdier days. Contrary voices would indeed bay, but they had no illusions about the impregnable bastions of the Catholic Church. They might have found shelter in a renegade priest or shepherd here or there, but those of that ilk were conspicuous in their paucity.

Blasphemy on such a grand scale as the Opening Ceremonies of the Paris Olympics would have been unthinkable. Yes, Napolean kidnapped Pope Pius VII in 1809, dragging him across the Alps in precarious health to Fontainebleau. And the Italian armies captured Rome in 1859, forcing Blessed Pius IX to flee the Eternal City to the city of Gaeta. But all these depredations could not approach the collapse that the Opening Ceremonies presage. While the Church was assaulted and the popes harassed, the foundations of human dignity and Western Civilization were not threatened. The Church, even with her popes in captivity, would see to that.

Enemies of all that is good and true and beautiful have found their opening in the decades-long attenuation of the Church's voice. They have seen all too clearly the Church's détente with the spirit of the world and exploited a perfect opportunity. It was the victory they awaited for so long, and now it was handed to them on a silver platter. How else to interpret Archbishop Paglia, president of the Pontifical Academy for Life, defending the Olympic Last Supper depiction "As revealing a profound question: everyone, absolutely everyone, wants to sit at that table where Jesus gives life to everyone and teaches love."

This is ambiguity and cowardice writ large.

Mankind's only wall against the encroachment of the barbarian is the Catholic Church. She alone can return a voice to the oppressed of the Woke Leviathan.

In A.D. 452, it was only one year after Pope Leo the Great valiantly defended the hypostatic union of Christ our Savior against the heretic Eutyches.

With that monumental task barely completed, he confronted still another crisis besetting the Roman world: the attack of Attila the Hun. His frightful hordes had decimated much of the former Roman Empire, with its legacy of high civilization and culture. Now that barbarian was at the very gates of Rome. All seemed to be lost. Pope Leo the Great, in solemn procession with priests, deacons, and acolytes swinging golden thuribles, went out to meet the bloodthirsty chieftain. Face-to-face, they spoke. After a brief conversation, Attila turned around and commanded his troops to retreat. Rome was saved. Christianity was saved. Civilization could breathe again.

And Leo became known to the ages as "The Great."

Only the Catholic Church can save mankind from the barbarians—whether it be from Attila or the Parisians of the 2024 Olympic Games.

So, we wait.

BILL IN THE HOTEL ROOM WITH PAULA

That whining you heard was from *Time* magazine. Their properly liberal columnist Margaret Carlson complained about the silly fuss over the sexual accusations of Paula Jones. Aren't we a laughingstock as the world watches Americans caviling over the sexual peccadilloes of the chief executive? When will this juvenile nation grow up and treat sex with the indifference that modern sophistication demands?

Carlson has not been alone in her crusade for sexual maturity. Catholic theologians have been at this campaign for some thirty years now. Back in those swinging seventies Marquette University's Daniel McGuire sternly scolded the Catholic Church for her pelvic preoccupation. Religion, don't you know, has no business in the bedrooms of adults. The Carlsons of the culture marched happily with the McGuires to create a winning team. Without them, and many others, the word adult could never have achieved detachment from its premodern associations of responsibility to its present suggestion of dark vice. Yet with all the Left has won, still it remains petulant. To their annoyance, a small but unbudging class of decent people cling to the notion that virtue, in general, and sexual chastity, in particular, have something to do with what a man is and what a man does. Quaint idea? Or is it something more?

Though man is a galaxy of physical parts and multiple powers, all those things operate together in stunning unity. That unity is produced by his rational soul. When a student passes an examination, he exclaims "I passed!" not "My brain passed." A husband expresses love for his wife not by whispering "My will loves you," but "I love you." Every act a man performs is all his own, and the graver the act, the more profound the mark it leaves on him. All these acts form the compass directing all that we do. All together we call this character.

Trying to say that sexual acts do not leave deep impressions on a man's personality violates the commonsense fact of man's unity. Moreover, the sexual powers are some of the most potent of man's nature and they link him to one of the most ennobling human pursuits, the family. The manner in which they are treated leaves a permanent cast on character. No matter how hard moderns try, sexual acts will never be a matter of indifference, only because they make such a difference. To be concerned about a man's chastity, especially if he is to take a position of importance, is a sharply relevant issue. Decisions and actions invariably are affected by it.

So, the bottom line is that we must care about Bill Clinton in the hotel room with Paula Jones. What he-no-doubt-did that day has a direct bearing on his behavior toward women, toward men, toward the Chinese, toward the unborn. Carlson would be the first to understand that even eating a bowl of ice cream has a fairly direct impact upon the thighs. Would that she could draw such a line from immoral act to immoral character.

Let me finish with St. Thomas Aquinas on the unbreakable linkage between chastity and truth, here in the words of the great Thomist Joseph Pieper.

> Since we nowadays think that all a man needs for acquisition of truth is to exert his brain more or less vigorously, and since we consider an ascetic approach to knowledge hardly sensible, we have lost the awareness of the close bond that links the knowledge of truth to the condition of purity. Thomas says that unchastity's first born daughter is blindness of spirit. Only he who wants nothing for himself, who is not subjectively 'interested,' can know the truth. On the other hand, an impure, selfishly corrupted will to pleasure destroys both resoluteness of spirit and the ability of the psyche to listen in silent attention to the language of reality.

OCCUPY HARVARD

Y ou probably think North Korea is thousands of miles away. Actually, it is as close as your nearest university. By and large most of our universities and colleges have become little North Koreas—sealed enclaves of repressive ideology, stifled speech, and rigid thought control. Students enthuse to this jailed status through daily dosages of Huxleyan *soma* in the form of Dionysian license with a sprinkling of MeToo puritanism.

Victor Hugo once cannily remarked, "A man can either make his soul a sanctuary or a sewer." That can also be said of our universities and colleges. Once-proud sanctuaries of truth have become sewers of agitprop fueling a chaotic makeover of America. This baneful circumstance has reached such a nadir that even the *hoi polloi* recognize it. Lacerating scenes of looting, vandalism, and killing in our major cities these past few months bring the problem of higher education into stark relief. Half of the rioters are white children nursed on privilege and entitlement, raised in the cloistered islands of caste wealth.

Whence these children's ferocious antipathy toward America, indeed the very pillars of Western civilization? The evidence of decades leads directly to the American classroom. For more than a half-century a surreptitious and altogether committed penetration of the entire education system has been accomplished. Its reigning *raison d'être* has been anti-Western in every aspect: economic, philosophical, historical, literary, and artistic. It's amazing that such a coup was effected with nary a whimper from ordinary Americans, as it was happily bankrolled by the very parents whose beloved beliefs it sought to plunder.

Only against the backdrop of burning cities, the desecration of cherished American monuments, and gratuitous violence has the country slightly awakened to its source in the rotted educational empire. Instances of this debasement could fill pages of old Manhattan telephone books. In 2020, California announced its mandate for K-12 students in a "model curriculum." It aims to build "possibilities for post-imperial life that promotes collective narratives of transformative resistance." Course outlines require "student political activities with approved topics on racism, LGBTQ rights, immigration rights, access to quality health care and income inequality." There's more. Students are assigned papers on U.S. events that "led to Jewish and Irish Americans gaining racial privilege." Are you incredulous? Simply read the state of California's Education Department web site.

Even more shocking is the 2020 piece of news from, of all places, the terribly woke *The Atlantic*. John McWhorter reports "Receiving missives since May almost daily from professors living in constant fear for their careers, because their opinions are incompatible with the current woke playbook." He chillingly continues, "I found it alarming how many of the letters sound as if they were written from Stalinist Russia or Maoist China." McWhorter then relates a typical episode in stomach-turning detail, "A professor who committed the sin of privileging the white male perspective in giving a lecture on the philosophy of the Founding Fathers, praised by Frederick Douglass, had to sit in a 'listening circle' in which his job was to remain silent while students explained how he hurt them." The journalist concludes, "This is a 21st-century-American version of a struggle session straight out of Mao's Cultural Revolution." Such hair-raising accounts should be enough to rouse armed rebellion. Where is the outrage? Instead we have silence – a silence that should be deeply concerning.

In the middle of the fourth century, St. Jerome famously remarked, "The world awoke and found itself Arian." Similarly, America is slowly awakening and finding itself in the teeth of a Marxist/Maoist revolution. For decades its progress was furtive but now it crackles with boastful hubris. To America's shock, our very primary and secondary schools, universities, colleges, and graduate schools have become the incubus for a New Bolshevism. Under this regime, children have become strangers to their parents and the nation's true history. Salutes to the flag are replaced by raised fists of defiant insurrection. Yes, homeschooling has become a desperate stop-gap measure, but it only educates 3.4 percent of the student population, which is hardly enough to stave off this national apocalypse. Yes, a handful of private colleges and universities have escaped the revolution's long arm, but out of 5,300, a paltry 27 boast a traditional curriculum. Not much consolation.

Despite the chilling statistics and evidence of our eyes, the indispensable importance of higher education cannot be slighted. As the scholastics taught, *abusus non tollit usum* (the abuse of a thing does not prohibit its use). Man's intellect only reaches its fulfillment in the systematic rigor of an educational system. From Plato's *Academy* and Aristotle's *Lyceum* to the great medieval universities, man has leapt to his greatness by being carefully led out of his darkness of ignorance (*educere* means "to lead out") into the light of truth (recall the ascent out of Plato's *cave*).

Josef Pieper reminds us in *Leisure: The Basis of Culture* that the word for school is derived from the ancient Greek word, σχολή (*skole*), meaning leisure. Man's only true rest arrives in the sedulous cultivation of the intellect. When crowned—as it was in the medieval universities—with the understanding that all knowledge is ultimately perfected in the knowledge of and union with God, education becomes revered, and is a culture's most precious boast. In a marvel of providential design, Plato's Academy was closed by Emperor Justinian in A.D. 529, and in that very year St. Benedict of Norcia founded his first Benedictine monastery at Monte Cassino.

As Pieper further reminds us, the purpose of true education is useless, in the sense that the wondrous worlds of wisdom are not for anything; they exist only for themselves—like beauty. Chesterton was touching upon this when he wrote, "The youngest children ought to learn the oldest things." That remark may seem peculiar, but it is the perfectly understandable truth that only the highest things should inform education's *studium*. Education must be useless in that its purpose is not to teach men a living, but how to live. The whole purpose of a liberal education (*liberales*, concerning the free) is to release man from the base servility of opinion and false ideas to the liberty of truth. The estimable medieval trivium and quadrivium was simply the toolbox of a well-disciplined mind preparing to scale the heights of wisdom. When man discovers what he is and where he is supposed to be going (i.e., his proper end), he is ready to become a happy man and a profitable citizen. When universities collapse into trade schools, man degenerates into *homo faber*, and his majesty as *homo sapiens* withers. Budding intellects should be filled with the pure gold of Plato's *Republic*, Aristotle's *Metaphysics*, and St. Thomas's *Summa Theologiae*, not the toxins of Critical Race Theory, Marxist analysis, and gender ideology.

Education is truly liberal when it looses man bondage to self and allows him to soar. It unfetters man so that he moves easily amongst his dreams. It swells man's soul so that he can burst with aspiration and ordered commitment. Education is properly liberal precisely when it makes smugness an embarrassment and wonder a prize. It fires souls with the insatiable hunger for truth and armors its charges with the steeliness that makes them unafraid to walk wherever truth can be found. Education becomes illiberal when it impales itself on the strange idea that truth does not exist or chokes itself on the still stranger idea that truth is only what you can see.

A truly liberal education does not ignore those strange ideas but carefully notes them, exactly because of their strangeness. It trains the soul to measure things not by itself, but by truth. Flannery O'Connor was once asked why she and her fellow Southern writers seemed to be obsessed with presenting such grotesque men and women in their literature. She replied, "Because we still know how to call something grotesque when we see it." Illiberal education teaches men how not to see. Merely admitting strangeness nowadays is taboo, and calling strange things strange is felonious hate speech or, in a more pretentious construal, "false consciousness." Ah, how Marx would dance!

A trenchant assessment of the current condition of higher education can nowhere be better found than in George Schuster. In an introduction to one of the editions of Newman's *Idea of a University*, he wrote:

> Newman foresaw, with remarkable prophetic realism, what the climate of culture would someday be – the climate to which Erich Heller has since given the label of disinherited mind – in which the springs of man's spirit would go dry, so that the soul which nurtured him would produce, as it were, no fruit or flower but only weird, often exhilarating chemical concentrates of literature and art... Newman's preview of these things... supplements the prophetic insights of the great Russian Christians Dostoevsky and Tolstoy... For the author of *The Brothers Karamazov* man's adoration of himself, taking the place of the worship of God, would spawn a race of demons whose pride would fully reveal the potential cruelty of the intelligence. And it was the vision of the barbarian turned engineer which in the end drove a frightened Tolstoy into monastic seclusion. For Newman, on the other hand, the

specter was that of the truncated inner life of the educated, product of the disuse of all the nobler muscles of the mind, unable any longer to give the masses an example suggesting better than the "holiday of resourceless ignorance."

Occupation might be an unseemly reaction for a moral people. Then let us settle for a re-occupation based on truth, wisdom and received tradition. In 1983, then—Secretary of Education William Bennet's office released the prescient white paper, *A Nation at Risk*, on the dire state of American education. Now, over thirty years later, a once merely impending risk has become a present nightmare. In another time, American heroism crushed the depraved totalitarianism of 1945 with *Operation Overlord* and the valor of Omaha Beach. Might it be time for another Operation Overlord of sorts?

One thing is certain, armchair tsk-tsking will no longer do.

SO MUCH FOR VERITAS

David Horowitz's name might not yet be a household word, but it should be. Some might remember him from his loony-left days when he edited the Sixties radical periodical *Ramparts*. Well, much water has gone under the bridge since then, including his *cri de Coeur*, *Radical Sons*, or his prickly monthly *Heterodoxy*, and his 1999 work of invective, *Hating Whitey* — each one a testament to his born-again conservatism expressed with the tart intelligence of an impatient convert.

Mr. Horowitz's latest crusade is against the proposal that every American citizen pay reparations for America's past toleration of black slavery. This issue has become de rigueur for the radical chic as well as the febrile preoccupation of America's first-tier universities. Many of them this year turned their campuses over to what they piously called Reparations Awareness Day. So much for Veritas.

All of this left an opening for the tweaking Mr. Horowitz does best. He wrote an irreverent (to the current liberal creeds) piece, "Ten Reasons Why Reparations for Slavery is a Bad Idea." It bristled with unassailable logic and withering wit. Mr. Horowitz submitted it as a paid ad to 35 college newspapers. Why an ad? Because hardly any college newspaper would have published it as an article, having long replaced free expression of ideas with *idées* fixes. Perhaps a cash ad could pry open the censorious door of political correctness. Alas, as Horowitz discovered, the new liberal dogmatism is impervious even to hard cash. Out of those 35 newspapers, only six decided to print it, and of those six, two papers apologized for doing so (Berkeley and the University of California-Davis). After the *Daily Californian* (Berkeley's student newspaper) ran the Horowitz ad, angry leftists stormed the editorial offices screaming and weeping. One protester shouted. "It hurt so much." "Indescribably hurtful," wailed another. They then fanned out over the campus stealing any remaining copies of the paper containing the offensive ad. A week later the *Daily Californian's* editor groveled, "I think the ad is inflammatory and inappropriate and we should not have run it." The paper issued a formal apology for allowing itself to become "An inadvertent vehicle for bigotry." If we didn't know better we would think it a script from a Stalin show trial, circa 1935; all of it slightly unsettling, all of it drearily familiar to Catholics.

While the specifics on Catholic college campuses are different, the stifling lack of freedom is not. Sure, freedom might exist to teach biology or chemistry, but not the truths of the Catholic Faith. Most Catholic universities have imposed a gag on the Catholic voice. Theology departments have become studios for a new designer religion, bearing little resemblance to historic Roman Catholicism and, in some cases, to revealed religion at all. They have reconstituted themselves as armed camps against the entrenched biases of Papism. These Dissenters brook no dissent. No Medieval Inquisitor prosecuted with more zest than they. The secular university walls blocking Mr. Horowitz's free speech are porous compared to these solid Catholic university walls erected against Catholic speech.

For almost ten years the Supreme Pontiff has tried to nudge this scandal into the open and redress it. His weapon was *Ex Corde Ecclesiae*, the document of 1991 demanding that professors in Catholic college teach only Catholic doctrine. Every teacher of theology would have to receive from his Bishop a *mandatum* (permission) that he was fit and willing to reach only the *Depositum Fidei*. Appears tame, doesn't it? Not to the entrenched Dissenters. They reacted with shock, and then immovable intransigence. Their supporters in the episcopate insisted on discussion; then suggested more discussion; and after ten years of impasse declared that the only path to resolution was still more discussion. Then came November 2000. In official session the Bishops voted on the demands of the Pontiff's *Ex Corde Ecclesiae*. That November meeting revealed a binding majority voting that the stipulations of *Ex Corde Ecclesiae* were to be considered by all bishops only a resource whose use was optional. Hegemony for Dissenters was secure. Catholic doctrine would continue to be as hard to come by at Catholic schools as the Horowitz ad is in college newspapers. Catholic universities are not the place for the free exercise of the Faith; for that, Catholic collegians have a better chance in Havana.

When questioned about the American bishops rendering null an explicit command of the Holy See, Archbishop Daniel Pilarczyk of

Cincinnati (chairman of the bishops' committee charged with the implementation of *Ex Corde Ecclesiae*) conceded that the bishops were surrendering any authority over theological teaching. Then in words philosophical, the Archbishop said, "There are lots of laws in the Church that one would contend don't have teeth." Even more disturbing was the remark of Bernard Cardinal Law: "Theologians have the freedom to be wrong." *Hmm.*

So the censorship of Catholic teaching in Catholic colleges proceeds apace. Of course, faced with the pallid stare of *theologie nouvelle* some Catholic universities have resorted to erecting separate Institutes of Catholic theology alongside their official Departments of Theology (or Religious Studies, as many now call themselves, so as to guarantee the furthest distance from even the appearance of sectarian Roman Catholicism, which would of course constitute unethical proselytism). But even that raises the white flag of surrender. For the clear message conveyed is that real Catholicism is the anti-Catholic dissent of the Theology Department, the Institute being only a campus museum of a fossilized past. Of course, where effective Institutes existed (and flourished) – for example, at the University of San Francisco and St. John's University in Queens – they have been suppressed owing to intense Theology Department pressure.

No less than a Berlin Wall now stands on most Catholic colleges. It separates Catholic students from the Faith as effectively as the historic one separated East Germans from their freedom. It must come down. The Supreme Pontiff tried and tried. Looks like he needs some help; just a few good Catholic men as daring as Horowitz.

Any takers?

HELL IN MANHATTAN[2]

I sit here writing this piece coughing on the fumes of hell. Though I sit some one hundred blocks from ground zero of Manhattan Island, the winds shift and billows of that smoke of death stretch all the way to my room at St. Agnes rectory. And to every one of you, wherever you sit in this beloved nation of ours, now supine before an Islamic monster. For the evil that growls at us now sits on the doorstep of every person in America, and of the world. More importantly, it proves to over intellectualized Americans that indeed evil exists. It kills. It corrupts. It demands a daily war against it, sometimes even requiring our blood.

This enormity presses upon us like a sumo wrestler sitting on a sparrow. No American can escape either its immediate horror or its irrepressible lessons. The numbing body count of over five thousand deaths has violently shaken Americans from their sybaritic slumber. America's eye, ever roaming for still more titillating satisfactions, has been forced to blink, only to open and focus again upon eternal truths, as though for the first time. America long trampling upon precious moral absolutes so that it could gorge itself on carnal delights might be coming to an end. A near Hiroshima at the tip of Manhattan Island might compel Americans to walk away from their orgiastic spasm, and see things as they are. Even the fatuous intellectuals who supplied cover for the unbridled hedonist may be given pause. To paraphrase Dr. Johnson, nothing focuses our attention more than the fact that any one of us may be next for the terrorist.

One awfully smart and terribly sophisticated television journalist asked an expert a question with childlike wonder, "Do you truly believe that God or religion can offer anyone solace at this time?" She was genuinely bewildered. It is a bewilderment

---

[2] This previously unpublished article was written on September 14, 2001 from the office of Fr. John A. Perricone at St. Agnes Rectory in Manhattan, some two miles away from Ground Zero. Much of the horror of that day has faded. Even more so, its urgent lessons. Much of America seems to have moved on to even greater follies.

born of non-stop decades of aggressive secularism settling in the souls of most of our cultural elites, a secularism that closeted religion and uncloseted vice. When Barbara Olson's parish priest preached the sermon at her Requiem Mass some days after her plane was crashed into the Pentagon, he spoke about Satan. One of the media commentators remarked rightly that Satan had not been mentioned with such seriousness in his recent memory. He was right. Words like sin, Satan, saintliness and virtue have all been made to sound slightly eccentric by secularism's totalizing reach. It is no surprise that it has tunneled deep within religion itself. More than a few priests are slightly embarrassed by the vocabulary of religion.

But this secularist house of cards was dealt a blow on Tuesday, September 11th. The effective swipe was not a dazzling *bon mot* by some academic but the silent gestures of New York City firemen. As they stumbled upon the dead bodies many removed their helmets and made the Sign of the Cross. That act of piety was louder than the sonic boom created by the World Trade Center's collapse. All at once it was not some atavistic tic of the cultural underclass, but a tower of strength envied by the cultural over class. The innocent journalist's query might well become the fossil of a time now past; of a hollow ideology, sterile and mendacious. September 11th proved that the future belongs to the simple godly men of the Sign of the Cross.

The death pit at the edge of Manhattan Island is not a pit at all. It is not, as the nihilist Nietzsche wrote, a matter of "Staring into the abyss, and the abyss staring at you back." It is a hill. It is Golgotha. Catholics need to teach this exquisite truth to the world. The death pit is Golgotha's hill because Christ hanging on Golgotha's cross saw September 11th, 2001. He saw it and hung there till His *consummatum est* would make it possible for each one of us to lay our crushed hearts in His. In the Divine alchemy of His sacred wounds, our wounds are transfigured into our strength. Our paralyzing fear is swallowed in the mighty words of the Word made Flesh commanding us, "Be not afraid." To the world's amazement, and the rage of wicked fanatics, the very catastrophes meant to decimate us only embolden us. Not by an Olympian show of will, as in Nietzsche, but through humble acceptance of grace, as in Christ's mercy. At Golgotha we are trained to fear nothing but sin, and even that we can conquer through the Cross. A conquest not obtained through the sheer grit of a warrior in the ancient Roman Imperium, but through the Christ's infinite benevolence showered upon us by His Roman Church.

Yes, it is only sin that is catastrophic, because only sin can take happiness from us—the happiness Who is God. Death cannot. Suffering cannot. Isolation cannot. Loss of loved ones cannot. Certainly 9/11 cannot. All of those things are dreadful, no doubt. But on the Cross dread is smothered by Love, and when eyes open after the tears have dried we meet the eyes of God. In those eyes there is only triumph. For none of those dreadful things are more powerful than Christ.

Alongside the victory of Golgotha, there is the glory of defiance. A defiant bravery that fears nothing. It gives vincible man a divine Invincibility. This is why saints laugh at the times when we cower. No time more than now do we require defiant bravery. Nothing on earth could deliver that. Only Golgotha. W. H. Auden expressed this elegantly:

> We can only do what it seems to us we were made for,
> look at this world with a happy eye
> but from sober perspective.

As I cover my nose now from the acrid fumes wafting over Manhattan I think of Aquinas's remark in the third part of the *Summa*. He is commenting on how Our Lord endured an assault upon all His senses on Calvary so that His sacrifice would be perfect. Even His sense of smell was invaded by the stench of Calvary, with its daily fare of rotting corpses torn down from their crosses by hungry dogs. Golgotha then, Golgotha now. America needs to know that triumphant truth of our Holy Faith.

Otherwise, that stench will never be anything but suffocating stench. That pit of evil will never stop staring back at us, as only evil, widening and widening, unbearably.

IN PRAISE OF LAND MINES

Y ou can stop holding your breath. That moment we await each year has come and gone. Phew, the Nobel Peace prize was announced. It went to Ms. Jody Williams and her organization The International Campaign to Ban Land Mines (ICBL). Actually, the solemn moment took place on October 10th, but don't you agree that the thrill takes many months to savor? Aside from an odd exception here and there (Mother Teresa in 1979 and Lech Walesa in 1983), the Nobel Peace prize has come to be the principal sideshow in the secular culture zoo. The *New York Times* photo of a shoeless Ms. Williams before a shabby wooden bungalow is 1960s *deja vu*. Not that we should ever judge a book by its cover, but in this case the cover begs to be tagged and that tag is unquestionably Woodstock chic.

Ms. Williams's trendy cause, as with all the enthusiasms of that ghastly decade, is part of a seamless garment of antinomian fervor. Ms. Williams's lineage confirms this. She first became politically active in protesting the Vietnam War and then focused her efforts on influencing American policy in Central America and providing aid there. The ICBL is not an isolated case but is one strand among a myriad in the web of the rigid liberal agenda.

Pause, therefore, before swallowing the ICBL estimates that 28,000 people are maimed or killed by land mines a year. After all, these are the same folks that brought you the 3,000,000 homeless figure in the 1980s (a 1984 study by Department of Housing & Urban Development put the population at a maximum of 250,000), or that 60,000,000 American women are beaten each year by either husbands or boyfriends (when the Census Bureau in 1993 estimated that only 56.8 million women in America even live with a man!) Researcher Richard Gelles in *Intimate Violence* revealed that 3% of women living with men suffer one act of violence a year, with only one third of 1 percent requiring medical help). Truth matters little to ideologues, only outcomes. How many distortions of public policy must we suffer before liberal gullibility is restrained.

But are there merits to ICBL's case that even one residual land mine claiming only one victim is sufficient reason for banning all of them? None whatsoever. Though we are moved deeply by these accidental tragedies, our reason cannot refrain from calm analysis. War is always unpleasant and frequently entails wholly unintended consequences which are tolerated by decent men for the achievement of the higher end of peace. Land mines in some conflicts are exactly what will deter aggressors. North Koreans would have long poured over the DMZ at the cost of thousands of American lives if not for thousands of land mines strewn there. While utopians like Ms. Williams would ban land mines, guaranteeing the slaughter of countless soldiers, sensible men utilize the weapon abundantly to save them. Who loves peace more?

Moreover, the consistent teaching of the Catholic Church confirms this common sense. Given the tragic necessity of war, nations have the right and obligation to use proportional force against an aggressor. This Just War Doctrine goes on to teach that as long as that force never directly intends the destruction of innocent non-combatants, a certain collateral harm to those non-combatants may be tolerated. In an imperfect world, this is the best that can be expected of decent men of good will. When possible they will go even further. The Defense Department has developed a smart land mine which does not remain active in the ground forever like the old dumb ones. They are of short duration, self-destructing and reliable (99.996 percent of the time). In use since 1994, not one civilian on earth has been injured by these smart mines.

Take note of that date again. 1994. These weapons were in development and use when ICBL was a mere twinkle in the eye of some sandaled peacenik simply proving that it is only men ready for war who truly love peace. Count this peace-lover for land mines.

I ♥ TEXAS

Travel from sea to shining sea or even across the fruited plain, and you will find no place better than Texas. Even folks who haven't been there say that. All you need to do is observe how Texas loves its citizens, the Judeo-Christian order of right and wrong, the common good and most importantly, peace. Texas bravely stands for the truth, beauty and goodness of every human life. Arguably, more than any other state in the union. To love Texas, all you have to know are a few statistics. In 2000 it executed 40 people, in 2018 it put 13 people to death (accounting for more than half of the 25 USA executions in that year), and Texas is responsible for three of the ten executions nationwide to date in 2019. That is not just talking love, that's doing love. When you love seriously, you don't wince at the serious things necessary to protect the people and values you love. Massachusetts or California may talk the talk about love. Texas walks the walk.

Executions demonstrate love?! Not always, surely. But they can, and in the case of Texas, they do. To the culture of death that sounds bizarre, for its moral eardrums has been shattered, making it impossible for them to pick up the textured sounds of true virtue. A moral tin ear only knows compassion as antinomianism, tolerance as permissiveness, moral uprightness as rigidity and accountability as a straightjacket. A culture that hails Ta Nahisi Coates as a moral beacon while vilifying Flannery O'Connor as a moral cretin cannot possibly understand why Texas stands for love. Texans stand closer to their humanity than the embalmed humanity of the coastal elites and its effete academicians. Those are the cretins, no longer grasping love or its wondrous parts, all of which make its presence so sweet – and so exacting.

C. S. Lewis writes that there is nothing as severe as love. Its severity is due to the generosity it summons and the justice it assumes. Leftists, and their rent-a-gang protesters frequently intone, "No justice, no peace." Ironically, they are quite right. Justice is the precondition of both peace and love, but not its sufficiency. If love is to radiate, its luster must be oblation. When it is, we understand Aristotle in the *Ethics*; "Where there is friendship, justice is not necessary." However, in the case of the state, we can only look to the presence of charity's spine, justice. Justice is that virtue which perpetually renders to a person exactly that which is his due. When a person has been deprived of his due – his life, his good name, his property – justice must restore it. And not to the aggrieved person alone, but to society in general. For when a person has been stripped of his right, the perpetrator of the crime has not only harmed that individual, but also the society to which he belongs. He has set himself above the law, indeed, as his own law. His crime is therefore not only against Mrs. Jones, but the entire society of which Mrs. Jones is a part. In harming Mrs. Jones, the criminal tacitly proclaims a willingness to harm everyone else. When Mrs. Jones is injured by the criminal, all the rest of society is as well. So in the court procedure of all fifty states, criminal trials begin with the announcement: "The People vs. Jack Smith."

So it is that the Church has always taught that among the purposes of punishment (retributive, protective and reparative), the principal one is retributive: "Punishment has the primary aim of redressing the disorder introduced by the offense."[3] As Dr Ralph McInerney wrote, "The criminal cannot be punished for what he might do (protective); he is in prison because of what he has already done." McInerney pointedly concludes, "But if there is no cause for retribution, punishment is unjust: All that would excuse it is the fear that someone might in the future harm us and that solitude might better his soul."[4] When retribution is execution, it is not only justified, but consoles the virtuous about the seriousness with which men guard these precious goods, as well as signaling to the wicked the swift and harsh punishment that will meet their violation. This triple cord produces the peace which cements society in place.

Hence, a society has the power to punish, whereas Mrs. Jones does not. When the state imposes punishment for an injustice, it is justice. If Mrs. Jones were to impose punishment for an injustice, it would be vengeance. The former is noble and charitable; the latter misguided and execrable. Clearly, a society is moved to

---

[3] *Catechism of the Catholic Church*, no. 2266.
[4] *Crisis*, September 2000, p. 60.

punish only insofar as it loves its citizens and the common good. Its punishments will be swift and proportionately severe. Passivity or hesitation before evil is the mark of a society in decline. Or as Chesterton put it, "The society that tolerates everything, is a society that believes in nothing." Hesitation in meting out the punishment a crime demands suggests a suspicion about the moral law itself. Therein lies great danger, because dangerous people are left to wander among the good.

Civilized societies are not the ones that clamor for the rights of the criminal, but for the rights of the innocent and weak. There is far more civility in nations like Taiwan that canes bad boys who vandalize property than one which remands them to therapists. The good society is not afraid to stoutly call evil, *evil*, rather than disease. Civility reigns where there is clear moral judgment, and fearlessness in maintaining it. When George Orwell remarked that there is no idea so absurd that an intellectual would believe it, he could be paraphrased to say that there is no excuse so flimsy as to sway a society besotted by secularism. Men of virtue keep their ear to the ground of reality; corrupted men keep their ear only to their own ideas. This is parlous, because when ideas become more important than people, terror descends.

So, Texas here I come. No, I can't pick up things and move down with you, but my heart already has. Call me an old softie, but I am just a pushover for a love story. Texas style.

IS OPPOSITION TO ILLEGAL IMMIGRATION A SIN?

To quickly answer the question asked by the title of this article: Of course not.
But listening to most Church leaders today, a Catholic would think that it is one of those sins that cry out to Heaven for vengeance (pardon that terribly antediluvian reference.)
In fact, opposition to it is a mandate of both the virtue of Justice and holy Charity. Before arguing that seemingly counterintuitive statement (considered so only against the noise of current nostrums), some background is in order.
It used to be that nothing was a sin. Today, almost everything is. The new catalogue of sins has not descended from Mt. Sinai but from Mt. Woke. Sinai's censures were of things like theft, lying, worship of idols, extra-marital sex, and murder. Today they are passe. For the properly illumined, it is Mt. Woke's new list: white privilege, heteronormativity, lookism, speciesism, intersectionality, pronoun insensitivity, and (dare I even mention it in this respected journal?) Green Indifference.
If the new proscriptions seem too erudite to comprehend, don't fret. They depend on obfuscation as their cachet. Part of the Gnostic playbook is entrée to a privileged knowledge that only a select few possess. The rest are, how shall we put it, restorationists.
Forgive me for an egregious omission germane to our purpose. One of the Woke sins is Bordered Nations. Its poison offspring, the dreaded obloquy, Illegal Immigrants. In the spanking New Woke World there are no nations. Only One World. No longer are there Americans, Samoans, French, or Romanians. Such cultural hegemony is a base evil. Now all are Citizens of the World.
Men of sound mind instantly recognize the lunacy of exchanging Mt. Sinai for Mt. Woke. Once upon a time, the greatest enemy to this Gnostic madness was the Roman Catholic Church. She stood like a mighty sentinel against all things offensive to Right Reason (Natural Law) or True Religion (Divine Revelation). In Chesterton's words, "Catholicism is sanity preached

to a planet of lunatics." Men of sound mind instantly recognize the lunacy of exchanging Mt. Sinai for Mt. Woke. Once upon a time, the greatest enemy to this Gnostic madness was the Roman Catholic Church.

The Church could always be depended upon to untangle the tangled; to show light where there was darkness; to set straight the unstraightened. She would shout over the din of specious inanities the sweet voice of reality. While the fallen world would spin out of control, she maintained control. And a grateful human race bowed gratefully before her poised reason and dazzling Depositum.

No longer.

Not a few of her shepherds now mimic the worst sectors of the Woke Left. They have become the lunatics. For the most part, the blessed few who are not hide beneath the safe cover of silence. They invoke prudence as their defense, even as they hear the shrieking of the Little Ones deprived of their bread. Their genteel courtesies remind one of the jolly aristocratic merrymakings of Paris 1789 as the peasants groveled.

They have before them a rent Church, like the one after the ravages of the Protestant Revolution and criminal episcopal/papal inaction of the medieval Church. So ruinous was the state of the Renaissance Church that it prompted Pope Clement VII, in 1537, to write a letter to the Holy Roman Emperor Charles V: "My dearest son, we look upon the Church today and see a corpse in shreds... St. Peter's is a stable."

Déjà vu?

At the conclusion of the Council of Trent, a certain sobriety settled upon the once insouciant episcopacy. It prompted the Cardinal of Lorraine to thunder at his fellow Council Fathers:

> Whom shall we accuse, my fellow bishops? Whom shall be declared to be the authors of such great misfortune? Ourselves! We must admit that much with shame and with repentance for our past lives. Storm and tempest have arisen on our account, my brethren, and because of this let us cast ourselves into the sea. Let judgment begin with the House of God. Let those who bear the sacred instruments of the Lord, be purged and reform.

We wait with bated breath to hear words of such affecting clarity today.

Returning to the matter at hand: What of opposition to illegal immigration as a mandate of justice? Let us begin with *The Compendium of the Social Doctrine of the Catholic Church*:

> A nation has a fundamental right to existence, to its own language and culture, through which a people expresses and promotes its fundamental spiritual sovereignty, to shape its life according to its own traditions and to build its future by providing an appropriate education for the younger generation.

This statement of the justice regarding nations should be understood in conjunction with the *Catechism of the Catholic Church*:

> Political authorities for the sake of the common good for which they are responsible, may make the exercise of the right to immigrate subject to various juridical conditions, especially regarding the immigrants' duties toward their country of adoption. Immigrants are obliged to respect with gratitude the material and spiritual heritage of the country that receives them, to obey its laws and to assist in carrying civic burdens. (no. 2241)

On February 2, 2001, Pope John Paul II addressed the 87th World Day of Migration, where he made even more explicit the imperatives of justice regarding immigration:

> Highly developed countries are not always able to assimilate all those who emigrate and that while the church strongly affirms the right to emigrate certainly, the exercise of such a right is to be regulated, because practicing it indiscriminately may do harm and be detrimental to the common good of the community that receives the migrant.

These authoritative statements underline not only the right of nations to enact laws that limit immigration but also emphasize that nations have as their principal obligation to assure the common welfare of first its own citizens. Overcrowded classrooms and packed emergency rooms are not examples of normative justice for a citizenry.

No doubt, justice clearly requires that nations welcome immigrants to their shores, but the reception must be strictly guided by the laws of nations. Legal immigrants are welcomed with open arms. Not illegal ones. Moreover, it is a gross miscarriage of justice to those who assume the painstaking requirements of the legal process of just immigration.

But what of the immigrants suffering at the hands of a callous homeland? While we pity them, we cannot house them when their entrance is illegal. Clerics who do are proselytizing law-breaking. Where does this carte blanche end? Do these pioneering clerics recognize that their theological gush opens a spiral of anarchy?

St. Thomas clarifies:

> Augustine says... "Since one cannot do good to all, we ought to consider those chiefly who by reason of place, time or any other circumstance, by a kind of chance are more closely united to us"... Now the order of nature is such that every natural agent pours forth its activity first and most all on the things which are nearest to it... But the bestowal of benefits is an act of charity towards others. Therefore, we ought to be most beneficent towards those who are most closely connected with us.
>
> Now one man's connection with another may be measured in reference to the various matters of which men are engaged together (thus the intercourse of kinsman is in natural matters, that of fellow citizens is in civic matters, that of the faithful is in spiritual matters, and so forth); and various benefits should be conferred in various ways according to these various connections, because we ought in preference to bestow on each one such benefits as pertain to the matter in which, speaking simply, he is most closely connected with us...
>
> For it must be understood that, other things being equal, one ought to succor those rather who are most closely connected with us.[5]

What of Holy Charity? For Catholics, St. Thomas's teaching above sheds light upon the subject. While all men deserve our charity, it is impossible to give all men our charity. Charity possesses its own order. Aquinas makes them eminently clear. Would the father of a house fulfill charity if he allowed into his home two dozen illegal immigrants while his children were neglected? No. Because he would be failing in charity those for whom he is bound first: his family. Under the roof of this faux charity there is grave sin.

When sentimentality replaces charity, chaos ensues. Charity flourishes within the boundaries of an ordered justice. It must be

---

[5] *Summa theologiae* II-II, Q. 31, art. 3.

remembered that the spine of charity is truth (justice), and the face of charity is oblation.

The present condition of illegal immigrants is a flagrant violation of charity. They are allowed entry into this country and then must suffer the indignity of being abandoned to substandard living conditions while a virtue-signaling elite assuages their Leftist conscience. This is not justice but the absolution of white liberal guilt.

Clerics are doing great injustice to justice by treating illegal immigration as though it were an article of Faith. These same clerics are preaching breaches of charity in the name of charity. By surrendering true charity to the *du jour* enthusiasms of the day, they make of charity a parody.

One prominent shepherd reproved Catholics protesting illegal immigrants. In tones of magisterial authority, he roared, "These are good people, I have baptized their babies!" How very touching. But that is not the point. This is dissembling at its worst. Rather like a man asking approval of his fornication because he is bringing beautiful children into the world.

A nation which is forced to give less to its citizens because it chooses to give priority to a promiscuous immigration policy is violating both justice and charity. These virtues are too grand to be dragged through the mud of secularism's (in George Orwell's apt phrase) "Smelly little orthodoxies."

Give the world and the Catholic faithful the full and robust teaching of the Catholic Church. Those teachings built Western Civilization and shall do so again.

In his *Essays of a Catholic*, Hilaire Belloc taught us well:

> One thing in this world is different from all other. It has a personality and a force. It is recognized, and (when recognized) most violently loved or hated. It is the Catholic Church. Within that household the human spirit has roof and hearth. Outside it, it is the night.

RADICAL CHIC REDUX

Only the gifted pen of a Tom Wolfe could have minted the generation-defining sobriquet, *radical chic*. It first appeared in a long monograph in *New York* magazine in 1970, where the author wrote a withering piece describing a fashionable cocktail party at the West Side apartment of Leonard Bernstein. The impresario had invited the glitterati of Manhattan's Café Society to fawn over a group of revolutionaries called the Black Panthers. It was a classic exercise in self-loathing. Here were the pacesetters of the culture pleading absolution of a deplorable underclass of violent black thugs. Wolf's depiction of the event's high pathos won his essay immemorial status in the annals of cultural criticism. Such imbecility would thenceforth never be able to hide beneath the skirts of respectable activism. Till now. Human nature being what it is always suffers the fate of moral amnesia. Lessons once thought to leave their indelible mark easily fade, but soon return to take advantage of easy dupes. Lenin called them "Useful idiots."

Welcome to the radical chic redux. Its dangerous enthusiasm can be seen today in the stance of not a few political leaders who have stood by and let our cities burn. Looters are elegized as avatars of a New Order of humanity. Their crudities are hailed as prophetic tokens of Brave New Worlds. Try digesting this sampling. Mind you, these are not radical outliers, but elected political leaders:

"What I don't want to hear is to be civil. Why does looting bother people?" asked Tammy Morales, a Seattle councilwoman.

"It is time to defund the police department and replace them with rapid response social workers," declared a *New York Times* editorial on June 1.

"A looter's statement is a once in a lifetime opportunity," observed Massachusetts attorney general Maura Healey. "Yes, America is burning, but that's how forests grow."

Meanwhile John Creuzot, Dallas's district attorney, has announced that he will not prosecute any looters.

Investigating the source of this fanaticism brings us quickly to our universities and colleges. Of the multiple examples, let it suffice to cite as typical Northwestern University's Professor of Journalism, Steven Thrasher, in a 2020 issue of *Slate:*

> The destruction of a police precinct is not only a tactically reasonable response to the crisis of policing, it is a quintessentially American response, and a predictable one. The uprising we have seen this week is speaking to the American police state in its own language up to and including the use of fireworks to mark a battle victory. Property destruction for social change is as American as the Boston Tea party.

This is the chilling stuff of 1789, 1848 or 1917. Truth to be told, its systematic chaos has been simmering in America for quite a time.

Norman Mailer's 1957 novel, *The White Negro*, was already tilling the soil for anarchic overthrow:

> It can of course be suggested that it takes little courage for two or three 18-year-old hoodlums, let us say, to beat the brains of a candy-store keeper... Still, courage of a sort is necessary, for one murders not only a weak 50-year-old man, but an institution as well, one violates private property, one enters into a new relation with the police and introduces a dangerous element into one's life. The hoodlum is therefore daring the unknown.

Simon Schama summarized this *cri de guerre* with perceptive insight in his masterpiece on the French Revolution, *Citizens:* "From the storming of the Bastille onward it was apparent that violence was not just an unfortunate side effect... It was the Revolution's source of collective energy. It was what made the Revolution revolutionary."

America coped with this type of organized terror in 1968 and imagined that, after a few years, it would eventually dissipate. It did not. Rather, it regrouped and discovered its natural petri dish in the universities. Much contempt for civilization in general, and Western civilization in particular, has been fueled by the mighty higher education establishment, to which parents have happily been paying their pound of flesh for decades now.

Within a short span, Sixties street radicals armed with Molotov cocktails became tenured radicals more effectively armed with blackboard and chalk. Given a few decades more to gestate, the university apparatus has become the assembly line for the Far Left to groom the young. A quick glance at the rioters reveals a rather large contingent of white-privileged youth, coddled by their parents' indulgence and weaponized by their universities.

An example is the Inclusive Communications Task Force at Colorado State University. Its latest speech guide directs students not to call people "American" because it "erases other cultures." Do not say, "you guys"—but, rather, "all folks." Of course, "male" and "female" are out; "man," "woman," and "gender non-binary" are in.

This argot would baffle even Huxley and Orwell, surpassing "newspeak" itself. More seriously, it threatens the very survival of the republic.

Then there are the journalists. While not quite parroting the sharp antinomian rantings of a Mailer, Ginsberg, or Thrasher, most of America's mainstream journalists couch them in a more palatable language. Hiding behind the atrocious murder of a black man, they deftly utilized it to peddle their disruptive agenda. More alarming is how readily the bourgeois upper class is anxious to be scolded and coaxed out of their common sense.

One of the major national news programs interviewed a prosperous fortyish gentleman. From his manner and dress, he could easily have been your typical hedge fund manager or *Fortune 500* CEO. He had decided to descend from his well-appointed East Side apartment with his two daughters, who looked school-aged and right out of a Nancy Drew novel. He confessed to the reporter that he felt he needed to teach his daughters the lessons of insurrection and protest, and the daughters nodded their heads, as though giving pious assent to a newly learned creed.

Add to this the uppermost layers of America's entertainment elite. A-list Hollywood stars and revered sports icons have publicly committed themselves to funding the struggles of rioters. Since our celebrities represent the new priestly class for many Americans, this is an ominous perfect storm.

The genealogy of this cultural suicide can be traced to Nietzsche's *transvaluation of values*. This was his prescription for the apotheosis of the abnormal. All the fixed verities of good and bad, and right and wrong, had to be bent into a hitherto unrecognizable form. Disequilibrium was the new normal. Its toxicity was to extend to every field, especially art and literature. All that was familiar had to be exorcised. Man must find himself and his world in a vertiginous free fall. The common sense normal was proscribed.

The success of Nietzsche's program can be traced in the rise of the censorious dicta of politically correct language, the rise of identity politics tribalism, and the new regimes of anti-free speech. For instance, the avant-garde of the 1970s decided that proper hospitalization for the mentally ill was actually a form of unjust incarceration. Psychiatric patients were post-haste released upon the streets, as a token of Nietzschean transvaluation. As a result, these poor unfortunates colonize our major cities, and our political leaders leave this desperate population to lie abandoned in our streets. They have become pawns in the cynical Left's strategy of convincing a once-sane American population that their sane norms of societal order were only instances of moral insanity.

This is of one cloth with the bizarre positions of the deconstructionist philosopher Michel Foucault in his *Discipline and Punish*, when he proposed the emptying of jails. The truly normal (he taught) were the jailed criminals. The abnormal are those who are *un*jailed – you and I.

As we have seen many times in the past two thousand years, it is only the Roman Catholic Church which can face such derangement and right it. Sadly, those Catholic tools lie buried in cobwebs. This momentous task is now left to the good Catholic faithful, who will rediscover those divine tools and wield them. For, I fear, too many Catholic leaders have fallen beneath the spell of the radical chic.

EPILOGUE

When I awake each morning, I grieve. I grieve the loss of the rapturous beauty that once was the Catholic Church before 1965. You see, I was born and raised during what must be called the Golden Age of Catholicism. That, in itself, is a sorrowful blessing—for those memories still swirl in my mind like a dream too sweet to end. But so much has changed. And so, I grieve.

Some of today's theological mandarins insist that this Golden Age was an illusion. Gary Wills, once a respected Catholic intellectual, rejoiced at its collapse in his Bare Ruined Choirs. Hans Urs von Balthasar, often hailed as a beacon in the postconciliar darkness, titled a work Razing the Bastions—and by that, he meant the Church itself as it had existed before 1965.

But while Wills and von Balthasar saw a moribund institution, most theologians of that era witnessed something altogether different. Seminaries and novitiates were full to bursting, missionary activity flourished across the globe, Catholic hospitals, schools, and colleges expanded with confidence, Masses overflowed with the faithful, and the Church basked in a golden age of letters and scholarship.

One wonders what exactly Father von Balthasar failed to see.

The sorrow over a dismembered Church pulses through every word I have written over the past thirty years. How could it not? We have witnessed self-inflicted ruin: the systematic doctrinal confusion of generations, religious orders gutted by the spirit of the age, the sacred liturgy dismantled, our churches looted, our youth betrayed—and bishops largely passive through it all. Even Pope Paul VI confessed in 1972, "from some fissure, the smoke of Satan has entered the temple of God."

But sorrow is not the end of the Catholic soul—it is never the end. Morning always follows the long night of lament. The virtue of hope stirs beneath the ashes. Every Catholic heart, even burdened, retains a bedrock conviction: Christ's conquering grace will always come to the rescue.

Every essay in this book is an elegy – and a promise. Each lament carries a call to arms. These pages are not mere memories; they are blueprints. They aim to awaken apostolic souls ready to rebuild – ready to recognize Christ's victory when it begins to take shape again.

Yes, the vineyard lies devastated. But new shoots are rising. You, dear reader, may be among them.

In 1542, when St. Ignatius received word that the Cardinal Archbishop of Toledo had denied his Jesuits permission to labor there, his companions were disheartened. But he consoled them, saying, "My dear Fathers, this trial was given to us by our Lord because He desires us to do great things for Him."

Are you ready to do great things for Christ – to lift your torch against the abyss?

SOURCES

"Abandon All Pride Those Who Seek the Kingdom," January 9, 2018, *Crisis Magazine*.
"Active Participation: Truths and Counterfeits," Christmas 2018, N/A.
"All About ME," 2014, *Latin Mass Magazine*.
"All of Vienna Is Giddy About Nanya," March 1, 1997, *Excelsis/Christifideles*.
"All You Need Is Love?," February 24, 2023, *Crisis Magazine*.
"Always the Same," November 1, 1996, *Excelsis/Christifideles*.
"Apocalypse or New Dawn?," Summer 2022, *Latin Mass Magazine*.
"Apologize? For What?," July 1, 1998, *Excelsis/Christifideles*.
"Archbishop Cordileone vs. Sisters of Perpetual Indulgence," June 6, 2023, *Crisis Magazine*.
"Archbishop Viganò's Letter: Now What?," March 1, 2020, N/A.
"Aren't We All Going to Heaven?," Fall 2021, *Latin Mass Magazine*.
"Awake in Paradise," June 1, 2020, N/A.
"(Bad) Business as Usual," August 1, 2002, *Excelsis/Christifideles*.
"The Bashfulness of Sin," December 15, 2017, *Crisis Magazine*.
"The Beginning of the End of Recreational Catholicism," September 20, 2024, *Crisis Magazine*.
"A Berlin Wall–Again," March 15, 2023, *Crisis Magazine*.
"Beware the Priest as Clown," July 11, 2025, *Crisis Magazine*.
"Bill in the Hotel Room with Paula," July 1, 1997, *Excelsis/Christifideles*.
"Black Lives Really Mattered to St. Peter Claver," October 6, 2017, *Crisis Magazine*.
"Black Power!," July 22, 2020, *Crisis Magazine*.
"Bless Me, Father, for I Have Sinned," March 20, 2018, *Crisis Magazine*.
"Cardinal Cupich's Uncertain Trumpet," April 1, 2018, *New Oxford Review*.
"Catholicism Is About Swords," February 29, 2024, *Crisis Magazine*.
"Catholicism, the World, and a Warrior Angel," October 17, 2017, *Crisis Magazine*.
"Catholicism's Ghost," December 2, 2024, *Crisis Magazine*.
"Catholics as 'Strangers,'" May 1, 2020, N/A.
"Censorship," February 1, 1999, *Excelsis/Christifideles*.
"Christ Was a Brown Jew," May 1, 1997, *Excelsis/Christifideles*.
"Christianity & Islam: Morally Equivalent?," April 2015, *New Oxford Review*.
"Christmas and Nietzsche's Abyss," December 25, 2017, *Crisis Magazine*.
"Clothing the Naked Catholic Square," November 25, 2017, *Crisis Magazine*.
"The Council of Nicaea at 1,700 Years Old," May 20, 2025, *Crisis Magazine*.
"Does Jesus Love You Just the Way You Are?," July 14, 2023, *Crisis Magazine*.
"Don't Look Away," April 10, 2020, *Crisis Magazine*.

"Down the Rabbit Hole of Synodality," September 30, 2021, *Crisis Magazine*.
"Easter: Launching the Revolution of the Cross," April 10, 2023, *Crisis Magazine*.
"The Ecstasy and Terror of Holy Thursday," April 14, 2022, *Crisis Magazine*.
"An Embarrassing Feast for a 'Reimagined Church,'" November 19, 2021, *Crisis Magazine*.
"An Embarrassment of Riches," 2018, *Latin Mass Magazine*.
"Escaping the Cross: The Ugliest Temptation," February 13, 2018, *Crisis Magazine*.
"Fable-Time in Chicago," Summer 2023, *Latin Mass Magazine*.
"Fathers, Rise to Your Greatness," June 14, 2024, *Crisis Magazine*.
"A Fearful Homage," May 1, 2013, N/A.
"A Friday Unlike Any Other," April 1, 2019, N/A.
"God Bless America?," August 7, 2019, *Excelsis/Christifideles*.
"Good Friday: The Start of a New Beginning," March 30, 2018, *Crisis Magazine*.
"The Greatness of the Priesthood," Fall 2017, *Latin Mass Magazine*.
"Haunted by Passiontide," Winter-Spring 2022, *Latin Mass Magazine*.
"Heaven is Only in Heaven," May 9, 2024, *Crisis Magazine*.
"Hell in Manhattan," September 14, 2021, *Crisis Magazine*.
"The Holy Family and Holy Families," January 2014, N/A.
"The Holy Spirit Makes Men of Steel," May 24, 2021, *Crisis Magazine*.
"How Long, O Lord?," Christmas 2017, *Latin Mass Magazine*.
"I ♥ Texas," October 7, 2019, N/A.
"In Praise of Heroic Priests," August 24, 2019, N/A.
"In Praise of Land Mines," January 1, 1998, *Excelsis/Christifideles*.
"In Praise of the (Former) Society of Jesus," August 2, 2022, *Crisis Magazine*.
"Is Christ a Magician?," May 20, 2024, *Crisis Magazine*.
"Is Opposition to Illegal Immigration a Sin?," September 27, 2023, *Crisis Magazine*.
"It's Not Your Education, Stupid," June 1, 2002, *Excelsis/Christifideles*.
"Joseph Cardinal Bernardin, R. I. P.," November 1, 1996, *Excelsis/Christifideles*.
"Latin in the Mass," Christmas 2017, *Latin Mass Magazine*.
"Lawmakers Declare War on the Church," January 19, 2021, *Crisis Magazine*.
"Lex Orandi, Lex Aedificandi," Spring 2002, *Excelsis/Christifideles*.
"Lift High the Cross," December 1, 2000, *Excelsis/Christifideles*.
"Looking Backward in the Diocese of Charlotte," June 10, 2025, *Crisis Magazine*.
"Love's Violence," October 1, 2020, N/A.
"Marin County Meets the Tiber," January 1, 2002, *Excelsis/Christifideles*.
"May Pope Francis Rest in Peace – And May Peace Return to Mother Church," April 22, 2025, *Crisis Magazine*.
"A Medieval Remedy for Modernity's Ills," September 21, 2017, *Crisis Magazine*.

"Mercy on the Cheap," Summer 2015, *Latin Mass Magazine*.
"Millstones Galore," 2002, *Excelsis/Christifideles*.
"Modernist Churches: Lies Set in Stone," Winter/Spring 2022, *Latin Mass Magazine*.
"Modernity's New Drink: Marriage on the Rocks," October 1, 2020, N/A.
"A Modest Proposal to End the Vocations Crisis," July 24, 2018, *Crisis Magazine*.
"Monsters at Hallmark," August 24, 2019, N/A.
"Mother Teresa: Loving the Poor Catholic Style," March 1, 2020, N/A.
"Motherhood and Civilization," May 11, 2018, *Crisis Magazine*.
"The Navel-Gazing of Synodal 'Listening,'" June 23, 2022, *Crisis Magazine*.
"Never Let a Crisis Go to Waste," March 2020, N/A.
"Not for Liturgists But for Men," September 1997, *Excelsis/Christifideles*.
"Nunsense, Redux," Christmas 2012, *Latin Mass Magazine*.
"Nunsense, Redux – Part II," 2012, N/A.
"O Death, Where Is Thy... Tickle?," November 14, 2023, *Crisis Magazine*.
"The Obsolete Human," 2015, *Latin Mass Magazine*.
"Occupy Harvard," September 23, 2020, *Crisis Magazine*.
"Of 'Healing Priests' and Other Strange Intrusions," February 15, 2024, *Crisis Magazine*.
"On Not Keeping the Poor Poor," Summer 2014, N/A.
"Our Brave New (Woke) World," 2022, N/A.
"Our Lepanto Moment," Fall 2016, *Latin Mass Magazine*.
"The Paradoxes of Auschwitz: Barbarity and Beatitude," August 9, 2023, *Crisis Magazine*.
"The Paris Olympics: Caligula Redux," August 2, 2024, *Crisis Magazine*.
"Paulist Fathers: Disassembling the Catholic Faith for Decades," May 19, 2023, *Crisis Magazine*.
"The Place of Joy in Times of Crisis," Fall 2022, *Latin Mass Magazine*.
"The Preferential Option for the Poor Sinner," April 3, 2023, *Crisis Magazine*.
"The Priest as Hercules," July 18, 2024, *Crisis Magazine*.
"The Properly Angry Catholic," July 2019, N/A.
"Purgatory," November 9, 2003, *Excelsis/Christifideles*.
"Radical Chic Redux," June 8, 2020, *Crisis Magazine*.
"A Radical Proposal for Eucharistic Revival," January 9, 2023, *Crisis Magazine*.
"'Re-enchanting' the World," Fall 2023, *Latin Mass Magazine*.
"The Remarkable Papacy of Pope Benedict XVI," Spring 2023, N/A.
"'Render unto Caesar...': To Vote or Not to Vote," October 30, 2024, *Crisis Magazine*.
"Resisting a Counterfeit Easter," April 7, 2021, *Crisis Magazine*.
"Returning to Our Knees," May 30, 2024, *Crisis Magazine*.
"RIP, DEI: The End of Our Captivity," February 11, 2025, *Crisis Magazine*.
"Rome, We Have a Problem," February 1, 2024, *Crisis Magazine*.
"A Rumbling," April 1, 1999, *Excelsis/Christifideles*.

"Saint Mychal Judge?," September 1, 2019, N/A.
"A Scene from Raphael," July 1, 2000, *Excelsis/Christifideles.*
"So Much for *Veritas*," June 1, 2001, *Excelsis/Christifideles.*
"Something to Apologize For," May 1, 2000, *Excelsis/Christifideles.*
"St. Mary Magdalene," March 1, 2020, N/A.
"St. Thomas Aquinas, Anyone?," December 19, 2019, N/A.
"The Strange Case of the Catholic Anti-Catholic," Winter/Spring 2013, *Latin Mass Magazine.*
"The Synodal Comedy: Act II," October 9, 2024, *Crisis Magazine.*
"Synodal Fallout: Putting Light Under Bushel Baskets," November 13, 2024, *Crisis Magazine.*
"Thank God, Governor Cuomo," April 24, 2020, *Crisis Magazine.*
"Three Cheers for Inequality," June 1, 2018, *Crisis Magazine.*
"Three Cheers for Smokers," January 17, 2022, *Crisis Magazine.*
"The Tightening Noose of Diversity Ideology," April 29, 2021, *Crisis Magazine.*
"The Time of Magical Thinking," January 16, 2024, *Crisis Magazine.*
"Together, Turning to God," Summer 2018, N/A.
"*Traditionis Custodes*: A Setback, not a Defeat," August 10, 2021, *Crisis Magazine.*
"The Tragedy of Legal Positivism," 1999, *Excelsis/Christifideles.*
"Union with God or Union with the World," April 8, 2025, *Crisis Magazine.*
"Vatican II at 60: Stop the Cheerleading," October 11, 2022, *Crisis Magazine.*
"Warning: This Music May Be Harmful to Your Soul," September 15, 2022, *Crisis Magazine.*
"What in the World is a 'Worship Space'?," March 14, 2019, *Crisis Magazine.*
"Whatever Happened to Lent?," March 20, 2024, *Crisis Magazine.*
"Where Eucharistic Revival Goes to Die," January 2, 2025, *Crisis Magazine.*
"Where is Today's Pope St. Pius X?," August 21, 2018, *Crisis Magazine.*
"Which Liturgy Appeals to Catholic Youth?," May 4, 2018, *Crisis Magazine.*
"Whither Our Catholic Churches?," Winter/Spring 2019, *Latin Mass Magazine.*
"Why I Love the *National Catholic Reporter*," March 30, 2021, *LifeSiteNews.*
"Why the Extraordinary Form is Truly Extraordinary," Christmas 2021, *Latin Mass Magazine.*
"Why the Walls of Notre-Dame Are Groaning," January 29, 2025, *Crisis Magazine.*
"Why Valentine's Day is Named After a Saint," February 13, 2019, *Crisis Magazine.*

N/A: publication source is unrecorded or undiscoverable.

ABOUT THE AUTHOR

A native of Jersey City, New Jersey, Fr. John A. Perricone earned his undergraduate degree from Seton Hall University and a master's in biblical studies from Immaculate Conception Seminary in Mahwah, New Jersey. He was ordained to the priesthood in 1976 at the Cathedral Basilica of the Sacred Heart in Newark. He later received a second master's degree in dogmatic theology from St. John's University in 1981, and was awarded a Ph.D. in medieval philosophy from Fordham University. In addition to his work as adjunct professor of philosophy at Iona University in New Rochelle, New York, Fr. Perricone has taught at St. Francis College (Brooklyn), La Salle University (Philadelphia), Dominican College (Orangeburg), and St. John's University (Queens).

In 1989, he founded ChristiFideles, a New York City-based apostolate dedicated to the spiritual and doctrinal formation of Catholics. In 1996, under his direction, ChristiFideles organized a landmark Solemn Pontifical High Mass at St. Patrick's Cathedral—the first celebration of the traditional Latin Mass by a curial cardinal in a major American archdiocese in over twenty-five years. From 1996 to 2008, he served as editor and publisher of *Excelsis*, a bi-monthly journal of theology, philosophy, and Catholic commentary rooted in the teachings of the Church and the thought of St. Thomas Aquinas. In 2002, Fr. Perricone co-founded The Montfort Academy in Mount Vernon, New York, a private Catholic high school grounded in a classical curriculum with the Catholic faith at its center.

His scholarly and popular writings have appeared in *St. John's Law Review*, *Crisis Magazine*, *Latin Mass Magazine*, *New Oxford Review*, and *The Journal of Catholic Legal Studies*. He has lectured at institutions including Harvard, Princeton, Columbia, Cornell, NYU, Georgetown, Boston College, Cambridge, and Loyola Marymount. His media appearances include EWTN, WNBC, WOR Radio, and several Catholic podcasts.

www.fatherperricone.com

www.ingramcontent.com/pod-product-compliance
Lightning Source LLC
Chambersburg PA
CBHW051614010526
44107CB00036B/1424/J